RISK MANAGEMENT IN EMERGING MARKETS

Issues, Framework, and Modeling

RISK MANAGEMENT IN EMERGING MARKETS

Issues, Framework, and Modeling

EDITED BY

SABRI BOUBAKER

Champagne School of Management, France

BONNIE BUCHANAN

Seattle University, USA

DUC KHUONG NGUYEN

IPAG Business School, France

Emerald

United Kingdom – North America – Japan
India – Malaysia – China

Emerald Group Publishing Limited
Howard House, Wagon Lane, Bingley BD16 1WA, UK

First edition 2016

British Library Cataloguing in Publication Data
A catalogue record for this book is available from the British Library

ISBN: 978-1-78635-452-5

Printed and bound by CPI Group (UK) Ltd, Croydon, CR0 4YY

Contents

About the Editors

Sabri Boubaker is Associate Professor of Finance at Champagne School of Management (Groupe ESC Troyes en Champagne, France) and Research Fellow at the Institut de Recherche en Gestion (University of Paris Est). He holds a Ph.D. in Finance from University of Paris Est (2006) and a HDR degree (Habilitation for Supervising Doctoral Research) in 2010 from the same university. He has recently published several academic papers in international refereed journals including *Journal of Corporate Finance, Journal of Banking and Finance, International Review of Financial Analysis, European Financial Management Journal, Review of Quantitative Accounting and Finance, Quarterly Review of Economics and Finance, Multinational Finance Journal, Global Finance Journal,* and *Journal of International Financial Markets, Institutions and Money.* Dr. Boubaker has also edited many books on corporate finance and financial markets and serves on editorial boards of several peer-reviewed finance journals. He is the co-founder (with Duc Khuong Nguyen) of the Paris Financial Management Conference.

Bonnie Buchanan is the Howard Bosanko Professor of Economics and Finance at the Albers School of Business and Economics, Seattle University. She was formerly the George Albers Professor between 2014 and 2017. She is Associate Professor of Finance and teaches undergraduate and graduate courses in International Finance, Financial Institutions and Markets and History of Financial Crises. Professor Buchanan has also served as Director for the Professional MBA program at Seattle University.

Her doctoral degree is from the Terry College of Business at the University of Georgia. Professor Buchanan has published in top-tiered journals such as *American Business Law Journal, Journal of Business Ethics* as well as *Review of Quantitative Finance and Accounting, International Review of Financial Analysis, Emerging Markets Review, Journal of Structured Finance, Review of International Business and Finance,* and *Journal of Financial Education*. Professor Buchanan's research interests include securitization, law and finance, emerging markets, and corporate governance. Prior to joining Seattle University, Professor Buchanan taught at the University of Georgia, Georgia State University, and the University of Melbourne. She was awarded the Outstanding Teaching Award, Honors Day, UGA in 2004 and the Dean's Teaching Certificate Award for Excellence at the University of Melbourne in 2006. Professor Buchanan has presented her work at national and international conferences and her co-authored work on shareholder proposals has been used in deliberations at the Securities and Exchange Commission (SEC) and cited in the *Financial Times*. Professor Buchanan has also received numerous grants throughout her career. Professor Buchanan is the Editor in Chief of *Journal of Risk Finance,* Associate Editor of *Research in International Business and Finance* and on the Editorial Advisory Board of Review in Behavioral Finance.

Duc Khuong Nguyen is Professor of Finance and Deputy Director for Research at IPAG Business School (France). He holds a Ph.D. in Finance from the University of Grenoble II (France) and a HDR (Habilitation for Supervising Scientific Research) degree in Management Science from University of Cergy-Pontoise (France), and completed an executive education program in "Leadership in Development" at Harvard Kennedy School (United States). He is also a Non-Resident Research Fellow at the School of Public and Environmental Affairs, Indiana University, and a Research Associate at the Department of Finance, Centre d'Economie de la Sorbonne, University Paris 1 Panthéon-Sorbonne. His research areas concern emerging markets finance, commodity finance, volatility modeling, and risk management in international capital markets. He published many articles in various refereed journals such as *Journal of Banking and Finance*, *Journal of International Money and Finance*, *Journal of International Financial Markets, Institutions and Money*, *Journal of Macroeconomics*, *Macroeconomic Dynamics*, and *Review of International Economics*. Dr. Nguyen has edited a dozen of books on corporate finance and financial markets issues and currently serves as subject and associate editors of several finance journals including *Emerging Markets Review*, *Finance Research Letters*, *International Review of Financial Analysis*, and *Journal of International Financial Markets, Institutions and Money*. He is the co-founder (with Sabri Boubaker) of the Paris Financial Management Conference.

About the Authors

Mahfod Aldoseri is Doctoral Candidate in the Department of Accounting, Finance, and Economics at Griffith University. His thesis, scheduled for completion in 2016 and supervised by his coauthor, Andrew C. Worthington, concerns the risk management practices of Islamic banks in Saudi Arabia. He holds a coursework master's degree in finance and a research master's degree on financial institution risk exposure, both from the University of Newcastle.

Mazin A.M. Al Janabi is Full Professor of Finance at the EGADE Business School, Tecnológico de Monterrey, Santa Fe Campus, Mexico City, Mexico. Before joining EGADE Business School, Prof. Al Janabi worked for 10 years as Full Professor of Finance & Banking at the College of Business and Economics, UAE University. He holds a Ph.D. degree from the University of London, UK, and has several years of real-world experience in financial markets and academic institutions and in many different roles. He has worked for top international financial groups (e.g., ING-Barings and BBVA-Bancomer) where he held several senior management positions, such as Director of Global Market Risk Management, Director of Asset & Liability Management, Head of Trading Risk Management, and Head of Trading of Financial Derivative Products. Professor Al Janabi has strong interest for research, publications, and developments within emerging economies. He has several publications in refereed international journals, books, and chapters in books. Moreover, he has participated as guest speaker and presenter in several international conferences and symposiums. He has served as consultant in finance & banking and as advisor for the creation of new financial markets within emerging economies. He has written extensively on contemporary topics in trading, market, and credit risk management besides modern portfolio management. His research interests and consulting activities address practitioners and regulatory issues in financial risk management, derivative securities, and portfolio management. Professor Al Janabi has published in top-tiered journals such as *International Review of Financial Analysis, Annals of Operations Research, Economic Modelling, Review of Financial Economics, Journal of Asset Management, Service Industries Journal, Studies in Economics and Finance, International Journal of Financial Engineering, Journal of Emerging Market Finance, Emerging Markets Finance and Trade, Review of Middle East Economics and Finance, Journal of Economic Research, Journal of Risk Finance, Journal of Banking Regulation, Annals of Nuclear Energy*, among others. He received several awards for excellence in teaching, research, and service and other awards in recognition of outstanding research publications output in A/A* ranked journals. His biography was cited and featured in the latest four editions of Who's Who in the World (2013–2016) and in the recent edition of Who's Who in Science and Engineering (2016–2017).

John R. Anchor is Professor of International Strategy in the University of Huddersfield Business School, UK. He is also Director of the Emerging Markets Research Group (EMERGE) within the School where he also has responsibility for European and Russian affairs. In addition he is Head of the Department of Strategy, Marketing and Economics.

Professor Anchor's research interests include the study of political risk and political risk assessment in emerging markets; strategic thinking, and implementation in emerging markets, especially in Central and Eastern Europe and the Middle East; and human capital theory, as applied to higher education policy, in both developed and emerging markets.

Professor Anchor has published in journals such as *International Business Review, Journal of Risk Research, Risk Management and International Journal of Project Management*. In addition he sits on the editorial board of Emerald Emerging Market Case Studies, as well as other journals. His Ph.D. is from the University of Manchester, UK, and he has supervised successfully more than 20 doctoral students of his own.

Professor Anchor is Visiting Professor in the Faculty of Economics, Technical University of Ostrava, and in the Faculty of Economics, Technical University of Liberec, both in the Czech Republic. He has received a number of awards ("medals") in recognition of his role in developing co-operation in research and education between Economics Faculties ("Business Schools") in Central and Eastern Europe and the University of Huddersfield.

Professor Anchor has been active in the European Union's Erasmus and Erasmus Mundus programmes and has been responsible for managing the mobility of large numbers of researchers and students within Europe, Central Asia, and Middle East/North Africa.

Francesca Battaglia is Assistant Professor of Banking and Finance at the Department of Management Studies and Quantitative Methods, University of Naples Parthenope (Italy). She holds a Ph.D. in Banking and Finance from the University of Roma Tor Vergata (2007) and a National Scientific Qualification as Associate Professor in Financial Markets and Institutions (2013). She has recently published several academic papers in international refereed journals, including *Applied Financial Economics, International Review of Financial Analysis, Journal of Business and Economics, Emerging Markets Review* and *Journal of Risk Finance*. She is author of several publications on financial institutions, including several chapters in Palgrave book editions ("Asset Pricing, Real estate and Public Finance over the Crisis"; "Advances in risk management"; "New issues in financial and credit markets"; "Governance, Regulation and Bank Stability"; "Bank Performance, Risk and Securitization").

Hana Benesova is Research Assistant of the Emerging Markets Research Group (EMERGE) at the Huddersfield Business School, University of Huddersfield, United Kingdom. Before joining EMERGE, she was an editorial assistant for the Emerald Emerging Markets Case Studies at Emerald Publishing, United Kingdom, and a lecturer at the University of Huddersfield. Her research interests include emerging markets and transition economies, collaboration of businesses, and corruption and trust.

She received a Bachelor in Business Economics and Administration from the Technical University in Liberec, Faculty of Economics, Czech Republic and a Bachelor degree in European Business from University of Huddersfield, Business School, United Kingdom. She was awarded a Master's degree in International Business with Financial Services (with distinction) before starting her Ph.D. titled "Corruption and Trust in Transition Context: the Case of the Czech Republic" at the University of Huddersfield.

She has lectured on international and European business, risk management and research methods in the United Kingdom, the Czech Republic, and Slovakia.

She is a member of several associations of researchers in international business and management such as the Academy of International Business, the British Academy of Management, and the Irish Academy of Management.

Emawtee Bissoondoyal-Bheenick is Senior Lecturer in the Department of Banking and Finance at Monash Business School. She holds a Ph.D. in Finance from RMIT University in December 2004. Banita's research interest is mainly in asset pricing, stock market volatility, stock markets analysis, mostly related to credit ratings — analysing the determinants of credit ratings, stock market impact and rating changes, structured finance products ratings and the Global Financial Crisis, and corporate ratings. Banita has published papers in the *Australian Journal of Management, Research in International Business and Finance, Emerging Markets Review, Global Finance Journal, Applied Financial Economics, Quantitative Finance and Pacific Basin Finance Journal.*

Maria Rosa Borges holds a Ph.D. in Economics (2001), from ISEG – Lisbon School of Economics and Management of the University of Lisbon. She is an Assistant Professor at ISEG, with tenure, and a member of the UECE – Research Unit on Complexity and Economics. She has authored and co-authored several books and book chapters in the fields of finance and microeconomics, and authored papers published in several academic refereed journals, including *Applied Economics, Applied Economics Letters, Atlantic Economic Journal, the Geneva Papers on Risk and Insurance, European Journal of Finance, and the Journal of Economic Studies*, among others. She won the NYSE Euronext Lisbon Award for the Best Scientific Research on Portuguese Capital Markets, in 2013. She was member of the Scientific Council of ISEG/ULisboa (2009–2014). She is a member of the Scientific Board of the M.Sc. in Monetary and Financial Economics ISEG/ULisboa, President of Pedagogical Council and Vice Dean of ISEG/ULisboa.

Luisa Bosetti is Assistant Professor of Business Administration in the Department of Economics and Management, University of Brescia (Italy), where she teaches graduate courses in Social reporting and Risk management and external control. She holds a Ph.D. in Corporate accounting and reporting. Her research interests include comparative corporate governance, internal control, risk management, CSR, and external disclosure. She has participated in several research projects; she has presented her works at national and international conferences; and she is author of many scientific papers published in books and journals. She serves as editorial board member and referee for international reviews and she actively cooperates with international institutes of management research.

Robert Brooks is Professor in the Department of Econometrics and Business Statistics and Deputy Dean, Education in Monash Business School. His primary area of research interest is in financial econometrics, with a particular focus on beta risk estimation, volatility modelling and the analysis of the impacts of sovereign credit rating changes on financial markets. Robert has published paper in *Journal of Econometrics, Journal of Banking Finance,*

Quantitative Finance, Journal of International Markets, Institutions and Money, International Review of Economics among others.

Alberto Burchi, Ph.D., is Assistant Professor of finance at the University of Perugia (Italy). He teaches undergraduate and graduate courses in Financial Market, Asset Management, Private Banking and Alternative Investments. His doctoral degree is from the Alma Mater Studiorum-University of Bologna (2006). Prior to joining the faculty at University of Perugia, Professor Burchi was assistant professor at SDABocconi School of Management (2003–2009). He has recently published several academic papers in international refereed journals including *Journal of Financial Regulation and Compliance, Journal of Financial Perspectives*. Professor Burchi's research interests include hedge funds, financial innovation, emerging markets, asset management, law and finance, risk valuation, and credit risk assessment. From 2015, he is a visiting professor at the University of Warmia and Mazury in Olsztyn (Poland) where he teaches Portfolio Management and Alternative Investments. He was awarded the 2015 Outstanding Reviewer for the *Journal of Risk Finance*.

Sherwood Clements, is Instructor of real estate and the William Carey Hulsey Faculty Fellow in the Economics, Finance and Legal Studies Department at the Culverhouse College of Commerce and Business Administration at the University of Alabama. He has taught undergraduate and graduate classes in real estate appraisal, development, finance, investment, and principles. He is active in scholarly research publishing in real estate journals such as the *Journal of Real Estate Research and the Journal of Property Research*. He earned a doctorate of philosophy in real estate from Georgia State University.

Edinson Cornejo was born in Chile. He studied Business at the Universidad Adventista de Chile, Master in Business Administration at the ILADES–Loyola University (Maryland) and is Ph.D. candidate at the Universidad Autónoma de Madrid. He was academic at the Faculty of Economy and Business of the University of Chile and also at the Universidad del Bío-Bío.

He was Academic Director of IEDE Business School (Chile) of the Laureate International Universities. Actually, he is academic of finance and accounting at the Faculty of Economics and Business at the University Santo Tomas in Chile.

Kevin Daly is Associate Professor (Economics and Finance) at Western Sydney University, Australia. Kevin's research passion revolves around applied finance and open economy macroeconomics; researching the effects of financial volatility on real economic activity. Related research publications have investigated the sustainability of foreign direct investment, Australia's portfolio investment, emerging markets financial development, global financial integration, finance and poverty and banking in Emerging Markets. I have consulted to state and local government, public enterprises and private corporations. Since joining UWS in 1997, I have over 80 publications in books, book chapters and refereed professional journal articles and have supervised 20 Ph.D. and DBA students to completion. Examples of collaborative research works cited in Scopus and Research Gate with colleagues from UWS, Chinese Academy of Social Science, Curtin University, Monash University, Sydney University, University of Economics – Hochiminh, Baptist University of Hong Kong, and the University of New South Wales. Current work includes a cross country study of High Net Wealth Individuals, Public Private Infrastructure Financing, Pension Fund Management, and Australia's Financial Deregulation.

Denis Davydov is Assistant Professor of Finance at the University of Vaasa (Finland). He is also a visiting Assistant Professor of Finance at the Stockholm University (Sweden). He teaches graduate and undergraduate courses in Investments, Corporate Finance, and Financial Analysis. His research interests are in corporate finance and financial institutions with the focus on emerging markets and his work includes papers on debt source choices and firm performance published in *Emerging Markets Review*. His Master's and Doctoral degrees are from the University of Vaasa.

Franco Fiordelisi holds Chair in Banking and Finance at the University of Rome III, Italy. He is also senior affiliated Faculty Member at the Bocconi Business School in Milan, Italy. Franco is also the President of the Financial Intermediation Network of European Studies (FINEST). His research revolves around different aspects of bank management and financial risk management. His work has been published in international academic journals such as the *Review of Finance, Journal of Corporate Finance, Journal of Banking and Finance, and Journal of International Money and Finance.* He is currently associate editor of the *European Journal of Finance, and member of the editorial board of the International Journal of Banking Accounting and Finance.*

Kenya Fujiwara is Professor at School of Business Administration, Kobe University. He received a Ph.D. from Kobe University in 1990. Before becoming a professor at Kobe University, he was a professor at Hiroshima University. Currently, he is a board member of the trustees of Kobe University. His major fields are Japanese banking behavior and the efficiency of the financial market, and restructurings and bankruptcy resolution for over-debt firms. He published academic articles in journals, such as *Pacific-Basin Finance Journal, Review of Monetary and Financial Studies,* and *International Journal of Business.*

Roland Füss is Full Professor of Real Estate Finance at the University of St.Gallen and Member of the Board of the Swiss Institute for Banking and Finance s/bf-HSG and of the School of Finance. He is also a Research Associate at the Centre for European Economic Research (ZEW), Mannheim, Germany. He studied economics at the University of Freiburg, Germany, from which he also obtained his doctoral degree and "habilitation." Prof. Füss is a member of the editorial board of several academic journals. His main research topics are in the field of asset pricing, portfolio optimization, real estate finance and economics, risk management, and applied financial econometrics. Prof. Füss has authored numerous articles in economics, finance, and real estate journals such as *Journal of Financial and Quantitative Analysis,*

Review of Finance, *Journal of Money, Credit and Banking*, *Journal of Banking and Finance*, *Public Choice*, and *Real Estate Economics*.

Francesca Gennari is Associate Professor of Business Administration in the Department of Economics and Management (DEM), University of Brescia (Italy) where she teaches Business Administration and Cost Accounting. She has a Ph.D. in Marketing, Management, and Assessment Statistical Method. Her major research fields concern corporate governance, management control, cost accounting, and corporate disclosure. She became involved in national and international researches and she has published many articles, books, book chapters, and scientific papers, presented at international and national conferences, about governance and management. She serves as referee and member of editorial board for international journals.

Jocelyn Grira is Assistant Professor of finance in the UAE University. He holds a Ph.D. degree in Finance from HEC Montreal (Canada) and a Master degree in Financial Engineering from Laval University (Canada). Before joining the UAE University, he was teaching quantitative finance in University of Sherbrooke in Canada.

Dr. Grira held several senior positions in international corporations based in Canada: KPMG Canada (Risk Consulting & Advisory Services), Desjardins Group (Risk Modeling), Industrial Alliance Group (Risk Analysis & Audit), Financial Markets Authority (Risk Modeling & Regulation), and the Ministry of Finance of Quebec (Financial Engineering & Portfolio Management). His research interests cover Sovereign Wealth Funds, Financial Regulation, Deposit Insurance, Corporate Governance, Portfolio Management, and Risk Management.

Dr. Grira's teaching interests cover Risk Management, Investment & Portfolio Management, Theoretical Finance, International Finance, Corporate Finance, Insurance, and Financial Engineering. Dr. Grira holds the Professional Risk Manager international designation (PRM) from the Professional Risk Manager International Association (PRMIA).

Mariya Gubareva is Assistant Professor at ISEG – Lisbon School of Economics and Management (University of Lisbon) and Adjunct Professor at ISCAL – Lisbon School of Accounting and Administration. She holds a Ph.D. in Economics from ISEG – Lisbon School of Economics and Management of the University of Lisbon (2013). She authored a book *Financial instability through the prism of Flight-to-Quality* and several chapters in books on emerging markets and risk management. She has published several working papers and articles in *Applied Economics*. Dr. Gubareva has presented her work at national and international conferences. She has also received numerous grants throughout her career.

Mayank Gupta is graduating from the joint Ph.D. program in Economics & Finance offered by the University of Venice Ca' Foscari, Padova & Verona in Italy. During his Ph.D. he has been a visiting fellow at Emerging Markets Group (EMG) Cass Business School City University London, UK, and Centre for Research in Econometric Analysis of Financial Time Series (CREATES) at Aarhus University in Denmark. His research is primarily focused on Emerging Markets in particular financial markets and banking crisis. He has previously published in the *Journal of Economics and Political Economy*. He has presented his work in various international conferences. Currently he is working on China's Shadow Banking System.

Haoshen Hu is Doctoral Student in finance and banking at the Carl von Ossietzky University of Oldenburg (Germany). His research interest lies mainly in the area of credit rating, with a focus on the analysis of capital market effects of credit rating announcements.

A. Can Inci is Professor of Finance at the College of Business, Bryant University. He teaches courses in Investments, Innovations in Finance, Financial Management, and International Finance. Professor Inci holds a Ph.D. in Business Administration – Finance from University of Michigan, Ann Arbor. He also has an MBA from Ohio State University, MSc in Control Systems from Imperial College – University of London, and a BSc in Electrical and

Electronics Engineering from Bogazici University. Professor Inci has published numerous research papers in international refereed journals including *Financial Management, European Financial Management, Corporate Governance: An International Review, Journal of Economic Dynamics & Control, Emerging Markets Finance and Trade, Global Finance Journal, Review of Financial Economics, Journal of International Financial Markets, Institutions and Money, Journal of Economics and Finance, and Research in International Business and Finance.* His research interests include Empirical Analysis of Currency Movements, Asset Pricing and Term Structures, Futures Markets, International Investments, Corporate Governance, Insider Trading and Information Asymmetry, Intraday Volatility. Prior to joining Bryant University, Professor Inci taught at Florida State University, and Sabanci University. He serves on editorial boards of several peer-reviewed finance journals. Professor Inci has received several Best Paper awards at academic conferences including Andima Best Paper in Fixed Income, Marie Curie International Reintegration Grant, and European Financial Management Top Download Award.

Toshiki Jinushi is Professor at the Graduate School of Economics, Kobe University. He received an M.A. from Kobe University in 1984 and a Ph.D. from Harvard University in 1989. Currently, he is a board member of the Japanese Association for Monetary Economics and the Japanese Economic Association. He has researched monetary policy, financial systems, and the economic influence of the disaster.

Dieter G. Kaiser is Co-founder and managing director of Robus Capital Management Limited, an alternative investment boutique focusing on mid-market corporate credit investments in Europe. Previously, from 2007 to 2011 he worked as Director at Feri AG and from 2003 to 2007 at Benchmark Capital Management GmbH in Frankfurt, Germany. Dr. Kaiser is the author of various publications on the topic of alternative investments and frequent speaker at industry conferences. Dr. Kaiser is Research Fellow at the Centre for Practical Quantitative Finance at the Frankfurt School of Finance and Management. He holds a degree in business administration (Diplom), a Master's degree in finance and a Ph.D. in finance.

Chiraz Labidi is currently Assistant Professor of finance at the College of Business and Economics, United Arab Emirates University where she has also served as Chairperson of the Department of Economics and Finance from 2010 to 2014. She has earned her Ph.D. from Dauphine University, France. She held various academic and Research positions at ESSEC Business School, Dauphine University, and Rouen Business School in France, HEC Lausanne in Switzerland, and IHEC Carthage in Tunisia. Before joining the UAEU, Dr. Labidi has visited Dickinson College in U.S. as a Fulbright visiting scholar.

Her main areas of teaching include Financial Management, Investment, Derivatives, International Finance, Portfolio Management, Interest Rates and Fixed Income Products, and Financial theory. She has been actively involved in executive educations programs. Her research has concentrated on International Financial Markets and more precisely on conditional dependence, information transmission processes, multivariate modeling and copula functions.

She has publications in reputable international journals such as *Journal of Futures Markets, Journal of Economics and Finance, International Review of Economics and Finance, Applied Financial Economics*, etc.

Yajing Liu is Assistant Professor in the Faculty of Economic Sciences, Hiroshima Shudo University, Hiroshima, Japan. She received a Ph.D. from Kobe University in March 2015. Her research is focused on small and medium enterprise finance in China. She also does comparative research on small and medium enterprise finance between China and other countries, such as Japan. She is a member of the Japan Society of Monetary Economics, and she peer reviews articles with the Singapore Economic Review.

Duccio Martelli, Ph.D., is Assistant Professor of finance at University of Perugia (Italy) and adjunct professor of finance at

University of Applied Sciences of Augsburg (Germany). He is also a summer school professor at Harvard University. He holds a Ph.D. in Banking and Finance from University of Rome "Tor Vergata." Dr Martelli has presented his research work at national and international conferences and has recently published several academic papers in international refereed journals, including *Journal of Economics and Business* and *Journal of Financial Management, Markets and Institutions*. He also serves as referee of several peer-reviewed finance journals. He teaches undergraduate and graduate courses in behavioral finance, corporate finance, private banking and financial markets, and his research interests include behavioral finance, financial literacy, asset management, and recently neuro finance.

Mónika Mátrai-Pitz is Assistant Research Fellow at the Faculty of Business and Economics at the University of Pécs, Hungary. After her graduation in Finances at the University of Pécs, and in Operations Research at the University of Hagen, she started her Ph.D. studies in Pécs with the pricing of FX loans of households as main research field. She further investigated the exposure of exchange rate movements, the validity of risk indicators during the crisis, and the effects of foreign direct investment in Hungary.

Takashi Matsuki is Professor of Economics at Osaka Gakuin University in Japan. He obtained his MA and Ph.D. in Economics from Osaka Prefecture University. His research interests are in econometric theory and applied econometrics, especially time series analysis and its applications. His research has been published in *Applied Economics, Applied Economics Letters, Economics Letters, Economic Modelling, Emerging Markets Review*, and *Empirical Economics*.

Jan Novotný is Visiting Lecturer and Research Fellow at the Cass Business School, City University London, and a Researcher at CERGE, Charles University. His research interests include financial econometrics, financial engineering, risk, finance, and econophysics. He has published papers in *Journal of Financial Markets, Emerging Markets Review, Monte Carlo Methods and*

Applications, and *Physica A*, and co-authored two chapters in books. He has co-authored number of papers in physics journals. He has a MSc. in experimental nuclear physics from Czech Technical University and a MA and Ph.D. in economics from Charles University.

Avni Önder Hanedar is a Researcher at Faculty of Business at Dokuz Eylül University (Izmir, Turkey). He holds Ph.D. in Economics at University of Essex. He did post-doctoral research at the Atatürk Institute for Modern Turkish History at Boğaziçi University in 2014. He was lecturer at the Turkish Military Academy in 2014–2015. Dr Hanedar conducted projects on economic and financial history at University of Essex and Dokuz Eylül University. He has recently published an academic paper in well-known economic history journal, that is, Historical Methods, on financial history of the Ottoman Empire and İstanbul bourse. Dr. Hanedar has other published papers in Borsa Istanbul Review, Review of Middle East Economics and Finance, International Trade Journal, as there are some forthcoming researches in Defence and Peace Economics and Research in Economic History.

Franco Parisi, Ph.D. Visiting Professor at Culverhouse College of Commerce and Business Administration at the University of Alabama. Visiting International Scholar Rawls College of Business Texas Tech University. Parisi was an Independent Presidential Candidate in Chile 2014 elections, obtaining more than 10% of preferences. Previously, I served as Dean at the Business School Universidad Europea de Madrid, Interin Dean and Associate Dean at Universidad de Chile, Business School with several publication in academic journal and books. Visiting Professor at Rice University, University of Alabama at Birmingham, University of Georgia, Universidad de Monterey, Universidad Nacional de Argentina Cordoba, Univerisdad del Bio Bio, among others.

Jörg Prokop is Professor of Finance and Banking at the Carl von Ossietzky University of Oldenburg (Germany). He holds a doctoral degree from University of Bremen (Germany), and he has recently published several papers in refereed journals such as

Journal of Risk Finance, *Quarterly Review of Economics and Finance*, and *Qualitative Research in Financial Markets*. His research interests include risk management, financial intermediation, business valuation, and financial market regulation.

Ornella Ricci is Assistant Professor of Banking and Finance at the Department of Business Studies, University of Roma Tre (Italy). She holds a Ph.D. in Banking and Finance from the University of Roma Tor Vergata (2009) and a National Scientific Qualification as Associate Professor in Financial Markets and Institutions (2012). She has recently published several academic papers in international refereed journals including *Journal of Corporate Finance*, *Journal of Banking and Finance*, *Journal of Financial Stability*, *European Journal of Finance*, *Applied Financial Economics*, and *Journal of Pension Economics and Finance*. Dr. Ricci has also edited books on bancassurance and corporate governance in the insurance industry, and serves as referee of several peer-reviewed finance journals.

Daniela M. Salvioni is Full Professor of Business Administration in the Department of Economics and Management (DEM) of Brescia University (Italy). She has also taught at Milan University, Bologna University, and L. Bocconi University. She is member of the Scientific Committee of the Ph.D. in "Institutions and firm: value, rules and social responsibility – Business and Law" of Brescia and Bergamo universities. Professor Salvioni is member of many scientific institutions, including: EBEN – European Business Ethics Network, Italian chapter (board of directors); IGS – Corporate Governance Institute; GBS – Study Group on Social Report, a national association for scientific research on social reporting; EBES – Eurasia Business and Economics Society; IMRA – International Management Research Academy; AIDEA – Italian Academy of Business Administration; SISR – Italian Society of Accounting History; SIDREA – Italian Society of Accounting and Business Administration Lectures. Professor Salvioni's research articles are published in various refereed international journals of governance and management, and she has also edited several books on corporate governance, internal control, financial communication, cost accounting, and financial control. She has coordinated international and national research projects on corporate communication, web reporting, corporate governance, and school governance. Professor Salvioni's research fields concern all the aspects of corporate governance, from direction and control to responsibility and accountability, with specific emphasis on companies operating in global markets. Due to her internationally recognised scientific reputation and competence, in 2012 she has been appointed by Ca' Foscari Venice University's Chancellor as referee for the local evaluation of scientific publications.

Zoltán Schepp is Associate Professor of Finance and Economics at the Faculty of Business and Economics of the University of Pécs where he has been the dean since July 2015. Dr. Schepp earned his Ph.D. degree in 2004 and the title Dr. Habil in 2011. His field of interest includes foreign exchange rate theory, international finance, and higher education policy. He teaches in this field on Bachelor, Master, and Ph.D. level, and published articles in Journals like *Applied Economics Letters, Hungarian Economic Review, Journal of Teaching and Education, Public Finance Quarterly* and *Szigma*. Dr. Schepp has dozens of international conference contributions (e.g. *Congresses of the European Economic Association, Future of Education Conference, INFINITI Conferences, Money, Macro and Finance Research Group Annual Conference* and *World Finance Conference*) and led several research groups, among them very recently the team of the University of Pécs in the *RAstaNEWS* project.

Felix Schindler is Professor for Real Estate Finance and Economics at the Center for Real Estate Studies (CRES) at the Steinbeis University Berlin (SHB) and Research Associate at the Centre for European Economic Research (ZEW). He holds a doctoral degree in Economics from the University of Freiburg and received the Habilitation for Business Administration at the University of Regensburg. Professor Schindler has recently published in journals such as *Review of Finance, Journal of International Money and Finance, Real Estate Economics* as well as *Journal of Real*

Estate Finance and Economics. His research interests include portfolio management, risk management, financial economics, real estate finance, and real estate economics. He has presented his research at several national and international conferences. For his research, he has received several awards such as the BlackRock Research Award, the Aareal Award of Excellence in Real Estate Research and the DTZ Research Institute Award for Academic Innovation. Professor Schindler is a member of the research network "Real Estate Markets and Capital Markets" (ReCapNet) and co-editor of the *German Journal of Real Estate Research*.

Kimiko Sugimoto is Associate Professor in the Hirao School of Management at Konan University in Japan. She lectures on development economics and international finance. She obtained her MA and Ph.D. in Economics from Osaka University. Before joining Konan University, she was an associate professor of Economics at Osaka Gakuin University. Her research interests are in the empirical analysis of monetary integration, financial transmission mechanism, stock market co-movement, and global liquidity, especially the macroeconomic and financial problems of Africa. Her research has been published in *Economics Letters, Economic Modelling, Emerging Markets Review, Histoire Economique Quantitative, Journal of African Economies, and Review of Development Economics*. She has also published a chapter in Japanese on the financial development and Economic Growth in Africa in the handbook "Contemporary African Economies".

Steve Swidler is the J. Stanley Mackin Professor of Finance at Auburn University. He has published articles on derivatives, financial engineering, housing, and financial institutions that have appeared in the *Journal of Finance, the Journal of Banking and Finance, the Journal of Financial and Quantitative Analysis* and other peer-reviewed journals. Prior to joining the faculty at Auburn, Professor Swidler taught at UT-Arlington, Southern Methodist University, UW-Milwaukee, and Rice University. He has also had summer appointments at Victoria University in New Zealand and the Oslo School of Business. Professor Swidler is the recipient of the W. Paul Green Memorial Award for Excellence in Teaching and was a Fulbright Scholar at Sogang University in Seoul, South Korea. In addition to his academic positions, Dr. Swidler previously worked at the Office of the Comptroller of the Currency and at Lexecon. He received his Bachelor's degree from Oberlin College and his Ph.D. from Brown University.

Hanh Thi My Phan has joined the University of Finance and Marketing (Vietnam) as a lecturer in the faculty of Finance and Banking since 2007. Hanh holds a BA Economics, and MA Economics University of Economics Hochiminh city. Hanh is a DBA student of University of Western Sydney. Examples of her research include an investigation of the relationship between inflation and exchange rate in Vietnam (*Journal of Economic Development*, 2011), an analysis of a vicious circle of inflation and exchange rate in Vietnam (Conference on Fiscal and Monetary Policy and Financial Market Development in Vietnam, 2011), examining bank competition in emerging Asian countries: prepost the global financial crisis (World Business and Social Science Research Conference, 2013), an analysis of factors affecting performance of Vietnamese commercial banks: testing SCP and ES hypotheses (*Journal of Economic Development*, 2014), investigating competition and concentration of banking in emerging Asian countries (World Finance & Banking Symposium, 2015). Current research interests focuses on banking and stock markets in emerging Asian countries.

Sirimon Treepongkaruna is Professor of Finance at UWA Business School. She holds a Ph.D. in Finance from the University of Queensland in October 2001. She has published a total of 40 refereed publications, a book chapter and a text book, including *Journal of Banking and Finance, International Review of Financial Analysis, Journal of International Financial Markets, Institutions and Money, Journal of Multinational Financial Management, Pacific-Basin Finance Journal, Australian Journal of Management, Review of Behavioral Finance, Applied Financial Economic, Accounting and Finance, and International Review of Finance*. Sirimon also serves on editorial board of Accounting and Finance and Review of Applied Economics.

Marvin Wee is Associate Professor at the UWA Business School, University of Western Australia. Dr Wee holds a Ph.D. in Finance from the University of Western Australia. He teaches undergraduate and graduate courses in Investments, Trading and Markets, and Research Methods in Accounting and Finance. Dr Wee was awarded the Excellence in Teaching Award by the UWA Business School in 2014. His research interests are in trading behaviour, financial market microstructure, firm disclosure, investor relations and information asymmetry within the stock market. Dr Wee has published academic papers in international journals, a book chapter and presented at leading international conferences. His research has been published in the *Australian Journal of Management, Accounting and Finance, European Financial Management, Journal of Consumer Affairs and Pacific Basin Finance Journal.* Dr Wee is also an editor at the *Accounting and Finance journal.*

Andrew C. Worthington is Principal Supervisor of his coauthor, Mahfod Aldoseri, and Professor of Finance in the Department of Accounting, Finance, and Economics at Griffith University. He holds master's degrees from the University of New South Wales and the University of New England, and obtained his doctorate from the University of Queensland. His previous career appointments comprise the University of New England, Queensland University of Technology and the University of Wollongong and his teaching interests encompass advanced corporate finance and finance theory. His published research includes financial and commodity markets, alternative investments, and household finance, while his research into Islamic finance covers banking and managed funds. He is the editor of the contributed volume "Contemporary Issues in Islamic Finance: Principles, Progress, and Prospects" published in 2014 and an editorial board member of *Managerial Finance* (Emerald) and the *Journal of Commodity Markets* (Elsevier).

Elmas Yaldız Hanedar is Assistant Professor of Economics at Yeditepe University (Istanbul, Turkey). She holds a Ph.D. in Economics and Management from University of Trento (2013). She has been visiting researcher at Bangor Business School (Bangor, UK) in 2011. She has published several academic papers in international refereed journals including *Historical Methods, Journal of Banking and Finance, Journal of Risk Finance, Borsa Istanbul Review, Financial Theory and Practice.* She has attended and presented papers at international conferences. Dr. Yaldız Hanedar served as referee for *North American Journal of Economics and Finance* and *Emerging Markets Finance and Trade.*

Ehab Yamani is Visiting Assistant Professor of Finance at Jackson State University (Jackson, Mississippi, USA) and Assistant Professor at Tanta University (Tanta, Egypt). He holds a Ph.D. in Finance from University of Texas at Arlington (2012). He has recently published several academic papers in international refereed journals including *Journal of International Financial Markets, Institutions and Money, Journal of International Finance and Economics, Journal of Applied Financial Research, and Academy of Business Journal.*

Nobuyoshi Yamori is Professor at the Research Institute for Economics & Business Administration, Kobe University. He received an M.A. from Kobe University in 1988 and a Ph.D. from Nagoya University in 1996. Before becoming a professor at Kobe University in 2014, he was a professor at Nagoya University. Currently, he is a member of Japan's FSA Financial System Council. He has published many academic articles in international journals, such as *Applied Financial Economics, Economics Letters, International Journal of Business, Journal of Banking and Finance, Journal of Financial Intermediation, Journal of Financial Research, Journal of Financial Services Research, Journal of International Financial Management and Accounting, Journal of International Financial Markets, Institutions and Money,* and *Journal of Risk and Insurance.*

Yushi Yoshida is Professor of Economics at Shiga University in Japan. Before joining Shiga University, he was a professor of Economics at Kyushu Sangyo University. He obtained his MA and Ph.D. in Economics from Osaka University. His research is in international finance, especially exchange rate pass-through, foreign exchange intervention, and international financial transmission.

He has also written on empirical international trade, including intra-industry trade and extensive margin of exports. His recent research has been published in the *Asia Pacific Business Review*, *Emerging Markets Review*, *IMF Staff Papers*, *International Review of Economics and Finance*, *North American Journal of Economics and Finance*, and *World Economy*. He is a researcher in the Pass-through Research Group at the Research Institute of Economics, Trade, and Industry (RIETI).

Preface

Academic finance research has shown that emerging markets still suffer from a myriad of risks such as credit, operational, market, legal, and exchange rate risks. The onset of the recent global financial crisis of 2007–2008 as well as the public debt crisis in the Eurozone has brought to the light a number of emerging markets facing tumbling currencies, rising inflation, slowing growth, heavy dependence on foreign capital, and high levels of vulnerability to external shocks due to increased market integration. The long swings in crude oil markets since June 2014 — which particularly arises from the complex geopolitical situations in the Middle East, low demand, and weak growth expectations — have been discouraging corporate investments, reducing corporate earnings, and consequently causing the plunge of stock markets around the world.

This context thus calls for not only a reconsideration of recent risk assessment models and risk management practices but also the improvement and innovation of these models and practices. Factors such as liquidity, tail dependence, comovement, contagion, and timescale interactions would definitively have to be part of an integrated risk assessment and management framework.

This book, composed of 21 high-quality exclusive chapters, provides insights into three main dimensions of risk management in emerging markets: (i) the state of the art and the effectiveness of risk management practices; (ii) current issues and challenges in risk assessment and modeling in emerging market countries;

(iii) the responses of emerging markets to the recent financial crises and the design of risk management models. Chapters are grouped into three parts. Part I proposes the general and integrated framework for risk management. Part II suggests suitable risk management applications for concrete cases. Part III discusses and sheds light on some future challenges, in terms of risk assessment and regulatory frameworks, facing risk managers, regulators, and policymakers.

Sabri Boubaker
Bonnie Buchanan
Duc Khuong Nguyen
Editors

Foreword

In the period immediately following the Global Financial Crisis (GFC) of 2007–2008, capital flows into emerging markets surged, as stock market investors chased returns of a staggering 79.02% in 2009 and 19.20% subsequently in 2010. Developed stock market returns during the same period, while certainly attractive at 30.78% and 12.34% respectively, seemed simply inadequate in comparison. The "risk-on" appetite of investors appeared insatiable in both equity and bond markets, with the latter seeing a significant narrowing in credit spreads. Since, then it has been quite a different story: emerging equity markets have declined approximately 18.23% in US dollar terms and much the same in local terms, while developed markets have risen more than 44.07%.[1]

The apparent weakness and subsequent underperformance of emerging versus developed stock and bond markets has become a common/frequent discussion point in the popular press. The obvious culprit was the withdrawal of excessive post-GFC stimulus and weaker demand internationally. Deflationary pressures persist now with the equally significant fall in the price of oil. Increased levels of financial market volatility appear to characterize all markets, with particular concern expressed over the worldwide impact of declines in the economic performance of China.

1. Based on analysis of MSCI indices returns. Please see: https://www.msci.com/resources/factsheets/index_fact_sheet/msci-world-index.pdf

It is in this broad context that the timely volume "Risk Management in Emerging Markets: Issues, Framework, and Modeling," edited by Sabri Boubaker, Bonnie Buchanan, and Duc Khuong Nguyen must be considered. The volume is broadly divided into three main parts with many excellent and carefully selected essays (chapters) contained within each that reflect the recent interest in managing risk — broadly defined — associated with investment in emerging markets. The first part consists of nine chapters that provide a framework for analyzing emerging market risk; the second consists of eleven chapters that address applications and case studies; while the third and final part contains four chapters that provide insights into mostly regulatory developments that are necessary to address the risk concerns addressed in earlier chapters, but with a particular focus on developments in banking markets. The contents of these chapters will now be briefly explained.

The first part begins with the analysis by Emawtee Bissoondoyal-Bheenick, Robert Brooks, Sirimon Treepongkaruna and Marvin Wee on realized exchange rate volatility and finds that increases in currency risks are associated with the variability of liquidity. Daniela M. Salvioni, Francesca Gennari and Luisa Bosetti then investigate the relationship between ethics, risks of compliance and find that a shared background of ethical principles is required to prevent the risk of compliance failure and limit the global risk exposure of a company. The chapter by Jan Novotný and Mayank Gupta then investigates the cross-sectional aspects of the dynamics of the valuation metrics across global stock markets including both developed and emerging markets, with their model providing early warning signs for asset mispricing in real time on a global scale and formation of asset bubbles.

This theme is then continued with a chapter by John R. Anchor and Hana Benešová that provides a new approach to political risk assessment in emerging markets, while Mariya Gubareva and Maria Rosa Borges reassess the economics of interest rate risk management in light of the global financial crisis by developing a derivative-based integrated treatment of interest rate and credit risk interrelation. Denis Davydov and Steve Swidler then undertake a forensic approach to audit the quality of accounting information reported by banks in emerging market countries, since the lack of financial standards and reporting transparency can ultimately lead to bank failures in many emerging nations. The chapter by Ehab Yamani identifies three crisis warning indicators driven from trading in emerging markets' carry trades, and determines if this allows the prediction of two major financial crises: The 1997–1998 Asian Crisis and the 2007–2008 GFC. The chapter by Mahfod Aldoseri and Andrew C. Worthington reviews the risks that Islamic financial institutions face in an emerging market context, including risk sharing in Islamic financing and Shari'ah (Islamic law) compliance. The final chapter in this part by Mazin A. M. Al Janabi then examines asset liquidity risk and obtains a Liquidity-Adjusted Value at Risk estimation for various equity portfolios.

The second part focuses on applications and provides insights from a series of case studies. The first chapter in this part is the work by Francesca Battaglia, Franco Fiordelisi and Ornella Ricci, who investigate enterprise risk management and bank performance in the context of Eastern Europe during the financial crisis. The next chapter by Haoshen Hu and Jörg Prokop assesses the market impact of credit rating changes in emerging stock markets by a group of six Chinese credit rating agencies and show that market reactions to rating signals are largely in line with observed behavior in Western stock markets.

The case study theme continues with Yajing Liu, Kenya Fujiwara, Toshiki Jinushi and Nobuyoshi Yamori investigating how relationship banking facilitates the management of funding risks in China, while Franco Parisi, Sherwood Clements and Edinson Cornejo assess risk management practice in the transitional economy of Chile. The study by Takashi Matsuki, Kimiko Sugimoto and Yushi Yoshida then considers the changing nature of regional integration and the implications for risk management of various African stock markets, while Zoltán Schepp and Mónika Mátrai-Pitz explore the interesting case of foreign currency borrowing in Hungary, which was used to fund housing loans. A. Can Inci then uses 5-minute (and 15-minute) intervals

Borsa Istanbul Stock Exchange data to undertake a microstructure analysis, while the final chapter in this part by Roland Füss, Dieter G. Kaiser and Felix Schindler determines whether diversification benefits accrue from adding emerging market hedge funds (EMHFs) to an emerging market bond/equity portfolio.

The final part in the volume "Looking Ahead" to expected developments, particularly with respect to banking markets. The first chapter in this part by Jocelyn Grira and Chiraz Labidi discusses the regulatory challenges that are faced by financial institutions in emerging countries, highlighting their idiosyncratic features compared with those in developed countries. The next chapter by Hanh Thi My Phan and Kevin Daly considers market concentration and bank competition in several emerging Asian countries and finds that there is generally a negative association between market concentration and bank competition. This is consistent with banks in concentrated markets colluding to generate higher profits. Alberto Burchi and Duccio Martelli then consider the possible unintended consequences of Basel III on emerging and developing economies and employ a Stressed Value at Risk (SVaR) to measure these effects. The final chapter in this volume is by Elmas Yaldõz Hanedar and Avni Önder Hanedar, who assess the financial constraints that small and medium size enterprises have experienced in emerging economies following the GFC demonstrating these effects are most significant on small- and medium-sized firms.

Overall, this excellent collection of essays provides key insights into the behavior of emerging financial markets and the risk associated with them.

Jonathan A. Batten

Part I
Framework

1

Realized Volatility of the Spread: An Analysis in the Foreign Exchange Market

Emawtee Bissoondoyal-Bheenick, Robert Brooks, Sirimon Treepongkaruna and Marvin Wee

Abstract

This chapter investigates the determinants of the volatility of spread in the over-the-counter foreign exchange market and examines whether the relationships differ in the crisis periods. We compute the measures for the volatility of liquidity by using bid-ask spread data sampled at a high frequency of five minutes. By examining 11 currencies over a 13-year sample period, we utilize a balanced dynamic panel regression to investigate whether the risk associated with the currencies quoted or trading activity affects the variability of liquidity provision in the FX market and examine whether the crisis periods have any effect. We find that both the level of spread and volatility of spread increases during the crisis periods for the currencies of emerging countries. In addition, we find increases in risks associated with the currencies proxied by realized volatility during the crisis periods. We also show risks associated with the currency are the major determinants of the variability of liquidity and that these relationships strengthen during periods of uncertainty. First, we develop measures to capture the variability of liquidity. Our measures to capture the variability of liquidity are non-parametric and model-free variable. Second, we contribute to the debate of whether variability of liquidity is adverse to market participants by examining what drives the variability of liquidity. Finally, we analyze seven crisis periods, allowing us to document the effect of the crises on determinants of variability of liquidity over time.

Keywords: Foreign exchange market; liquidity; realized volatility; realized skewness; bid-ask spreads; financial crisis

Introduction

The liquidity squeeze following the collapse of Lehman Brothers during the 2007–2008 Global Financial Crisis (GFC) adversely affected the global financial markets (Brunnermeier, 2009). The GFC highlighted the importance of liquidity and brought to our attention the risks associated with illiquidity in the financial markets. The foreign exchange (FX) market is the world's most liquid market where average daily turnover has grown from US$1.7 trillion in 1998 to US$3.98 trillion in April 2010 (Bank of International Settlements, 2010). As the FX market trades continuously and is connected globally, research has shown that contagion and spillover effects are of significant concerns to FX market participants (Fratzscher, 1998; Horen, Jager, & Klaassen, 2006). Given the concerns with the lack of liquidity during the recent crises such as the GFC and the size of the FX market, it is pertinent to examine the extent to which liquidity provision fluctuates and better understand the determinants of these fluctuations in the FX market. In this chapter, we investigate whether the risk associated with the currencies quoted (i.e., information) or trading activity affects the variability of liquidity provision in the FX market and examine whether the crisis periods have any effect on the relationships we document in the non-crisis periods.

In our analysis, the quoted bid-ask spread is used as a proxy for liquidity. The bid-ask spreads in the FX market determine the transaction and hedging costs and are important as they affect trade, the effectiveness of macroeconomic policy and represents real costs to the economy (Becker & Sy, 2006). Many prior studies (Bollerslev & Melvin, 1994; Glassman, 1987; Huang & Masulis, 1999; Koutmos & Martin, 2011) have examined the determinants of the bid-ask spread in the FX market. Most have found that spreads are related to their past values as well as the risk associated with the currencies that are quoted. The risk of a currency is often proxied, in prior studies, by the variance of the spot rate (Glassman, 1987) or the estimated conditional variance (Bollerslev & Melvin, 1994). While the bid-ask spread, itself, is an important cost to participants on the currency market, the variability of the bid-ask spread represents the availability of liquidity to the participants. For example, a sufficiently liquid currency pair with a modest spread on average may allow traders to more easily take or unwind their positions in that currency. However, the average spread does not indicate whether liquidity is consistently available to the traders. The proliferation of high frequency trading in recent years has drawn attention to the variability of liquidity where market participants have complained that liquidity seemingly vanishes when they place a large order against the quote. We argue that when the bid-ask spread is more variable, the participants encounters more risk when completing a round-trip transaction.

Although the variability of liquidity represents an aspect of risk that is important to market participants, only very few studies (Bollerslev & Melvin, 1994; Koutmos & Martin, 2011) have examined the volatility of liquidity (i.e., variability of the bid-ask spread). Koutmos and Martin (2011), a study closely related to ours, examine the effect of spread volatility on the level of the spread in a GARCH setting.[1] In our analysis, we develop new measures of the volatility of liquidity and explicitly examine the relationship between these measures and the determinants of the volatility of liquidity in the foreign exchange (FX) market. We also examine the relationships under stressed market conditions as prior research has documented changes to the dynamics of the currency bid-ask spreads during crisis periods such as the 1997 Asian crisis (Kallberg, Liu, & Pasquariello, 2005; Koutmos & Martin, 2011).

While there is only scant literature on the volatility of liquidity in the foreign exchange market, a number of studies have examined the volatility of liquidity and returns on the equities market. For example, Chordia, Subrahmanyam, and Anshuman (2001) conjecture that risk averse investors dislike variability in liquidity and thus demand higher expected returns for stocks with higher variability in liquidity. Contrary to their conjecture, Chordia et al. find that stocks with higher volatility of liquidity command lower expected returns. Hasbrouck (2009) argues that the findings are surprising and that it may be due to the use of turnover instead of the bid-ask spread as the proxy for liquidity.[2] In more recent work, Pereira and Zhang (2010) suggest that the effect of the volatility of liquidity on stock returns is not well understood and offers a model to explain the puzzling results in Chordia et al. (2001). Pereira and Zhang posit that higher liquidity volatility provides more opportunity for the investor to time her trades and thus leads to a lower required liquidity premium.

Given the limited research on what are the determinants of the volatility of liquidity in the FX markets, we seek to provide insight into this important research question. In particular, we extend the work (such as by Koutmos & Martin, 2011) that has previously

1. The volatility of spread is expressed as a function of lag terms of the errors and variance from the spread model and also of the time periods.

2. The comments on the findings from Chordia et al. (2001) appeared in the working paper, but not published, version of Hasbrouck (2009).

examined the volatility of liquidity in modeling of the effect of risk on the provision of liquidity. We do so by examining if factors that have been shown in prior studies to affect liquidity also affect the volatility of liquidity. Specifically, we are interested in the risk faced by the liquidity providers, that is, the currency dealers. The general level of risk associated with the exchange rate that currency dealers bear is proxied by the realized volatility and the down-side risk is proxied by the realized skewness of returns. In addition, we include trading activities measures such as the number of quotes posted and the number of quoters in the market as control variables in our model. These measures allow us to test whether periods with high volatility in liquidity are associated with greater levels of trading activity. While not directly examining the issue, the analysis allows some insight into whether currency pairs with higher levels of volatility in liquidity provide traders with more opportunities to time their trades.

Finally, we examine whether the relationship between the determinants and volatility of liquidity persist during the financial crises in our sample period. We posit that the relationship between the determinants and the volatility of liquidity may be different during the crisis and non-crisis periods. Understanding what causes the variability of liquidity and how volatility of liquidity behaves during the crisis versus non-crisis periods can assist policy makers or central bankers in making decisions regarding FX policies and central bank interventions.

We compute the measures for the volatility of liquidity by using bid-ask spread data sampled at a high frequency of five minutes. By examining 11 currencies over a 13-year sample period, we find that volatility of liquidity is positively associated with our measure of risk, that is, realized volatility. These findings suggest that not only does exchange rate risk affect the magnitude of the bid-ask spread as documented in prior studies, it also affects the volatility of the spread. In addition, we find liquidity suppliers adjust their spreads more frequently thus increasing the variability of liquidity when the exchange rate moves unfavorably, that is, measured by realized skewness.

After controlling for the effects of the financial crises, we find the effect of the risk measure (i.e., realized volatility) on the volatility of liquidity to be stronger than the trading activity proxies during non-crisis periods. During periods such as the Argentinean and Brazilian crises, the relationship between the realized volatility of the spread and the risk measures are much stronger suggesting a heightened awareness of the risks in the market place.

This chapter contributes to the existing literatures in several ways. First, we develop measures to capture the variability of liquidity. Our measures are non-parametric and model-free variable hence it does not rely on any assumptions like volatility measures derived from the GARCH-type models (Andersen, Bollerslev, Diebold, & Ebens, 2001). Second, we contribute to the debate of whether variability of liquidity is adverse to market participants by examining what drives the variability of liquidity. Finally, our sample covers seven crisis periods, allowing us to document the effect of the crises on determinants of variability of liquidity. In our analysis, we are able to examine the effect of each crisis separately as it is likely the effects and severity of each crisis on the currency markets differs.

The remainder of this chapter is organized as follows. The section "Literature Review and Propositions Development" provides a brief review of the literature on spread dynamics and develops our propositions. The section "Data and Methodology" describes the data and research design. The section "Empirical Results" discusses our findings and the section "Conclusion" concludes the chapter.

Literature Review and Propositions Development

There is a body of literature on the dynamics of the bid-ask spread in the FX markets. The seminal paper by Glassman (1987) develops a model of the exchange rate bid-ask spread and attributes the bid-ask spread to (1) the overhead costs of the transaction, (2) the profit to the market maker for the provision of liquidity, and (3) the compensation to the market maker for assuming an open position and facing the risk that the exchange rate will move unfavorably while the position is held. The third component in Glassman's (1987) model is most relevant to our analysis. She refers to this component as the risk component and finds the exchange rate volatility to be an important factor in explaining variations in the risk component of spreads over time.

Research that follows offers empirical and theoretical analyses of the determinants of the bid-ask spread. For example, Bollerslev and Melvin (1994) presents a simple asymmetric information model where the size of the bid-ask spread in the foreign exchange market is positively related to the underlying exchange rate uncertainty. Bollerslev and Melvin suggest the magnitude of the spread is unlikely to change in the presence of unambiguous "good" or "bad" news as both the bid and the ask prices should adjust in the same direction in response to reflect the particular news event. Using Deutschemark/dollar quotes and measuring exchange rate volatility as the conditional variance of the ask price estimated by a GARCH model, they find greater uncertainty regarding the future spot rate (proxied by the volatility measure) results in a widening of the spread.

In earlier studies that have examined the bid-ask spread, most assume that the variance of the spread is time invariant (Glassman, 1987). The study by Bollerslev and Melvin (1994) is an obvious exception where they model the variance of the spread as a function of the current conditional variance of the exchange rate and the lagged spread. More recently, Koutmos and Martin (2011) allow the variance of spread in their model to be conditionally heteroscedastic in their study of the dynamics of the currency bid-ask spread and the Asian crisis. In allowing the variance of the spread to be time variant, Koutmos and Martin were able to examine how the variance of the spread varies during the crisis and post-crisis periods. While not the main focus of their paper, the results on the volatility of the spreads reinforced the findings from examining spreads alone. The results show that volatility of the spreads decreased for developed markets such as Canada, Switzerland and the United Kingdom but increased for most emerging markets. Koutmos and Martin suggest that this finding is a reflection of the flight to quality where capital flowed from the Southeast Asian region to more developed countries.

While the papers above infer the effects of risk on the volatility of liquidity, none have examined the effects directly. We propose the hypothesis that the volatility of liquidity is affected by the risk of the exchange rate and also the down-side risk of the exchange rate. While dealers are likely to widen their spreads in the presence of market risk, they are also likely to revise their quotes more frequently. We also propose that the revisions will be more frequent and the spreads be more variable in the periods with heightened down-side volatility as the risk to the currency will be relatively higher. Following from the research by Koutmos and Martin, we propose the relationships between the volatility of the spread and its determinants will be stronger during the crisis periods as liquidity is likely to be withdrawn from the market and the dealer's provision of liquidity will be more sensitive to the risk associated with the currency.

Data and Methodology

The sample period includes a number of crises and the dates of the crises are presented in Table 1. While we acknowledge that there is no consensus in the literature as to the dating of a crisis, we use the dates adopted by prior studies such as Dungey, Fry, Martin, Tang, and González-Hermosillo (2010) and Fry, Hsiao, and Tang (2011). Fry et al. (2011) suggest defining the crisis periods based on some trigger events where the trigger event marks the beginning of the crisis, and where possible, an event or a policy reform marks the end of the crisis. We include the following crises in our analyses: Asia, Russian, Long Term Capital Management (LTCM), Brazilian, Dot-com, Argentinean and the Global Financial Crisis (GFC).

Similar to Yiu, Ho, and Choi (2010), we define the period July 2, 1997 to December 31, 1998 as the Asian crisis. In July 1997, the Thai Government stopped defending the value of the Thai Baht. This is followed by the Taiwanese decision to depreciate

Table 1: Crisis Period Dates.

Crisis	Start of Period	End of Period	Literature
Asia	July 2, 1997	December 31, 1998	Yiu et al. (2010)
Russia	August 17, 1998	December 31, 1998	Fry, Hsiao, and Tang (2011)
LTCM	September 23, 1998	October 15, 1998	
Brazil	January 7, 1999	February 25, 1999	
Dot-com	February 28, 2000	June 7, 2000	
Argentina	October 11, 2001	March 3, 2005	
GFC	July 26, 2007	December 31, 2010	

This table reports the start and end dates of the seven crises examined in this chapter. The data sources of these crises dates are also provided.

the Taiwanese dollar to increase the attractiveness of its export in October of the same year. The Taiwanese decision was met by large-scale attacks on the Asian currencies.

We define the other crisis periods using the triggers identified by Fry et al. (2011). The Russian crisis is dated based on the decision by the Russian government to defer bond repayments. The LTCM crisis is nested within the Russian crisis and is dated based on the decision by the Federal Reserve of New York to bail out LTCM. The end date of the LTCM crisis coincides with the inter-FOMC interest cut. The relatively short Brazilian crisis is dated based on the currency devaluation due to the loss of substantial foreign reserves and its end is triggered by a revised International Monetary Fund (IMF) program. The Dot-com crisis is identified based on the decline in the equity returns. The introduction of the partial deposit freeze and capital controls in Argentina is used to define the Argentinean crisis. The GFC is defined to have begun with the heightened risk aversion and falls in liquidity in the financial markets in July 2007. We examine the seven crisis periods collectively and in further analyses examine the effects of each crisis separately as the severity of the effects on the foreign currency markets are likely to differ (e.g., Russian, LTCM, Dot-com).

The dataset used in this chapter consists of the tick-by-tick bid-ask quotes for the following 11 currencies traded in the Over-the-Counter (OTC) market: Australian dollar (AUD), Canadian dollar (CAD), Swiss Franc (CHF), Euro (EUR), British Pound (GBP), Hong Kong dollar (HKD), Indonesian Rupiah (IDR), Japanese Yen (JPY), Korean Won (KRW), Singaporean dollar (SGD) and Thai Baht (THB). Our sample period is from January 1, 1996 to December 31, 2010 and the bid-ask quotes are extracted from the Thomson Reuters Tick History database provided by the Securities Industry Research Centre of Asia-Pacific (SIRCA). To account for the difference in the magnitude of the quotes across the currencies examined, we calculate the spread for each currency i relative to its midpoint:

$$s = \frac{2 \times (\text{ask}_i - \text{bid}_i)}{(\text{ask}_i + \text{bid}_i)} \tag{1}$$

where ask_i is the ask price in US dollars for currency i and bid_i is the bid price in US dollars for currency i.

In filtering the data, we exclude currency-day observations where there are fewer than 24 quotes for the day (i.e., less than a quote for each hour) to mitigate the effects of non-trading (i.e., public holidays). Similar to Boehmer, Saar, and Yu (2005), we exclude quotes with non-positive ask or bid prices, or where the bid price is higher than the ask. We eliminate a quote if the bid (ask) is greater (less) than 150 percent (50 percent) of the bid (ask) of the previous quote. In addition, we require that the difference between the bid and the ask be smaller than 25 percent of the quote midpoint.

Dependent Variable — Volatility of Liquidity

In prior studies that have examined the volatility of liquidity, the common approach is to model the spread (Koutmos & Martin, 2011) or the proportional change in the spread (Bollerslev & Domowitz, 1993) as a function of their lag values. The volatility of the spread is then measured by the variance of the error term from the spread model. However, the validity of such measures should be questioned as they are not model-free. Similar questions were raised in the modeling of the volatility of returns (Andersen et al., 2001). We propose a new measure, realized volatility of the spread, to proxy for the volatility of liquidity where the construction of this measure is similar to that of the measure of realized volatility developed by Andersen et al. (2001). For each currency, the realized volatility of the spread on day t is computed as follows.

$$\mathrm{RVS1}_t = \sum_{d=1}^{D} s_{d,t}^2 \tag{2}$$

where $s_{d,t}$ denotes the dth five-minute proportional bid-ask spread during day t and D denotes the total number of five-minute intervals during trading day t.[3]

In addition, due to concerns with the non-zero value for the average spread, we also use the daily standard deviation of the spread as an alternative proxy for the volatility of the spread:

$$\mathrm{RVS2}_t = \frac{\sum_{d=1}^{D}\left(s_{d,t}^2 - \bar{s}_t\right)}{D-1} \tag{3}$$

where $\bar{s}_t$ denotes the daily average of the proportional bid-ask spreads taken at five-minute intervals during day t.

Independent Variables

The two measures that are used to proxy for risk are realized volatility and realized skewness. Similar to Andersen et al. (2001), we compute these measures based on the five-minute returns series constructed from the logarithmic difference between the mid

3. Because the second order effects (i.e., serial correlations of intraday returns) are insignificant, realized volatility measure has been used successfully in the modeling of stock return volatility. However, spreads are typically more persistent than stock returns and as such, we run additional robustness test where we include serial correlations of intraday spread when calculating RVS1 (Du Toit & Conradie, 2006 for the detailed formulae). Our results are robust to whether we adjust for the serial correlation in RVS1.

quote recorded at or immediately before the corresponding five-minute mark. The mid quote, which is the midpoint quote between the bid and ask quote, is employed to minimize the effect of the bid-ask bounce (Roll, 1984). From the intraday return, we then construct the realized measures (our key independent variables). For each currency, the daily realized volatility is computed as proposed by Andersen, Bollerslev, Diebold, and Labys (2003):

$$\mathrm{RV}_t = \sum_{d=1}^{D} r_{d,t}^2 \tag{4}$$

where $r_{d,t}$ denotes the dth five-minute return during day t and D denotes the total number of five-minute return intervals during any trading day.

Following Chen, Hong, and Stein (2001) and Hutson, Kearney, and Lynch (2008), we also compute the daily realized skewness for day t as follows:

$$\mathrm{RSKW}_t = -\frac{D(D-1)^{3/2}\left(\sum_{d=1}^{D} r_{d,t}^3\right)}{(D-1)(D-2)\left(\sum_{d=1}^{D} r_{d,t}^2\right)^{3/2}} \tag{5}$$

This is the negative of the third moment of returns divided by the cubed standard deviation of returns to standardize for differences in variances. The negative sign is included to facilitate ease of interpretation — that is an increase in the daily skewness corresponds to a stock having a more left-skewed distribution (Chen et al., 2001). Therefore, this formula allows us to focus on the importance of the down-side risk in analyzing the volatility of liquidity.

In addition, we include the level of the spread, that is, daily average proportional bid ask spread (SPRD), in our model given previous evidence on the relationship between the size of the bid-ask spread and the underlying exchange rate uncertainty (Bollerslev & Melvin, 1994). Prior studies have examined the effects of order flow on the dynamics of spread on the FX market and have found trading activity to have a strong positive effect on the conditional variance of the spread process (Bollerslev & Domowitz, 1993).

The results from Bollerslev and Domowitz suggest that transaction costs on the FX market are more uncertain when market activity increases. Evans and Lyons (2002) were the first to augment the macroeconomic models with variables from the microstructure finance literature. They established a strong relationship between cumulative order flow and exchange rates. Order flow is defined as "the net of buyer-initiated and seller initiated orders" (Evans & Lyons, 2002, p. 171). In more recent work, McGroarty, ap Gwilym, and Thomas (2009) shows that, while generally at a low level, the bid-ask spreads on an electronic interdealer FX market varies with the flow of trading activity during the day. The spread is highest when the expected volume falls and is lowest when the expected volume increases. The research cited above suggests the importance in controlling for market activity in our modeling of the dynamics of the bid-ask spread.

We include the following control variables that are proxies for trading activity — specifically, number of quotes per day (QUOTE) and number of quoters per day (QUOTERS). The inclusion of these trading activities allows us to examine whether the variability of liquidity is associated with the number of unique banks providing quotes and the total number of quotes posted by the dealers. As our sample contains several crises, we also include dummy variables for the different crises periods as shown in Table 1. In order to control for the effects associated with the exchange regime such as the tight currency management by the Hong Kong currency board, the exchange rate regimes are classified into three categories based on Bubula and Ötker-Robe (2002), Koutmos and Martin (2011) and data provided by the IMF. Type 1 (TIGHT) regimes include, amongst others, the use of another currency as legal tender, currency union and/or the pegging of the currency to another currency or to a basket.[4] Type 2 includes the following systems: pegged within a horizontal band, forward-looking crawling band, backward-looking

4. Type 1 regime includes EUR during the period January 1, 1999–April 30, 2008, HKD during the period January 1, 1996–December 31, 2010 and THB during the period January 1, 1996–May 31, 1997. Type 2 regime includes IDR, KRW and SGD during the period January 1, 1996–May 31, 1997. All other currency periods fall under Type 3 regime.

crawling peg, backward-looking crawling band, tightly managed float. Type 3 (LOOSE) includes other managed floating and independently floating regimes.

Methodology

We begin by conducting both panel and individual unit root tests for all variables included in this chapter. Overall, we do not find unit root processes in our variables.[5] All variables in this chapter are I(0) and it is unlikely that we will encounter the problem of endogeneity in our dynamic panel regression.[6] We use a balanced dynamic panel regression model with the following specification in our analyses:

$$y_{it} = \alpha_{it} + \sum_{e=1}^{n} \beta_e X_{it,e} + u_{it} \tag{6}$$

where X is a matrix of realized volatility, realized skewness, and the other control variables discussed in the sections "Dependent Variable — Volatility of Liquidity" and "Independent Variables". We normalize the continuous variables for each currency by its mean and standard deviation to ensure comparability across currencies. Due to the inclusion of 11 currencies, we also include fixed effects to account for country-specific effects with our spread volatility measures.

Empirical Results

Descriptive Statistics

Table 2 reports the descriptive statistic for the 11 currencies classified into developed and emerging countries. The most liquid

5. For the sake of brevity, we do not report the results from the unit root tests. These results are available from the authors upon request.

6. Nevertheless, we conduct the Arellano and Bond (1991) dynamic panel regression as a robustness test. The results are qualitatively similar to our main findings and are available upon request.

Table 2: Descriptive Statistics for Individual Countries.

		RVS1	RVS2	RV	RSKW	SPRD	QUOTES	QUOTERS
Panel A: Developed Countries								
AUD	Mean	0.0170	0.0192	0.0096	–0.0236	0.0699	16,096	39
	Stdev	0.0179	0.0112	0.0631	1.2070	0.0254	19,785	9
CAD	Mean	0.0073	0.0155	0.0039	0.0897	0.0469	14,436	30
	Stdev	0.0033	0.0080	0.0047	1.2709	0.0092	15,934	7
CHF	Mean	0.0077	0.0145	0.0057	0.0154	0.0473	22,501	42
	Stdev	0.0047	0.0074	0.0052	1.4313	0.0148	22,513	14
EUR	Mean	0.0054	0.0159	0.0211	0.0121	0.0360	39,612	76
	Stdev	0.0075	0.0116	0.6464	1.5366	0.0156	23,005	28
GBP	Mean	0.0046	0.0114	0.0286	0.0000	0.0358	25,625	55
	Stdev	0.0032	0.0051	1.5233	1.2267	0.0132	23,060	16
HKD	Mean	0.0005	0.0054	0.0000	–0.0615	0.0102	2,959	23
	Stdev	0.0007	0.0039	0.0004	1.3392	0.0034	3,615	6
JPY	Mean	0.0073	0.0175	0.0061	0.0217	0.0453	31,175	67
	Stdev	0.0043	0.0051	0.0089	1.3665	0.0140	27,026	23
SGD	Mean	0.0166	0.0226	0.0035	–0.0095	0.0654	4,857	28
	Stdev	0.0212	0.0151	0.0126	1.2234	0.0293	6,427	11

Table 2: (*Continued*)

		RVS1	RVS2	RV	RSKW	SPRD	QUOTES	QUOTERS
Panel B: Emerging Countries								
IDR	Mean	2.4247	0.1879	0.1901	−0.2805	0.4160	252	19
	Stdev	11.2154	0.3148	1.3902	3.2937	0.7423	385	7
KRW	Mean	0.3175	0.1097	0.0202	0.0207	0.1650	4,266	6
	Stdev	1.7085	0.1849	0.1679	5.7757	0.1985	4,523	2
THB	Mean	0.2872	0.1042	0.5203	−0.0739	0.1861	264	30
	Stdev	0.7633	0.1400	2.0779	1.3700	0.1911	195	7

This table reports the average values (Mean) and standard deviations (Stdev) of daily realized volatility of spread (RVS1), standard deviation of spread (RVS2), realized volatility of return (RV), realized skewness of return (RSKW), daily average spread (SPRD), number of quotes per day (QUOTES), and number of quoters per day (QUOTERS). Panel A (B) presents the statistics for the developed (emerging) countries.

currency is EUR with an average of 39,612 quotes made per day with an average of 76 dealers providing quotes on the currency. The least liquid currency is IDR with an average of 252 quotes made per day with an average of 19 dealers providing quotes on the currency. In general, the currencies of the emerging countries (i.e., Indonesia, Korea, and Thailand) and Asian developed countries (i.e., Hong Kong and Singapore) have lower activity as shown by the less number of banks quoting the currency (QUOTERS) and less average number of quotes per day (QUOTES). The liquidity in the emerging countries are lower where average spread (SPRD) for the emerging countries ranging from 0.17 percent to 0.41 percent compared to the developed countries (of which Australia has the highest average spread of 0.07 percent). Similarly, the currencies of the emerging country are riskier with the risk measure (RV) being higher for the emerging countries than the developed countries. In addition, our measures of liquidity volatility (RVS1 and RVS2) are higher in the emerging countries with RVS1 ranging from 0.29 to 2.42 compared to the developed countries (of which Australia has the highest at 0.02).

Table 3 presents the difference in the liquidity volatility (RVS1 and RVS2) and risk measures (RV and RSKW) between crisis and non-crisis periods. Similar to Koutmos and Martin (2011), we find spread increases in the crisis periods for the emerging countries and also the Asian developed countries (i.e., Hong Kong and Singapore). In contrast, spreads drop significantly for the other developed countries. Koutmos and Martin (2011) describe this phenomenon as the "flight to quality" where market participants rebalance their portfolios to contain investments denominated in developed country currencies. We also find realized volatility (RV) increases significantly during the crises for eight of the 11 currencies. Untabulated results shows there are surprisingly more quotes during the crisis periods provided by a smaller number of quoters. The changes in liquidity volatility (RVS1 and RVS2) is similar to the changes in spread where significant increases are seen for the emerging countries and also the Asian developed countries (i.e., Hong Kong and Singapore).

Table 3: Comparison of Spread Variability and Risk Measures between Crisis and Non-Crisis Periods.

	ΔRVS1	ΔRVS2	ΔRV	ΔRSKW	ΔSPRD
Panel A: Developed Countries					
AUD	−0.002	−0.002[a]	0.007[a]	0.028	−0.004[a]
CAD	−0.001[a]	−0.001[a]	0.003[a]	−0.051	−0.001
CHF	−0.001[a]	0.002[a]	0.001[a]	0.047	−0.002
EUR	0.000	−0.001	0.001	0.039	−0.003[b]
GBP	−0.001[a]	−0.002[a]	−0.053	0.010	−0.004[a]
HKD	0.000[a]	0.001[a]	0.000[b]	−0.019	0.001[a]
JPY	−0.002[a]	−0.003[a]	0.002[a]	0.076	−0.005[a]
SGD	0.010[a]	0.008[a]	0.003[a]	0.023	0.014[a]
Panel B: Emerging Countries					
IDR	2.893[a]	0.048[a]	0.247[a]	−0.214[b]	0.188[a]
KRW	0.054	0.021[a]	0.017[a]	0.185	0.066[a]
THB	0.146[a]	0.020[a]	0.099	−0.076	0.065[a]

This table presents the difference in the daily realized volatility of spread (RVS1), standard deviation of spread (RVS2), realized volatility of return (RV), realized skewness of return (RSKW) between crisis and non-crisis periods. For example, $\Delta RVS1 = RVS1_{Crisis} - RVS1_{Non\text{-}crisis}$. Panels A and B presents the changes for the developed and emerging countries respectively.

[a]Indicates significance at one percent.

[b]Indicates significance at five percent.

Table 4 presents the correlation matrix of the variables. The two measures of volatility of the spread, RVS1 and RVS2, are highly correlated at 0.70 (0.79) during the crisis (non-crisis) periods. The high correlation suggests the concerns with the zero mean assumption in the computation of RVS may be unwarranted. The high correlation between the average spread (SPRD) and both RVS and RVS1 suggests currencies with a higher spreads are associated with greater uncertainty with respect to liquidity provision.

Table 4: Correlation Matrix for Balanced Sample.

	RVS1	RVS2	RV	RSKW	SPRD	QUOTES
Panel A: Crisis periods						
RVS2	0.701					
RV	0.427	0.451				
RSKW	−0.006	−0.011	−0.001			
SPRD	0.877	0.884	0.447	−0.010		
QUOTES	−0.059	−0.177	−0.065	0.010	−0.169	
QUOTERS	−0.044	−0.164	−0.035	0.014	−0.131	0.422
Panel B: Non-crisis periods						
RVS2	0.785					
RV	0.104	0.208				
RSKW	−0.058	−0.030	0.000			
SPRD	0.675	0.785	0.187	−0.027		
QUOTES	−0.072	−0.165	−0.033	0.018	−0.225	
QUOTERS	−0.086	−0.181	−0.022	0.013	−0.172	0.273

This table reports the correlation matrix of the daily realized volatility of spread (RVS1), standard deviation of spread (RVS2), realized volatility of return (RV), realized skewness of return (RSKW), daily average spread (SPRD), number of quotes per day (QUOTES) and number of quoters per day (QUOTERS). Panel A presents the matrix for the crisis periods and Panel B presents the matrix for the non-crisis periods.

Consistent with our expectations, the relationship between liquidity volatility, RVS1 and RVS2, and risk (RV) are heightened during the crisis periods with the correlation increasing from 0.10 and 0.21 to 0.42 and 0.45, respectively.

Dynamic Panel Regression Results

The results for the two models (Panels A and B) reported in Table 5 are from our panel regressions where the dependent

Table 5: Impact of Realized Volatility and Realized Skewness on Realized Volatility of Spread and Standard Deviation of Spread.

Variable	All Countries		Developed Countries		Emerging Countries	
	Coeff	*t*-stat	Coeff	*t*-stat	Coeff	*t*-stat
Panel A: Normalized RVS1 as dependent						
C	0.0362	(10.17)[a]	0.0291	(7.90)[a]	0.060	(7.16)[a]
RV	0.0493	(20.56)[a]	0.0319	(13.24)[a]	0.105	(16.34)[a]
RSKW	–0.0072	(–3.09)[a]	0.0001	(0.05)	–0.028	(–5.08)[a]
SPRD	0.8411	(295.32)[a]	0.8396	(275.81)[a]	0.879	(122.65)[a]
QUOTES	0.0183	(5.88)[a]	0.0128	(3.65)[a]	0.054	(8.38)[a]
QUOTERS	–0.0006	(–0.23)	–0.0055	(–1.91)	0.013	(2.26)[b]
ASIA	–0.0423	(–4.17)[a]	0.0684	(6.58)[a]	–0.402	(–15.79)[a]
ARGENTINA	–0.0797	(–12.66)[a]	–0.0955	(–14.42)[a]	0.019	(1.28)
BRAZIL	–0.1863	(–7.64)[a]	–0.0625	(–2.48)[b]	–0.488	(–8.58)[a]
Dot-com	–0.0416	(–2.45)[b]	–0.0451	(–2.58)[b]	0.028	(0.69)
GFC	–0.0501	(–6.79)[a]	–0.0633	(–8.02)[a]	–0.066	(–4.06)[a]

LTCM	0.0389	(1.04)	0.0659	(1.70)*	−0.023	(−0.27)
RUSSIA	−0.0750	(−4.18)[a]	−0.0137	(−0.73)	−0.215	(−5.21)[a]
TIGHT	−0.0095	(−2.14)[b]	0.0479	(7.79)[a]	−0.038	(−5.28)[a]
LOOSE	−0.0322	(−4.65)[a]	−0.1107	(−12.12)[a]	0.076	(6.69)[a]
Adj R^2	0.768		0.810		0.702	
n	41,024		30,289		10,735	
Panel B: Normalized RVS2 as dependent						
C	0.007	(1.30)	−0.001	(−0.21)	0.028	(3.36)[a]
RV	0.077	(20.84)[a]	0.031	(6.83)[a]	0.166	(28.91)[a]
RSKW	0.001	(0.34)	0.004	(0.84)	−0.005	(−0.99)
SPRD	0.660	(148.19)[a]	0.639	(112.82)[a]	0.767	(110.78)[a]
QUOTES	0.104	(21.21)[a]	0.175	(26.56)[a]	−0.030	(−4.79)[a]
QUOTERS	0.024	(5.78)[a]	0.058	(10.82)[a]	0.053	(9.22)[a]
ASIA	0.219	(13.79)[a]	0.280	(14.45)[a]	−0.114	(−4.64)[a]
ARGENTINA	−0.102	(−10.25)[a]	−0.052	(−4.15)[a]	−0.067	(−4.60)[a]
BRAZIL	−0.182	(−4.79)[a]	−0.099	(−2.11)[b]	−0.361	(−6.50)[a]

Table 5: (*Continued*)

Variable	All Countries		Developed Countries		Emerging Countries	
	Coeff	*t*-stat	Coeff	*t*-stat	Coeff	*t*-stat
Dot-com	–0.030	(–1.11)	0.069	(2.09)[b]	–0.122	(–3.11)[a]
GFC	–0.008	(–0.68)	–0.066	(–4.47)[a]	0.023	(1.44)
LTCM	0.078	(1.32)	0.182	(2.50)[b]	–0.119	(–1.38)
RUSSIA	–0.014	(–0.48)	0.013	(0.37)	0.098	(2.42)[b]
TIGHT	–0.030	(–4.32)[a]	0.008	(0.69)	–0.030	(–4.37)[a]
LOOSE	–0.006	(–0.51)	–0.137	(–8.00)[a]	0.110	(10.00)[a]
Adj R^2	0.467		0.408		0.698	
n	41,611		30,477		11,134	

This table reports the results from the dynamic panel regression, estimated using Generalized Method of Moments. The sample period is from January 1, 1996 to December 31, 2010. The dependent variables are the daily realized volatility of spread (RVS1) in Panel A and the daily standard deviation of spread (RVS2) in Panel B. The independent variables are realized volatility of return (RV), realized skewness of return (RSKW), daily average spread (SPRD), number of quote per day (QUOTES), and number of quoters per day (QUOTERS). The continuous variables are normalized to ensure comparability across different currencies. The dummy crisis variables (the periods are defined in Table 1) are included and so are the dummy variables indicating the tight and loose foreign policy regime. The models are presented for (1) all 11 countries, (2) the developed countries and (3) the emerging countries.

[a]Indicates significance at one percent.

[b]Indicates significance at five percent.

variables are the realized volatility of the bid-ask spread (RVS1) and standard deviation of the spread (RVS2). We also run the models separately for the developed and emerging countries. The model specification seems to fit well with the Adjusted R^2 of 47 percent and 81 percent. The results (Panel A) for the model using RVS1 as the dependent variable indicate a positive relation between the realized volatility of spread and our proxy for risk, that is, realized volatility (RV). Consistent with our expectations, currency dealers are more cautious of the risk of holding a position during volatile periods, hence the bid and ask quotes are adjusted more frequently and this causes more variability in the spread. However, we do not find the volatility of liquidity to be higher during periods associated with higher down-side risk. The results (RSKW = –0.007) suggests dealers adjust their quotes less frequently when the market is declining compared to when the market is rallying. This negative relationship is driven by the emerging countries and not the developed countries and could be explained by the general withdrawal of liquidity from the emerging countries.

The realized volatility of spread also has a positive relationship with all the control variables except for number of quoters (QUOTERS). The daily average spread (SPRD) has a positive relationship with the volatility of the spread. Again, as dealers increase their bid-ask spread when they are uncertain about the direction of the market and to avoid being hit, this has the effect of increasing the volatility in the spread.

The numbers of quotes per day (QUOTES) has a positive relationship with the volatility of liquidity and a standard deviation increase in the number of quotes increases RVS1 by 0.018. This is compared to the effects of the risk variable where a standard deviation increase in RV increases RVS1 by 0.49. The results suggest the risk associated with the currency plays an economically significant role in determining the variability of the spread and not the trading activity.

The variables for the exchange regime (TIGHT and LOOSE) shows the countries with tight (Type 1) and loose (Type 3) regimes have lower liquidity volatility compared to Type 2 regimes.

The results (for all countries and developed countries) are counter-intuitive and may be associated with the classification of the regimes as they are not necessarily classified with respect to the US dollar (Koutmos & Martin, 2011). The dummy variables (TIGHT and LOOSE) document the expected relationship for the emerging countries and are likely due to the variables capturing the tight monetary control exerted by the Hong Kong currency board.

With regard to the crises, the negative coefficients on most of the dummy variables indicate a decline in the liquidity volatility during the crisis periods. The results from the sub-sample analysis indicate (consistent with the results from Table 2) the decline is mostly in the developed countries and not the emerging countries.

The results for the dynamic panel regression (Panel B) using RVS2 as the independent variable are similar for most of the independent variables (all countries sample). With regard to the two risk measures, they are in the predicted direction but the realized skewness variable is not statistically significant. The coefficients on the crisis dummy variables are negative except for the Asian crisis and are significant for three of the seven crisis periods.

Augmented Dynamic Panel Regression Results

Given the significance of many of our crisis dummy variables in Panel A of Table 5, we further investigate the impact of financial turmoil and exchange regime on the determinants of volatility of liquidity. Table 6 reports the dynamic panel regression results with an augmented model that includes interaction terms of the crisis dummy variables on all independent variables. The augmented model allows us to examine the relationship during the crisis versus non-crisis periods and also for countries under tight and loose exchange regimes. Our model specification (see Panel A of Table 6) using the RVS1 as the independent variable appears to work well with the Adjusted R^2 of 79.3 percent.

Overall, we find the variable RVS1 has significant and positive relationships with RV, and SPRD during the non-crisis periods. These results are similar to our findings in Table 5 in that we find that higher risks associated with the currency (proxied by our realized returns measure) during non-crisis periods are associated with the dealers' propensity to adjust their positions and vary the liquidity they provide to the market. Also, similar to the findings shown in Table 5, the relationship between RV and the trading activities proxy (QUOTES) is positive and statistically significant during the non-crisis periods.

In addition, we find the dummy variables for the crisis periods are negative and significant. Similar to the results reported in Table 5, we find that TIGHT and LOOSE dummy variables do not document the expected relationship. That is liquidity volatility is higher in a tight (Type 1) regime and lower in a loose (Type 3) regime.

Panel A of Table 6 also reports the coefficients on the interaction terms of the crisis dummy variables on all independent variables, along with the two joint tests of (1) the significance of the crisis variables and exchange regime on each independent variable (*F*-statistics reported in the last column of the table) and (2) the significance of each crisis and exchange regime variable on all independent variables (*F*-statistics reported in the third last row of the panel). Overall, results indicate that each included crisis dummy variables jointly impact all independent variables except for LTCM. All included crisis variables also jointly impact all independent variables.

More pertinently, in examining the impact of financial turmoil on the relationship between RVS1 and RV, we find the relationship strengthens during the Argentinean and Brazilian crisis periods. In contrast, the relationship weakens between the RVS1 and RV during the Dot-com and GFC and Russian crisis periods. Anecdotal evidence suggests the Argentinean and Brazilian crises affected the currency markets more so than, for example, the Dot-com crisis. As expected, we find the relationship between RVS1 and RV weakens during the tight (Type 1) exchange regimes but we do not find significant changes during the loose (Type 3) exchange regimes.

The effects of down-side risk on the volatility of spread are not significantly different in most of the crisis periods other than during the GFC and the Asian crisis. The interaction term RSKW*ASIA (RSKW*GFC) has a negative (positive) and significant coefficient at the one percent significance level. The generally weaker effect of the crises on the RVS1 and RSKW relationship compared to the effect of the crises on the relationship between RVS1 and RV may be explained by the generally weak relationship between down-side risk and spread volatility (Tables 5 and 6).

The relationship between RVS1 and SPRD is weakened during the crisis periods (negative and significant for ARGENTINA, Dot-com and GFC). The results are surprising given the increase in the correlation between RVS1 and SPRD during the crisis periods shown in Table 5. The *F*-statistic shows the crisis periods and the exchange regimes are jointly significant in their effects on the relationship between QUOTES and RVS1 and also between QUOTERS and RVS1. In general, the crisis weakens the positive relationship between spread volatility and the number of quotes. In contrast, the relationship between the number of quoters and spread volatility is strengthened, albeit only three of the four interaction terms are significant. Overall, the results suggest the frequency at which quotes are placed and the number of quoters in the market plays a less important role in affecting the volatility of the spread observed during the crisis periods.

The results of the augmented model using RVS2 as the independent variable is presented in Panel B of Table 6. The main results are similar to those shown in Panel A in that the crisis periods are found to affect the relationship between RV and RVS2 (*F*-statistic = 72.9). Similar to the results presented in Table 6 Panel A, the relationship is significantly stronger during the Argentinean and Brazilian crises.

In general, our augmented dynamic panel regression results are consistent with the findings that risk-based factors and trading activities factors are drivers of the variability of liquidity. This relationship between the liquidity volatility and the risk-based factors strengthens during some crises such as the Argentinean and Brazilian crises.

The sample period in our chapter does not cover the recent events associated with the Eurozone crisis. However it is worth

Table 6: Impact of Financial Turmoil and Exchange Regime on the Relation between Realized Measures and the Volatility of Liquidity.

Variable	Coeff	*t*-stat	Change due to									
			TIGHT	LOOSE	ASIA	ARGENTINA	BRAZIL	Dot-com	GFC	LTCM	RUSSIA	*F*-stat
Panel A: RVS1 as dependent												
C	0.031	(8.75)[a]										
RV	0.049	(10.07)[a]	−0.018[a]	0.005	0.003	0.209[a]	0.119[a]	−0.084[b]	−0.058[a]	0.014	−0.037[a]	85.36[a]
RSKW	−0.011	(−3.02)[a]	−0.012[b]	−0.003	−0.025[a]	0.004	−0.003	0.004	0.018[a]	0.055	0.019	3.42[a]
SPRD	0.869	(194.68)[a]	0.110[a]	−0.076[a]	0.159[a]	−0.248[a]	0.068	−0.105[a]	−0.182[a]	0.018	0.014	418.42[a]
QUOTES	0.034	(8.25)[a]	0.111[a]	0.030[b]	−0.823[a]	−0.110[a]	−0.508[a]	−0.153[b]	−0.081[a]	−0.233	−0.203[a]	142.84[a]
QUOTERS	−0.005	(−1.54)	−0.005	−0.026[a]	0.125[a]	0.054[a]	0.005	−0.055[b]	0.047[a]	0.041	0.037	35.16[a]
ASIA	−1.046	(−31.98)[a]										
ARGENTINA	−0.086	(−11.21)[a]										
BRAZIL	−0.666	(−8.46)[a]										
Dot-com	−0.063	(−1.21)										
GFC	−0.036	(−3.35)[a]										
LTCM	−0.200	(−1.35)										
RUSSIA	−0.240	(−3.40)[a]										

Table 6: (*Continued*)

Variable	Coeff	*t*-stat	Change due to									
			TIGHT	LOOSE	ASIA	ARGENTINA	BRAZIL	Dot-com	GFC	LTCM	RUSSIA	*F*-stat
TIGHT	0.093	(9.61)[a]										
LOOSE	−0.001	(−0.05)										
F-stat			72.34[a]	21.76[a]	220.61[a]	286.52[a]	15.20[a]	5.69[a]	101.92[a]	1.15	3.86[a]	
Adj R^2	0.793											
n	41,024											
Panel B: RVS2 as dependent												
C	0.019	(3.29)[a]										
RV	0.187	(24.13)[a]	0.022[b]	−0.021	−0.167[a]	0.095[a]	0.346[a]	0.250[a]	−0.196[a]	−0.002	0.034	72.90[a]
RSKW	−0.007	(−1.17)	−0.005	0.005	0.030[b]	−0.002	−0.055	0.010	0.017	0.060	−0.020	1.31
SPRD	0.616	(86.26)[a]	−0.044[a]	−0.136[a]	−0.064[a]	−0.047[a]	−0.314[a]	−0.235[a]	0.345[a]	0.198[a]	0.239[a]	132.54[a]
QUOTES	0.112	(16.76)[a]	−0.144[a]	−0.151[a]	0.290[a]	−0.098[a]	−0.022	−0.623[a]	−0.016	−0.067	0.511[a]	24.57[a]
QUOTERS	0.055	(9.80)[a]	0.114[a]	0.206[a]	−0.097[a]	0.129[a]	0.058	0.022	0.000	−0.014	−0.112[a]	74.68[a]
ASIA	0.597	(11.41)[a]										
ARGENTINA	−0.047	(−3.85)[a]										

BRAZIL	−0.050	(−0.40)									
Dot-com	−0.365	(−4.39)[a]									
GFC	0.185	(10.64)[a]									
LTCM	−0.244	(−1.03)									
RUSSIA	0.074	(0.66)									
TIGHT	−0.145	(−9.42)[a]									
LOOSE	−0.161	(−8.10)[a]									
F-stat			69.67[a]	139.23[a]	36.80[a]	26.25[a]	12.48[a]	25.36[a]	210.15[a]	2.48[a]	22.28[a]
Adj R^2	0.500										
n	41,024										

This table reports the results from the dynamic panel regression, estimated using Generalized Method of Moments. The sample period is from January 1, 1996 to December 31, 2010. The dependent variables are the daily realized volatility of spread (RVS1) in Panel A and the daily standard deviation of spread (RVS2) in Panel B. The independent variables are realized volatility of return (RV), realized skewness of return (RSKW), daily average spread (SPRD), number of quote per day (QUOTES), and number of quoters per day (QUOTERS). The continuous variables are normalized to ensure comparability across different currencies. The dummy crisis variables (the periods are defined in Table 1) are included and so are the dummy variables indicating the tight and loose foreign policy regime. The dummy variables are interacted with the continuous variables to examine the interaction effect. For the sake of brevity, the *t*-statistics for the interaction terms are not reported.

[a]Indicates significance at one percent.

[b]Indicates significance at five percent.

discussing some of the recent literature on how both the Global Financial crisis and Eurozone crisis have impacted the foreign exchange markets and how this relates to our chapter. Both Melvin and Taylor (2009) and Banti, Phylaktis, and Sarno (2012) provide an analysis of how the global financial crisis impacted foreign exchange markets. Both studies show that spreads widened as market makers provided greater liquidity to the market in response to the increased risk and volatility and also show that spreads widened significantly after the Lehman collapse. In addition they both also find that the spreads became much more volatile. De Bock and de Carvalho Filho (2015) provide an extended analysis of foreign currency markets during so called "risk-off" periods which are termed as periods when risk aversion levels change and many traders seek to synchronously alter their specific currency exposures. De Bock and de Carvalho Filho (2015) find that post the Lehman collapse and the onset of problems in Greece that investors are more likely to take on currency positions creating greater volatility and liquidity exposure. King, Osler, and Rime (2013) provide a survey paper on the operation of market microstructure in the foreign exchange market identifying a positive relationship between volume and volatility due to private information effects. King et al. (2013) find a widening of spreads and increased volatility is characteristic of the behavior around previous crisis events and based on their review the findings of Melvin and Taylor (2009), Banti et al. (2012) and De Bock and de Carvalho Filho (2015) are consistent with this behavior for more recent crisis events. These findings are also consistent with the key findings of our empirical research.

Conclusion

While the liquidity in the foreign exchange market has been widely examined in prior research, the volatility of liquidity has undeservedly attracted less attention. The important role of liquidity risk in the recent GFC and the size and uniqueness of the FX market motivated us to examine the role played by liquidity in the FX market. The existing literature on volatility of liquidity on stock returns does not provide insight into whether the variability of liquidity is a function of the risk associated with the underlying currencies or the trading activity that is associated with the currencies. Hence, this chapter investigates what drives variability of liquidity in the FX market and whether the crisis periods have any impact on these drivers of variability of liquidity.

We find that the volatility of liquidity proxied by our measures, RVS1 and RVS2, is associated with the general level of risk proxied by realized volatility. The association between the volatility of liquidity and realized volatility is strengthened during some crisis periods in our sample period. In contrast, the relationship between trading activity and volatility of liquidity weakens during the crisis periods. Our findings are important to policy makers, central bankers and investors as it suggests that drivers of variability of liquidity are risk. Policy makers or central bankers may wish to take into consideration the effects of liquidity risk when setting foreign exchange policy or attempting to intervene in the market.

References

Andersen, T. G., Bollerslev, T., Diebold, F. X., & Ebens, H. (2001). The distribution of realized stock return volatility. *Journal of Financial Economics, 61*(1), 43–76.

Andersen, T. G., Bollerslev, T., Diebold, F. X., & Labys, P. (2003). Modeling and forecasting realized volatility. *Econometrica, 71*(2), 579–625.

Arellano, M., & Bond, S. (1991). Some tests of specification for panel data: Monte Carlo evidence and an application to employment equations. *The Review of Economic Studies, 58*(2), 277–297.

Bank of International Settlements. (2010). *Triennial Central Bank Survey.* Report on global foreign exchange market activity.

Banti, C., Phylaktis, K., & Sarno, L. (2012). Global liquidity risk in the foreign exchange market. *Journal of International Money and Finance, 31*(2), 267–291.

Becker, T., & Sy, A. (2006). Were bid-ask spreads in the FX market excessive during the Asian crisis? *International Review of Financial Analysis, 15*(4–5), 434–449.

Boehmer, E., Saar, G., & Yu, L. (2005). Lifting the Veil: An analysis of pre-trade transparency at the NYSE. *The Journal of Finance, 60*(2), 783–815.

Bollerslev, T., & Domowitz, I. (1993). Trading patterns and prices in the interbank foreign exchange market. *The Journal of Finance, 48*(4), 1421–1443.

Bollerslev, T., & Melvin, M. (1994). Bid-ask spreads and volatility in the foreign exchange market. An empirical analysis. *Journal of International Economics, 36*(3–4), 355–372.

Brunnermeier, M. K. (2009). Deciphering the liquidity and credit crunch 2007–2008. *Journal of Economic Perspectives, 23*(1), 77–100.

Bubula, A., & Ötker-Robe, I. (2002). *The evolution of exchange rate regimes since 1990: Evidence from de facto policies (EPub).* IMF Working Papers No. 02/155. International Monetary Fund.

Chen, J., Hong, H., & Stein, J. C. (2001). Forecasting crashes: Trading volume, past returns, and conditional skewness in stock prices. *Journal of Financial Economics, 61*(3), 345–381.

Chordia, T., Subrahmanyam, A., & Anshuman, V. R. (2001). Trading activity and expected stock returns. *Journal of Financial Economics, 59*(1), 3–32.

De Bock, R., & de Carvalho Filho, I. (2015). The behavior of currencies during risk-off episodes. *Journal of International Money and Finance, 53*(0), 218–234.

Du Toit, C., & Conradie, W. (2006). A realised volatility measurement using quadratic variation and dealing with microstructure effects. Paper presented at the Journal Article.

Dungey, M., Fry, R., Martin, V. L., Tang, C., & González-Hermosillo, B. (2010). *Are financial crises alike?* IMF Working Papers No. 10/14.

Evans, M. D. D., & Lyons, R. K. (2002). Order flow and exchange rate dynamics. *The Journal of Political Economy, 110*(1), 170–180.

Fratzscher, M. (1998). Why are currency crises contagious? A comparison of the Latin American crisis of 1994–1995 and the Asian crisis of 1997–1998. *Weltwirtschaftliches Archiv, 134*(4), 664–691.

Fry, R., Hsiao, Y. L., & Tang, C. (2011). *Actually this time is different centre for applied macroeconomic analysis.* Working Paper No. 12. The Australian National University.

Glassman, D. (1987). Exchange rate risk and transactions costs: Evidence from bid-ask spreads. *Journal of International Money and Finance, 6*(4), 479–490.

Hasbrouck, J. (2009). Trading costs and returns for U.S. equities: Estimating effective costs from daily data. *The Journal of Finance, 64*(3), 1445–1477.

Horen, N.v., Jager, H., & Klaassen, F. (2006). Foreign exchange market contagion in the Asian crisis: A regression-based approach. *Review of World Economics/Weltwirtschaftliches Archiv*, *142*(2), 374–401.
Huang, R., & Masulis, R. (1999). FX spreads and dealer competition across the 24-hour trading day. *Review of Financial Studies*, *12*(1), 61–93.
Hutson, E., Kearney, C., & Lynch, M. (2008). Volume and skewness in international equity markets. *Journal of Banking and Finance*, *32*(7), 1255–1268.
Kallberg, J. G., Liu, C. H., & Pasquariello, P. (2005). An examination of the Asian crisis: Regime shifts in currency and equity markets. *The Journal of Business*, *78*(1), 169–211.
King, M. R., Osler, C. L., & Rime, D. (2013). The market microstructure approach to foreign exchange: Looking back and looking forward. *Journal of International Money and Finance*, *38*(0), 95–119.
Koutmos, G., & Martin, A. D. (2011). Currency bid-ask spread dynamics and the Asian crisis: Evidence across currency regimes. *Journal of International Money and Finance*, *30*(1), 62–73.
McGroarty, F., ap Gwilym, O., & Thomas, S. (2009). The role of private information in return volatility, bid-ask spreads and price levels in the foreign exchange market. *Journal of International Financial Markets, Institutions and Money*, *19*(2), 387–401.
Melvin, M., & Taylor, M. P. (2009). The crisis in the foreign exchange market. *Journal of International Money and Finance*, *28*(8), 1317–1330.
Pereira, J. P., & Zhang, H. H. (2010). Stock returns and the volatility of liquidity. *Journal of Financial and Quantitative Analysis*, *45*(04), 1077–1110.
Roll, R. (1984). A simple implicit measure of the effective bid-ask spread in an efficient market. *The Journal of Finance*, *39*(4), 1127–1139.
Yiu, M. S., Ho, A. W.-Y., & Choi, D. F. (2010). Dynamic correlation analysis of financial contagion in Asian markets in global financial turmoil. *Applied Financial Economics*, *20*(4), 345–354.

2

Global Responsibility and Risks of Compliance Failure in Emerging Markets

Daniela M. Salvioni, Francesca Gennari and Luisa Bosetti

Abstract

The aim of this chapter is to investigate the relationship between ethics, risks of compliance failure and strategic value of global responsibility for BRICS companies. The first part of the chapter adopts a theoretical approach: it introduces and analyzes the key role of compliance risk management for sustainable and successful development of companies. The second part of the chapter uses an empirical approach, based on the case study method. The chapter focuses on the BRICS. The chapter demonstrates that mere formal compliance with laws, recommendations, and internal codes is not sufficient for companies that want to be responsible and attract stakeholders' consent and resources. A shared background of ethical principles is required for a proper understanding of the rules, in order to prevent the risk of compliance failure and limit the global risk exposure of a company. Due to the business perspective adopted in the research, this chapter leaves out the sociological aspects regarding how to create, spread, and strengthen the culture of compliance within a company. The chapter encourages companies to connect ethical principles and compliance with the rules. Indeed, a lack of ethics in business operations, obscured by formal compliance, often results in indirect negative impacts on stakeholder relationships, so it is only a futile attempt to act responsibly. The originality of the chapter consists in suggesting the adoption of a responsibility-oriented approach for compliance risk management.

Keywords: Corporate governance; sustainability; corporate culture; risk of compliance failure; integrated risk management; BRICS

Introduction

Company competitiveness in globalized markets benefits from a clear focus on sustainable growth as the basis for risk minimization, and from the adoption of a proactive risk management model. This model requires a broad approach, intended for considering the impact of all types of risks (preventable, strategy, and external risks); however, it can only be really effective when ethical principles and values are clearly defined and an appropriate compliance control exists.

The corporate orientation toward global responsibility emphasizes compliance control as a prerequisite for the effectiveness of the entire risk management system. This situation is crucially important for the companies of emerging markets, which can attract international investors by complying with high and internationally recognized standards of corporate governance. In particular, compliance with the rules should not be intended only in the short term, but it should be a premise to a shared risk culture and the basis for managing any kind of corporate responsibility-related risks.

Our study is positioned in the literature that goes beyond the traditional notion of compliance. Compliance has long been considered a system of formal structures and processes that a company implements to oversee the risk of violating laws, regulations, and internal codes. A new approach has also emphasized the ethical aspects of observing the rules (Clarke, 1995; Milroy, 1992; Murphy, 2004; Rowe & Cadzow, 2014; Verschoor, 2006; Weber & Wasieleski, 2012). Successful corporate compliance in the long term should be based on a real culture of compliance linked to ethical core values. Implementing a high number of rules is not a guarantee of effective risk minimization and a company's success in the long run. Organizational culture is the real determinant of behavior in companies; moreover, it is the basis for the development of a culture of compliance which goes beyond the declared rules and guides the conduct of the individual.

The frequent and recent cases of irresponsible corporate behavior demonstrate that in companies lacking a real culture of compliance, formal and structured compliance processes can only reduce the risks in the short term. This is particularly true for the BRICS (Brazil, Russia, India, China, and South Africa), which have often emulated corporate governance standards developed in other countries, under increasing pressure to attract foreign investment and sustain their GDP.

Long-term value creation and sustainable development require that formal corporate structures, such as a compliance function and chief officer, be the visible side of a spread culture of compliance. This culture should be based on the core values of the company and its individuals, inspired by ethics and honesty.

Despite the limitation related to the lack of sociological considerations (e.g., the way leaders can spread a culture of compliance in their organizations), our research contributes to the existing studies. It highlights the vulnerability of well-structured risk management compliance functions when compliance is considered simply as a way of observing rules and not as a way of life in the organization. The case studies reported in this chapter encourage companies to invest in their organizational culture. This is necessary to create and boost a set of core values that influence individual behaviors and improve the effectiveness of internal control procedures (Ahrens & Khalifa, 2015).

In light of the above, the chapter is structured as set out below.

The second section illustrates the role of compliance risk management for corporate development and underlines the importance of a culture of compliance in creating sustainable value over time. Compliance with the rules is the basic condition for minimizing corporate risks; however, it is not enough to sustain all stakeholders' expectations in the long run: there must be a culture of compliance recognized at individual level.

The third section introduces the causes of compliance failure risks in the BRICS, in relation to the ambition to quickly narrow the corporate governance gap with old industrialized economies. Although high quality corporate governance standards can be adopted in a relatively short amount of time, the reinforcement of a culture of compliance matures gradually and in a different way in every organization.

The fourth section summarizes the key elements of internal control and risk management in the BRICS. According to the international best practices for listed companies, each of the five countries has promoted a reform of corporate governance involving different positions and processes. The board of directors plays a leading role in risk monitoring, while specific bodies and officers implement risk management procedures across the organization.

The fifth section describes five selected cases of compliance failure in BRICS companies. The investigation provided evidence about the existence of formal compliance with the laws, recommendations and internal regulations. However, the unethical and irresponsible conduct exposed proved that the companies lacked a genuine culture of compliance.

The chapter's last section contains our final considerations on the relationship between corporate responsibility, risk management, culture of compliance, and corporate effectiveness.

Global Responsibility and Compliance Risk

Corporate debacles and the global financial and economic meltdown over the last two decades were often described as crises of corporate governance systems. All over the world these crises inspired reforms that were primarily focused on risk management. The gradual fall of space and time barriers to the circulation of information, goods and capital due to globalization caused more wide-scale confrontation between old industrialized and emerging countries (Brondoni, 2009; Salvioni, 2005; Salvioni, Bosetti, & Almici, 2013; Salvioni, Gennari, Bosetti, & Almici, 2015). This situation induced companies to make continuous, fast changes that needed to be addressed with a clear and concrete perception and management of all possible risks.

Over time, companies started to recognize the value of interacting with all major stakeholders (stakeholder relations management), by adopting a broader concept of responsibility based on the connection between economic, social, and environmental goals (Carroll, 2004; Freeman, 2010; Galbreath, 2006; Kanji & Chopra, 2010; Porter & Kramer, 2006; Salvioni & Bosetti, 2014; Salvioni & Gennari, 2014). This change took place slowly and in different ways in various countries and involved amendments to the corporate governance approach.

In the global context, achievement of successful conditions in terms of competitive advantage, economic results and social and environmental outcomes, depends on the adoption, maintenance and strengthening of governance systems. These should comply with international best practices and enable management of both the complexity of the business and the major conditions for sustainable development (Eccles, Ioannou, & Serafeim, 2011; Perrini & Vurro, 2010).

The challenges posed by the global economy for corporations, in terms of risks related to the environment, trade, internal processes and reliability of information, prompted the emergence of a risk management-oriented governance approach in the interest of all stakeholders (Boubaker & Nguyen, 2015; Kaplan & Mikes, 2012; Salvioni, 2012). Risks are indeed better managed and the ability to limit negative effects is greater in companies that support their own path of sustainable development with appropriate internal control systems.

The origin of corporate risk management is frequently connected with a partial approach focused on key variables for the maintenance of development conditions. In this sense, many companies in the past used to associate risk management with compliance control, and would adopt a "silos-by-silos" approach, that is, risks were managed separately in each autonomous unit, without coordination. However, such behavior made firms vulnerable to strategy execution and external risks. Neither rules-based compliance nor functional risk silos helped companies avoid disasters such as the global financial crisis or environmental catastrophes (e.g., the BP Deepwater Horizon rig explosion) (Mikes & Kaplan, 2014).

The evolution of the competitive environment, however, has provoked progressive development of a proactive and integrated approach to risk management. This is in accordance with the changes in the corporate key factors connected to the economic, social, and competitive dimensions (Gandini, Gennari, & Cassano, 2014). Indeed, the acceptance of a global concept of responsibility must include the legal, economic, social and environmental commitment areas and implies an integrated approach to risk management (Figure 1).

However, the legal aspects must be emphasized: legal responsibility is the basis of the entire system of corporate responsibility.

An advanced concept of risk management should focus on a number of variables that a company has to monitor, the correct composition of which affects the ability to create value for stakeholders. In other words, the correct setting of a corporate governance system requires observation of the individual dimensions of

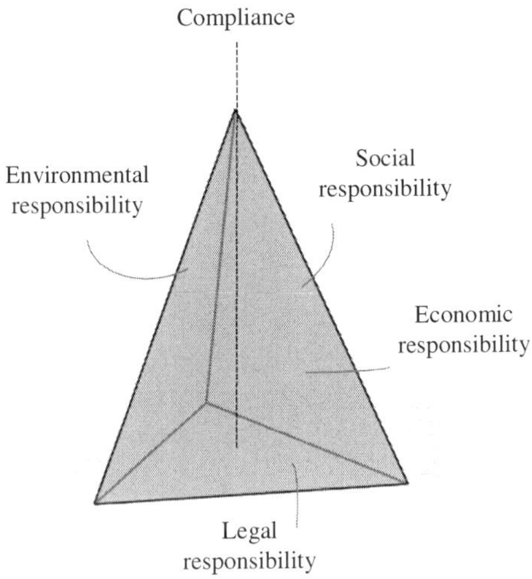

Figure 1: The Dimensions of Corporate Responsibility. *Notes*: The system of corporate responsibility is composed of legal responsibility, which is the basis for operating in a legal area; economic responsibility, which guarantees the business's autonomy by balancing economic and financial values; environmental and social responsibilities toward the environment and the community. Compliance can be considered as a cross element that assures correct corporate behavior respecting the stakeholders' interests in all corporate responsibility areas.

the above-mentioned responsibility; moreover, the said dimensions should be considered in the context of specific and transitional priorities, in relation to the related potential risks.

All firms should develop an effective risk management system based on the integration of strategic and operational goals, key success factors and key risks; this should guarantee corporate success in the long term, satisfying the company's stakeholders at the same time. Indeed, a well-functioning risk management system should permit the company to anticipate, reduce or transfer the negative effects of events monitored and to reach goals in line with stakeholders' expectations.

In this context, compliance is both an element to be monitored by firms and a prerequisite of management effectiveness; moreover, it increases the possibilities of creating sustainable value. As managers become more aware of the importance of risks, there is a progression along a broad risk spectrum toward greater sophistication in risk management and appreciation of its link to stakeholder value in the long term. First of all, by managing the risks associated with compliance and prevention, companies should progress naturally toward the minimization of uncertainty; they should then move to a higher level of risk management, in which opportunities are caught in order to increase sustainable value (FMAC & PWC, 1999).

The broader source of compliance risk, now more than ever, is embedded throughout business activities (Batchelor, 1999). The adoption of behavior that does not comply with binding or self-imposed external or internal rules constitutes a risk that companies should proactively govern: this should enable them to avoid both immediate sanctions and future consequences associated with the loss of stakeholders' support, which are difficult to quantify.

The value of compliance should be embedded in the corporate culture (D'Arcy & Greene, 2014), as a shared principle that guides the behavior of the entire organization and constitutes the basis for managing any type of risks connected to corporate responsibility. Compliance risk management should also be consistent and continuous, because compliance control is inefficient and unnecessarily expensive when exercised sporadically or as a one-off. The board of directors and the compliance leaders (such as the chief compliance officer) should continuously promote compliance on a permanent basis at all levels of the organization, establishing, and sustaining a culture of compliance which employees can observe (Griffin & Hu, 2013; Rowe & Cadzow, 2014; Sobol, 2009). In this sense, compliance is a cross-cutting activity that covers the observation of all rules, both external and internal, self-regulatory and prescriptive, and behavioral and organizational.

For proper compliance risk management, the company should analyze its strategic and organizational complexity. It should then map all areas that are currently or potentially subject to risks. Finally, it should resolve situations of non-compliance or implement appropriate protective measures to prevent them.

Appropriate compliance risk management favors the creation of long-term value and actively contributes to the implementation of development paths inspired by sustainable growth. Indeed

- greater risk awareness (risk culture) reduces the possibility of non-compliant behavior, which could cause economic and/or reputational damage with immediate or future impact;
- the most credible companies in global markets are the ones which submit themselves to stricter rules than those imposed by the regulators.

In a classification of risks based on the degree of predictability, controllability, management and magnitude of their consequences to the enterprise, compliance risk can be positioned at the bottom level of the hierarchy, as it is connected with routine, standardized and predictable processes. Since these risks are predictable and avoidable, internal control mechanisms should permit companies to have zero defects and 100 percent compliance in this level's processes (Kaplan, 2009).

Based on the above considerations, we can argue that all companies should govern the risk of compliance failure. Indeed, the respect of rules and procedures is the basic condition in order to achieve minimum standards when performing operational activities, facing the competition on global markets and satisfying all stakeholders. This situation makes the company primarily focused on strategic risks. Unfortunately, compliance risk is not always governed opportunely. This especially happens in companies characterized by a lack of risk culture and dominated, in general, by a substantial absence of ethics in internal and external relationships.

Compliance Risk in the BRICS

The recent evolution of the economic system has emphasized the need to improve corporate governance, in order to accomplish the company's mission in a sustainable way. In such a context, a firm's success depends on two main conditions: firstly, the respect of both laws and ethics in all internal and external relationships (compliance), as stated above; secondly, the ability to innovate the managerial approach to take care of economic, ecological, and social issues. So, corporate effectiveness primarily depends on the compliance of behavior with both mandatory and self-discipline rules (such as laws, recommendations, codes of corporate governance, codes of ethics, codes of conduct, and operational and organizational procedures), covering the different dimensions of global responsibility (legal, economic, environmental, and social aspects) and in accordance with a broad vision of risk management.

The global economic crisis has considerably raised the importance of emerging markets for western companies. The latter are interested in competing in global areas where they can reduce operational costs, as the prospect for macroeconomic growth in mature markets is forecast to be less than 3 percent over the next two decades (Peters, Miller, & Kusyk, 2011).

The BRICS are a diverse group of nations in terms of economic development, political systems, and cultural traditions; however, they present similarities in relation to their large economies and rapid growth (Li, Qiu, & Gu, 2010).

Despite the great opportunities offered by emerging markets, large-scale investments by old industrialized countries have slowed: one of the reasons of this reluctance is the absence of effective corporate governance mechanisms that could protect the investors of mature markets. As emerging countries are likely to be the driving force of the global economy in the decades to come (Table 1), the improving development of corporate governance issues should be understood as being in the general interest of developing, as well as developed, countries.

The BRICS have improved their corporate governance systems recently (Aguilera, Kabbach-Castro, Lee, & You, 2012; Ararat & Dallas, 2011; Boubaker & Nguyen, 2014; Gibson, 2002; Székely-Doby, 2011) in order to introduce international best practices; such practices should help their companies reach a leading position in

Table 1: GDP of the BRICS (Expressed in Billions of US Dollars) (2000–2014).

	Brazil	China	India	Russia	South Africa	Total
2000	644.734	1,192.854	476.636	259.702	132.967	2,706.893
2001	554.185	1,317.236	493.934	306.583	118.564	2,790.502
2002	506.043	1,455.560	523.768	345.125	111.357	2,941.853
2003	552.383	1,650.514	618.369	430.289	168.217	3,419.772
2004	663.734	1,944.674	721.589	591.177	219.419	4,140.593
2005	882.044	2,287.258	834.218	763.704	246.951	5,014.175
2006	1,089.255	2,793.159	949.118	989.932	261.176	6,082.640
2007	1,366.853	3,504.605	1,238.478	1,299.703	285.805	7,695.444
2008	1,653.539	4,547.716	1,223.206	1,660.846	273.453	9,358.760
2009	1,622.311	5,105.769	1,365.343	1,222.645	285.416	9,601.484
2010	2,142.905	5,949.648	1,708.541	1,524.915	365.165	11,691.174
2011	2,474.636	7,314.482	1,880.102	1,904.790	404.343	13,978.353

Table 1: (*Continued*)

	Brazil	China	India	Russia	South Africa	Total
2012	2,247.745	8,386.677	1,858.748	2,017.469	382.340	14,892.979
2013	2,246.037	9,469.124	1,876.811	2,096.774	350.800	16,039.546
2014	2,244.131	10,355.350	2,047.811	2,057.301	341.216	17,145.809
Total	20,890.535	67,274.626	17,916.672	17,470.955	3,947.189	127,499.977

Source: International Monetary Fund, World Economic Outlook Database October 2014.
Despite a slowdown, the trend of GDP in the BRICS indicates increasing value over the years, making these countries the driving force of the global economy in the decades to come.

global markets, acquiring the "know-how" for advanced activities from old economies.

Many organizations affirm the importance of sound corporate governance based on effective risk management as a key factor to compete in the global markets, spreading internationally accepted principles.[1] Corporate governance reforms in the BRICS are driven by the necessity to align the regulations of the country with the internationally accepted standards of governance in order to attract international investors. Such reforms share some similar features, such as the transit from a closed, opaque and relation-based governance system to a more open, transparent and rule-based governance one (Charles, Fries, & Buiter, 2003). This behavior tends to reduce the gap with old industrialized economies, nurturing a formal convergence path in terms of corporate governance systems (Lattemann, 2014; Yoshikawa & Rasheed, 2009).

According to Peters et al. (2011), emerging markets are characterized by some common factors that create similar situations when it comes to corporate governance:

- reliance on informal institutions and inclination to favor relation-based rather than rule-based governance. This situation can be explained by the fact that the enforceability of the law is generally lower and institutions tend to be less developed than those in industrially advanced economies (Fan, Lau, & Young, 2007; Young, Peng, Ahlstrom, Bruton, & Jiang, 2008). Nevertheless, the boards of emerging markets'

1. For example, we only need to mention the OECD Principles of Corporate Governance (2004), which stress the central role of an adequate internal control system for proper risk management and the need of transparent information to the market as concerns foreseeable risks. In addition, the Green Paper on "The EU Corporate Governance Framework" (2011) suggests the importance of an adequate risk culture and arrangements to effectively manage the wide variety of external and internal risks by companies. This Paper defines corporate governance as one of the means to curb harmful short-termism and excessive risk-taking. Finally, the UN Global Compact "Guide to Corporate sustainability" (2014) invites companies to move beyond traditional approaches based largely on narrow risk assessments toward a wider vision of global risks and opportunities.

companies are concerned about making it known that the firms they run respect the rules and are accountable, posing themselves as trusty partners;

- presence of controlling shareholders (family-run companies) and "principal-principal" rather than "principal-agent" problem (Claessens, Djankov, Fan, & Lang, 1999; La Porta, Lopez-De-Silanes, Shleifer, & Vishy, 2000). It can be assumed that the concentrated ownership structure in emerging markets is a response to the lack of contract enforcement mechanisms;
- defect of enough leverage to develop their own forms of governance and standards. This situation induces the adoption of rules defined in other countries that are difficult to transplant quickly in a different context, because of the so-called path dependence (Alston, 1999; Wong, 2008; Young et al., 2008). Some authors indicated that emerging markets need a different structure of corporate governance from that of developed ones, suggesting a different point of view to analyze the phenomenon (Choudhury & Hoque, 2006; Fauver, Houston, & Naranjo, 2003; Grais & Pellegrini, 2006; Li & Nair, 2009; Wanyama, Burton, & Helliar, 2009);
- prior need to establish effective corporate governance measures (both legally binding and self-regulating) as a way to attract foreign investment and achieve higher performance.

The BRICS policymakers have made efforts to promote business practices that may reduce the gap with old industrialized economies. However, the persistent weaknesses of their legal systems prompt the BRICS companies to symbolically express their adherence to advanced corporate governance standards, with a view to competing better on global financial markets. For this reason, voluntary regulation is rapidly growing thanks to the initiative of markets' regulators and authorities.

Despite the institutional and legal context in which they are embedded, individual firms wish to attract international investors through their corporate governance practices and disclosure (Chipalkatti, Le, & Rishi, 2007). Therefore, a company's adherence to a code of self-discipline is the expression of its will to govern corporate conduct by respecting requirements that are even more stringent than those required by the laws. The considerations above underline the importance of internal control systems and risk management: the company's board should ensure effective mechanisms of control in order to guarantee compliance between the behaviors and the rules, thereby preventing any possible compliance risk.

If we assume compliance with the binding standards (legal responsibility), then self-discipline codes function as a guide. However, these codes cannot solve ethical problems: in other words, in the absence of an ethical corporate culture, any type of rule can be bypassed, with both immediate economic damage (sanctions, reimbursements, etc.) and the loss of stakeholders' consent in the long term.

Therefore, the creation of national self-regulatory corporate governance codes, inspired by internationally accepted guidelines or rules in force in the old industrialized countries, is not a guarantee of sound governance. The formal adoption of these codes implies the enforcement of standards that may be recognized by large investors; however, such standards are not always supported by an adequate system of risk management. Formal compliance is only a declaration of intent, which can initially be a source of financial resources from the markets, but does not protect the company from the actual risks. In the short term, the need to adapt corporate governance to the competitive requirements of financial markets can produce a formal compliance that is a risk factor in itself, if it does not evolve into a culture of compliance. It follows that the compliance risk is far to be removed, especially in those countries that have gained experience in codified corporate governance more quickly than others. In other words, the pressure for the BRICS companies to adhere to the international corporate governance standards for attracting investors does not guarantee the minimization of risks in the long term. Value-based compliance can be much more effective than the ever growing number of external and internal rules a company decides voluntarily to respect. Therefore, it is necessary to go beyond the traditional concept of compliance and include an ethical dimension at individual level, which may overlap with corporate ethics (Murphy, 2004; Rowe & Cadzow, 2014; Verschoor, 2006). In fact, an effective culture of compliance requires that all the members of the firm respect ethical core values: the continuous reiteration of frauds and irresponsible conduct by companies, notwithstanding the existence of legally binding rules to prevent them, demonstrate the ineffectiveness of internal controls when the individuals do not share common ethical values and do not practise self-control behavior.

Corporate Governance, Internal Control, and Risk Management in the BRICS: Legislative and Regulatory Framework

This section highlights the most important laws and regulations on corporate governance, internal control, and risk management that are currently in force in the BRICS. These rules have inspired the self-regulatory codes, procedures, and mechanisms adopted by the companies.

Even if specific laws and recommendations may consider different types of risks, it is sufficient to mention here only the most significant rules with which the BRICS have outlined their national framework.

Brazil

According to the *Code of Best Practice of Corporate Governance* released by the Instituto Brasileiro de Governança Corporativa in 2009, the board of directors is responsible for monitoring the company's risks. An audit committee established within the board should discuss risk assessment methods and findings with the independent auditors. It should also monitor the high-risk areas affecting the company's financial statements. For this reason, the audit committee should include members with experience in identifying and controlling risks.

The board of directors should also ensure that the management identify in advance and list the main risks to which the company is exposed, their probability of occurrence, and the measures to prevent or minimize them.

Russia

The *Russian Code of Corporate Governance*, issued by the Moscow Exchange and OECD Russia in 2014, recommends that listed companies establish an efficient risk management and internal control system. This system should provide reasonable confidence that the corporate goals will be achieved.

The risk management and internal control system should also ensure a fair and clear view of the current conditions and prospects of the company, and guarantee the integrity and transparency of accounts and reports.

The board of directors should determine the basic principles and approaches of risk management and internal control, while the executive bodies should ensure the establishment and continuing operation of the system.

Independent internal auditors should evaluate the reliability and efficiency of the system on a regular basis.

India

According to the Indian *Corporate governance voluntary guidelines* (2009), the board of directors, the audit committee and the executive management should collectively identify the risks impacting on the company's business. They should then document the process of risk identification, risk minimization and risk optimization as part of a risk management policy or strategy.

The board of directors should also affirm and disclose in its report that it has put in place a critical risk management framework across the company, which it oversees once every six months. The disclosure should also include a statement of the risk factors that may threaten the existence of the company. Similar rules are contained in *Clause 49* of the *Listing Agreement*, published by the Securities and Exchange Board of India in 2000 and continually revised.

China

The Chinese regulation is contained in the so-called China SOX, published by the Chinese Government and comprising the *Basic Standard for Enterprise Internal Control* (2008) and the *Supporting Guidelines* (2010). According to the China SOX, all listed companies are required to adopt an internal control system including risk assessment procedures. Such procedures should permit the company to identify and analyze risks related to the achievement of company objectives. Non-listed companies are also invited to do the same.

South Africa

According to the *King III Code of Governance* (2009), the board of directors is responsible for risk governance: the board should identify the level of risk tolerance, promote the development of a policy and a plan for risk management, and ensure and monitor their continuous implementation.

A risk committee or an audit committee should assist the board in carrying out its responsibilities.

The board should delegate to managers the responsibility to design, implement and monitor the risk management plan: the managers are in charge of assessing risks, selecting and implementing risk responses, and providing assurance to the board that the risk management plan is integrated in the daily activities of the company.

Compliance Failure in the BRICS Companies: Selected Case Studies

Through a selection of case studies, this section aims to supplement the theoretical analysis carried out in the previous paragraphs of the chapter. According to Yin (2003), a case study is an "empirical inquiry that investigates a contemporary phenomenon within its real-life context."

This empirical research shows that formal compliance with external and internal laws, regulations and ethical principles is not enough to make companies responsible, sustainable, and successful: companies that lack a shared culture of compliance may suffer indirect impacts on stakeholder relations, with dangerous consequences in the long term.

This section contains five case studies: we analyzed one company for each BRICS country. The selection of companies was based on the evidence of previous research and surveys. Moreover, the dimension of such companies and the diversity of the stakeholder interests that they were expected to protect made these cases highly significant for the topic investigated.

For each company, we collected information using the Internet in March and April 2015, considering both the official websites of the five companies and other websites divulging business information. Most events reported in the chapter happened in the last five years.

Vale SA (Brazil)

At the time of the investigation, Vale SA was a global mining company with headquarters in Brazil. It was the world leader in the production of iron ore and the second largest producer of nickel. Due to its activity, the company needed access to natural resources and lands, so its operations could produce a significant impact on the environment and the lives of local people. For example, this used to be the case when the company demanded territories originally intended for agricultural and land reform purposes.

Vale had operating units on all five continents and was listed on several stock exchanges (São Paulo, Madrid, NYSE, Euronext and Hong Kong). Despite Vale's privatization in 1997, the Brazilian government still held golden shares in the company, associated with the ownership of preferred shares (5.2 percent of the total capital at September 30, 2014). The golden shares entitled the government to veto any proposal concerning changes in the company's name, location of the head office, corporate purposes as regards mining activities, liquidation, and rights assigned to golden share owners by the company's by-law.

According to Vale's mission statement, the company had embraced a path of responsible growth in order "to transform natural resources into prosperity and sustainable development." Moreover, Vale's vision consisted in being "the first global natural resources company in creating long term value, through excellence and passion for people and the planet." To do so, Vale used to take into account social and environmental care in all phases of its activities, from project design through to completion.

According to the company's *2013 Sustainable Report*, Vale's social and environmental management was based on the company's values and official regulations, such as the *Code of Ethics and Conduct*, the *Social Action Policy*, the *Community Relations Guide* and *Manual*, and the *Issues and Stakeholder Model*.

The aforesaid documents stated the rules governing both internal and external relationships. Specifically, they emphasized Vale's commitment to observe all legal obligations in force in those countries where it operated; furthermore, they explained Vale's contribution to local development in relation to health, education, and creation of jobs and wealth.

In this regard and according to Vale's code of ethics, all directors, employees, contractors and partners were expected to:

- pursue sustainable development and respect environmental legislation locally (Rule 1.12);
- act in accordance with social responsibility and respect human dignity (Rule 1.13);

– perform daily activities complying with health and safety rules set by the company (Rule 1.14).

To improve strategic decision-making and the effectiveness of governance, Vale recognized the importance of stakeholder engagement, which it applied through different mechanisms and channels: among others, the company declared that it involved the community in a dialogue to create a unified view of critical matters and to promote a good relationship.

Vale's corporate governance, internal control and risk management system was organized to offer proper support to the development of social and environmental management. Indeed, the company had established dedicated bodies to identify priority issues and analyze the ways to reduce the negative impacts of activities and to enhance positive effects.

The board of directors had set up an internal technical and advisory committee, named the governance and sustainability committee, in charge of discussing and reviewing social and environmental-related issues. The committee had to prepare reports for the board concerning the company's social and environmental performance with respect to the policies proposed by the executive directors. Moreover, the committee was responsible for making improvements to the code of ethics.

Vale had also established an ethics and conduct office, which was responsible for promoting continuous advancement in ethical awareness. It also received and dealt with stakeholders' complaints when a company's director, manager, employee, partner, or contractor violated the code of ethics.

Vale's internal control system was supported by enterprise-wide risk management processes to identify, prevent and control all relevant risk factors that could affect the company's growth. An executive risk management committee had been appointed by the board of directors to handle risk management issues. The committee would classify the main risks into market risks, credit risks, operational risks and political risks, and regularly monitor them to ensure that the overall corporate risk stayed within an acceptable range of tolerance, in line with the board's risk appetite and the company's risk policies.

As reported by the company in its *2013 Annual Report*, Vale was subject to the risk of disagreements with the local communities where it operated, and it consequently suffered an adverse impact on both business and reputation. Such a risk existed in spite of Vale's contribution to local development by means of taxes, royalties, employment and business opportunities, and social programs.

According to the company's disclosure, risk management procedures related to this risk consisted in two main techniques: on the one hand, the involvement of local people in natural resource management; on the other hand, consultation and negotiation with landowners, local communities, and the government about measures to limit the impact of operations or obtain access to lands.

Despite Vale's commitment statement to sustainability, the company has often been accused of irresponsible behavior. Since 2012 Vale has repeatedly faced protests and open opposition to its activities in different countries, due to violation of human rights and workers' rights, environmental exploitation and pollution, and attempts of tax avoidance (Business & Human Rights Resource Centre, 2013; Halifax Initiative, Both Ends, CounterCurrent, Fórum Suape, & Ríos Vivos, 2015; RepRisk, 2012).

In Mozambique, Vale was held responsible for the displacement of about 1300 families: many of them did not receive the compensation promised by the company in exchange for their land (RepRisk, 2012); many others were displaced to zones where farming-work was difficult due to poor quality of land and scarcity of water (Human Rights Watch, 2013; Kabemba & Nhancale, 2011). In order to solve some of the problems provoked by its conduct, Vale signed a Memorandum of Understanding with the Mozambican government in July 2012, to improve the living conditions of the displaced families (Human Rights Watch, 2013).

In Brazil, Vale was criticized by NGOs for having increased greenhouse gas emissions, violating its previous commitment to reduce them (RepRisk, 2012). In the same country, Vale tried to extend a railway track near its mines, but the law court stopped the company because of risks of soil, air and water contamination, risks for public health and risks of injury or death of inhabitants hit by the trains. In 2012, Vale and three government agencies agreed to cooperate for enhancing community safety in the area of the railway; however, two years later their commitment was still unfulfilled (Halifax Initiative, Both Ends, CounterCurrent, Fórum Suape, & Ríos Vivos, 2015).

Moreover, a former employee of Vale made heavy accusations at the Labour Court of Espirito Santo and the Federal Public Ministry of Rio de Janeiro against the company. He reported the company for forcing him to spy on the employees and place infiltrators in social movements. The company defined such accusations as unfounded and due to the discomfort of the former employee for having previously been dismissed for just cause (Business & Human Rights Resource Centre, 2013).

Gazprom (Russia)

When we carried out the research, Gazprom was a Russian joint stock company operating in the energy sector, the main business of which concerned natural gas, gas condensate and oil exploration, production, transportation, storage, processing, and sales. Gazprom was the largest extractor of natural gas in the world and owned 72 percent of Russian gas reserves and 18 percent of the world's gas reserves. The company was also among Russia's five largest oil producers and possessed 17 percent of the total installed capacity of the national energy system.

Founded by the Soviet Ministry of Gas Industry in 1989 and then privatized, Gazprom was listed on three stock exchanges (Moscow, London and Frankfurt), but was still controlled by the Russian Government through a majority share (50.23 percent at May 8, 2014). A board of directors comprising Government representatives led the company, assisted by an audit committee responsible for monitoring business operations and the completeness, timeliness and fairness of the financial statements.

As an energy company, Gazprom's activity was subject to many mandatory rules on the use of natural resources and the impact of activities on the environment. Moreover, the firm was expected to behave ethically toward all shareholders, investors, customers and other parties, and to disclose transparent information to the market, public authorities and other stakeholders.

In order to strengthen ethics in the personnel's conduct, Gazprom had adopted a *Code of Corporate Ethics*; moreover, it had created a hotline for employees and third parties who had questions on the company's ethics. Gazprom had also established a corporate ethics commission that would help the company respect the principles and rules stated in the code of ethics. Compliance with the code was also reviewed by the audit committee on behalf of the board of directors.

Verifying compliance with existing laws and corporate regulations was a key function of the company's internal control and auditing system, and a conduct consistent with the rules was required of all Gazprom's people, bodies, operating units and subsidiaries.

Gazprom's business was subject to the environmental legislation of the Russian Federation, but not only. The company had therefore applied all the commonly accepted principles of environmental impact mitigation and natural resource conservation. Such rules and principles were stated in the *Code of Corporate Ethics* and reflected in the *Gazprom Environmental Policy*, which all the firms belonging to Gazprom Group were recommended to adopt.

Within its *Environmental Management System*, certified under ISO 14001:2004, Gazprom had established a corporate environmental inspectorate and hired many environmental experts. All of them were responsible for implementing preventive environmental protection measures and reviewing the corporate projects to guarantee their compliance with all the environmental rules, laws and regulations, both internal and external.

According to Gazprom's *2013 Annual Report* and *2013 Environmental Report*, risks of damage to the environment, human health and private property, due to violation of environmental protection laws, were critical for the company. Indeed, such damage could entail legal implications, including the suspension of corporate activities, financial costs for sanctions and compensation for damages, and loss of reputation.

In order to preserve the climate and biological diversity and to prevent environmental risks, the company carried out pre-design environmental surveys. It also assessed the environmental impact of planned activities and ran environmental due diligence of projects. Furthermore, facilities were constructed, operated, updated, and decommissioned in line with environmental laws and corporate standards. Insurance agreements were also in force to cover the costs that would originate from environmental damage and consequent effects.

Gazprom's formal attention to the environment was also proved by its commitment in programs focused on this matter. In this regard, the company launched an initiative in 2014 to increase environmental awareness among the population and to provide environmental education to its employees and contractors.

The nature of state-owned company and the type of activities developed made it important for Gazprom to adopt internal anti-corruption measures, which were stated in the *Code of Corporate Ethics*. The document also described how the company had to interact with governmental and political organizations.

Even if Gazprom seemed to monitor and manage internal and external risk factors capable of provoking violation of mandatory laws and corporate provisions, the company and its subsidiaries had been repeatedly accused of much irresponsible or even illegal conduct (RepRisk, 2012).

As regards environmental issues, WWF Russia expressed concern about the Group's lack of transparency, when a subsidiary denied access to its environmental impact assessment for a project. Another subsidiary started exploratory drilling despite explicit prohibition by the Russian authorities.

According to the German Society for Threatened Peoples, a company controlled by Gazprom destroyed the way of life of nomadic Nenets people (ILO, 2012).

Furthermore, environmentalists claimed that Gazprom provoked detrimental impact to the marine ecosystem by using old-model drilling platforms in the Arctic region. Irreversible damage also hit a UNESCO World Heritage Site in Siberia, sacred to indigenous people.

With regard to competitive practices, Gazprom was investigated by the European Commission, which opened a formal proceeding against the company in September 2012: allegations comprised monopolistic conduct in the supply, transmission and storage of gas in Eastern Europe (European Commission, 2012). According to the European Commission's *Statement of Objections* sent to the company on April 22, 2015, "Gazprom [was] breaking EU antitrust rules by pursuing an overall strategy to partition Central and Eastern European gas markets with the aim of maintaining an unfair pricing policy in several of those Member States. Gazprom [implemented] this strategy by (i) hindering cross-border gas sales, (ii) charging unfair prices, and (iii) making gas supplies conditional on obtaining unrelated commitments from wholesalers concerning gas transport infrastructure" (European Commission, 2015).

Gazprom has also been accused of bribing politicians and members of the Russian government, establishing companies in tax havens, attempting to manipulate media communications and intimidating business partners (Roth, 2012).

Maruti Suzuki (India)

At the time of writing, Maruti Suzuki was an Indian car manufacturing company controlled by Japanese motorbike producer Suzuki. Maruti Suzuki's shares were traded on the main financial markets in India: the Bombay Stock Exchange and the National Stock Exchange of India.

Maruti Suzuki's corporate culture fostered ethics, integrity, transparency, accountability and compliance with laws and regulations. The company required that all directors, managers and employees respect those core values, which were also stated in the corporate *Code of Conduct*. An ad-hoc *Whistle Blower Policy* protected employees who reported to the Ombudsman any instance of unethical conduct, irregularities and frauds they had witnessed or suspected.

This system derived from the conviction that ethical behavior should support the company's sustainable growth and the satisfaction of all the stakeholders.

Specifically, Maruti Suzuki stated that it paid attention to the needs of its regular and contractual employees, because their welfare and progress were considered critical for long-term sustainability. Even if the Indian legislation regulated labor practices, the company had adopted specific mechanisms to take care of its employees and strengthen their protection in the workplace. For example, Maruti Suzuki had established a hospitalization policy for employees with dependent children and parents, as well as better maternity leave than the one guaranteed by the national *Maternity Benefit Act*. The company had also set up medical centers providing health check-ups for the workers.

Occupational health and safety was one of the priorities of Maruti Suzuki, as a large part of the company's personnel carried out manufacturing operations. According to the company's *2013–2014 Sustainability Report*, Maruti Suzuki used to verify that the business was managed in accordance with all relevant health and safety legislations, standards and internal policies. In this regard, the company had introduced a formally structured *Occupational Health and Safety Management System*. Furthermore, Maruti Suzuki's risk management comprised a detailed *Hazard Identification and Risk Assessment*, applied in each corporate area. According to the *Indian Factories Act*, the company had also established an apex safety committee, which was composed of an equal number (eight) of employees and managers. Finally, Maruti Suzuki declared that it encouraged its suppliers to face all safety issues properly, by adopting appropriate management systems.

As reported in Maruti Suzuki's *2013–2014 Sustainability Report*, the company recognized employees' freedom of association, as well as collective bargaining for all regular workers. In accordance with the statutory requirements, workers elected internal and independent labor union representatives, who operated at the company's plants and examined with the board all policy changes that could affect the employees. Moreover, Maruti Suzuki had formally established an employee relations development committee to ensure constructive discussions between the unions and the corporate officials on a monthly basis. This was a stakeholder engagement tool adopted by the company in order to involve the personnel in decision-making; another tool was participative formulation of human resources policies.

Despite the fact that Maruti Suzuki largely informed the public about its commitment to employee protection and involvement, the company has been repeatedly accused of violating fundamental labor and human rights guaranteed by the conventions of the International Labour Organization (ILO).

One of the most notorious cases happened in 2012, when activists alleged that Maruti Suzuki had dismissed many employees and detained them without trial because of their effort to create a labor union. The company was also alleged to have sent security guards to attack the employees: that episode was also marked by the death of a human resources manager who sympathized with the workers (RepRisk, 2012).

In that occasion a delegation of experts set up by the International Commission for Labor Rights (ICLR) investigated the facts, ascertaining the following (ICLR, 2013, 2014):

- physical and psychological pressure on the workers due to operational activity, and lack of adequate rest time during the day;
- an unfair wage structure, marked by manifest disadvantages for employees in case of illness;
- unpaid overtime;
- reliance on a highly precarious workforce, largely composed of contractual workers, trainees and apprentices, who earned dramatically less than full time workers and had no job security or benefits.

Previously, an investigation of the Labour Department had already focused on Maruti Suzuki: in 2011, the company had been accused of violating the agreements with the employees for the creation of a Grievance Redressal Committee and a Labour Welfare Committee to handle with their complaints (RepRisk, 2012). Attempts of corrupting some union leaders were also associated with the company (RepRisk, 2012).

China National Petroleum Corporation (China)

China National Petroleum Corporation (CNPC), a state-owned integrated energy company, was established in 1988 to replace the Chinese Ministry of Petroleum Industry. As the largest oil and gas producer in China at the time of the research, CNPC had 1.5 million employees and its line of business included oilfield services, engineering and construction, equipment manufacturing, financial services, and new energy development. CNPC controlled PetroChina, one of the largest companies in the world and listed on Hong Kong and New York stock exchanges.

According to CNPC's stated mission, the company aimed to achieve harmonious relationships between operations and safety, energy and the environment, corporate and community interests, and employers and employees. In doing so, CNPC was inspired by the following corporate values: a dynamic nature, loyalty, honesty, commitment, and achieving excellence through innovation and integrity. Such values were formalized in the company's internal rules and policies and put into action by means of adequate management systems.

As a state-owned company, CNPC had significant social responsibilities toward both the employees and the community. Moreover, as an oil and gas giant, the company was also expected to monitor and limit the potentially catastrophic impact of its operations on the environment. Hence, socially and environmentally responsible behavior was a priority for CNPC.

Such premises help us understand CNPC's *Health, Safety and Environment (HSE) Management Principles*. The company had formal HSE guidelines and plan, which were the fundamentals of the HSE management system implemented, assessed and reviewed on a regular basis by the top management. CNPC highly recommended that all its subsidiaries and contractors adopted social and environmental management systems, too.

The *HSE Management Principles* strengthened the respect of the national legislation on social and environmental matters. In this regard, such principles required that the company took into account all HSE risks when it made decisions about strategic planning, project investment and operations management. After identifying HSE risks with the contribution of the relevant workers, the company had to adopt appropriate risk treatment measures to ensure safe and clean development of business.

With regard to health, CNPC declared that it followed policies and used measures intended to offer a sanitary and pleasant workplace to the personnel. The company complied with the *Code of Occupational Disease Prevention of the People's Republic of China*; it had also implemented an internal health care system to prevent occupational diseases in the long term, and a convalescence system that was considered very important for production workers.

Safety was a major concern for CNPC too, so both CNPC and its employees were expected to do their best to maximize the effectiveness of the company's HSE management system: the employees had to comply with safety rules and regulations, while the company had to promote safety training and review the employees' safety awareness, skills and performance.

CNPC also put the environment at the top of its agenda. The company therefore affirmed strict compliance with all laws and regulations on environmental conservation, climate change, biodiversity, energy saving and emission reduction. In particular, the company's HSE management system controlled and tried to limit the impact of operations on environmental areas like deserts, wetlands, and natural reserves.

According to CNPC's core values, the commitment to socially and environmentally responsible conduct also brought the company to launch public initiatives, such as the "Safety and Environmental Protection Year" campaign, and to participate in public welfare undertakings, such as disaster relief and cultural and educational projects.

Finally, the company stated that it operated in conformity with relevant laws and regulations requiring the respect of human and labor rights. In this sense, CNPC had introduced a human resources management system based on the following principles:

- treating all the employees equally;
- promoting the employment of women, minorities and local people;
- providing insurance coverage for unemployment, healthcare, work injury and maternity;
- forbidding child labor, forced labor and discrimination in any form throughout the company.

Since 2010, however, CNPC has often been alleged of breaking the rules in different countries, where it was operating directly or indirectly (RepRisk, 2012): it appears that CNPC and its main subsidiaries have violated the laws on human rights, labor, the environment and anti-corruption.

CNPC-AktobeMunaiGaz joint venture in Kazakhstan was charged with a fine of $ 4.4 million because of water and soil pollution and mass mortality of birds (Business & Human Rights Resource Centre, 2014; citing Tengrinews). Moreover, serious environmental damage resulted from the loss of crude oil due to the explosion of two pipelines at the port of Dalian in China (RepRisk, 2012). In 2011, environmental organizations observed that CNPC's activities in Siberia for the construction of pipelines in partnership with the Russian Gazprom could provoke irreversible damage to a UNESCO World Heritage Site sacred to local people (RepRisk, 2012).

Finally, corruption scandals have often involved executives and managers of the CNPC group (Sheng, Zhao, & Yang, 2015). A recent case has regarded the company's former vice-chairman: on 16 March 2015, CNPC announced to PetroChina that its vice-chairman was "currently under investigation by the relevant authorities on suspicion of severe breach of discipline and violating the relevant laws" (PetroChina, Investor FAQs). Allegations claimed that the director might be involved in a corruption case.

Harmony Gold Mining Ltd (South Africa)

At the time of this study, Harmony was a gold-mining and exploration company operating in two of the most important gold mining regions in the world: South Africa, where the company had its headquarters, and Papua New Guinea. In 2014, Harmony was the third largest producer of gold in South Africa and the eleventh in the world.

Harmony owned nine underground mines, one open pit operation, and several surface sources in South Africa; it also held a 50 percent share in a Papua New Guinean firm, through which it exploited an open-pit gold and silver mine.

The company was listed on Johannesburg, New York, and Berlin Stock Exchanges.

Harmony recognized that its activities could produce impacts on people's lives, the environment and the communities surrounding its mines. For this reason it founded its strategy on responsible behavior and sustainable development. In this regard, safety in operations, accountability and honesty in both business dealings and stakeholder communication were among the values shared by Harmony's top management and employees to achieve strategic goals.

As stated in the company's *Code of Ethics*, the chief executive officer was responsible for the ethics and culture of the company. The CEO was supported by the heads of departments and an ad-hoc committee established by the board, named the social and ethics committee. According to the *Terms of Reference*, this committee had to be composed of non-executive directors, in majority independent, and it had to:

– assist the Board in "ensuring that the Harmony and the other entities in the Group [were and remained] committed and socially responsible corporate citizens by creating a sustainable business and having regard to the company's economic, social and environmental impact on the communities in which it [operated]" (Rule 2.1, in compliance with the *King III Code*);

- oversee "the company's activities in sustainable social and economic development which, inter alia, [included] public safety, HIV/Aids, environmental management, corporate social investment, consumer relationships, labor and employment, the promotion of equality and ethics management" (Rule 2.2);
- check the compliance of the company's activities with all applicable laws, regulations, codes, standards and principles concerning social, environmental and economic matters, including the UN Global Compact and the OECD recommendations against corruption (Rule 1.1 of *Annexure A*);
- be informed on sustainability risks (Rule 1.2.8 of *Annexure A*, in compliance with the *King III Code*);
- review the company's integrated annual and sustainable development reports, on an annual basis (Rule 1.2.9).

Harmony's ethical and responsible conduct involved safety of people, respect of the environment and eradication of corruption. In this regard, all directors, managers, employees, and contractors were expected to comply with the internal policies, frameworks, programs and management systems that the company had adopted to guide their behavior.

As described in the company's *Integrated Annual Report 2014*, Harmony's occupational health and safety policies and management systems were aligned with South African and Papua New Guinean legislations for the mining sector. Moreover, the company's health and safety management system was certified in accordance with the OHSAS 18001 standard.

Harmony used many procedures to implement health and safety principles and rules. For example:

- it promoted internal initiatives to coach the employees, in cooperation with the trade unions;
- it formally reported the incidents and assessed the company's safety performance;

- it provided medical care to the personnel, especially in relation to occupational diseases;
- it monitored the risks associated with the employees' safety and health.

Furthermore, Harmony recognized the possible negative effects of its operations on the ecosystem, so it committed itself to avoiding, mitigating, managing and limiting such impacts. In this sense, the company had implemented an environmental management system, which was certified in accordance with the ISO 14001 standard. The company's environmental policies covered all relevant issues: resource usage, energy, climate change, water, land, effluents, and waste.

In summary, Harmony seemed to have adopted satisfactory rules of conduct and well-structured management systems in order to comply with the legislation and recommended principles. However, in recent years the company has faced convictions and allegations for incorrect and unfair behavior.

Harmony's workers have often been in danger, due to lack of safety and contraction of occupational diseases.

In February 2015, almost 500 workers remained trapped in a mine 2300 meters below ground level, probably because of a fire begun during maintenance of an air cooler (Business & Human Rights Resource Centre, 2015). Similar events had already happened a year before, as a consequence of seismic activity (RepRisk, 2014): in that instance 17 workers were trapped underground and half of them died, perhaps due to inadequate refuge chambers. Moreover, the company was alleged of non-compliance with the safety laws and regulations: indeed, some mineworkers revealed that the safety rules were often discussed within the company, but not always applied.

In December 2012, Harmony was one of 30 mining companies alleged of causing the lung disease silicosis in employees. About 17,000 former mineworkers took part in a class action against the companies: according to the workers, the companies were aware of the risks they were running by exposing them to silica dust, but they failed to take effective measures to protect the personnel. Since November 2014 an expert group, established by the companies accused, has been studying appropriate measures to prevent occupational lung disease, even if the companies have repeated their innocence.

From 2003 to 2008, Harmony's activities also gave rise to water pollution, due to the exploitation of a mine without implementing adequate operational and control systems. The Court condemned Harmony as being responsible for pollution and ordered it to contribute to rehabilitation costs. However, in December 2013 Harmony was still refusing to pay: indeed, the company did not feel guilty of environmental damage, because it had sold that mine to another owner in 2008.

Conclusion

In order to carry out effective business processes, all the companies analyzed in the chapter introduced board committees and officers and implemented mechanisms and procedures in conformity with the laws, regulations and internal codes. In other words, the five companies formally fulfilled their duty of compliance.

Compliance should involve tangible conduct intended to safeguard all the economic, social, and environmental interests of the stakeholders. However, all the companies investigated have been alleged of irresponsible behavior and unsustainable operations: we may describe such circumstances as failure to comply with the ethical values defined by the companies as essential for obtaining stakeholders' approval and long-term corporate success.

The lack of a culture of compliance prevents the companies from embracing a path of sustainable development that may attract consent and resources. Indeed, sustainable growth usually accompanies multidimensional corporate success, based on legal responsibility (i.e., respect of principles and rules) and involving economic, social and environmental aspects.

To conclude, any company should face the risk of compliance failure from two different perspectives. On the one hand, this risk needs to be specifically monitored and managed, as with any other type of risk. On the other hand, it influences the global risk exposure of the company, with significant implications for other types of risks (e.g., risks related to health and safety, safeguarding of assets, reporting, technology, integrity, and corporate reputation).

References

Aguilera, R. V., Kabbach-Castro, L. R., Lee, H. J., & You, J. (2012). Corporate governance in emerging markets. In G. Morgan & R. Whitley (Eds.), *Capitalisms and capitalism in the 21st century* (pp. 319–344). Oxford: Oxford University Press.

Ahrens, T., & Khalifa, R. (2015). The impact of regulation on management control: Compliance as a strategic response to institutional logics of university accreditation. *Qualitative Research in Accounting & Management, 12*(2), 106–126. doi:10.1108/QRAM-04-2015-0041

Alston, P. (1999). Transplanting foreign norms: Human rights and other international legal norms in Japan. *European Journal of International Law, 10*(3), 625–632.

Ararat, M., & Dallas, G. (2011). Corporate governance in emerging markets: Why it matters to investors – And what they can do about it? *Private Sector Opinion, 22*, 1–24.

Batchelor, D. (1999). Risk-based compliance monitoring. *Journal of Financial Regulation and Compliance, 7*(1), 22–26. doi:10.1108/eb024993

Boubaker, S., & Nguyen, D. K. (Eds.). (2014). *Corporate governance in emerging markets: Theories, practices and cases*. New York, NY: Springer Science & Business Media.

Boubaker, S., & Nguyen, D. K. (Eds.). (2015). *Corporate governance and corporate social responsibility: Emerging markets focus*. Singapore: World Scientific Publishing.

Brondoni, S. M. (2009). Market-driven management, competitive customer value and global networks. *Symphonya. Emerging Issues in Management, 1*, 8–25. doi:10.4468/2009.1.02brondoni

Business & Human Rights Resource Centre. (2013, April). Brazil: Former manager accuses Vale of spying on employees and infiltrating social and environmental movements; company response provided.

Business & Human Rights Resource Centre. (2014, April). *CNPC AktobeMunaiGas fined $4.4 million [Kazakhstan].*

Business & Human Rights Resource Centre. (2015). South Africa: 500 Harmony Gold miners emerge unscathed from underground fire, February, 22.

Carroll, A. B. (2004). Managing ethically with global stakeholders: A present and future challenge. *Academy of Management Executive, 18*(2), 114–120.
Charles, O., Fries, S., & Buiter, W. (2003). *Corporate governance in developing, transition and emerging-market economies*. Policy Brief No. 23, OECD Development Centre. Paris: OECD.
Chipalkatti, N., Le, Q. V., & Rishi, M. (2007). Portfolio flows to emerging capital markets: Do corporate transparency and public governance matter? *Business and Society Review, 112*, 227–249.
Choudhury, M. A., & Hoque, M. Z. (2006). Corporate governance in Islamic perspective. *Corporate Governance, 6*(2), 116–128.
Claessens, S., Djankov, S., Fan, J. P. H., & Lang, L. H. P. (1999). *Corporate diversification in East Asia: The role of ultimate ownership and group affiliation*. Working Paper No. 2089. World Bank, Washington, DC.
Clarke, M. (1995). What is compliance? The moral dimension. *Journal of Financial Regulation and Compliance, 3*(2), 123–125. doi:10.1108/eb024834
D'Arcy, J., & Greene, G. (2014). Security culture and the employment relationship as drivers of employees' security compliance. *Information Management & Computer Security, 22*(5), 474–489. doi:10.1108/IMCS-08-2013-0057
Eccles, R. G., Ioannou, I., & Serafeim, G. (2011). *The impact of a corporate culture of sustainability on corporate behavior and performance*. Harvard Business School Working Paper No. 12-035.
European Commission. (2011). Green Paper. The EU Corporate Governance Framework. COM (2011) 164 final. Brussels.
European Commission. (2012, September 4). *Antitrust: Commission opens proceedings against Gazprom*. IP/12/937. Brussels: Press release.
European Commission. (2015). Antitrust: Commission sends statement of objections to Gazprom for alleged abuse of dominance on central and Eastern European gas supply markets. IP/15/4828. Fact Sheet, 22 April.
Fan, D. K. K., Lau, C., & Young, M. (2007). Is China's corporate governance beginning to come of age? The case of CEO turnover. *Pacific-Basin Finance Journal, 15*(2), 105–120.
Fauver, L., Houston, J., & Naranjo, A. (2003). Capital market development, international integration, legal systems, and the value of corporate diversification: A cross-country analysis. *The Journal of Financial and Quantitative Analysis, 38*(1), 135–157.
FMAC, & P W C. (1999). *Enhancing shareholder wealth by better managing business risk*. New York, NY: International Federation of Accountants (IFAC).
Freeman, R. E. (2010). *Strategic management: A stakeholder approach*. Cambridge: Cambridge University Press.

Galbreath, J. (2006). Corporate social responsibility strategy: Strategic options, global considerations. *Corporate Governance: The International Journal of Business in Society*, *6*(2), 175–187. doi:10.1108/14720700610655178

Gandini, G., Gennari, F., & Cassano, R. (2014). Global responsibility and strategic risk management. *Journal of Business Management and Applied Economics*, *3*(5), 1–13.

Gibson, M. S. (2002). *Is corporate governance ineffective in emerging markets? Finance and economics discussion series. Division of research & statistics and monetary affairs*. Washington DC: Federal Reserve Board.

Grais, W., & Pellegrini, M. (2006). *Corporate governance and stakeholders' financial interests in institutions offering Islamic financial services*. World Bank Policy Research Working Paper No. 4053.

Griffin, M. A., & Hu, X. (2013). How leaders differentially motivate safety compliance and safety participation: The role of monitoring, inspiring, and learning. *Safety Science*, *60*, 196–202. doi:10.1016/j.ssci.2013.07.019

Halifax Initiative, Both Ends, CounterCurrent, Fórum Suape, & Ríos Vivos. (2015). Export credit agencies and human rights. Failure to protect.

Human Rights Watch. (2013). *"What is a house without food?" Mozambique's coal mining boom and resettlements*. Human Rights Watch.

International Commission for Labor Rights (ICLR). (2013). *Merchants of menace. Repressing workers in India's new industrial belt*. ICLR, New York, NY.

International Commission for Labor Rights (ICLR). (2014). Shiny car, shattered dreams. ICLR, New York, NY.

International Labor Organization (ILO). (2012). Lums Model United Nations, Lumun IX – Annual Conference, December 25–29.

Kabemba, C., & Nhancale, C. (2011). *Coal versus communities: Exposing poor practices by vale and rio tinto in mozambique*. Southern Africa Resource Watch.

Kanji, G. K., & Chopra, P. K. (2010). Corporate social responsibility in a global economic. *Total Quality Management & Business Excellence*, *21*(2), 119–143. doi:10.1080/14783360903549808

Kaplan, R. S. (2009). *Risk management and the strategy execution system.* Balanced Scorecard Report. Harvard Business Publishing, November–December.

Kaplan, R. S., & Mikes, A. (2012). Managing risk: A new framework. *Harvard Business Review*, *90*(6), 48–61.

La Porta, R., Lopez-De-Silanes, F., Shleifer, A., & Vishy, R. (2000). Investor protection and corporate governance. *Journal of Financial Economics*, *58*(1–2), 3–27.

Lattemann, C. (2014). On the convergence of corporate governance practices in emerging markets. *International Journal of Emerging Markets, 9*(2), 316–332.

Li, S., & Nair, A. (2009). Asian corporate governance or corporate governance in Asia? *Corporate Governance: An International Review, 17*(4), 407–410.

Li, W. A., Qiu, A. C., & Gu, Z. H. (2010). Dual corporate governance environment, political connections preference and firm performance-study on governance transition of China's private listed firms. *China Industrial Economy, 6*, 85–95.

Mikes, A., & Kaplan, R. S. (2014). *Towards a contingency theory of enterprise risk management*. Harvard Business School Working Paper No. 13-063.

Milroy, P. (1992). Setting the right compliance culture. *Journal of Financial Regulation and Compliance, 2*(2), 155–159. doi:10.1108/eb024803.

Ministry of Finance, China Securities Regulatory Commission, National Audit Office, China Banking Regulatory Commission, & China Insurance Regulatory Commission. (2008). Basic standard for enterprise internal control. People's Republic of China.

Ministry of Finance, China Securities Regulatory Commission, National Audit Office, China Banking Regulatory Commission, & China Insurance Regulatory Commission. (2010). Supporting guidelines. People's Republic of China.

Murphy, K. (2004). The role of trust in nurturing compliance: A study of accused tax avoiders. *Law Human Relations, 28*(2), 187–209.

Perrini, F., & Vurro, C. (2010). Corporate sustainability, intangible assets accumulation and competitive advantage constraints. *Symphonya. Emerging Issues in Management*, (2), 25–38. doi:10.4468/2010.2.03perrini.vurro

Peters, S., Miller, M., & Kusyk, S. (2011). How relevant is corporate governance and corporate social responsibility in emerging markets? *Corporate Governance: The International Journal of Business in Society, 11*(4), 429–445.

Porter, M. E., & Kramer, M. R. (2006). Strategy and society: The link between competitive advantage and corporate social responsibility. *Harvard Business Review, 84*(12), 78–92.

RepRisk. (2012, December). *The most controversial companies in Brazil, Russia, India and China*. BRIC report.

RepRisk. (2014, August). Most controversial mining projects. RepRisk special report.

Roth, J. (2012). Gazprom – Das unheimliche imperium (Gazprom – The uncanny empire, *in German)*. Frankfurt am Main: Westend Verlag GmbH.

Rowe, J., & Cadzow, R. (2014). Core values are the bedrock of a culture of compliance in health care agencies. *Home Health Care Management & Practice*, *26*(3), 163–166. doi:10.1177/1084822313518557

Salvioni, D. M. (2005). Corporate governance, management control and global competition. *Symphonya. Emerging Issues in Management*, (1), 39–51. doi:10.4468/2005.1.03salvioni

Salvioni, D. M. (2012). Governance, risk management and business effectiveness in global firms. In D. Tipuric & M. Dabic (Eds.), *Management, governance, and entrepreneurship – New perspectives and challenges*. Darwen: Access Press UK.

Salvioni, D. M., & Bosetti, L. (2014). Sustainable development and corporate communication in global markets. *Symphonya. Emerging Issues in Management*, (1), 32–49. doi:10.4468/2014.1.03salvioni.bosetti

Salvioni, D. M., Bosetti, L., & Almici, A. (2013). Board independence and internal committees in the BRICs. *Chinese Business Review*, *12*(8), 521–539.

Salvioni, D. M., & Gennari, F. (2014). Corporate governance, sustainability and capital markets orientation. *International Journal of Management and Sustainability*, *3*(8), 469–483.

Salvioni, D. M., Gennari, F., Bosetti, L., & Almici, A. (2015). The Audit Committee in the EU emerging countries. In S. Boubaker & D. K. Nguyen (Eds.), *Corporate governance and corporate social responsibility. Emerging markets focus* (pp. 211–234). Singapore: World Scientific Publishing.

Sheng, H., Zhao, N., & Yang, J. (2015). *Administrative monopoly in China: Causes, behaviors, and termination*. Singapore: World Scientific Publishing.

Sobol, R. (2009). Conversations at the top: The tone of the independent chief compliance officer. *Journal of Investment Compliance*, *10*(4), 10–15. doi:10.1108/15285810911007336

Székely-Doby, A. (2011). The EU's external relations: The case of BRIC countries with special emphasis on China. *Economic Studies Journal*, (2), 69–79.

Verschoor, C. (2006). Interactions between compliance and ethics. *Strategic Finance*, *87*(12), 23–24.

Wanyama, S., Burton, B., & Helliar, C. (2009). Frameworks underpinning corporate governance: Evidence on Ugandan perceptions. *Corporate Governance: An International Review*, *17*(2), 159–175.

Weber, J., & Wasieleski, D. M. (2012). Corporate ethics and compliance programs: A report, analysis and critique. *Journal of Business Ethics*, *112*(4), 609–626.

Wong, L. (2008). An end of history for corporate governance? The resilience of culture. *International Finance Review*, *9*, 495–520.

Yin, R. K. (2003). *Case study research: Design and methods* (3rd ed.). Thousand Oaks, CA: Sage.

Yoshikawa, T., & Rasheed, A. A. (2009). Convergence of corporate governance: Critical review and future directions. *Corporate Governance: An International Review, 17*(3), 388–404.

Young, M. N., Peng, M. W., Ahlstrom, D., Bruton, G. D., & Jiang, Y. (2008). Corporate governance in emerging economies: A review of the principal-principal perspective. *Journal of Management Studies, 45*(1), 196–220.

3

The Dynamics of Value Comovement across Global Equity Markets

Jan Novotný and Mayank Gupta

Abstract

The ratio between share price and current earnings per share, the Price Earning (PE) ratio, is widely considered to be an effective gauge of under/overvaluation of a corporation's stock. Arguably, a more reliable indicator, the Cyclically Adjusted Price Earning ratio or CAPE, can be obtained by replacing current earnings with a measure of permanent earnings i.e. the profits that a corporation is able to earn, on average, over the medium to long run. In this study, we aim to understand the cross-sectional aspects of the dynamics of the valuation metrics across global stock markets including both developed and emerging markets. We use a time varying DCC model to exploit the dynamics in correlations, by introducing the notion of value spread between CAPE and the respective Market Index from 2002 to 2014 for 34 countries.

Value spread is statistically significant during the 2008 crisis for asset allocation. The signal can be utilized for better asset allocation as it allows one to interpret the common movements in the stock market for under/overvaluation trends. These estimates clearly indicate periods of misvaluation in our sample. Furthermore, our simulations suggest that the model can provide early warning signs for asset mispricing in real time on a global scale and formation of asset bubbles.

Keywords: Asset pricing; PE ratio; CAPE; financial crisis; value portfolio; equity markets

JEL classifications: C58; G11; G15; G17

Introduction

The value strategy represents one of the most commonly used investment strategies pursued in the investment world and in particular in the emerging markets (see Cronqvist, Siegel, & Yu, 2015; Van der Hart, Slagter, & Van Dijk, 2003). For instance, Warren Buffet one of the most well-known value investor, chooses a low value and high-quality firms while making investments (see Gray & Carlisle, 2012 for more information). The typical approach of a value investor is to assess the intrinsic value of the assets in the opportunity set based on some valuation metric. A quality metric will then be used to determine which assets are undervalued and are worth investing.

The ratio between the share price and current earnings per share, the PE ratio, is widely considered to be an adequate gauge of under/overvaluation of a corporation's stock. Arguably, a more reliable indicator, the Cyclically Adjusted Price Earning ratio (CAPE), can be obtained by replacing current earnings with a measure of *Permanent Earnings*, that is, the profits that a corporation can earn, on average, over the medium to long run. In this study, we aim to understand the cross-sectional aspects of the dynamics of valuation metrics across global equity markets including both developed and emerging markets. Valuation measures involve various accounting ratios based on economic fundamentals — Piotroski score (Piotroski, 2000) is a representative example. An alternative is the CAPE, or Shiller PE, an inflation-adjusted price-to-earning ratio defined as a price divided by a moving average of the earnings, evaluated in real terms (see Campbell & Shiller, 1987). A compelling reason for using CAPE is that it goes deep into history, and tends to remove the business cycle effect of the economy and focuses more on the long run historical average of real earnings to better forecast present value of future dividends, as summarized by Molodovsky (1995). It further means that[1] higher than average CAPE values means lower expected long-term returns. Therefore, an undervalued equity stock is one that has a CAPE value which is below its long-term historical value. Even though CAPE values are not intended to act as a leading indicator to foresee discontinuity in asset prices shortly, however, higher CAPE values have often been associated with impending market corrections.

The advantage of the CAPE approach is that it can be employed to evaluate entire markets through the underlying traded benchmark index. Nowadays, the value-based investment strategy is becoming increasingly popular for asset allocation (see, for instance, Meb Faber's new GVAL ETF). Employing such an approach, however, gives rise to a new and challenging question, namely, when CAPE ratio can be used to make an investment decision for a portfolio of country-specific indices, how such a portfolio correlates across all the individual equity indices. In particular, the CAPE is a variable derived from price; however, it is fundamentally different to price. Thus, the correlation matrices based on the price of country-specific indices and the derived CAPE is in theory linked but not identical. The question becomes palpable in the case of emerging markets, which at present based

1. See, for instance, Asness, Moskowitz, and Pedersen (2013) for discussion of the details of value and momentum strategies.

on a benchmark market cap approach have an allocation of more than 12% in MSCI All-Country World Index (ACWI).[2] In light of this discussion, in this work, we contribute to the existing literature in the following ways: We focus on the correlation matrix of CAPE for a list of 34 global economies including both developed and emerging economies and use the DCC GARCH model to capture the dynamics of the correlation. We then define the value spread in the correlation matrix as a difference between the DCC GARCH calculated correlation for the CAPE and the one obtained from the prices. We discuss the value spread to global economic events and assess it concerning value risk.

The concept of value risk is based on the premise that long-term investors are seeking and holding undervalued assets, while managing the risk using the price of the assets. The price itself, however, does not adequately capture the cross-sectional dynamics in value as the price in an efficient market world should reflect the long-term earning potential of the assets with respect to all available information. However, this does not say anything about the valuation metric that investors are using to value assets, and sharp decline is asset prices with the sudden onset of a heightened degree of risk aversion, which in most cases is preceded by a financial crisis. It is during these periods of euphoria and fear when asset prices can be detached from their intrinsic value and can be under/overvalued until prices come back to equilibrium. Therefore, investors following a value-based strategy are exposed to a value risk wherein the valuation metric they are employing to forecast the long-term earning potential may not be adequate. The CAPE metric, for instance, considers that historical earnings and inflation, that is, adjusting for business cycle effects, are a good forecast of future returns. In this chapter, we focus on this discrepancy and analyze this difference using empirical data. Thus, value investors may use our method as an advanced metric to evaluate the changes in the overall value of the entire portfolio and accurately estimate the corresponding risk.

2. MSCI via FactSet as of December 31, 2012.

To further expand the scope of this study, we have analyzed the evolution of the dynamic correlations across these markets, by computing correlations and covariance matrix in a Multivariate GARCH framework. One of the bigger challenges that these family of models has faced is an exponential increase in the number of parameters while computing the dynamics of the covariance of multiple assets. Bollerslev (1990) made the first attempt to address this problem by suggesting to keep the correlations constant over time and proposed the Constant Conditional Correlation (CCC) GARCH model. Engle (2002) proposed Dynamic Conditional Correlation (DCC) GARCH model which considered a time varying unconditional correlation matrix of the standardized residuals (see also Bollerslev, Chou, & Kroner, 1992; Ding & Engle, 2001). These models allow one to see the change in correlations for a given pair of markets over time, and thereby enable us to better understand the dynamics of covariances arising in these markets. These dynamics can be attributed to a sudden change in expectations of market participants, and how shocks are transmitted across different markets, over time. As discussed earlier, there have been multiple approaches to the DCC model. However, for this study, we will be restricting ourselves to the Asymmetric Dynamic Conditional Correlation (A-DCC GARCH) by Cappiello, Engle, and Sheppard (2006). Our choice for A-DCC GARCH model rests on the assumption that asymmetric volatility arises because of the leverage effect and because of time-varying risk premium (volatility feedback) (Black, 1976; Christie, 1982). However, Bekaert and Wu (2000) have shown that leverage effect alone does not adequately explain the changes in volatility after a decrease in the asset price. Another stream of literature that has provided a plausible explanation of time-varying risk premium for asymmetries in return volatility is by focusing on the asymmetric response to joint bad news (negative returns for both assets) in correlations. This reasoning stems from the fact that a systematic negative shock induces downward pressure on the returns, in any given pair of assets and thereby will increase the variances of these securities. In a CAPM world, if betas do not change, the covariances will increase, and if idiosyncratic variances do not proportionally change, correlations will also increase as well. In the end, correlations can, therefore, be higher after a negative innovation, than after a positive innovation of the same magnitude.

We use DCC GARCH models to understand the dynamics of correlations in the given markets, as we are specifically interested in the value spread of the correlations obtained by taking a difference of the CAPE and return correlations. The value spread intuitively captures the effect of liquidity spillover from a given market to other markets in the same region, and how the markets have deviated from their historic cyclically adjusted earnings growth. These deviations can further shed light on the valuation risk for any given market as it helps in identifying ex ante when a given market is undervalued/overvalued with reference to a particular asset pricing equilibrium model. On the other hand, the measure of value spreads are heavily skewed toward historical growth. Therefore, its predictions can be underpinned by a sudden revision in the future growth outlook especially in light of the recent central bank actions taken after the 2008 financial crisis. During this period, with the infusion of unprecedented amounts of liquidity in global financial markets, the historical growth rates have in a sense lost their relevance as most of the advanced economies are running below their projected long-term trend growth and with significant output gap.

Our results show that, for the U.S. market, there is nearly no impact on the dynamics of the valuation metrics during the financial crisis thus affecting price and value in the same way. On the other hand, for the remaining two subsets, the financial crisis affected both price and the value of the respective markets differently, and thus investors, when valuing financial assets, should take this into consideration and adjust their valuation risk measure. Further, our results suggest that findings made for the U.S. market, or for the portfolio with the U.S. market as its component, cannot be generalized globally. Additionally, the value spreads also provide crucial information concerning market liquidity, and allows financial market regulators to foresee sudden changes in market liquidity and the spillover direction of hot money from other equity markets. Last but not the least, the European debt crisis does not reveal any significant impact on the value spreads. It thus suggests that the equity markets, which are considered for this study, were not primarily affected by the national budget imbalances, and the crisis was wholly contained in other asset classes, namely in the sovereign bond market.

The remainder of the chapter is structured as follows: In the next section, we describe our dataset. After this, we specify the methodology we use to assess the dynamic correlation and to estimate the value spreads between price and CAPE. In the section "Results," we provide results of the empirical exercise. In the section "Value Portfolio: The Risk Angle," we examine the results through the value investor. We briefly present the conclusion in the last section.

Data

We use a panel of 34 countries, wherein for each country we use the MSCI stock market index. The choice of the MSCI indices, as opposed to the local indices, is because MSCI indices are often tracked by ETFs, which can be directly traded. Therefore, our results have direct trading consequences. For each index, we record both the index level and the earnings per share for the index as it is available from Bloomberg. We accompany the data with the CPI time series from Morningstar to adjust prices in real terms. Our data covers the period from 2002 to 2014 using weekly frequency. The weekly data allows us to ignore the different time zones and addresses the issue of financial market synchronicity. At the same time, the weekly frequency is sufficient enough to capture the dynamics in the ever-changing financial world. We use the following list of countries (in alphabetical order): Australia, Austria, Belgium, Brazil, Canada, Chile, China, Colombia, Finland, France, Germany, Hong Kong, India, Ireland, Israel, Italy, Japan, Malaysia, Mexico, Netherlands, Norway, Peru, Philippines, Poland, Portugal, Russia, South Africa, South Korea, Spain, Sweden, Switzerland, Taiwan, UK, and USA.

Constructing the CAPE

We employ Shiller's CAPE which is defined for a given stock market index I at time t as:

$$\mathrm{CAPE}^{I}_{M;t} = \frac{rP^{I}_{t}}{\mathrm{Avg}_{M;t}\left[r\mathrm{EPS}^{I}_{t\prime}\right]} \tag{1}$$

where the numerator, rP^{I}_{t}, is the price level of the index I at time t expressed in real terms as:

$$rP^{I}_{t} = P^{I}_{t} \cdot \frac{\mathrm{CPI}^{I}_{T}}{\mathrm{CPI}^{I}_{t}}$$

where CPI^{I}_{t} is the last published consumer price index at the domestic country to index I at time t, T is the reference date taken as the last time in the sample and P^{I}_{t} is the price level of the index, and the denominator, $\mathrm{Avg}_{M;t}\left[r\mathrm{EPS}^{I}_{t\prime}\right]$, is the average of the earnings per share, expressed in real terms, over a past window M.[3]

Let us remark, that we tacitly assume that $\mathrm{Avg}_{M;t}\left[r\mathrm{EPS}^{I}_{t\prime}\right] > 0$, which is not always the case. As $\mathrm{Avg}_{M;t}\left[r\mathrm{EPS}^{I}_{t\prime}\right] \to 0+$, the $\mathrm{CAPE}^{I}_{M;t}$ is diverging, where for negative average earnings, the CAPE is negative as well. In fact, our choice of indices was driven by the fact that we consider only those indices, for which $\mathrm{Avg}_{M;t}\left[r\mathrm{EPS}^{I}_{t\prime}\right] > 0$, and thus CAPE is well defined.

We further consider the weekly log-returns from the CAPE and the price level itself, both in real terms:

$$p^{I}_{t} = \log\left(\frac{rP^{\mathrm{I}}_{\mathrm{t}}}{rP^{\mathrm{I}}_{\mathrm{t}}}\right)$$

$$c^{I}_{M;t} = \log\left(\frac{\mathrm{CAPE}^{I}_{M;t}}{\mathrm{CAPE}^{I}_{M;t-1}}\right)$$

3. EPSj is published as 12-month trailing average.

Descriptive Statistics

Tables A1 and A2 provide the descriptive statistics for price-based and CAPE-based returns. Besides, we also document the mean, minimum, and maximum of price and CAPE levels. First, the CAPE-based returns clearly show that CAPE ratio in itself is a dynamic variable with first four moments being comparable to those of returns, though, with lower kurtosis. Second, the value strategies are based on CAPE levels. The range of the CAPE levels suggests large variation over time, which is in line with the reasoning that CAPE itself is a non-stationary variable. Thus, we work with log-returns for both variables to ensure that we have a stationary time series.[4]

Methodology

To capture the time-varying correlation between the assets,[5] Cappiello et al. (2006) proposed a generalized autoregressive conditionally heteroskedastic process, AGDCC-GARCH, which allows for the asymmetric generalized dynamic conditional correlation. Such an approach is an extension of the multivariate DCC-GARCH model by Engle (2002), and it allows for series-specific news impact and smoothing parameters and permits conditional asymmetries in correlation dynamics. ADCC-GARCH model is suitable to assess the correlation dynamics among the different asset classes, which is, in fact, the case when considering stock markets at the different development level. In this chapter, we employ the scalar version of the AGDCC GARCH model, which is numerically more feasible to be used for large-dimensional problems.

4. CAPE-based strategies usually work with levels. Such an approach has to be carefully reviewed as it is based on the non-stationarity of the time series.

5. We chose GARCH models as it's a stylized fact that financial time series data exhibit Conditional Heteroskedasticity.

Let us consider an N-dimensional vector of time series $\mathbf{X}_t$, we then consider the dynamics of log-returns to be driven by the following equations:

$$\mathrm{X}_t = \varepsilon_t \tag{2}$$

$$\varepsilon_t = \mathrm{H}_t^{1/2} v_t \tag{3}$$

$$\mathrm{H}_t = \mathrm{D}_t^{1/2} \mathrm{R}_t \mathrm{D}_t^{1/2} \tag{4}$$

$$\mathrm{R}_t = \mathrm{diag}(\mathrm{Q}_t)^{-1/2} \mathrm{Q}_t \, \mathrm{diag}(\mathrm{Q}_t)^{-1/2} \tag{5}$$

$$\begin{aligned}\mathrm{Q}_t = {} & (\overline{\mathrm{R}} - a^2\overline{\mathrm{R}} - b^2\overline{\mathrm{R}} - g^2\overline{\mathrm{N}}) + a^2\tilde{\varepsilon}_{t-1}\tilde{\varepsilon}'_{t-1} + g^2(I[\tilde{\varepsilon}_t < 0]\circ\tilde{\varepsilon}_t)(I[\tilde{\varepsilon}_t < 0]\circ\tilde{\varepsilon}_t)' \\ & + b^2\mathrm{Q}_{t-1}\end{aligned} \tag{6}$$

$$\overline{\mathrm{R}} = E\left[\tilde{\varepsilon}_t\tilde{\varepsilon}'_t\right] \tag{7}$$

$$\overline{\mathrm{N}} = E\left[(I[\tilde{\varepsilon}_t < 0]\circ\tilde{\varepsilon}_t)(I[\tilde{\varepsilon}_t < 0]\circ\tilde{\varepsilon}_t)'\right] \tag{8}$$

$$\tilde{\varepsilon}_t^{(i)} = x_t^{(i)} / \sqrt{h_t^{(i)}} \tag{9}$$

with $h_t^{(i)}$ being the standardized residuals from the univariate model.

As we see, Eqs. (1–8) show the modeling of asset return and subsequently fitting an asymmetric DCC-GARCH model. The matrix $\mathbf{H}_t$ provides a time-varying variance-covariance matrix. In particular, the element $\{\mathbf{H}_t\}_{ij}$ captures the covariance between i-th and j-th component at time t.

Value Spreads

Let us further denote the time-varying covariance matrix $\mathbf{H}_t$ estimated from the vector of the log-returns of price, $p_t = \{p_t^I\}_{I\in\mathrm{Indices}}$, and the vector of the log-returns of CAPE, $c_{M,t} = \left\{c_{M,t}^I\right\}_{I\in\mathrm{Indices}}$, as

$\mathbf{H}_t^p$ and $\mathbf{H}_t^{c,M}$, respectively. The difference between the p_t^I and $c_{M;t}^I$ comes through the slowly varying process of $\mathrm{Avg}_{M;t}\left[r\mathrm{EPS}_{t'}^I\right]$. Such a process should not have a very significant contribution to the dynamics at the weekly frequency as it is an M-year average across a large number of underlying companies. Consequently, the matrices $\mathbf{H}_t^p$ and $\mathbf{H}_t^{c,M}$ should be similar to each other both in the diagonal and the off-diagonal terms

$$\mathbf{H}_t^p \cong \mathbf{H}_t^{c,M} \tag{10}$$

The matrix $\mathbf{H}_t^p$ enters directly into the mean-variance optimization exercises, when an investor tries to optimize her portfolio. The matrix captures the covariance across markets and thus reflects the risk contagion, where the large off-diagonal elements suggest a strong channel for the value spread of the market shocks. On the other hand, $\mathbf{H}_t^{c,M}$ itself does not have a priori usage as the CAPE is used as a metric to value assets for the purpose of the Value investment. It is believed by practitioners that $\mathrm{CAPE}_{M;t}^I$ is properly normalized price, which allows one to set a threshold to determine the (low) value of the asset/index. The $\mathrm{CAPE}_{M;t}^I$-based valuation of markets is conventionally done on the univariate basis.

We, therefore, focus on the understanding the difference between $\mathbf{H}_t^p$ and $\mathbf{H}_t^{c,M}$ to assess whether the value investment strategies reflect both univariate price variation and the covariance features across markets. In particular, if the off-diagonal terms differ the $\mathrm{CAPE}_{M;t}^I$-based valuation is not from the portfolio perspective anymore similar to normalized price and may lead to different cross-sectional properties.

For that purpose, we define the matrix of the covariance value spreads as:

$$\mathbf{S}_t = \mathbf{H}_t^{c,M} - \mathbf{H}_t^p \tag{11}$$

where $\{\mathbf{S}_t\}_{ij}$ denotes the time-varying difference between the $\mathrm{CAPE}_{M;t}^I$-based and the price-based covariances between indices i and j.

Results

We use the weekly data for 34 stock market indices and calculate the $CAPE^I_{7;t}$, the cyclically adjusted price-to-earnings ratio based on the 7-year moving average of the inflation-adjusted earnings per share.[6] For the weekly time series, we have estimated the matrices $\mathbf{H}^p_t$ and $\mathbf{H}^{c,M}_t$, respectively.[7] To overcome the significant numerical burden with the convergence of the full maximum likelihood model with 34 countries, we have split the sample into three regional subsets; the splitting has been based on the stock exchange opening times with respect to the GMT.

Subset No. 1: America — *USA*, Brazil, Canada, Chile, Colombia, Mexico, and Peru.

Subset No. 2: Europe — *UK*, Austria, Belgium, Finland, France, Germany, Ireland, Italy, Netherlands, Norway, Portugal, Poland, Spain, Sweden, and Switzerland.

Subset No. 3: Asia — *Japan*, Australia, China, Hong Kong, India, Israel, Malaysia, Philippines, Russia, South Africa, South Korea, and Taiwan.

The European subset in our sample is based on the strong economic and financial integration of the EU member states. It is due to this reason why we left Russia for the Asia subset, as well as South Africa, which is highly linked through the commodity channel to China and Japan. Each of three subsets contains a large number of correlations. Further, in the Asia subset, there are 66 correlation pairs. To simplify the numerical estimations and make the system more tractable, we consider the biggest financial center for each region to act as a reference center. The first country in each of the subset, denoted by italics, is the benchmark for the given

6. We have considered the range of values between 5 and 10 years and all of them shows similar quantitative results.
7. We have used Matlab Financial ToolBox.

region, and all the correlations are computed concerning the given stock index.

Benchmark

To evaluate the time-varying correlation, we relate them to the benchmark based on the standard correlation. We use the standard Pearson correlation coefficient, ρ, for which we calculate the sample standard error: $\sigma_\rho = \sqrt{\frac{1-\rho^2}{N-2}}$ where N is the size of the sample. We estimate the static correlation for both the price-based and $\text{CAPE}^I_{7;t}$-based log-returns.

Correlations

We calculate both the static and dynamic correlations for each of the three regions separately, where we focus on the correlation between the respective financial center and other markets. Our primary objective is to understand the difference between the dynamics of the prices and the cyclically adjusted price-to-earnings ratio. Cyclically adjusted earnings per share, $\text{Avg}_{M;t}\left[r\text{EPS}^I_{t'}\right]$, as defined in Eq. (1), are not a smooth function even though we use a 7-year moving average. Figure 1 depicts the 7-year cyclically adjusted earnings per share, $\text{Avg}_{7;t}\left[r\text{EPS}^I_{t'}\right]$, based on the 12-month trailing average, for three major financial centers. The figure confirms the intuition that earnings per share, even when using the 7-year average are not smooth. Thus, the $\text{CAPE}^I_{7;t}$ is a normalized price with a denominator being a rapidly varying variable. The denominator, however, is not an independent variable with the numerator as the price of an asset is a function of the present value of future expected earnings.

We now focus our attention on the dynamics of the pair-wise correlations. Figures 2–4 depict the pair-wise correlations between the financial centers and the respective countries. The dash straight line depicts the static correlation between the price-based returns, where the shaded region enveloping the static correlation corresponds to 95% confidence interval; the solid straight line represents the static correlation between the $\text{CAPE}_{7;t}$-based

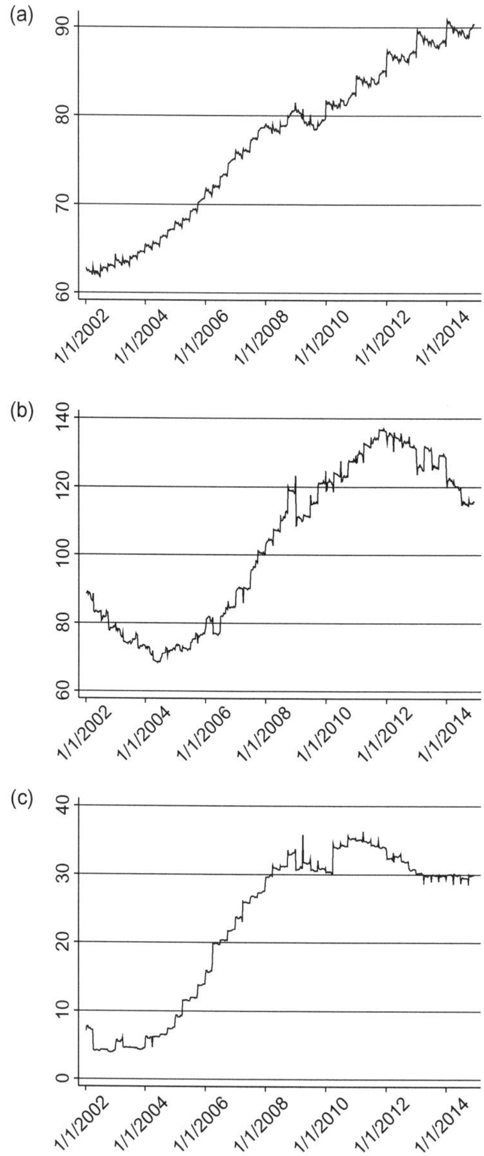

Figure 1: 7-Year Cyclically Adjusted Earnings per Share: (a) USA, (b) UK, (c) Japan. *Note*: It depicts the 7-year cyclically adjusted earnings per share, $\text{Avg}_{7;t}[r\text{EPS}^{I}_{t'}]$ based on the 12-month trailing average.

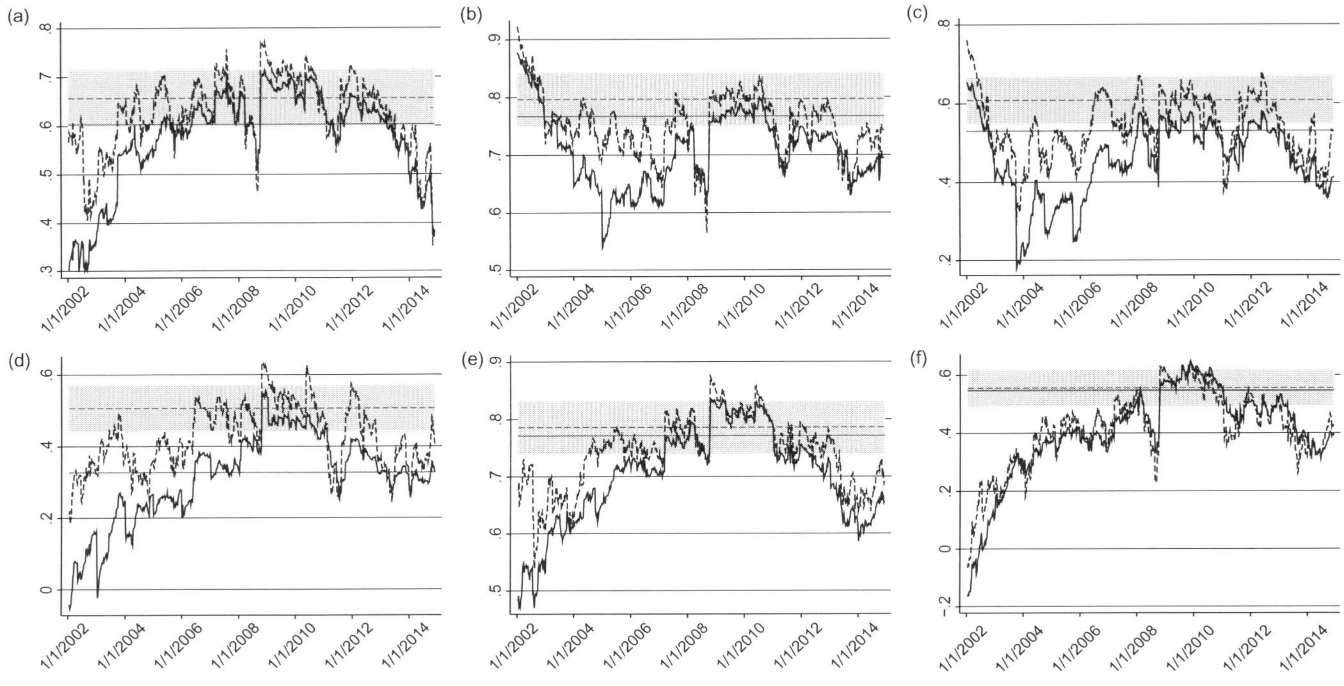

Figure 2: Correlations: America. (a) USA-Brazil, (b) USA-Canada, (c) USA-Chile,. (d) USA-Colombia, (e) USA-Mexico, (f) USA-Peru.

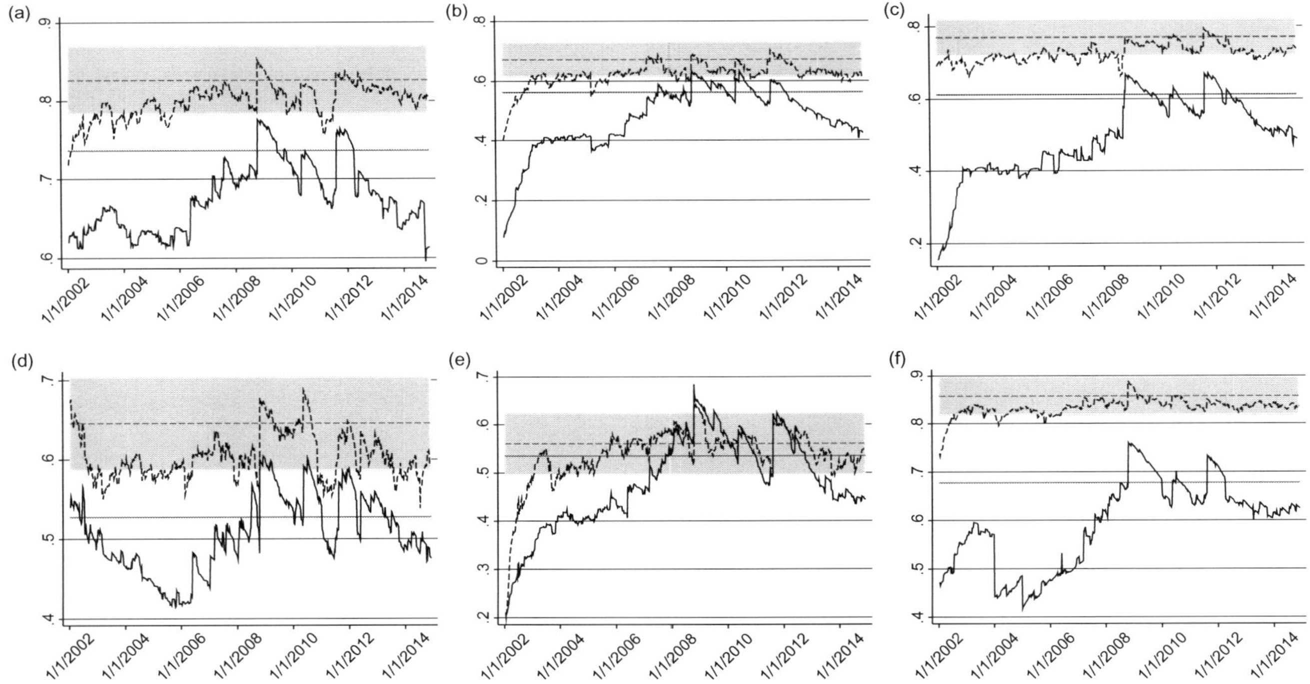

Figure 3: Correlations: Europe. (a) UK-Sweden, (b) UK-Ireland, (c) UK-Norway, (d) UK-Portugal, (e) UK-Poland, (f) UK-Switzerland, (g) UK-Finland, (h) UK-Austria, (i) UK-Belgium, (j) UK-Spain, (k) UK-Italy, (l) UK-Netherlands, (m) UK-France, (n) UK-Germany. *Note*: The solid black and gray lines depict the dynamic and the static correlations between the $\mathrm{CAPE}^{I}_{7;t}$ and $\mathbf{H}^{c,7}_{t}$, respectively; the dashed black and gray lines illustrates the dynamic and the static correlation between the price levels, $\mathbf{H}^{p}_{t}$, respectively. The shaded region shows the 95% confidence interval for the static correlation of the price levels, which serves as a benchmark.

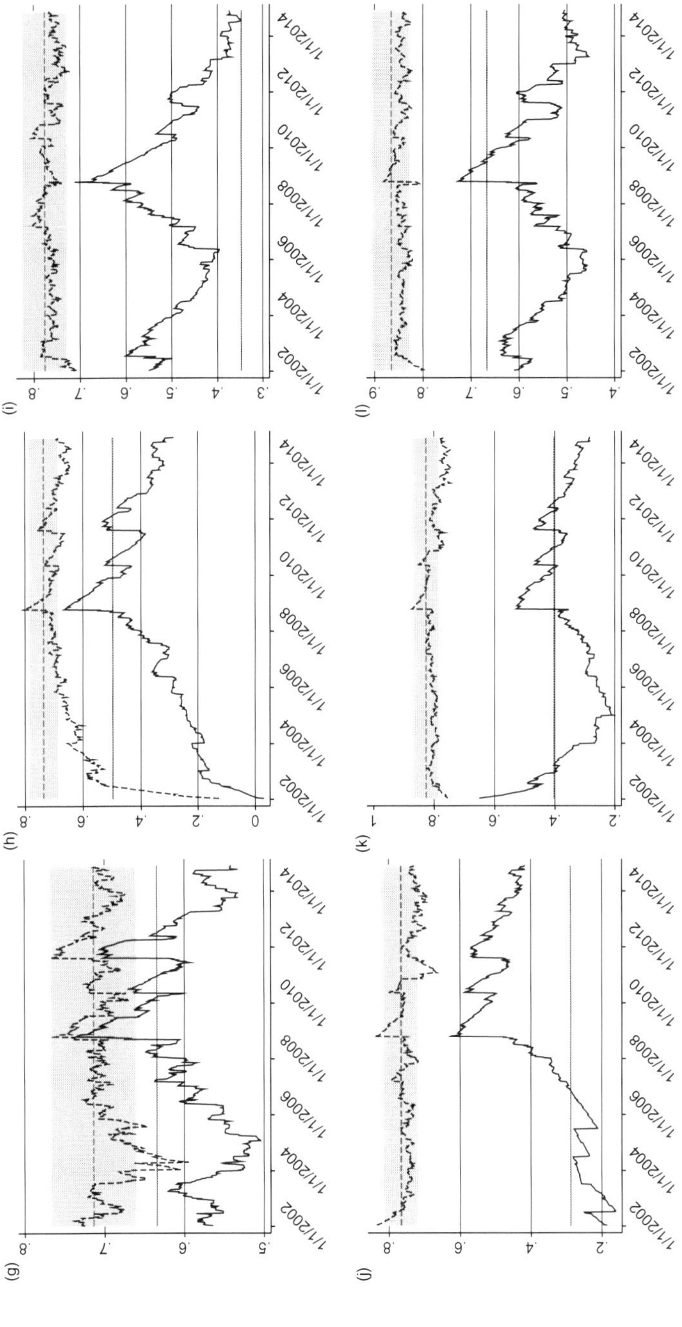

Figure 3: (Continued)

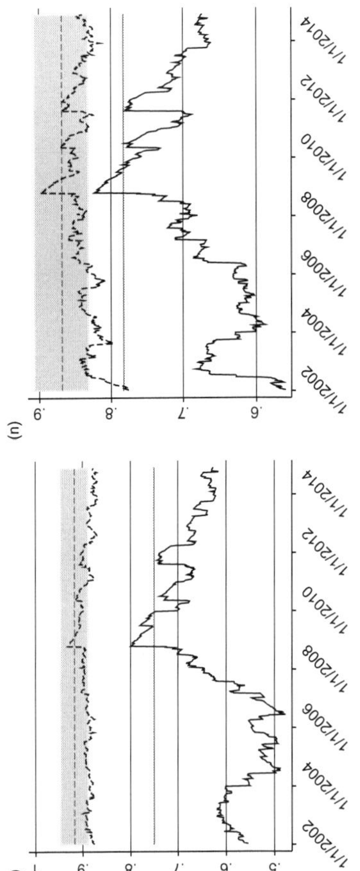

Figure 3: *(Continued)*

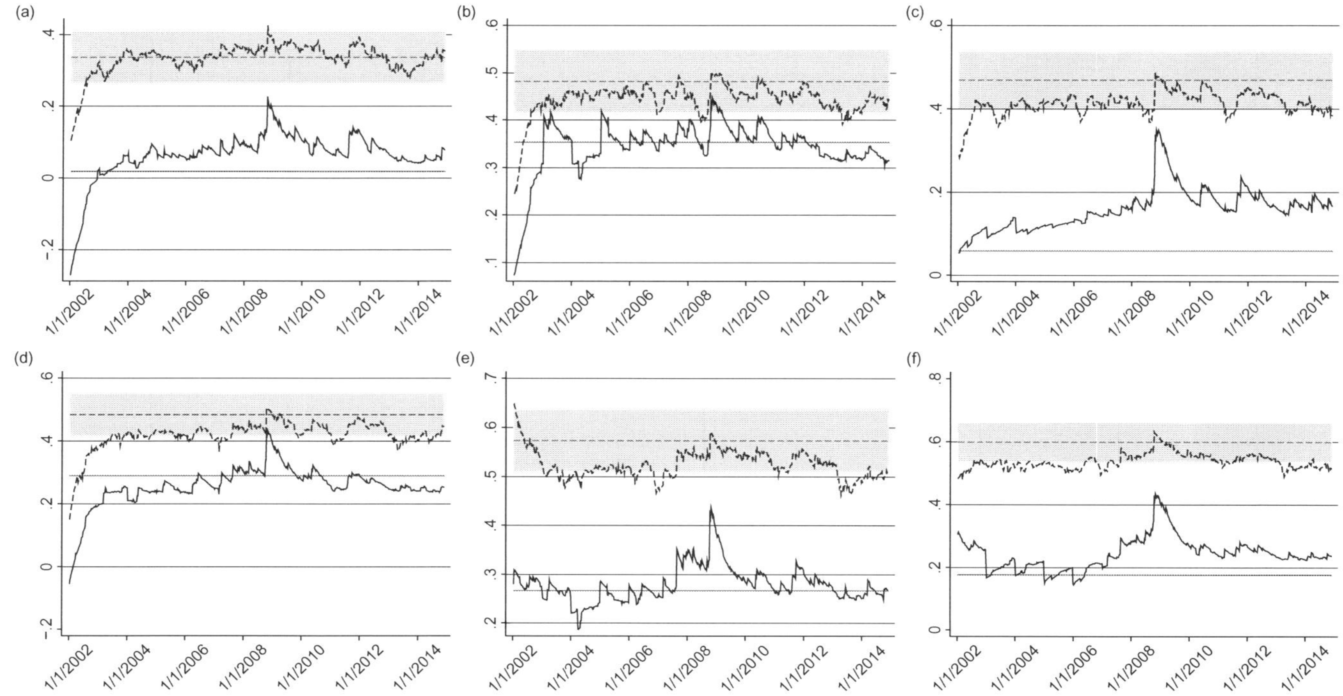

Figure 4: Correlations: Asia. (a) Japan-Israel, (b) Japan-South Africa, (c) Japan-Russia, (d) Japan-India, (e) Japan-China, (f) Japan-Hong Kong, (g) Japan-Malaysia, (h) Japan-Philippines, (i) Japan-Taiwan, (j) Japan-Australia, (k) Japan-South Korea. *Note*: The solid black and gray lines depict the dynamic and the static correlations between the $\text{CAPE}^{I}_{7;t}$ and $\mathbf{H}^{c,7}_{t}$, respectively; the dash black and gray lines illustrates the dynamic and the static correlation between the price levels, $\mathbf{H}^{p}_{t}$, respectively. The shaded region shows the 95% confidence interval for the static correlation of the price levels, which serves as a benchmark.

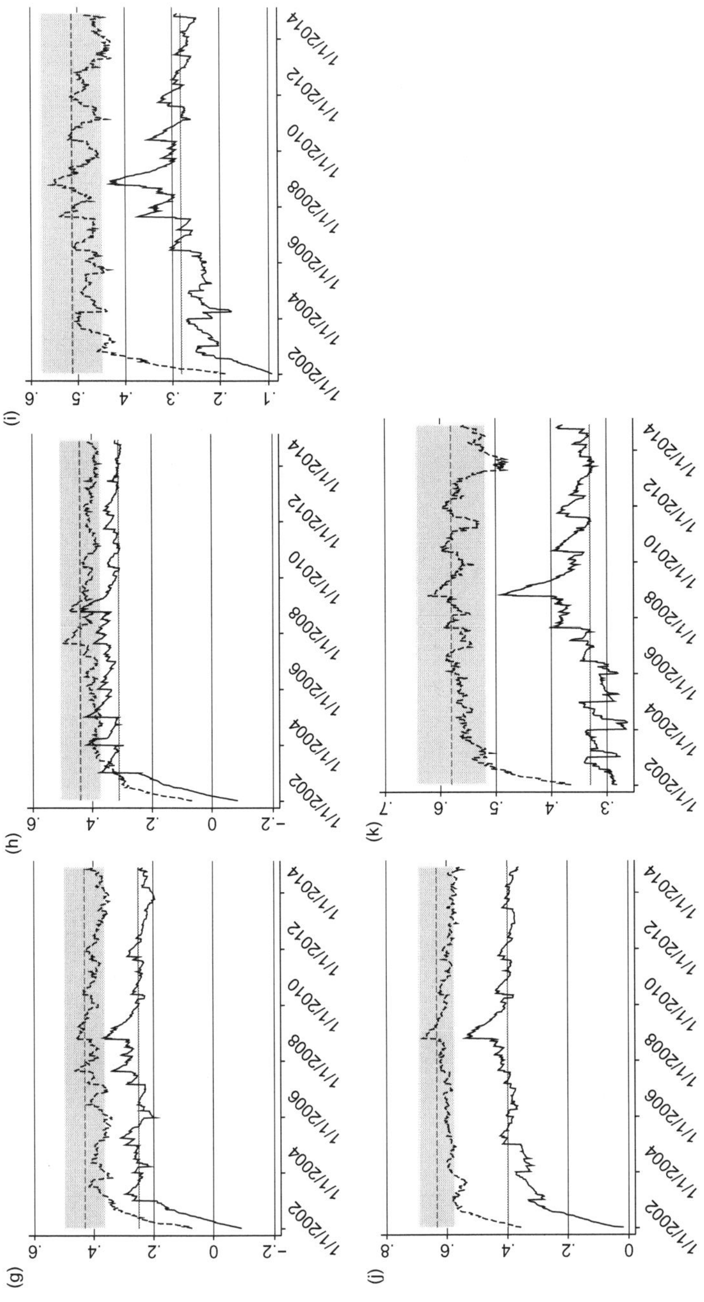

Figure 4: (Continued)

log-returns; the time-varying dash line corresponds to the dynamic correlation of the price-based log-returns, and the solid time-varying line corresponds to the dynamic correlation between the $CAPE_{7;t}$-based log-returns.

The variance in earnings thus brings a new dynamic component into the price process. The earnings itself relates to the economic performance of a given stock market, and, consequently, the country. Thus, both the price and the $CAPE_{7;t}$ are two related measures which track the economic performance of a country. As we do not want to consider a priori state, as to which one is more accurate, we rather proceed with a pair-wise comparison of the two measures across the countries. The first hypothesis is thus to assess whether the static correlation between the two measures is statistically significant or not. Given that we can calculate the confidence interval for the static correlation, we may answer the question accurately. By the second hypothesis, we aim to understand how the dynamic correlation is different with the static one and in particular when the static price-based correlation can act as a benchmark.

America

Figure 2 captures the pair-wise correlation for USA-Brazil, USA-Canada, USA-Chile, USA-Colombia, USA-Mexico, and USA-Peru. First, except in the case of Colombia and Peru, the static correlations are not statistically distinguishable from each other as we can see from the confidence levels presented in the figure. Thus, even though we use the unsmoothed denominator, the overall impact on the correlation is not severe. Second, the dynamic correlations are following closely each other, except in 2002, where we see an opposite trend for the case of Brazil and Mexico, which presumably is due to the post dot-com bubble correction.

Europe

Figure 3 captures the pair-wise correlation for UK-Sweden, UK-Ireland, UK-Norway, UK-Portugal, UK-Poland, UK-Switzerland, UK-Finland, UK-Austria, UK-Belgium, UK-Spain, UK-Italy, UK-Netherlands, UK-France, and UK-Germany. Compared to the case of America, there is a significant discrepancy in the static correlations between the two measures. It suggests that the two measures are capturing different economic effects and are not integrated in the same way. Second, the dynamic correlations further stress the difference between the two measures, namely, the dynamic price-based correlation in most of the cases is close to the static one. Thus, the dynamic effects do not play such a significant role. However, the $CAPE_{7;t}$-based dynamic correlation shows the shift in level — an effect linked to both the absolute difference between the static correlations — and the different patterns. For instance, during 2002 and 2003 the UK-Italy pair shows a different trend in the dynamic correlations. Such a pattern is present in other countries as well. Thus, for European Union (EU) — which is a union of economically integrated countries — there exists greater discrepancy in the valuation metric based on the two measures than countries in the American continent.

Asia

Figure 4 captures the pair-wise correlation for Japan-Israel, Japan-South Africa, Japan-Russia, Japan-India, Japan-China, Japan-Hong Kong, Japan-Malaysia, Japan-Philippines, Japan-Taiwan, Japan-Australia, and Japan-South Korea. First, the difference between the two static correlations is statistically significant for all country pairs. It suggests that the two valuations are capturing different economic factors. Second, the dynamic correlations show a different pattern. For pairs like Japan-Malaysia and Japan-Philippines, the dynamic correlations are tightly connected and evolve in a similar manner, presumably because of a higher integration in the set of economic factors both exogenous as well as endogenous influencing these markets. On the other hand, for pairs like Japan-China and Japan-Russia, there is disentanglement between the dynamic of the two measures. This further shows that even though the set of exogenous factors affecting these markets remains similar, the set of idiosyncratic endogenous variables has a big impact on these markets.

In conclusion, the two measures tend to capture the value of financial markets, and, in particular, the dynamics of the economic integration in a significantly different ways. Such a difference is more pronounced outside the American continent, or, rather for all the pairs except those with the USA. Our use of dynamic correlations further amplifies this difference. Consequently, the stylized fact about the link between the price — or the value of a market — and the financial distress is not necessarily preserved when using other valuation metrics, even for those which are popular for the value investment. In the following section, we focus more closely on the value spreads between the dynamic correlations, $\mathbf{S}_t$, as defined in Eq. (11).

Value Spreads

We calculate the value spreads between the dynamic correlations for measures as defined in Eq. (11). To assess the econometric significance of the value spread, we set the confidence bounds based on the static correlations. That is, for a given pair of countries, we estimate the static correlations using price-based and $\mathrm{CAPE}_{7;t}$-based log-returns. For both the correlations, we calculate the error:

$$\sigma_\rho = \sqrt{\frac{1-\rho^2}{N-2}}$$

Then, we set the confidence bounds for the value spreads as $\sigma_S = \sqrt{\sigma_P^2 + \sigma_{\mathrm{CAPE}}^2}$. Thereby, we can benchmark the value spreads against the static case and assess the significance of the difference between the dynamics of the two valuation measures.

In Figures 5–7, we depict the dynamics of the value spread $S_t^{(i,j)}$ between the two countries, the dotted line, together with the static value spreads, the dashed line, as well as the shaded region corresponding to the 95% confidence interval based on the static value spreads. Therefore, every time the dynamic value spread lies outside the shaded area, we will consider that the pair-wise dynamics of the two valuation metrics is statistically different from each other.

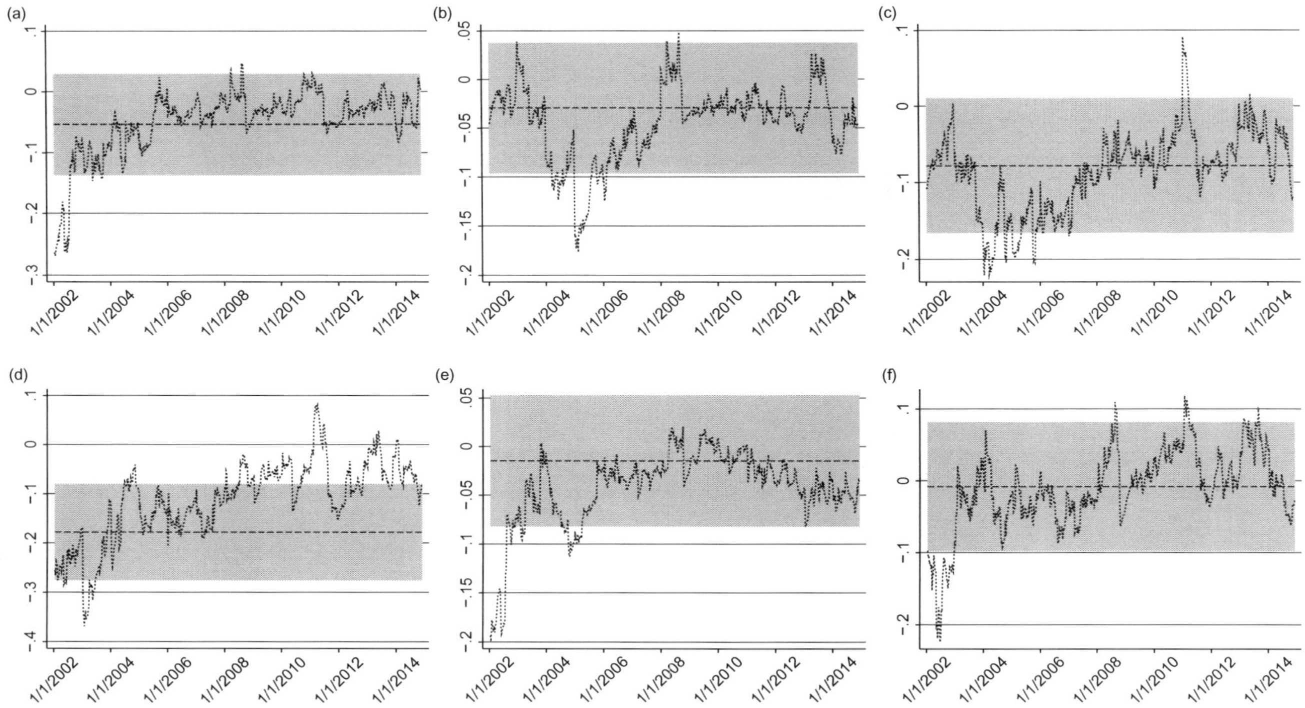

Figure 5: Value spreads: America. (a) USA-Brazil, (b) USA-Canada, (c) USA-Chile, (d) USA-Colombia, (e) USA-Mexico, (f) USA-Peru. *Note*: The dashed line depicts the value spread between the static correlations of the price-based and $CAPE^{I}_{7;t}$-based valuation measures, the shaded region corresponds to the 95% confidence interval of the static value spreads, and the dotted line corresponds to the dynamic value spreads $\mathbf{S}_t$.

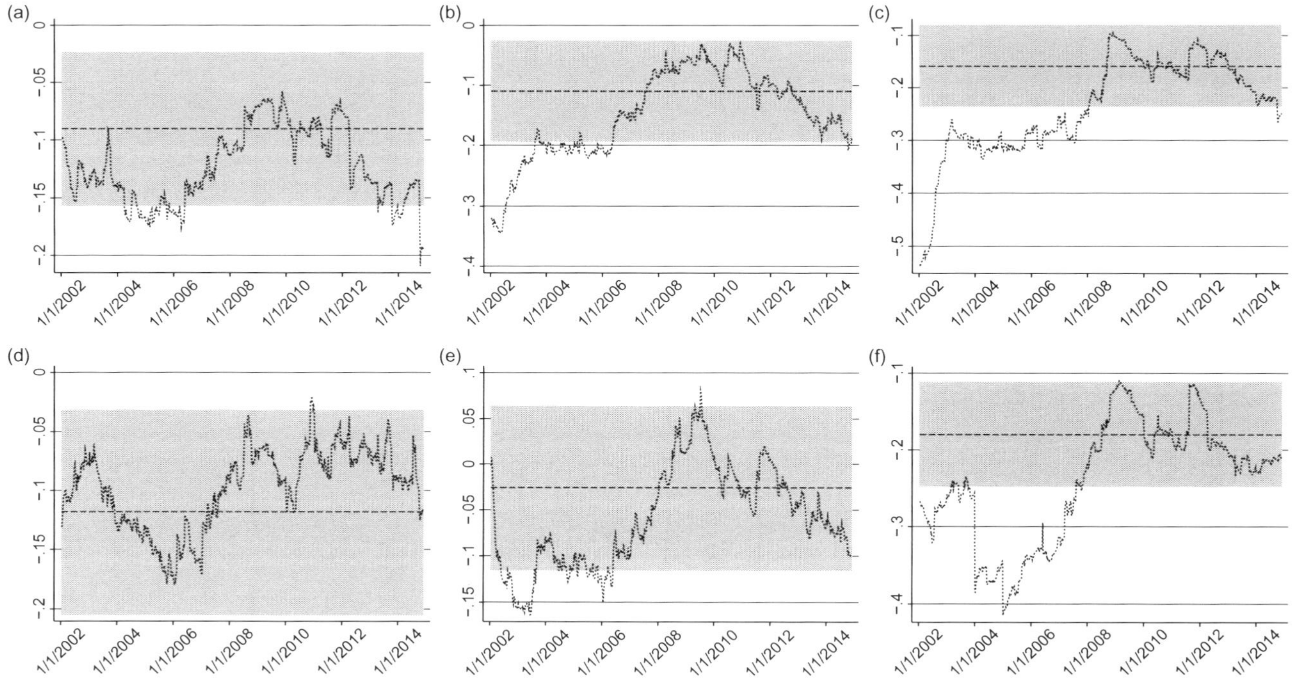

Figure 6: Value Spreads: Europe. (a) UK-Sweden, (b) UK-Ireland, (c) UK-Norway, (d) UK-Portugal, (e) UK-Poland, (f) UK-Switzerland, (g) UK-Finland, (h) UK-Austria, (i) UK-Belgium, (j) UK-Spain, (k) UK-Italy, (l) UK-Netherlands, (m) UK-France, (n) UK-Germany. *Note*: The dashed line depicts the value spread between the static correlations of the price-based and $CAPE^{I}_{7;t}$-based valuation measures, the shaded region, corresponds to the 95% confidence interval of the static value spreads, and the dotted line corresponds to the dynamic value spreads $\mathbf{S}_t$.

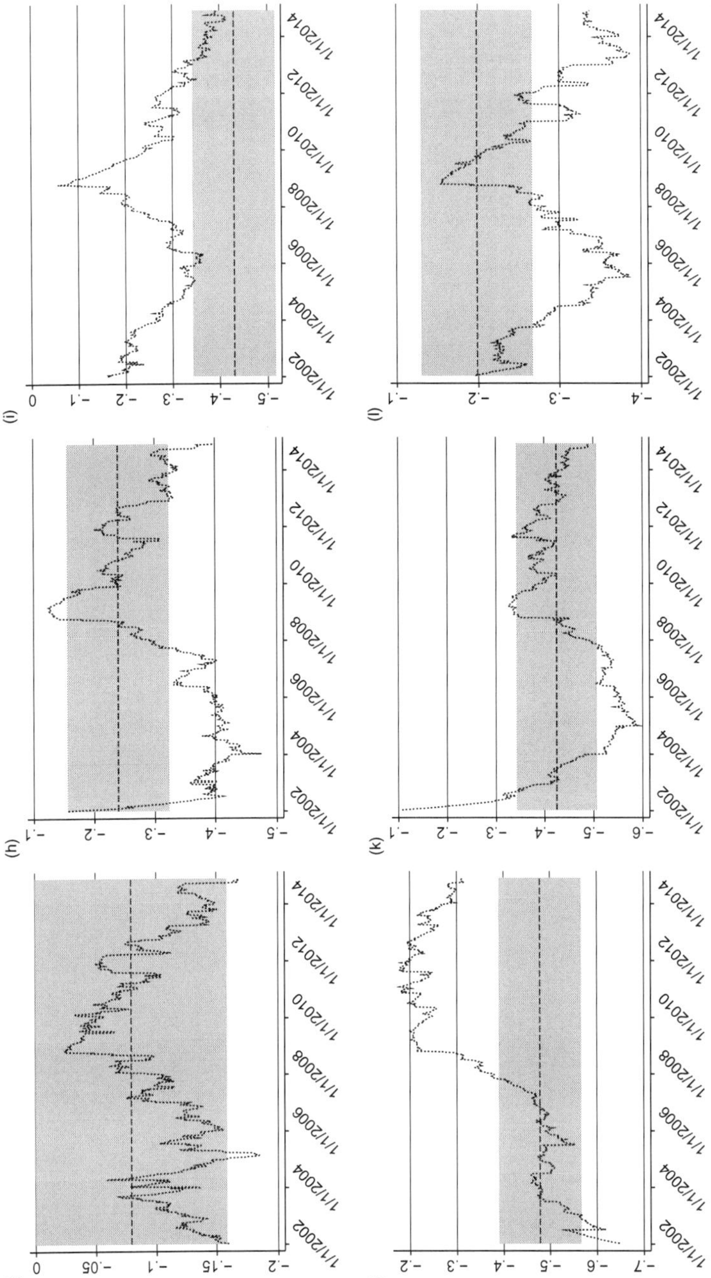

Figure 6: (Continued)

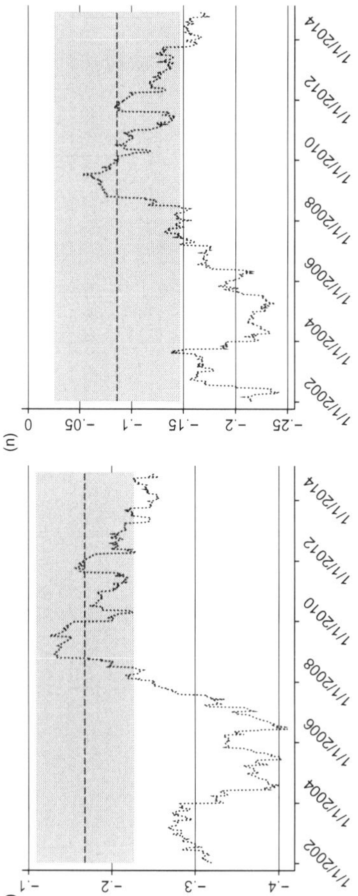

Figure 6: *(Continued)*

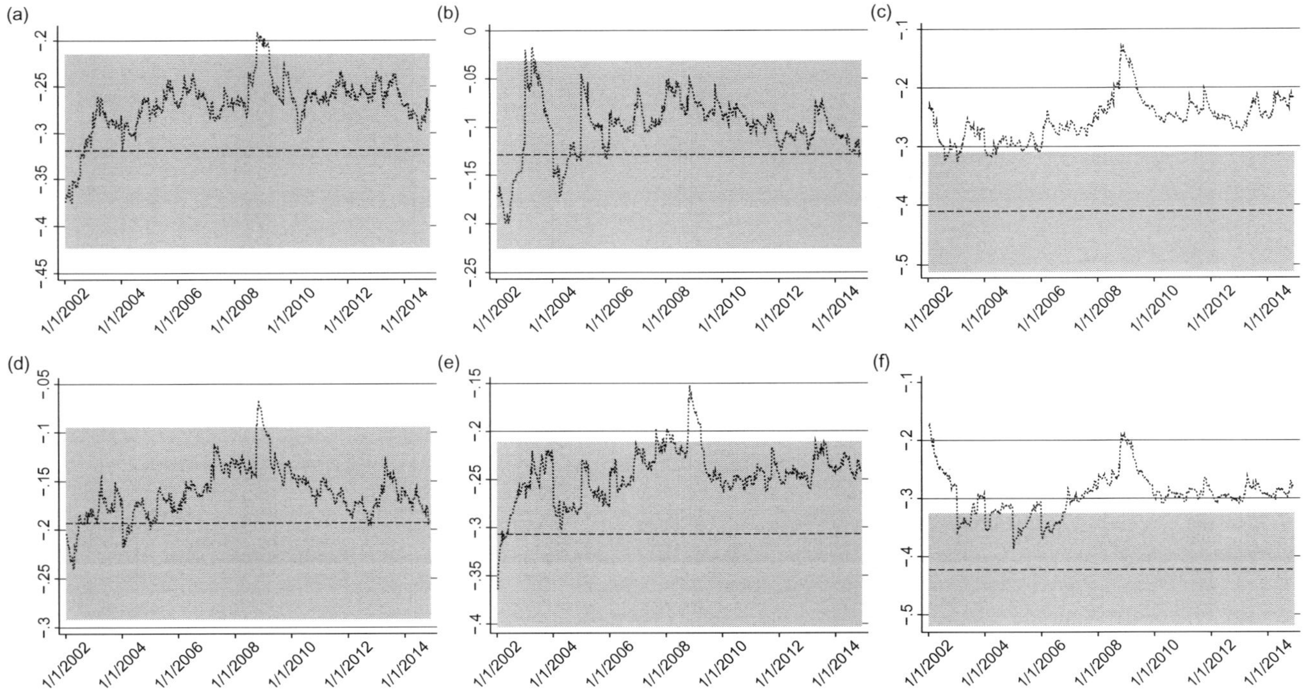

Figure 7: Value Spreads: Asia. (a) Japan-Israel, (b) Japan-South Africa, (c) Japan-Russia, (d) Japan-India, (e) Japan-China, (f) Japan-Hong Kong, (g) Japan-Malaysia, (h) Japan-Philippines, (i) Japan-Taiwan, (j) Japan-Australia, (k) Japan-South Korea. *Note*: The dashed line depicts the value spread between the static correlations of the price-based and $CAPE^{I}_{7;t}$-based valuation measures, the shaded region corresponds to the 95% confidence interval of the static value spreads, and the dotted line corresponds to the dynamic value spreads $\mathbf{S}_t$.

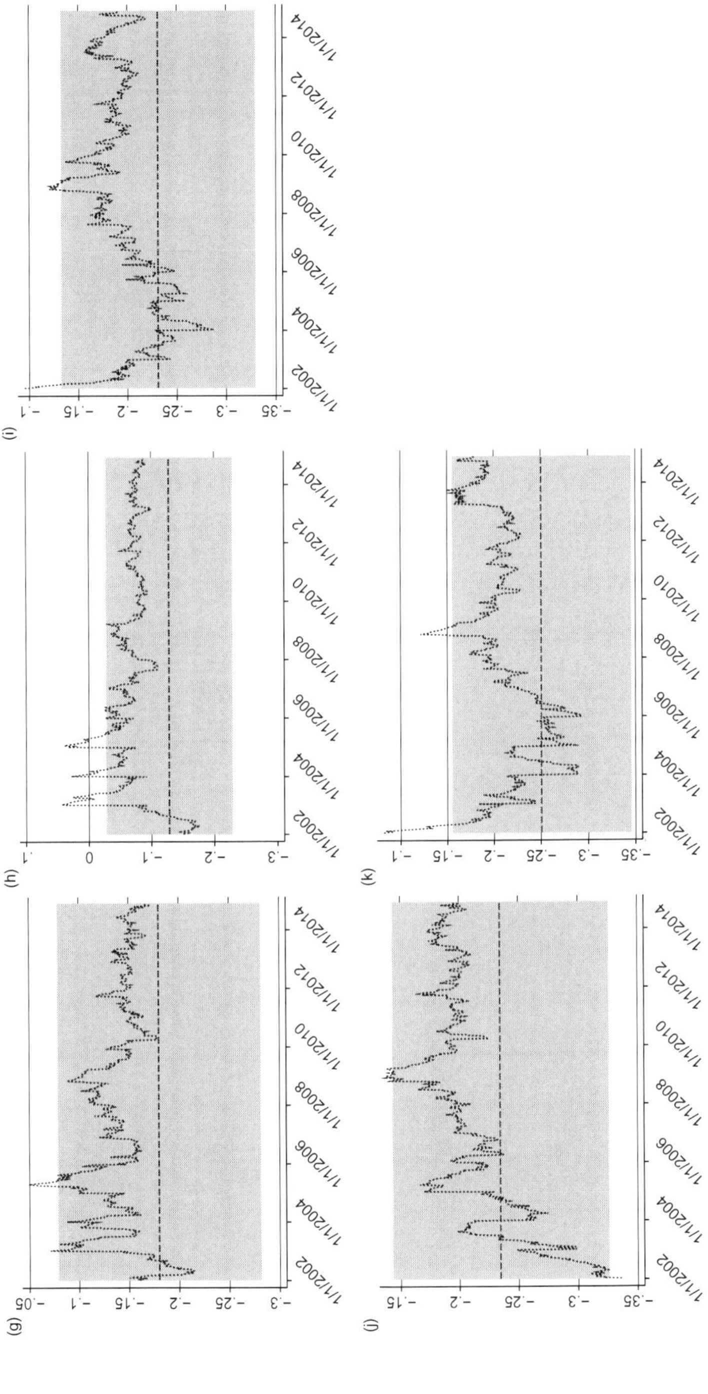

Figure 7: (Continued)

America

Figure 5 captures the pair-wise value spreads for USA-Brazil, USA-Canada, USA-Chile, USA-Colombia, USA-Mexico, and USA-Peru. Overall, the value spreads between dynamic correlations are rather indistinguishable from each other as most of the time; the value spreads do not leave the shaded region. The value spreads tend to be negative meaning that the $CAPE_{7;t}$-based returns are less correlated than prices. The figure shows that in the post dot-com bubble period, the value spreads tend to leave confidence interval, and is often in the negative territory. Therefore, the market prices were not in equilibrium as proposed by the CAPE measure capturing the historical long-term growth. This deviation can be inferred as a sign of panic or exuberance in the market. For instance post dot-com bubble the earnings estimate of Brazil, Colombia, Mexico, and Peru got detached from their historical earnings with the only exception of Canada and Chile. It further suggests that there was liquidity spillover from the USA equity markets, as all the correlations are referenced to USA, and, therefore, suggests the influx of hot money into the financial markets of these economies. This deviation of prices from their long-term earnings can explain that market participants were driven by euphoria, and asset prices deviated from their equilibrium prices. Furthermore, post 2008 crisis we can see that prices again got disentangled from their historical earnings in Colombia, Peru, and Chile and for a short interval from Brazil and Canada. However, in this case, money was flowing out of these economies; market participants were driven by a state of panic and were severely penalizing these markets by rapidly discounting the earnings far greater than suggested by the historical trend.

Europe

Figure 6 captures the pair-wise value spreads for UK-Sweden, UK-Ireland, UK-Norway, UK-Portugal, UK-Poland, UK-Switzerland, UK-Finland, UK-Austria, UK-Belgium, UK-Spain, UK-Italy, UK-Netherlands, UK-France, and UK-Germany. Compared to the case of America, the value spreads tend to be larger in absolute value, suggesting much greater valuation discrepancy among countries.

This is, in fact, surprising, as one would expect that Europe is composed of the countries, which are highly economically and financially integrated, more than the countries across the North and South America. Further, in most of the European pairs, we see a spike around the default of Lehman Brothers, suggesting that the impact of the financial crisis was transmitted through the relative value of financial assets in European capital markets. On the other hand, the European debt crisis, which started in Europe, does not seem to have such a severe effect on the dynamics of market valuations vis-à-vis with the financial crisis post-Lehman bankruptcy.

Asia

Figure 7 captures the pair-wise value spreads for Japan-Israel, Japan-South Africa, Japan-Russia, Japan-India, Japan-China, Japan-Hong Kong, Japan-Malaysia, Japan-Philippines, Japan-Taiwan, Japan-Australia, and Japan-South Korea. The value spreads across Asia resemble more closely to Europe than when compared to America. We see a significant discrepancy between Japan and Russia and Japan and Hong Kong. Otherwise, the valuation metrics between the countries across the last subset of countries is rather similar. For the first pair of countries, the discrepancy is not so surprising as Japan and Russia are not tightly linked — strictly in an economic, financial, or political sense. Similar to Europe, we see an impact of the financial crisis on the dynamics of valuations as the value spreads tend to move away from the static bounds.

Value Portfolio: The Risk Angle

We now summarize the results from an investor's standpoint using a value-based investment strategy with the opportunity set being individual stock markets across the globe. Such investments with minimal transaction costs can be carried out through Exchange Traded Funds (ETFs), which track the performance of an underlying tradable broad market index. Among those Indices, the MSCI family is in particular very common and is therefore used in this chapter.

Such a strategy works as follows: Investor operates with the opportunity set consisting of stock market indices, or the corresponding ETFs, where for each of the indices the investor continuously assesses the valuation metric. Thus, at every point in time, the investor can rank the markets based on its value. Also, the valuation metrics can be used to assess the cardinal value of the markets. Based on the results of the valuation metric, the investor can form a respective trading strategy.[8] Thus, the investor uses the valuation metric to screen the investment universe and to make investment decisions. While making an investment decision on the optimal mix of assets in the portfolio, the investor puts the valuation metric aside and focuses on the under/overvaluation of the assets for a given risk-return metric. In this stage, the relative performance of a valuation metric across assets plays a central role.

Our results clearly demonstrate that using a static correlation, which is the most intuitive choice, does not provide real-time information concerning the comovements between markets during the crisis period. For instance, during the post dot-com bubble period, we can observe that the correlation between the markets across the American continent were very volatile. Therefore, an investor relying solely on static correlation for asset allocation cannot take into account the misvaluation period during the formation of an asset bubble. In fact, the need for dynamic correlation can be illustrated in all three subsets during the recent financial crisis. Further, our empirical results for the value spreads suggest that the pair-wise dynamics of the valuation metric vary significantly across countries. For the subset of countries from American continents, the valuation metric closely resembles the price process, even for seemingly unrelated countries like USA and Brazil. On the other hand, the economically and financially integrated

8. Particular choices are long-short portfolio based on buying long highly undervalued and going short on overvalued assets, thereby allowing prices to fall in equilibrium. Alternatively, a long only strategy on the most undervalued assets anticipating that prices will rise in future to their intrinsic value.

countries in Europe show significantly different pair-wise dynamics from the price process, as we can see from the value spreads. The difference among European countries is far more significant than for the countries from the Asian subset.

Conclusions

In this work, we have introduced the notion of value spread as a measure of cross-sectional dynamics between price ratio and the CAPE, which serves as an alternative measure for asset pricing. The value spread helps investors to identify periods of asset mispricing and highlights the cross-sectional differences in valuation dynamics for all the major financial centers especially during the financial crisis. We have divided the given set of countries in our sample into three subsets: America, Europe, and Asia. For each region, we have calculated pair-wise dynamics between the financial center of that region and other countries. The subset of the U.S. market shows nearly no impact on the dynamics of the valuation metrics thus affecting price and value in the same way. On the other hand, for the remaining two subsets, the financial crisis affected both price and the value of the respective markets differently. This valuation metric shows different properties for different countries, and thus investors when valuing a financial asset should take this into consideration and adjust their valuation risk measure. Such an observation has direct consequence for valuation of financial assets in emerging economies as the capital markets in these economies are still evolving, compared to capital markets in advanced economies.

In particular, our results suggest that the findings made for the U.S. market, or for the portfolio with the U.S. market as its component, cannot be generalized globally. Our results demonstrate that the recent financial crisis was not related to asset mispricing, as opposed to the dot-com era, which we capture at the beginning of our sample. During the dot-com period, asset prices were detached from their intrinsic value as the markets were driven by irrational euphoria; however, during the post-bubble period, one can observe that the value dynamics were converging toward the price dynamics. Additionally, the value spreads also provide crucial information concerning market liquidity, and allows financial market regulators to foresee sudden changes in market liquidity and the spillover direction of hot money from other equity markets. Finally, the European debt crisis does not reveal any significant impact on the value spreads. It thus suggests that the equity markets, which are considered for this study, were not primarily affected by the national budget imbalances, and the crisis was wholly contained in other asset classes, namely in the sovereign bond market. Therefore, we may consider that the severity of such a crisis spilling over to global equity markets was considerably small.

Note: The solid black and gray lines depict the dynamic and the static correlations between the $\text{CAPE}^{I}_{7;t}$ and $\mathbf{H}^{c,7}_{t}$, respectively; the dash black and gray lines illustrate the dynamic and the static correlation between the price levels, $\mathbf{H}^{p}_{t}$, respectively. The shaded region shows the 95% confidence interval for the static correlation of the price levels, which serves as a benchmark.

Acknowledgments

Jan Novotný acknowledges funding from the European Community's Seventh Framework Program FP7-PEOPLE-2011-IEF under grant agreement number PIEF-GA-2011-302098 (Price Jump Dynamics), the Centre for Econometric Analysis and GAČR P402/12/G097 — DYME. Both the authors thank Robert Shiller, Marco Pagano, Thierry Foucault, and seminar participants at ISEO 2015. Any errors or omissions remain the sole responsibility of the authors.

References

Asness, C. S., Moskowitz, T. J., & Pedersen, L. H. (2013). Value and momentum everywhere. *The Journal of Finance*, *68*(3), 929–985.

Bekaert, G., & Wu, G. (2000). Asymmetric volatility and risk in equity markets. *Review of Financial Studies*, *13*(1), 1–42.

Black, F. (1976). Studies in stock price volatility changes. *Proceedings of the 1976 business meeting of the business and economics statistics section.* American Statistical Association, 177–181.
Bollerslev, T. (1990). Modelling the coherence in short run nominal exchange rates: A multivariate generalized arch approach. *Review of Economic Studies, 72*, 498–505.
Bollerslev, T., Chou, R. Y., & Kroner, K. F. (1992). Arch modeling in finance: A review of the theory and empirical evidence. *Journal of Econometrics, 52*(1), 5–59.
Campbell, J., & Shiller, R. (1987). Stock prices, earnings and expected dividends. *The Journal of Finance, 43*(3), 661–676.
Cappiello, L., Engle, R. F., & Sheppard, K. (2006). Asymmetric dynamics in the correlations of global equity and bond returns. *Journal of Financial Econometrics, 4*(4), 537–572.
Christie, A. A. (1982). The stochastic behavior of common stock variances: Value, leverage and interest rate effects. *Journal of Financial Economics, 10*(4), 407–432.
Cronqvist, H., Siegel, S., & Yu, F. (2015). Value versus growth investing: Why do different investors have different styles? *Journal of Financial Economics, 117*(2), 333–349.
Ding, Z., & Engle, R. F. (2001). *Large scale conditional covariance matrix modeling, estimation and testing*. NYU Working Paper (Fin-01-029).
Engle, R. (2002). Dynamic conditional correlation: A simple class of multivariate generalized autoregressive conditional heteroskedasticity models. *Journal of Business & Economic Statistics, 20*(3), 339–350.
Gray, W. R., & Carlisle, T. E. (2012). *Quantitative value: A practitioner's guide to automating intelligent investment and eliminating behavioral errors*. New York, NY: Wiley.
Molodovsky, N. (1995). A theory of price-earnings ratios. *Financial Analysts Journal, 51*(1), 29–43.
Piotroski, J. D. (2000). Value investing: The use of historical financial statement information to separate winners from losers. *Journal of Accounting Research, 38*, 1–41.
Van der Hart, J., Slagter, E., & Van Dijk, D. (2003). Stock selection strategies in emerging markets. *Journal of Empirical Finance, 10*(1), 105–132.

Appendix

Table A1 presents the descriptive statistics for log-returns for each stock market index observed at the weekly frequency. Also, we provide necessary information about the price levels. Table A2 documents the descriptive statistics for log-returns based on CAPE for each stock market index observed at a weekly frequency. Further, we provide the mean, min and max for CAPE as many value strategies are based directly on the level of the CAPE itself despite being obviously a non-stationary time series.

If we focus on the levels of both price and CAPE, we see that the range of prices and the range of CAPE values are not in all cases in line. For instance, levels of CAPE for Belgium varies between 4.447 and 1153.587, that is, by nearly a three orders of magnitude while prices of the index are in the range between 28.690 and 120.720. This further stresses the fact that prices and CAPEs may have different dynamics and CAPE, being a price normalized by permanent income, may vary significantly. A similar disparity between prices and CAPE can be observed in Russia also.

Table A1: Descriptive Statistics: MSCI Market Indices.

	Panel A: Price levels				Panel B: Price log-returns				
	Mean	Min	Max	Mean	Std.	Skewness	Kurtosis	Min	Max
Australia	909.034	548.270	1363.610	0.0007	0.1591	−0.9797	9.3399	−0.1649	0.0973
Austria	158.642	73.580	348.870	0.0000	0.2711	−1.9573	18.8110	−0.3605	0.1742
Belgium	68.952	28.690	120.720	0.0001	0.2224	−1.5534	11.8074	−0.2175	0.1020
Brazil	2156.354	285.720	4664.740	0.0018	0.3791	−0.6810	8.1804	−0.3306	0.2562
Canada	1414.901	731.910	1981.460	0.0010	0.1719	−0.9358	11.9164	−0.1697	0.1413
Chile	1577.873	389.060	2921.800	0.0016	0.2475	−1.7553	20.6362	−0.3466	0.1913
China	46.489	13.160	100.820	0.0019	0.2741	−0.3179	6.1388	−0.2229	0.1776
Colombia	644.737	53.270	1393.460	0.0042	0.2709	−1.2531	11.2543	−0.2902	0.1278
Finland	104.827	58.470	195.220	−0.0007	0.2813	−0.4659	4.6065	−0.1672	0.1234
France	108.407	67.910	162.940	−0.0001	0.2157	−1.1115	10.6410	−0.2450	0.1228
Germany	95.915	46.520	140.700	0.0003	0.2336	−0.7784	9.0982	−0.2385	0.1564
Hong Kong	8714.399	3946.570	13494.679	0.0012	0.2042	−0.3260	5.7529	−0.1730	0.0981
India	525.425	124.660	1045.250	0.0029	0.2319	−0.5804	6.4157	−0.1900	0.1366

Table A1: (*Continued*)

	Panel A: Price levels			Panel B: Price log-returns					
	Mean	Min	Max	Mean	Std.	Skewness	Kurtosis	Min	Max
Ireland	56.186	18.710	126.180	−0.0013	0.2854	−1.7631	17.6180	−0.3767	0.1705
Israel	197.773	84.570	302.410	0.0008	0.2001	−0.5378	4.5174	−0.1247	0.0900
Italy	75.382	38.530	128.650	−0.0007	0.2333	−1.3467	10.3030	−0.2512	0.1025
Japan	689.748	433.820	1146.700	0.0004	0.2087	−0.9496	8.3987	−0.2232	0.0964
Malaysia	442.750	234.310	667.950	0.0014	0.1345	−0.5525	6.4794	−0.1024	0.0764
Mexico	4602.442	1307.990	7683.990	0.0020	0.2805	−0.8570	13.6156	−0.3068	0.2255
Netherlands	81.131	44.800	116.530	0.0001	0.2212	−1.6827	16.4452	−0.2968	0.0939
Norway	2108.751	785.370	3474.929	0.0011	0.2403	−1.2146	10.8746	−0.2461	0.1534
Peru	884.150	143.810	1887.540	0.0032	0.3021	−0.6556	8.7490	−0.2936	0.2206
Philippines	606.535	203.620	1245.319	0.0021	0.2227	−0.5674	6.6154	−0.1960	0.1252
Poland	1597.544	751.750	2690.310	0.0008	0.2301	−0.3784	5.7641	−0.1670	0.1608
Portugal	69.680	38.890	125.120	−0.0011	0.1989	−1.0454	7.8495	−0.1898	0.0778
Russia	749.904	237.470	1618.319	0.0012	0.3775	−0.1366	12.5633	−0.2806	0.4275

South Africa	650.738	216.240	1309.080	0.0020	0.1897	0.0586	6.4076	−0.0970	0.1626
South Korea	414.013	159.530	629.100	0.0014	0.2445	−0.4064	7.3841	−0.2140	0.1882
Spain	110.286	62.570	179.370	0.0002	0.2407	−0.9328	8.3558	−0.2411	0.1200
Sweden	7234.157	3128.550	10805.889	0.0008	0.2268	−0.8630	8.5443	−0.2267	0.1260
Switzerland	873.908	504.010	1248.870	0.0005	0.1858	−1.5044	18.8001	−0.2479	0.1230
Taiwan	272.479	155.860	376.690	0.0004	0.2163	−0.2923	5.5171	−0.1148	0.1722
UK	1617.446	1042.840	2025.689	0.0003	0.1793	−1.3372	17.2138	−0.2343	0.1255
USA	1273.067	683.380	2052.750	0.0008	0.1785	−0.8597	11.3135	−0.2008	0.1136

Note: This table reports the descriptive statistics for prices for each of the 34 stock market indices. Panel A captures the properties of the price levels while Panel B captures log-returns based on prices for 34 countries observed at a weekly frequency. Std. stands for the standard deviation expressed in annualized terms.

Table A2: Descriptive Statistics: CAPEs.

	Panel A: CAPE levels			Panel B: CAPE log-returns					
	Mean	Min	Max	Mean	Std.	Skewness	Kurtosis	Min	Max
Australia	18.361	10.653	25.313	−0.0005	0.1759	−0.8520	7.1649	−0.1649	0.0947
Austria	18.119	4.695	39.085	−0.0009	0.3671	−0.9724	13.4189	−0.3606	0.3105
Belgium	41.585	4.447	1153.587	0.0035	0.8711	8.1573	139.3207	−0.8079	2.0418
Brazil	13.416	3.349	33.311	0.0001	0.4296	−1.0034	10.8721	−0.4114	0.2789
Canada	20.199	12.342	27.521	−0.0004	0.1828	−1.0293	10.5705	−0.1702	0.1365
Chile	25.161	9.508	43.769	0.0001	0.2764	−1.2375	14.2081	−0.3449	0.1849
China	17.425	5.194	49.047	0.0009	0.3193	0.6205	8.8247	−0.2229	0.2717
Colombia	26.020	4.922	77.041	0.0017	0.4103	−1.0724	18.2424	−0.3987	0.4224
Finland	16.1164	7.400	38.745	−0.0009	0.3047	−0.4185	4.4418	−0.1756	0.1250
France	20.212	8.877	36.545	−0.0010	0.2659	−0.3420	10.3162	−0.2437	0.2322
Germany	18.896	10.255	29.217	−0.0006	0.2538	−0.6685	8.2174	−0.2380	0.1502
Hong Kong	15.355	8.488	31.158	−0.0002	0.2882	−1.2641	16.1666	−0.2619	0.2074
India	20.676	10.918	41.826	0.0006	0.2375	−0.5312	5.7043	−0.1866	0.1381

Ireland	11.120	3.221	21.485	0.0001	0.3208	−0.7462	14.3632	−0.3756	0.2694
Israel	22.179	11.573	36.074	−0.0003	0.2378	−0.0911	5.8980	−0.1330	0.1631
Italy	14.684	5.473	31.300	0.0000	0.4308	−0.7082	35.5276	−0.5159	0.4642
Japan	51.161	13.270	171.782	−0.0018	0.3151	0.7001	21.0139	−0.2853	0.3886
Malaysia	20.441	12.183	29.629	−0.0002	0.1555	−0.5547	6.3291	−0.1115	0.0799
Mexico	17.983	8.309	31.458	0.0008	0.2849	−0.7697	12.8277	−0.3051	0.2255
Netherlands	15.453	7.823	25.926	0.0004	0.2606	−0.7497	10.2093	−0.2919	0.1449
Norway	15.622	7.691	29.675	−0.0001	0.2970	−0.7442	8.0652	−0.2459	0.1834
Peru	14.760	4.660	29.632	0.0016	0.3183	−0.4704	8.3147	−0.2930	0.2577
Philippines	20.843	9.319	44.159	0.0013	0.3834	0.2979	26.1250	−0.4026	0.4369
Poland	15.6691	7.804	29.515	0.0000	0.2451	−0.2492	5.3329	−0.1650	0.1608
Portugal	13.888	6.801	24.761	−0.0007	0.2305	−1.2951	12.2555	−0.2647	0.1441
Russia	6.393	0.039	16.476	0.0036	1.4479	8.1806	150.2212	−1.7843	3.2509
South Africa	16.072	9.763	23.234	0.0003	0.2099	−0.0541	6.2787	−0.1163	0.1630
South Korea	17.052	7.759	41.279	−0.0016	0.2798	−0.6531	7.3192	−0.2189	0.1902
Spain	12.637	5.426	23.570	−0.0006	0.6122	−1.2237	60.4374	−0.7864	0.7048

Table A2: (*Continued*)

	Panel A: CAPE levels			Panel B: CAPE log-returns					
	Mean	Min	Max	Mean	Std.	Skewness	Kurtosis	Min	Max
Sweden	18.872	10.332	31.429	−0.0004	0.2443	−0.7297	7.7379	−0.2261	0.1287
Switzerland	20.646	12.807	29.328	0.0000	0.2260	−1.0579	12.0801	−0.2370	0.1568
Taiwan	19.210	9.5868	26.693	−0.0001	0.2325	−0.1121	5.3047	−0.1140	0.1691
UK	19.439	10.995	30.006	−0.0006	0.2068	−0.3965	14.5088	−0.2332	0.2054
USA	18.703	9.474	24.965	−0.0001	0.1827	−0.7277	10.4383	−0.2012	0.1148

Note: This table reports the descriptive statistics for CAPE. Panel A captures the properties of the CAPE levels while Panel B captures log-returns based on CAPE for 34 countries observed at weekly frequency. Std. stands for the standard deviation expressed in annualized terms.

4

The Adoption of Political Risk Assessment in Emerging Markets

John R. Anchor and Hana Benesova

Abstract

This chapter seeks to conceptualize a new approach to the identification of the factors influencing the adoption of a political risk assessment (PRA) function. By making use of firm value maximization and risk aversion and considering the rationale for risk management activities, a number of determinants are identified which can be deployed in future PRA studies. A model for predicting the PRA adoption decision is proposed. Geographical contextualization in one or more emerging markets (EMs) provides a further dimension of originality as well as reflecting an increasingly important international business phenomenon. Political risk (PR) and political risk assessment (PRA) are of increasing importance in the context of the growth and development of emerging markets (EMs). The latter provide opportunities for inward investment from more developed economies. There has also been a rapid growth in outward foreign direct investment (OFDI) from emerging markets to other economies. This chapter adds to the current understanding of PRA by examining this issue in emerging markets (EMs) through the model developed here.

Keywords: Political risk; country risk; risk assessment; enterprise risk management; emerging markets

Introduction

Any firm is subject to political exposure, whether directly or indirectly, and political risk (PR) is an ever-present threat. Just like any other risk, PR is magnified in the context of the international business environment and in globalized markets. Political risk has evolved over the past few decades and different types have emerged. Its main focus has changed from nationalization and expropriation to other issues such as license cancellation, tax restrictions, changes in investment agreements, delayed profit repatriation, and terrorism. Given the recent developments in the global business arena, particularly after the global economic downturn in 2007, it has been suggested that the post-crash period is a new era for PR with new threats and increased uncertainties (MIGA, 2009).

Moreover political risk has become an increasingly salient issue with the growing rate of firms' internationalization by foreign direct investment (FDI) into emerging markets (Clark & Tunaru, 2001; UNCTAD, 2014; World Bank, 2014). According to the World Investment and Political Risk 2013 report, "there has been explosive FDI growth since the turn of the century; however political risk has been a major concern for multinational firms operating in developing countries" (World Bank, 2014, p. 5). This is because political risk increases the transaction costs of investing in these markets, thereby making it one of the key influences on firms' internationalization to emerging markets (Althaus, 2013; Baek & Qian, 2011; Brink, 2004; Jiménez, Luis-Rico & Benito-Osorio, 2014; Keillor, Hauser, & Griffin, 2009).

Political risk in emerging markets has been evolving over the past few decades and different types have emerged. At one time, the main concerns were nationalization and expropriation. Subsequently, issues such as license cancellation, tax restrictions, changes in investment agreements, delayed profit repatriation and terrorism have come to the fore (Baek & Qian, 2011; Birău, Busuioc, & Stoia, 2010; Clark & Tunaru, 2005; Jiménez et al., 2014; Sottilotta, 2013; Tölö, 2010; World Bank, 2013, 2014). The evolutionary nature of political risk makes it increasingly difficult to analyze as well as to comprehend. This has resulted in a range of consequences for multinational firms (Ferrari & Rolfini, 2008; Kesternich & Schnitzer, 2010). However, firms have different types of international involvement and different degrees of internationalization (Agarwal & Feils, 2007; Kesternich & Schnitzer, 2010). This suggests that the influence of political risk on firms will depend on their degree of internationalization and that multinational firms will perceive political risk differently according to their type of international involvement.

Political risk affects FDI more than other types of international involvements (Agarwal & Feils, 2007; Filipe, Ferreira, Coelho, & Moura, 2012; Rios-Morales, Gamberger, Smuc, & Azuaje, 2008; World Bank, 2013, 2014). FDI provides more investment opportunities and developing countries are becoming increasingly known as emerging market destinations due to their high returns on investment (Clark & Tunaru, 2001; Ramamurti, 2004; UNCTAD, 2012, 2013, 2014; World Bank, 2013, 2014). However, many emerging markets have evolving political climates, with unstable governments and frequent policy changes (Asiedu, 2002, 2006; Baek & Qian, 2011; Jensen, 2008; Morisset, 2000; Tarzi, 2005). Emerging markets are known to be heterogeneous in their level of development and environmental surroundings. Each manifests different starting points or different stages of development, even within the same geographical region (Bianchi, 2014; Hoskisson, Eden, Lau, & Wright, 2000). One of the main characteristics of these regions is unstable political and economic environments (Bilson, Brailsford, & Hooper, 2002; MIGA, 2009; Nganga & Curo, 2008; Rao, 2012).

The last decade has also seen an increase in internationalization by emerging market multinationals (EMNCs) via outward foreign direct investment (OFDI) (Cavusgil, 1980; Hoskisson et al., 2000; Jormanainen & Koveshnikov, 2012). In 2013, investment from emerging economies increased to 39 percent of global OFDI, compared with only 12 percent in 2000 (UNCTAD, 2014). This trend is consistent across different emerging market sub-regions, as organizations which are investing substantially are doing so not only from large emerging economies like China, India, Brazil, and Russia, but also from a number of new emerging economies in Asia, Latin America, and Africa (Gammeltoft, Pradhan, & Goldstein, 2010; Goldstein & Bonaglia, 2007). Emerging markets (EM) are seen generally as low income, rapid growth countries using economic liberalization as their primary engine of growth (Hoskisson et al., 2000). The economic liberalization or open policies adopted by these emerging markets during the last two decades has led organizations from these economies to internationalize or seek other markets. As a consequence, it has become more important for EMNCs to adopt a more sophisticated approach to risk management.

Since the existing literature on risk focuses predominantly on risk management in general or, more recently, on enterprise risk management (ERM) in which PR is already implemented in a risk management conceptual framework (Altunas, Berry-Stolzle, & Hoyt, 2011; Golshan & Rasid, 2012; Lai & Samad, 2001; Liebenberg & Hoyt, 2003; Yazid, Razali, & Hussin, 2012), we know only a little about the role of PR itself within firms. There have been some studies conducted which are concerned with PR and PRA (Al Khattab, Anchor & Davies, 2008; Hashmi & Baker, 1988; Hashmi & Guvenli, 1992; Jenney, 2001; Kettis, 2004; Pahud De Mortanges & Allers, 1996; Stapenhurst, 1992; Wyper, 1995). However, the outcomes of these studies have identified a limited number of determinants of PRA adoption, for example, firm size (Al Khattab et al., 2008; Hashmi & Baker, 1988; Kettis, 2004; Stapenhurst, 1992), degree of internationalization (Al Khattab et al., 2008; Hashmi & Baker, 1988;

Hashmi & Guvenli, 1992), ownership (Al Khattab et al., 2008), and industry type (Al Khattab et al., 2008; Jenney, 2001; Kettis, 2004; Pahud De Mortanges & Allers, 1996; Stapenhurst, 1992; Wyper, 1995). We believe that an expansion of the PRA adoption determinants and a more in-depth analysis of the PRA function are necessary if we are to obtain a clearer understanding of these processes.

In order to conceptualize further the determinants of PRA adoption, we make use of firm value maximization theory and the theory of risk aversion, which are both linked closely to the theory of shareholders' value maximization and their ultimate goal of profit generation as a rationale for risk management (RM) and by extension political risk management (PRM). Although these theories usually prepare the ground for studies aimed at corporate risk hedging (Ameer, 2010; Ephraim & Amrit, 2008; Nance, Smith, & Smithson, 1993), since hedging activities are included within RM activities in the majority of firms, they can be used to identify some of the determinants of PRA adoption (Dionne & Garand, 2003; Liebenberg & Hoyt, 2003).

The above mentioned arguments have been used to determine the factors which influence the adoption of enterprise risk management (ERM) in a firm (Altunas et al., 2011; Golshan & Rasid, 2012; Lai & Samad, 2001). Even though ERM is a broader concept than PRA and PRM we argue that, as part of ERM, the determinants of PRM and by extension PRA adoption can also be examined using the theories of risk aversion and the value maximization hypothesis under which the activities of risk management in general are justified by (i) reducing the expected costs of financial distress; (ii) reducing the risk premiums payable to various partners; (iii) increasing investment possibilities; (iv) reducing expected tax payments.

Risk, Uncertainty, Political Risk, and Political Risk Assessment

The theoretical rationale behind political risk and political risk assessment studies are the distinction and relationship between risk and uncertainty. The following sections will discuss the nature of all these phenomena. Hypotheses for model development will be derived based on these discussions.

Risk and Uncertainty

Sometimes the terms uncertainty and risk are used interchangeably. There is however a clear distinction between these two: uncertainty is the state of knowing that something might happen in the future but not knowing what exactly it is going to be and risk provides the information on its degree and its likelihood (Fabozzi & Peterson, 2003; Golshan & Rasid, 2012; Vaughan & Vaughan, 1995). While uncertainty is not measurable (McLean & McMillan, 2003), risk can be defined using a simplified model as the probability of an adverse event occurring times its magnitude (Pinheiro, Cranor, & Anderson, 2011). In terms of political risk assessment, it is the process of converting the uncertainty arising from politics into "quantifiable" risk.

Political Risk and Country Risk

Attempts to quantify political risk are often to be found in studies of political risk in the context of FDI or portfolio returns (Guerin & Manzocchi, 2009; Haksoon, 2010; Jimenez, 2011; Krifa-Schneider, & Matei, 2010; Meon & Sekkat, 2012; Palacios & Griffin, 2011; Vadlamannati, 2012). In these studies, political risk usually overlaps with country risk. Therefore a distinction between political risk and country risk needs to be made (Al Khattab et al., 2008).

Country risk is often referred to as encompassing all the social, cultural, political and economic risks faced by a firm when operating in that country whereas political risk is directly linked to government actions or to actions aimed against a government. This is however a very simplistic delimitation of PR. An exact definition would depend on many factors: the insurance industry for example divides PR "into (i) currency convertibility and transfer, (ii) expropriation, (iii) political violence, (iv) breach of contract by a host government, and (v) the non-honoring of sovereign financial obligations [and is only aimed at the host country]" (MIGA, 2009, p. 28). In management research, PR is usually defined as the likelihood of a deterioration in the political climate in a host country (Rios-Morales et al., 2008) or simply as an action of a political institution — both voluntary and/or involuntary — that would threaten the objectives of a firm (Howell, 2001; Nawaz & Hood, 2005). Given that the priority of a profit making firm is profit generation the definition provided by Inkster who describes PR as "threats to profitability which are external to the business and which arise from government action or inaction" (Inkster, 2008, p. 162) seems to be an appropriate one.

Although the exact definition of PR is sometimes unclear, the determination of the elements constituting a political risk is an even more controversial topic. Even after more than four decades of intense discussion, academics still struggle to determine what exactly PR consists of and to what extent it influences other risks faced by firms. Nevertheless, they agree on the fact that given the nature of political risk it should be of major concern to any firm and its management and that they would benefit from the implementation of a PRA function within their risk management activities (Blank, Basek, Kobrin, & LaPalombara, 1980; Burmester, 2000; Hashmi & Baker, 1988; Hood & Nawaz, 2004; Kobrin, 1981, 1982; Kobrin, Basek, Blank, & LaPalombara, 1980; Pahud De Mortanges & Allers, 1996; Rice & Mahmoud, 1990; Stapenhurst, 1992; Wyper, 1995).

Political Risk Assessment

Political risk assessment (PRA) is the process of analyzing and evaluating political risk often in the context of undertaking international business activities. The political risk literature has suggested a variable standard of PRA undertaken by international firms. However the political risk literature also suggests that political risk is assessable and that international firms are aware of their exposure to political risk and consider political risk assessment to be one of the most important risks for their international business activities (Al Khattab et al., 2008; Blank et al., 1980; Burmester, 2000; Hashmi & Baker, 1988; Hood & Nawaz, 2004; Kobrin, 1981, 1982; Kobrin et al., 1980; Pahud De Mortanges & Allers, 1996; Rice & Mahmoud, 1990; Stapenhurst, 1992; Wyper, 1995).

The diversity of political risk and differences in a firm's exposure to it may lead to different approaches to PRA. A firm's exposure to political risk is related to its characteristics. The literature on political risk suggests that the extent to which international firms are involved in PRA is correlated with a number of organizational characteristics such as firms' size (Al Khattab et al., 2008; Hashmi & Baker, 1988; Kettis, 2004; Stapenhurst, 1992); firms' degree of internationalization (Al Khattab et al., 2008; Hashmi & Baker, 1988; Hashmi & Guvenli, 1992); firms' industry (Al Khattab et al., 2008; Jenney, 2001; Kettis, 2004; Pahud De Mortanges & Allers, 1996; Stapenhurst, 1992; Wyper, 1995); and firms' ownership (Al Khattab et al., 2008).

Firms benefit from the adoption of PRA by decreasing the uncertainty arising from the political environments in which they operate. The adoption of effective and appropriate mitigation tools can increase a firm's stability; hence this can lead to a decrease in the volatility of its performance in general and its cash flow in particular. Therefore, in this chapter we build upon the concept of PRA adoption in firms. In view of the theory of firm value maximization and risk aversion we attempt to contribute to the existing literature on the determinants of PRA adoption by enlarging the number of these determinants of the PRA adoption decision; that is, the decision whether or not to assess formally a firm's political risks.

The Determinants of the Adoption of Political Risk Assessment

The literature on both risk management implementation and the determinants of firms' hedging behavior suggests that the most appropriate determinants are firm size, industry and complexity, the level of a firm's internationalization, liquidity, managerial ownership, institutional ownership, past performance, location of headquarters and subsidiaries, liquidity, growth options, cash flow volatility, tax losses, return on assets, CAPEX, dividend yield, industrial diversification, type of auditors, independence of board of directors, assets opacity, and stock price volatility (Allayannis & Ofek, 2001; Altunas et al., 2011; Ameer, 2010; Dionne & Triki, 2004; Golshan & Rasid, 2012; Khediri & Folus, 2010).

Given the nature of many emerging market business environments and, in particular, the fact that not all firms operating and/ or based in these countries are publically listed, and that the availability of information on these firms is sometimes an issue we propose to examine the literature relating to the following determinants of PRA adoption in this context: (i) firm size; (ii) firm complexity; (iii) level of internationalization; (iv) ownership; (v) location of subsidiaries; (vi) leverage; (vii) growth options; (viii) auditor type; and (ix) industry.

Firm Size

Firm size influences the nature and the extent of risks threatening business as well as the structure of a firm. It is one of the variables included in almost every study where firm-specific determinants are tested. The bigger a company is the more likely it is to identify any potential risks and also the more resources it has to mitigate its risks (Kobrin, 1982). However, there is an argument that managers may be overwhelmed by their workload, and hence not have the capacity to conduct PRA (Al Khattab et al., 2008; Albright, 2004). Moreover, smaller firms are also much more adaptable and flexible and therefore in the event of an emergency they are likely to deal with these situations much more quickly (Al Khattab et al., 2008). In addition large firms have a greater volatility in operating cash flows and risk of financial distress; due to which the likelihood of PRA adoption is greater (Golshan & Rasid, 2012; Pagach & Warr, 2011). In previous studies the main indicators used are (i) number of employees and (ii) logarithm of firm's total assets as a measure of firm's size.

Firm Complexity

The complexity variable which is usually employed in studies of ERM implementation (Golshan & Rasid, 2012; Gordon, Loeb, & Tseng, 2009; Pagach & Warr, 2011). Doyle, Ge, and McVay (2007) suggest that a firm's complexity can be measured by the number of its business segments; the more segments a firm has the more complex it is. In line with previous studies, we argue that the more segments a firm has, the more difficult it is to align its activities and hence the more likely it is to employ a risk management unit and, by extension, a PRA function.

Level of Internationalization

The more activities a firm engages in abroad the more it is exposed to host-country risks including political risks (Al Khattab et al., 2008; Blank et al., 1980; Hashmi & Baker, 1988; Keillor, Boller, & Ferrell, 1997; Keillor, Wilkinson, & Owens, 2005; Kobrin, 1982; Oetzel, 2005; Pahud de Mortanges & Allers, 1996; Rice & Mahmoud, 1990; Wyper, 1995). In previous studies, the usual indicators of firms' level of internationalization are (i) number of years in international business; (ii) number of countries of functioning; and (iii) percentage of revenue from international business activities. Although these methods are all used to determine and indicate firms' level of internationalization their relationship with PRA adoption is not explicit.

For example, in the case of *years in international business*, higher values would suggest higher levels of exposure. However it has been pointed out by Kobrin (1982) and Oetzel (2005) that the experience will result in a reduction in risk perceptions over time. The results for *number of operating countries* and *foreign revenues* suggest a significant positive relationship with PRA implementation for both of these variables (Al Khattab et al., 2008). However, the diversification of firms' activities across multiple markets can lead to the offsetting of losses and gains by portfolio diversification in which case the effect of the *number of operating countries* may be disputable (Iankova & Katz, 2003). Nevertheless, previous studies have found that both *international revenues* and *number of countries of operation* are positively correlated with PRA adoption (Al Khattab et al., 2008; Hashmi & Baker, 1988; Hashmi & Guvenli, 1992; Keillor et al., 1997).

Ownership

In some emerging markets, stock-exchanges have not developed significantly. Nevertheless there will usually be a mixture of both publicly listed and private firms. The legal structure of a firm rather than the percentage of managerial and/or institutional ownership may be the crucial issue. More formal risk management can be expected to be implemented in firms with a higher percentage of ownership by external stakeholders who require information about a firm's activities and the amount and nature of its risks (Liebenberg & Hoyt, 2003; Pagach & Warr, 2011). This trend may have been magnified by the events of 2007–2009.

Ownership affects significantly firms' tolerance and attitude towards risk. Firms owned by government are usually more risk-averse than private ones (Yazid, 2001). This is caused mainly by the different objectives of their managers since the primary goal of private organizations is to generate profit whereas public ones may try to ensure that they serve the public interest (Freeman, Wicks, & Parman, 2004; Jensen, 2002; Sundaram & Inkpen, 2004). The ownership structure of publicly listed versus private firms appears to influence how companies perceive and tackle risks. Publicly traded companies may need to ensure that they will meet their shareholders' expectations which — in most cases — are profits. Therefore these companies are much more likely to monitor and assess potential risks stemming from the environments in which they operate — including the political ones (Al Khattab et al., 2008).

Location of Subsidiaries

The standard of risk management is higher in developed economies than in emerging markets (Golshan & Rasid, 2012). Indeed

ERM frameworks have been invented and developed in the United Kingdom and adopted mainly in the United States, Canada, Australia, and New Zealand (Beasley, Clune, & Hermanson, 2005; Golshan & Rasid, 2012; Liebenberg & Hoyt, 2003). The fact that these countries have rules and regulations in their legal systems which put an emphasis on corporate risk management (e.g., the 4360 standard or the Sarbanes Oxley Act) pushes firms operating within these countries towards a more responsible approach to risk management and risk in general. Therefore firms with subsidiaries in these countries will be more inclined to adopt risk management procedures and they will be more likely to adopt PRA than firms whose subsidiaries are located elsewhere.

Leverage

Leverage is linked directly to the costs of financial distress. A firm with a large percentage of debt compared to its assets will face issues relating to its ability to repay its debt. In order to ensure that a firm will have enough resources to cover its liabilities, it will need to ensure steady cash flows; that is, such a firm will seek to reduce the volatility of its cash flows. However reducing cash flow volatility is only one of the justifications for the adoption of a risk management function. The hedging literature (Ameer, 2010; Heaney & Winata, 2005; Khediri & Folus, 2010; Nance et al., 1993) also suggests that the more a firm is leveraged, the more likely it is to hedge. From the financial management perspective, leverage leads to an interest rate risk to a firm linked — directly or indirectly — to politics (Shapiro, 2010). Therefore, firms from more stable economies are generally more likely to be leveraged (Brown & Toft, 2002; Ephraim & Amrit, 2008).

Investment Opportunities

The rationale behind making use of investment opportunities as a means of PRA adoption is identical with the one for leverage — the reduction of cash flow volatility. In firms with more opportunities for investment, such as research and development or expansion, managers need to make sure that the firms will be able to finance these investments (Bishop, 1996). Therefore, expenditure on research and development has been used in previous studies as a proxy for firms' investment opportunities (Bishop, 1996; Khediri & Folus, 2010; Nance et al., 1993).

Auditor Type

It has been suggested that the type of a firm's auditor affects a firm's risk management (Beasley et al., 2005). Golshan and Rasid (2012) investigated this hypothesis and found that the presence of a "Big Four" (KPMG, Deloitte, Price Waterhouse Coopers, Ernst & Young) auditor increases the likelihood of ERM implementation. The "Big Four" acknowledge PR as one of the major threats for firms and suggest that PRA should be undertaken by all firms, especially those operating internationally. It is logical to assume, therefore, that the presence of one of these auditors will influence the process of PRA adoption (DiPiazza & Bremmer, 2006; Ernst & Young, 2009; MIGA, 2009).

Industry

Many approaches to the treatment of this variable have been developed in previous studies; these distinguish mostly between (i) primary, secondary and tertiary sectors; (ii) industrial and manufacturing, service and financial companies; and (iii) many specific industrial branches. The existing literature on PRA suggests that there are significant differences between companies which are tightly linked to the host-country governments in which they operate, such as construction, military or extracting companies, whose activities are of a contractual nature and sectors over which host- country governments have little control. Firms in the latter category are not likely to worry as much about the potential risks stemming from the host-country political environment as much as the first group. However it is not suggested that companies from "low-profile" sectors are not exposed to political risks at all. However, the nature of the PR to which these sectors are exposed is macro environmental, rather than industry-specific (Al Khattab et al., 2008; Jenney, 2001; Kettis, 2004; McKellar, 2010; Pahud De Mortanges & Allers, 1996; Stapenhurst, 1992; Wyper, 1995).

Conclusion

The aim of this chapter has been to propose a new approach to the examination of the determinants of PRA adoption. From a review of appropriate literature on political risk (PR) and its assessment (PRA), risk management, ERM adoption, and corporate hedging incentives, the following determinants of the adoption of a PRA function have been identified: firm size, complexity, industry, leverage, investment opportunities, type of auditor, ownership, level of internationalization, and location of firms' subsidiaries. The growth in importance of emerging markets adds a further, and increasingly important, dimension to this approach.

The mitigation of political risk is a thorny issue, but one of considerable importance. The adoption of political risk assessment is by no means a straightforward process. The identification of the key influences upon PRA adoption therefore has considerable utility associated with it. It may be expected that there may be a significant economic pay off to companies and to emerging market economies if the processes associated with PRA adoption can be better understood and then enhanced. Governments in emerging market economies and elsewhere may be interested in the possibility of policy interventions which may promote good practice and/or effective outcomes in this context. This literature survey attempts to provide insights which can lead to these outcomes.

References

Agarwal, J., & Feils, D. (2007). Political risk and the internationalization of firms: An empirical study of Canadian-based export and FDI firms. *Canadian Journal of Administrative Sciences/Revue Canadienne des Sciences de l'Administration*, 24(3), 165–181.

Al Khattab, A., Anchor, J. R., & Davies, E. M. M. (2008). The Institutionalisation of Political Risk Assessment (IPRA) in Jordanian international firms. *International Business Review, 17*(6), 688–702.

Albright, K. (2004). Environmental scanning: Radar for success. *Information Management Journal, 38*(3), 38–45.

Allayannis, G., & Ofek, E. (2001). Exchange rate exposure, hedging and the use of currency derivatives. *Journal of International Money and Finance, 20*(2), 273–296.

Althaus, C. (2013). *Calculating political risk*. Abingdon: Routledge.

Altunas, M., Berry-Stolzle, T. R., & Hoyt, R. E. (2011). *Dynamic determinants of enterprise risk management adoption in the property-liability insurance industry: Evidence from Germany*. Retrieved from http://www.wu.ac.at/egrie2011/programme/papers/v.b1.altuntas.pdf

Ameer, R. (2010). Determinants of corporate hedging practices in Malaysia. *International Business Research, 3*(2), 120–130.

Asiedu, E. (2002). On the determinants of foreign direct investment to developing countries: is Africa different? *World Development, 30*(1), 107–119.

Asiedu, E. (2006). Foreign direct investment in Africa: The role of natural resources, market size, government policy, institutions and political instability. *World Economy, 29*(1), 63–77.

Baek, K., & Qian, X. (2011). An analysis on political risks and the flow of foreign direct investment in developing and industrialized economies. *Economics, Management, and Financial Markets, 6*(4), 60–91.

Beasley, M., Clune, R., & Hermanson, D. (2005). Enterprise risk management: An empirical analysis of factors associated with the extent of implementation. *Journal of Accounting and Public Policy, 25*(6), 521–531.

Bianchi, C. (2014). Internationalisation of emerging market firms: An exploratory study of Chilean companies. *International Journal of Emerging Markets, 9*(1), 54–78.

Bilson, C. M., Brailsford, T. J., & Hooper, V. C. (2002). The explanatory power of political risk in emerging markets. *International Review of Financial Analysis, 11*(1), 1–27.

Birău, C. R., Busuioc, A., & Stoia, A. C. (2010). Determinants of political risk in the context of the contemporary economic crisis. Financial and monetary stability in emerging countries, FABBV 11th international conference, Bucharest (pp. 586–593).

Bishop, M. (1996). To hedge or not to hedge? *Economist, 338*(7952), 10–11.

Blank, S., Basek, J., Kobrin, S., & LaPalombara, J. (1980). *Assessing the political environment: An emerging function in international companies*. New York, NY: Conference Board Inc.

Brink, C. H. (2004). *Measuring political risk: Risks to foreign investment*. Aldershot: Ashgate Publishing Limited.
Brown, G. W., & Toft, K. B. (2002). How firms should hedge. *Review of Financial Studies*, *15*(4), 1283–1324.
Burmester, B. (2000). Political risk in international business. In M. Tayeb (Ed.). *International business: Theories, policies and practices* (pp. 247–272). London: Prentice Hall.
Cavusgil, T. S. (1980). On the internationalization process of firms. *European Research*, *8*(6), 273–281.
Clark, E. A., & Tunaru, R. (2001). Emerging markets: Investing with political risk. *Multinational Finance Journal*, *5*(3), 155–173.
Clark, E. A., & Tunaru, T. (2005). The evolution of international political risk 1956–2001. Paper presented at the Paper provided by Money Macro and Finance Group in its Series Money Macro and Finance (MMF) Research Group Conference.
Dionne, G., & Garand, M. (2003). Risk management determinants affecting firms' values in the gold mining industry: New empirical results. *Economic Letters*, *79*(1), 43–52.
Dionne, G., & Triki, T. (2004). *On risk management determinants: What really matters?* Retrieved from http://papers.ssrn.com/sol3/papers.cfm?abstract_id=558761
DiPiazza, S. A., & Bremmer, I. (2006). *PricewaterhouseCoopers: Integrating political risk into enterprise risk management*. Retrieved from http://www.pwc.com/gx/en/political-risk-consulting-services/integrating-poitical-risk-into-enterprise-risk-management.jhtml
Doyle, J., Ge, W., & McVay, S. (2007). Determinants of weaknesses in internal control over financial reporting. *Journal of Accounting and Economics*, *44*(1/2), 193–223.
Ephraim, C., & Amrit, J. (2008). The determinants of foreign currency hedging: Does foreign debt induce a bias? *European Financial Management*, *14*(3), 445–469.
Ernst & Young. (2009). *The 2009 Ernst & young business risk report: The top 10 risks for global business*. Retrieved from http://www.google.cz/url?sa=t&rct=j&q=&esrc=s&source=web&cd=4&sqi=2&ved=0CD8QFjAD&url=http%3A%2F%2Fwww.ey.com%2FPublication%2FvwLUAssets%2FNewsletter_Business_Risk_English%2F%24FILE%2FBusiness_Risk-Media_and_Ent_2009-E.pdf&ei=r3sHUaGxEdCM0wWW0oGACQ&usg=AFQjCNFS2S-L_48Mf97IWgVoMBV0-VAAJw&sig2=KJf5Zd5KpSeJaj_RljKz2Q&bvm=bv.41524429,d.d2k
Fabozzi, F. J., & Peterson, P. P. (2003). *Financial management and analysis*. New York, NY: Wiley.
Ferrari, F., & Rolfini, R. (2008). *Investing in a dangerous world: A new political risk index*. SACE Working Paper No. 06. SACE Group.

Filipe, J. A., Ferreira, M. A. M., Coelho, M. P., & Moura, D. (2012). FDI political risks: The new international context. *International Journal of Latest Trends in Finance and Economic Sciences*, *2*(2), 117–124.

Freeman, R. E., Wicks, A. C., & Parman, B. (2004). Stakeholder theory and "the corporate objective revisited". *Organization Science*, *15*(3), 364–369.

Gammeltoft, P., Pradhan, J. P., & Goldstein, A. (2010). Emerging multinationals: Home and host country determinants and outcomes. *International Journal of Emerging Markets*, *5*(3/4), 254–265.

Goldstein, A., & Bonaglia, F. (2007). Accelerated internationalization by emerging markets' multinationals: the case of the white goods sector. *Journal of World Business*, *42*(4), 369–383.

Golshan, N. M., & Rasid, S. A. (2012). Determinants of enterprise risk management adoption: An empirical analysis of Malaysian public listed firms. *International Journal of Social and Human Sciences*, *6*, 119–126.

Gordon, L. A., Loeb, M. P., & Tseng, C. Y. (2009). Enterprise risk management and firm performance: A contingency perspective. *Journal of Accounting and Public Policy*, *28*(4), 301–327.

Guerin, S. S., & Manzocchi, S. (2009). Political regime and FDI from advanced to emerging countries. *Review of World Economics*, *145*(1), 75–91.

Haksoon, K. (2010). Political stability and foreign direct investment. *International Journal of Economics and Finance*, *2*(3), 59–71.

Hashmi, A., & Baker, J. (1988). Political risk assessment models and techniques: Analysis of the experience of MNCs. *International Trade Journal*, *3*(2), 187–202.

Hashmi, A., & Guvenli, T. (1992). Importance of political risk assessment functions in U.S. multinational corporations. *Global Finance Journal*, *3*(2), 137–144.

Heaney, R., & Winata, H. (2005). Use of derivatives by Australian companies. *Pacific-Basin Finance Journal*, *13*(4), 411–430.

Hood, J., & Nawaz, M. S. (2004). Political risk exposure and management in multi-national companies: Is there a role for the corporate risk manager? *Risk Management: An International Journal*, *6*(1), 7–18.

Hoskisson, R. E., Eden, L., Lau, C. M., & Wright, M. (2000). Strategy in emerging economies. *Academy of Management Journal*, *43*(3), 249–267.

Howell, L. D. (2001). *Handbook of country and political risk analysis* (3rd ed.). East Syracuse, NY: Political Risk Services Group.

Iankova, E., & Katz, J. (2003). Strategies for political risk mediation by international firms in transition economies: The case of Bulgaria. *Journal of World Business*, *38*(3), 182–203.

Inkster, N. (2008). Assessing political risk. *Adelphi Papers, 48*(400–401), 161–166.
Jenney, F. (2001). Breach of contract coverage in infrastructure projects: Can investors afford to wait for arbitration? In T. Moran (Ed.). *International political risk management: Exploring new frontiers* (pp. 45–56). Washington, DC: World Bank Group.
Jensen, M. C. (2002). Value maximization, stakeholder theory, and the corporate objective function. *Business Ethics Quarterly, 12*(2), 235–256.
Jensen, N. (2008). Political risk, democratic institutions, and foreign direct investment. *Journal of Politics, 70*(4), 1040–1052.
Jimenez, A. (2011). Political risk as a determinant of southern European FDI in neighbouring developing countries. *Emerging Markets, Finance & Trade, 47*(4), 59–74.
Jiménez, A., Luis-Rico, I., & Benito-Osorio, D. (2014). The influence of political risk on the scope of internationalization of regulated companies: Insights from a Spanish sample. *Journal of World Business, 49*(3), 301–311.
Jormanainen, I., & Koveshnikov, A. (2012). International activities of emerging market firms. *Management International Review, 52*(5), 691–725.
Keillor, B., Boller, G., & Ferrell, O. (1997). Firm-level political behaviour in the global marketplace. *Journal of Business Research, 40*(2), 113–126.
Keillor, B., Hauser, W., & Griffin, A. (2009). The relationship between political risk, national culture and foreign direct investment as a market entry strategy: Perspectives from US firms. *Innovative Marketing, 5*(1), 48–54.
Keillor, B., Wilkinson, T., & Owens, D. (2005). Threats to international operations: Dealing with political risk at the firm level. *Journal of Business Research, 58*(5), 629–635.
Kesternich, I., & Schnitzer, M. (2010). Who is afraid of political risk? Multinational firms and their choice of capital structure. *Journal of International Economics, 82*(2), 208–218.
Kettis, M. (2004). *The challenge of political risk: Exploring the political risk management of Swedish multinational corporations*. PhD Thesis. Stockholm University, Sweden.
Khediri, K. B., & Folus, D. (2010). Does hedging increase firm value? Evidence from French firms. *Applied Economics Letters, 17*(10), 995–998.
Kobrin, S. (1981). Political assessment by international firms: Models or methodologies? *Journal of Policy Modeling, 3*(2), 251–270.
Kobrin, S. (1982). *Managing political risk assessment: Strategic response to environmental change*. California, CA: University of California Press.

Kobrin, S., Basek, J., Blank, S., & LaPalombara, J. (1980). The assessment and evaluation of noneconomic environment by American firms: A preliminary report. *Journal of International Business Studies, 11*(1), 32–47.

Krifa-Schneider, H., & Matei, I. (2010). Business climate, political risk and FDI in developing countries: Evidence from panel data. *International Journal of Economics and Finance, 2*(5), 54–65.

Lai, F. W., & Samad, F. A. (2001). *Enterprise risk management framework and the empirical determinants of its implementation.* Retrieved from http://www.google.cz/url?sa=t&rct=j&q=&esrc=s&source=web&cd=1&ved=0CDUQFjAA&url=http%3A%2F%2Fwww.ipedr.com%2Fvol1%2F73-G10003.pdf&ei=WGsHUfPzBu6a1AXwxoHwCA&usg=AFQjCNGbmB9SAK1-P0tEwv8Cmm11W-Be4g&sig2=HV8S3oiWLz8dHgpo6HZHUg&bvm=bv.41524429,d.d2k

Liebenberg, A. P., & Hoyt, R. E. (2003). The determinants of enterprise risk management: Evidence from the appointment of chief risk officers. *Risk Management and Insurance Review, 6*(1), 37–52.

McKellar, R. (2010). *Short guide to political risk.* Farnham: Gower.

McLean, I., & McMillan, A. (2003). *Concise Oxford dictionary of politics* (2nd ed.). Oxford: Oxford University Press.

Meon, P. G., & Sekkat, K. (2012). FDI waves, waves of neglect of political risk. *World Development, 40*(11), 2194–2205.

MIGA. (2009). *Multilateral investment guarantee agency: World investment and political risk.* Retrieved from www.miga.org/documents/WIPR11.pdf

Morisset, J. (2000). Foreign direct investment in Africa: Policies also matter. World Bank Publications. Retrieved from http://www.oecd.org/daf/inv/investmentstaticsandanalysis/2408225.pdf.

Nance, D. R., Smith, C. W., & Smithson, C. W. (1993). On the determinants of corporate hedging. *Journal of Finance, 48*(1), 267–284.

Nawaz, M. S., & Hood, J. (2005). Managing international business risk – Political, cultural and ethical dimensions: A case study approach. *Journal of Insurance Research and Practice, 20*(1), 16–24.

Nganga, C., & Curo, E. (2008). *Assessing extreme values in political risk estimates.* Retrieved from http://ieeexplore.ieee.org/xpl/login.jsp?tp=&arnumber=4559730&url=http%3A%2F%2Fieeexplore.ieee.org%2Fiel5%2F4550722%2F4559674%2F04559730.pdf%3Farnumber%3D4559730

Oetzel, J. (2005). Smaller may be beautiful but is it more risky?: Assessing and managing political and economic risk in Costa Rica. *International Business Review, 14*(6), 765–790.

Pagach, D., & Warr, R. (2011). The characteristics of firms that hire chief risk officers. *Journal of Risk and Insurance, 78*(1), 185–211.

Pahud De Mortanges, C., & Allers, V. (1996). Political risk assessment: Theory and the experience of Dutch firms. *International Business Review, 5*(3), 303–318.

Palacios, A., & Griffin, T. (2011). Country risk and FDI: Empirical evidence from Latin American countries. *Journal of International Business Research*, *10*(1), 9–25.

Pinheiro, A., Cranor, B. D., & Anderson, D. O. (2011). Assessing risk: A simplified methodology for prejob planning in oil & gas production. *Professional Safety*, *56*(9), 34–41.

Ramamurti, R. (2004). Developing countries and MNEs: Extending and enriching the research agenda. *Journal of International Business Studies*, *35*(4), 277–283.

Rao, S. (2012). *Analysis: Politics store risk for emerging market yield-seekers.* Retrieved from http://www.reuters.com/article/2012/10/04/us-emerging-politics-risk-idUSBRE8930OL20121004

Rice, G., & Mahmoud, E. (1990). Political risk forecasting by Canadian firms. *International Journal of Forecasting*, *6*(1), 89–102.

Rios-Morales, R., Gamberger, D., Smuc, T., & Azuaje, F. (2008). Innovative methods in assessing political risk for business internationalization. *Research in International Business and Finance*, *23*(2), 144–156.

Shapiro, A. C. (2010). *Multinational financial management* (9th ed.). Hoboken: John Wiley.

Sottilotta, C. E. (2013). *Political risk: Concepts, definitions, challenges.* SOG-WP6/2013. Rome: Luiss School of Government.

Stapenhurst, F. (1992). The rise and fall of political risk assessment. *Management Decision*, *30*(5), 54–57.

Sundaram, A. K., & Inkpen, A. C. (2004). The corporate objective revisited. *Organization Science*, *15*(3), 350–363.

Tarzi, S. (2005). Foreign direct investment flows into developing countries: Impact of location and government policy. *Journal of Social, Political, and Economic Studies*, *30*(4), 488–497.

Tölö, M. (2010). Political risk: Literature review. *Proceedings of the 2009 Academy of Marketing Science (AMS) annual conference*, (pp. 118–122).

UNCTAD. (2012). *World investment report: Towards a new Generation of investment policies.* United Nations conference on trade and development.

UNCTAD. (2013). *World Investment Prospects Survey 2013–2015*, United Nations conference on trade and development.

UNCTAD. (2014). *World Investment Report: Investing in the SDGs: An Action Plan*. United Nations conference on trade and development.

Vadlamannati, K. C. (2012). Impact of political risk on FDI revisited – An aggregate firm-level analysis. *International Interactions*, *38*(1), 111–139.

Vaughan, E. J., & Vaughan, T. M. (1995). *Essentials of insurance: A risk management perspective*. New York, NY: Wiley.

World Bank. (2013). *World investment and political risk 2012-multilateral investment guarantee agency*. Washington, DC: World Bank.

World Bank. (2014). *World investment and political risk 2013-multilateral investment guarantee agency*. Washington, DC: World Bank.

Wyper, C. (1995). The extent of usage of political risk analysis in UK multinational organisations. MPhil Thesis. University of Strathclyde.

Yazid, A. (2001). *Perceptions and practices of financial risk management in Malaysia*. PhD Thesis. Glasgow Caledonian University.

Yazid, A. S., Razali, A. R., & Hussin, M. R. (2012). Determinants of Enterprise Risk Management (ERM): A proposed framework for Malaysian public listed companies. *International Business Research*, *5*(1), 80–86.

5

Rethinking Framework of Integrated Interest Rate and Credit Risk Management in Emerging Markets

Mariya Gubareva and Maria Rosa Borges

Abstract

This chapter reassesses the economics of interest rate risk management in light of the global financial crisis by developing a derivative-based integrated treatment of interest rate and credit risk interrelation. The decade-long historical data on credit default swap spreads and interest rate swap rates are used as proxy measures for credit risk and interest rate risk, respectively. An elasticity of interest rate risk and credit risk, considered a function of the business cycle phases, maturity of instruments, economic sector, creditworthiness, and other macroeconomic parameters, is investigated for optimizing economic capital. This chapter sheds light on how financial institutions may address hedge strategies against downside risks implementing the proposed derivative-based integrated treatment of interest rate and credit risk assessment allowing for optimization of interest rate swap contracts. The developed framework of integrated interest rate and credit risk management is of special importance for emerging markets heavily dependent on foreign capital as it potentially allows emerging market banks to improve risk management practices in terms of capital adequacy and Basel III rules. Analyzing diversification versus compounding effects, it allows enhancing financial stability through jointly optimizing Pillar 1 and Pillar 2 economic capital.

Keywords: Emerging markets; integrated risk modeling; interest rate risk; credit risk; downside risk management; economic capital

Introduction

Credit risk and interest rate risk management is among the main challenges faced by fixed-income portfolio managers and regulators. These risks are usually analyzed separately and not through a holistic approach that considers aggregate changes in bond yields. A theoretical justification of a split of liquidity, credit and interest rate risk descends from Black's (1970) economic thinking: "... a long term corporate bond could actually be sold to three separate persons. One would supply the money for the bond; one would bear the interest rate risk, and one would bear the risk of default. The last two would not have to put up any capital for the bond, though they might have to post some sort of collateral." Thus, Black (1970) anticipated two derivative instruments: interest rate swaps (IRS) and credit default swaps (CDS).

Nowadays, the most common types of the derivative instruments are IRS and CDS. IRSs and CDSs have become important components of financial markets, playing important role in the understanding of economics, management, and regulation of interest rate risk and credit risk, respectively.

While financial regulation continues to address the risk components of fixed-income banking portfolios, such as credit risk and interest rate risk, in a separate way, much of recent academic research turns to analyzing interrelations between these components, compounding a yield of a bond, while emphasizing an importance of understanding such interrelation for fixed-income portfolio allocation and hedging decisions in the context of economic conjuncture. For instance, Tang and Yan (2010) demonstrate that credit spreads are counter-cyclical. They also observe negative correlation between interest rate and credit spreads.

On the side of the regulatory perspective, under Basel II/III rules, for banking books composed of liquidly traded securities, predominantly bonds, banks are expected to estimate their economic capital for credit risk and interest rate risk in a segregate manner. This exercise is referred to as an internal capital adequacy assessment process (ICAAP). According to the existing regulation, credit risk and interest rate risk even enter into different economic capital pillars, namely, Pillar 1 for credit risk and Pillar 2 for the interest rate risk in the banking book (IRRBB).

Despite this segregated regulatory perspective, the correlation of credit risk with interest rate changes had already attracted considerable attention as for instance in Kiesel, Perraudin, and Taylor (2002). It is widely recognized that issue of interest rate risk and credit risk interaction is complex (Chen, Cheng, & Wu, 2013 and references therein) suggesting that it is worthwhile to move from the independent analyses of risks to an integrated approach.

In fact, Alessandri and Drehmann (2010) model bank economic capital, though their modeling is performed simply under an arbitrary assumption that these risks amplify one another. They assume that borrowers are more likely to default when interest rates are high. Such assumption is not always corroborated by results of other researchers which depending on the geography, sector, creditworthiness, and time horizons arrive at conclusions that credit risk spreads do not act as interest rates risk enhancers.

In general, hypothetically speaking, credit spreads may widen as interest rates rise, but historically they have not. For instance, Bonfim and Soares (2013) do not confirm "an increase in the likelihood of default in the aftermath of a period of lower monetary policy rates." Thus, revisiting this issue is highly desirable.

The interrelation between interest rate and credit risk differs between expansion and contraction phases of a business cycle. Especially important in comprehending mechanisms of this interaction are the flight-to-quality phenomena when capital flies from risky to risk-free assets, augmenting credit risk spreads of the former and diminishing the yields of the latter (Gubareva, 2010). It was especially so during the recent financial crisis, when interest rates dropped and simultaneously the average creditworthiness of debt issuers, being banks, corporates, or sovereigns, deteriorated too. Our contribution to the new economic thinking of integrated interest rate and credit risk management is that such joint dynamics of interest rate and credit risks do not represent an exceptional case but rather common and expectable circumstances, as crashes and recessions usually always coincide with downward tendency in interest rate dynamics (Gubareva, 2014; Gubareva & Borges, 2014).

Relations between credit and interest rate risk have been attracting attention of academic research both, from empirical (Bonfim & Soares, 2013; Boulkeroua & Stark, 2013; Landschoot, 2008; Lin & Sun, 2007), and theoretical (Jermann & Yue, 2013; Miloudi & Moraux, 2009; Neal, Rolph, Dupoyet, & Jiang, 2013; Piazzesi, & Schneider, 2010) perspectives. The common finding is that credit and interest rate risks are intrinsically related to each other and hardly separable. The above-mentioned works address integrated risks dynamics analyzing individual bond yields or bond indexes data.

However, less attention is paid to study an interrelation of credit and interest rate risks based on CDS spreads (Barbosa & Costa, 2010; Garcia & Yang, 2009; Tang & Yan, 2010). Following these studies, our chapter seeks to further advance the use of the derivative instruments such as CDS and IRS in researching the interaction of the credit and interest rate risk. We apply our approach to a selected universe of emerging market (EM) countries. What essentially distinguishes our chapter from other works in this field is that we address interrelations of risks from the perspective of quantifying economic capital, which bank must allocate to their fixed-income portfolios in order to be able to cover unexpected losses in the event of crystallization of downside risks.

It is of a special importance for emerging markets as they are heavily dependent on foreign capital for integrated interest rate and credit risk management potentially allows emerging market banks to improve risk management practices and optimize economic capital in terms of complying with capital adequacy and Basel III rules.

We revisit the economics of interest rate risk management in fixed-income banking books of liquidly traded bonds focusing on the interrelation between credit and interest rate risks. Our approach is based on historical VaR methodology, the first widely used in banking industry (Pérignonand & Smith, 2010), which allows for uncovering empirical complexities of interest rate and credit spread dynamics. The main objectives of our chapter are presented below.

First, our chapter focuses on interrelation between interest rate and credit risk using CDS spreads and IRS rates as proxies for credit default risk and interest rate risk related components in bonds yields. More than a decade-long historic CDS data regarding sovereign debt of EM countries is employed.

The second objective of our chapter is the study of a capital-wise elasticity of interest rate risk and credit risk, that is, an elasticity of interest rate risk and credit risk impacts analyzed through the prism of economic capital quantification. We demonstrate that such elasticity is a function of the considered time windows and, hence, depends on the phases of business cycle; either expansion or contraction, as they affect the risk-free interest rate level, the creditworthiness of obligors, and other parameters which in their turn influence IRS rates and CDS spreads.

Third, based on values of historical elasticity between interest rate and credit risk, we analyze potential hedge strategies against downside risk, which could be developed based either on usage of

IRS, or on usage of CDS, or on joint usage of both IRS and CDS instruments. We discuss possible outcomes of such strategies from the point of view of economic capital optimization.

The fourth objective of our work is a comparison of a derivative-based integrated approach with a similar historic VaR approach, widely employed in banking sector, which is based on sovereign bond yields. As a result of this comparison, we are able to quantify economic capital overcharge or undercharge, intrinsically present in the yield-based methodology as a result of the existence of a liquidity component in a bond yield.

And last but not least, the derivative-based model for economic capital undergoes a process of calibration based on comparison of its results country by country with the outcome of the regulatory Basel II/III formula for economic capital under the internal ratings based (IRB) Foundation approach. It is demonstrated that the proposed capital requirements metrics based on integrated treatment of interest rate and credit risk allows for optimizing bank economic capital and, hence, seeking to unleash resources needed to accelerate economic growth for diverse emerging market geographies.

The proposed and applied here derivative-based integrated downside risk assessment further advances the use of derivative instruments such as CDS and IRS to research the interaction of credit and interest rate risk. In this way the original risk-split idea of Black (1970) gains a new application in an aggregation of the split risks through analysis of interest rate and credit risk derivative instruments. The interaction of these risks is assessed within the flight-to-quality time windows linked to the business cycle and also over the periods of recovery from flights-to-quality.

Scope and Data

Our chapter is focused on EM countries. And as there is a lot of heterogeneity between developing economies we decide to firstly address those countries for which the available data are more extensive and reliable. We align our selection with the most recent

FTSE Global Equity Index Series Country Classification, as of September 2014, available at the beginning of our analyses (FTSE International Limited, 2014), which distinguishes four EM statuses, namely, Advanced Emerging, Secondary Emerging, Frontier, and Unclassified. Our attention herein is centered on Advanced Emerging markets that comprise 10 countries: Brazil, Czech Republic, Hungary, Malaysia, Mexico, Poland, South Africa, Taiwan, Thailand, and Turkey. As for Taiwan there is no CDS data, and for Czech Republic the history of CDS spreads is shorter than for other countries, we focus on the remaining eight markets.

To make the scope of our chapter more restricted, we focus on five year (5Y) point in the term structures of yields and spreads, as this is the most tradable and the most liquid term. We use CDS quotes for USD-denominated instruments due to the following; first, such instrument are much more liquid than CDS denominated in other currencies, and, second, our choice facilitates comparison of credit risks data and results across diverse countries, as they are quoted in the same basis. As a proxy for the USD-denominated risk-free interest rate we use an interest rate swap (IRS) rate at 5Y point (Bloomberg ticker: USSW5).

For the sake of comparative analyses based on USD-denominated bonds yields for selected key countries, we use actual Bloomberg Valuation (BVAL) curves, which recently substituted the well-known Bloomberg Fair Market Curves (FMC). For sovereign zero coupon yield 5Y the respective Bloomberg tickers that we use are the following: Brazil — F80205Y (FMC802), Mexico — C8045Y (BV050804), and Turkey — F85005Y (I24905Y (IYC)).

Methodology

Historical VaR Modeling of Economic Capital

Our derivative-based approach to integrated measure of interest rate and credit risk is built upon the widely used technique of Value at Risk (VaR). VaR describes the maximum loss, which is not exceeded in a given time period, called holding period, with a given quite elevated probability, denominated confidence level.

In mathematical terms, VaR is a percentile of the loss distribution. In general, VaR can be calculated for different holding periods and different confidence levels. But as we are focused on the ICAAP process, whose horizon is one-year forward, we use a one-year holding period, that is, 260 banking days, to achieve consistency between our VaR estimates and achievable ICAAP conclusions.

The main conclusion that regulators expect from ICAAP reports is whether a bank allocates sufficient economic capital to withstand negative outcomes in a year to come with a certain degree of probability. As generally speaking a probability of default (PD) for investment grade (entities) is expected to be below 0.1 percent, banks usually choose the 99.9 percent confidence level for their ICAAP exercises, and, hence, the 99.9 percent confidence interval in their VaR calculations. Such practice is also consistent with the confidence level of 99.9 percent determined by the Second and Third Basel accords for VaR-based model under the IRB approach. Thus, we opt for 99.9 percent confidence level in our VaR calculations and economic capital estimates.

As to the length of historical data to be employed in our VaR calculations, we use four different data arrays, namely, of 5, 7, 10 and 12 years. It is worth noting that the regulatory minimum is five years, while seven years series represent an advisable choice, widely used within the financial sector. Longer historical series are rather rare to be seen in practice, as they demand additional data storage and computing power capacities. Nevertheless, we include 10 and 12 years long data series in our analyses as potentially insightful for the research objectives.

To quantify economic capital we consider a model bond portfolio with book value of USD80 million, with USD10 million dollar exposure to each of eight above-mentioned EM countries.

Derivative-Based Segregated Approach to Risk Assessment

Following the segregated approach to risk assessment, the impact of the variation of interest rates, that is, the interest rate risk VaR, for the banking book, is calculated with a confidence level of

99.9 percent, using as a proxy for the risk-free interest rate the USD-denominated IRS rate. The impact in value of a 5Y maturity bond caused by one-year move in interest rate could be written as

$$\Delta \text{Value}_{260d_{\text{IR}}}(t) = \frac{[1+\text{yield}(t)]^5}{[1+\text{yield}(t)+\Delta \text{USSW5}_{260d}(t)]^5} \times \$10\text{mln} \quad (1)$$

where $\Delta\text{USSW5}_{260d}(t)$ stands for USSW5(t)–USSW5 ($t-260$), representing the change in the USD 5Y swap rate, calculated over the holding period of 260 banking days. The above formula for $\Delta\text{Value260}_{d\_\text{IR}}$ (t) represents a result of capitalization into the future at the rate yield(t) followed by discounting of the future value to the present moment at the rate yield $(t)+$ $\Delta\text{USSW5}_{260d}(t)$ that incorporates the change in USSW5.

Moving along time, over a chosen time window, and calculating $\Delta\text{Value}_{260d\_\text{IR}}$ (t) for an array of consecutive dates we receive the corresponding array of the value impacts, that is, Array [$\Delta\text{Value}_{260d\_\text{IR}}(t)$]. Using this array, the economic capital requirements for interest rate risk (IRR) with a confidence level of 99.9 percent could be written as follows:

$$\text{EC}_{\text{IRR}} = \text{Percentile}_{99.9\%}\left\{\text{Array}\left[-\Delta\text{Value}_{260d\_\text{IR}}(t)\right]\right\} \quad (2)$$

which is but the modulus of the negative impact whose probability to occur is less than 1 out of 1000.

Similarly, following the segregated approach to risk assessment, the impact in value of a 5Y maturity bond caused by one-year move in credit spread could be written as:

$$\Delta\text{Value}_{260d\_\text{spread}}(t) = \frac{[1+\text{yield}(t)]^5}{[1+\text{yield}(t)+\Delta\text{Spread}_{260d}(t)]^5} \times \$10\text{mln} \quad (3)$$

where $\Delta\text{Spread260}_d(t)$ stands for Credit_Spread(t)–Credit_Spread ($t-260$), representing the change in a chosen country CDS 5Y spread, calculated over the holding period of 260 banking days. Constructing the array of the value impacts, the economic capital requirements for credit risk regarding a chosen bond with a confidence level of 99.9 percent could be written as follows:

$$EC_{\text{Credit Risk}} = \text{Percentile}_{99.9\%}\left\{\text{Array}\left[-\Delta\text{Value}_{260d\_\text{Spread}}(t)\right]\right\} \quad (4)$$

which is the modulus of the negative impact whose probability to occur is less than 1 out of 1000.

Thus, under the segregated risk approach the total economic capital to be hold for IRR and credit risk under this approach is:

$$EC_{\text{Compounded}} = EC_{\text{IRR}} + EC_{\text{Credit Risk}} \quad (5)$$

Derivative-Based Integrated Approach to Risk Assessment

On the other hand, under the integrated risk approach, the impact in value of a 5Y maturity bond caused by the joint dynamics of the one-year interest rate and one-year credit spread moves could be written as:

$$\Delta\text{Value}_{260d\_\text{integrated}}(t) = \frac{[1+\text{yield}(t)]^5}{[1+\text{yield}(t)+\Delta\text{Spread}_{260d}(t)+\Delta\text{USSW5}_{260d}(t)]^5} \times \$10\text{mln} \quad (6)$$

In this way, the economic capital to be held in order to withstand the joint impact of IRR and country credit risk is:

$$EC_{\text{Integrated}} = \text{Percentile}_{99.9\%}\left\{\text{Array}\left[-\Delta\text{Value}_{260d\_\text{Integrated}}(t)\right]\right\} \quad (7)$$

The comparison of $EC_{\text{Compounded}}$ and $EC_{\text{Integrated}}$ is capable of shading light on interrelation between interest rate risk and credit risk for any chosen geography. Of course, it is expectable that $EC_{\text{Integrated}}$ is supposed to be inferior to the $EC_{\text{Compounded}}$ due to the risk diversification effect. The origins of risk diversifications for interest rate risk and credit risk reside in a possibility of the most value destroying 260 days moves in the interest rate and credit spread to occur over different time windows, attenuating, hence, the dynamics of their composition. It is also worth noting that the difference between $EC_{Compounded}$ and $EC_{Integrated}$ varies as a function of a length of the historical data series considered for the economic capital quantification. The outcomes of our integrated approach and its comparison to the segregated approach will be discussed in more detail while addressing our results.

Capital-Wise Elasticity of Interest Rate Risk and Credit Risk

To study cross-elasticity of interest rate risk and credit risk impacts, we analyze a problem of minimizing economic capital by augmenting or diminishing a joint sensitivity of a bond and its tailor-optimized hedge by IRS contract. In mathematical terms, we construct a hypothetical yield using an expression:

$$\text{Hypo Yield} = \text{USSW5} \times \text{Elasticity\_Coefficient} + \text{CDS\_Spread} \quad (8)$$

The value of the elasticity coefficient, which corresponds to the minimum possible economic capital, defines a possible downside risk hedge strategy from the capital optimization point of view. Thus if Elasticity_Coefficient is equal to 1, it means that from capital minimization perspective no hedge is needed, as joint dynamics of the interest rate and credit spread already results in the minimum possible capital requirements.

If Elasticity_Coefficient is equal to a value r, greater than 1, it means that in order to diminish exposure to downside risk we may need to augment exposure to the interest rate risk by contracting pay-float receive-fixed IRS with notional, equal to \$10mln × $(r-1)$. On the other hand, if Elasticity_Coefficient is equal to a value r, smaller than 1, it means that in order to diminish exposure to downside risk we may need to diminish exposure to the interest rate risk by contracting pay-fixed receive-float IRS with notional, equal to \$10mln × $(1-r)$.

Of course many other aspects need to be taken into account while evaluating a necessity of IRS-based hedging contracts, such as regulatory limits of the maximum possible impacts of parallel shifts of interest rate curves, overall profitability of the portfolio, among others. Still an issue of targeting economic capital minimization through downside risk hedging, addressed herein, seems to be undeservedly overlooked by both, academics and practitioners.

Components of a Bond Yield

In order to highlight a theoretical base of our approach, we discuss here a structure of a yield of a bond. In accordance with Black's (1970) view, there could be identified three major components, namely, credit risk, interest rate risk, and liquidity components. In an ideally perfect market the credit risk component of a chosen maturity bond is to be equal to the spread of the respective CDS. The interest rate related part of the yield ought to be equal to the reward of bearing interest rate risk, represented in the case of USD-denominated securities by the USD swap rate for the chosen term. The difference between the sum of these two components and the yield is nothing but liquidity premium, serving as a reward for the money supplied for the bond.

Figure 1 gives a schematic representation of a generic bond yield composed by three major contributions: the cost of bearing the risk of default loss, the cost of bearing the interest rate risk, and the cost of supplying money for the bond.

As a proxy for a credit spread of a chosen bond the respective CDS spread is used. This part of the bond yield is required so that investors earn sufficient return for their risk of losses in case of

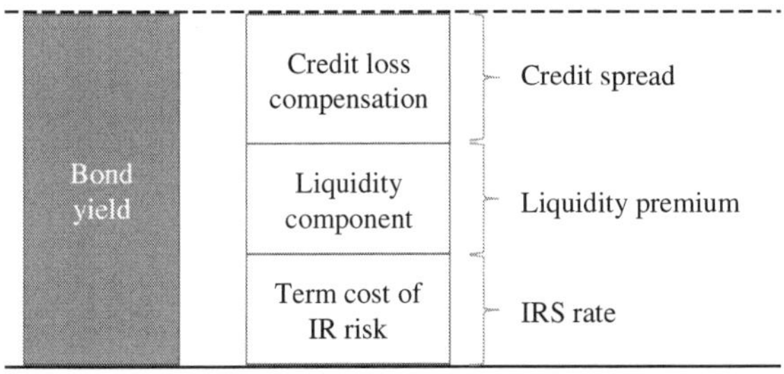

Figure 1: Components of a Bond Yield: Credit Spread, Liquidity Premium, and IRS Rate.

default. As a proxy for a term cost of interest rate risk (IRR) the respective maturity IRS rate is employed. This part of the bond yield is required so that investors earn sufficient return for bearing the IRR. As this study is focused on interest rate and credit risk, the third component, called here liquidity premium, serves as an adjustment to the bond yield. The meaning of this liquidity premium is a compensation for investors for being invested in the bond and, hence, not having money at hand.

Yield-Based Integrated Approach to Risk Assessment

It is worth noting that one of the methods employed across the financial sector to quantify economic capital for fixed-income portfolio is based on calculating VaR using historical series of a yield. Under this yield-based aggregated approach, the impact in value of a 5Y maturity bond caused by one-year yield move could be written as:

$$\Delta \text{Value}_{260d\_\text{yield}-\text{based}}(t) = \frac{[1+\text{yield}(t)]^5}{[1+\text{yield}(t)+\Delta\text{yield}_{260d}(t)]^5} \times \$10\text{mln} \quad (9)$$

where $\Delta\text{yield}260_d(t)$ stands for yield(t) – yield(t–260), representing the change in a chosen bond yield, calculated over the holding period of 260 banking days. Constructing the array of the value impacts, the economic capital requirements regarding a chosen bond with a confidence level of 99.9 percent could be written as follows:

$$\text{EC}_{\text{yield-based}} = \text{Percentile}_{99.9\%}\left\{\text{Array}\left[-\Delta\text{Value}_{260d\_\text{yield based}}(t)\right]\right\} \quad (10)$$

Although such approach may seem to present benefit of relative simplicity in comparison to the proposed derivative-based integrated approach, it also presents a certain weakness from the theoretical point of view, as possible impacts originated by interest rate and credit spread moves could be disguised, that is, reduced or amplified, by the liquidity component present in the yield. It is worth noting, that it is widely acknowledged by regulators and industry players that capital is rather a not appropriate instrument to mitigate liquidity risk that ought to be managed by diverse techniques, including, among others, maintenance of high quality liquid assets (HQLA) as a certain percent of fixed-income portfolios.

Thus, the implicit consideration of the liquidity component in capital quantification potentially implies eventual misallocation of economic capital. For a chosen set of countries, Brazil, Mexico, and Turkey, we show that the liquidity component makes bonds to appear either excessively risky, as for Brazil and Turkey, or to mask their real riskiness as in the case of Mexico.

Estimating Liquidity Component

The proposed herein derivative-based approach to risk assessment offers a possibility to track historical behavior of the liquidity component of the yield, that is to quantify the bond specific liquidity risk, although with no intention of capital allocation. Plotting the sum of IRS rate and the CDS spread we depict a proxy for a liquidity-free yield. The difference between the observable bond yield and the liquidity-free yield, constructed from IRS rates and CDS spread based inputs, is nothing but liquidity premium, serving as a reward for the money supplied for the bond.

IRB Foundation Approach to Unexpected Loss Assessment

The outcomes of the derivative-based model for economic capital are compared to results of capital requirements quantification based on comparison of its results country by country with outcomes of the regulatory Basel II/III formula for economic capital under the internal ratings based (IRB) Foundation approach as defined by CRR — Capital Requirements Regulation (Regulation (EU) No 575/2013 of the European Parliament, Article 153). Under this approach, using the risk-weighted factor of 8 percent, capital requirements for exposures to corporates, institutions, and central governments shall be calculated according to the following formulae:

$$\text{EC} = \text{exposure value} \times \left[\text{LGD} \times N\left(\frac{1}{\sqrt{1-R}} \times G(\text{PD}) + \sqrt{\frac{R}{1-R}} \times G(0.999) \right) - \text{LGD} \times \text{PD} \right] \times \frac{1+(M-2.5)b}{1-1.5b} \times 1.06 \tag{11}$$

where $N(x)$ is the cumulative distribution function for a standard normal random variable (i.e., the probability that a normal random variable with mean zero and variance of one is less than or equal to x); $G(Z)$ denotes the inverse cumulative distribution function for a standard normal random variable (i.e. the value x such that $N(x) = z$); R denotes the coefficient of correlation, is defined as:

$$R = 0.12 \times \frac{1-e^{-50\times\text{PD}}}{1-e^{-50}} + 0.24 \times \left(1 - \frac{1-e^{-50\times\text{PD}}}{1-e^{-50}}\right) \tag{12}$$

and b stands for the maturity adjustment factor: $b = (0.11852 - 0.05478 \times \ln(\text{PD}))^2$.

We use a regulatory value of 45 percent for the senior debt LGD (loss given default) parameter. To assess PD (probability of default) parameter we use a Basel rating (second best rating) based on two rating agencies Moody's and Standard & Poor's. Then, according to the country Basel rating, the second best one, we attribute to the country a PD equal to the average of long term default frequency calculated by Moody's (2014) over the years 1983–2013 (Moody's Annual Default Study Corporate Default and Recovery Rates, 1920–2013) and of long term default frequency calculated by Standard & Poor's (2014) over the years 1981–2013 (S&P's Default, Transition, and Recovery: 2013 Annual Global Corporate Default Study and Rating Transitions).

It can be demonstrated that the results of derivative-based integrated approach to risk assessment are consistent with the described above IRB Foundation approach. Still being more issuer specific our derivative-based approach to integrated treatment of interest rate and credit risk seems to be more comprehensive and hence allowing for better optimizing bank economic capital.

Results and Discussion

Derivative-Based Integrated versus Segregated Approach to Risk Assessment

We start the discussion of our results presenting our findings focused on interrelation between interest rate and credit risk. Using CDS spreads and IRS rates as proxies for the credit default risk and the interest rate risk related components in bonds yields we quantify EC requirements with 99.9 percent confidence level as of December 31, 2014, based on four different lengths of time series analyzed by the historical VaR technique, namely 12Y, 10Y, 7Y, and 5Y. We compare composed EC requirements with the EC requirements quantified following the integrated approach to risk assessment, and present potentially disposable fund as a difference between these two estimates in Tables 1–4. We perform this analysis on a country-by-country basis, and also on the whole portfolio basis evidencing in this way a presence of a diversification benefit due to diversity of geographies.

As could be seen from these tables the length of the VaR analyses window impacts significantly EC estimations, but still some common patterns arise. Thus, analyzing the requirements for the model portfolio for all lengths of VaR series, the EC under integrated approach is significantly lower that under the segregated one, being the former on average roughly equal to 53 percent of the latter; varying between 45 percent for 7Y VaR history and 58 percent for 10Y of VaR history into the past.

As the historical data sample becomes more distant from the apogee of the world financial crisis between September 2008 and March 2009, the EC quantification by the historical VaR method, as expected, results in lower figures. We observe that for 12Y and

Table 1: Integrated versus Segregated Approach to EC as of December 2014 with 12Y VaR History.

Country	Position Book Value, US$ mln	IRR EC Requirements, %	Credit Risk EC Requirements, %	Compounded EC Requirements, %	Integrated Approach EC Requirements, %	Potentially Disposable EC, %
		A	B	C = A + B	D	E = C − D
Brazil	10	8.54	19.70	28.24	15.21	13.03
Hungary	10	9.19	20.94	30.13	16.99	13.14
Malaysia	10	9.14	15.79	24.93	12.29	12.64
Mexico	10	9.07	20.21	29.28	15.89	13.39
Poland	10	9.18	15.07	24.25	10.19	14.06
South Africa	10	9.10	21.73	30.83	18.53	12.30
Thailand	10	9.16	14.98	24.14	11.43	12.71
Turkey	10	8.55	23.29	31.84	19.56	12.28
Portfolio	*80*	*8.98*	*17.98*	*26.96*	*14.26*	*12.70*

Compounded EC requirements minus integrated approach EC requirements represent potentially disposable EC. Results presented for each country individually and for the portfolio as a whole.

Table 2: Integrated versus Segregated Approach to EC as of December 2014 with 10Y VaR History.

Country	Position Book Value, US$ mln	IRR EC Requirements, %	Credit Risk EC Requirements, %	Compounded EC Requirements, %	Integrated Approach EC Requirements, %	Potentially Disposable EC, %
		A	B	C = A + B	D	E = C − D
Brazil	10	7.18	19.83	27.01	15.82	11.19
Hungary	10	7.39	21.68	29.07	17.96	11.11
Malaysia	10	7.38	17.22	24.60	13.54	11.06
Mexico	10	7.34	20.31	27.65	16.26	11.39
Poland	10	7.39	15.12	22.51	10.3	12.21
South Africa	10	7.36	22.56	29.92	19.17	10.75
Thailand	10	7.38	16.36	23.74	12.59	11.15
Turkey	10	7.22	23.92	31.14	20.34	10.80
Portfolio	*80*	*7.33*	*19.07*	*26.40*	*15.36*	*11.04*

Compounded EC requirements minus integrated approach EC requirements represent potentially disposable EC. Results presented for each country individually and for the portfolio as a whole.

Table 3: Integrated versus Segregated Approach to EC as of December 2014 with 7Y VaR History.

Country	Position Book Value, US$ mln	IRR EC Requirements, %	Credit Risk EC Requirements, %	Compounded EC Requirements, %	Integrated Approach EC Requirements, %	Potentially Disposable EC, %
		A	B	C = A + B	D	E = C − D
Brazil	10	5.28	11.98	17.26	8.89	8.37
Hungary	10	5.15	19.81	24.96	15.98	8. 98
Malaysia	10	5.29	10.30	15.59	7.02	8.57
Mexico	10	5.29	15.31	20.60	11.58	9.02
Poland	10	5.27	15.17	20.44	10.43	10.01
South Africa	10	5.27	13.80	19.07	9.6	9.47
Thailand	10	5.28	9.49	14.77	7.22	7.55
Turkey	10	5.26	12.08	17.34	10.08	7.26
Portfolio	*80*	*5.26*	*13.15*	*18.41*	*8.31*	*9.12*

Compounded EC requirements minus integrated approach EC requirements represent potentially disposable EC. Results presented for each country individually and for the portfolio as a whole.

Table 4: Integrated vs. Segregated Approach to EC as of Dec-2014 with 5Y VaR History.

Country	Position Book Value, US$ mln	IRR EC Requirements, %	Credit Risk EC Requirements, %	Compounded EC Requirements, %	Integrated Approach EC Requirements, %	Potentially Disposable EC, %
		A	B	C = A + B	D	E = C – D
Brazil	10	5.29	4.95	10.24	8.84	1.40
Hungary	10	5.16	16.17	21.33	12.86	8.47
Malaysia	10	5.3	5.91	11.21	7.08	4.13
Mexico	10	5.3	4.57	9.87	6.45	3.42
Poland	10	5.29	8.52	13.81	7.31	6.50
South Africa	10	5.29	5.25	10.54	9.6	0.94
Thailand	10	5.29	6.60	11.89	7.29	4.60
Turkey	10	5.27	8.94	14.21	10.2	4.01
Portfolio	*80*	*5.27*	*6.72*	*11.99*	*6.58*	*5.41*

Compounded EC requirements minus integrated approach EC requirements represent potentially disposable EC. Results presented for each country individually and for the portfolio as a whole.

10Y lengths of data series, the EC requirements are substantially higher than for 7Y and more than two times higher for 5Y long data histories that do not capture the full history of the crisis.

We also observe that EC requirements under the integrated approach are consistently lower than the segregated approach EC requirements solely for credit risk. This fact clearly indicates that for all lengths of the considered VaR series, the interest rate downtrend dynamics mitigate the credit spread widening. We discuss this in more detail in one of the following sections while addressing the interest rate elasticity.

Derivative-Based Studies of Expansion and Contraction Phases of Business Cycle

Interrelations of interest rate and credit risk differ between expansion and contraction phases of business cycle. A great importance in comprehending mechanisms of this interaction will play the flight-to-quality phenomena when capital flies from risky to risk-free assets, augmenting credit risk spreads of the former and diminishing the yields of the latter (Gubareva, 2014). It was especially so during the recent financial crisis, when interest rates dropped and simultaneously the average creditworthiness of debt issuers, being banks, corporates, or sovereigns, deteriorated too. Although this situation could appear counterintuitive, the novel contribution of this chapter to the new economic thinking is that it is not an exceptional case but rather common and expectable circumstances, as crashes and recessions usually always coincide with downward tendency in interest rate dynamics (Gubareva & Borges, 2014).

To address this issue, in Table 5 we present our results for the two very distinctive time windows in the recent history, namely, before and after the apogee of the global financial crisis in September 2008/March 2009.

As we observe for the period before the crisis, if treated separately, credit risk requirements are almost three times higher than IRR requirements. On the contrary, for the period after the crisis they are roughly 50 percent above the IRR requirements. Due to

Table 5: Integrated versus Segregated Approach to EC with 5Y VaR; December 2008 and December 2013.

Country/VaR history	Position Book Value, US$ mln	IRR EC Requirements, %	Credit Risk EC Requirements, %	Compounded EC Requirements, %	Integrated Approach EC Requirements, %	Potentially Disposable EC, %
		A	B	C = A + B	D	E = C − D
Brazil/2004–2008	10	7.42	20.38	27.80	16.72	11.08
Brazil/2009–2013	10	5.29	4.95	10.24	8.84	1.40
Hungary/2004–2008	10	7.81	22.86	30.67	19.31	11.36
Hungary/2009–2013	10	5.16	16.17	21.33	12.86	8.47
Malaysia/2004–2008	10	7.79	18.34	26.13	14.47	11.66
Malaysia/2009–2013	10	5.30	5.91	11.21	7.08	4.13
Mexico/2004–2008	10	7.75	21.93	29.68	18.33	11.35
Mexico/2009–2013	10	5.30	4.57	9.87	6.45	3.42
Poland/2004–2008	10	7.80	11.51	19.31	8.20	11.11
Poland/2009–2013	10	5.29	8.53	13.82	7.31	6.51
South Africa/2004–2008	10	7.75	23.73	31.48	20.17	11.31
South Africa/2009–2013	10	5.29	5.25	10.54	9.60	0.94

Thailand/ 2004–2008	10	7.80	17.57	25.37	13.75	11.62
Thailand/2009–2013	10	5.29	6.60	11.89	6.3	5.59
Turkey/2004–2008	10	7.56	24.99	32.55	21.62	10.93
Turkey/2009–2013	10	5.27	8.94	14.21	9.64	4.57
Portfolio/2004–2008	*80*	*7.71*	*20.19*	*27.90*	*16.44*	*11.46*
Portfolio/2009–2013	*80*	*5.27*	*7.62*	*12.89*	*6.22*	*6.67*

Compounded EC requirements minus integrated approach EC requirements represent potentially disposable EC. For the two selected time intervals 2004–2008 and 2009–2013 the results are presented separately for the sake of comparison of EC requirements and potentially disposable EC for the pre-crisis and post-crisis economic environments.

these circumstances, the diversification benefits of the integrated treatments of this pair of risks are bigger for the pre-crisis period.

Still, the proposed herein derivative-based aggregated approach accounts correctly for the higher riskiness of the pre-crisis period. On the other hand, one could infer that if exposure to the interest rate risk in the pre-crisis period would be bigger, the diversification benefits could be also bigger, reducing in this manner integrated approach EC requirements. In the next section, we discuss in more detail the economic capital-wise elasticity of interest rate risk and credit risk.

Derivative-Based Capital-Wise Elasticity of Interest Rate Risk and Credit Risk

We study the cross-elasticity of interest rate risk and credit risk impacts analyzed through the prism of economic capital quantification. We minimize hypothetical EC requirements with 99.9 percent confidence level as of December 31, 2014, based on four different length of the historical VaR data samples, namely 12Y, 10Y, 7Y, and 5Y. For this purpose we construct a hypothetical yield as a sum of USSW5 rate multiplied by elasticity coefficient and CDS spread. In Tables 6–9 we present the values of elasticity coefficient minimizing EC and the values of the minimal EC achievable for a joint combination of a bond and its hedge by the appropriate IRS contract.

As expected, we observe that EC-wise elasticity is a function of the considered time windows. As we approach the apogee of the global financial crisis, we see at the aggregate portfolio level that the interest rate risk and credit risk start to present a strong negative correlation. For example, the highest value of the EC-wise elasticity coefficient is found to correspond to the 10Y long VaR data sample, while shorter lengths of VaR data arrays of 7Y and 5Y result in smaller values of the coefficient, indicating that this EM portfolio after the apogee of the crisis in the sense of capital minimization behaves as roughly insensitive to the changes in the interest rate, and thus not needing the interest rate hedge by pay-fixed receive-float IRS contracts.

Table 6: EC-Wise IR Elasticity and Possible Gain in EC as of December 2014 under 12Y VaR.

Country	Position Book Value, US$ mln	Integrated Approach EC Requirements, %	EC-wise Interest Rate Elasticity Coefficient	Corresponding Minimum of EC %	Gain in EC under Downside Risk Hedging, %
		α		β	$\gamma = \alpha - \beta$
Brazil	10	15.21	1.49	12.64	2.57
Hungary	10	16.99	1.55	14.72	2.27
Malaysia	10	12.29	1.29	11.12	1.17
Mexico	10	15.89	1.43	13.64	2.25
Poland	10	10.19	1.12	9.79	0.40
South Africa	10	18.53	1.71	15.71	2.82
Thailand	10	11.43	1.15	10.82	0.61
Turkey	10	19.56	1.99	15.69	3.87
Portfolio	*80*	*14.26*	*1.49*	*12.28*	*1.98*

The difference between integrated approach EC requirements corresponding to historically observed yield and minimal EC corresponding to the least volatile hypothetical yield represents a potentially attainable gain in EC under downside risk hedging by optimized IRS contracts.

Table 7: EC-Wise IR Elasticity and Possible Gain in EC as of December 2014 under 10Y VaR.

Country	Position Book Value, US$ mln	Integrated Approach EC Requirements, %	EC-Wise Interest Rate Elasticity Coefficient	Corresponding Minimum of EC %	Gain in EC under Downside Risk Hedging, %
		α		β	$\gamma = \alpha - \beta$
Brazil	10	15.82	1.95	12.7	3.12
Hungary	10	17.96	1.88	14.74	3.22
Malaysia	10	13.54	1.61	11.7	1.84
Mexico	10	16.26	1.84	12.8	3.46
Poland	10	10.3	1.19	9.47	0.83
South Africa	10	19.17	2.01	15.21	3.96
Thailand	10	12.59	1.47	11.21	1.38
Turkey	10	20.34	2.10	16.13	4.21
Portfolio	*80*	*15.36*	*1.78*	*12.65*	*2.71*

The difference between integrated approach EC requirements corresponding to historically observed yield and minimal EC corresponding to the least volatile hypothetical yield represents a potentially attainable gain in EC under downside risk hedging by optimized IRS contracts.

Table 8: EC-Wise IR Elasticity and Possible Gain in EC as of December 2014 under 7Y VaR.

Country	Position Book Value, US$ mln	Integrated Approach EC Requirements, %	EC-Wise Interest Rate Elasticity Coefficient	Corresponding Minimum of EC %	Gain in EC under Downside Risk Hedging, %
		α		β	$\gamma = \alpha - \beta$
Brazil	10	8.89	0.82	8.65	0.24
Hungary	10	15.98	2.06	12.16	3.82
Malaysia	10	7.02	0.89	6.93	0.09
Mexico	10	11.58	1.48	9.66	1.92
Poland	10	10.43	1.68	7.5	2.93
South Africa	10	9.6	0.95	9.56	0.04
Thailand	10	7.22	0.75	6.50	0.72
Turkey	10	10.08	0.68	9.29	0.79
Portfolio	*80*	*8.31*	*1.25*	*8.14*	*0.17*

The difference between integrated approach EC requirements corresponding to historically observed yield and minimal EC corresponding to the least volatile hypothetical yield represents a potentially attainable gain in EC under downside risk hedging by optimized IRS contracts.

Table 9: EC-Wise IR Elasticity and Possible Gain in EC as of December 2014 under 5Y VaR.

Country	Position book value, US$ mln	Integrated Approach EC Requirements, %	EC-wise Interest Rate Elasticity Coefficient	Corresponding Minimum of EC %	Gain in EC under Downside Risk Hedging, %
		α		β	$\gamma = \alpha - \beta$
Brazil	10	8.84	−0.02	4.95	3.89
Hungary	10	12.86	1.26	12.07	0.79
Malaysia	10	7.08	0.63	5.37	1.71
Mexico	10	6.45	0.45	3.92	2.53
Poland	10	7.31	1.04	7.29	0.02
South Africa	10	9.6	−0.07	5.16	4.44
Thailand	10	7.29	0.65	6.07	1.22
Turkey	10	10.2	0.39	8.03	2.17
Portfolio	*80*	*6.58*	*0.81*	*5.91*	*0.67*

The difference between integrated approach EC requirements corresponding to historically observed yield and minimal EC corresponding to the least volatile hypothetical yield represents a potentially attainable gain in EC under downside risk hedging by optimized IRS contracts.

On the country-by-country basis, values of EC-wise elasticity coefficient varies a lot. Nevertheless, for 12Y and 10Y lengths of VaR data, all the individual country coefficients present values above one meaning that in long run including financial turmoil an additional exposure to the interest rate risk would benefit EC requirements. Such exposure could be reached by contracting a pay-float receive-fixed IRS contracts with notional values equal to *Position_book_value* × (*Elasticity_Coefficient* – 1). Such downside risk hedging could be performed either on individual level, or on the integrated portfolio level.

For the 7Y and 5Y long VaR samples we observe quite a few positions with EC-wise elasticity coefficient values below 1. It means that such positions have a positive sensitivity to the interest rate and could be hedged against the downside risk, and partially against the interest rate risk, by contracting in such cases a pay-fixed receive-float IRS contracts with notional values equal to *Position_book_value* × (1 – *Elasticity_Coefficient*). Of course many other aspects, such as profit targets and regulatory limits of exposure to IRR need to be taken into account while evaluating a necessity of IRS-based hedging strategy.

Derivative-Based Integrated Approach versus Yield-Based Approach to Risk Assessment

One of non-derivative methods employed across the financial sector to jointly quantify Pillar 1 plus Pillar 2 economic capital for fixed-income portfolio is based on calculating VaR using historical series of bond yields. In Table 10 we present a comparison of the EC figures calculated according to the yield-based methodology and proposed herein derivative-based approach in its both modalities employing either segregated or integrated risk treatment.

Comparing the derivative-based integrated EC requirements with the yield-based EC requirements, we observe that liquidity component in the yield of the bonds make results differ from those purely based on integrated treatment of interest rate and credit risk. As in principal, the liquidity risk is not supposed to be mitigated by holding additional capital the value added of our

Table 10: EC Estimates through Derivative-Based Approach versus Yield-Based Approach.

Country	Position Book Value, US$ mln	Derivative-Based compounded EC Requirements, %	Derivative-Based Integrated EC Requirements, %	Yield-Based EC Requirements, %
12Y VaR				
Brazil	10	28.24	15.21	17.03
Mexico	10	29.28	15.89	14.01
Turkey	10	31.84	19.56	29.28
10Y VaR				
Brazil	10	27.01	15.82	17.04
Mexico	10	27.65	16.26	14.15
Turkey	10	31.14	20.34	29.33
7Y VaR				
Brazil	10	17.26	8.89	8.65
Mexico	10	20.60	11.58	6.82
Turkey	10	17.34	10.08	13.45
5Y VaR				
Brazil	10	10.24	8.84	8.70
Mexico	10	9.87	6.45	6.49
Turkey	10	14.21	10.20	11.77

Derivative-based compounded EC, derivative-based integrated EC, and yield-based EC for the selected set of countries and for diverse lengths of the employed VaR samples.

derivative-based integrated approach is a possibility to eliminate impacts of liquidity conditions and consider joint impacts of changes in interest rate and in credit spreads, represented by derivative instruments: IRS rates and CDS spreads, respectively.

We observe that differences between the derivative-based integrated EC requirements and the yield-based EC requirements become smaller as the length of VaR historical data becomes shorter. Still bonds of different countries are being impacted by liquidity conditions in different ways. For example, for Turkey one could conclude that the liquidity risk acts rather as an amplifier of the impacts of two other interest rate and credit spread components, substantially increasing in this manner the yield and augmenting a perceived riskiness of Turkish debt.

For Brazil, for the longer VaR data series of 12Y and 10Y, the impact of liquidity is found to be similar to that of Turkey, but much more moderated in the degree. On the other hand, for the shorter VaR data series of 7Y and 5Y on Brazilian debt, we observe no material impact on the yield-based EC requirements from liquidity conditions as figures are very closed to the derivative-based integrated EC requirements.

For Mexico, for the longer VaR data series of 12Y, 10Y, and 7Y, liquidity seems to play the role of masquerading credit risk. Our guess would be that this geography used to be a favorable destination of US investment, and hunting for the yield, the demand for Mexico debt seems to make prices rise and yields come down. Alternatively one could argue that CDS market for protection of Mexican debt was overheated and, hence, rather speculative, resulting in too wide CDS spreads representing higher costs of debt protection. Of course, to precisely solve this enigma further detailed research is needed. But still our results allow us to infer that yield-based analyses, under certain conditions, could result into better than real creditworthiness, and hence to misallocation, here undercharge, of EC.

Additionally, the proposed herein derivative-based approach could be useful not only for EC analysis, but also for disentangling liquidity components and tracking it on a daily basis.

Estimating Liquidity Component

For the same selected set of EM countries, Brazil, Mexico, and Turkey, we plot the sum of IRS rate and the CDS spread, representing but a proxy for a liquidity-free yield. The difference between the observable bond yield and the liquidity-free yield, constructed from IRS rates and CDS spread based inputs, is nothing but liquidity premium, serving as a reward for the money supplied for the bond.

In Figure 2 we plot generic sovereign zero coupon yield of Brazilian 5Y maturity debt as represented by the Bloomberg curve F80205Y along with the liquidity-free yield proxy constructed as a sum of USD-denominated IRS rate at 5Y point, namely, the USSW5 curve and the Brazil CDS spread for 5Y maturity debt according to the data available on Bloomberg terminal (ticker: CBRZ1US). In Figure 3, we plot a 5Y liquidity component in the Brazilian sovereign debt yield as a difference between the generic 5Y bond yield and the derivatives-based liquidity-free proxy.

A few comments are relevant. We suggest that the negativity of the liquidity component in 2003 is ascribable to the recovery from

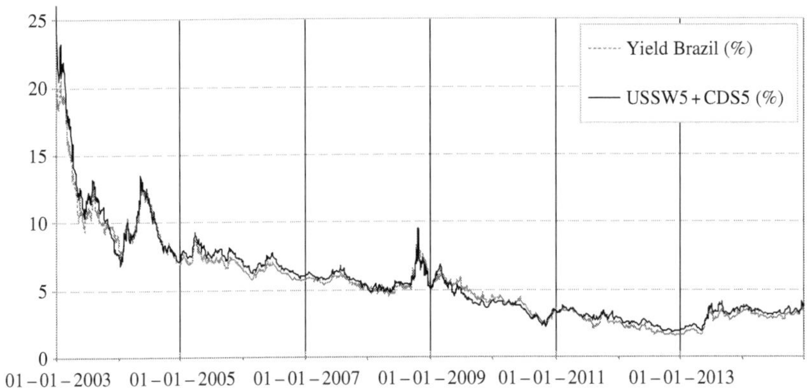

Figure 2: Generic 5Y Yield of Brazilian Debt versus Derivative-Based Liquidity-Free Proxy. *Source*: Bloomberg, authors' calculations. *Note*: The spread between the two curves measures liquidity component contained in the yield of the Brazilian government bonds. See also Figure 3.

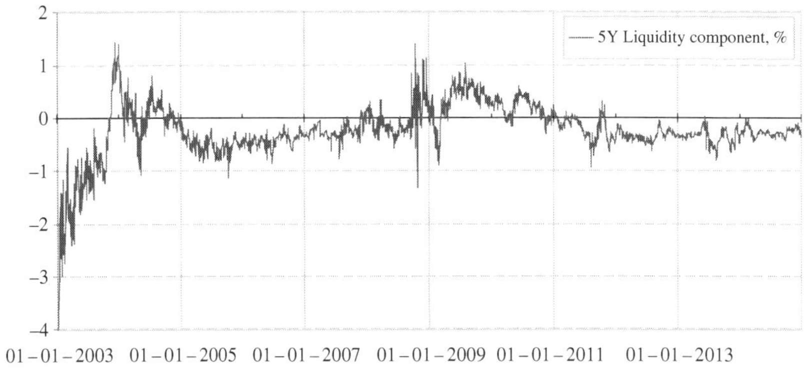

Figure 3: 5Y Liquidity Component in the Brazilian 5Y Debt Yield, January 2003–December 2014. *Source*: Bloomberg, authors' calculations.

the so-called Brazilian crisis of autumn of 2002, linked to the elections whose winner was Mr. Lula da Silva, of whom financial markets were notably afraid, at the beginning. But evidencing no disrupt in economic policies, Brazilian debt became strongly demanded by the investor in order not to lose a train of debt prices recovery, resulting thus in negative liquidity premium.

Here one can also notice an excess of liquidity prior to the global financial crisis, and a lack of liquidity during the three years following this financial turmoil. The last three years present a negative liquidity component likely reflecting high investors interest in Brazilian debt.

In Figure 4 we plot generic sovereign zero coupon yield of Mexican 5Y maturity debt as represented by the Bloomberg curve C8045Y along with the liquidity-free yield proxy constructed as a sum of USD-denominated IRS rate at 5Y point, namely, the USSW5 curve and the Mexico CDS spread for 5Y maturity debt according to the data available on Bloomberg terminal (ticker: CMEX1US). In Figure 5 we plot a 5Y liquidity component in the Mexican sovereign debt yield as a difference between the generic 5Y bond yield and the derivatives-based liquidity-free proxy.

We see a positive spike in the derivative-based liquidity-free proxy in 2009, which results in a negative spike in the liquidity component. The discussion of what was the cause of the spike in

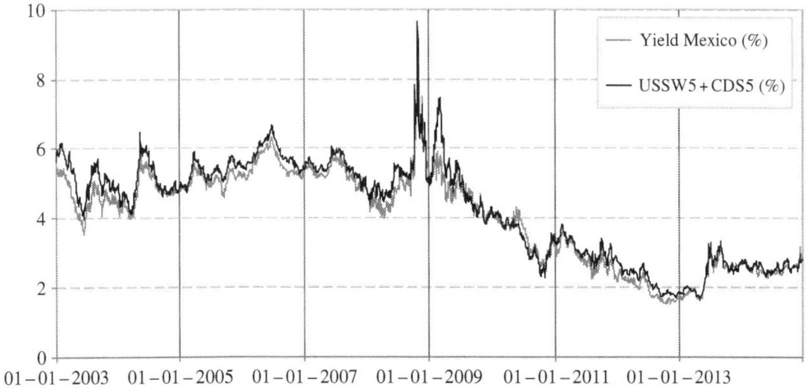

Figure 4: Generic 5Y Yield of Mexican Debt versus Derivative-Based Liquidity-Free Proxy. *Source*: Bloomberg, authors' calculations. *Note*: The spread between the two curves measures liquidity component contained in the yield of the Mexican government bonds. See also Figure 5.

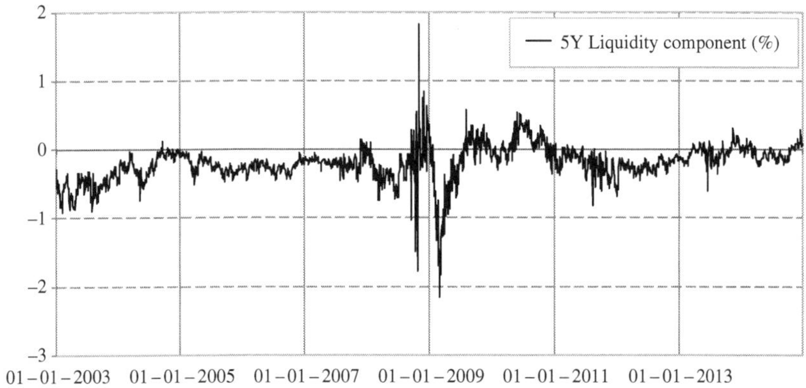

Figure 5: 5Y Liquidity Component in the Mexican 5Y Debt Yield, January 2003–December 2014. *Source*: Bloomberg, authors' calculations.

the 5Y Mexican debt CDS spreads in 2009 stays beyond the scope of this research, but it serves as an indication of the usefulness of our derivative-based integrated approach for revealing eventual discrepancies between yield-based and derivative-based data, and hence allowing for better mutual calibration of diverse methodologies for assessing EC requirements.

In Figure 6 we plot generic sovereign zero coupon yield of Turkish 5Y maturity debt as represented by the Bloomberg curve F80505Y along with the liquidity-free yield proxy constructed as a sum of USD-denominated IRS rate at 5Y point, namely, the USSW5 curve and the Turkey CDS spread for 5Y maturity debt according to the data available on Bloomberg terminal (ticker: CTURK1US). In Figure 7 we plot a 5Y liquidity component in the Turkish sovereign debt yield as a difference between the generic 5Y bond yield and the derivatives-based liquidity-free proxy.

For Turkey, Figure 7 clearly shows that prior to the apogee of the world financial crisis between September 2008 and March 2009 the liquidity component for Turkish sovereign debt was negative, certifying in this way an excess liquidity in the financial markets. After this, due to a lack of liquidity in the markets the liquidity premium for 5Y Turkish debt becomes positive, and continues positive through the recent past increasing in this manner the yields an diminishing bond prices, most likely due to specific

Figure 6: Generic 5Y Yield of Turkish Debt versus Derivative-Based Liquidity-Free Proxy. *Source*: Bloomberg, authors' calculations. Note: The spread between the two curves measures liquidity component contained in the yield of the Turkish government bonds. See also Figure 7.

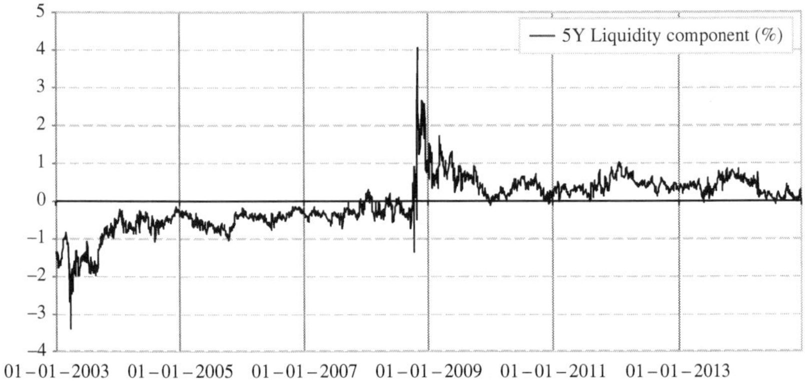

Figure 7: 5Y Liquidity Component in the Turkish 5Y Debt Yield, January 2003–December 2014. *Source*: Bloomberg, authors' calculations.

turbulence experiences by Turkish state at least over the last two years.

Benchmarking the Derivative-Based Integrated Approach against the Basel III Regulation

The outcomes of the derivative-based model for economic capital are compared to results of capital requirements quantification based on comparison of its results country by country with outcomes of the regulatory Basel II/III formula for economic capital under the internal ratings based (IRB) Foundation approach. In Table 11 we present our results for both methodologies.

Comparing the last two columns one could observe that capital requirements for credit risk computed according to the regulatory formula are well below the CDS-based estimates for EC in regard to credit risk. This result is quite expectable as we used the long run default frequencies as proxies for probabilities of default. Under the regulatory approach, it is an admissible procedure both by market participants and regulators.

But going one step further at this point we calculate the total compounded EC represented by a sum of the regulatory Pillar 1 credit risk requirements and the Pillar 2 IRS-based IRR

Table 11: Basel III Foundation Approach Regulatory Credit Risk Requirements versus CDS-Based Credit Risk Requirements as of December 2014.

Country	Position Book Value, US $ mln	Moody's Foreign Currency LT Debt Rating	S&P's Foreign Currency LT Debt Rating	Basel Rating in S&P Notation	Basel III Foundation Regulatory Credit Risk Requirements, %	CDS-based Credit Risk Requirements, %
Brazil	10	Baa2	BBB –	BBB –	4.52	4.95
Hungary	10	Ba1	BB	BB	6.89	16.17
Malaysia	10	A3	A –	A –	2.04	5.91
Mexico	10	A3	BBB +	BBB +	3.15	4.57
Poland	10	A2	A –	A –	2.04	8.52
South Africa	10	Baa2	BBB –	BBB –	4.52	5.25
Thailand	10	Baa1	BBB +	BBB +	3.15	6.60
Turkey	10	Baa3	BB +	BB +	6.17	8.94

Calculations of the Basel III Foundation regulatory credit risk requirements based on the Basel (second best) rating are compared to CDS-based credit risk requirements assessed using historic 5Y VaR methodology.

requirements and compare this compounded EC to the EC estimated following the derivatives-based integrated approach to risk assessment. In Table 12 we explicitly show the delta between the results of these two approaches.

Hence, it is empirically demonstrated that the results of derivative-based integrated approach to risk assessment are consistent with the Basel III IRB Foundation approach. The average delta is about 0.63 percent certifying that proposed herein approach is competitive in the sense of its outcomes with the alternative use of regulatory formula under segregated risk treatment. Additionally, being more issuer specific our derivative-based approach to integrated treatment of interest rate and credit risk seems to be more comprehensive and, thus, allowing for better optimizing of economic capital to be held by a bank in order to withstand the joint impact of IRR and specific country credit risk.

Derivative-Based Modeling of Economic Capital for the 2007–2014 Period

To study how the EC calculated following the proposed herein derivative-based approach behaves along the time, we perform our modeling for all the years for which we have a regulatory minimum of 5Y history for VaR analysis. Figure 8 depicts dynamics of EC following the integrated approach to the risk assessment. For the sake of comparison we also plot the EC calculated under the segregated assumption regarding the risks treatment. These calculations are made directly on the portfolio level and thus benefited from credit risk diversification.

Figure 8 evidences that integrated approach to risk assessment permits optimizing EC. It is important that all these calculations could be drilled down in order to understand all the components impacting final results. For example, an apparently strange plato-behavior of EC under integrated approach, in fact, has a simple and convincing explanation. While time window of VaR analysis contains the maximum yearly increase in credit spreads due to the global financial crises, the percentile analysis returns the very same values for four consecutive years.

Table 12: Compounded Basel III Foundation Regulatory Credit Risk Plus IRS-Based IRR Requirements versus EC Calculated according to Derivative-Based Integrated Approach to Risk Assessment as of December 2014.

Country	Position Book Value, US$ mln	IRS-based IRR EC Requirements, %	Basel III Foundation Regulatory Credit Risk Requirements, %	Total Compounded Pillar 1 Credit risk + Pillar 2 IRR EC, %	Derivative-Based Intergrated Approach EC, %	Delta, %
		A	B	C = A + B	D	E = C − D
Brazil	10	5.29	4.52	9.81	8.84	0.97
Hungary	10	5.16	6.89	12.05	12.86	−0.81
Malaysia	10	5.30	2.04	7.34	7.08	0.26
Mexico	10	5.30	3.15	8.45	6.45	2.00
Poland	10	5.29	2.04	7.33	7.31	0.02
South Africa	10	5.29	4.52	9.81	9.60	0.21
Thailand	10	5.29	3.15	8.44	7.29	1.15
Turkey	10	5.27	6.17	11.44	10.2	1.24

Pillar 1 credit risk requirements plus Pillar 2 interest rate risk requirements exceed (except for Hungary) EC requirements calculated according to the proposed herein derivative-based integrated approach to risk assessment using 5Y VaR methodology.

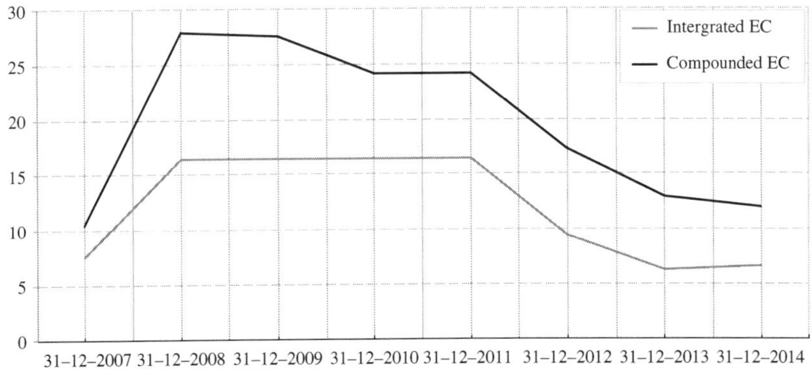

Figure 8: Derivative-Based EC under Integrated versus Segregated Approach to Risk Assessment through 5Y Long VaR Analysis for Year-Ends between 2007 and 2014. *Source*: Bloomberg, authors' calculations. *Note*: (For all years between 2007 and 2014, integrated EC line is observed below compounded EC line that potentially allows for EC optimization).

The fact that the increase in the EC under integrated approach is attenuated in comparison to the EC under segregated approach is also plausible and understandable through the diversification mechanisms between the interest rate and credit risk. The behavior of the EC calculated under integrated approach to risk assessment seems to be consistent with the dynamics of the real riskiness of obligors, especially EM obligors, as during the global financial crisis and its aftermath, there was observed only slight increase in default occurrences, with exception of financial and energy sector participants.

Conclusion

This chapter addresses a regulatory perspective of interest rate and credit risk integration. Analyzing such risk integration results and focusing on diversification versus compounding effects this study represents a long needed attempt to define a common basis for discussion between banking industry and financial markets regulators. Examining rules for asset sensitivity or non-sensitivity to interest rate and providing an integrated treatment of interest rate and credit risk potentially allows for optimizing bank economic capital. This research contributes to the advancement of the discussion on the emerging markets cross-geographies alignment of the Pillar 2 methodologies under Basel III capital accord.

Using sovereign CDS data covering eight emerging countries, we conclude that the interest rate downtrend dynamics mitigates the credit spread widening, as for all lengths of the considered VaR series EC requirements under the integrated approach are consistently lower than the segregated approach EC requirements solely for credit risk. Thus, the hedging of downside risk could be based on augmenting exposure to the interest rate risk.

We analyze cross-elasticity of interest rate risk and credit risk impacts through the prism of economic capital quantification. For exposures with interest risk elasticity above one the downside risk could be hedged by pay-float receive-fixed IRS contracts, while the downside risk of positions with EC-wise elasticity below one could be hedged by pay-fixed receive-float IRS contracts. We demonstrate that EC-wise elasticity is a function of the considered phase of a business cycle.

The proposed herein derivative-based integrated approach is compared to the yield-based approach to risk assessment. Such comparison results in disentangling liquidity components present in bond yields.

Finally, we benchmark the derivative-based integrated approach against the Basel III regulation using Basel II/III formula for economic capital under the internal ratings based (IRB) Foundation approach. It is shown that the proposed herein approach is consistent with the benchmark.

Looking ahead, we can affirm that the applicability of the integrated derivative-based approach is considerably wider than emerging market sovereign debt. It can be applied to diverse portfolios containing several types of assets, more sophisticated than bonds, such as loans, credit-linked notes, and total return swaps, among others. Thus, further research in this field is highly desirable for positively impacting overall efficiency of financial system.

It potentially allows financial institution to improve their risk assessment and economic capital management.

References

Alessandri, P., & Drehmann, M. (2010). An economic capital model integrating credit and interest rate risk in the banking book. *Journal of Banking and Finance*, *34*(4), 730–742.

Barbosa, L., & Costa, S. (2010). *Determinants of sovereign bond yield spreads in the euro area in the context of the economic and financial crisis*. Economic Bulletin and Financial Stability Report Articles, Bank of Portugal.

Black, F. (1970). *Fundamentals of liquidity*. Internal Memo. Graduated School of Business, University of Chicago, Chicago, IL.

Bonfim, D., & Soares, C. (2013). *Is there a risk-taking channel of monetary policy in Portugal?* Economic Bulletin and Financial Stability Report Articles, Bank of Portugal.

Boulkeroua, M., & Stark, A. (2013). On the determinants of the sensitivity of the yield spread of corporate bonds to changes in the level and slope of the yield curve. In N. Apergis (Ed.), *Proceedings of the IV world finance conference* (pp. 118/167).

Chen, R., Cheng, X., & Wu, L. (2013). Dynamic interactions between interest-rate and credit risk: theory and evidence on the credit default swap term structure. *Review of Finance*, *17*(1), 403–441.

European Parliament. (2013). *Regulation (EU) N° 575/2013*. Retrieved from http://www.eur-lex.europa.eu

FTSE International Limited. (2014). *FTSE country classification process*. Retrieved from http://www.ftse.com

Garcia, A., & Yang, J. (2009). Understanding corporate bond spreads using credit default swaps. *Bank of Canada Review*, *4*, 27–35.

Gubareva, M. (2010). Flight-to-quality analysis for financial stability enhancements. In: C. Prachlias (Ed.), *Proceedings of the 7th international conference on applied financial economics* (pp. 270–279).

Gubareva, M. (2014). *Financial instability through the prism of flight-to-quality*. Germany: Lambert Academic Publishing.

Gubareva, M., & Borges, M. (2014). Typological classification, diagnostics, and measurement of flights-to-quality. In J. Vieito (Ed.), *Proceedings of the V world finance conference* (pp. 177/295).

Jermann, U., & Yue, V. (2013). *Interest rate swaps and corporate default*. Working Paper Series No. 1590. European Central Bank. AU.

Kiesel, R., Perraudin, W., & Taylor, A. (2002). Credit and interest rate risk. In M., Dempster & H., Moffatt (Ed.), *Risk management: Value at risk and beyond* (pp. 129–144). Cambridge: Cambridge University Press.

Landschoot, A. (2008). Determinants of yield spread dynamics: Euro versus US dollar corporate bonds. *Journal of Banking and Finance, 32*(12), 2597–2605.

Lin, W., & Sun, D. (2007). Diversification with idiosyncratic credit spreads: a pooled estimation on heterogeneous panels. *Taiwan Banking and Finance Quarterly, 8*(2), 1–24.

Miloudi, A., & Moraux, F. (2009). Relations between corporate credit spreads, treasury yield and the equity market. *International Journal of Business, 14*(2), 105–122.

Moody's. (2014). Annual default study corporate default and recovery rates, 1920–2013.

Neal, R., Rolph, D., Dupoyet, B., & Jiang, X. (2013). Interest rates and credit spread dynamics. In: N. Apergis (Ed.), *Proceedings of the IV world finance conference* (pp. 17–69).

Pérignonand, C., & Smith, D. (2010). The level and quality of Value-at-Risk disclosure by commercial banks. *Journal of Banking and Finance, 34*(4), 362–377.

Piazzesi, M., & Schneider, M. (2010). Interest rate risk in credit markets. *American Economic Review, 100*(2), 579–584.

Standard & Poor's. (2014). *Default, transition, and recovery: 2013 Annual global corporate default study and rating transitions.* Retrieved from http://www.standardandpoors.com/ratingsdirect

Tang, D. Y., & Yan, H. (2010). Market conditions, default risk and credit spreads. *Journal of Banking and Finance, 34*(4), 743–753.

6

Auditing Bank Financial Statements in Emerging Market Countries: The Use of the Benford Distribution

Denis Davydov and Steve Swidler

Abstract

The analysis considers the use of Benford's Law as a forensic tool to audit the quality of accounting information reported by banks in emerging market countries. History suggests that lack of financial standards and reporting transparency can ultimately lead to bank failures in these nations. We use the Benford Distribution to analyze the first digits of bank financial statement entries and show the value of accounting standards in producing information of high quality. Benford's Law maintains that the first digits of an unconstrained, large array of numbers might follow a lognormal pattern. It can be applied, for example, to financial statements issued by banks to infer their data integrity. To illustrate the importance of accounting standards and reporting transparency, the analysis utilizes Russian bank statement data from 2001 to 2011. The main finding is that accounting standards matter. After the Russian Central Bank required all banks to adopt International Financial Reporting Standards in 2004, the financial statement data largely conformed to Benford's Law. While the Benford distribution can be used to infer the overall quality of bank financial statement data in emerging market countries, it is less effective in spotting troubled banks that commit reporting fraud. One possible reason is that the Benford distribution is scale invariant, and violation of Benford's Law is a sufficient but not necessary condition for accounting irregularities.

Keywords: Benford's Law; emerging market accounting standards; bank financial statement irregularities; fraud detection

A report by the International Monetary Fund (Laeven & Valencia, 2008) finds that there have been 124 episodes of systemic banking crises over the period 1970–2007. The vast majority of these events occurred in emerging market countries and led to a rise in bank failures. Of 27 emerging market countries in the IMF study, 17 experienced at least one episode of a systemic crisis between 1970 and 2007. In total, there were 734 cases of bank failures in these countries representing roughly 90 percent of total bank failures for the period (Table 4, Laeven & Valencia, 2008). While the financial crisis of 2008–2009 started in the United States, a decline in international bank loans played a significant role in transmitting the crisis from industrialized to emerging market countries (Deutsche Bundesbank, 2010). Thus, episodes of financial crises and resulting bank failures have occurred in emerging market countries throughout the last half century.

Caprio and Klingebiel (1996) argue that bank insolvency is more costly in the developing world as losses form a greater share of income. Whereas macroeconomic events often appear to be a root cause of bank insolvency, Caprio and Klingebiel suggest that lax regulatory oversight and discretionary accounting contribute to any crisis. For example, of 51 emerging market countries that responded to a bank survey, 13 (25.5 percent) permitted accrued unpaid interest or principal to enter the income statement while the loan is non-performing (Barth, Caprio, & Levine, 2013). The same survey reports that 45 of 180 countries do not mandate either U.S. Generally Accepted Accounting Principles (U.S. GAAP) or International Financial Reporting Standards (IFRS) at both the individual bank and consolidated levels.

The lack of accounting transparency and the resulting number of bank failures in emerging market countries suggests that it is important to employ effective monitoring methods. One possible auditing technique is to see whether bank financial data conform to the Benford distribution (Benford, 1938). Benford's Law presumes that the collection of first digits from an array of numbers follows a logarithmic pattern. The main idea is that if accounting data does not follow the Benford distribution, it is of lower quality and suggests fraud or inaccuracies.

The first to use Benford's Law to analyze accounting data was Carslaw (1988). He finds that when company earnings are just below psychological boundaries, firms tend to round the numbers up. Later, Nigrini and Mittermaier (1997) show how the Benford distribution can be employed by auditors to determine the quality of accounting information.

While a number of authors have used Benford's Law to examine the quality of firm financial statements, there has been little investigation of its specific use to monitor emerging market banking activity. Nigrini (2012, p. 213) provides one possible reason when he submits that it is not clear "whether accounting numbers from companies in emerging markets will conform to Benford's Law in their emerging stages or whether conformity comes about only in mature markets." In the following analysis, we consider the use of Benford's Law to examine the quality of emerging market banks' financial data, specifically focusing on Russian bank data. The reason for looking at Russian banks is twofold. First, Russian banks experienced a regime change in financial accounting practices in 2004 so that it is possible to use the Benford distribution to test whether accounting standards matter. Second, examining the case of a failed Russian bank cited for providing false financial statements enables us to test whether the Benford distribution can be used in real time to uncover accounting fraud. Early warning supervisory tests are particularly important in Russia where banks accounted for more than 50 percent of all failed banks in emerging market countries during the 1970–2007 period. Before examining the Russian bank data, we begin with a discussion of the Benford distribution and how it may be used to audit financial statement data.

The Benford Distribution

The Benford distribution describes the frequency of first digits in an array of numbers. Data sets expected to conform to the Benford distribution are those collections that represent the size of facts or events, for example, the population of cities in the United States, the market value of companies on the New York Stock Exchange or entries from company financial statements. Furthermore, the distribution is more likely to obtain when the set of numbers span several magnitudes. On the other hand, data sets with value ranges constrained (child care deductions on the federal income tax) or that include identification numbers (zip codes and social security numbers) cannot be presumed to conform to Benford's Law.

The exact form of the Benford distribution can be described as

$$P(D=d)=\log_{10}\left(1+\frac{1}{d}\right) \text{ for } d\in\{1,2,\cdots 9\} \tag{1}$$

where $P\ (D = d)$ is the probability that the first digit of numbers in a collection equal the value d from the set that includes the integers from 1 through 9. As a matter of course, if a number is negative, then the observation equals the absolute value of the first digit. In the analysis below, we follow the absolute value rule. Eq. (1) describes the distribution in Figure 1 which illustrates a highly skewed set of numbers with the frequency of the first digit of 1 occurring 30.1 percent of the time and monotonically decreasing to 9 appearing in 4.58 percent of the sample.

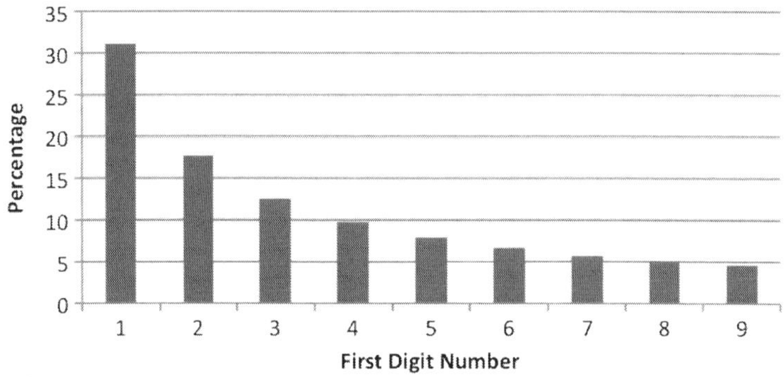

Figure 1: The Benford Distribution.

Negrini (2011, p. 96) states that the conventional wisdom "is that authentic data should follow Benford's Law and deviations from Benford's Law could signal irregularities." In the context of our study, if financial statement data deviate significantly from the Benford distribution, this implies unintended mistakes, manipulation of data or outright fraud. One way to examine whether the observed sample deviates significantly from Benford is to perform a chi-square test on the sum of squared deviations of the observed first digit frequencies from the Benford values:

$$\text{Sum of Squared Deviation} = \sum_{d=1}^{9} \left(\hat{P}(d) - \log_{10}\left(1 + \frac{1}{d}\right)\right)^2 \tag{2}$$

For large chi-square values we can reject the null hypothesis of high quality accounting data and instead accept that the reported values are irregular and have been manipulated or contain errors. This is a particularly powerful test, especially when the sample size is large (greater than 1000), and one typically employed in the forensic accounting literature.

Russian Bank Accounting Practices

As of January 1, 2004, the Central Bank of Russia required that all Russian banks adopt International Financial Reporting Standards

(IFRS). The move was largely a result of Russia moving from a centrally planned economy to one more integrated with markets in the rest of the world. Prior to 2004, lax accounting standards contributed to manipulation of accounting entries in order to meet certain Central Bank requirements. For example, banks would artificially inflate liquidity ratios by obtaining loans from a correspondent bank and depositing the funds in a nostro account (Davydov & Swidler, 2016).

To see whether accounting standards matter, Davydov and Swidler (2016) examine 39 entries from a bank's financial statements (18 from the income statement, 21 from the balance sheet) for more than one thousand banks. The data is annual for the period 2001–2011 and appears in the Bureau Van Dijk's BankScope. All numbers are in rubles, although units should have little bearing on the results as numbers that conform to the Benford distribution are scale invariant. We return to an important implication of this attribute later in the analysis. The final sample consists of 272,606 book entries throughout the entire sample period.

Figure 2 charts the annual sum of squared deviations described in Eq. (2). The picture illustrates the dramatic change in financial statement reporting after Russian banks adopted IFRS. Starting in 2004, the financial data more closely follows the Benford distribution and suggests that uniform and transparent accounting standards lead to higher quality information.

On an ex post basis, it is clear that accounting standards matter. Without transparency, it appears that financial data was prone to manipulation; however, once accounting standards were implemented in 2004, the quality of information improved. The next question then is whether the Benford distribution can be used in real time to identify failing banks.

Identifying Failing Banks in Real Time

Haynes (2012) first considers the idea that Benford's Law may be used as an early warning indicator of financial reporting fraud. He examines the municipal failures of Jefferson County, Orange

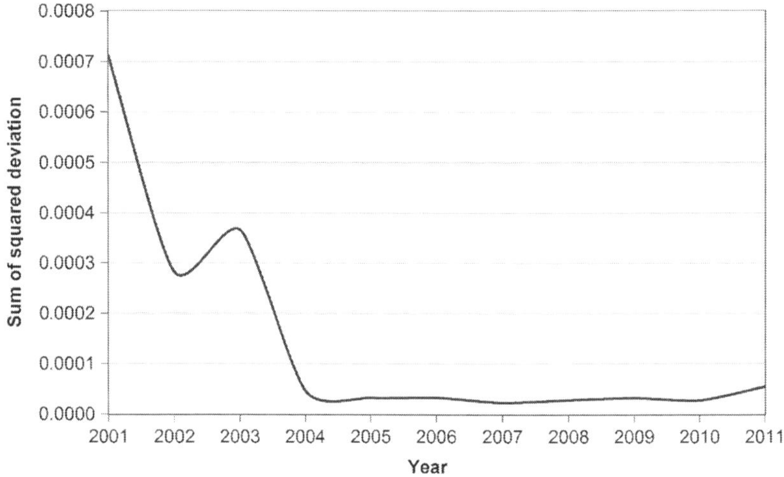

Figure 2: Deviation from the Benford Distribution by Year. *Source*: Davydov and Swidler (2016). *Notes*: The figure plots the sum of squared deviation (Eq. 2) of the first digits' distribution from the Benford distribution on a year by year basis. The data include financial statements of Russian commercial banks for the period 2001–2011. The distribution is based on 39 variables from the income statement (18) and balance sheet (21) of 1,187 commercial banks.

County and the city of Vallejo and argues that had Benford "been applied in real time to those financial statements, (it) would have been able to detect that something was amiss." Despite his empirical findings, Haynes (2012, p. 22) moderates his view of real time use and concludes that accounting firms might use Benford's Law as an initial "smell test." He further cites Nigrini (2012) who cautions that distribution characteristics alone cannot conclusively identify fraud.

The question of whether the Benford distribution can be added as a tool to uncover problem banks in the early stages of financial distress is potentially of great interest to regulators. One example of regulators' interest to identify troubled banks is the U.S. Office of the Comptroller of the Currency's Canary Early Warning System (Comptroller of the Currency, 2001). In a Bank for International Settlements (BIS) paper, Sahajwala and Van den Bergh (2000) point out that a bank's financial condition correlates to a set of financial variables covering capital adequacy, asset quality, profitability and liquidity. They further state, "a large number of ratios relating to these variables are used in various financial ratio and peer group analysis systems." Thus, the quality of this financial information is crucial if it is to be used in the supervisory process. Conversely, if regulators detect accounting fraud, that may be reason enough to suspect bank financial distress. To examine the effectiveness of Benford's Law in uncovering financial distress and possible accounting fraud, we turn to an example of a failed Russian bank.

The Central Bank of Russia revoked the license of Universal Credit on October 10, 2014, stating that the bank had been consistently issuing false financial statements. Knowing that financial fraud had been committed, an investigation of the bank's quarterly statements leading up to the closure provides insight into the real time use of the Benford distribution as an early warning indicator. If fraudulent reporting occurred, one might expect that squared deviations from the Benford distribution will increase the closer the quarterly statements are to the Central Bank's suspension of Universal Credit's license. Moreover, the squared deviations from Benford should be statistically significant for the quarters closest to the October 2014 closure.

Figure 3, Panel A graphs the squared deviations from the Benford distribution of Universal Credit's income statement variables by quarter. The first observation is that squared deviations from Benford do not seem to increase over time. Moreover, while deviations from the distribution are statistically significant one year prior to bank closure, that is the only quarter that is significant.

Figure 3, Panel B tells a similar story looking at entries from the bank's balance sheet. Specifically, there is no upward trend in deviations from Benford over time. Furthermore, in only 3 of 13 quarters are deviations from Benford statistically significant.

Taken together, the income and balance sheet statement data yield little support for identifying troubled banks in real time.

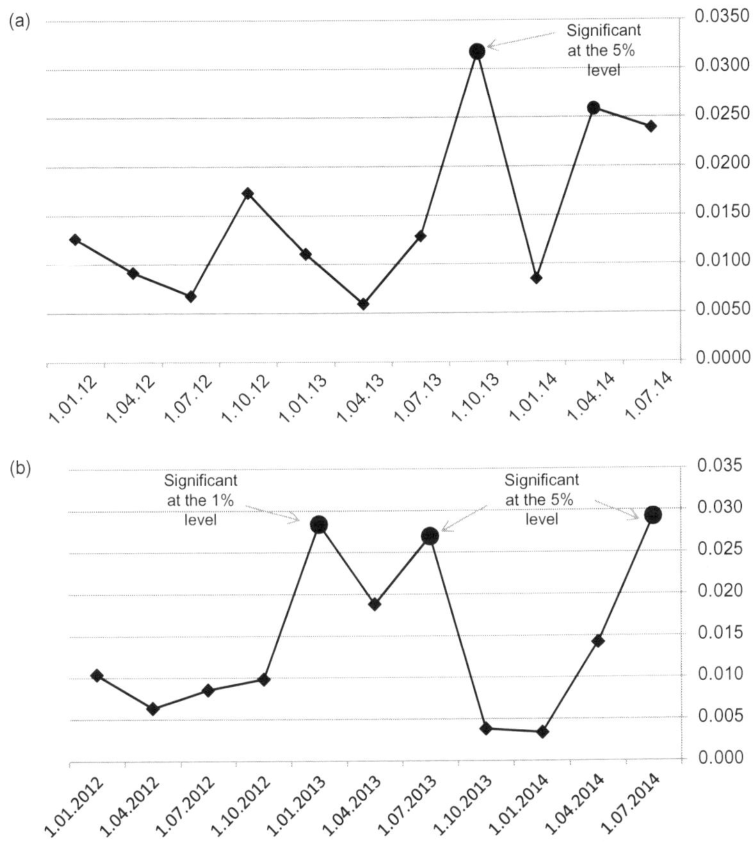

Figure 3: Deviation from the Benford Distribution by Quarter for Failed Bank. (a) Income Statement The analysis is based on the quarterly income statement reports of the Universal Credit Bank starting from the January 2012 quarter and until the last available report, July 2014. In total, the sample includes 11 quarterly reports. Income statements include detailed information on a maximum of 60 (minimum of 43) raw accounts both from income and expenses sides. Sum of Squared Deviations from the Benford Distribution (Eq. 2) by quarter. (b) Balance Sheet The analysis is based on the quarterly income statement reports of the Universal Credit Bank starting from the January 2012 quarter and until the last available report, July 2014. In total, the sample includes 11 quarterly reports. Balance Sheet statements include detailed information on a maximum of 76 (minimum of 71) raw accounts. Sum of Squared Deviations from the Benford Distribution (Eq. 2) by quarter.

Moreover, in this example, we know that the bank was not only failing, but also issued false statements. Thus, if we know the data is misstated, why does the financial data conform to the Benford distribution in the majority of quarters?

Any of a number of possible reasons explains the ineffectiveness of Benford's Law in capturing manipulated data of a failing bank. The first reason is sample size. With fewer than 100 observations in a sample, the power of the chi-square test is very low and it is difficult to reject the null hypothesis that the distribution conforms to Benford. This problem can be addressed by the regulator if detailed financial data exists for individual branch banks. Still, the fact that there is no pattern of increasing deviations from the Benford distribution over time suggests that it may be difficult for regulators to use the Law as a means to detect data manipulation in real time.

Yet another possibility is that bad banks issue financial statements that imitate good bank financial statements. Given that the banking industry is regulated, bad banks already know the minimum regulatory capital requirements, and it maybe that they are able to, in effect, work backwards in building their seemingly healthy balance sheet and income statements. While either of the above explanations may explain the ineffectiveness of Benford's Law detecting irregular accounting data in real time, a third possible reason is that doctored data may follow the Benford distribution. This can occur because the Benford distribution is scale invariant so that if we start with an array whose first digits conform to Benford's Law, then increasing or decreasing all numbers in the set by a constant will yield first digits that also follow the Benford distribution.

Implications of Scale Invariance

Pinkham (1961) first proved that the Benford distribution is scale invariant. In other words, if you begin with a set of first digits that conform to the Benford distribution, multiplying the original array of numbers by a constant will also yield first digits that follow the Benford distribution. Thus, if the bank accounting data in our sample denominated in rubles obeys Benford's Law, translating the data into U.S. dollars (i.e., multiplying by the dollar/ruble exchange rate) will yield a set of first digits that also conforms to the Benford distribution.

This attribute of scale invariance has a potentially important implication for using Benford's Law in real time to identify irregularities in bank reported data. Suppose that a failing bank faithfully follows acceptable accounting practices and reports its financial statements accordingly. It is entirely possible that the entries of the bad bank's financials follow the Benford distribution. If however, the failing bank wishes to disguise its financial position, it might begin to shade its numbers in some systematic way. For example, on the earnings statement, the bank might increase all of its revenues by 10 percent and decrease its expenses by 10 percent, and in doing so, implicitly inflate earnings by 10 percent. If the original (correct) entries follow Benford's Law, the new set of inflated earnings will also conform to the Benford distribution.

To illustrate the thought experiment of the distributional effect from inflating reported earnings, Table 1 begins with the actual distribution of first digits from the 2007 annual reports of Russian Banks. The analysis considers 2007 as it was the year in our sample that had the smallest deviation from Benford's Law. Given a relatively healthy economic environment, one might further expect that the vast majority of banks reported financial statements following IFRS. Column 1 shows the true Benford distribution, while column 2 reports the actual distribution of first digits from the 2007 earnings statements (Figure 2). Sixteen earnings statement entries of 947 banks (15,152 observations) yield the actual percentages of the first digits in column 2. The similarity of percentages in columns 1 and 2 and the low chi-square measure based on deviations from the distribution both imply Benford conformity.

Now suppose that we increase all 9 income variables 10 percent and decrease the 7 expense variables by 10 percent. The resulting distributions of the income and expense variables appear in columns 3 and 4. Both look remarkably like the Benford distribution and according to the chi-square test statistics are not

Table 1: Scalar Invariance.

	Benford's	Actual	Income +10%	Expenses −10%	Income +10% & Expenses −10%
	(1)	(2)	(3)	(4)	(5)
1	*0.301*	0.299	0.301	0.298	0.299
2	*0.176*	0.175	0.174	0.176	0.175
3	*0.125*	0.124	0.124	0.125	0.124
4	*0.097*	0.100	0.098	0.099	0.097
5	*0.079*	0.081	0.082	0.082	0.083
6	*0.067*	0.064	0.067	0.063	0.066
7	*0.058*	0.059	0.056	0.058	0.055
8	*0.051*	0.051	0.050	0.052	0.051
9	*0.046*	0.046	0.048	0.047	0.049
	Sq. Diff.	0.00002	0.00003	0.00004	0.00004
	X^2	4.05	5.29	7.31	9.06

The simulation are based on 16 variables from the Income statement (9 from the income side and 7 from expenses) of 947 commercial banks in the year of 2007.

significantly different. Reassembling all 16 earnings variables again yields a distribution that conforms to Benford's Law, the results appearing in column 5. The final outcome is that if a bank starts with earnings entries that follow the Benford distribution, systematically inflating those earnings figure by a scalar will again produce first digits that conform to Benford's Law.

The property of scalar invariance makes it less likely that Benford can be used as an auditing tool in real time to identify failing banks that manipulate their financial statements. It must be remembered that a breach of Benford's Law suggests fraud or irregularities in reported accounting data. However, the lack of finding a violation does not provide a clear signal. We have just shown how you can shade earnings and yet still produce numbers that conform to Benford's Law. Scale invariance may be another reason why the majority of Universal Credit's quarterly statements still produced first digits that followed the Benford distribution even though regulators cited the bank for accounting fraud. Thus, a final conclusion is that violation of Benford's Law is a sufficient condition for signaling accounting irregularities but it is not a necessary condition.

Concluding Lessons

In emerging market countries, it is paramount that accounting practices be transparent. Too often in these countries, accounting irregularities lead to or contribute to bank failures which have dire consequences for the welfare of the nation. To mitigate these reporting problems, it is important that banks follow some acceptable accounting standard, either U.S. GAAP or IFRS. In the context of Benford's Law, an examination of Russian Banks witnessed a drop in financial statement fraud after the imposition of International Financial Reporting Standards.

The effective use of Benford's Law as a real time auditing tool is less clear. As noted in a BIS study, supervisors regularly rely on the veracity of a bank's accounting statements to infer financial health. While a violation of the Benford distribution is sufficient to show reporting irregularities and thus suspect financial distress, it is not a necessary condition. Indeed we have shown that systematic manipulation of data may still conform to Benford's Law. The results suggest that the Benford distribution alone cannot uncover failing banks in real time. More conventional auditing methods must be used in conjunction with Benford' Law to uncover troubled banks.

References

Barth, J. R., Caprio, G., & Levine, R. (2013). *Bank regulation and supervision in 180 countries from 1999 to 2011*. National Bureau of Economic Research Working Paper No. 18733.

Benford, F. (1938). The law of anomalous numbers. *Proceedings of the American Philosophical Society*, *78*(4), 551–572.

Caprio, G., & Klingebiel, D. (1996). *Bank insolvencies: Cross country experience*. The World Bank, Policy Research Working Paper No. 1620.

Carslaw, C. (1988). Anomalies in income numbers: Evidence of goal oriented behavior. *Accounting Review*, *63*(2), 321–327.

Comptroller of the Currency. (2001). *Problem bank identification, rehabilitation and resolution: A guide for examiners*. Washington, DC: OCC Publication.

Davydov, D., & Swidler, S. (2016). *Reading Russian tea leaves: Assessing the quality of bank financial statements with the Benford distribution*. Review of Pacific Basin Financial Markets and Policies, forthcoming.

Deutsche Bundesbank. (2010). *Emerging markets in the financial crisis: The effect of cross-border bank loans*. DEUTSCHE BUNDESBANK Monthly Report, April, 35–50.

Haynes, A. (2012). *Detecting fraud in bankrupt municipalities using Benford's Law*. Scripps Senior Theses Paper No. 42.

Laeven, L., & Valencia, F. (2008). *Systemic banking crises: A new database*. IMF Working Paper No. 08/224.

Nigrini, M. (2011). *Forensic analytics: Methods and techniques for forensic accounting investigations*. Hoboken, NJ: Wiley.

Nigrini, M. (2012). *Benford's law: Applications for forensic accounting, auditing, and fraud detection*. Hoboken, NJ: Wiley.

Nigrini, M., & Mittermaier, L. (1997). The use of Benford's law as an aid in analytical procedures. *Auditing – A Journal of Practice & Theory*, *16*(2), 52–67.

Pinkham, R. (1961). On the distribution of first significant digits. Annals of Mathematical Statistics, *32*(4), 1223–1230.

Sahajwala, R., & Van den Bergh, P. (2000, December). *Supervisory risk assessment and early warning systems*. Basel Committee on Banking Supervision Working Paper Series No. 4.

7

Emerging Markets Carry Trades and Financial Crises

Ehab Yamani

Abstract

This chapter identifies three crisis warning indicators driven from trading in emerging markets' carry trades, and empirically examines whether these indicators could predict two major financial crises that hit the global financial markets in the last decades — The 1997–1998 Asian crisis and the 2007–2008 global crisis. The probit regression is used to examine the power of the three indicators in forecasting financial crises, using data from eight Asian emerging countries which serve as proxies for emerging markets, independent of the origination of the crisis. I use both fixed effect and random effect estimation to measure crisis impacts. The empirical results show that financial crises could have been predicted. Probit estimation show that carry trade returns can predict a financial crisis, and the estimation results are robust to both panel level and country-level analysis. These three indicators are by no means an exhaustive list of all possible predictors of financial crisis. The literature suggests other fundamental indicators of financial crises such as the current account deficit and foreign debt. However, this chapter cannot fully consider these indicators for lack of data at this point in time. Although financial crisis may be better predicted by the well-known fundamental indicators, the contribution of this chapter is simply that carry trade-related indicators can help in predicting crises.

Keywords: Interest rate parity; carry trade; liquidity risk; default risk; exchange rate; financial crisis

Introduction

Carry trade has been a very popular speculative strategy for currency investors for more than three decades (Gagnon & Chaboud, 2007; Galati, Heath, & McGuire, 2007). This strategy consists of borrowing in low-interest rate currencies (funding currencies) and investing in high interest rate currencies (investment currencies), betting that the foreign exchange rate will not change so as to offset the profits made on the interest rate differential. Such profitable carry trade strategy exploits the failure of the uncovered interest rate parity (UIP). While the UIP predicts that exchange rate changes will eliminate any arbitrage opportunities arising from interest rate differentials between countries, there is overwhelming empirical evidence that reverse holds, namely the low-interest rate currency tend to depreciate while the high interest rate currency tend to appreciate.[1]

Emerging markets' carry trades involves borrowing in a low-interest currency, such as the US dollar, and investing in the higher yielding domestic debt of emerging markets. The onset of the recent financial crises in the last few decades has brought to

1. For a survey on the failure of the UIP, see Froot and Thaler (1990), Engel (1996), Obstfeld and Rogoff (2001).

the light that emerging markets face higher risks than developed markets. When thinking of investing in emerging markets, risks may take on a different flavor due to the unique nature of the emerging markets such as pegged exchange rates, crawling peg or currency boards, reliance on central banks for providing liquidity, limited resources of central banks, small capital markets, lack of transparency, and counterparties unwilling to share information.

All of these factors, among others, increase the degree of financial vulnerability of emerging markets and thus leave them more vulnerable to risks during times of tension. Emerging markets carry trades thus is a double-sword edge. During periods of 'booms', the emerging market carry trade strategy works well since it leads to the arrival of huge capital inflows to emerging markets. Conversely, when a financial crisis hits any region in the world with fears of contagion, emerging market carry traders rush to liquidity and quality and the "capital inflow reversal" process starts, and severe losses occur as evidenced by several crises in the last few decades.

Motivated by these insights, the goal in this chapter is to investigate the link between carry trade and the probability of financial crisis. In particular, I use the probit model to empirically examine whether trading in emerging markets carry trade could predict two major financial crises that hit the global financial markets in the last two decades — the 1997–1998 Asian crisis and the 2007–2008 global crisis. I identify three carry trade-related warning indicators of a crisis, which are carry trade excess returns, JP Morgan EM-VXY index, and JP Morgan GBI-EM index, and then I use data from eight Asian emerging countries to empirically examine the ability of these indicators to forecast financial crises.

The empirical results of the probit estimation show that both the 1997–1998 Asian crisis and the 2007–2008 global crisis could have been predicted using carry trade-related indicators. The results are robust to both country-level and panel data and to both fixed and random effect estimations. These three indicators are by no means an exhaustive list of all possible predictors of financial crisis. To the best of the author's knowledge, however, this chapter is the first attempt to predict crises using indicators driven by trading in emerging market carry trades.

This chapter is organized as follows. The section "Introduction" presents a brief literature review on the interest rate parity and the speculative carry trade strategies. The section "Interest Rate Parity and Carry Trades" discusses the risks and threats associated with investment in emerging markets' carry trades during financial crises. The section "Emerging Markets' Carry Trade: Opportunities and Threats" presents the results of the empirical investigation of the link between emerging carry trades' and the probability of occurring financial crises. The section "Conclusion" concludes.

Interest Rate Parity and Carry Trades

Theoretically, interest rate parity (IRP)[2] generally predicts zero profit on the carry trade strategy, because the exchange rate changes will eliminate any arbitrage opportunities arising from interest rate differentials between countries. As far as emerging markets' carry trade strategy is concerned, the IRP predicts that the return on the higher yielding domestic debt of emerging markets will just equal the return on the low-interest home currency, as follows:

$$1 + r_h = \frac{1}{S_t}\left(1 + r_f\right)S_{t+1} \tag{1}$$

where S_t denotes the nominal spot exchange rate denominated in units of the foreign currency per home currency unit, and r_h and r_h

2. The IRP is considered the theoretical framework for the relation between interest rates and foreign exchange rates. The IRP also is the benchmark for the efficient market hypothesis in the FX markets (Ahmad, Rhee, & Wong, 2012; Baillie & Bollerslev, 1989, 2000; Fama, 1984; Frankel & Poonawala, 2010; Froot & Thaler, 1990). According to IRP, FX market is efficient if the interest rate differentials are unbiased predictors of changes in exchange rates. In other words, the high interest rate currency should depreciate against the low-interest rate currency by the same amount as the interest rate differential.

refer to the nominal interest rate in the home and the foreign emerging country, respectively. If we rearrange Eq. (1), we get

$$\frac{S_{t+1}}{S_t} = \frac{1 + r_h}{1 + r_f} \tag{2}$$

If we subtract Eq. (1) from Eq. (2), we get

$$\begin{aligned} \frac{S_{t+1} - S_t}{S_t} &= \frac{r_h - r_f}{1 + r_f} \\ \frac{S_{t+1} - S_t}{S} &\approx r_h - r_f \end{aligned} \tag{3}$$

The IRP theory states that the expected exchange rate S_{t+1} differs from the spot rate S_t at equilibrium by an amount equal to the interest differential $r_h - r_f$ between two countries. The IRP can also be expressed in a regression form by regressing exchange rate changes on interest rate differentials

$$E_t[S_{t+1} - S_t] = \alpha_0 + \beta_1 \left(r_{f,t} - r_{h,t}\right) \tag{4}$$

According to the IRP condition, Eq. (4) should produce a slope coefficient (β) of one since we should expect a depreciation of the high interest rate currency against the low-interest rate currency by the same amount as the interest rate differential. In practice, however, there is overwhelming empirical evidence that reverse holds, namely the low-interest rate currency tend to depreciate while the high interest rate currency tend to appreciate.

As a result, carry trade strategy exploits the failure of the covered interest rate parity (CIRP). Such profitable currency strategy has been very popular for currency investors for more than three decades. This strategy involves trading in the forward market, betting that the foreign exchange rate will not change so as to offset the profits made on the forward premium or discount differential. If the foreign currency is at forward discount (i.e., $f_t < S_t$), currency traders long the foreign currency (or equivalently short the dollar) in the forward market in period t, and then short the foreign currency (or equivalently long the dollar) in the spot market in period $t + 1$. The net currency excess log returns dominated in dollars, ($CRET_{t+1}$), thus equals the log forward rate f_t minus the expected spot rate S_{t+1}. Alternatively, $CRET_{t+1}$ can be measured as forward discount ($f_t - S_t$) minus the rate of the appreciation of the home currency ($\Delta s_{t+1} = s_{t+1} - s_t$)

$$\mathrm{CRET}_{t+1} = f_t - s_{t+1} = (f_t - s_t) - \Delta s_{t+1} = f_t - s_{t+1} \quad (5)$$

The carry trade strategy is a double-edged sword. In other words, carry trades have a risk-return profile that is consistent with a Wall Street adage that "exchange rates go up by the stairs and down by the elevator." During periods of "booms" associated with high risk appetite and low volatility, carry trades are very profitable to currency traders (Brunnermeier, Nagel, & Pedersen, 2008; Clarida, Davis, & Pedersen, 2009). When market conditions deteriorate, however, carry trades are problematic. During times of market tension, risk aversion increases and hence low (high) interest rate currencies appreciate (depreciate) since they are seen as safe-haven (risky) currencies. As a result, a reversal process starts and currency traders tend to unwind carry trades (i.e., selling high interest currencies and buying low-interest rate currencies) and severe losses occur (Brunnermeier et al., 2008; Coudert, Couharde, & Mignon, 2011; Mancini, Ranaldo, & Wrampelmeyer, 2013).[3]

This phenomenon is especially obvious during the recent 2007–2008 financial crisis, since there was a major carry trade unwinds in August 2007 in the wake of the turbulence in the global financial markets. This risk-return behavior shows that carry trade returns are subject to crash risk that is exchange rate movements between high-interest-rate and low-interest-rate currencies predict negative skewness, which has been documented in the literature (Brunnermeier et al., 2008; Rafferty, 2011). Figure 1 supports such crash risk behavior by showing the time-series data

3. According to the IMF data (IMF, 1999–2001), the net capital flows to emerging markets decreased from about $225 billion in 1996 to only $37 billion dollars in 1999 as a result of the Asian and later the Russian crises.

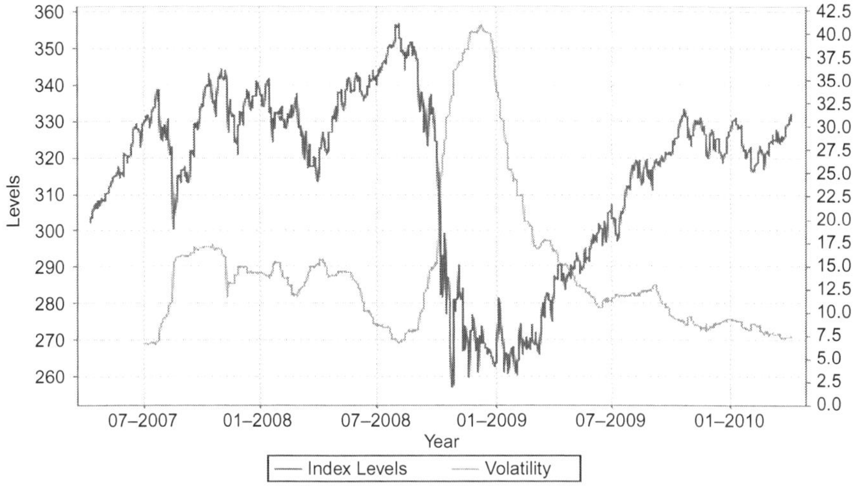

Figure 1: Balanced Currency Harvest Funded USD. *Notes*: This figure shows the balanced currency harvest index which is developed by Deutsche Bank Currency to track the performance carry trades. The balanced index tracks the performance of a portfolio that systematically invests in the five highest yielding currencies, funded by a diversified basket of the five lowest yielding currencies from the whole currency pool.

of the balanced currency harvest index[4] from January 2007 till June 2010. It is clear from Figure 1 that carry trade yields dropped significantly during periods of the recent financial crisis, and in particular during late 2008 reflecting the collapse of Lehman Brothers, while the index volatility skyrocketed during the same period.

Emerging Markets' Carry Trade: Opportunities and Threats

Emerging markets' carry trades involves borrowing in a low-interest currency, such as the US dollar, and investing in the

4. The balanced currency harvest index is developed by Deutsche Bank Currency to track the performance carry trades. In particular, the balanced index tracks the performance of a portfolio that systematically invests in the five highest yielding currencies, funded by a diversified basket of the five lowest yielding currencies from the whole currency pool.

higher yielding domestic debt of emerging markets. Emerging market carry trade strategies present opportunities to both emerging economies that rely on carry trade inflows as well as the currency traders. The Emerging market carry trade strategies are beneficial to the recipient emerging economies because emerging market governments look increasingly toward their domestic market for sources of finance, and these carry trading strategies lead to the arrival of huge capital inflows to emerging markets. Although the magnitude of these inflows is unknown, estimates suggest that carry trade inflows equal about $2 trillion invested in emerging market debt (Kynge, 2015).

Emerging market carry trade strategy is profitable also for international investors with an appetite for higher risk who are looking more closely at local markets in search for higher yield and greater diversification. As a part of diverse portfolio, they seek to borrow in a low-interest rate currency (such as the US dollar) and invest in high yield emerging debt, betting that the foreign exchange rate will not change so as to offset the profits made on the interest rate differential. Such increase in investor appetite toward emerging markets' local currency bond markets can be visible in the clearly upward trend in Figure 2, which graphically reports the JP Morgan government bond index (GBI) emerging markets (EM) composite. The JPM GBI-EM is a local currency bond index that tracks emerging market debt issued by emerging market governments.

High returns, however, do not come without high risk. When thinking of investing in emerging markets, risks may take on a different flavor due to the unique nature of the emerging markets such as pegged exchange rates, crawling peg or currency boards, reliance on central banks for providing liquidity, limited resources of central banks, small capital markets, lack of transparency, and counterparties unwilling to share information. The risks of investment in emerging markets include, among others, interest rate risk, foreign exchange risk, liquidity risk, and default risk.

The *interest rate risk* is the uncertainty associated with the fluctuations in the level of interest rates. Emerging markets face a unique set of challenges that act as severe constraints on implementing their interest rate policies. The interest rate policy in

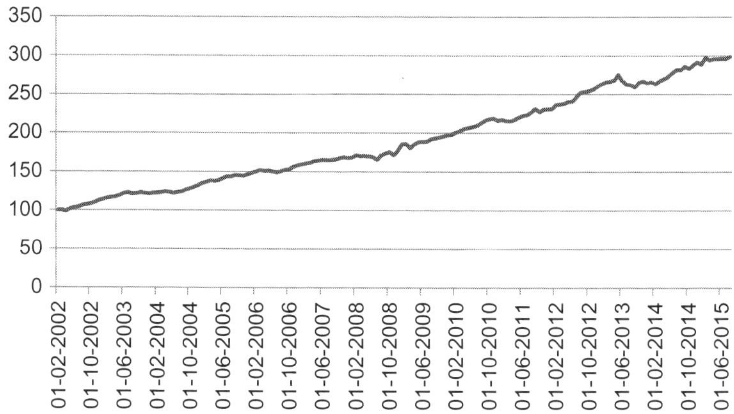

Figure 2: JP Morgan GBI-EM Index. *Notes*: This figure shows the monthly data for JP Morgan GBI-EM Index from January 2002 to August 2015. The GBI-EM index is a local currency bond index that tracks emerging market debt issued by emerging market governments. The GBI-EM index was developed by JP Morgan in response to the increased interest of investors in emerging markets' local currency debt.

emerging markets is hampered by the underdevelopment of the financial system which takes the form of illiquid capital markets, fragile banking system, and politically dependent central banks. The lack of deep and liquid capital markets in emerging countries hamper the effectiveness of the interest rate policy, because there is no or weak feedback signals from the domestic capital markets through which the central banks in emerging countries can measure the impact of their interest rate policy on investors' sentiments. In addition, the banking system in emerging markets is fragile and this means that large interest rates changes associated with aggressive interest rate policy might lead to the bankruptcy of weak banks. The absence of central bank independence in emerging markets is another challenge that undermines the effectiveness of the interest rate policy. The central banks in many emerging countries are subject to political forces, especially from the finance ministry. Although the dual role for central banks is primarily price stability and financial stability, the political pressure may take the form of the central bank being responsible for other roles such as promoting output and employment growth.

The *foreign exchange rate risk* is the uncertainty that arises from the changes in currency exchange rates. The foreign exchange rate policy in emerging markets faces greater challenges than developed markets. These challenges arise from the fixed exchange rate regimes used by the central banks in most of the emerging countries, as compared to the floating exchange rate regimes used by most developed countries. Under the floating exchange rate regime, the central bank does not intervene in the foreign exchange market and the foreign exchange rate is determined by the demand and supply mechanism. Conversely, central banks in most of emerging countries use several "currency pegs" (i.e., fixed exchange rate arrangements) to manage their nominal exchange rates. There is a vast choice of pegs which can be classified into soft pegs (such as the conventional pegged exchange rates and crawling pegs) and hard pegs (such as currency boards and dollarization). Pegged exchange rate arrangement means maintaining a fixed rate against one currency or a basket of currencies, and crawling peg refers to the permanent daily domestic currency devaluation/appreciation to maintain a fixed real exchange rate. These soft peg mechanisms prevailed in several Asian emerging countries before the 1997 Asian crisis and in many Latin American countries (such as Brazil until 1999). Under a currency board regime, central banks issue domestic currency at a fixed rate in exchange for foreign exchange reserves. Currency boards have been adopted by several emerging economies such as Hong Kong (1983), Argentina (1991), Bulgaria (1997), and Bosnia (1998). The extreme case of pegs is dollarization which means that a country completely abandons its own currency and adopts a stronger foreign currency. Panama, Ecuador and El Salvador are examples of countries that use the US dollar as a domestic currency.

Liquidity risk is the risk arising from inability to meet contractual obligations resulting from a lack of available currency. It is worth noting that emerging markets are more vulnerable to liquidity risk than developed countries during financial crises, since most of the emerging currencies are illiquid. The lack of liquidity in emerging currencies is due to several factors related to the domestic conditions in emerging countries. For example, most of the emerging markets rely significantly on their central banks for providing liquidity given that these central banks may have limited resources particularly during times of crises. In addition, emerging markets suffer from lack of or small capital markets as these markets are usually dominated by family businesses that usually offer only a small proportion of stock. Capital markets allow investments to be liquid and marketable. Without an active capital market, therefore, there will not be adequate capital available for the economic activity.

When a financial crisis occurs in any region in the world, risk-averse investors tend to rebalance their portfolios toward more liquid currencies (i.e., flight-to-liquidity). Emerging market carry traders rush to liquidity by trying to get rid of illiquid emerging currencies and replacing them with more liquid currencies, and as a result the unwinding of carry trades occurs. The role of liquidity risk in unwinding carry trades during market crashes is documented in several studies (Brunnermeier et al., 2008; Mancini et al., 2013). Both studies show that liquidity risk is a priced risk factor that explains the returns to carry trades. In particular, low (high) yielding currencies tend to be more (less) liquid and exhibit lower (higher) liquidity sensitivities, and thus offer insurance against (exposure to) liquidity risk. During periods of booming financial markets, low (high) interest rate currencies tend to depreciate (appreciate) because of low (high) liquidity sensitivities, and thus the deviation from the IRP increases. When foreign exchange liquidity dries up, however, liquidity betas tend to have opposite signs and therefore low (high) yielding currencies tend to appreciate (depreciate), which leads to the unwinding of carry trades.

The high liquidity risks facing emerging markets during times of market tension and the associated unwinding of carry trades leads to huge capital flow reversals in emerging markets, and thus leaves them more vulnerable to liquidity crises. The two major liquidity crises that hit the emerging world in the last few decades were the 1994 Mexican and the 1997 Thai crises. In both Mexican and Thai cases, the liquidity crises were due to exchange rate overvaluation caused by exchange rate appreciation that the Mexican Peso and the Thai Baht had undergone as a result of the large capital inflows. The exchange rate overvaluation in both countries absorbed valuable liquid dollar assets of the Central Bank balance sheet through the loss of liquid foreign exchange reserves. On the liability side, the failure of external creditors to roll over short-term debt increased short-term (liquid) dollar liabilities. The combination of such maturity mismatches (i.e., lengthening the maturity of central bank's assets and shortening that of its liabilities) and very high domestic interest rates in Mexico and Thailand resulted in liquidity crises in both countries since the large short-term external debt was unlikely to be serviced.

There is also a counterparty *default risk* to be considered when investment in emerging markets. Default risk is the risk that the counterparty will default, by failing to perform an obligation when it falls due. Currency traders typically use a prime broker to obtain financing required to implement carry trades, and they also use the creditworthiness of their prime broker to back their trades in the face of their counterparties. Given the important role played by the prime broker in currency trading, currency traders are exposed to credit risk if the prime broker went bankrupt (Melvin & Taylor, 2009). The default spread typically tends to widen during deteriorating market conditions.

When thinking of emerging markets, the default risk is more extreme than in developed countries due to many factors such as limited disclosure, lack of transparency, counterparties unwilling to share information, and political uncertainty. Emerging market carry traders rush to quality during times of market tension by trying to replace risky emerging currencies with safe-haven currencies. The counterparty default risk thus plays a major role in unwinding carry trades during periods of market stress, since carry trade involves using leverage to finance the investment in the high-yielding currency in emerging countries. The role of default risk in unwinding carry trades during market crashes is documented in Coudert and Mignon (2013) who show that sovereign credit risk affects carry trades asymmetrically across booming and crisis periods. In particular, default betas (i.e., sensitivity of excess returns to carry trades to default risk) tend to be positive during booming periods, which means that carry trade gains are higher for high default currencies. Conversely, default betas are negative during crisis period which implies that carry trade losses are deeper when invested in countries with higher default risk.

In contrast to the 1994 Mexican and 1997 Thai crises, the international debt crisis of the 1980s has been default crisis where the "capital flow reversals" occurred because of debtor default. The international debt crisis officially started on August 15, 1982 when Mexico declared its inability to pay its debt obligations. The major debtors in the crisis were concentrated in Latin American countries, such as Mexico, Argentina, Brazil, Bolivia, Ecuador, Peru, and Venezuela. Consequently, investors began to withdraw their investments from the Latin American market to safer markets. Although several of the world's largest banks faced the prospect of major loan defaults and failure as a consequence of the crisis, it was obvious that the US banks' exposure was the highest. In particular, the largest Latin American countries (Mexico, Brazil, Venezuela, and Argentina) owed the eight largest US banks $37 billion that constituted 147% of their capital and reserves at the end of 1983. The size of such debt coupled with the overexposure (lending in excess of capital assets) gave rise to a fear of financial collapse to the largest American banks such as Citibank, Bank of America, Chase Manhattan, and Morgan Guaranty (FDIC, 1997).

The above discusses how large swings in capital flows in emerging countries during crises were driven by deteriorating conditions (such as liquidity and default problems) in the recipient emerging economies. However, the "capital inflow reversal" problem may be driven also by contagion (spillover effects) which is unrelated to fundamentals. The motivation draws primarily from a common phenomenon of the last few decades where financial crises rapidly spread from one country to another.

Contagion risk is the risk that an event at the country level will trigger unexpected consequences at the regional or the global level, which are not obviously related to the original source of the disturbance. Contagion is a common feature of the financial crises that have engulfed emerging markets over the last few decades.[5] For example, the international debt crisis originally began in Mexico in August 1982 and, by the end of the year, intra-regional contagion took place since difficulties in interest payments were evident in most of the Latin American countries for 40 countries such as Argentina, Brazil, Bolivia, Ecuador, Peru, and Venezuela.

The most prominent evidence of contagion comes from the 1997 to 1998 Asian crisis that started in Thailand in July 1997 with the collapse of the Thai Baht and then spread rapidly into neighboring countries such as Indonesia, Malaysia, South Korea, and (to a lesser degree) the Philippines. One year later, the crisis spread to Russia due to the Russian default on domestic debt on August 17, 1998, and thereafter the collapse of the Russian stock market. The crisis moved next to Brazil and then to Argentina when both countries started facing liquidity problems in late 1998 and mid-1999.

To sum up, higher interest rate and foreign exchange risks in emerging markets leave the emerging economies more vulnerable to speculation, given the fact that interest rates and exchange rates are very likely to move significantly together with little warning. These unique set of challenges give rise to increased risks in emerging markets relative to developed markets. When a financial crisis occurs in any region in the world with fears of contagion (spillover effect) which is unrelated to fundamentals, risk aversion increases and carry traders tend to rebalance their portfolios toward more liquid (i.e., flight-to-liquidity) and less risky securities (i.e., flight-to-quality). As a result, emerging market carry trades unwind and consequently the "capital inflow reversal" process starts, and severe losses occur which might threaten growth

5. Interest in investigating the impact of global crises on co-movement among international stock markets has arisen primarily since the October crash of 1987. On Black Monday (October 19, 1987), the S&P 500 composite index dropped by 22.9 percent on the second highest volume ever recorded (604 million shares) and the DJIA fell by 22.6 percent. Such decline was the largest one-day percentage decline in the history of the markets. On October 13, 1989, the index dropped 7 percent accompanied by a 50 percent increase in volume (Gallant, Rossi, & Tauchen, 1992).

in emerging economies that rely on carry trade inflows and leave them vulnerable to banking and currency crises.[6]

Forecasting Financial Crises: Can Emerging Markets Carry Trades Help?

As far as all the risks and threats associated with investment in emerging market carry trades during financial crises are concerned, it would be most useful if a number of indicators could be identified that might predict the probability of the occurrence of financial crisis. This section identifies three crisis warning indicators, and empirically examines their forecasting power in predicting a financial crisis.

Methodology: I propose three crisis warning indicators motivated by the trading in emerging markets' carry trades. These indicators are carry trade excess returns, the JP Morgan volatility index, and the JP Morgan GBI index. Let me explain each of these indicators briefly:

1. *Carry trade returns*, denoted as CRET_{it}, is the currency excess returns to buying a foreign currency in the forward market and then selling it in the spot market after one month, and it is defined in Eq. (5) (*i.e.*, $\text{CRET}_{it} = f_{it-1} - s_{it}$).[7] The exchange

6. The key measure of a country's vulnerability to the carry trade flow withdrawal is the differential between local and US dollar interest rates when judged against currency futures prices.

7. I measure the currency excess returns using forward markets. Alternatively, the excess return to investing in the carry trade while funded in USD can be measured as the difference between interest rate differential and exchange rate changes, as follows: $\text{CRET}^*_{i,t} = (i^*_t - i_t) - \Delta s_t$. The interest rate differential $(i^*_t - i_t)$ is the interest rate difference between the foreign country and the United States, where i^*_t is the foreign interest rate in units of foreign currency and i_t is the nominal interest rate in US currency. As in Lustig, Roussanov, and Verdelhan (2011, 2014), the merit of focusing our attention to investments in forward markets (compared to investment in interest rates) is that forward contracts are subject to low default risk. In addition, the data on forward exchange rates are easily available.

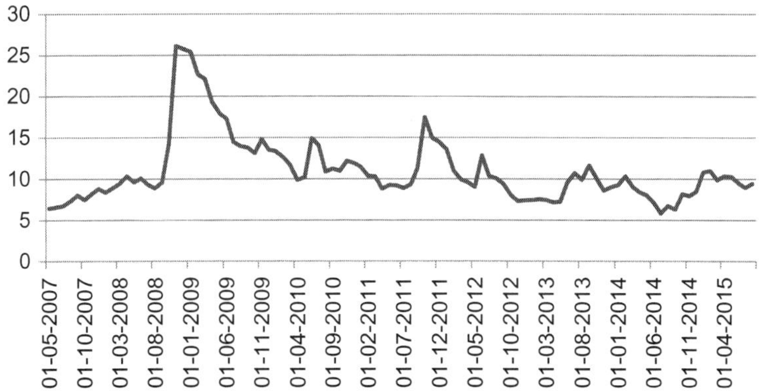

Figure 3: JP Morgan EM-VXY Index. *Notes*: This figure shows the monthly data for JP Morgan EM-VXY index from May 2007 to August 2015. The JP Morgan EM-VXY index tracks volatility in emerging market currencies. The EM-VXY index follows aggregate volatility in currencies through a turnover-weighted index of emerging market volatility, based on three-month at-the-money forward options. The index is designed to measure aggregate risk premiums in currency markets.

rates are measured as the number of units of the emerging currency per one US dollar.[8]

2. *JP Morgan EM-VXY index*, denoted as $JPMVOLAT_t$, is an index that tracks volatility in emerging market currencies. The EM-VXY index follows aggregate volatility in currencies through a turnover-weighted index of emerging market volatility, based on three-month at-the-money forward options. The index is designed to measure aggregate risk premiums in currency markets, as seen in Figure 3.

3. *JP Morgan GBI-EM index*, denoted as $JPMGBI_t$, is a local currency bond index that tracks emerging market debt issued by emerging market governments. The GBI-EM index was developed by JP Morgan in response to the increased interest of investors in emerging markets' local currency

8. Note that returns are dated by the time they are known. Thus, the change in exchange rates between t and $t + 1$ is dated $t + 1$.

debt. Figure 2 shows the graphical representation of GBI-EM index.

It is crucial to note that these three indicators are motivated by trading in emerging markets' carry trade. Since carry trade strategy is a speculative currency strategy that exploits the empirical violation of the IRP relation which shows a theoretical relation between interest rates and exchange rates, I use CRET_{it} to measure excess currency returns from carry trades; $\mathrm{JPMVOLAT}_t$ to measure the volatility in exchange rates of emerging currencies measured as the number of units of the emerging currency per one US dollar; and JPMGBI_t to track the investors' interest in the merging markets' local currency debt. These indicators are by no means an exhaustive list of all possible predictors of financial crisis. The literature suggests other fundamental indicators of financial crises such as the current account deficit and foreign debt.[9] However, this chapter cannot fully consider these indicators for lack of data at this point in time.

In order to empirically examine the power of these indicators in forecasting financial crises, I use a probit regression model that is a limited dependent variable approach specifically suited for estimation where the dependent variable is only partially observed over some range. The Probit model and the predicted effect is estimated as follows:

$$\begin{aligned}\mathrm{Crisis}_t^* = \beta_0 + \beta_{\mathrm{CRET}}\mathrm{CRET}_{it} + \beta_{\mathrm{JPMVOLAT}}\mathrm{JPMVOLAT}_t \\ + \beta_{\mathrm{JPMGBI}}\mathrm{JPMGBI}_t + \varepsilon_{it} \qquad (6)\end{aligned}$$

where Crisis_t^* is an indicator function that takes on the value of 1 if a country actually had a financial crisis during the sample period and zero otherwise. The indicator variable Crisis_t^* measures the underlying propensity for a given country to have a financial crisis for each country in the sample. For notational purposes, I use t as

9. For a survey for an exhaustive list of proposed indicators of financial crises previously used in the literature, see Kaminsky, Lizondo, and Reinhart (1998).

an index for time in general, and i as an indication for country/currency-level variables. A persistent challenge in examining financial crises is to identify the precise beginning and ending of a crisis, that is to pinpoint the source of the crisis (identify the major triggering event). I use the chronology of both the 1997–1998 Asian crisis and the 2007–2008 global financial crisis to define crisis period for each of these two crises. For the Asian crisis, $\text{Crisis}_t^* = 1$ from July 1, 1997 to December 31, 1998, and zero otherwise.[10] For the global financial crisis, $\text{Crisis}_t^* = 1$ from January 1, 2008 to December 31, 2009 and zero otherwise.[11]

Data: I use data from eight Asian emerging countries which serve as proxies for emerging markets, independent of the origination of the crisis. The sample countries are Hong Kong, Indonesia, Philippines, Russia, Singapore, South Korea, Taiwan, and Thailand. The data span the period from January 1997 to August 2015

10. According to the International Monetary Fund (1998), the Asian crisis began July 2, 1997 when the bank of Thailand devalued the baht by roughly 20 percent. On March, 1999, the Asian crisis had ended when the IMF approved a $1 billion increase in its emergency loan package for Indonesia, and the DJIA closed above the 10,000 level for the first time in its history. Therefore, we define the 'Asian crisis period' from July 1997 to March 1999.

11. The 2007–2008 global financial crisis hit the financial markets as a result of the implosion of the US mortgage market and reversal of the housing boom. The first indications of a credit crunch appeared on July 17, 2007 when the credit spreads soar as a result of Bear Sterns announcement that two if its hedge funds with subprime exposure has released losses of $1.5 billion (more than 90 percent of their value). Two weeks later after the announcement, on July 31 2007, these two hedge funds filed for Chapter 15 bankruptcy. On October 25, 2007, Merrill Lynch reports the biggest quarterly loss in the company's history ($2.24 billion), resulting from its huge write downs on subprime mortgages ($7.9 billion). Specifically, the credit crunch gets much worse on January 15, 2008 when Citigroup (the largest bank in the United States) reports a $9.83 billion loss as a result of its $18.1 billion write down, followed by an announcement by Wells Fargo (the fifth largest US bank) of a 37 percent loss in net income and by Merrill Lynch of a $7.8 billion net loss. Although the first indications of the 2008 crisis appeared on January 15 when news of a sharp drop in profits of Citigroup, September 2008 is considered a historic month and a new phase of the crisis since it witnessed the bankruptcy of Lehman Brothers which is considered the largest bankruptcy filing in the US history. Lehman's bankruptcy in September 2008 led to profound effects on the equity and bond market. On September 15 2008 — the day the Lehman Brothers filed for bankruptcy, the DJIA witnessed the largest drop in a single day since the September 11, 2001 attack (–4.4 percent). Also, the price volatility of investment grade bonds reached unprecedented levels during September 2008 (Longstaff, 2010).

although the sample period varies by currency. This time span is long enough to study the effects of two major recent global crisis periods: the 1997–1998 Asian crisis and the 2008–2008 global financial crisis. The raw currency dataset consist of daily and monthly observations for spot exchange rates and one month forward exchange rates. All exchange rates are denominated in units of foreign currency unit per one US dollar (FCU/USD). All spot and forward exchange rates in addition to EM-VXY and GBI-EM indices are obtained from Datastream, with Reuters as the underlying source. Table 1 reports the descriptive summary statistics of the study variables.

Results: In order to investigate the predictability power of these indicators, I estimate the parameters of the probit model in Eq. (6) using two different approaches. First, I measure trades conducted on a currency by currency basis against the US dollar. Second, I run a panel regression model. Both analyses are conducted using both daily and monthly data.

Table 1: Descriptive Statistics.

Variable	Mean	Standard Deviation
Panel A: Daily data		
$CRET_{Hong\ Kong}$	−0.0000661	0.00115
$CRET_{Indonesia}$	9441	2014
$CRET_{Phillippines}$	0.00338	0.00611
$CRET_{Russia}$	0.00459	0.01097
$CRET_{Singapore}$	−0.0006726	0.00408
$CRET_{South\ Korea}$	0.0009800	0.00720
$CRET_{Taiwan}$	0.00190	0.00352
$CRET_{Thailand}$	−0.0007139	0.00724
JPMVOLAT	10.98541	4.20700
JPMGBI	189.39479	58.45040

Table 1: (*Continued*)

Variable	Mean	Standard Deviation
Panel B: Monthly data		
$CRET_{Hong\ Kong}$	−0.0001119	0.00149
$CRET_{Indonesia}$	0.01392	0.08747
$CRET_{Phillippines}$	0.00105	0.02398
$CRET_{Russia}$	−0.0008285	0.04230
$CRET_{Singapore}$	−0.0006720	0.01825
$CRET_{South\ Korea}$	0.00175	0.03414
$CRET_{Taiwan}$	−0.00140	0.01617
$CRET_{Thailand}$	0.0006879	0.03105
JPMVOLAT	10.98850	4.11094
JPMGBI	189.27172	58.82710

This table presents descriptive statistics for daily and monthly country-level data in panels A and B, respectively. The sample consists of eight currencies over the period from January 1, 1997 until August 7, 2015. The table shows statistics for three variables — carry trade returns (CRET), JP Morgan EM-VXY index (JPMVOLAT), and JP Morgan GBI-EM index (JPMGBI). The carry trade returns, CRET, is measured as the log one-month forward rate (f_t) minus the log spot exchange rate of the foreign currency against the USD (s_t), measured as the number of units of the foreign currency per one US dollar. The JP Morgan GBI-Emerging Markets index, JPMVOLAT, is a benchmark that tracks volatility in emerging market currencies. The JP Morgan GBI-Emerging Markets index, JPMGBI, is a benchmark that tracks local currency bonds issued by Emerging market governments.

First, I estimate the probit model in Eq. (6) using country-by-country analysis, so that the probability of a crisis is calculated for each country in the sample. Tables 2 and 3 report the results of the probit regression using country-by-country analysis using daily and monthly data, respectively. The propensity for a country to have a financial crisis is determined by the carry trade returns for each individual currency $CRET_{it}$, in addition to the $JPMVOLAT_t$ and $JPMGBI_t$. The $\beta^{w/o}_{CRET}$ is the parameter estimate of a simple regression of the $Crisis^*_t$ variable on individual currency excess returns $CRET_{it}$, while β^{w}_{CRET} measures the sensitivity of the $Crisis^*_t$

Table 2: Probit Estimation of Crises Using Country-Level Analysis: Daily Data.

Country	$\beta^{w/o}_{\text{CRET}}$	β^{w}_{CRET}	β_{JPMVOLAT}	β_{JPMGBI}
Hong Kong	−940.921***	−850.471***	−3.0228***	0.4908
Indonesia	0.0001***	−0.0016**	−2.7396***	0.4376***
Philippines	−74.2374***	−74.8147***	−2.8823***	0.4594***
Russia	−51.5942***	−73.0411***	−2.8209***	0.4519***
Singapore	−50.7874***	−102.816***	−2.8630***	0.4588***
S Korea	47.1198***	−135.251***	−3.2260***	0.5159***
Taiwan	4.2420***	−366.313	−3.0768***	0.4937***
Thailand	−51.2184***	−75.3811*	−2.8970***	0.4580***

This table reports the results of the underlying propensity for a given country to have a financial crisis conditional on the daily data of the three warning indicators — carry trade returns, JP Morgan EM-VXY index, and JP Morgan GBI-EM index. The table shows the slope coefficients from two regressions. Panel A reports the slope coefficients from the following probit simple regression

$$\text{Crisis}^*_t = \beta_0 + \beta^{w/o}_{\text{CRET}}\text{CRET}_{it}$$

Crisis^*_t is an indicator function that takes on the value of 1 if a country actually had a financial crisis during the sample period and zero otherwise. For the Asian crisis, $\text{Crisis}^*_t = 1$ from July 1, 1997 to December 31, 1998, and zero otherwise. For the global financial crisis, $\text{Crisis}^*_t = 1$ from January 1, 2008 to December 31, 2009 and zero otherwise. The CRET is the daily currency excess return measured as the log forward rate minus the log expected spot rate.

Panel B shows the slope coefficients from the following probit multiple regression

$$\text{Crisis}^*_t = \beta_0 + \beta^{w}_{\text{CRET}}\text{CRET}_{it} + \beta_{\text{JPMVOLAT}}\text{JPMVOLAT}_t + \beta_{\text{JPMGBI}}\text{JPMGBI}_t$$

The JPMVOLAT is the JP Morgan emerging markets volatility index which is a benchmark that tracks volatility in emerging market currencies. The JPMGBI is the JP Morgan GBI-emerging markets index that tracks local currency bonds issued by emerging market governments.

*Significance at 10% level.

**Significant at 5% level.

***Significant at 1% level.

Table 3: Probit Estimation of Crises Using Country-Level Analysis: Monthly Data.

Country	$\beta^{w/o}_{\text{CRET}}$	β^{w}_{CRET}	β_{JPMVOLAT}	β_{JPMGBI}
Hong Kong	−385.495***	−19.9521	−4.4845**	0.7595**
Indonesia	4.0333**	−102.319	−8.6229*	1.4850*
Philippines	14.0525**	−8.0511	−4.5054**	0.7617**
Russia	−3.0927	−14.7664	−4.2994**	0.7215**
Singapore	5.6403	−21.9341	−4.4825**	0.7539**
S Korea	11.6082*	−13.0543	−4.5917**	0.7773**
Taiwan	14.2762	−6.4580	−4.4116**	0.7482**
Thailand	4.0353	−50.1152	−4.7891**	0.8117**

This table reports the results of the underlying propensity for a given country to have a financial crisis conditional on the monthly data of the three warning indicators — carry trade returns, JP Morgan EM-VXY index, and JP Morgan GBI-EM index. The table shows the slope coefficients from two regressions. Panel A reports the slope coefficients from the following probit simple regression

$$\text{Crisis}_t^* = \beta_0 + \beta^{w/o}_{\text{CRET}}\text{CRET}_{it}$$

For the Asian crisis, $\text{Crisis}_t^* = 1$ from July, 1997 to December, 1998, and zero otherwise. For the global financial crisis, $\text{Crisis}_t^* = 1$ from January, 2008–December, 2009 and zero otherwise. The CRET is the monthly currency excess return measured as the log forward rate minus the log expected spot rate. Panel B reports country-level results from the following probit multiple regression:

$$\text{Crisis}_t^* = \beta_0 + \beta^{w}_{\text{CRET}}\text{CRET}_{it} + \beta_{\text{JPMVOLAT}}\text{JPMVOLAT}_t + \beta_{\text{JPMGBI}}\text{JPMGBI}_t$$

The JPMVOLAT is the monthly JP Morgan Volatility Index Emerging Markets, and the JPMGBI is the monthly JP Morgan GBI-Emerging Markets index that tracks local currency bonds issued by Emerging market governments.
*Significant at 10% level
**Significant at 5% level
***Significant at 1% level.

variable to CRET_{it} in the presence of JPMVOLAT_t and JPMGBI_t in a multiple regression.

The results of country-by-country analysis, given in Tables 2 and 3, provide support for using the three indicators to forecast a financial crisis. All the three indicators are significant at 1% level for most of the sample countries. In particular, the $\beta^{w}_{\mathrm{CRET}}$ has the correct signs and are statistically significant for all seven out of eight countries. The negative sign of the excess currency returns coefficients means that a drop in the currency excess returns increases the predicted probability of crisis. However, the $\mathrm{JPMVOLAT}_t$ have the wrong sign, and the standard errors of the estimated coefficients (not reported) using country-by-country data are very high.

To further check the findings from the country-by-country analysis, therefore, I run estimations using panel regression (i.e., cross-sectional combined with time-series data) using both random effect and fixed effect estimation. Tables 4 and 5 report the results of panel regression using daily and monthly data, respectively. Each two out of three indicators are included in a separate regression in lines 1 and 2 to avoid multicollinearity, and the three indicators are included in the same regression in line 3. Panel (A) shows the results of fixed effect estimation, and panel (B) reports the results of random effect estimation. The results of the probit estimation, given in Tables 4 and 5, provide support for using the three indicators to forecast a financial crisis. The three variables are significant at 1% percent level in the three regressions using both fixed and random effects, and the standard errors are very small in all regression.

Conclusion

This chapter presents the first attempt to predict financial crises using indicators driven by trading in emerging market carry trades. This chapter identifies three crisis warning indicators driven by trading in the emerging markets carry trade — carry trade returns, JP Morgan EM-VXY index, and JP Morgan GBI-EM index. The empirical results show that both the 1997–1998 Asian crisis and the 2007–2008 global crisis could have been predicted using these three indicators. These indicators show high significant power in forecasting crises whether the analysis is conducted on a

Table 4: Probit Estimation of Crises Using Panel Analysis: Daily Data.

	β_{CRET}	β_{JPMVOLAT}	β_{JPMGBI}
Panel A: Fixed effect estimation			
1	−0.00002***	0.057007***	
	(5.659E-6)	(0.000657)	
2	0.000109***		−0.00642***
	(5.607E-6)		(0.000067)
3	0.000073***	0.040145***	−0.00488***
	(5.006E-6)	(0.000605)	(0.000064)
	β_{CRET}	β_{JPMVOLAT}	β_{JPMGBI}
Panel B: Random effect estimation			
1	−0.00001***	0.057003***	
	(4.552E-6)	(0.000656)	
2	0.000107***		−0.00642***
	(5.558E-6)		(0.000067)
3	0.000071***	0.040174***	−0.00487***
	(4.93E-6)	(0.000605)	(0.000064)

This table reports the panel results of probit regression using daily data for the crisis indicator variable, Crisis^*_{it}, on carry trade returns, JP Morgan EM-VXY index, and JP Morgan GBI-EM index, as follows

$$\text{Crisis}^*_t = \beta_0 + \beta_{\text{CRET}}\text{CRET}_{it} + \beta_{\text{JPMVOLAT}}\text{JPMVOLAT}_t + \beta_{\text{JPMGBI}}\text{JPMGBI}_t$$

For each regression, the slope coefficients β are reported using both cross-sectional fixed effect (Panel A) and random effect estimation (Panel B).
***Significant at 1% level.

currency by currency basis against the US dollar, or on a panel basis. It appears that carry trade variables might be important determinants of crises and deserve more attention in future research. Although financial crisis may be better predicted by the well-known fundamental indicators, the contribution of this

Table 5: Probit Estimation of Crises using Panel Analysis: Monthly Data.

	β_{CRET}	$\beta_{JPMVOLAT}$	β_{JPMGBI}
Panel A: Fixed effect estimation			
1	0.861487**	0.057681***	
	(0.4544)	(0.00313)	
2	−0.82721**		−0.00617***
	(0.4263)		(0.000282)
3	0.023661	0.039024***	−0.00478***
	(0.3889)	(0.00286)	(0.000273)
	β_{CRET}	$\beta_{JPMVOLAT}$	β_{JPMGBI}
Panel B: Random effect estimation			
1	0.861275**	0.05768***	
	(0.4523)	(0.00312)	
2	−0.82718**		−0.00617***
	(0.4244)		(0.000281)
3	0.023655	0.039024***	−0.00478***
	(0.3871)	(0.00285)	(0.000272)

This table report the results of probit regression using monthly for the crisis indicator variable, Crisis_t^*, on carry trade returns, JP Morgan EM-VXY index, and JP Morgan GBI-EM index, as follows:

$$\text{Crisis}_t^* = \beta_0 + \beta_{\text{CRET}}\text{CRET}_{it} + \beta_{\text{JPMVOLAT}}\text{JPMVOLAT}_t + \beta_{\text{JPMGBI}}\text{JPMGBI}_t$$

For each regression, the slope coefficients β are reported using both cross-sectional fixed effect (Panel A) and random effect estimation (Panel B).
**Significant at 5% level.
***Significant at 1% level.

chapter is simply that carry trade-related indicators can help in predicting crises. Although these indicators are by no means an exhaustive list of all possible predictors of financial crisis, but future research needs to include these three indicators to include a more complete set of crisis warning indicators.

References

Ahmad, R., Rhee, S. G., & Wong, Y. M. (2012). Foreign exchange market efficiency under recent crises: Asia-Pacific focus. *Journal of International Money and Finance, 31*, 267–291.

Baillie, R. T., & Bollerslev, T. (1989). Common stochastic trends in a system of exchange rates. *The Journal of Finance, 44*, 167–181.

Baillie, R. T., & Bollerslev, T. (2000). The forward premium anomaly is not as bad as you think. *Journal of International Money and Finance, 19*, 471–488.

Brunnermeier, M. K., Nagel, S., & Pedersen, L. H. (2008). Carry trades and currency crashes. *NBER Macroeconomics Annual, 23*, 313–347.

Clarida, R., Davis, J., & Pedersen, N. (2009). Currency carry trade regimes: Beyond the Fama regression. *Journal of International Money and Finance, 28*, 1375–1389.

Coudert, V., Couharde, C., & Mignon, V. (2011). Exchange rate volatility across financial crises. *Journal of Banking and Finance, 35*(11), 3010–3018.

Coudert, V., & Mignon, V. (2013). The forward premium puzzle and the sovereign default risk. *Journal of International Money and Finance, 32*, 491–511.

Engel, C. (1996). The forward discount anomaly and the risk premium: A survey of recent evidence. *Journal of Empirical Finance, 3*, 123–192.

Fama, E. F. (1984). Forward and spot exchange rates. *Journal of Monetary Economics, 14*, 319–338.

Federal Deposit Insurance Corporation (FDIC). (1997). The LDC debt crisis. *An examination of the banking crises of the 1980s and early 1990s* (Vol. 1, pp. 191–210), Chapter 5. Washington, DC: FDIC

Frankel, J., & Poonawala, J. (2010). The forward market in emerging currencies: Less biased than in major currencies. *Journal of International Money and Finance, 29*, 585–598.

Froot, K. A., & Thaler, R. H. (1990). Anomalies: Foreign exchange. *Journal of Economic Perspectives, 4*, 179–192.

Gagnon, J., & Chaboud, A. (2007). *What can the data tell us about carry trades in Japanese Yen?* International Finance Discussion Paper No. 899. Board of Governors of the Federal Reserve System.

Galati, G., Heath, A., & McGuire, P. (2007). Evidence of carry trade activity. BIS Quarterly Review, 27–41.

Gallant, R., Rossi, P., & Tauchen, G. (1992). Stock prices and volume. *Review of Financial Studies, 5*, 199–242.

International Monetary Fund. (1998). *World economic and financial surveys: International capital markets developments, prospects and key policy issues*. Washington, DC: International Monetary Fund.

International Monetary Fund (IMF). (1999–2001). *World economic outlook*. IMF, Washington, DC.

Kaminsky, G., Lizondo, S., & Reinhart, C. (1998). Leading indicators of currency crises. *IMF Staff Papers*, *45*(1), 1–45.

Kynge, J. (2015). Surging US dollars threatens emerging markets' carry trades. *Financial Times*, Prentice Hall. Retrieved from http://www.ft.com/cms/s/0/27a516d8-47e4-11e4-be7b-00144feab7de.html

Longstaff, F. A. (2010). The subprime credit crisis and contagion in financial markets. *Journal of Financial Economics*, *97*, 436–450.

Lustig, H., Roussanov, N., & Verdelhan, A. (2011). Common risk factors in currency markets. *Review of Financial Studies*, *24*(11), 3731–3777.

Lustig, H., Roussanov, N., & Verdelhan, A. (2014). Countercyclical currency risk premia. *Journal of Financial Economics*, *111*(3), 527–553.

Mancini, L., Ranaldo, A., & Wrampelmeyer, J. (2013). Liquidity in the foreign exchange market: Measurement, commonality, and risk premiums. *The Journal of Finance*, *5*, 1805–1841.

Melvin, M., & Taylor, M. P. (2009). The crisis in the foreign exchange market. *Journal of International Money and Finance*, *28*, 1317–1330.

Obstfeld, M., & Rogoff, K. (2001). The six major puzzles in international macroeconomics: Is there a common cause. In B. Bernanke & K. Rogoff (Eds.), *NBER macroeconomics annual 2000* (Vol. 15, pp. 339–412). Cambridge, MA: Cambridge MIT Press.

Rafferty, B. (2011). The returns to currency speculation and global currency realignment risk, manuscript. Duke University.

8

Risk Management in Islamic Banking: An Emerging Market Imperative

Mahfod Aldoseri and Andrew C. Worthington

Abstract

The purpose of this chapter is to review the risks Islamic financial institutions face in an emerging market context, including risk sharing in Islamic financing and Shari'ah (Islamic law) compliance risk. We explore current risk management practices and establish the link between risk management and the financial performance of banks and the efficiency and effectiveness of financial sectors in emerging markets. Because of their distinctive risk profile, Islamic finance institutions face challenges in risk management. We show that Islamic banking is riskier in emerging markets because of the presence of immature money markets, limitations in the availability of lender of last resort facilities, and deficiencies in market infrastructure. There is also no evidence that Islamic banks have developed effective solutions for managing the risks conventional banks face as well as their own unique risks. We suggest that the countries that do this best are those that prioritize the structure of risk management knowledge and capabilities in a single financial regulator.

Keywords: Islamic banking; risk management; Shari'ah compliance; risk sharing; credit risk; liquidity risk; operational risk; emerging markets; *Murāba'ah*; *Salam*; *Istisnā*; *Sukuk*

Introduction

Financial institutions have evolved various methods to mitigate risk and improve their overall performance. Risk management is one such practice used by financial institutions to reduce risk of various kinds. Like their conventional counterparts, Islamic banks face a wide range of important risks, even though the business approach used in Islamic banking is quite different. In sum, the unique characteristics and nature of Islamic banking, specifically the profit sharing approach to banking, completely alters the extent of any risks they face. Further, compared with conventional banks, Islamic banks deal with many products not found in conventional banking, with unique and sometimes significant risks. For this reason, it is extremely important for Islamic banks to use risk management techniques to mitigate any present and potential risks (Rahman, Rahman, & Azad, 2015).

Currently, there are more than 400 financial institutions worldwide with operations conducted according to *Shari'ah* (Islamic law). These institutions provide an extensive range of services and products with assets currently in excess of US$1 trillion. The burgeoning popularity of Islamic finance has encouraged many countries to award licenses to financial institutions so that they can commence operations according to *Shari'ah*. These licensed firms are now present in more than 75 countries, including Muslim states such as Bahrain, Kuwait, Malaysia, and the United Arab

Emirates (UAE), and others like Singapore, along with some 50 Islamic financial institutions in Europe, 30 of them currently operating in the United Kingdom, and another 20 Islamic financial institutions in the United States (Al-Hares, AbuGhazaleh, & El-Galfy, 2013).

Risk management for Islamic banking financial products and services is one of the greatest challenges that many conventional, as well as Islamic banks, face today. The central issue is the implications of *Shari'ah* compliance on the risk management system. Since its conception 40 years ago, Islamic banking and finance has enjoyed impressive growth and has demonstrated it is a feasible and viable form of finance. The benefit to users of Islamic financial products, as well as a notable rate of innovation in these products has meant this sector has presented itself as a practical alternative to conventional finance. Today Islamic finance and banking deserves recognition as a valuable constituent in the global financial system (Bitar, 2015).

Risk management practices are particularly important for Islamic banks in emerging markets. Islamic banks in most of these markets are rapidly increasing their market share. For example, Pakistan currently offers the fastest growing market for *Shari'ah* compliant products and that Islamic banking in Pakistan has been growing at over 30 percent for the last five years. Currently, more than 1,200 branches spread over 80 districts offer *Shari'ah* compliant products and services. However, Islamic banks currently only represent about 10 percent of banking assets and deposits in Pakistan. Analysis of the industry shows that it has a bright future, and it intends to double its market share by 2020.

Globally, Islamic banking has likewise achieved substantial growth worldwide, with cumulative assets of about US$ 1.3 trillion in 2011, expected to surpass US$2.8 trillion by the end of 2015. Two of the most important elements to realize further substantial development in the Islamic banking industry are product development and the standardization of regulatory practices. The banking industry also requires the development of human capital and marketing. Recent studies show that Islamic banking have ventured into other banking areas such as investment banking, project finance, capital market, as well as microfinance. However, the most immediate thing Islamic banks need to do is to develop products that can enhance their liquidity (Zamir, 2014).

Following the global financial crisis, some scholars contested that Islamic banks were more stable than conventional banks because they were relatively unaffected. However, others have refuted this claim by arguing that Islamic banks are an integral part of the international financial system, and therefore it is not possible to exclude them from the crisis. The contention is that Islamic banks, although in their infancy, are nonetheless obliged to participate in existing market risks. As a result, Islamic banks and institutions were affected, but they were found to be more stable than the conventional counterparts because they engaged in *Shari'ah*-compliant activities. A report provided by Islamic banks and Global Stability Report (2010) indicated that during the crisis, the Islamic banks experienced 38.2 percent asset growth and 20 percent profit growth. In contrast, conventional banks experienced only 16.3 percent asset growth and -6.1 percent profit growth between 2007 and 2008 (IFSB-IDB-IRTS, 2010). These findings clearly show that Islamic banks are apparently safer and better performing than conventional banks. However, this can also be attributed to their structure of their products, mainly asset-backed financing. Most studies evaluating the performance of banks during the financial crisis show that Islamic banks performed well when compared with conventional banks (Ahmed, Asutay, & Wilson, 2013).

Furthermore, the current globalization and liberalization movement in capital markets is encouraging the development of improved risk management measures for Islamic banks, especially in emerging markets. While extensive risk management is common in conventional financial institutions and markets, it is less common and relatively immature in Islamic financial institutions and markets. Moreover, because of their sometimes limited resources (especially in terms of appropriately trained staff, but also suitable risk management software and procedures), Islamic banks are often unable to afford high-cost management information systems or the technology to assess and monitor risks in a timely fashion. With arguably weaker management and a lack of proper risk-monitoring systems, the risk exposure of Islamic banks is potentially higher (Mokni, Echchabi, Azouzi, & Rachdi, 2014).

The chapter is organized as follows. The section "The Nature of Risk in Islamic Banking" describes risk in Islamic banks. The section "Unique Counterparty Risks in Islamic Modes of Finance" explains the counterparty risks in Islamic modes of finance. The section "Bank Risk Management Practices in Emerging Markets" describes bank risk management in emerging markets. Finally, the section "Conclusion" summarizes our findings.

The Nature of Risk in Islamic Banking

There is a substantial difference in the concepts and practices used in Islamic and conventional banking systems (Gait and Worthington (2014) for a useful introduction). Both styles of banking differently recognize and manage the differing risk exposure associated with these differences. Moreover, Islamic banks with different characteristics of assets and liabilities face very different kinds of risks not experienced by most conventional banks, including especially risk sharing and *Shari'ah* compliance risk. In addition, Islamic banks are also exposed to the usual risks faced by conventional commercial banks, such as credit, liquidity, and interest rate risk. However, these risks typically take on different forms based on the differences in the products and services offered in the two types of banks, which in turn affects the characteristics of the assets and liabilities held by the bank (Greuning & Iqbal, 2009).

Credit Risk

Credit risk is the potential exposure to risk which occurs when one of the parties to a deal makes a payment, as in *Salam* (sale by advance payment for the future delivery) or *Istisnā* (contract for manufacture) contract, or with the delivery of assets, as in *Murāba'ah* (sale on goods with markup) contract, before receipt of funds. In the case of finance based on profit sharing, as in *Murāba'ah* and *Mushārakah* (profit and loss sharing), credit risk arises when the business owner/entrepreneur fails to pay the bank its share of profits when due. This generally occurs when banks have insufficient information (an asymmetric information problem) about the actual profit of the enterprise owing them money. *Murāba'ah,* basically trading contracts subject to counterparty credit risk, potentially arise because of nonperforming trading partners. The sources of such nonperformance can be of an external systematic nature (Al-Wesabi & Ahmad, 2013).

Benchmark Risk

Islamic banks may appear immune to market risk caused by interest rate changes in that their deals do not overtly depend on interest rates. However, in contrast to widely held opinion, market interest rate changes do affect Islamic financial institution earnings, as Islamic financial institutions still typically price against a benchmark interest rate. A case in point is the *Murāba'ah* contract where a markup adds a fixed risk premium for the duration of the contract to the benchmark rate (usually the London Interbank Offered Rate or LIBOR). This results in an increase in credit risk for Islamic banks because they usually cannot adjust the markup rate, if the benchmark rate changes (Zepeda, 2013).

Liquidity Risk

Difficulties in borrowing money at a reasonable rate or selling assets at a reasonable cost give rise to liquidity risk. In either case, this is critical for Islamic banks because *Shari'ah* does not permit loans based on interest and hence borrowing funds to overcome a liquidity problem is not an option for Islamic banks. Moreover, the sale of debt is also prohibited by *Shari'ah* unless it is at face value, thus making it impossible for Islamic banking institutions to sell debt-based assets in order to improve liquidity (Paldi, 2014).

Operational Risk

Given the unique nature of Islamic banks, operational risk can arise because of human resource risk. This is a very significant risk for Islamic financial institutions because they may not have enough sufficiently qualified personnel to carry out their relatively new and unique financial operations. In addition, the nature of business in Islamic banks does not make it easy to use off the shelf computer software, thus introducing it may be associated with the adaptation of existing software or the wholesale development of new software (Archer & Karim, 2013).

Legal Risk

Islamic banks require the use of nonstandard financial contracts and hence are also subject to additional risks associated with documentation and enforcement. Islamic banks have to prepare specific contracts to suit their various financial dealings and instruments based on their needs, their concerns, and their own understanding of *Shari'ah* and local laws. This leaves Islamic banks open to increased legal risks due to the lack of litigation systems dealing with problems arising from the enforceability of contract, related to the Islamic contractual agreement, by the counterparty (Archer & Karim, 2013).

Withdrawal Risk

Where the rates of return on savings, investments, or deposits are variable, they introduce uncertainty regarding the real value of deposits. In turn, the risk of loss associated with a lower rate of return, and the need to preserve the value of assets, affects decisions by depositors concerning withdrawal. As far as the Islamic banks themselves are concerned, this possibility of a relatively lower rate of return than conventional financial institutions constitutes withdrawal risk (Abedifar, Molyneux, & Tarazi, 2013).

Fiduciary Risk

A lower rate of return than that in the general market will cause depositors and investors to believe that the low rate of return is an indication of mismanagement of the funds by the bank and/or a potential breach of their investment contract. Banks not being fully compliant with the *Shari'ah* requirements of the contract entered into is one example of a breach of contract that can cause a fiduciary risk, as Islamic banks have no option other than full and strict compliance with *Shari'ah* or else face serious confidence problems arising from the withdrawal of deposits (Abedifar et al., 2013).

Displaced Commercial Risk

This risk arises when banks forgo part of their profit subject to commercial pressure and pay depositors in order to prevent withdrawals triggered by a low level of return. This is, in fact, a transfer of withdrawal risk to equity holders. Displaced commercial risk means that although the bank may have operations that are fully compliant with the requirements of *Shari'ah*, it will underperform relative to other Islamic banks and other peers by paying less than competitive rates of return causing investors to withdraw their deposits. The bank is then not in the position where it can pay competitive rates of return compared with other Islamic banks and other bank competitors. Depositors will again have the incentive to seek withdrawal. In order to prevent such withdrawals, banks need to forgo to depositors a portion of their own profit (Abedifar et al., 2013).

Operation of Islamic Banks in Emerging Markets

Notwithstanding the diversity and extensiveness of risk inherent in Islamic banking, a number of additional factors make the operations of Islamic banks even riskier, and consequently potentially less profitable, in emerging markets. These are:

- Immature money markets are more challenging for Islamic financial institutions. Therefore, it is important to implement systemic liquidity in Islamic money markets (domestic and international) that should comply with *Shari'ah*.

- Lender of last resort (LOLR) features are of limited availability for Islamic banks and other financial institutions because of the prohibition of discount rates. Therefore, one way to solve this limitation for Islamic banks and other financial institutions in emerging markets is to establish a practical approach to provide liquidity according to *Shari'ah* compliance by the central banks.
- Limitations of market infrastructure and legal uncertainties limit the availability of hedging instruments. The absence of a legal context can increase operational risks and weaken market development. For example, derivatives can potentially serve to reduce the risk of Islamic financial transactions. However, the way forward in this area is still not clear (Chattha & Halim, 2014).

Furthermore, foreign exchange and equity risks are some of the major risks that investors in Islamic markets may undertake in these emerging markets, despite these markets often having fewer financial instruments to create common hedges for such financial exposure. In emerging markets, investment portfolios have the potential for higher returns. However, the associated risks, including currency and equity risks can be significant. For instance, many of the standard tools used to hedge currency risk, such as futures, swaps and options contracts, are either unavailable in emerging markets or, where available, are traded in illiquid and inefficient markets, making the overall process of hedging and unwinding a hedge difficult. The lack of adequate foreign exchange and equity risk measurement/management tools is one of the contributing factors leading to major financial losses among national/multinational corporations in emerging countries. As a result, foreign exchange and equity risk management has become an important theme in Islamic markets (Al-Janabi, 2008).

Unique Counterparty Risks in Islamic Modes of Finance

As discussed, Islamic banks with their differently characterized assets and liabilities face different kinds of risks, primarily profit sharing risk and *Shari'ah* compliant risk. In addition, they are exposed to the risks faced by conventional commercial banks such as operational, market, credit, liquidity, and interest rate risk, but these take another form because of the profound differences in the products offered by these two types of banks. This in turn affects the characteristics of assets and liabilities. The risks inherent in particular Islamic banking products and services are as follows.

Murāba'ah Financing

The most commonly used Islamic financial contract is *Murāba'ah*. Its risk characteristics are in fact very similar to interest-based financing if standardized, and *Murāba'ah* is approved as recognized method of finance in many regulatory jurisdictions because of its close resemblance, at least in terms of its risk features, to standard interest-based contracts. Nevertheless, this kind of standardized contract is not acceptable to all *Figh* (Islamic jurisprudence) scholars. Furthermore, there is an absence of complete consistency in *Figh* viewpoints as the contract stands at present. The diverse viewpoints can be a cause of major counterparty risks because of the prospect for litigation.

The major problem is that *Murāba'ah* is in fact only a relatively modern contract, created by mixing many different existing Islamic finance contracts. However, there is a consensus among nearly all *Figh* scholars that it is a type of deferred trading. Its cogency relies on the fact that the bank first ought to purchase the asset (become owner) and following that transfer the ownership right to the customer. The order placed by the customer is then simply a promise to purchase and not a sale contract. A promise can be binding on one party alone, as determined by the Organization of the Islamic Conference's (OIC) *Figh* Academy resolution. The Accounting and Auditing Organization for Islamic Financial Institutions (AAOIFI) and OIC *Fiqh* Academy, and nearly all Islamic banks treat the promise to purchase as binding on the customer. Nevertheless, some scholars are of the view that the contract is not binding on the customer, such that the customer, even after placing an order and paying the commitment fee, can withdraw from the contract. The most significant counterparty risk particular to *Murāba'ah* emerges because of this in that Islamic banks cannot usually charge anything in addition to the agreed upon cost for late payment by the counterparty. Consequently, late payments of dues during the stated period by the counterparty directly imply bank loses (Siti Nor Amira et al., 2014).

Salam Financing

Salam financing is subject to at least two key counterparty risks. First, counterparty risks can result from the failure to supply goods, be they on time or at all, or a failure to supply the goods with the quality contractually agreed. In addition, as the *Salam* contract is primarily for agricultural purposes and knowing that agricultural outcomes are prone to natural conditions that may prevent the client, who may have an excellent credit history, from meeting the contractual obligations, without having anything to do with the actual breaching of the contract. This causes the *Salam* contract to bear more than normal counterparty risk. Second, as *Salam* contracts require the bank to take ownership and physical delivery of the actual goods, these incur costs unique to Islamic banks associated with inventory, storage and other related price risks (Alrukhayyes, Grove, & Feldman, 2014).

Istisnā Financing

Istisnā finance exposes the capital of the bank to a multitude of specific counterparty risks. These include:

- The bank dealing under the *Istisnā* contract faces counterparty risks similar to those for *Salam* contracts. Contract failure relating to quality and the time of delivery may exist. However, the *Istisnā* contract has more control over the counterparty and is less prone to natural calamities. Hence, the *Istisnā* counterparty risk although substantially high, is not as severe as that involved in *Salam*.

- The buyer's default risk, such as a delay in making full and timely payment, is of only a general nature.
- Should the *Istisnā* contract be nonbinding, as required by some *Fiqhī* jurisdictions, the supplier is able to rescind the contract and this would constitute counterparty risk.
- Where in the case of *Istisnā* contract, the client is allowed to rescind the contract, as is the case in the *Murāba'ah* contract, and refuse to take delivery of the goods when due, this would introduce further risks, as the Islamic bank executing an *Istisnā* contract assumes responsibility for any subcontractors. It therefore has to take full responsibility for these subcontractors, be they trades people, builders, manufacturers or service providers as the bank cannot possibly act in all these capacities itself (Alrukhayyes et al., 2014).

Mushārakah (Profit and Loss Sharing) *Mudārabah* (Profit Sharing) (M-M) Financing

Numerous academic and banking strategy-oriented works regard that the distribution of funds by Islamic banks based on *Mushārakah* and *Mudārabah* is better than the fixed returns methods associated with *Murābadah*, leasing and *Istisnā'*. However, in practical terms, the use of M-M modes by Islamic banks is minimal, largely because of the extremely high credit risk involved. The credit risk is extremely high because of no need (at least as far as the contract is concerned) for collateral. There is also a high degree of moral hazard and adverse selection and the existing competencies of Islamic banks in project evaluation may be limited. One probable way to decrease the risks in profit sharing methods of financing is for Islamic banks to act as universal banks, providing both equity and conventional debt loans. This would simply mean Islamic banks providing financing solely through the *Mushārakah* method. The bank would of course need to undertake a full feasibility study prior to investing in projects, but universal banks can avoid many of the risks involved by becoming more engaged in the decision-making and management of the company by holding equity positions (Greuning & Iqbal, 2009; Iqbal, 2013).

Consequently, the bank will be capable of monitoring the use of funds by the project more closely and decrease the problem moral hazard. Nevertheless, some economists contend that banks are not actually benefiting from portfolio variation and thus, taking on more risks instead of avoiding risks by not choosing these modes. However, the application of M-M methods on both sides of the balance sheet by the bank could provide a benefit in that any shocks on the asset side will be absorbed on the credit side. It is also contended that well-matched contracts can be formulated that can decrease the impact of the moral hazard and adverse selection associated with these contracts. Nevertheless, these disregard the fact that banks essentially should specialize in managing credit portfolios not credit and equity portfolios. In addition, as the use by Islamic banks of current liabilities (deposits) is extremely high (even more so than conventional banks), shocks on the asset side may not be matched. Thus, greater application of M-M on the asset side could actually lead to systemic instability (Greuning & Iqbal, 2009; Iqbal, 2013).

Sukuk Financing

AAOIFI defines investment "*Sukuk*" as "certificates of equal value representing undivided shares in ownership of tangible assets, infrastructure and services or in the ownership of the assets of particular projects or special investment activity however, this is true after the receipt of the value of the *Sukuk*, the closing of the subscription and employment of funds received for the purpose for which the *Sukuk* were issued"(AAOIFI, 2004, p. 1). *Sukuk* have to be capable of being owned and sold lawfully, in compliance with *Shari'ah*. *Sukuk* finance models include different risks. These risks comprise both an idiosyncratic risk factor arising from Islamic finance and a systemic market risk factor. The idiosyncratic risk comprises factors such as *Shari'ah* compliance risk, institutional risk, credit risk and operational risk, while the systemic market risk contains factors such as interest rate risk, equity price risk, foreign exchange risk and commodity price risk (Najeeb, 2013; Tariq & Humayon, 2007).

Counterparty Risk in Emerging Markets

Despite the growth in Islamic banking, Islamic capital markets generally are not very well established. The sector needs to improve the sophistication and variety of the instruments on offer. Consistency across Islamic markets is also desirable, with many pronounced differences in those emerging markets practicing Islamic banking. For example, the trading of derivatives and speculation are obviously not acceptable under *Shari'ah*, but in Malaysia, the secondary market trades only debt contracts, and not equity contracts. Most *Shari'ah* scholars also agree that stock investment is permissible, but they face certain standards designed to reduce activities not permitted in *Shari'ah*, and these can vary by market. Emerging markets especially display significant variations in regulation and market behavior. Typical prohibitions include the trade in unethical services and goods, such as wineries and tobacco, the receipt of earnings from a loan (*Riba* or interest), excessive uncertainty in contracts or any business (*Gharar*), gambling and other forms of games, transactions in debt agreements at a discount, and forward exchange contracts (Fenech & Watson, 2009). The challenge is that eliminating these entirely from an equity portfolio could be virtually impossible, especially in low-depth and -breadth emerging markets. While *Shari'ah* scholars continuously review the jurisprudences to arrive at uniform rulings on investment procedures, the improvement of equity markets generally in Muslim countries would assist this, especially in relation to market rules, company disclosure and market information.

Bank Risk Management Practices in Emerging Markets

The existing literature identifies a number of features of applied risk management practices in the banking sector in emerging markets, whether Islamic or conventional banking. Essentially, we can divide the literature into four basic streams. The first stream of research discusses risks that are currently prevalent in the conventional banking system. Shafiq and Nasr (2010) contacted their study in Pakistan conventional banks and emphasized on risk management practices applied in these banks. They used primary and secondary data sources and claim that the there is a vast difference between the application of risk management features of public sector commercial banks and local private banks. In addition, for each type of commercial bank, the financial security indicators differed prominently. Even though the staff of commercial banks have an overall perceptive about risk(s) and its management, still it is important for commercial banks to plan training courses/workshops.

With respect to the practice of risk management in commercial banks in the UAE region, Al-Tamimi (2002) found that the two main methods of risk identification are inspection by bank managers and analysis of financial statements. The most common techniques exercised in risk management are benchmarking, credit score, credit worthiness analysis, risk rating, and collateral. More recently, Al-Tamimi and Al-Mazrooei (2007) examined UAE's national and foreign banks, putting focus mainly on their risk management practices. They concluded that the three most prominent categories of risks encountered by UAE's commercial banks are foreign exchange risk (being the highest), credit risk, and operating risk (being the lowest). Moreover, they found that there is not much difference between the local and foreign banks of UAE. They concluded that banks operating in UAE were able to determine possible risks related to their objectives and goals.

Alam and Masukujjaman (2011) likewise examined risk management practices of conventional banks operating in Bangladesh.

They selected date from 25 respondents across five banks with a five-point Likert scale as a measurement tool. The basic purpose of the study was to scrutinize the risk management practices of Bangladeshi banks, specifically the types of risks faced by the bank and the procedure(s) and techniques used to mitigate this risk. The study also observed the extent to which banks follow the rules and regulations set by the central bank (the Bangladesh Bank) regarding risk management. The results showed that bankers across three levels of management judged credit, market, and operational risks as the major risks. They also found that in terms of bank governance, the board of directors performed the responsibility of the main risk oversight, with the monitoring of risks done by the executive committee whereas the audit committee supervised the operations of the bank. In the context of opinions regarding the usage of risk management methods, they found that bankers considered the internal rating system less important and the risk-adjusted rate of return on capital more important.

A second stream of research explores the risk management practices applied to Islamic banks. Ahmed, Akhtar, and Usman (2011) examined the risk management practices of Islamic banks of Pakistan by specifying credit, operational and liquidity risks as dependent variables and size, leverage, the nonperforming loan (NPL) ratio, capital adequacy and asset management as explanatory variables over a period from 2006 to 2009. The results showed that bank size has a positive and statistically significant relationship with credit and liquidity risks, but a negative relation with operational risk. A positive and significant relationship was observed between asset management, liquidity, and operational risks. The debt equity ratio and NPL ratio had a negative but important relationship with liquidity and operational risks. Moreover, capital sufficiency had negative and significant relationship with credit and operational risks, whereas it had positive relation with liquidity risk. More recently, Khalid and Amjad (2012) evaluated the extent to which Pakistan's Islamic banks use risk management practices (RMPs) and methods in dealing with different types of risk. A questionnaire was distributed which focused on six features: understanding risk and risk management (URM), risk assessment and analysis (RAA), risk identification (RI), risk-monitoring (RM), credit risk analysis (CRA) and RMPs. The study concluded that Pakistani Islamic banks efficiently managed most aspects of risk, with URM, RM and CRM the keys factors determining RMPs.

The third stream of risk management research explores the link between risk management and the financial performance of banks, which has been mostly theoretical in nature. Schroeck (2002) and, Nocco and Stulz (2006) examined the significance of 'good' risk management practices resulting in the maximization of overall value. This literature clearly showed that there is a strong relationship between good risk management practices and improved financial performance. More specifically, they suggested that prudent risk management practices lessen the volatility in banks' operating income, earnings, firm's market value, share return, and return on equity. Furthermore, Schroeck (2002) advised that banks could achieve increased earnings by ensuring best-practice activities in risk management. However, there is generally little empirical evidence of the link between risk management practices and bank's financial performance. That said, work by Drzik (2005) found that investments in risk management by banks during the 1990s were useful in protecting earnings during the 2001 recession.

A similar study by Pagach and Warr (2007) observed factors that influence risk management practices. They concluded that the more leveraged the firms are, the more unpredictable their earnings. Angbazo (1997) studied the relationship between risk management and financial performance from a different perspective by testing the influence of risk factors in determining bank profitability. He found that default risk was a key determinant of a bank's net interest margin (NIM) and the NIMs of super-regional banks and regional banks were sensitive to interest rate risk as well as default risk. Saunders and Schumacher (2000) provided further support to the importance of mitigating risks as a way of smoothing financial performance by examining the determinants of NIM for 614 banks in European countries (both developed and merging) and the United States between 1988 and 1995. They concluded that interest rate volatility has a significant positive impact on bank profitability.

Hakim and Neami (2001) employed a similar approach and examined the link between credit risk and performance for banks in Egypt and Lebanon. The results indicated a positive relation between credit risk and profitability, but an insignificant relation between liquidity and profitability. Ariffin and Kassim (2011) also evaluated the logical connection between risk management practices and financial performance of the Islamic banks in Malaysia following the approach used by Hakim and Neami (2001) and, Saunders and Schumacher (2000) and using both primary data from questionnaires and secondary data from annual reports. They found that Islamic banks need to employ the more advanced risk management techniques common in conventional banks such as value-at-risk (VaR), estimates of worst-case scenarios, stress testing and simulation techniques to measure different types of risks. However, they also concluded that Islamic banks have generally good strategies for risk management practices.

In the final stream of research in this area, some studies have compared Islamic and conventional banks in relation to risk management practices. Tafri, Rahman, and Omar (2011) carried out a survey, the main purpose of which was to explore current practices and future trends in risk management techniques of Islamic and commercial banks in Malaysia. Their results clearly identified the difference in usage of risk management techniques between Islamic and conventional banks, including market VaR, stress testing results, credit risk mitigation methods, and operational risk management tools. The main reason was these risk management tools were new and thus relatively underutilized in many Islamic banks.

Most recently, Nazir, Daniel, and Nawaz (2012) compared the conventional banking system with Islamic banks in Pakistan, with that the suggestion that the method used for credit risk analysis should inherently differ for both sets of banks. They concluded that the lack of innovation in risk management practices tailored to Islamic banking required the wholesale adoption of risk management practices more appropriate for their conventional counterparts. Several extant studies have also wondered whether the lack of conventional-type risk management tools in Islamic banks was primary because of a lack of expertise. For example, the presence of IT professionals who have expertise in the field of risk analytics, IT systems to tackle Islamic styles of risk management, and experienced banking professionals in Islamic banking. Hence, more product development and innovation was required for Islamic banks so that they can improve risk management.

Many researchers believe that the risks involved in Islamic banking systems in emerging markets are both complicated as well as unique. Ullah and Chowdhury (2013) listed four common problems policymakers generally faced with Islamic finance in this regard, especially in emerging markets. The legal framework is the first, with significant differences from country to country. Some countries have chosen to have separate regulations for Islamic finance, while other countries have chosen to modify existing regulations. Transparency and clarity are vital for the legal framework to guarantee a level playing field among financial institutions in the market and to raise consumer confidence. The second is supervision and the regulation of an operational environment where both Islamic and conventional finance can coexist. This task is complex, as well as facilitated by an early identification of the requirement to develop, and plan for, instruments to manage liquidity and financial policy control. The second is the appropriate choice of a distribution channel for Islamic financial services and products to reach as many consumers as possible. Finally, there is *Shari`ah* structure governance that needs to be clearly addressed, whether in a centralized framework or a more decentralized form.

There is also a recognition that building risk management capabilities in financial institutions, as well as in central banks at a whole of economy level, requires the setting of clear priorities over the medium-term for the growth of *Shari`ah*-compliant markets and the diversity of instruments. The emerging markets most successful in terms of the sustained growth of Islamic banking are those that have prioritized the structure, capabilities, and knowledge in their central bank. Islamic finance in terms of these concerns needs to converge via mutual recognition and harmonization on an expanding range of issues. Cross-fertilization between countries in their experiences with risk management practices in Islamic banks is also taking place as countries adapt and learn from their own experiences and from the experiences of others (Ullah & Chowdhury, 2013).

Conclusion

In this chapter, we discussed the various risks that Islamic financial institutions, primarily banks, have faced through their financing activities, to provide a clear picture of the risks facing these institutions including the unique counterparty risks involved in Islamic finance and banking. Due to a distinctive risk profile, Islamic finance institutions have made risk management, especially in an emerging market context, extremely challenging. The final section of this chapter emphasized the risk management practices in both Islamic and conventional banks. Essentially, we divided the literature into four basic streams. The first stream of research discussed risks currently prevalent in the conventional banking system. The second stream explored the risk management practices in Islamic banks. The third stream explored the link between risk management and the financial performance of banks. Lastly, the final stream compared Islamic and conventional banks in relation to risk management practice.

The implications of risk management in Islamic banks in emerging markets are clearly of critical importance. We showed that there are numbers of factors that make Islamic banks even riskier in emerging markets. These include immature money markets, limitations in the availability of lender of last resort facilities, and limitations in market infrastructure. Other problems, more or less common to Islamic and conventional banks, include foreign exchange and equity risks. However, many of the standard tools used to manage currency risk, such as futures, swaps and options contracts, are either not available in emerging markets or, where available, are traded in illiquid and inefficient markets, making the overall process of hedging and unwinding of a hedge a difficult task.

Despite the idealism of Islamic banking principles and practices and the earnest endeavors of Islamic banks to compete with their conventional counterparts, until now Islamic banks have not provided evidence they have developed effective solutions for managing the same risks that conventional banks face as well as their own unique risks. We suggested that countries that do this best are those that prioritize the structure of risk management knowledge and capabilities in the central bank. Islamic banks need to converge via mutual recognition and harmonization on an expanding range of issues. Fortunately, cross-fertilization between countries in terms their experiences of risk management practices in Islamic banks is taking place as countries adapt and learn from their own experiences, and from the experiences of others.

References

AAOIFI. (2004). *Accounting, auditing & governance standards for Islamic financial institutions.* Shari'ah Standards for Financial Institutions Bahrain. Accounting and Auditing Organization of Islamic Finance Institutions.

Abedifar, P., Molyneux, P., & Tarazi, A. (2013). Risk in Islamic banking. *Review of Finance, 17*(6), 2035–2096.

Ahmed, H., Asutay, M., & Wilson, R. (2013). *Islamic banking and financial crisis: Reputation, stability and risks.* Edinburgh: Edinburgh University Press.

Ahmed, N., Akhtar, M. F., & Usman, M. (2011). Risk management practices and Islamic banks: An empirical investigation from Pakistan interdisciplinary. *Journal of Research in Business, 1*(6).

Al-Hares, O. M., AbuGhazaleh, N. M., & El-Galfy, A. M. (2013). Financial performance and compliance with Basel III capital standards: Conventional vs. Islamic banks. *The Journal of Applied Business Research, 29*(4), 18.

Al-Janabi, M. A. M. (2008). Proactive risk management in emerging and Islamic financial markets: Evidence from the Moroccan financial markets. *Humanomics, 24*(2), 20.

Al-Tamimi, H. (2002). Risk management practices: An empirical analysis of the UAE commercial banks. *Finance India, 16*(3), 1045–1057.

Al-Tamimi, H., & Al-Mazrooei, M. (2007). Banks' risk management: A comparison study of UAE national and foreign banks. *The Journal of Risk Finance*, *8*(4), 394.

Al-Wesabi, H. A. H., & Ahmad, N. H. (2013). Credit risk of Islamic banks in GCC countries. *International Journal of Banking and Finance*, *10*(2), 97–112.

Alam, M. Z., & Masukujjaman, M. (2011). Risk management practices: A critical diagnosis of some selected commercial banks in Bangladesh. *Journal of Business and Technology (Dhaka)*, *6*(01), 15–35.

Alrukhayyes, Z., Grove, H., & Feldman, J. (2014). Islamic banks risk management case. *Online Journal of International Case Analysis*, *5*(2), 1.

Angbazo, L. (1997). Commercial bank net interest margins, default risk, interest rate risk, and offbalance sheet banking. *Journal of Banking and Finance*, *21*(1), 55–87.

Archer, S., & Karim, R. A. A. (2013). *Operational risk exposures of Islamic banks* (pp. 133–152). Singapore: Wiley.

Ariffin, M., & Kassim, H. (2011). Risk management practices and financial performance of Islamic banks. Paper presented at the Malaysian Evidence Paper presented at the 8th International Conference on Islamic Economics and Finance. National Convention Center, Qatar. Retrieved from http://conference.qfis.edu.qa/app/media/271

Bitar, B. A. (2015). *Risk management under Shariah law: Products, techniques and competitiveness* (p. 64). Berlin: Anchor Academic Publishing.

Chattha, J. A., & Halim, W. N. W. A. (2014). *Strengthening the financial safety net: The role of Sharia'h Compliant Lender-Of-Last-Resort (SLOLR) facilities as an emergency financing mechanism*. IFSB Working Paper Series. Retrieved from http://www.ifsb.org/docs/WP-01_(2014%20April)%20Working%20Paper%20on%20SLOLR.pdf

Drzik, J. (2005). New directions in risk management. *Journal of Financial Econometrics*, *3*(1), 26–36.

Fenech, J. P., & Watson, J. (2009). The use of fixed income in emerging markets: Empirical evidence. *Banks and Bank Systems*, *4*(1), 11–18.

Gait, A., & Worthington, A. C. (2014). A primer on Islamic finance. In A. C. Worthington (Ed.), *Contemporary issues in Islamic finance: Principles, progress, and prospects* (pp. 7–29). New York, NY: Nova Publishing.

Greuning, H. V., & Iqbal, Z. (2009). Risk analysis for Islamic banks. *J.KAU: Islamic Economics*, *22*(1), 7.

Hakim, S., & Neami, S. (2001). *Performance and credit risk in banking: A comparative study of Egypt and Lebanon*. ERF Working Paper Series, Working Paper No. 0137. Retrieved from http://www.erf.org.eg/CMS/uploads/pdf/0137.pdf

IFSB-IDB-IRTS. (2010, April). *Islamic finance and global financial stability report 2010*. Kuala Lumpur: Islamic Financial Services Board.

Iqbal, M. (2013). Islamic finance: An attractive new way of financial intermediation. *International Journal of Banking and Finance, 10*(2), 25.
Khalid, S., & Amjad, S. (2012). Risk management practices in Islamic banks of Pakistan. *The Journal of Risk Finance, 13*(2), 148–159.
Mokni, R. B. S., Echchabi, A., Azouzi, D., & Rachdi, H. (2014). Risk management tools practiced in Islamic banks: Evidence in MENA region. *Journal of Islamic Accounting and Business Research, 5*(1), 77–97. doi:10.1108/JIABR-10-2012-0070
Najeeb, S. F. (2013). Managing business and financial risks of Sukuk: An Islamic risk management perspective. *Journal of Islamic Business and Management, 3*(2), 26.
Nazir, M. S., Daniel, A., & Nawaz, M. M. (2012). Risk management practises: A comparison of conventional and Islamic banks in Pakistan. *American Journal of Scientific Research, 68*, 114–122.
Nocco, W., & Stulz, R. (2006). *Enterprise risk management: Theory and practice*. Ohio State University working paper. USA. Retrieved from http://ssrn.com/abstract=921402 or http://dx.doi.org/10.2139/ssrn.921402
Pagach, D. P., & Warr, R. S. (2007). *An empirical investigation of the characteristics of firms adopting enterprise risk management*. Retrieved from http://papers.ssrn.com/sol3/papers.cfm?abstract_id=1010200
Paldi, C. (2014). Capital adequacy, liquidity, and risk: Is Islamic banking too expensive? *Journal of Islamic Banking and Finance, 2*(1), 407–411.
Rahman, M. M., Rahman, M. A., & Azad, M. A. K. (2015). Risk management practices in Islamic and conventional banks of Bangladesh: A comparative analysis. *Asian Social Science, 11*(18), 153–163.
Saunders, A., & Schumacher, L. (2000). The determinants of bank interest rate margins: An international study. *Journal of International Money and Finance, 19*(6), 813–832.
Schroeck, G. (2002). *Risk management and value creation in financial institutions*. Canada: Wiley.
Shafiq, A., & Nasr, M. (2010). Risk management practices followed by the commercial banks in Pakistan. *Journal of International Review of Business Research Papers, 6*(2), 308–325.
Siti Nor Amira, M., Mohamad, B., Muhammad Ridhwan, A.-A., Khairil, K., Mazlynda, Y., & Hisham, S. (2014). Islamic credit risk management in Murabahah financing-the study of Islamic banking in Malaysia. *Australian Journal of Basic and Applied Sciences, 8*(6), 318–323.
Tafri, F. H., Rahman, R. A., & Omar, N. (2011). Empirical evidence on the risk management tools practised in Islamic and conventional banks. *Qualitative Research in Financial Markets, 3*(2), 86–104.

Tariq, A. A., & Humayon, D. (2007). Risks of Sukuk structures: Implications for resource mobilization. *Thunderbird International Business Review*, *49*(2), 20.

Ullah, M. M., & Chowdhury, M. S. A. (2013). Prospects of Islamic banking in Bangladesh. Published Paper. Presented at the Proceedings of 3rd Asia-Pacific Business Research Conference, Kuala Lumpur, Malaysia. Retrieved from http://www.wbiworldconpro.com/uploads/malaysia-conference-2013/banking/611-Shahnur.pdf

Zamir, I. (2014). Post-crisis regulatory environment and implications for Islamic financial services industry. *Journal of Islamic Banking and Finance*, *31*(1), 10.

Zepeda, R. (2013). Enhancing Islamic finance through risk benchmarking. *The Capco Institute Journal of Financial Transformation*, *38*(1), 17–34.

9

Value at Risk Prediction under Illiquid Market Conditions: A Comparison of Alternative Modeling Strategies

Mazin A. M. Al Janabi

Abstract

Given the rising need for measuring and controlling of financial risk as proposed in Basel II and Basel III Capital Adequacy Accords, trading risk assessment under illiquid market conditions plays an increasing role in banking and financial sectors, particularly in emerging financial markets. The purpose of this chapter is to investigate asset liquidity risk and to obtain a Liquidity-Adjusted Value at Risk (L-VaR) estimation for various equity portfolios. The assessment of L-VaR is performed by implementing three different asset liquidity models within a multivariate context along with

GARCH-M method (to estimate expected returns and conditional volatility) and by applying meaningful financial and operational constraints. Using more than six years of daily return dataset of emerging Gulf Cooperation Council (GCC) stock markets, we find that under certain trading strategies, such as short selling of stocks, the sensitivity of L-VaR statistics are rather critical to the selected internal liquidity model in addition to the degree of correlation factors among trading assets. As such, the effects of extreme correlations (plus or minus unity) are crucial aspects to consider in selecting the most adequate internal liquidity model for economic capital allocation, especially under crisis condition and/or when correlations tend to switch sings. This chapter bridges the gap in risk management literatures by providing real-world asset allocation tactics that can be used for trading portfolios under adverse markets' conditions. The approach to computing L-VaR has been arrived at through the application of three distinct liquidity models and the obtained results are used to draw conclusions about the relative liquidity of the diverse equity portfolios.

Keywords: Asset allocation; emerging markets; financial risk management; liquidity risk; portfolio management; Liquidity-Adjusted Value at Risk (L-VaR)

Introduction and Motivation

Techniques for assessing trading (or market) risk have been well established in the academic alongside the banking/financial industry. In contrast, asset liquidity risk has gained less attention, maybe since it is less important in developed financial markets where most of the market risk management methods were coined. Nevertheless, the recent rapid expansion of emerging markets' financial trading activities besides the frequent turbulences in those markets has driven liquidity trading risk to the forefront of financial risk management research and development (Al Janabi, 2008, 2013).

Asset liquidity trading risk is an all-embracing apprehension for anyone holding a portfolio of any type of trading assets and liquidity crises proved to be imperative in the failure of many well-known financial entities. In general, asset liquidity trading risk arises from situations in which a party interested in trading certain assets cannot do it because no one in the market wants to trade those assets. Asset liquidity risk becomes for the most part significant to financial market participants who are about to hold or currently hold certain assets, as it influences their capacity to trade or unwind (close-out) the trading positions. Insolvencies often arise because financial institutions cannot get out or unwind their holdings successfully and hence the liquidation value of trading assets may differ considerably from their current mark-to-market values (Al Janabi, 2011a, 2011b). For all financial entities that are market-makers in financial securities, the question propounded for managing financial risk as well as for regulators is: What is your ability to close-out the trading position fully, or as a minimum to hedge its exposure effectively?

In fact, the traditional Value at Risk (VaR) methodology to assessing market (or trading) risk of a portfolio does not consider explicitly liquidity trading risk. Mainstream VaR models assess the worst change in mark-to-market portfolio value over a given time horizon but do not account for the actual trading risk of liquidation. As such, conventional fine-tunings are made on an ad hoc basis. At the most, the liquidation horizon (or holding period) over which the VaR figures are considered is tweaked to ensure the enclosure of liquidity risk. As a result, liquidity risk can be roughly factored into VaR valuations by assuring that the liquidation interval is as a minimum larger than an orderly liquidation horizon (Al Janabi, 2011a, 2011b). Likewise, the same close-out period is applied to all trading asset classes, albeit certain assets may be more liquid than others. Undoubtedly, overlooking liquidity risk can lead to an underestimation of the total market risk and misuse of capital cushion (i.e., economic capital) for the safety and soundness of financial institutions. In emerging financial markets, which are fairly regarded as illiquid, ignoring the liquidity risk can induce substantial underestimation of the VaR estimate, mainly under severe market conditions (Al Janabi, 2008, 2011a, 2011b, 2013). As a result, the growth in trading of equities in emerging markets demands a reassessment of current market and liquidity risk management techniques and methods, specifically for investment funds with trading portfolios of either long-only positions or a combination of long/short trading positions.

To measure the different risks involved in their trading operations, major financial entities are increasingly using VaR techniques. Since financial institutions differ in their particular traits, a tailor-made internal risk models are more suitable. Moreover, the increase in the relative importance of trading risk in financial institutions' portfolios has obliged regulators to reconsider the system of capital requirements as outlined in the previous Basel Capital Accords. Fortunately, and in line with the latest Basel Capital Accord (so-called Basel II and Basel III), financial institutions are allowed to build their own internal risk models for the purposes of risk measurement and to set thereafter the required regulatory capital cushion to contain unforeseen markets turmoil. Furthermore, internal risk models can be used in the determination of economic capital that financial institutions must hold to endorse their trading of securities (Al Janabi, 2011a, 2011b, 2013).[1]

In line with Basel II and Basel III capital adequacy accords, financial entities can develop their own internal risk management models with the objective of assessing the amount of regulatory and economic capital (risk capital) necessary to back their diverse proprietary trading actions. However, different internal risk models will certainly produce different capital adequacy and the question that may arise is: which internal asset liquidity market risk model is the most suitable one and under what market condition its performance can be assessed? To this end, this chapter attempts

1. For further discussion on economic capital and its assessment, we refer the readers to Al Janabi (2013) research paper.

to answer this question by comparing three distinct asset liquidity risk multipliers (or asset liquidity risk model factors) and determines the impact of liquidating trading assets during the unwinding period on the economic capital that financial institutions are required to retain in order to absorb unexpected market shocks. The three asset liquidity models that are used in this research are the *RiskMetrics*^{TM} (Morgan Guaranty Trust Company, 1994), and the two asset liquidity multipliers developed by Al Janabi (2007, 2008, 2011a, 2011b, 2013).

Set against this background, the emphasis of this chapter is on asset liquidity trading risk assessment using a multivariate L-VaR methodology that centers on the measurement of L-VaR under the notion of different unwinding horizons and correlation factors, trading volumes, and forecasted conditional volatility and expected returns with a generalized autoregressive conditional heteroscedasticity in mean (GARCH-M) technique. This chapter is focused on defining a practical technique for asset liquidity risk management; with a specific focus on multiple assets portfolios (within a long/short trading framework) and subject to applying realistic financial and operational boundary limits. With the aim of establishing a doable risk management structure, it examines four questions:

(1) How can asset liquidity trading risk be well-defined and determined? (2) How much a financial entity can lose under adverse illiquid market circumstances? (3) How can a financial institution select the most appropriate internal trading risk model? (4) What is the impact of undesirable events on the economic capital of different internal asset liquidity models?

Literature Review and Underlying Principle of the Chapter

Literatures Associated with Liquidity-Adjusted Value at Risk (L-VaR) Modeling

The blend of the rapid growth of emerging markets' proprietary trading events and the continuing turbulences in those developing markets has prompted asset liquidity risk to the frontline of market risk research and development. As such, Jarrow and Subramanian (1997), offer a market impact model of liquidity by allowing for the optimal liquidation of a portfolio over a fixed time horizon and within a VaR framework. By supposing that the time horizon until liquidation is set as an exogenous factor, they develop the optimal execution scheme by defining the assets sales schedule that can maximize the expected total sales values. While the applied model is relatively uncomplicated, it has certain problems for its implementation in the practical world (Al Janabi, 2011a, 2012).

Other authors, such as Bangia, Diebold, Schuermann, and Stroughair (2002), approach the liquidity risk from another angle by focusing on the assessment of transactions cost liquidity risk and by providing a methodology of VaR tailored for exogenous liquidity. Bangia et al. (2002) method consists of assessing exogenous liquidity risk through the use of the observed distributions of bid-ask spreads and then incorporating it into a typical VaR structure. Indeed, their model does not accommodate endogenous liquidity — which varies across market participants and is mainly driven by the size of the position (Al Janabi, 2011a, 2012). The Bangia et al. (2002) correction to VaR is appropriate only for continuously traded markets such as currencies.

In a different vein, Almgren and Chriss (2001) derive a certain method for developing the optimal execution strategy using a mean-variance technique. In fact, their method has a high promise for practical use (Al Janabi, 2011a). Unlike Almgren and Chriss (2001), Hisata and Yamai (2000) and Dubil (2002) extend the previous framework in order to endogenize the final liquidation horizon. Both approaches consider the risk of a liquidation strategy in a VaR setup and assume a constant speed of trading. Indeed, the two frameworks basically differ in the way they specify the dynamics of the asset price process and in the parameterization of the impact function, yet they derive similar results.

Recently, in his research papers, Al Janabi (2008, 2011a, 2011b, 2013) examines the measures of the risk of adverse price impact and, hence, establishes a practical technique for the assessment of market risk. The impacts of asset liquidity, that are central traits of emerging markets, are also integrated into the risk assessment methodologies. These literatures offer practical risk management methods and tactics that can be applied to trading and investment portfolios in emerging financial markets.

Furthermore, in a previous paper, Al Janabi (2007) derives a simple, however different, liquidity multiplier that focuses on the liquidation of trading asset. In his paper, the author proposes a linear liquidation model of the trading asset; or in other words, the trader can proceed by selling equal fractions of each asset every day till the last trading day, where the entire asset is fully sold. The essence of this model is based on the assumption that the remaining unsold fractions are the only *"left-over"* amounts of the trading asset that can be influenced, during the next trading day, by the time-varying volatility of the illiquid asset. In this manner, if the asset position is liquidated in equal parts during each trading day, the trader faces an increase in the asset liquidity risk factor on a 1-day holding period by ($1/t$) of the total position, a 2-day holding period on a fraction ($2/t$) of the position, a 3-day holding period on a fraction ($3/t$) of the position and so forth. Evidently, the additional asset liquidity risk factor depends only on the number of days (t) needed to sell an illiquid trading position linearly. As such, the proposed asset liquidity multiplier can also be used to calculate L-VaR for any specific time horizon.

Underpinnings and Particular Objectives of Present Research Study

Indeed, despite the growing position of the Gulf Cooperation Council (GCC) financial markets, there is a very limited published research literatures in this regard and above all within the context of asset liquidity risk assessment. Likewise, to the best of our knowledge, no work has been published yet on asset liquidity risk management in any international literature that considers the GCC zone as a case study using a comparison of different liquidity modeling techniques. This chapter makes the following contributions to the academic literature in this particular asset liquidity risk management field. Firstly, it describes one of the limited number of empirical research studies that investigates asset liquidity risk management applying real financial dataset of the six GCC financial markets. Secondly, a dataset of the six GCC states stock markets indices is used whose performance is apparently more diverse than if equity assets of any certain stock market had been applied. Thirdly, different to other empirical studies in this specific field, this chapter applies a systematic and reliable risk estimation models that consider risk assessment under normal and severe illiquid market settings and by using the GARCH-M technique for the appraisal of time-varying conditional volatility. Fourthly, this chapter implements and compares three distinct asset liquidity multipliers for minimizing the amount of economic capital within L-VaR context. To this end, a robust L-VaR process is presented to allocate equity assets by minimizing L-VaR subject to imposing certain meaningful financial and operational constraints. The focus on L-VaR as the competent measure of economic capital allows risk managers and fund managers to allocate the preferred liquidity horizon and to distribute long and short trading assets in proportion to rational market trading situations. In this sense, the present work is closer to the actual actions of fund managers who apply, in some relevant way, active asset allocation trading strategies subject to maximum L-VaR trading boundaries (i.e., risk-budgeting).

To this end, this empirical research study shows that the amount of economic capital as measured by L-VaR depends on the designated internal asset liquidity model, degree of correlation among assets under unfavorable market outlooks, expected returns and conditional volatility as estimated by the GARCH-M model, the volume of long/short-sales trading positions, the liquidity unwinding periods of each trading asset, and the proportions allocated to each asset (i.e., portfolio weights). Furthermore, in this chapter, the comparative performance of the different selected L-VaR models is evaluated within an active asset allocation context. The main aim of active asset allocation is to find the least amount of economic capital (of each internal asset liquidity multiplier) at which L-VaR is minimized conditional on the implementation of certain financial and operational constraints, which are justified by underlying asset management practices.

The empirical analyses are provided using daily database of the six GCC countries' stock markets for the period 2004–2009.[2] Several empirical case studies are carried out with the objective of assessing L-VaR under adverse illiquid market conditions. The L-VaR estimates have been obtained for various equity trading portfolios in the GCC stock markets through the application of an amended closed-form parametric L-VaR methodology and by employing three different asset liquidity models. The obtained empirical results show that our method functions much better than the typical mean-variance (i.e., Markowitz, 1959) VaR technique in terms of determining the amount of economic capital and in shaping the portfolio manager's active trading and/or investment portfolios.

The rest of the chapter proceeds as follows. The following section discusses the quantitative infrastructure of L-VaR, its limitations, and the incorporation of asset liquidity risk into a parametric trading risk infrastructure. First, we show that L-VaR can be derived for a single-asset portfolio and then we derive a general and broad model that incorporates the effects of multiple illiquid assets in daily market risk management (by simply scaling the multi-assets' L-VaR matrix) and by implementing three distinct internal asset liquidity models. Finally, we demonstrate, by applying L-VaR measures to the GCC stock markets, to what extent the quantified liquidity effects can affect conventional assessment of trading risk by putting into practice the three different asset liquidity models. The results of empirical analysis are included in the final section together with conclusions and recommendations.

2. The 2004–2009 time horizon includes the impact of the most severe period of the latest sub-prime financial crisis on the GCC's financial market.

Incorporating Asset Liquidity Risk into Parametric Trading Risk Modeling[3]

Statistical Foundation of a Coherent L-VaR Approach

A streamlined calculation process for the estimation of VaR's risk factors (using a closed-form parametric method) for a single and multiple assets' trading positions is illustrated as follows (Al Janabi, 2011a, 2011b, 2013):

We begin by defining one-day asset return at time t, $R_{i,t}$ to be the log difference of mid-prices:

$$R_{i,t} = \ln(P_{i,t}) - \ln(P_{i,t-1}) = \ln\left[\frac{(P_{i,t})}{(P_{i,t-1})}\right] \tag{1}$$

where $R_{i,t}$ is the daily return of asset i, ln is the natural logarithm; $P_{i,t}$ is the current price level of asset i, and $P_{i,t-1}$ is the previous day asset price. Accordingly, by taking a one-day horizon over which the change in asset value is considered, and assuming that one-day returns are Gaussian, the worst VaR of a single asset in monetary terms is:

$$\text{VaR}_i = \alpha^* \text{Mark-to-Market Value of Equity}_i{}^* \text{Fx}_i{}^* \sigma_i \tag{2}$$

where α is the confidence level (or in other words, the standard normal variant at confidence level α) and σ_i is the conditional volatility of the return of the equity asset and can be assessed, for instance, by using a GARCH-M technique. The *"Mark-to-Market Value of Equity"* specifies the amount of cash investment in equity asset i (henceforth A_i) and Fx_i indicates the unit foreign exchange rate of equity asset i. Without a loss of generality, we have assumed in the above formula that the expected value of daily returns $E\,[R_{i,t}]$ is zero. Though Eq. (2) includes some simplifying

3. This risk modeling section is a concise outline of detailed technical methodologies and is largely drawn from Al Janabi (2007, 2008, 2011a, 2011b, 2013) research papers.

suppositions, yet it is consistently used by researchers and practitioners in financial markets for the assessment of VaR for a single equity trading position.

Asset trading risk in the presence of multiple risk factors is determined by the combined effect of individual risk factors. As such, the extent of the total risk is determined not only by the magnitudes of the individual risks but also by their interrelated movements. For multiple assets, VaR is a function of individual security's risk factors and the correlation factor $[\rho_{i,j}]$ between the expected returns of the different securities as follows:

$$\mathrm{VaR}_P = \sqrt{\sum_{i=1}^{n}\sum_{j=1}^{n} \mathrm{VaR}_i \, \mathrm{VaR}_j \, \rho_{i,j}} = \sqrt{|\mathrm{VaR}|^T |\rho| |\mathrm{VaR}|} \qquad (3)$$

Equation (3) is a general formula for the estimation of VaR_P for any portfolio irrespective of the number of trading assets. It is important to emphasize that the second term of Eq. (3) is rewritten in terms of vectors. The vectors presentation is indeed a useful form to circumvent mathematical complication, can aid in streamlining the programming process and can enable easy integration of short-sales trading operations in the risk assessment route.

In effect, VaR technique is only one tactic of assessing market risk and it is primarily related to the appraisal of the maximum expected portfolio losses under normal market outlooks. It is indeed not an absolute measure of risk, as the real amount of loss may be bigger than the given VaR figures under adverse market environments. In extreme circumstances, VaR methods do not perform properly. To this end, financial entities should enhance VaR assessment with scenario-analysis and stress-testing techniques. In this chapter, a risk management process is established to evaluate possible event risk under the notion of several unwinding periods, different correlation parameters and by implementing three different liquidity assessment models.

Modeling Asset Liquidity Trading Risk in L-VaR Context

The simplest way to account for liquidity trading risk is to extend the holding period of illiquid positions to reflect a suitable liquidation period. An adjustment can be made by adding a multiplier to the VaR measure of each trading asset type, which at the end depends on the liquidity of each individual security. Nonetheless, the weakness of this method is that it allows for subjective estimation of the liquidation period. Furthermore, the typical assumption of a one-day horizon (or any inflexible time horizon) within VaR framework, neglects any calculation of trading risk related to liquidity effect (i.e., when and whether a trading position can be sold and at what price). A broad VaR model should incorporate an asset liquidity premium (or asset liquidity risk factor). This can be worked out by formulating a method by which one can unwind a position, not at some ad hoc rate, but at the rate that market conditions is optimal, so that one can effectively set a risk value for the liquidity effects. In general, this will raise significantly the VaR, or the amount of economic capital to support the trading position (Al Janabi, 2012).

In fact, if returns are independent and they can have any elliptical multivariate distribution, then it is possible to convert the VaR horizon parameter from daily to any t-day horizon. The variance of a t-day return should be t times the variance of a 1-day return or $\sigma^2 = f(t)$. Thus, in terms of standard deviation (or volatility), $\sigma = f(\sqrt{t})$ and the daily or overnight VaR can be adjusted for any t-day horizon as:

$$\left(L - \mathrm{VaR}_{\mathrm{adj}}\right)_{\mathrm{RM}} = \mathrm{VaR}\sqrt{t} \tag{4}$$

Equation (4) was suggested by *J.P. Morgan* in their former *RiskMetrics™* technique (1994), hereafter *RM* asset liquidity model. This approach indirectly supposes that asset liquidation happens in one block sale at the end of the unwinding period (holding horizon) and that there is one close-out period for all trading assets, irrespective of their liquidity composition. In fact, this technique does not take into consideration real-life proprietary trading circumstances, where traders can unwind certain amounts of their holding assets on a daily basis (Al Janabi, 2012).[4] In order to perform the calculation of VaR under illiquid market conditions, Al Janabi (2007) proposes a linear liquidation modeling approach (henceforth AJ(1) asset liquidity model) in which one can sell equal parts of each asset every day till the last trading day, where the entire asset is fully sold. The same approach can also be used to calculate the L-VaR for any specific time horizon and as follows:

$$\left(L - \mathrm{VaR}_{\mathrm{adj}}\right)_{\mathrm{AJ}(1)} = \mathrm{VaR}\sqrt{\frac{(t+1)}{2}} \tag{5}$$

where t is the number of liquidation days (t-day to liquidate the entire asset fully). Under this daily liner-liquidation approach, one can define two separate VaR components. The first VaR represents Value at Risk under liquid market conditions and the second $\left(L - \mathrm{VaR}_{\mathrm{adj}}\right)_{\mathrm{AJ}(1)}$ represents Value at Risk under illiquid market conditions using AJ(1) model. Consequently, the difference between $\left[\left(L - \mathrm{VaR}_{\mathrm{adj}}\right)_{\mathrm{AJ}(1)} - \mathrm{VaR}\right]$ should equal to the residual market risk due to the illiquidity of any asset under illiquid markets settings.

While the above approach represents an important practical improvement on the square root of time method (i.e., *RiskMetrics*™ (1994)), in recent studies Al Janabi (2008, 2011a, 2011b, 2013) proposes an alternative asset liquidation model.

4. Although the RiskMetrics model implicitly assumes that financial markets participants may liquidate their assets only at the end of the close-out period (i.e., it is a more conservative approach and could perhaps overestimate the amount of economic capital), it is still has its use within the financial market industry. Indeed, the RiskMetrics group was listed in 2008 on the New York Stock Exchange (NYSE) and was acquired thereafter in the year 2010 by MSCI group. In 2006, a new methodology for modeling risk factor returns was introduced (namely; RM2006). The new RM2006 method to evaluate market risks is devised to be more accurate than existing techniques as it has the ability to forecast long risk horizons. For further details on RiskMetrics models, we refer the readers to Zumbach (2007) and the following web-link: https://en.wikipedia.org/wiki/RiskMetrics

The new model is based on a different re-engineered approach for calculating a closed-form parametric VaR with explicit treatment of liquidity trading risk. The essence of the model relies on the assumption of a stochastic stationary process and some rules of thumb, which can be of crucial value for more accurate overall trading risk assessment during market stress periods when liquidity dries up. To this end, a practical framework of a methodology (within a simplified mathematical approach) is proposed by Al Janabi (2008, 2011a, 2011b, 2013) for the incorporation of assets' daily L-VaR. The end result of his technique is a realistic mathematical expression of time and it is certainly quite different from the square root of time function that is used by certain risk managers based on *RiskMetrics*^{TM} (1994) practices. Furthermore, the proposed methodology can also be used to assess L-VaR for any close-out period. With the purpose of performing a realistic estimation of VaR under illiquid market settings, Al Janabi (2008, 2011a, 2011b, 2013) defines the following (henceforth AJ(2) asset liquidity model):

$$\left(L-\mathrm{VaR_{adj}}\right)_{\mathrm{AJ(2)}}=\mathrm{VaR}\sqrt{\frac{(2t+1)(t+1)}{6t}} \tag{6}$$

where VaR = Value at Risk under liquid market conditions, $\left(L-\mathrm{VaR_{adj}}\right)_{\mathrm{AJ(2)}}$ = Value at Risk under illiquid market conditions using AJ(2) model, and t = number of liquidation days (i.e., t-days to unwind any particular equity asset completely). The former equation also specifies that $\left(L-\mathrm{VaR_{adj}}\right)_{\mathrm{AJ(2)}} > \mathrm{VaR}$, and for the exceptional case when the close-out period equals one trading day, Eq. (6) is reduced to $\left(L-\mathrm{VaR_{adj}}\right)_{\mathrm{AJ(2)}} = \mathrm{VaR}$. As a result, the spread between $\left(L-\mathrm{VaR_{adj}}\right)_{\mathrm{AJ(2)}} - \mathrm{VaR}$ should be equivalent to the remaining market risk associated with the illiquidity of any particular asset under adverse markets environments. In fact, by choosing any t-days to liquidate the assets positions, the AJ(2) model, once compared with the RM and AJ(1) models, should intuitively produce lower asset liquidity risk than the other two models. As such, the AJ(2) model could even lead to an additional decrease in the total portfolio market risk; and thus in the required total sum of regulatory capital and/or economic capital, as stated by Basel II and Basel III capital adequacy requirements. Nevertheless, as we will deduce later on, this is not always the case mainly under adverse market conditions, in which the correlation between the risk factors increases to unity or otherwise switches signs.

In order to calculate L-VaR, implementing any of the three asset liquidity risk multipliers as discussed above [i.e., Eqs. (4), (5) or (6)], for the entire trading portfolio under illiquid market conditions ($L-\mathrm{VaR}_{\mathrm{P}_{\mathrm{adj}}}$), the above mathematical formulation can be extended with the aid of Eq. (3) into a matrix-algebra form to yield the following:

$$L-\mathrm{VaR}_{\mathrm{P}_{\mathrm{adj}}} = \sqrt{\left|L-\mathrm{VaR}_{\mathrm{adj}}\right|^{T}\left|\rho\right|\left|L-\mathrm{VaR}_{\mathrm{adj}}\right|} \qquad (7)$$

It should be noted that when reporting individual L-$\mathrm{VaR}_{\mathrm{adj}}$ these figures are always taken as positive, even though they represent a loss (which conventionally has a negative sign). In assessing the portfolio $L-\mathrm{VaR}_{P_{\mathrm{adj}}}$ the sign of each trading asset "A_i" must be incorporated into the $\left|L-\mathrm{VaR}_{\mathrm{adj}}\right|^{T}$ and $\left|L-\mathrm{VaR}_{\mathrm{adj}}\right|$ vectors. That is, if the asset position is held long (i.e., you own it), then the $A_i > 0$, but if the asset has been sold short, then $A_i < 0$.

Worst-case $L-\mathrm{VaR}_{P_{\mathrm{adj}}}$ (or undiversified $L-\mathrm{VaR}_{P}$) can be deduced as a special case of Eq. (7) under the assumption that asset returns are perfectly positively correlated ($\rho = +1$) and that there are positive amounts of each asset. This indeed will give the worst-case scenario, since there are no benefits from diversification by holding multiple assets. Thus, the maximum value $L-\mathrm{VaR}_{P_{\mathrm{adj}}}$ can take is given by setting $\rho = +1$ in Eq. (7), which gives:

$$\begin{aligned}\text{Worst case } L-\mathrm{VaR}_{P_{\mathrm{adj}}} &= L-\mathrm{VaR}_{\mathrm{adj}_1} + L-\mathrm{VaR}_{\mathrm{adj}_2} + \cdots\cdots + L-\mathrm{VaR}_{\mathrm{adj}_n} \\ &= \sum_{i=1}^{n} L-\mathrm{VaR}_{\mathrm{adj}_i} \qquad (8)\end{aligned}$$

Hence, in a worst-case scenario the $L-\mathrm{VaR}_{P_{\mathrm{adj}}}$ is simply the sum of the individual $L-\mathrm{VaR}_{\mathrm{adj}_i}$. In real-world practices it is unlikely that the correlations parameters between the returns of assets are perfectly correlated (i.e., $\rho = +1$). However, under severe or crisis periods, it is often the case that correlation factors increase in value, and the worst-case $L - \text{VaR}_{P_{\text{adj}}}$ provides a high figure that may be representative of these crisis periods. Indeed, in real-world risk management practices, risk and fund managers usually look at both the diversified $L - \text{VaR}_{P_{\text{adj}}}$ [Eq. (7)] and the worst-case $L - \text{VaR}_{P_{\text{adj}}}$ [Eq. (8)]. Indeed, this gives the risk and fund managers a realistic view of what would happen if historical correlations did not stay the same but rather increase in value during a crisis period. Moreover, it is worth noting that if $\rho = +1$ and one or more of the constituent trading assets is a short-sales position (i.e., $A_i < 0$), then there will be some risk offset and hence the worst-case scenario $L - \text{VaR}_{P_{\text{adj}}}$of Eq. (8) cannot be held as a representative of the maximum loss of the trading portfolio.

Furthermore, the above mathematical structure of Eq. (7) (in the form of two vectors and one matrix, $|L - \text{VaR}_{\text{adj}}|$, $|L - \text{VaR}_{\text{adj}}|^T$and $|\rho|$) can facilitate the programming process so that the trading risk manager can specify different liquidation days for the whole portfolio and/or for each individual trading security according to the necessary number of days to liquidate the entire asset fully.

On another front, the above mathematical design can aid in the establishment of optimal L-VaR limits, minimum economic capital, and proper asset allocation of trading portfolios by imposing rational financial and operational boundaries (constraints) based on underlying investment principles, detailed as follows.

From Eqs. (4), (5), and (6) and based on the definition of the three asset liquidity multipliers, we can define three asset-liquidity-horizon-factor (ALHF_i) for any trading asset i as:

$$(\text{ALHF}_i)_{\text{RM}} = \sqrt{t_i} \tag{9}$$

$$(\text{ALHF}_i)_{\text{AJ}(1)} = \sqrt{\frac{(t_i + 1)}{2}} \tag{10}$$

$$(\text{ALHF}_i)_{\text{AJ}(2)} = \sqrt{\frac{(2t_i + 1)(t_i + 1)}{6t_i}} \tag{11}$$

To compute maximum L-VaR trading limits, employing any of the above three asset liquidity risk multipliers, we can solve for the following quadratic linear-programming formulation (i.e., objective function) with the aid of Eq. (7), to yield:

$$\text{Maximize: } L-\mathrm{VaR}_{P_{\mathrm{adj}}} = \sqrt{\left|L-\mathrm{VaR}_{\mathrm{adj}}\right|^{T}\left|\rho\right|\left|L-\mathrm{VaR}_{\mathrm{adj}}\right|} \tag{12}$$

On the other hand, to compute optimal portfolios and proper asset allocation weight factors besides minimum economic capital, we can resolve the following quadratic linear-programming objective function via Eq. (7), to yield:

$$\text{Minimize: } L-\mathrm{VaR}_{P_{\mathrm{adj}}} = \sqrt{\left|L-\mathrm{VaR}_{\mathrm{adj}}\right|^{T}\left|\rho\right|\left|L-\mathrm{VaR}_{\mathrm{adj}}\right|} \tag{13}$$

Indeed, both maximization and minimization algorithms can be resolved conditional on applying certain meaningful financially and operationally budget constraints and boundary limits, when are available, on the L-VaR optimization algorithm, detailed along these lines:

$$\sum_{i=1}^{n} R_i x_i = R_P;\, l_i \le x_i \le u_i \quad i = 1, 2, \ldots, n \tag{14}$$

$$|\mathrm{LHF}| \ge 1.0;\, \forall_i \quad i = 1, 2, \ldots, n \tag{15}$$

$$\sum_{i=1}^{n} x_i = 1.0;\, l_i \le x_i \le u_i \quad i = 1, 2, \ldots, n \tag{16}$$

$$\sum_{i=1}^{n} V_i = V_P \quad i = 1, 2, \ldots, n \tag{17}$$

where R_P and V_P indicate the mean return of the target portfolio and total trading volume respectively, and x_i the asset allocation weight for each asset class. The values l_i and u_i, $i = 1, 2, \ldots, n$

denote the lower and upper constraints for the portfolio weights x_i. If we choose $l_i = 0$, $i = 1, 2,..., n$, then we have the condition where no short-sales are permitted. Furthermore, |LHF| denotes an (nx1) vector for all $i = 1, 2,..., n$. The logic of enforcing the above constraints and boundary limits is to conform with contemporary international regulations. These regulations (such as, Basel II and III capitalization rules) impose capital adequacy requirements on investment companies according to the estimated overall VaR and/or L-VaR of trading portfolios in addition to other operational constraints (for example, volume trading boundaries).

Comparing and Testing the Performance of L-VaR Models — Empirical Analysis of the GCC Stock Markets

In this research study, datasets of daily price returns of the six GCC stock markets' main indicators (indices), for the period October 17, 2004–May 22, 2009, are gathered, filtered, and adequately adapted as inputs for the calculation of all risk factors within an L-VaR framework. These datasets are drawn from Reuters 3000 Xtra Hosted Terminal Platform and Thomson's Datastream database. In fact, the selected 2004–2009 time horizon includes the impact of the most severe period of the latest subprime financial crisis on the GCC's financial market.

Because the objective of this chapter is to examine risk analysis and portfolio management under crisis market condition, the historical datasets for the period 2004–2009 fall within the most critical period of the latest global financial crunch.[5] To this end,

5. Our selected dataset ends in 2009 and ironically it coincides with a new era of another major financial markets turmoil, namely the European sovereign debt crisis. As such, the Eurozone crunch is a multi-year sovereign debt crisis that has been going on in several Eurozone countries since the end of 2009. This crisis was erupted following the recession of late 2009 and is regarded as a situation of accelerating high debt levels along with severe government deficits. While the European debt crisis is also an interesting natural experiment (with different nature and amplitude), it is beyond the scope of our research study.

the overall number of indices that are examined in this work are nine indices; seven local indices for the six GCC stock markets (including two indices for the UAE markets) and two benchmark indices, detailed as follows: DFM General Index (United Arab Emirates, Dubai Financial Market General Index), ADX Index (United Arab Emirates, Abu Dhabi Stock Market Index), BA All Share Index (Bahrain, All Share Stock Market Index), KSE General Index (Kuwait, Stock Exchange General Index), MSM30 Index (Oman, Muscat Stock Market Index), DSM20 Index (Qatar, Doha Stock Market General Index), SE All Share Index (Saudi Arabia, All Share Stock Market Index), Shuaa GCC Index (Shuaa Capital, GCC Stock Markets Benchmark Index), and Shuaa Arab Index (Shuaa Capital, Arab Stock Markets Benchmark Index).

Moreover, in this work index returns are defined as $R_{i,t} = \ln(P_{i,t}) - \ln(P_{i,t-1})$ where $R_{i,t}$ is the daily return of index i, ln is the natural logarithm; $P_{i,t}$ is the current level of index i, and $P_{i,t-1}$ is the previous day index level. Furthermore, for this particular research study we have chosen a confidence interval of 95 percent (or 97.5 percent with "one-tailed" loss side) and several liquidation time horizons to compute L-VaR. The examination of datasets and analysis of pertinent results and empirical findings are described as follows:

Estimation of Conditional Volatility with GARCH-M (1,1) Technique

To investigate the nexus between expected returns and volatility of the different stock market indices, we apply a conditional volatility tactic to determine the required risk parameters based on GARCH technique (Bollerslev, 1986; Engle, 1982, 1995; Engle & Kroner, 1995).

In this regard, and by implementing GARCH-M (1,1) model, Table 1 shows the daily conditional volatility of all stock market indices under normal and severe (crisis) market settings.[6] In this chapter, crisis market conditional volatilities are estimated by

6. In this chapter, crisis market settings stand for unpredicted adverse market circumstances at which aggregate portfolio losses are several times bigger than losses under normal conditions.

Table 1: Risk Analysis Dataset: Daily and Annual Volatility and Sensitivity Factor.

Stock Market Indices	Daily Volatility (Normal Market)[a]	Daily Volatility (Severe Market)[a]	Annual Volatility (Normal Market)[a]	Annual Volatility (Severe Market)[a]	Sensitivity Factor
DFM General Index	1.81%	12.2%	29.2%	196.0%	0.58
ADX Index	1.32%	7.1%	21.4%	114.1%	0.40
BA All Share Index	0.58%	3.8%	9.4%	60.8%	0.06
KSE General Index	0.71%	3.7%	11.5%	60.2%	0.14
MSM30 Index	0.79%	8.7%	12.8%	140.3%	0.10
DSM20 Index	1.48%	8.1%	23.9%	130.2%	0.31
SE All Share Index	1.86%	11.0%	30.0%	177.9%	0.98
Shuaa GCC Index	1.30%	8.1%	20.9%	130.6%	1.05
Shuaa Arab Index	1.15%	7.6%	18.5%	122.1%	1.00

Source: Al Janabi (2011a, 2011b, 2013) research papers.
Notes: This table illustrates the daily conditional volatility of each of the sample indices under normal and crisis market conditions and by implementing GARCH-M (1,1) model. This table also includes the sensitivity risk factor (beta systematic risk).
Table is produced and designed by the author.
[a]Denotes estimation of conditional volatility using GARCH-M model.

applying the maximum historical losses of each stock market. This downside-risk tactic can assist in solving some of the restrictions of normal distribution and can offer a superior analysis of L-VaR, particularly under illiquid market scenarios. This table also includes the sensitivity risk factor (i.e., the beta systematic risk parameter).

Statistical Analysis and Testing for Non-Normality

Statistical tests of asymmetry (i.e., non-normal distribution) are applied to the different stock market indices using the Jarque-Bera (JB) test. In the first empirical analysis, testing for kurtosis and skewness patterns are carried out on all indices. The outcomes of this analysis are described in Table 2. By and large, we can conclude that all stock market indices have shown certain asymmetric patterns although with different degrees. The outcomes of common patterns of non-normality are also validated with the Jarque-Bera test. The appealing conclusion of this empirical test stresses the need of unifying L-VaR appraisals with other techniques such as scenario-analysis and stress-testing to get a detailed view of other residual risks (e.g., the effects of fat-tails in the distribution of asset's returns).

Liquidity Trading Risk Management — A Comparison of Alternative L-VaR Modeling Strategies

In this section, several case studies are carried out to emphasize the importance of asset liquidity trading risk management reports for daily risk-taking practices. Tables 4–6 illustrate the output simulation reports of three empirical results for the analysis of L-VaR of certain equity portfolios consisting of several indices of the GCC stock markets and by implementing three asset liquidity models RM, AJ(1) and AJ(2), respectively. Furthermore, in this work all risk tests are carried out at a one-tailed confidence level of 97.5 percent over distinct close-out periods and by applying the empirical correlation factors as indicated in Table 3.

Table 2: Risk Analysis Dataset: Descriptive Statistics of Daily Returns, Skewness, Kurtosis, and Jarque-Bera Test of Normality.

Stock Market Indices	Maximum	Minimum	Arithmetic Mean	Expected Return[a]	Skewness	Kurtosis	Jarque-Bera (JB) Test
DFM General Index	9.9%	−12.2%	0.12%	0.14%	0.01	7.86	955**
ADX Index	6.6%	−7.1%	0.07%	0.07%	0.12	7.26	734**
BA All Share Index	3.6%	−3.8%	0.05%	0.04%	0.43	10.24	2142**
KSE General Index	5.0%	−3.7%	0.09%	0.08%	−0.18	8.38	1173**
MSM30 Index	5.2%	−8.7%	0.12%	0.10%	−0.57	18.40	9617**
DSM20 Index	6.2%	−8.1%	0.06%	0.07%	−0.11	5.59	273**
SE All Share Index	9.4%	−11.0%	0.03%	0.01%	−0.97	8.47	1361**
Shuaa GCC Index	11.1%	−8.1%	0.06%	0.08%	−0.66	14.00	4949**
Shuaa Arab Index	9.4%	−7.6%	0.07%	0.10%	−0.61	13.79	4758**

Source: Al Janabi (2011a, 2011b, 2013) research papers.
Notes: Table 2 illustrates certain descriptive statistics and the test for non-normality (asymmetry) using the Jarque-Bera (JB) test. Table is produced and designed by the author.
[a]Denotes estimation of expected return using GARCH-M model.**Denotes statistical significance at the 0.01 level.

Table 3: Risk Analysis Dataset: Correlation Matrix of Stock Market Indices.

	DFM General Index	ADX Index	BA All Share Index	KSE General Index	MSM30 Index	DSM20 Index	SE All Share Index	Shuaa GCC Index	Shuaa Arab Index
DFM General Index	100%								
ADX Index	56%	100%							
BA All Share Index	12%	8%	100%						
KSE General Index	17%	16%	12%	100%					
MSM30 Index	12%	17%	11%	11%	100%				
DSM20 Index	18%	23%	12%	12%	20%	100%			
SE All Share Index	20%	20%	7%	16%	11%	10%	100%		
Shuaa GCC Index	37%	35%	13%	19%	13%	26%	62%	100%	
Shuaa Arab Index	39%	36%	12%	24%	15%	26%	60%	93%	100%

Source: Al Janabi (2011a, 2011b, 2013) research papers.
Notes: Table 3 depicts the empirical correlation factors among the different market indices.
Table is produced and designed by the author.

In this research, L-VaR analysis and asset allocation are done under the notion that local stock market indices are precise substitutes of diversified structured portfolios for each stock market respectively. The simple logic is that country stock market indices may have additional predictable pattern due to aggregation than using individual stocks. In the first set of structured case studies (as illustrated in Tables 4–6 respectively), total portfolio volume is assumed to be AED 1000 million (UAE Dirham) with various long/short asset allocations and different unwinding liquidity horizons. Likewise, Tables 4–6 show the special effects of stress-testing and the impact of unlike correlations on daily L-VaR assessment. The L-VaR simulation risk report shows also the overnight conditional volatilities and expected returns using GARCH-M technique. The special effects of short-sales (though at this time short selling of stocks is not allowed in the GCC zone) are described in these tables too.

The L-VaR simulation outcomes are estimated under normal and crisis (severe) market circumstances by taking into consideration dissimilar correlation parameters (i.e., empirical, zero and negative/positive unity correlations factors among the different risk components). For the empirical case, the correlation parameters are assessed via a variance/covariance matrix and presented in Table 3 accordingly.

As a result, with 97.5 percent level of confidence and by using as an illustrative example the AJ(2) asset liquidity model, the structured portfolio can be expected to have a decrease in value no bigger than AED 31,741,339 over a one-day timeframe as indicated in Table 6. If the real losses surpass the L-VaR estimation, then this could be considered a violation to the assessment process.

In addition, the examination of L-VaR under illiquid market settings is implemented using four unlike correlation parameters (i.e., empirical correlations, zero correlations and positive/negative unity correlations) and for both long and short-sales structured portfolios. The reason behind including different correlation factors is due to the fact that prevailing tendencies in correlation parameters could change signs or breakdown under

Table 4: Asset Liquidity Market Risk Management with RM Model.

Stock Market Indices	Market Value in AED	Asset Allocation	Liquidity Holding Horizon	Daily Volatility (Normal)	Daily Volatility (Severe)	Sensitivity Factor	Expected Return	Undiversified L-VaR in AED (Normal)	Undiversified L-VaR in AED (Severe)
DFM General Index	500,000,000	50.0%	2	1.81%	12.16%	0.58	0.14%	12,824,404	85,964,851
ADX Index	200,000,000	20.0%	3	1.32%	7.08%	0.40	0.07%	4,588,923	24,510,377
BA All Share Index	(200,000,000)	−20.0%	4	0.58%	3.77%	0.06	0.04%	2,323,366	15,072,630
KSE General Index	400,000,000	40.0%	3	0.71%	3.74%	0.14	0.08%	4,936,256	25,886,979
MSM30 Index	(400,000,000)	−10.0%	4	0.79%	8.70%	0.10	0.10%	1,585,345	17,397,975
DSM20 Index	400,000,000	40.0%	3	1.48%	8.07%	0.31	0.07%	10,256,014	55,939,239
SE All Share Index	(400,000,000)	−20.0%	2	1.86%	11.03%	0.98	0.01%	5,254,284	31,205,741
Shuaa GCC Index	-	0.0%	1	1.30%	8.10%	1.05	0.08%	–	–
Shuaa Arab Index	-	0.0%	1	1.15%	7.57%	1.00	0.10%	–	–
Total Portfolio Value in AED	1,000,000,000	100%					0.13%		
Expected Return and Risk-Adjusted Return									
Trading Portfolio Expected Return									0.13%
Risk-Adjusted Expected Return (Normal)									3.00%
Risk-Adjusted Expected Return (Severe)									0.50%

Table 4: (*Continued*)

Daily Liquidity-Adjusted Value at Risk (L-VaR) in AED			
[Normal Market Conditions]			
Correlation = Empirical	Correlation = 1	Correlation = 0	Correlation = −1
42,035,294	46,885,202	37,448,357	24,627,964
4.20%	4.69%	3.74%	2.46%
Diversification Benefits			
4,849,908		11.54%	
Daily Liquidity-Adjusted Value at Risk (L-VaR) in AED			
[Severe Market Conditions]			
Correlation = Empirical	Correlation = 1	Correlation = 0	Correlation = −1
252,169,137	257,250,199	230,596,793	200,429,781
25.22%	25.73%	23.06%	20.04%
Diversification Benefits			
5,081,062		2.01%	
Overall Sensitivity Factor: Portfolio of Stock Indices			
0.335			

Notes: Table 4 demonstrates a full report for asset allocation and Liquidity-Adjusted Value at Risk (L-VaR) parameters using RM model. The table includes empirical risk analysis under normal and severe markets conditions.
Table 4 also illustrates the diversification benefit for each case, the impact of undiversified L-VaR along with the overall sensitivity factor (beta systematic risk factor) for the entire trading portfolio. Finally, it includes an analysis of expected return and risk-adjusted return of the overall portfolio.
Table is produced and designed by the author.

Table 5: Asset Liquidity Market Risk Management with AJ(1) Model.

Stock Market Indices	Market Value in AED	Asset Allocation	Liquidity Holding Horizon	Daily Volatility (Normal)	Daily Volatility (severe)	Sensitivity Factor	Expected Return	Undiversified L-VaR in AED (Normal)	Undiversified L-VaR in AED (Severe)
DFM General Index	500,000,000	50.0%	2	1.81%	12.16%	0.58	0.14%	11,106,259	74,447,744
ADX Index	200,000,000	20.0%	3	1.32%	7.08%	0.40	0.07%	3,746,840	20,012,639
BA All Share Index	(200,000,000)	–20.0%	4	0.58%	3.77%	0.06	0.04%	1,836,782	11,915,960
KSE General Index	400,000,000	40.0%	3	0.71%	3.74%	0.14	0.08%	4,030,436	21,136,630
MSM30 Index	(100,000,000)	–10.0%	4	0.79%	8.70%	0.10	0.10%	1,253,326	13,754,307
DSM20 Index	400,000,000	40.0%	3	1.48%	8.07%	0.31	0.07%	8,374,001	45,674,197
SE All Share Index	(200,000,000)	–20.0%	2	1.86%	11.03%	0.98	0.01%	4,550,344	27,024,965
Shuaa GCC Index	-	0.0%	1	1.30%	8.10%	1.05	0.08%	–	–
Shuaa Arab Index	-	0.0%	1	1.15%	7.57%	1.00	0.10%	–	–
Total Portfolio Value in AED	1,000,000,000	100%					0.13%		
Expected Return and Risk-Adjusted Return									
Trading Portfolio Expected Return									0.13%
Risk-Adjusted Expected Return (Normal)									3.57%
Risk-Adjusted Expected Return (Severe)									0.59%

Table 5: (*Continued*)

Daily Liquidity-Adjusted Value at Risk (L-VaR) in AED			
[Normal Market Conditions]			
Correlation = Empirical	Correlation = 1	Correlation = 0	Correlation = −1
35,351,629	39,234,169	31,585,207	21,352,532
3.54%	3.92%	3.16%	2.14%
Diversification Benefits			
38,82,540			10.98%
Daily Liquidity-Adjusted Value at Risk (L-VaR) in AED			
[Severe Market Conditions]			
Correlation = Empirical	Correlation = 1	Correlation = 0	Correlation = −1
213,083,489	217,151,958	195,319,037	170,716,372
21.31%	21.72%	19.53%	17.07%
Diversification Benefits			
4,068,468			1.91%
Overall Sensitivity Factor: Portfolio of Stock Indices			
0.335			

Notes: Table 5 demonstrates a full report for asset allocation and Liquidity-Adjusted Value at Risk (L-VaR) parameters using AJ(1) model.
The table includes empirical risk analysis under normal and severe markets conditions. Table 5 also illustrates the diversification benefit for each case, the impact of undiversified L-VaR along with the overall sensitivity factor (beta systematic risk factor) for the entire trading portfolio. Finally, it includes an analysis of expected return and risk-adjusted return of the overall portfolio.
Table is produced and designed by the author.

Table 6: Asset Liquidity Market Risk Management with AJ(2) Model.

Stock Market Indices	Market Value in AED	Asset Allocation	Liquidity Holding Horizon	Daily Volatility (Normal)	Daily Volatility (severe)	Sensitivity Factor	Expected Return	Undiversified L-VaR in AED (Normal)	Undiversified L-VaR in AED (Severe)
DFM General Index	500,000,000	50.0%	2	1.81%	12.16%	0.58	0.14%	10,138,581	67,961,182
ADX Index	200,000,000	20.0%	3	1.32%	7.08%	0.40	0.07%	3,304,402	17,649,489
BA All Share Index	(200,000,000)	−20.0%	4	0.58%	3.77%	0.06	0.04%	1,590,700	10,319,524
KSE General Index	400,000,000	40.0%	3	0.71%	3.74%	0.14	0.08%	3,554,511	18,640,755
MSM30 Index	(100,000,000)	−10.0%	4	0.79%	8.70%	0.10	0.10%	1,085,412	11,911,579
DSM20 Index	400,000,000	40.0%	3	1.48%	8.07%	0.31	0.07%	7,385,174	40,280,856
SE All Share Index	(200,000,000)	−20.0%	2	1.86%	11.03%	0.98	0.01%	4,153,877	24,670,305
Shuaa GCC Index	-	0.0%	1	1.30%	8.10%	1.05	0.08%	–	–
Shuaa Arab Index	-	0.0%	1	1.15%	7.57%	1.00	0.10%	–	–
Total Portfolio Value in AED	1,000,000,000	100%					0.13%		
Expected Return and Risk-Adjusted Return									
Trading Portfolio Expected Return									0.13%
Risk-Adjusted Expected Return (Normal)									3.98%
Risk-Adjusted Expected Return (Severe)									0.66%

Table 6: (*Continued*)

Daily Liquidity-Adjusted Value at Risk (L-VaR) in AED			
[Normal Market Conditions]			
Correlation = Empirical	Correlation = 1	Correlation = 0	Correlation = −1
31,741,339	35,105,360	28,414,671	19,555,070
3.17%	3.51%	2.84%	1.96%
Diversification Benefits			
33,64,021			10.60%
Daily Liquidity-Adjusted Value at Risk (L-VaR) in AED			
[Severe Market Conditions]			
Correlation = Empirical	Correlation = 1	Correlation = 0	Correlation = −1
191,856,074	195,261,747	176,150,549	154,696,096
19.19%	19.53%	17.62%	15.47%
Diversification Benefits			
3,405,672			1.78%
Overall Sensitivity Factor: Portfolio of Stock Indices			
0.335			

Notes: Table 6 demonstrates a full report for asset allocation and Liquidity-Adjusted Value at Risk (L-VaR) parameters using AJ(2) model. The table includes empirical risk analysis under normal and severe markets conditions.

Table 6 also illustrates the diversification benefit for each case, the impact of undiversified L-VaR along with the overall sensitivity factor (beta systematic risk factor) for the entire trading portfolio. Finally, it includes an analysis of expected return and risk-adjusted return of the overall portfolio.

Table is produced and designed by the author.

adverse market conditions, triggered by unexpected financial or political crunch. In theory, the particular case of correlation +1 should provide the highest L-VaR figures (AED 35,105,360 and AED 195,261,747 under normal and adverse markets conditions respectively) owing to the fact that under these perspectives the overall portfolio L-VaR is simply the weighted average of the specific L-VaRs of individual trading positions. Likewise, the results of diversified L-VaR (that is, the degree of risk-diversification) can simply be determined as the change in monetary value of the two extreme L-VaRs — explicitly the L-VaR of correlation +1 as opposed to the L-VaR with empirical correlations (i.e., AED 3,364,021 (or 10.60 percent) and AED 3,405,672 (or 1.78 percent) for normal and adverse market circumstances respectively). Furthermore, the L-VaR risk analysis report includes the total beta sensitivity factor as well as expected returns and risk-adjusted expected returns.

In another relevant empirical study we compare the three asset liquidity models under different operational constraints and determine the amount of economic capital for each model under the notion of different correlation factors. Following the definition of the three asset-liquidity-horizon-factor ($ALHF_i$) in Eqs. (9), (10) and (11), intuitively it is obvious to deduce that the RM model should produce the highest economic capital figure followed by AJ(1) and AJ(2) models, respectively. For instance, if we assume 10-days to unwind an asset or a portfolio of assets fully, then the asset liquidity risk factors are 3.162, 2.345, and 1.962 by using Eqs. (9), (10) and (11) respectively. However, there are certain operational circumstances at which correlation factors can increase dramatically to unity ($\rho = +1$) or otherwise to switch signs to negative unity ($\rho = -1$). Certainly, under such dramatic operational circumstances the amount of minimum economic capital is rather sensitive to the selection of the most adequate internal asset liquidity model. As such, Tables 7–9 depict three distinct active portfolios and illustrate the amount of trading volume in each trading asset and its unwinding period. In each of these three tables, the minimum amount of economic capital is calculated and compared accordingly by implementing the three internal

Table 7: Fund Manager Market Portfolio [1] (Case Analysis of Long and Short Trading Positions).

Market Index	Liquidation Period (in Days)	Market Value in AED	Asset Allocation per Market
DFM General Index	10	100,000,000	−50%
ADX Index	1	(200,000,000)	100%
BA All Share Index	10	100,000,000	−50%
KSE General Index	1	(200,000,000)	100%
MSM30 Index	10	100,000,000	−50%
DSM20 Index	1	(200,000,000)	100%
SE All Share Index	10	100,000,000	−50%
Total Portfolio Value in AED		(200,000,000)	100%

Daily L-VaR in AED Under Normal Market Conditions

Asset Liquidity Model	$\rho =$ Empirical	$\rho = +1$	$\rho = 0$	$\rho = -1$
RM	17,818,216	17,836,206	19,480,755	20,996,891
AJ(1)	13,469,560	9,592,251	15,517,497	19,737,632
AJ(2)	11,682,738	5,727,245	13,781,634	18,629,694

Daily L-VaR in AED under Severe Market Conditions

Asset Liquidity Model	$\rho =$ Empirical	$\rho = +1$	$\rho = 0$	$\rho = -1$
RM	122,794,188	149,972,072	128,231,306	101,955,448
AJ(1)	90,422,012	91,703,057	99,870,679	107,419,060
AJ(2)	76,366,426	64,384,840	87,190,273	105,161,208

Notes: This table illustrates the asset allocation of fund manager market portfolio [1]. It also compares the three liquidity models and determines the amount of economic capital for each model under the notion of different correlation factors and for both normal and severe markets conditions.
Table is produced and designed by the author.

Table 8: Fund Manager Market Portfolio [2] (Case Analysis of Long and Short Trading Positions).

Market Index	Liquidation Period (in Days)	Market Value in AED	Asset Allocation per Market
DFM General Index	10	400,000,000	200%
ADX Index	1	(200,000,000)	–100%
BA All Share Index	10	(600,000,000)	–300%
KSE General Index	1	400,000,000	200%
MSM30 Index	10	(200,000,000)	–100%
DSM20 Index	1	600,000,000	300%
SE All Share Index	10	(200,000,000)	–100%
Total Portfolio Value in AED		200,000,000	100%

Daily L-VaR in AED under Normal Market Conditions

Asset Liquidity Model	$\rho =$ Empirical	$\rho = +1$	$\rho = 0$	$\rho = -1$
RM	53,216,537	*8,481,121*	60,164,655	84,661,928
AJ(1)	41,068,918	*10,983,244*	46,477,284	64,804,662
AJ(2)	35,642,552	12,156,312	40,310,467	55,696,423

Daily L-VaR in AED under Severe Market Conditions

Asset Liquidity Model	$\rho =$ Empirical	$\rho = +1$	$\rho = 0$	$\rho = -1$
RM	352,432,850	*13,454,070*	397,119,219	561,450,209
AJ(1)	267,855,859	*35,422,867*	302,859,663	426,840,920
AJ(2)	229,501,791	45,722,481	259,868,080	364,653,661

Notes: This table illustrates the asset allocation of fund manager market portfolio [2]. It also compares the three liquidity models and determines the amount of economic capital for each model under the notion of different correlation factors and for both normal and severe markets conditions.
Table is produced and designed by the author.

Table 9: Fund Manager Market Portfolio [3] (Case Analysis of Long and Short Trading Positions).

Market Index	Liquidation Period (in Days)	Market Value in AED	Asset Allocation per Market
DFM General Index	10	300,000,000	100%
ADX Index	1	(100,000,000)	−33%
BA All Share Index	10	100,000,000	33%
KSE General Index	1	(100,000,000)	−33%
MSM30 Index	10	100,000,000	33%
DSM20 Index	1	(100,000,000)	−33%
SE All Share Index	10	100,000,000	33%
Total Portfolio Value in AED		300,000,000	100%

Daily L-VaR in AED under Normal Market Conditions

Asset Liquidity Model	ρ = Empirical	$\rho = +1$	$\rho = 0$	$\rho = -1$
RM	38,028,883	47,812,243	37,129,929	21,708,354
AJ(1)	27,719,077	33,640,792	27,681,480	20,020,634
AJ(2)	22,912,910	26,996,802	23,275,087	18,831,676

Daily L-VaR in AED under Severe Market Conditions

Asset Liquidity Model	ρ = Empirical	$\rho = +1$	$\rho = 0$	$\rho = -1$
RM	259,644,280	341,522,939	249,376,003	87,970,815
AJ(1)	189,736,615	243,520,586	185,569,943	97,827,051
AJ(2)	157,073,993	197,574,219	155,757,510	97,392,155

Notes: This table illustrates the asset allocation of fund manager market portfolio [3]. It also compares the three liquidity models and determines the amount of economic capital for each model under the notion of different correlation factors and for both normal and severe markets conditions.
Table is produced and designed by the author.

liquidity RM, AJ(1) and AJ(2) models respectively. As expected, in almost all cases, the AJ(2) model produces the minimum amount of economic capital. However, there are certain extreme operational conditions at which the RM and AJ(1) models can produce lower economic capital than the AJ(2) model. Indeed, these extreme conditions can be attained if and only if the correlation factors increase dramatically to unity or otherwise switch signs to negative unity. The dark gray cells in Tables 7–9 indicate certain violations to the assumption that the RM model should produce always the highest economic capital.

In summary, the above empirical findings indicate that the amount of economic capital as measured by L-VaR rely on the chosen internal liquidity risk model, extent of correlation parameters under severe market situation, expected return and conditional volatility as estimated by the GARCH-M model, the total volume of long/short-sales assets, liquidity horizons (close-out periods) of each asset, and asset allocation (i.e., the set of portfolio weights). Moreover, the empirical outcomes denote that the risk tolerance in the L-VaR context is time varying and strongly have to do with the choice of the close-out liquidity periods, trading volume in each asset along with the effect of the degree of correlation parameters, particularly under adverse market settings.

Furthermore, one of the motivating outcomes of this empirical analysis is the manner in which L-VaR figures have declined under adverse market scenarios. It is appealing to remark here that there are certain operational circumstances at which L-VaR figures with correlation +1 is lower than L-VaR under the assumption of empirical correlations. Indeed, this effect is attributed to the influence of short-selling of assets. This observation can perhaps be justified by the means in which the total structured assets portfolio is financed — that is, long assets trading positions have been financed with the short selling of other assets and as a result have generated a cutback of the total portfolio risk exposure.

Summary and Concluding Remarks

The traditional VaR approaches to assessing trading risk of multi-assets portfolios do not consider directly liquidity risk, rather it assumes perfect market where an investor can buy or sell any amount of securities without initiating a sizable price change. At most, the holding liquidation period over which the VaR number is calculated is adjusted to take care of liquidity risk. In emerging markets such as the Gulf Cooperation Council (GCC), which are comparatively illiquid, overlooking liquidity trading risk can lead to considerable underestimation of actual VaR figures. Our results demonstrate that in emerging financial markets such as the GCC zone, asset liquidity risk can form a significant proportion of total L-VaR figures and hence it should not be ignored. Further, in this analysis, we have considered three different asset liquidation models in an attempt to remedy the above shortcoming and to estimate separately the trading risk and asset liquidity risk of different equity portfolios.

To examine the statistical characteristics of the datasets, we have calculated the log-returns of each time-series. However, it is a stylized fact that the distributions of many financial assets returns are non-normal, with pervasive skewness and kurtosis behaviors. As such, it would therefore be more desirable to focus on a measure for risk that is able to incorporate any non-normality in the return distributions of financial assets. For all examined cases, the analysis of some primary statistics permits us, by and large, to deduce that all time-series of the GCC stock market indices are characterized by non-normality (asymmetry) and excessive leptokurtosis. Likewise, the normality proposition was rejected for all time-series with the application of the Jarque-Bera (JB) test. In view of that, the application of normal distribution, which is the case in a mean-variance method (i.e., Markowitz, 1959), tends to provide insignificant evidence of what is perceived in reality in our daily returns time-series. With the aim of overcoming this disadvantage, in this chapter we have used the empirical distribution of historical assets returns and the conditional volatility is estimated via GARCH-M model. This tactic has assisted in presenting a superior analysis of L-VaR and economic capital, mainly under crisis and illiquid market outlooks.

The ability to focus on additional moments in the return distribution with the possibility of allowing for skewed or leptokurtotic distributions enables additional risk factors (along with the use of conditional volatility) to be included into the determination of the minimum amount of economic capital. To this end, in this chapter we present a systematic analysis for the calculation of the minimum economic capital cushion using three different internal models of asset liquidity trading risk management and for multiple-assets' portfolios. This is with the objective of predicting L-VaR under illiquid market conditions and within a multivariate context. Using more than 6 years of daily returns datasets (for the years 2004–2009) of emerging GCC financial markets, we analyze different trading portfolios and determine the risk exposure under different illiquid and adverse market conditions and correlation factors. Our results suggest that ignoring liquidity trading risk can produce substantial underestimates of overall trading risk, particularly in emerging markets securities. Finally, asset liquidity trading risk should be included in any performance evaluation as part of returns adjusted for risk compensation. Likewise, it should be induced in the process of setting of maximum trading limits and risk-budgeting.

To this end, quite a few structured case studies for the measurement of L-VaR are accomplished to validate how different internal asset liquidity models can be implemented in determining the minimum required amount of economic capital. The empirical findings indicate that in almost all operational cases the AJ(2) internal asset liquidity approach performs adequately across the whole sampling period and among different investment prospects. Nevertheless, there are certain adverse operational circumstances — when correlations among risk factors tend to cluster to unity or otherwise to switch signs to negative unity — at which the RM or AJ(1) models can produce lower economic capital. Our empirical testing results also indicate that the amount of economic capital (as measured by L-VaR technique) depends on the chosen internal liquidity risk model, degree of correlation among assets under unfavorable market outlooks, expected returns and conditional volatility as estimated by the GARCH-M model, the volume of long/short-sales trading positions, the liquidity unwinding periods of each trading asset, and the proportions allocated to each asset (i.e., portfolio weights).

The obtained empirical results are appealing in terms of theoretical foundations in addition to its practical uses and applications. The theoretical foundations and empirical tests can have many uses for portfolio management purposes as well as in complying with contemporary risk management regulations.

Acknowledgment

Some aspects of this chapter are partially based on a conference paper entitled "Integrating Liquidity Risk Factor into a Parametric Value at Risk Method," which I have presented at the 57th annual conference of the Midwest Finance Association (MFA), San Antonio, Texas, USA, March, 2008.

References

Al Janabi, M. A. M. (2007). Equity trading risk management: The case of Casablanca stock exchange. *International Journal of Risk Assessment and Management*, *7*(4), 535–568.

Al Janabi, M. A. M. (2008). Integrating liquidity risk factor into a parametric value at risk method. *Proceedings of the 57th annual conference of the Midwest Finance Association (MFA)*, San Antonio, TX.

Al Janabi, M. A. M. (2011a). Economic capital allocation under coherent market liquidity constraints. *Journal of Economic Research*, *16*(2), 147–186.

Al Janabi, M. A. M. (2011b). Dynamic equity asset allocation with liquidity-adjusted market risk criterion: Appraisal of efficient and coherent portfolios. *Journal of Asset Management*, *12*(6), 378–394.

Al Janabi, M. A. M. (2012). Optimal commodity asset allocation with a coherent market risk modeling. *Review of Financial Economics*, *21*(3), 131–140.

Al Janabi, M. A. M. (2013). Optimal and coherent economic-capital structures: Evidence from long and short-sales trading positions under

illiquid market perspectives. *Annals of Operations Research, 205*(1), 109–139.
Almgren, R., & Chriss, N. (2001). Optimal execution of portfolio transaction. *Journal of Risk, 3*(Winter), 5–39.
Bangia, A., Diebold, F., Schuermann, T., & Stroughair, J. (2002). Modeling liquidity risk with implications for traditional market risk measurement and management. In S. Figlewski & R. M. Levich (Eds.), *Risk management: The state of the art, The New York university Salomon center series on financial markets and institutions* (Vol. 8, pp. 3–13). New York, NY: Springer.
Bollerslev, T. (1986). Generalized autoregressive conditional heteroscedasticity. *Journal of Econometrics, 31*, 309–328.
Dubil, R. (2002). Optimal liquidation of large security holdings in thin markets. In Y. Shachmurove (Ed.), *Research in international entrepreneurial finance and business ventures at the turn of the third millennium.* Academy of Entrepreneurial Finance. Special proceedings issue.
Engle, R. (1982). Autoregressive conditional heteroscedasticity with estimates of the variance of UK inflation. *Econometrica, 50*, 987–1008.
Engle, R. (1995). *ARCH selected readings, advanced texts in econometrics.* Oxford: Oxford University Press.
Engle, R., & Kroner, K. (1995). Multivariate simultaneous generalized ARCH. *Econometric Theory, 11*, 122–150.
Hisata, Y., & Yamai, Y. (2000). *Research toward the practical application of liquidity risk evaluation methods.* Discussion Paper, Institute for Monetary and Economic Studies, Bank of Japan.
Jarrow, R., & Subramanian, A. (1997). Mopping up liquidity. *Risk, 10*(12), 170–173.
Markowitz, H. (1959). *Portfolio selection: Efficient diversification of investments*. New York, NY: Wiley.
Morgan Guaranty Trust Company (1994). *RiskMetrics-technical document.* New York, NY: Morgan Guaranty Trust Company, Global Research.
Zumbach, G. (2007). *The RISKMETRICS 2006 methodology*. New York, NY: RiskMetrics Group.

Part II
Applications and Case Studies

10

Enterprise Risk Management and Bank Performance: Evidence from Eastern Europe during the Financial Crisis

Francesca Battaglia, Franco Fiordelisi and Ornella Ricci

Abstract

Does the adoption of the Enterprise Risk Management (ERM) improve bank profitability? Does ERM also reduce bank risk? By analyzing a sample of banks located in European emerging markets between 2005 and 2013, the aim of this chapter is to empirically investigate the determinants of firm performance, both in terms of bank profitability and risk, with respect to the adoption of Enterprise Risk Management (ERM). In order to capture the effect of the ERM program adoption on banks' performance, we both use market-based measures as well as accounting-based indexes. Following the seminal literature on the topic (Aebi, Sabato, & Schmid, 2012; Eckles et al., 2014; Ellul & Yerramilly, 2013; Hoyt & Liebenberg, 2003, 2011; Lin, Wen, & Yu, 2012; Pagach & Warr, 2010), we adopt a binary proxy variable, that is, the appointment of a Chief Risk Officer (CRO), to define whether the firm is currently undertaking an ERM program. Our results show that a post-ERM firm experiences an increase in the risk-adjusted profits and a reduction of the overall risk.

Keywords: Enterprise Risk Management (ERM); risk governance; European emerging markets; bank performance; financial crisis; Chief Risk Officer (CRO)

Introduction

In 2004, the Committee of Sponsoring Organizations of the Treadway Commission (COSO) issued the Enterprise Risk Management Integrated Framework and proposed the following definition of ERM: "*Enterprise risk management is a process, effected by an entity's board of directors, management, and other personnel, applied in strategy setting and across the enterprise, designed to identify potential events that may affect the entity, and manage risk to be within its risk appetite, to provide reasonable assurance regarding the achievement of entity objectives.*" As argued by Hull (2015), the previous definition of ERM assumes several points, such as the board involvement in ERM, the ERM contribution to a company's strategy, the identification of potential adverse events and the company definition of its risk appetite and of its related risk management. According to this point of view, ERM should help a company achieve its objectives and be a core part of strategic planning and strategic execution processes.

ERM can be considered as an attempt to take a holistic approach to risk management. The central idea is that business units within the financial institution should be part of an integrated, strategic, and enterprise-wide risk management system, in which the management of different types of risks in different business units is consistent with the overall risk appetite framework, defined at the top and approved by the board.

A financial institution's risk appetite statement should define how much risk the organization is going to take in pursuit of its objectives. It has to be converted into directives for the risks taken by business units. Suitable restrictions are then set on trading risk: how concentrated the financial institution's portfolio can become, how much credit risk can be taken, and so on. The financial institution should continually monitor the risks being taken to ensure that they are consistent with its risk appetite.

An essential part of ERM is concerned with developing a good risk culture (Fraser & Simkins, 2010; Hull, 2015). A key element of the risk culture is ensuring that medium- to long-term risks are considered when opportunities that offer short-term profits are estimated. If the risk culture is good, all decisions are made in a disciplined way, with a particular attention to possible outcomes, weighing risks and rewards. In practice, risks are considered in relation both to potential rewards and to the risk appetite of the financial institution.

The 2008 financial turmoil showed that managerial excellence is critical for banks' survival and it is not surprising the increasing effort of policy makers to set rules with the aim of improving bank management. In its recent papers dealing with "lessons from the financial crisis," the OECD (2009, 2010) put great emphasis on four specific areas: remuneration schemes, risk management practices, board performance, and shareholder rights. With reference to risk management practices, some technical assumptions of risk management models have proven to be unrealistic, leading to unreliable predictions, despite the high level of sophistication. The inadequacy of risk management models was exacerbated by at least two other circumstances: information about risk exposure did not always reach top management, and when it did, it was not always fully understood. If the inadequacy of risk models is not a corporate governance issue, the correct flow of information inside the firm and the professional requirements of senior managers certainly are.

In recent years, the Enterprise Risk Management (ERM) approach is being implemented by an increasing number of corporations, especially banks, in order to improve their risk management. To the extent that risk management decreases the volatility of cash flows and earnings (Beasley, Pagach, & Warr, 2008; Cumming & Hirtle, 2001; Lam, 2001; Meulbroek, 2002; Miccolis & Shah, 2000), it also enables investors and regulators to better assess and monitor banks' performance, both in terms of risk-taking and risk-adjusted performance. It is generally recognized that firms adopting ERM programs create shareholder value by allowing them to achieve a more optimized risk-return trade-off. This leads us to the following research questions: Does the adoption of the Enterprise Risk Management (ERM) approach improve bank performance? Does ERM also reduce bank risk? Our empirical analysis shows that the ERM approach produces positive effects on bank management by increasing risk-adjusted profits and reducing risk.

Following Nocco and Stulz (2006), who define ERM as an approach under which "all risks (are) viewed together within a coordinated and strategic framework," we consider ERM as a process that identifies, evaluates and manages individual risks within a coordinated framework. In other words, the ERM adoption implies a shift from the traditional way of managing risks separately to managing them collectively. Also Sabato (2014) states that banks engaging in a good ERM program should be able to better understand the aggregate risk of the whole organization and, as a result, they should have a more objective basis for the allocation of the resources among different business units. He points out that by doing so banks improve capital efficiency and maximize the shareholder wealth, because they should have an amount of capital that exceeds their regulatory requirements. Consistently with the existing literature, we adopt a binary proxy variable, that is, the appointment of a Chief Risk Officer (CRO), to define whether the firm is currently undertaking an ERM program (Aebi, Sabato, & Schmid, 2012; Eckles, Hoyt, & Miller, 2014; Ellul & Yerramilli, 2013; Hoyt & Liebenberg, 2003, 2011; Lin, Wen & Yu, 2012; Pagach & Warr, 2010).

Our empirical investigation focuses on the ERM adoption by European banks located in emerging markets over the period 2005–2013, because of the fast growth of their banking systems and the large variety of their institutional and regulatory framework (e.g., differences between EU and non-EU countries), by assuming that banks implementing ERM are more effective in monitoring and advisory terms. Consistent with previous researches (Aebi et al., 2012; Eckles et al., 2014; Ellul & Yerramilli, 2013), our analysis show that banks that have undertaken an ERM program experience a better performance, both in terms of higher profitability and lower risk. In final, our findings provide empirical support to recent regulatory and market pressure on the implementation of ERM, supporting the idea that the structure and the organization of the risk management function is not only crucial for compliance and loss mitigation issues, but also to render the strategy and the culture of the entire bank more consistent with its risk appetite and its long-term objectives.

Our chapter contributes to previous literature in various ways. At our knowledge, there are only two studies (Aebi et al., 2012; Ellul & Yerramilli, 2013) assessing the performance impact of the ERM adoption in a sample of banks, both dealing with the United States and the 2007–2008 financial crisis. With respect to this study, we provide a focus on European emerging markets and, by investigating the period 2005–2013, we consider all three stages of the financial crisis: the U.S. subprime crisis, the global financial crisis, and the sovereign debt crisis.

This chapter is structured as follows. Section 2 reviews the academic literature dealing with ERM, while section 3 presents our data. Section 4 explains our methodology, section 5 comments our main results and section 6 concludes.

Literature Review

Empirical studies on ERM are limited and their results are quite mixed, reflecting the newness of the topic, which is still relatively young.

Current research on the value implications of ERM-adopting firms is relatively limited. This is not surprising given that the formalized discipline of ERM has only been in existence for just over a decade. Furthermore, as a result of the lack of ERM disclosure requirements, research to date has been limited in terms of the shortage of an appropriate measurement of the ERM adoption by firms. We specify that the relevant works on the topic adopt a binary proxy variable, such as the appointment of a Chief Risk Officer (CRO) or public ERM-related announcement, to show whether the firm is currently undertaking an ERM program (Aebi et al., 2012; Eckles et al., 2014; Ellul & Yerramilli, 2013; Hoyt & Liebenberg, 2003, 2011; Lin et al., 2012; Pagach & Warr, 2010).

Early empirical studies on ERM investigate why firms adopt ERM programs and several researches employ survey data. The first work by Colquitt, Hoyt, and Lee (1999) analyzes the characteristics and extent of integrated risk management by surveying 397 risk managers. Their findings show that political risk, exchange rate risk, and interest rate risk are the three most common nonoperational risks handled by the risk management department. The study of Kleffner, Lee, and McGannon (2003) surveys Canadian Risk and Insurance Management Society members about ERM programs' implementation. The authors find that 31 percent adopt ERM and that the primary reasons for that adoption are risk manager influence, board encouragement and stock exchange guidelines.

Other early works on ERM focus on the determinants of ERM. The paper of Liebenberg and Hoyt (2003) is one of the first studies in this area. They investigate a sample composed of all U.S. firms that announce the appointment of a CRO between 1997 and 2001 and, by perform a logistic regression, they compare firms that announce the appointment of a chief risk officer to a matched sample. Their results show that companies appointing a chief risk officer are more likely to be financially leveraged and they conclude that further research is necessary to understand ERM determinants. A related but more recent investigation is that of Pagach and Warr (2011). By analyzing the announcements of senior risk officers for a period between 1992 and 2005, their results corroborate previous findings regarding firm size and leverage. In particular, they find that such appointments are positively associated with size, leverage, volatility and the number of business segments.

Other works on ERM examine additional determinants of ERM adoption. They make it clear that ERM adoption may be related to various firm characteristics. Desender (2007) studies 100 randomly selected pharmaceutical companies in 2004 and explores the link between ERM implementation and board composition. He finds an association between a separate chairman and CEO and the degree of ERM implemented by the company. Another paper related to ERM determinants is Beasley, Clune, and Hermanson (2005). By analyzing 123 organizations in 2004, the authors survey internal auditors and their views on factors associated with ERM implementation. Their results show that ERM adoption is positively associated with board independence, the presence of a CRO, explicit calls from CEO or CFO for internal audit involvement in ERM, size and industry group (banking, education, and insurance). It is interesting to note that they also find U.S. companies are not advanced in their ERM implementation.

In a more recent study, Beasley et al. (2008) extend the ERM literature by moving beyond the ERM adoption question and examine aspects of whether ERM adds value. For the purpose of this chapter, we focus on this stream of literature, that analyze the effects of the ERM implementation. The authors measure the equity market response to the hiring announcements of senior executives in charge of risk management, by splitting data into two groups: financial firms and nonfinancial firms. The investigated sample is composed of 120 firms announcing the appointment of a chief risk officer over the period 1992–2003. They perform an event study and measure the ERM benefit for shareholders by examining the abnormal returns surrounding the date of the CRO assignment. The results show that among the financial firms, only the slack variable is found to be significantly associated with the market reaction to announcements of appointments of senior executive officers supervising risk. For nonfinancial firms, there is no statistical association between the announcement period returns and growth.

Also Pagach and Warr (2010) find no support for the proposition that ERM creates shareholder value. They examine the effect of the ERM adoption on firms' long-term performance, by analyzing how both financial and market characteristics change around the date of ERM adoption. Using a sample of 106 firms announcing the appointment of a chief risk officer, they find little and very limited evidence of risk reduction in the earnings of firms undertaking ERM programs.

Unlike the two previous studies, Gates, Nicolas, and Walker (2009) show that a good ERM environment, better communication of ERM missions, and explicit risk tolerance levels positively influenced better decision making. A better ERM environment. Moreover, they find that explicit risk tolerance levels along with the number of employees devoted to ERM process appear to have an impact on profitability.

In a later study, Hoyt and Liebenberg (2011) analyze a sample composed of 275 U.S. insurance firms for the period 1998–2005, to investigate both the determinants of ERM and the effect of ERM adoption on firm value, proxied by Tobin's Q. In their empirical analysis, they use the dummy variable ERM to indicate an insurer engaged in ERM in any given year during the investigated period. To avoid the potential endogeneity bias arising from the construction of their model, they use a maximum-likelihood treatment effects approach, that jointly estimates the decision to engage in ERM and the effect of that decision (or treatment) on Q in a two-equation system. Their findings show that ERM adoption is associated with higher firm value, indicated by a Tobin's Q premium of roughly 20%.

More recently, Aebi et al. (2012), Ellul and Yerramilli (2013), Farrell and Gallagher (2014) and Eckles et al. (2014) find evidence that banking and insurance firms adopting ERM create shareholder value, by reducing earnings volatility and improving performance, especially during periods of financial distress.

Aebi et al. (2012) analyze a sample of 573 U.S. banks and test whether risk management-related corporate governance mechanisms, such as the presence of a CRO in the executive board of a bank and the line of reporting of the CRO, at the end of the year

2006 are associated with a positive bank performance during the 2007–2008 financial crisis. They use four alternative measures of bank performance: the banks' buy-and-hold returns over the investigated period, the alphas from Carhart (1997) multifactor model and two accounting-based profitability measures, ROA and ROE. In their model, they employ two key risk governance variables: CRO in executive board, to indicate whether the CRO is a member of the executive board and the dummy variable risk committee, which is equal to one if the bank has a risk committee and zero otherwise. Moreover, for banks with a risk committee, they additionally collect data on the number of times the risk committee met in 2006, the number of its directors and the percentage of its independent directors. Their findings show that banks in which the CRO reports directly to the board of directors perform significantly better, while those in which the CRO reports to the CEO perform significantly worse than other banks in the sample. Moreover, they do not find a significant relationship between banks' performance during the crisis and standard corporate governance variables (i.e., CEO ownership, board independence, or shareholder rights).

Ellul and Yerramilli (2013) focus on a sample of 74 large U.S. holding companies during the financial turmoil and analyze whether a strong and independent risk management is significantly related to bank performance, both in terms of risk taking and profitability. To this end, they build up a Risk Management Index (RMI), composed by the following variables: "CRO Executive," a dummy variable identifying if the CRO is an executive officer of the bank or not, "CRO-Top5," a dummy variable signaling if the CRO is among the five highest paid executives at the investigated bank or not, "CRO Centrality," measured as the ratio of the CRO's total compensation to the CEO's total compensation, "Risk Committee Experience," a dummy variable identifying whether at least one of the grey or independent directors of the risk committee has banking experience and the dummy variable "Active Risk Committee," to consider if the bank's risk committee met more frequently during the year compared to the average risk committee across all the investigated banks. Their findings show that banks with a high RMI value in 2006 had lower exposure to private-label mortgage-backed securities, were less active in trading off-balance sheet derivatives, had a smaller fraction of non-performing loans, had lower downside risk, and a higher Sharpe Ratio during the crisis years 2007–2008.

The study of Farrell and Gallagher (2014) analyzes the valuation implications of 225 publicly listed firms, across various sectors and countries, that have reached mature levels of ERM over the 2006–2011 period. To this end, the authors collect data from the industry leading Risk and Insurance Management Society Risk Maturity Model over the period from 2006 to 2011, which scores firms on a five-point maturity scale. Following the two-step model proposed by Heckman (1979), in order to avoid the selection bias, in the first-stage specification the authors use a probit model, estimated with time and industry fixed effects. In the second stage, the inverse Mills ratio, generated in the first step, is included in the adopted firm value model as an explanatory variable to correct for selection bias. Their results suggest that firms characterized by mature levels of ERM exhibit a higher firm value, as measured by Tobin's Q. Moreover, the authors find a statistically significant positive relation to the magnitude of 25 percent. Upon decomposition of the maturity score, results show that firms having successfully integrated the ERM process into both their strategic activities and everyday practices display superior ability in uncovering risk dependencies and correlations across the entire enterprise and, as a result, increase their value when reaching ERM maturity.

Eckles et al. (2014) analyze the impact of the ERM adoption on a sample of 354 U.S. insurance companies from 1992 to 2008. In particular, they investigate whether firms adopting ERM will exhibit a reduction in risk and if the risk reduction post-ERM adoption is associated with an increase of the insurance risk-adjusted profits. From our perspective, this paper, even if dealing with a different industry, is very interesting, since it considers firm performance, both in terms of profitability and risk, also taking into consideration the potential problem of ERM endogeneity. To test their research hypotheses, the authors specify two models with banks' profitability and risk, respectively, as dependent variables; then they regress the insurance companies performance on a set of independent variables, including the ERM adoption dummy (as the key independent variable) and other controls, that potentially influence firm performance. Moreover, by addressing the potential endogeneity concern in their analysis, related to the omitted variables bias, Eckles et al. employ the Heckman two-step procedure to estimate the impact of ERM implementation on both bank profitability and risk. Their findings show that firms adopting ERM experience a reduction in stock return volatility and that the reduction in return volatility experienced by ERM adopters becomes stronger over time. Furthermore, the authors find that the insurance companies risk-adjusted performance, proxied by the operating profits per unit of risk (ROA/return volatility), increases post-ERM adoption.

So, consistently with the most relevant stream of research on the topic, our main hypothesis is that banks in which there is a Chief Risk Officer in charge of the risk committee should experience a lower enterprise risk and/or a higher risk-adjusted performance. The underlying idea is that, given the increasing complexity of banking institutions the risk-taking behavior of traders and security desks within banks cannot be contained through either regulatory supervision or traditional external market discipline from bondholders or stockholders (Acharya et al., 2009). In order to monitor, to correctly identify and estimate the banks' risk exposure, we believe that a strong and independent risk management function is necessary (Stulz, 2008). As a result, the formal specifications of the hypotheses we are going to test are the following:

Hypothesis 1 (H1). All else equal, the ERM adoption is associated with a reduction in the overall bank risk.

Hypothesis 2 (H2). All else equal, the ERM adoption is associated with an increase in the bank risk-adjusted performance.

Data

Our initial sample is drawn from the Bankscope database, specifying the following selection criteria: the bank is active (i.e., not bankrupt, in liquidation or dissolved by a merger), is a listed institution, has consolidated financial statements, and operates in an Eastern Europe country (Bulgaria, Croatia, Czech Republic, Hungary, Lithuania, Macedonia, Montenegro, Poland, Republic of Moldova, Romania, Russian Federation, Serbia, Slovakia, Slovenia, and Ukraine). We specify that we consider Emerging Europe as all countries listed by Bankscope under Eastern Europe. We observe a nine-year period, from 2005 to 2013. These criteria result in a panel data of 67 banks*9 years = 603 observations. While financial data are drawn from Bankscope, stock market prices are obtained from Bloomberg. The list of banks is reported in the Appendix. The information regarding the presence of a CRO is collected by consulting every single annual report downloadable from banks' institutional websites. Unfortunately, this information is available only for about half of the sample (specifically, for 339 observations). Only 15 banks out of 67 have adopted the ERM approach (one in Czech Republic, one in Montenegro, five in Poland, five in Russian Federation, one in Slovakia, and two in Ukraine).

Methodology

In order to test our first research hypothesis (H_1: *All else equal, the ERM adoption is associated with a reduction in the overall bank risk*), we specify a model in which overall risk is the dependent variable and a dummy indicating ERM adoption is our main interest variable. Other regressors are included to control for other banks' characteristics potentially able to influence overall risk.

Our methodology is based on the study of Eckles et al. (2014) dealing with a large sample of U.S. listed insurance companies. With respect to this paper, we specify a more parsimonious model with partially different variables, since we examine a small sample of listed institutions operating in emerging Europe, and we analyze the banking industry rather than the insurance one. In Eckles et al. (2014), overall risk is measured using stock market data, as the annualized standard deviation of daily returns (*Stock return volatility*). Since we analyze a sample of listed banks operating in emerging Europe, for which liquid and continuous daily price series are not always available, we also try an alternative measure of overall risk. Using accounting information, we define the *RWA_ratio*, as the ratio between risk-weighted assets and total assets. This alternative accounting indicator, like the stock return volatility, is a global measure, which allows incorporating all main risks implied by the banking activity. Nevertheless, with respect to the stock return volatility, it presents some advantages and drawbacks. On the one hand, it is available for a larger number of observations with respect to the market-based measure; in addition, the riskiness of assets is assessed based on the indications set out in the prudential regulation, and therefore according to parameters shared by supervisory authorities. On the other hand, it has a lower variability than stock returns and it is influenced by the methodology adopted by banks to define risk weights (i.e., there may be significant differences across banks using different internal models).

The main problem arising from the model specified to test hypothesis H_1 is that the decision to adopt ERM is likely to be endogenous and driven by omitted variables influencing also the level of overall risk. In order to overcome this limitation, we apply the same methodology suggested by Eckles et al. (2014). We first run a probit model estimating the probability to adopt ERM; secondly, we run our main model including the inverse mills ratio to control for the endogeneity of treatment.

In our first step, the dependent variable is *ERM_adoption*, equal to 1 if the firm adopts the ERM methodology in the considered year, and 0 otherwise. As explained in the literature review section, we consider the ERM approach as implemented when a Chief Risk Officer is present in the bank's organizational chart, consistently with several previous studies (see the section "Literature Review"). Following Eckles et al. (2014), our probit model includes several control variables:

- *Size*, measured as the natural logarithm of total assets, since there is past evidence that larger firms are more likely to adopt an holistic risk management approach, such as the ERM;

- *Diversification*, measured as the ratio between other operating income and total assets. In this way, we consider the income not classified as net interest revenue, generated by activities different from the traditional credit intermediation (e.g., deriving from fees and commissions). We do not have a specific expectation on the sign assumed by this variable: on the one hand, banks with a more complex and diversified business may be more likely to adopt ERM; on the other hand, more diversified firms may be less risky and then less incentivized to adopt this more demanding approach;
- *Cost income*, measured as the ratio between total operating costs and total operating income, since more efficient firms may have more resources to devote to the implementation of a more sophisticated risk management approach, such as the ERM;
- *Lagged_risk*, measured as the annualized standard deviation of daily stock returns during the previous year, following the idea that riskier banks may have greater incentive to adopt the ERM methodology.[1] However, it is also possible that more adverse-risk banks are more likely to adopt an approach able to better control and hence reduce the overall risk;
- *NO_EU*, a dummy taking the value of 1 for countries out of the European Union (i.e., Macedonia, Montenegro, Republic of Moldova, Russian Federation, Serbia and Ukraine), and 0 otherwise (i.e., Bulgaria, Croatia, Czech Republic, Hungary, Lithuania, Poland, Romania, Slovakia and Slovenia). This variable should account for institutional differences between

1. Eckles et al. (2014) use the standard deviation over the previous three years. However, the use of such a time interval would have caused a severe restriction of our number of observations, due to the scarce availability of liquid and continuous price series for our sample of banks operating in emerging Europe.

countries belonging or not to the EU. This is also strongly correlated with the application of Basel principles, which may have fostered the ERM adoption, since the only non-EU country that is member of the Bank for International Settlement is the Russian Federation.

In addition, we also control for a set of *j* year dummies, taking into account time differences (e.g., it is likely that the ERM adoption is more common after the recent global financial crisis, showing the weaknesses of traditional silo-based risk management approaches). Our first step probit model is represented in Eq. (1):

$$\begin{aligned}\Pr\left(\text{ERM\_adoption}_{i,t}=1\right) = \alpha + \beta_1 \text{Size}_{i,t} + \beta_2 \text{Diversification}_{i,t} \\ + \beta_3 \text{Cost income}_{i,t} + \beta_4 \text{Lagged\_risk}_{i,t} \\ + \beta_5 NO\_EU_i + Sd_j \text{year\_dummy}_j + \varepsilon_{i,t}\end{aligned} \tag{1}$$

In our second step, we estimate an OLS model in which the dependent variable is *Bank_risk*. Our main interest variables are:

- *ERM_bank*, a dummy taking the value of 1 if the bank has ever adopted the ERM methodology during the investigated period, and 0 otherwise;
- *ERM_bank*ERM_adoption*, that is the interaction between *ERM_bank* and *ERM_adoption*. As outlined in Eckles et al. (2014), the inclusion of both *ERM_bank* and *ERM_bank* ERM_adoption* allows to (1) control for any potential structural differences between the group of banks implementing or not implementing the ERM approach during the investigated period and (2) measure the incremental impact of ERM adoption in the considered year;
- *Mills*, that is the selection hazard obtained from the first step probit model and correcting for the potential endogeneity of the decision to adopt ERM.

In addition to these variables, we also include all the regressors used in the first step, excluding *Lagged Risk*. Finally, as in the first step, we also include a set of year dummies. Our second step regression model is represented in Eq. 2:

$$\begin{aligned}\text{Firm\_Risk}_{i,t} = \alpha + \beta_1 \text{ERM\_bank}_i + \beta_2 \text{ERM\_bank}_i \times \text{ERM\_adoption}_{i,t} \\ + \beta_3 \text{Mills}_{i,t} + \beta_4 \text{Size}_{i,t} + \beta_5 \text{Diversification}_{i,t} \\ + \beta_6 \text{Cost income}_{i,t} + \beta_7 \text{NO\_EU}_i + \text{Sd}_j \text{year\_dummy}_j + \varepsilon_{i,t}\end{aligned} \quad (2)$$

In order to conduct a further robustness check, as suggested by Eckles et al. (2014), we also run a panel fixed effect model accounting for possible omitted variables causing time-invariant banks heterogeneity. In this model, all time-invariant regressors (*ERM_bank* and *NO_EU*) are omitted.

To test our second research hypothesis (H_2: *All else equal, the ERM adoption is associated with an increase in the bank risk-adjusted performance*), we use a very similar methodology with respect to the one adopted for testing our first hypothesis. The only difference is that the dependent variable of our main regression model is a risk-adjusted performance measure (RAPM). Consistently with the study of Eckles et al. (2014), our main RAPM is given by the ratio between ROA (i.e., Return on Asset) and the annualized standard deviation of daily stock returns. As an alternative, we also calculate a RAPM based on accounting information, defined as the ratio between total operating income and risk-weighted assets.

Summary statistics for our main variables (excluding dummies) are reported in Table 1.

Since our dependent variables, both indicators of overall bank risk and risk-adjusted performance measures, show a very large variability, we decide to winsorize them at the 1% level. All control variables (except dummy variables) are included in regression models as standardized values.

Empirical Results

Table 2 shows our results for testing H_1, using stock return volatility as a measure of the overall bank risk. From the first-stage

Table 1: Summary Statistics.

	Obs	Mean	Std. Dev.	Min	Max
Measures of overall bank risk					
Stock_volatility	278	0.4027	0.1670	0.0873	1.1142
Rwa_ratio	406	0.7645	0.3308	0.1104	6.4308
Risk-adjusted performance measures					
ROA/stock return volatility	236	0.0333	0.0498	−0.4399	0.2794
Operating income/ RWA	406	0.0793	0.0332	−0.0173	0.2551
Other bank variables					
Total assets	509	9,378,254	18,100,000	49,994	194,000,000
Cost-income	508	0.6339	0.3347	0.2338	6.5676
Diversification	509	0.0262	0.0344	−0.0372	0.5658

Source: Authors' elaboration on Bankscope and Bloomberg. All values are in units, except than for total assets (in Euros).

probit regression, we can observe that *Size* has a positive coefficient, statistically significant at the 1% level, indicating that larger firms are more likely to adopt ERM, as expected and consistent with the large-scale hypothesis. Neither *Diversification* nor the lag of *Stock return volatility* show a statistically significant coefficient. This may be due to the existence of several opposite effects: on the one hand, it could be that more diversified firms have a more complex business and hence a greater incentive to adopt ERM; on the other hand, more diversified firms are also less risky and this could decrease such incentive. A similar argument may be raised also for the past level of firm risk: ERM firms may be more risk-adverse and hence less volatile, but riskier firms may have a greater advantage in adopting a holistic risk management approach. As expected, institutions located in *NO_EU* countries

Table 2: Impact of ERM Adoption on Bank Overall Risk — Stock Return Volatility.

First Stage Regression	Probit (1)	Second Stage Regression	(2) Group FE	(3) Firm FE
Determinants of ERM Adoption		Y = Stock Return Volatility		
Y = ERM_adoption = 1				
Size	0.56338***	Size	0.03146	−0.05610
	(0.19397)		(0.02354)	(0.06810)
Diversification	−0.79133	Diversification	−0.05741**	−0.09341
	(0.50161)		(0.02859)	(0.08970)
Cost income	−0.59230*	Cost income	0.02662***	0.02538***
	(0.33311)		(0.00341)	(0.00755)
NO_EU	−0.96325***	NO_EU	−0.00503	
	(0.30157)		(0.03495)	
Stock return volatility$_{t-1}$	−0.57334			
	(0.84309)			
Constant	−0.54403			
	(0.42785)			
		ERM_bank	−0.02339	
			(0.03860)	

		ERM_bank*ERM_adoption	−0.19644*	−0.19844
			(0.10195)	(0.20476)
		Mills	0.13328**	0.14241
			(0.06062)	(0.13820)
		Constant	0.33172***	0.36436***
			(0.02620)	(0.03300)
Year dummies	YES	Year dummies	YES	YES
Observations	187	Observations	183	183
Psuedo R-Squared	0.1866	R-squared	0.52763	0.57937
		Number of firm_id		30
Robust standard errors in parentheses		Robust standard errors in parentheses		

*** $p < 0.01$, ** $p < 0.05$, * $p < 0.1$.

This table reports the result of a two-step model analyzing bank overall risk. The first step (1) is a probit model explaining the probability to adopt ERM. The second step is a regression model in which the dependent variable is the bank's overall risk measured in terms of Stock return volatility. The regressors are indicator variables related to the ERM adoption, a set of bank-specific control variables, and a correction with the selection hazard estimated from the first step. Model (2) is a group FE regression, including a dummy variable (ERM_bank) indicating firms implementing or not ERM in the investigated period. Model (3) is a firm FE estimation, including firm fixed effects. The sample period is 2005–2013. All regressors are standardized. Financial data are drawn from Bankscope; market data from Bloomberg.

thave a lower probability to adopt ERM (the coefficient is negative and statistically significant at the 1% level). Finally, banks with a lower *Cost-income* ratio are more likely to adopt ERM (the coefficient is negative and statistically significant at the 10% level), probably because their higher level of operational efficiency allows devoting more resources to sophisticated risk management processes. From the second stage regression, using a group fixed effect model, we can observe that there are no structural differences in the level of overall risk between banks adopting or not ERM over the investigated period (consistently with the findings of the first step): *ERM_bank* shows a coefficient that is not statistically significant at the 10% confidence level or less. However, there is some evidence that the ERM approach is able to reduce overall risk after its implementation (the coefficient for *ERM_bank*ERM_adoption* is negative and significant at the 10% level). In addition to this, the selection hazard (*Mills*) appears in the regression with a significant coefficient (at the 5% level), showing that it is important to control for the endogeneity problem. These results are not confirmed when we move to a firm fixed effect model, in which both *ERM_bank*ERM_ adoption* and *Mills* are no more significant. Other control variables present intuitive results: more diversified and more efficient banks are less volatile (while *Diversification* shows a negative and statistically significant coefficient only in Model 2, *Cost income* is positive and statistically significant in both Models 2 and 3).

Moving to the alternative specification, in which the overall firm risk is measured by the risk-weighted asset ratio (see Table 3), we can see that results from the first stage are quite similar to the previous one: large banks are more likely to adopt ERM, and the same is evident for ones that are more efficient. Being out of the EU lowers the probability to adopt ERM, while the coefficient for lagged risk is not statistically significant at the 10% level or less. Differently from the model presented in Table 2, *Diversification* seems to be inversely related to the ERM adoption (the coefficient is negative and statistically significant at the 1% confidence level); this provides support to the idea that less diversified firms are more risky and then more incentivized to adopt ERM. In this case,

Table 3: Impact of ERM Adoption on Bank Overall Risk — Rwa Ratio.

First Stage Regression	Probit (1)	Second Stage Regression	(2) Group FE	(3) Firm FE
Determinants of ERM Adoption		Y = Rwa Ratio		
Y = ERM_adoption = 1				
Size	0.31072**	Size	0.06660***	0.10743
	(0.15394)		(0.02156)	(0.09781)
Diversification	–1.03540***	Diversification	–0.03444	0.02720
	(0.37244)		(0.04373)	(0.03062)
Cost income	–0.78642**	Cost income	–0.02091***	–0.01651***
	(0.30985)		(0.00748)	(0.00467)
NO_EU	–0.57595**	NO_EU	0.06318*	
	(0.23153)		(0.03466)	
Rwa $ratio_{t-1}$	–0.87002			
	(0.77015)			
Constant	–0.14113			
	(0.58659)			

Table 3: (*Continued*)

First Stage Regression	Probit (1)	Second Stage Regression	(2) Group FE	(3) Firm FE
Determinants of ERM Adoption		Y = Rwa Ratio		
Y = ERM_adoption = 1				
		ERM_bank	0.00329	
			(0.03703)	
		ERM_bank*ERM_adoption	−0.46529***	−0.42069*
			(0.12838)	(0.21434)
		Mills	0.24496***	0.11654
			(0.07762)	(0.09686)
		Constant	0.78042***	0.79388***
			(0.03861)	(0.04510)
Year dummies	YES	Year dummies	YES	YES
Observations	210	Observations	206	206

Psuedo R-Squared	0.1619	R-squared	0.26551	0.13468
		Number of firm_id		45
Robust standard errors in parentheses		Robust standard errors in parentheses		

*** $p < 0.01$, ** $p < 0.05$, * $p < 0.1$.
This table reports the result of a two-step model analyzing bank overall risk. The first step (1) is a probit model explaining the probability to adopt ERM. The second step is a regression model explaining bank overall risk measured in terms of Rwa ratio. The regressors are indicator variables related to the ERM adoption, a set of bank-specific control variables, and a correction with the selection hazard estimated from the first step. Model (2) is a group FE regression, including a dummy variable (ERM_bank) indicating firms implementing or not ERM in the investigated period. Model (3) is a firm FE estimation, including firm fixed effects. The sample period is 2005–2013. All regressors are standardized. Financial data are drawn from Bankscope; market data from Bloomberg.

the second stage regression shows findings in favor of hypothesis H_1 more robust with respect to the model considering stock return volatility. The group fixed effect model does not reveal structural risk differences between firms adopting or not ERM during the investigated period (consistently with the findings of the first step). However, the ERM adoption results to lower bank overall risk. A negative coefficient for *ERM_bank*ERM_adoption* is statistically significant at the 1% level in Model 2 and remains significant, even though only at a lower 10% level, also in Model 3. When we use firm fixed effects, the only control variable remaining determinant is the level of *Cost income*, with a counterintuitive result (i.e., less efficient banks, with a higher cost income, show a lower level of risk).

Overall, we can conclude that H_1: *All else equal, the ERM adoption is associated with a reduction in the overall firm risk* is confirmed. With respect to the paper of Eckles et al. (2014), our results provide a less strong evidence of the risk reduction impact; however, if we consider that our sample is significantly smaller and that we deal with emerging markets rather than with the United States, our models provide important findings about the effects of the ERM implementation. These findings have important policy implications since provide support for the recent regulatory attention on this issue. For example, the CRD IV Directive explicitly requires the presence of an independent senior manager with distinct responsibility for the risk management function and devotes an entire section to "Technical criteria concerning the organization and treatment of risks."

We now focus on findings obtained testing H_2, starting from the model in which the risk-adjusted performance is measured as the ratio between ROA and stock return volatility, as in Eckles et al. (2014) (see Table 4). The first stage is the same used in Table 2 for testing H_1. From the second stage regression, using a group fixed effect model (including *ERM_bank*), we can observe that there are no structural differences in risk-adjusted performance between firms ever adopting the ERM approach or not. However, firms introducing ERM are able to increase their overall risk-adjusted performance (the coefficient for *ERM_bank*ERM_adoption* is positive

Table 4: Impact of ERM Adoption on Risk-Adjusted Performance — ROA/Stock Return Volatility.

First Stage Regression	Probit (1)	Second Stage Regression	(2) Group FE	(3) Firm FE
Determinants of ERM Adoption		Y = ROA/Stock Return Volatility		
Y = ERM_adoption = 1				
Size	0.56338***	Size	−0.00069	0.02197
	(0.19397)		(0.00456)	(0.03343)
Diversification	−0.79133	Diversification	0.03266***	0.01884
	(0.50161)		(0.00984)	(0.01527)
Cost income	−0.59230*	Cost income	−0.00259**	−0.00089
	(0.33311)		(0.00123)	(0.00178)
NO_EU	−0.96325***	NO_EU	0.00972	
	(0.30157)		(0.00848)	
Stock return volatility$_{t-1}$	−0.57334			
	(0.84309)			
Constant	−0.54403			
	(0.42785)			

Table 4: (*Continued*)

First Stage Regression	Probit (1)	Second Stage Regression	(2) Group FE	(3) Firm FE
Determinants of ERM Adoption		Y = ROA/Stock Return Volatility		
Y = ERM_adoption = 1				
		ERM_bank	−0.00790	
			(0.00702)	
		ERM_bank*ERM_adoption	0.07849***	0.06908
			(0.02479)	(0.05920)
		Mills	−0.04144***	−0.03454
			(0.01488)	(0.03702)
		Constant	0.05704***	0.04617***
			(0.00622)	(0.01476)
Year dummies	YES	Year dummies	YES	YES
Observations	187	Observations	183	183

Psuedo R-Squared	0.1866	R-squared	0.48415	0.34530
		Number of firm_id		30
Robust standard errors in parentheses		Robust standard errors in parentheses		

*** $p < 0.01$, ** $p < 0.05$, * $p < 0.1$.

This table reports the result of a two-step model analyzing bank risk-adjusted performance. The first step (1) is a probit model explaining the probability to adopt ERM. The second step is a regression model explaining bank risk-adjusted performance measured as the ratio between ROA and stock return volatility. The regressors are indicator variables related to the ERM adoption, a set of bank-specific control variables, and a correction with the selection hazard estimated from the first step. Model (2) is a group FE regression, including a dummy variable (ERM_bank) indicating firms implementing or not ERM in the investigated period. Model (3) is a firm FE estimation, including firm fixed effects. The sample period is 2005-2013. All regressors are standardized. Financial data are drawn from Bankscope; market data from Bloomberg.

and statistically significant at the 1% level); in addition to this, the selection hazard (*Mills*) appears in the regression with a significant coefficient (at the 1% level), showing that it is important to control for the endogeneity problem. Control regressors suggest that banks that are more diversified and more efficient overperform their competitors. Nevertheless, these results are not confirmed when we move to a firm fixed effect model (both *ERM_bank*ERM_adoption* and *Mills* are no more significant). Control regressors also lose their significance and the model shows a much lower explanatory power.

Moving to the alternative model in which the risk-adjusted performance is measured by the ratio between total operating income and risk-weighted assets (reported in Table 5), we can find more robust results in favor of H_2. In this case, the first stage regression is the same used for testing H_1 in Table 3. The group fixed effect model suggests that banks adopting the ERM during the investigated period are on average less performant than their competitors. However, there is quite a strong evidence that the ERM approach is able to increase risk-adjusted performance after its implementation. A positive coefficient for *ERM_bank*ERM_adoption* is statistically significant at the 1% level in Model 2 and remains significant, at the same level, also in Model 3. The selection hazard is also statistically significant in both models (at the 1% level in Model 2 and at the 5% level in Model 3), confirming the importance to account for the endogeneity problem. When we use firm fixed effects, the only control variables remaining determinant are the level of *Diversification* (more diversified banks overperform their competitors) and the level of *Cost income* (presenting in this model a counterintuitive sign, suggesting that less efficient banks have a higher level of risk-adjusted performance). As for the case of risk, we can observe than models for risk-adjusted performance based on accounting indicators provide more significant results with respect to the ones based on market measures.

Overall, we can conclude that H_2: *All else equal, the ERM adoption is associated with an increase in the bank risk-adjusted performance* is confirmed. With respect to the paper of Eckles et al. (2014), our results provide similar evidence of the positive impact on the

Table 5: Impact of ERM Adoption on Risk-Adjusted Performance — Total Operating Income/ Risk-Weighted Assets.

First Stage Regression	Probit (1)	Second Stage Regression	(2) Group FE	(3) Firm FE
Determinants of ERM Adoption		Y = Total Operating Income/ Risk Weighted Assets		
Y = ERM_adoption = 1				
Size	0.31072**	Size	−0.00812**	−0.02148
	(0.15394)		(0.00344)	(0.01702)
Diversification	−1.03540***	Diversification	0.04916***	0.04213***
	(0.37244)		(0.00767)	(0.00742)
Cost income	−0.78642**	Cost income	0.00153*	0.00175**
	(0.30985)		(0.00079)	(0.00072)
NO_EU	−0.57595**	NO_EU	0.02629***	
	(0.23153)		(0.00654)	
Rwa ratio$_{-1}$	−0.87002			
	(0.77015)			
Constant	−0.14113			
	(0.58659)			

Table 5: (*Continued*)

First Stage Regression	Probit (1)	Second Stage Regression	(2) Group FE	(3) Firm FE
Determinants of ERM Adoption		Y = Total Operating Income/ Risk Weighted Assets		
Y = ERM_adoption = 1				
		ERM_bank	–0.02180***	
			(0.00720)	
		ERM_bank*ERM_adoption	0.08812***	0.08748***
			(0.02192)	(0.02949)
		Mills	–0.04053***	–0.03393**
			(0.01252)	(0.01317)
		Constant	0.06337***	0.07252***
			(0.00696)	(0.00764)
Observations	210	Observations	206	206

Psuedo R-Squared	0.1619	R-squared	0.33632	0.25729
		Number of firm_id		45
Robust standard errors in parentheses		Robust standard errors in parentheses		

*** $p < 0.01$, ** $p < 0.05$, * $p < 0.1$.

This table reports the result of a two-step model analyzing bank risk-adjusted performance. The first step is a probit model explaining the probability to adopt ERM. The second step is a regression model explaining bank risk-adjusted performance measured as the ratio between total operating income and risk-weighted assets. The regressors are indicator variables related to the ERM adoption, a set of bank-specific control variables, and a correction with the selection hazard estimated from the first step. Model (2) is a group FE regression, including a dummy variable (ERM_bank) indicating firms implementing or not ERM in the investigated period. Model (3) is a firm FE estimation, including firm fixed effects. The sample period is 2005–2013. All regressors are standardized. Financial data are drawn from Bankscope; market data from Bloomberg.

risk-adjusted performance. Considering these findings together with those regarding H_1, it is possible to affirm that despite the use of a small sample and of parsimonious regression models, there is quite a strong evidence that the ERM adoption has been positive for banks operating in emerging Europe, similarly to what has happened in more developed financial systems. The positive effect is not only in terms of risk reduction, but also in terms of performance enhancement, lending support to the idea that ERM is crucial not only for regulatory, compliance and loss mitigation issues, but also to transforming risk as part of the strategy process, informing discussion and deliberations at all levels (McKinsey & Company, 2013).

Conclusions

Does the adoption of the Enterprise Risk Management (ERM) approach reduce bank risk? Does ERM also improve bank risk-adjusted performance? Our analysis shows that the ERM adoption helps banks operating in European emerging markets to improve their profits and reduce risks.

Specifically, we posit the following research hypotheses: H_1: All else equal, the ERM adoption is associated with a reduction in the overall bank risk; H_2: All else equal, the ERM adoption is associated with an increase in the bank risk-adjusted performance. To investigate our research hypotheses, we specify a model in which the dependent variable is the overall bank risk (to test H_1) and then a risk-adjusted performance measure (to test H_2), the independent variables are a dummy indicating ERM adoption (this is our main interest variable) and various control variables. To address a potential endogeneity concern (due to an omitted variables bias), we follow Eckles et al. (2014) and we also employ the Heckman two-step procedure to estimate the impact of ERM implementation on both bank profitability and risk.

A critical issue in our study is the measurement of the ERM. Following previous literature (Aebi et al., 2012; Eckles et al., 2014; Ellul & Yerramilli, 2013; Hoyt & Liebenberg, 2003, 2011;

Pagach & Warr, 2010; Lin et al., 2012), we use a binary proxy variable (i.e., the appointment of a Chief Risk Officer) to define whether the firm is currently undertaking an ERM program. Next, we measure bank risk as the annualized standard deviation of daily stock returns and bank profits as risk-adjusted performance (i.e. the ratio between the ROA and the stock return volatility). As a robustness check, we also use accounting-based indicators, measuring bank risk as the risk-weighted asset ratio and bank profits as the ratio between total operating income and risk-weighted assets. Previous studies in the field are very rare and deal with the U.S. banking (Aebi et al., 2012; Ellul & Yerramilli, 2013) or insurance (Eckles et al., 2014) industries during the financial crisis.

At our knowledge, our study is the first analysis providing empirical evidence in European emerging markets and considering a period that covers all three stages of the financial crisis (i.e., the U.S. subprime crisis, the global financial crisis and the sovereign debt crisis).

We find a quite strong evidence that ERM has a positive impact on both reducing risk and enhancing risk-adjusted performance. We believe to be particularly important the focus on European emerging markets due to the fast growth of their banking systems and the large variety of their institutional and regulatory frameworks (e.g., differences between EU and non-EU countries). Banks operating in these markets have experienced an unprecedented growth in the past decade; this growth will probably continue, but at a slower pace: for example, in a recent study, McKinsey & Company (2014) reports for Eastern Europe banks a CAGR of revenue pools after risk cost equal to 16.2% over 2002–2012 and estimated at 8.8% for 2012–2020. This implies that risk management has now moved to the top of their agenda, as previously happened for U.S. and Western Europe banks.

In final, our analysis provides empirical support to recent regulatory and market pressure on the implementation of ERM, supporting the idea that the structure and the organization of the risk management function is not only crucial for compliance and loss mitigation issues, but also to render the strategy and the culture of the entire bank more consistent with its risk appetite and its long-term objectives.

Acknowledgments

Franco Fiordelisi and Ornella Ricci wish to gratefully acknowledge the support of the Czech Science Foundation within the project GAČR 13-03783S "Banking Sector and Monetary Policy: Lessons from New EU Countries after Ten Years of Membership."

References

Acharya, V., Carpenter, J. N., Gabaix, X., John, K., Richardson, M., Subrahmanyam, G., ... Zemel, E. (2009). Corporate governance in the modern financial sector. In V. Acharya & M. Richardson (Eds.), *Restoring financial stability*. Hoboken, NJ: Wiley Finance.

Aebi, V., Sabato, G., & Schmid, M. (2012). Risk management, corporate governance, and bank performance in the financial crisis. *Journal of Banking & Finance, 36*, 3213–3226.

Beasley, M. S., Clune, R., & Hermanson, D. R. (2005). Enterprise risk management: An empirical analysis of factors associated with the extent of implementation. *Journal of Accounting and Public Policy, 24*, 521–531.

Beasley, M., Pagach, D., & Warr, R. (2008). Information conveyed in hiring announcements of senior executives overseeing enterprise-wide risk management processes. *Journal of Accounting, Auditing & Finance*, 311–332.

Carhart, M. M. (1997). On persistence of mutual fund performance. *Journal of Finance, 52*, 57–82.

Colquitt, L., Hoyt, R. E., & Lee, R. B. (1999). Integrated risk management and the role of the risk manager. *Risk Management and Insurance Review, 2*, 43–61.

Cumming, C. M., & Hirtle, B. J. (2001). The challenges of risk management in diversified financial companies. *FRBNY Economic Policy Review, 7*, 1–17.

Desender, K. A. (2007). *The influence of board composition on enterprise risk management implementation*. Working Paper. Retrieved from http://papers.ssrn.com/sol3/papers.cfm?abstract%20id=1025982

Eckles, D. L., Hoyt, R. E., & Miller, S. M. (2014). The impact of enterprise risk management on the marginal cost of reducing risk: Evidence from the insurance industry. *Journal of Banking & Finance, 43*, 247–261.
Ellul, A., & Yerramilli, V. (2013). Stronger risk controls, lower risk: Evidence from U.S. bank holding companies. *The Journal of Finance, 68*, 1757–1803.
Farrell, M., & Gallagher, R. (2014). The valuation implications of enterprise risk management maturity. *The Journal of Risk Finance, 15*, 1–33.
Fraser, J., & Simkins, B. J. (2010). *Enterprise risk management: Today's leading research and best practices for tomorrow's executives*. Hoboken, NJ: Wiley.
Gates, S., Nicolas, J. L., & Walker, P. L. (2009). *Perceived value of enterprise risk management*. University of Virginia Working Paper.
Heckman, J. J. (1979). Sample selection bias as a specification error. *Econometrica, 47*, 153–161.
Hoyt, R. E., & Liebenberg, A. P. (2003). Determinants of enterprise risk management: Evidence from the appointment of chief risk officers. *Risk Management and Insurance Review, 6*, 37–52.
Hoyt, R. E., & Liebenberg, A. P. (2011). The value of enterprise risk management. *The Journal of Risk and Insurance, 78*, 795–822.
Hull, J. C. (2015). *Risk management and financial institutions*. Hoboken, NJ: Wiley.
Kleffner, A. E., Lee, R. B., & McGannon, B. (2003). The effect of corporate governance on the use of enterprise risk management: Evidence from Canada. *Risk Management and Insurance Review, 6*, 53–73.
Lam, J. (2001). The CRO is here to stay. *Risk Management, 48*, 16–20.
Liebenberg, A. P., & Hoyt, R. E. (2003). The determinants of enterprise risk management: Evidence from the appointment of chief risk officers. *Risk Management and Insurance Review, 6*, 37–52.
Lin, Y., Wen, M., & Yu, J. (2012). Enterprise risk management: Strategic antecedents, risk integration, and performance. *North American Actuarial Journal, 16*, 1–28.
McKinsey & Company. (2013). *Getting to ERM. A roadmap for banks and other financial institutions*. McKinsey Working Papers on Risk No. 43, March.
McKinsey & Company. (2014). *Risk in emerging markets. The way forward for leading banks*. McKinsey Working Papers on Risk No. 56, June.
Meulbroek, L. K. (2002). Integrated risk management for the firm: A senior manager's guide. *Journal of Applied Corporate Finance, 14*, 56–70.
Miccolis, J., & Shah, S. (2000). *Enterprise risk management: An analytic approach*. New York, NY: Tillinghast-Towers Perrin Monograph.
Nocco, B. W., & Stulz, R. M. (2006). Enterprise risk management: Theory and practice. *Journal of Applied Corporate Finance, 18*, 8–20.

Organization for Economic Co-operation and Development (OECD). (2009). Corporate governance and the financial crisis. Key findings and main messages, June.

Organization for Economic Co-operation and Development (OECD). (2010). Corporate governance and the financial crisis. Conclusions and emerging good practices to enhance implementation of the Principles, 24 February.

Pagach, D., & Warr, R. (2010). *The effects of enterprise risk management on firm performance*. World WideWeb. Retrieved from http://ssrn.com/abstract=1155218. Accessed on April 10.

Pagach, D., & Warr, R. (2011). The characteristics of firms that hire chief risk officers. *The Journal of Risk and Insurance*, *78*, 185–211.

Sabato, G. (2014). *Financial crisis: Where did risk management fail?* doi: 10.2139/ssrn.1460762.

Stulz, R. M. (2008). Risk management failures: What are they and when do they happen? *Journal of Applied Corporate Finance*, *20*, 39–48.

Appendix

Table A1: List of Analyzed Banks (in Alphabetical Order).

AK Bars Bank	RUSSIAN FEDERATION
Alfa Bank PJSC	UKRAINE
Alior Bank Spólka Akcyjna	POLAND
Banca Comerciala Carpatica SA	ROMANIA
Banca de Economii a Moldovei	REPUBLIC OF MOLDOVA
Banca Sociala SA	REPUBLIC OF MOLDOVA
Bank BPH SA	POLAND
Bank Handlowy w Warszawie S.A.	POLAND
Bank Millennium	POLAND
Bank Ochrony Srodowiska SA – BOS SA-Bank Ochrony Srodowiska Capital Group	POLAND
Bank of Khanty-Mansiysk	RUSSIAN FEDERATION
Bank Petrocommerce	RUSSIAN FEDERATION
Bank Polska Kasa Opieki SA-Bank Pekao SA	POLAND
Bank Saint-Petersburg	RUSSIAN FEDERATION
Bank UralSib	RUSSIAN FEDERATION
Bank Zachodni WBK S.A.	POLAND

Table A1: (*Continued*)

Bank Zenit	RUSSIAN FEDERATION
BC Unibank SA	REPUBLIC OF MOLDOVA
BNP Paribas Bank Polska SA	POLAND
BRD-Groupe Societe Generale SA	ROMANIA
Chelindbank Group-Chelindbank – Chelyabinsk Joint Stock Commercial Bank	RUSSIAN FEDERATION
Corporate Commercial Bank AD	BULGARIA
DZ Bank Polska SA	POLAND
Eurostandard Banka ad Skopje	MACEDONIA
Finance and Credit Bank	UKRAINE
First Investment Bank AD	BULGARIA
First Ukrainian International Bank	UKRAINE
Gazprombank Open Joint-Stock Company	RUSSIAN FEDERATION
Getin Noble Bank SA	POLAND
ING Bank Slaski S.A. – Capital Group	POLAND
Joint Stock Bank Avangard	RUSSIAN FEDERATION
Joint Stock Commercial Bank – Bank of Moscow	RUSSIAN FEDERATION
Joint-Stock Commercial Bank for Social Development – Ukrsotsbank	UKRAINE
JSC Rosbank	RUSSIAN FEDERATION
Komercijalna Banka A.D. Beograd	SERBIA

Table A1: (*Continued*)

Komercijalna Banka A.D. Skopje	MACEDONIA
Komercni Banka	CZECH REPUBLIC
mBank SA	POLAND
MDM Bank	RUSSIAN FEDERATION
Moldova Agroindbank SA	REPUBLIC OF MOLDOVA
Moscow Industrial Bank	RUSSIAN FEDERATION
NLB Montenegrobanka ad Podgorica	MONTENEGRO
Nova Kreditna Banka Maribor d.d.	SLOVENIA
OJSC Promsvyazbank	RUSSIAN FEDERATION
Open Joint Stock Company UniCredit Bank	UKRAINE
Open Joint-Stock Company MTS Bank	RUSSIAN FEDERATION
OTP Bank Plc	HUNGARY
Pivdennyi Joint-Stock Bank	UKRAINE
Podravska Banka	CROATIA
Privredna Banka Zagreb d.d-Privredna Banka Zagreb Group	CROATIA
Probanka d.d. Maribor	SLOVENIA
Probusiness Bank	RUSSIAN FEDERATION
Public Joint-Stock Company 'Bank Otkritie Financial Corporation'	RUSSIAN FEDERATION

Table A1: (*Continued*)

Raiffeisen Bank Aval	UKRAINE
SDM Bank JSC	RUSSIAN FEDERATION
Siauliu Bankas	LITHUANIA
Slatinska Banka dd	CROATIA
Tatra Banka a.s.	SLOVAKIA
Teximbank-PEB Texim AD	BULGARIA
Transilvania Bank-Banca Transilvania SA	ROMANIA
Urals Transport Joint-Stock Bank – UralTransBank	RUSSIAN FEDERATION
VABank-Vseukrainsky Aktsionerny Bank	UKRAINE
Vozrozhdeniye Bank	RUSSIAN FEDERATION
Vseobecna Uverova Banka a.s.	SLOVAKIA
VTB Bank, an Open Joint-Stock Company (JSC)	RUSSIAN FEDERATION
West Siberian Commercial Bank-Zapsibcombank	RUSSIAN FEDERATION
Zagrebacka Banka dd	CROATIA

11

The Informational Content of Issuer Credit Rating Changes in Emerging Stock Markets: Evidence from China

Haoshen Hu and Jörg Prokop

Abstract

We study the information content of issuer credit rating changes announced by a group of six Chinese credit rating agencies. We conduct an event study, and we use multivariate regression analyses to identify factors driving abnormal stock returns. Our results confirm prior findings for Western countries that downgrades are associated with significant negative abnormal returns. However, upgrades and positive or negative rating outlooks do not seem to have information content. While we cannot find differences in information content conditional on which rating agency issues the downgrade, we find that abnormal returns may vary with the target firm's industry. In addition, the magnitude of stock price reactions to rating downgrades seems to be related to the business cycle to some extent. With respect to the role of the industry in explaining the information content of rating changes, our results may be biased due to small sample size. Nevertheless, they illustrate that the role the industry plays in explaining investor behavior may deserve special attention in future research. Our findings imply that new rating information seems to be processed quickly in the Chinese stock market, and that market reactions to rating signals are largely in line with what has been observed for Western stock markets. Both observations lend credibility to observable stock prices. The chapter sheds new light on the relevance of Chinese credit rating agencies from an equity investor's perspective and confirms similarities between the Chinese and Western stock markets with respect to the way rating signals are processed by investors.

Keywords: Abnormal returns; China; credit rating agency; credit risk; event study; rating outlook

JEL classifications: G14; G24

Introduction

In spite of China's rich history in international trade, and its current position as both one of the leading emerging markets and the world's second largest economy, the emergence of its credit rating industry is a rather recent phenomenon. Starting in 1987, the People's Bank of China was one of the country's first official providers of credit rating services, acting mainly on behalf of the Chinese government. In the early 1990s, China Cheng X in Credit Management Co., Ltd. (CCXI) was founded as the first independent credit rating agency (CRA), followed by the emergence of other local CRAs, such as Dagong and Lianhe. In order to improve their rating methodology's quality, and to foster international acceptance, China's local CRAs soon entered into cooperation agreements with leading international CRAs, as evidenced by the acquisition of 49 percent of CCXI's shares by Moody's in 2006, and of 49 percent of Lianhe's shares by Fitch in 2007. However, compared to ratings issued by (Western) international CRAs, their Chinese counterparts are often considered less informative, and more prone to positive biases due to weaker capital market regulation, lower investor sophistication, and higher government involvement.[1] In this chapter, our aim is to scrutinize this alleged lack of information content using the impact of six Chinese CRAs' issuer credit rating changes on stock prices as an indicator. Our final sample consists of 51 downgrades, 208 upgrades, and 137 rating outlooks, and covers a period from 2003 to 2014.

The results confirm our hypothesis regarding an asymmetric market reaction to rating changes: while downgrades lead to significantly negative abnormal stock returns in almost all event windows, there is no significant stock market reaction to upgrades. Moreover, positive and negative rating outlooks — serving as mid-term indicators of future rating changes — do not induce significant abnormal stock returns either. In a cross-sectional regression analysis, we show that downgrades issued by Xinhua Far East (allegedly one of the most independent CRAs) do not induce stronger market reactions than downgrades issued by other Chinese CRAs. Finally, abnormal returns associated with downgrades of the firms classified as "industrials" seem to be significantly larger than abnormal returns following downgrades in other industries, and the information content of downgrades seems to be conditional on the economic cycle at least to some extent.

The remainder of this chapter is organized as follows: The section "Literature Review and Hypothesis Development" reviews relevant literature and develops our test hypotheses. The section "Data and Methodology" presents the data and the test methodology. The section "Event Study Results" discusses the event study's results, and the section "Regression Analysis" contains the multivariate regression analysis. The final section concludes.

---

1. Kennedy (2003), Kennedy (2008), Rong, Ye, and Wang (2010), Wilson (2006).

Literature Review and Hypothesis Development

Literature Background

A credit rating is an opinion on the (relative) creditworthiness of an entity, or of a financial instrument. The effect of rating changes on the underlying firm's stock prices has been studied extensively for the US capital market, and these studies typically find that stock markets react significantly negative to rating downgrades, while market reactions to rating upgrades are often insignificant.[2] In addition, there is also a considerable number of studies in this area covering other developed markets, with their results usually being consistent with prior findings for the United States.[3] However, most of these studies are based on data from one or more of the big three international credit rating agencies, namely Fitch, Moody's, and Standard & Poor's. By contrast, evidence on the information content of rating signals by other CRAs relating to firms in emerging markets is rather scarce.

China's bond market has experienced rapid growth since its emergence in the mid-1980s. It started with 20 bond issues and an issued volume of about 13 billion RMB in 1990, and reached a historical peak in terms of the number of new issues in 2010. In 2014, there were 1458 new issues with an issued volume of almost 6000 billion RMB.[4] In August 2014, the size of the bond market even exceeded the size of the Chinese stock market in terms of total market capitalization.[5] However, despite its growing

2. Griffin and Sanvicente (1982), Holthausen and Leftwich (1986), Ederington and Goh (1998), Goh and Ederington (1999), Norden and Weber (2004), Li, Shin, and Moore (2006), Kim and Nabar (2007) find significant stock price responses to bond rating downgrades, but not to upgrades. By contrast, a few papers such as Stickel (1986), Hsueh and Liu (1992), Jorion, Liu, and Shi (2005), Jorion and Zhang (2007) find significant stock market reactions to both downgrades and upgrades.

3. Barron, Clare, and Thomas (1997), Li et al. (2006), Creighton, Gower, and Richards (2007), Chan, Edwards, and Walter (2009).

4. China Central Depository & Clearing Co., Ltd. (2015).

5. China Securities Regulatory Commission (2015).

importance China's bond market has often been criticized for an apparent lack of reliable credit risk indicators. One of the main reasons for this is an alleged informational irrelevance of the credit ratings issued by China's domestic credit rating agencies. For instance, Kennedy (2008) claims that when making investment decisions, institutional or private investors pay little attention to ratings issued by Chinese CRAs since they expect them to be biased upwards due to a lack of CRA independence. This view is supported by Rong et al. (2010) who argue that Chinese CRAs tend to be less experienced than their international competitors, and rely on immature rating methodologies, which on average leads to exaggerated credit ratings.

While these arguments may seem plausible, our aim is to challenge their validity by testing empirically the information content of rating changes issued by Chinese CRAs. To the best of our knowledge, there are only very few empirical studies focusing on the impact of credit ratings on China's stock market. For instance, Poon and Chan (2008a, 2008b) study the significance of both the certification effect of initial ratings and the signaling effect of rating downgrades based on a sample provided by Xinhua Far East China Credit Rating for the period January 2002–July 2006. In addition, Poon and Chan (2008a, 2008b) confirm that credit ratings and rating outlooks by Xinhua Far East do have significant effects on stock returns, and that some firm-specific variables such as profitability or past stock performance are relevant in explaining ratings and outlooks. Finally, Poon, Chan, and Firth (2013) show that unsolicited ratings by Xinhua Far East mitigate underpricing problems in seasoned equity offerings by Chinese listed firms.

In our view, the main limitations of previous empirical studies in this area are twofold: Firstly, they cover only an early time period, typically ending well before 2009. However, the emerging Chinese capital market in general, and the Chinese bond market in particular have recently undergone substantial changes with respect to regulation, competitiveness, and market structure. For instance, on March 4, 2014 Shanghai Chaori Solar Energy Science & Technology Co. announced a partial default on its corporate bond "11 Chaori."[6] Being the very first default announcement that ever occurred in China's bond market, this event marks the end of an impeccable debt service record, and casts a new light on the relevance of credit risk in the Chinese market. Secondly, prior studies are mostly based on credit ratings provided by Xinhua Far East due to its alleged independence. However, in terms of coverage Xinhua Far East was only a small player in the Chinese rating industry, and it even largely shut down its bond rating activities after the so-called "Fuxi Short-term Financing Bill Event" in 2006.[7] As a consequence, we argue that Xinhua Far East's ratings alone are not an ideal basis for evaluating the role credit ratings play in the Chinese capital market today, and that observations drawn from a richer set of sources may provide additional insights.

In the light of these limitations, we perform a comprehensive event study to analyze the information content of both changes in issuer credit ratings, and rating outlook placements announced by a group of six Chinese leading CRAs for a period ranging from 2003 to 2014. We thereby extend prior research by Poon and Chan (2008a, 2008b) with regard to both time horizon and market coverage. In addition, we perform a multivariate regression analysis to provide new evidence on potential idiosyncratic and systematic drivers of abnormal stock market returns. Regarding the latter, Amato and Furfine (2004) show that credit ratings issued by Standard & Poor's tend to exhibit a certain degree of positive covariation with the business cycle, but do not seem to be overly sensitive to the respective firms' macroeconomic environment. However, based on a theoretical model taking into account CRAs' reputational concerns, Bar-Isaac and Shapiro (2013) argue that ratings quality — and thus informativeness — should be rather countercyclical. With a focus on bank ratings, Hau, Langfield, and Marques-Ibanez (2013) confirm this result empirically, and

6. http://www.bloomberg.com/news/2014-03-07/chaori-solar-fails-to-make-interest-payments-on-bond-wsj-says.html

7. http://www.dagongxypj.com/credit.php?pid=4960&tid=118

conclude that "bank ratings are a better predictor of credit risk during a financial crisis than in normal times" (p. 313). Tying in with this idea, we control for the state of the economy in our study using a diffusion index. Following Gatfaoui and Girardin (2015), we employ the CEMAC-Goldman Sachs Economic Climate Coincident Index as a proxy for the state of the Chinese business cycle.[8]

Hypotheses

Based on prior findings for both developed countries and the Chinese economy, our test hypotheses are as follows:

> **Hypothesis 1.** Stock price reactions to rating downgrades are significantly negative.
>
> **Hypothesis 2.** Rating upgrades are not associated with significant stock price reactions.
>
> **Hypothesis 3.** Positive or negative outlook announcements are associated with significant stock price reactions.
>
> **Hypothesis 4.** Downgrades issued by Xinhua Far East do not lead to significantly more negative abnormal stock returns than those issued by the Big Five CRAs.
>
> **Hypothesis 5.** The stock market effect of issuer rating downgrades varies depending on certain idiosyncratic and systematic factors.

Data and Methodology

Data

China's domestic credit rating industry consists of both full-service CRAs, and small CRAs which are active in selected market

8. The China Economic Monitoring and Analysis Center (CEMAC) and Goldman Sachs provide three types of economic diffusion indexes: a leading index, a coincident index, and a lagging index. The CEMAC-Goldman Sachs Economic Climate Coincident Index incorporates a number of economic variables, which include industrial corporate profits, fixed asset investment, government tax revenues and industrial labor supply (http://www.cemac.org.cn/Cyzzs.html). As Yamasawa (2008) shows, CEMAC diffusion indexes allow for the identification of peaks and troughs in China's business cycles.

Table 1: Corporate Bond Market Shares of China's Local CRAs for 2014.

Agency	Total Value of Bonds Issued	Market Share by Bond Value (%)	Total Number of Bond Issues	Market Share by Issue Number (%)
Brilliance	81,100	9.12	74	10.48
CCXI	214,840	24.15	121	17.14
Dagong	160,140	18.00	97	13.74
Lianhe	134,320	15.10	110	15.58
Pengyuan	247,468	27.82	253	35.84
Others	51,700	5.81	51	7.22
Total	889,568	100.00	706	100.00

Notes: This table shows corporate bond market shares of China's local CRAs by notional values of bonds issued and total number of bond issues, respectively, for the year 2014. The total value of bond issued is given in millions of RMB. Only corporate and enterprise bonds issued during 2014 which received an initial rating from at least one rating agency are included. Xinhua Far East does not appear in this table since it was not involved in any bond issurance in 2014.

segments only. Based on data drawn from Wind Financial, Table 1 summarizes market shares of the five largest Chinese CRAs as of year-end 2014.

Based on total number of corporate and enterprise bond issues that received at least one issue rating from rating agencies,[9] Pengyuan (Pengyuan Credit Rating) has the highest market share of 35.84 percent, followed by CCXI (China Cheng Xin International Credit Rating, 17.14 percent), Lianhe (China Lianhe Credit Rating, 15.58 percent), Dagong (Dagong Global Credit Rating, 13.74 percent), and Brilliance (Shanghai Brilliance Credit Rating & Investors Service, 10.48 percent). The total market share

9. Issuers of enterprise bonds are state-owned enterprises (SOE), while issuers of corporate bonds can be corporations, joint ventures and limited liability companies according to Chinese Company Law (Chapter 1, Article 2, and Chapter 7, Article 154).

of these "Big Five" CRAs in China amounts to 92.78 percent in corporate and enterprise bond markets. In comparison with market shares by number of bond issues in 2008 reported by He and Jin (2010), we observe a rapid rise of Pengyuan since 2008, and a decline in market position for Xinhua Far East, which did not rate any newly issued corporate or enterprise bond in 2014.

Our sample contains all available issuer credit ratings issued by the "Big Five." To avoid potential biases, we do not include ratings issued by small agencies which only offer rating services in selected market segments. However, since ratings issued by Xinhua Far East were widely used in previous research, and since this CRA was also very active during the first part of our sample period, we also include rating observations for Xinhua Far East in our sample.

We focus on long-term issuer ratings. Unfortunately, although Wind is one of China's leading financial data providers, the rating history available pre-2008 is incomplete. Therefore, in addition to data collected from Wind we also use rating data drawn from Bloomberg and drop any duplicates. We then manually match the resulting rating sample with a stock price dataset obtained from the CSMAR Financial Database. Following Li et al. (2006), we retain only firms for which we have a time series of daily stock returns ranging from 200 days before to five days after the rating event. As a result, we arrive at the full sample with 62 downgrades, 291 upgrades, and 163 outlook placements. Other financial data, such as the Shanghai and Shenzhen Composite Indices' time series, are collected from CSMAR as well. Moreover, we use the monthly Economic Climate Coincident Index published by China Economic Monitoring Center.

We convert the Chinese CRAs' letter ratings into a cardinal scale. For all rating agencies except for Brilliance, the scale starts with a numerical value of "1" for the highest level ("AAA"), and ends with a value of "19" for the lowest level ("C"). In case of Brilliance, which is the only CRA using the letter rating "AAA−" we deviate from this "normal" conversion scheme, and assign a value of "2" to the letter rating "AAA−." As a consequence, a value of "20" reflects Brilliance's lowest rating level ("C"). Thus, as Table 2 shows, if for instance an issuer rated "AA" by CCXI is downgraded to "A+," it is subject to an across-class rating change from the initial rating level of 3 to the new level of 5.

In the next step, we draw on information provided by Wind Financial to eliminate observations from our sample which coincide with potentially confounding corporate events within a [−5, +5] window.[10] In this vein, we get an unbiased sample consisting of 51 downgrades, 208 upgrades and 137 outlook placements. Table 3 summarizes the characteristics of both the initial ("full") and the final ("unbiased") sample.

Panels A and B of Table 3 show the distribution of rating events by industry and by year, respectively. We observe a high concentration of rating changes in the category "industrials" according to CSMAR's primary industry classification system. Besides, more than 50 percent of the rating downgrades occur after 2013, while the distribution of upgrades seems to be uniform since 2009. When differentiating according to the stock exchanges at which the rated firms are listed, we find that about 58 percent of downgrades and upgrades are issued for firms listed at the Shanghai Stock Exchange (Panel C). Panel D shows the distribution of rating changes across all six CRAs.[11]

Methodology

We perform a standard event study based on the market model approach advocated by Brown and Warner (1985). Hence, the abnormal return (AR_{it}) for the common stock of firm i on day t is defined as follows.

---

10. Confounding corporate events include the announcement of earnings levels, mergers or acquisitions, management board changes, stock splits, analyst forecast revisions, public or government financing, dividends, capital structure changes, or seasoned equity offerings, or of being classified as a "Special Treatment" (ST, *ST), or "Particular Transfer" (PT) firm. The latter applies to firms which have reported losses for two (ST) or more (PT) consecutive years.

11. Given the frequency of downgrades and upgrades, Panel D seems to substantiate the critique of Wilson (2012) regarding Dagong's ratings, since Dagong has not issued any rating downgrade for listed companies in the past 12 years.

Table 2: Rating Categories and Definitions.

Normal	Brilliance	Normal_19	Brilliance_20	Class	Rating Definitions
AAA	AAA	1	1	1	Highest quality, smallest risk
.	AAA−	.	2	1	Highest quality, smallest risk
AA+	AA+	2	3	2	High quality, very low credit risk
AA	AA	3	4	2	High quality, very low credit risk
AA−	AA−	4	5	2	High quality, very low credit risk
A+	A+	5	6	3	Upper-medium grade, low credit risk
A	A	6	7	3	Upper-medium grade, low credit risk
A−	A−	7	8	3	Upper-medium grade, low credit risk
BBB+	BBB+	8	9	4	Moderate credit risk

Table 2: (*Continued*)

Normal	Brilliance	Normal_19	Brilliance_20	Class	Rating Definitions
BBB	BBB	9	10	4	Moderate credit risk
BBB –	BBB –	10	11	4	Moderate credit risk
BB +	BB +	11	12	5	Questionable credit quality
BB	BB	12	13	5	Questionable credit quality
BB –	BB –	13	14	5	Questionable credit quality
B +	B +	14	15	6	High credit risk, generally poor credit quality
B	B	15	16	6	High credit risk, generally poor credit quality
B –	B –	16	17	6	High credit risk, generally poor credit quality
CCC	CCC	17	18	7	Very high credit risk, extremely poor credit quality

Table 2: (*Continued*)

Normal	Brilliance	Normal_19	Brilliance_20	Class	Rating Definitions
CC	CC	18	19	8	Highly speculative, potential recovery value low
C	C	19	20	9	Default

Notes: This table shows the six Chinese rating agencies' letter rating scales and their conversion into numerical scales. The rating agencies CCXI, Pengyuan, Dagong, Lianhe, and Xinhua Far East use the same letter scale (labeled "normal"), while Brilliance adds "AAA−" as an additional rating step between "AAA" and "AA+" (labeled "Brilliance"). The respective numerical scale starts with "1" for the highest level ("AAA") and ends with "19" for the lowest level ("C"). For Brilliance, the numerical scale also starts with "1" for the letter rating "AAA," but ends with "20" for the letter rating "C." The column "class" assigns numerical values to the overall rating classes net of potential modifiers (±). The highest rating class ("AAA") is assigned the value "1," the lowest one ("C") is assigned the value "9."

$\mathrm{AR}_{it} = R_{it} - (\alpha_i + \beta_i R_{mt})$ where R_{it} is the logarithmic rate of return on common stock of firm i on day t. We winsorize the underlying stock market returns at the 1st and 99th percentile to account for potential biases due to extreme observations. The market model's parameters (α_i, β_i) are estimated against the benchmark market return (R_{mt}), which is proxied by the Shanghai and Shenzhen Composite Indices for firms listed at the respective stock exchanges. Our estimation period spans 200 trading days and ends 10 days before the rating announcement.

After the estimation of abnormal returns for each firm, cumulative abnormal returns (CARs) are computed for six different event windows, namely [0, +1], [−1, 0], [−1, +1], [−2, +2], [−3, +3], and [−5, +5]. Day 0 is defined as the announcement date of a rating change recorded in Wind or Bloomberg. To test the null hypothesis that the CARs for a specific event window are equal to zero, we conduct the standardized cross-sectional test by Boehmer, Masumeci, and Poulsen (1991) (BMP). We choose the

Table 3: Sample Characteristics.

Industry	Downgrades				Upgrades			
	Full Sample		Unbiased Sample		Full Sample		Unbiased Sample	
	Obs.	Fraction (%)	Obs.	Fraction (%)	Obs.	Fraction (%)	Obs.	Fraction (%)
Panel A: Distribution of rating downgrades and upgrades by industry								
Commercials	5	8.06	3	5.88	30	10.31	23	11.06
Financials	0	0.00	0	0	14	4.81	12	5.77
Industrials	52	83.87	43	84.31	174	59.79	122	58.65
Properties	2	3.23	2	3.92	24	8.25	14	6.73
Services	2	3.23	2	3.92	2	0.69	2	0.96
Utilities	1	1.61	1	1.96	47	16.15	35	16.83
Total	62	100.00	51	100.00	291	100.00	208	100.00
Panel B: Distribution of rating downgrades and upgrades by year								
Year								
2003	5	8.06	4	7.84	2	0.69	1	0.48
2004	3	4.84	3	5.88	0	0.00	0	0.00

2005	4	6.45	4	7.84	5	1.72	4	1.92
2006	9	14.52	6	11.76	4	1.37	3	1.44
2007	0	0.00	0	0.00	6	2.06	4	1.92
2008	2	3.23	2	3.92	17	5.84	11	5.29
2009	2	3.23	0	0.00	35	12.03	26	12.50
2010	0	0.00	0	0.00	46	15.81	36	17.31
2011	0	0.00	0	0.00	44	15.12	27	12.98
2012	4	6.45	3	5.88	55	18.90	38	18.27
2013	17	27.41	15	29.41	40	13.75	29	13.94
2014	16	25.81	14	27.45	37	12.71	29	13.94
Total	62	100.00	51	100.00	291	100.00	208	100.00
Panel C: Distribution of rating downgrades and upgrades by stock exchange								
Stock exchange								
Shanghai	38	61.29	30	58.82	172	59.11	120	57.69
Shenzhen	24	38.71	21	41.18	119	40.89	88	42.31
Total	62	100.00	51	100.00	291	100.00	208	100.00

Table 3: (*Continued*)

Industry	Downgrades				Upgrades			
	Full Sample		Unbiased Sample		Full Sample		Unbiased Sample	
	Obs.	Fraction (%)	Obs.	Fraction (%)	Obs.	Fraction (%)	Obs.	Fraction (%)
Panel D: Distribution of rating downgrades and upgrades by rating agency								
Rating agency								
Brilliance	1	1.61	1	1.96	37	12.71	28	13.46
CCXI	13	20.97	12	23.53	123	42.27	83	39.90
Dagong	0	0.00	0	0.00	42	14.43	33	15.87
Lianhe	7	11.29	5	9.80	70	24.05	51	24.52
Pengyuan	18	29.03	16	31.37	6	2.06	3	1.44
Xinhua Far East	23	37.10	17	33.33	13	4.48	10	4.81
Total	62	100.00	51	100.00	291	100.00	208	100.00

Notes: The "full" sample consists of 62 downgrades and 291 upgrades of listed firms between January 2003 and December 2014. The "unbiased" sample contains only rating changes not accompanied by other corporate events during Day –5 to + 5. Panel A illustrates the summary statistics of downgrade and upgrades events by industry. Panel B describes the distribution of rating downgrade and upgrades for each year of the sample period. Panel C shows the number of rating events by stock exchange. Panel D shows the distribution of observations across credit rating agencies.

BMP test since it is robust to event-induced variance increases of stock returns. Furthermore, we report the proportion of negative abnormal returns and implement a non-parametric generalized sign test proposed by Cowan (1992) under the null hypothesis that the portion of negative abnormal returns over the event window is not statistically different from zero.

Finally, the cross-sectional regression analysis uses individual CARs as dependent variable and both firm-specific and market-level factors as independent variables. Following Jorion and Zhang (2009), we conduct ordinary least squares regressions and compute t-statistics based on clustered standard errors to account for potential event clustering.

Event Study Results

Following Hand, Holthausen, and Leftwich (1992), Jorion et al. (2005), we perform separate event studies for the "full" and for the "unbiased" samples to see whether our results are robust to the elimination of confounding events. Focusing on Hypothesis 1 first, Table 4 shows the event study results for the two downgrade subsamples. The event date ($t = 0$) is defined as the publication date of an issuer rating change. On the left-hand side of Table 4, the cumulative average abnormal return (CAAR) of –0.68 percent (z-statistic = –2.83) over a two-day window [0, +1] is significant at the one percent level with a significant fraction of negative CARs of 69.35 percent. Moreover, for the longer event windows CARs associated with rating downgrades are also negative and significant at the one or five percent level, respectively.

With respect to the unbiased downgrade subsample, Table 4 confirms the existence of significantly negative mean CARs. For instance, while the CAAR of –0.62 percent (z-statistic = –2.49) over the [0, +1] window is slightly lower than the one for the same window in the full sample, it is still significant at the one percent level. Similarly, CAARs over the other event windows are also consistently negative and significant at the 1, 5, or 10 percent level, respectively.

Table 4: Abnormal Equity Returns for Firms with Issuer Rating Downgrades.

	Full sample ($N = 62$)			Unbiased sample ($N = 51$)		
	Mean CAR	Median CAR (%)	% of CAR <0	Mean CAR	Median CAR (%)	% of CAR <0
[0, +1]	−0.68%	−0.48%	69.35%***	−0.62%	−0.48%	68.63%**
	(−2.83)***			(−2.49)***		
[− 1, 0]	−0.65%	−0.72%	62.90%	−0.86%	−1.18%	66.67%*
	(−2.19)**			(−2.61)***		
[− 1, +1]	−1.04%	−0.85%	67.74%**	−1.15%	−0.89%	70.59%**
	(−3.29)***			(−3.29)***		
[− 2, +2]	−1.09%	−1.56%	69.35%***	−0.95%	−1.56%	70.59%**
	(−2.66)***			(−2.27)**		
[− 3, +3]	−1.94%	−2.70%	66.13%**	−2.09%	−2.53%	66.67%*
	(−3.18)***			(−3.09)***		
[− 5, +5]	−1.47%	−1.21%	59.68%	−1.43%	−0.81%	56.86%
	(−2.22)**			(−2.01)*		

Notes: This table displays mean and median cumulative abnormal returns for firms with issuer rating downgrades for different event windows. Abnormal returns are calculated against the market model using the Shanghai Composite Index and the Shenzhen Composite Index as benchmarks for firms listed at the respective stock exchanges. To test the null hypothesis that CARs are equal to 0, we use the standardized cross-sectional test by Boehmer, Musumeci, and Poulsen (1991). z-statistics are given in parentheses directly below the mean CAR. The percentage of negative CARs is reported on the basis of the generalized sign test by Cowan (1992).
Asterisks indicate significance at the 10% (*), 5% (**), and 1% (***) level, respectively.

As a consequence, our results are robust to whether confounding events are included or not, and strongly confirm Hypothesis 1. However, when repeating the above analysis for the subsample of rating upgrades, we do not find significant CAARs in any of the event windows considered. Thus, we conclude that rating upgrades are not associated with abnormal returns in the Chinese market, which is in line with our Hypothesis 2.[12]

In the next step, we conduct the same analysis to study the impact of both negative and positive rating outlook announcements. However, similar to rating upgrades these indicators are also not associated with any significant stock market reaction, which is at odds with both prior findings by Poon and Chan (2008a, 2008b) and our Hypothesis 3.[13]

Regression Analysis

Independent Variables

To scrutinize Hypothesis 4 and Hypothesis 5, we conduct a multivariate regression analysis using the CARs for our unbiased downgrade subsample as dependent variables, and several firm-specific and market-level variables as independent variables. In particular, we expect the magnitude of negative stock market reactions to issuer rating downgrades to depend on the following factors:

- *Across versus within rating class changes (ACCLA):* Drawing on Table 2, we classify all rating downgrades as either "across class" or "within class" conditional on whether the downgrade moves the respective firm into a lower letter rating class (net of potential "±"-modifiers) or not.[14]

12. Detailed results for the upgrade subsample are available from the authors upon request.
13. Again, detailed results are not reported here, but available from the authors upon request.
14. See Holthausen and Leftwich (1986), Goh and Ederington (1999), Jorion and Zhang (2007).

- *Absolute degree of rating change (RCHANGE):* We expect stronger rating downgrades to induce stronger stock market reactions. The magnitude of a rating downgrade is measured based on the respective numerical rating scale shown Table 2. For instance, if an issuer rated AAA by CCXI is downgraded to AA, the magnitude of this rating change is two notches.
- *Age of the issuer (AGE):* As investors might have more trust in the creditworthiness of firms with a longer track record in the stock market, we control for potential effects of firm age on abnormal returns by using the logarithm of the number of days between the respective firm's IPO date and the event date as an explanatory variable.
- *Industry of the issuer (INDUSTRY):* As most of the downgrades in our sample occur for firms classified as "industrials," we include an industry dummy in our regression that is equal to 1 for these observations to control for a potential industry bias.
- *Firm size (SIZE):* The value relevance of firm size as an idiosyncratic risk factor is well documented in the finance literature. Thus, we control for potential size-effects using the logarithm of the downgraded firm's market capitalization on the announcement date as an independent variable.
- *Rating agency effect (CRA):* Poon and Chan (2008a, 2008b) use a sample of Xinhua Far East's ratings and argue that Xinhua is "a serious rating agency" adhering to "international rating standards." However, if the other five CRAs issued rating signals of lesser quality, these signals should be considered less informative by stock market investors. Thus, to corroborate Hypothesis 4 we define an agency dummy variable that is equal to 1 if the rating downgrade is announced by Xinhua Far East, and 0 otherwise.
- *Impact of economic cycle (ECOCLIM):* As argued earlier, the quality of credit ratings may be expected to covary with the business cycle. However, if this is the case then the effect

of downgrades on abnormal stock returns may be conditional on the business cycle as well. We use the Economic Climate Coincident Index provided by the China Economic Monitoring Center as a proxy to control for this effect.[15]

- *Effect of Chaori's default announcement (CHAORI):* With the announcement of a partial default on the corporate bond "11 Chaori" on March 4, 2014, the Chinese bond market's impeccable debt service record came to an end. However, surprisingly on October 23, 2014, this event was nullified by the announcement that Chaori would benefit from a debt guarantee by two mainland "bad banks."[16] However, since between these two dates market participants had to assume that Chaori really was in default, we use a dummy variable which is equal to 1 during the apparent default period, and 0 otherwise to test whether this extreme event has had an effect on the information content of rating changes from an equity investor's perspective.

Regression Models

Table 5 shows the correlation matrix for all independent variables, and indicates that while most of the correlations are low, the variables ECOCLIM and CRA seem to be highly correlated (Pearson's $r = 0.8196$). We use Variance Inflation Factors (VIF) to test all independent variables for multicollinearity, and based on the criterion suggested by Allison (1998), we confirm collinearity between ECOCLIM (VIF = 3.63) and CRA (VIF = 4.50). Thus, to avoid biases in our results we use either the one or the other in the following regression models, but not both at the same time.

---

15. The Economic Climate Coincident Index takes into account various economic factors such as industrial production, employment, income, and demand, and should hence provide a comprehensive view of the firms' respective macroeconomic environment (http://www.cemac.org.cn/Cyzzs.html).

16. http://www.scmp.com/business/china-business/article/1612441/chaori-solar-energy-gets-debt-guarantee-mainland-bad-bank

Table 5: Correlation Matrix for Independent Variables.

	ACCLA	RCHANGE	AGE	INDUSTRY	SIZE	CRA	ECOCLIM	CHAORI
ACCLA	1.0000							
RCHANGE	0.3732	1.0000						
AGE	−0.0573	−0.0415	1.0000					
INDUSTRY	−0.1509	−0.0091	0.3310	1.0000				
SIZE	−0.1872	−0.2649	0.0929	−0.2320	1.0000			
CRA	0.3622	0.3588	−0.1063	0.1906	−0.3414	1.0000		
ECOCLIM	0.2301	0.1866	−0.2038	0.0103	−0.2504	0.8196	1.0000	
CHAORI	−0.1312	−0.1212	−0.1232	−0.0150	0.0075	−0.3922	−0.3812	1.0000

Notes: The independent variables are defined as follows:
ACCLA = dummy variable that is equal to 1 for across-class downgrades (e.g., from AA− to A+), and 0 otherwise.
RCHANGE = absolute magnitude of the rating change based on our numerical scales.
AGE = logarithm of the number of days since the downgraded firm's IPO.
INDUSTRY = dummy variable that is equal to 1 if the company is classified as "industrial," and 0 otherwise.
SIZE = logarithm of the downgraded firm's market capitalization on the announcement date.
CRA = dummy variable that is equal to 1 if the downgrade is announced by the rating agency Xinhua Far East, and 0 otherwise.
ECOCLIM = level of Economic Climate Coincident Index in the month of the downgrade announcement.
CHAORI = dummy variable that is equal to 1 if the downgrade is published after the press release of 11 Chaori Debt's default (March 4, 2014) but before the public announcement of its bailout plan (October 23, 2014), and 0 otherwise.

Our regression models are specified as follows:

$$\text{Model 1: } CAR_{ij} = \alpha_j + \beta_{1j}ACCLA_i + \beta_{2j}RCHANGE_i + \beta_{3j}AGE_i + \beta_{4j}INDUSTRY_i + \beta_{5j}Size_i + \beta_{6j}CRA_i + \beta_{7j}CHAORI_i + \epsilon_j$$

$$\text{Model 2: } CAR_{ij} = \alpha_j + \beta_{1j}ACCLA_i + \beta_{2j}RCHANGE_i + \beta_{3j}AGE_i + \beta_{4j}INDUSTRY_i + \beta_{5j}Size_i + \beta_{6j}ECOCLIM_i + \beta_{7j}CHAORI_i + \epsilon_j$$

where CAR_{ij} is the CAR of downgraded firm i over a specific window j.

Regression Results

We conduct linear ordinary least squares regressions for each of our six event windows. Following Jorion and Zhang (2009), *t*-statistics are computed based on clustered standard errors to account for potential event clustering. Table 6 shows the respective results.

Overall, we find that our hypothesis regarding the explanatory power of idiosyncratic and systematic factors (Hypothesis 5) is confirmed only for very few of the variables considered in our regression models. Since the coefficient for RCHANGE and the coefficient for ACCLA are weakly significant only for the [0, +1] and [−3, +3] event window, respectively, these two factors do not seem to play a substantial role in explaining abnormal stock returns. Similarly, firm age and size have no explanatory power in any of the event windows either. With respect to the CRA dummy, we find that its coefficients are positive for all event windows, but only (weakly) significant for the [−1, +1] as well as the [−2, +2] window, and insignificant otherwise. Overall, we take this as a confirmation of Hypothesis 4, that is, our expectation that the information content of rating downgrades by Xinhua is not higher than in case of the other Chinese credit rating agencies.

With respect to the INDUSTRY dummy, we observe negative and significant coefficients for the [−1, 0], [−1, +1], [−2, +2], and [−3, +3] windows for both model specifications. This finding suggests that downgrades of firms classified as "industrials" lead to more negative abnormal stock returns than downgrades of firms belonging to other industries. Although admittedly, the

Table 6: Regression Analysis of Cumulative Abnormal Stock Returns Associated with Rating Downgrades.

Independent variables	Event window	[0, +1]		[−1, 0]		[−1, +1]		[−2, +2]		[−3, +3]		[−5, +5]	
		Model 1	Model 2	Model 1	Model 2	Model 1	Model 2	Model 1	Model 2	Model 1	Model 2	Model 1	Model 2
ACCLA	Coeff.	−0.011	−0.009	−0.011	−0.009	−0.016	−0.014	−0.028	−0.026	−0.039	−0.035	−0.004	−0.004
	t-statistics	(−1.396)	(−1.245)	(−1.111)	(−1.014)	(−1.437)	(−1.363)	(−1.596)	(−1.561)	(−1.679)*	(−1.668)	(−0.202)	(−0.211)
RCHANGE	Coeff.	0.004	0.004	−0.002	−0.002	0.002	0.003	0.001	0.002	0.002	0.003	−0.003	−0.002
	t-statistics	(1.711)*	(1.897)*	(−1.145)	(−0.745)	(−0.96)	(−1.21)	(−0.34)	(−0.71)	(−0.38)	(−0.69)	(−0.596)	(−0.549)
AGE	Coeff.	0.002	0.002	0.007	0.007	0.004	0.006	0.008	0.011	0.015	0.017	0.008	0.010
	t-statistics	(−0.28)	(−0.28)	(−1.06)	(−1.22)	(−0.45)	(−0.68)	(−0.53)	(−1.04)	(−0.87)	(−1.12)	(−0.50)	(−0.65)
INDUSTRY	Coeff.	−0.027	−0.024	−0.031	−0.027	−0.042	−0.038	−0.065	−0.058	−0.066	−0.056	−0.040	−0.038
	t-statistics	(−1.825)*	(−1.555)	(−2.393)**	(−2.193)**	(−2.605)**	(−2.347)**	(−3.225)***	(−3.126)***	(−2.169)**	(−2.112)**	(−1.359)	(−1.480)
SIZE	Coeff.	0.007	0.007	0.000	0.000	0.008	0.008	0.013	0.015	0.018	0.018	0.016	0.016
	t-statistics	(−1.34)	(−1.34)	(−0.0595)	(−0.0567)	(−0.98)	(−1.10)	(−1.00)	(−1.19)	(−1.18)	(−1.26)	(−1.09)	(−1.13)
CRA	Coeff.	0.012		0.018		0.020		0.033		0.034		0.009	
	t-statistics	(−1.49)		(−1.55)		(1.695)*		(1.959)*		(−1.35)		(−0.41)	
ECOCLIM	Coeff.		0.003		0.005		0.007		0.013		0.011		0.005
	t-statistics		(−1.28)		(1.949)*		(1.930)*		(2.265)**		(1.742)*		(−0.73)
CHAORI	Coeff.	0.015	0.015	0.006	0.007	0.014	0.017	0.017	0.023	0.024	0.025	0.021	0.024
	t-statistics	(−1.58)	(−1.64)	(−0.59)	(−0.70)	(−1.17)	(−1.49)	(−0.93)	(−1.40)	(−0.96)	(−1.05)	(−0.77)	(−0.85)

Dependent variable = CAR

INTERCEPT	Coeff.	−0.116	−0.400	−0.029	−0.532	−0.132	−0.815	−0.217	−1.551	−0.346	−1.428	−0.272	−0.750
	t-statistics	(−1.360)	(−1.566)	(−0.278)	(−1.849)*	(−1.141)	(−2.016)**	(−1.242)	(−2.296)**	(−1.687)*	(−1.998)*	(−1.136)	(−1.060)
No. of obs.		51	51	51	51	51	51	51	51	51	51	51	51
R^2		0.26	0.25	0.15	0.16	0.24	0.27	0.29	0.37	0.24	0.26	0.11	0.12
F-statistics		1.17	1.21	1.26	1.34	1.47	1.35	2.76	2.26	1.40	1.47	1.24	1.40

Notes: This table reports results of the regression analyses for different event windows. In Model 1 individual CARs are regressed against ACCLA, RCHANGE, AGE, INDUSTRY, SIZE, CRA, and CHAORI. In Model 2 individual CARs are regressed against ACCLA, RCHANGE, AGE, INDUSTRY, SIZE, ECOCLIM, and CHAORI.

ACCLA = dummy variable that is equal to 1 for across-class downgrades (e.g., from AA− to A+), and 0 otherwise.
RCHANGE = absolute magnitude of the rating change based on our numerical scales.
AGE = logarithm of the number of days since the downgraded firm's IPO.
INDUSTRY = dummy variable that is equal to 1 if the company is classified as "industrial," and 0 otherwise.
SIZE = logarithm of the downgraded firm's market capitalization on the announcement date.
CRA = dummy variable that is equal to 1 if the downgrade is announced by the rating agency Xinhua Far East, and 0 otherwise.
ECOCLIM = level of Economic Climate Coincident Index in the month of the downgrade announcement.
CHAORI = dummy variable that is equal to 1 if the downgrade is published after the press release of 11 Chaori Debt's default (March 4, 2014) but before the public announcement of its bailout plan (October 23, 2014), and 0 otherwise.

Asterisks indicate significance at the 10 percent (*), 5 percent (**), and 1 percent (***) level, respectively.

number of observations in the latter group is too small to make a strong point regarding industry-specific differences in the information content of credit ratings in China, we conclude that the role the industry plays in explaining investor behavior may deserve special attention in future research.

Moreover, the positive coefficient for ECOCLIM, which is significant for several event windows at the 5 percent or 10 percent level, respectively, indicates that the stock market reaction to rating downgrades may be cyclical to some extent: CARs on rating downgrades are higher (i.e., less negative) during booms than during more tense economic periods, which is in line with what we expected based on the aforementioned findings regarding ratings' quality by Hau et al. (2013).

Interestingly, and contrary to expectations, the coefficient for the dummy variable "CHAORI" is insignificant across all event windows. Thus, our results suggest that in spite of its uniqueness the Chaori default cannot be classified as a paradigm-changing event with respect to the information content of Chinese CRAs credit ratings.

Finally, it is worth noting that the significance of all regression coefficients fades for the long [−5, +5] event window in both model specification. This observation ties in nicely with the [−5, +5] CAAR of −1.43 percent being only weakly significant (as reported in Table 4). Thus, abnormal returns associated with rating downgrades seem to occur only within a small period of time, which supports the notion that while rating downgrades constitute new information to investors in the Chinese stock market, this information is processed rather quickly.

Conclusion

We analyze the information content of issuer credit rating changes using a comprehensive sample of ratings issued by a group of six leading Chinese CRAs for a period ranging from 2003 to 2014. On the basis of 51 downgrades and 208 upgrades, our results strongly support the well-documented observation that rating downgrades lead to significantly negative abnormal returns on the stock of the downgraded firm (confirming Hypothesis 1), while upgrades have no significant information content with respect to the upgraded firm's stock price (confirming Hypothesis 2). Moreover, based on a sample of 137 rating outlooks, our results show that positive and negative rating outlooks do not induce significant abnormal stock returns (rejecting Hypothesis 3).

Due to an alleged lack of both sophisticated rating methods and experience, Chinese CRAs are often suspected of issuing low-quality ratings with only poor informational content. As a consequence, previous studies typically focus on ratings issued by Xinhua Far East's, allegedly one of the most independent Chinese CRAs. Our results challenge the validity of this critique by showing that downgrades issued by other Chinese CRAs also do have information content, and that Xinhua's rating signals do not seem to be considered more relevant than other CRAs' ratings by stock market investors (confirming Hypothesis 4).

Regarding Hypothesis 5, we find that the stock market reaction to rating downgrades seems to be cyclical to some extent. In addition, the information content of a rating downgrade also seems to depend on the industry the rated firm belongs to. However, as our results regarding the latter may be spurious due to small sample size, further research in this area is needed. Finally, and contrary to our expectation, we find that the so-called "Chaori event" — that is, the very first default of a top-rated corporate bond in the Chinese bond market — did not seem to have an effect on how stock market investors react to rating signals issued by Chinese CRAs.

Acknowledgments

The authors gratefully acknowledge research assistance provided while Haoshen Hu was a visiting researcher with Everbright Securities Co., Ltd., and they thank the editors for their valuable comments on the chapter.

References

Allison, P. D. (1998). *Multiple regression: A primer* (1st ed.). Thousand Oaks, CA: Pine Forge Press.

Amato, J. D., & Furfine, C. H. (2004). Are credit ratings procyclical? *Journal of Banking & Finance, 28*(11), 2641–2677. Retrieved from http://doi.org/10.1016/j.jbankfin.2004.06.005

Bar-Isaac, H., & Shapiro, J. (2013). Ratings quality over the business cycle. *Journal of Financial Economics, 108*(1), 62–78. Retrieved from http://doi.org/10.1016/j.jfineco.2012.11.004

Barron, M. j., Clare, A. d., & Thomas, S. h. (1997). The effect of bond rating changes and new ratings on UK stock returns. *Journal of Business Finance & Accounting, 24*(3), 497–509. Retrieved from http://doi.org/10.1111/1468-5957.00117

Boehmer, E., Masumeci, J., & Poulsen, A. B. (1991). Event-study methodology under conditions of event-induced variance. *Journal of Financial Economics, 30*(2), 253–272. Retrieved from http://doi.org/10.1016/0304-405X(91)90032-F

Brown, S. J., & Warner, J. B. (1985). Using daily stock returns: The case of event studies. *Journal of Financial Economics, 14*(1), 3–31. Retrieved from http://doi.org/10.1016/0304-405X(85)90042-X

Chan, P. T., Edwards, V., & Walter, T. (2009). The information content of Australian credit ratings: A comparison between subscription and non-subscription-based credit rating agencies. *Economic Systems, 33*(1), 22–44. Retrieved from http://doi.org/10.1016/j.ecosys.2008.09.002

China Central Depository & Clearing Co., Ltd. (2015, January 5). *Statistics of bond issurance of December 2014*. Retrieved from http://www.chinabond.com.cn/Channel/18205883. Accessed on January 28.

China Securities Regulatory Commission. (2015, January 20). *Securities market statistics in December 2014*. Retrieved from http://www.csrc.gov.cn/pub/csrc_en/marketdata/. Accessed on January 28.

Cowan, A. R. (1992). Nonparametric event study tests. *Review of Quantitative Finance and Accounting, 2*(4), 343–358. Retrieved from http://doi.org/10.1007/BF00939016

Creighton, A., Gower, L., & Richards, A. J. (2007). The impact of rating changes in Australian financial markets. *Pacific-Basin Finance Journal, 15*(1), 1–17. Retrieved from http://doi.org/10.1016/j.pacfin.2006.04.003

Ederington, L. H., & Goh, J. C. (1998). Bond rating agencies and stock analysts: Who knows what when? *The Journal of Financial and Quantitative Analysis, 33*(4), 569–585. Retrieved from http://doi.org/10.2307/2331132

Gatfaoui, J., & Girardin, E. (2015). Comovement of Chinese provincial business cycles. *Economic Modelling, 44*, 294–306. Retrieved from http://doi.org/10.1016/j.econmod.2014.10.015

Goh, J. C., & Ederington, L. H. (1999). Cross-sectional variation in the stock market reaction to bond rating changes. *The Quarterly Review of Economics and Finance, 39*(1), 101–112. Retrieved from http://doi.org/10.1016/S1062-9769(99)80006-4

Griffin, P. A., & Sanvicente, A. Z. (1982). Common stock returns and rating changes: A methodological comparison. *The Journal of Finance, 37*(1), 103–119. Retrieved from http://doi.org/10.1111/j.1540-6261.1982.tb01098.x

Hand, J. R. M., Holthausen, R. W., & Leftwich, R. W. (1992). The effect of bond rating agency announcements on bond and stock prices. *The Journal of Finance, 47*(2), 733–752. Retrieved from http://doi.org/10.2307/2329121

Hau, H., Langfield, S., & Marques-Ibanez, D. (2013). Bank ratings: What determines their quality? *Economic Policy, 28*(74), 289–333. Retrieved from http://doi.org/10.1111/1468-0327.12009

He, P., & Jin, M. (2010). On the impact of credit rating on bond market of China. *Journal of Financial Research, 358*(04), 15–28.

Holthausen, R. W., & Leftwich, R. W. (1986). The effect of bond rating changes on common stock prices. *Journal of Financial Economics, 17*(1), 57–89. Retrieved from http://doi.org/10.1016/0304-405X(86)90006-1

Hsueh, L. P., & Liu, Y. A. (1992). Market anticipation and the effect of bond rating changes on common stock prices. *Journal of Business Research, 24*(3), 225–239. Retrieved from http://doi.org/10.1016/0148-2963(92)90020-C

Jorion, P., Liu, Z., & Shi, C. (2005). Informational effects of regulation FD: Evidence from rating agencies. *Journal of Financial Economics, 76*(2), 309–330. Retrieved from http://doi.org/10.1016/j.jfineco.2004.05.001

Jorion, P., & Zhang, G. (2007). Information effects of bond rating changes: The role of the rating prior to the announcement. *Journal of Fixed Income, 16*(4), 45–59.

Jorion, P., & Zhang, G. (2009). Credit contagion from counterparty risk. *The Journal of Finance, 64*(5), 2053–2087. Retrieved from http://doi.org/10.1111/j.1540-6261.2009.01494.x

Kennedy, S. (2003). China's credit rating agencies struggle for relevance. *China Business Review, 30*(6), 36–40.

Kennedy, S. (2008). China's emerging credit rating industry: The official foundations of private authority. *The China Quarterly, 193*, 65–83. Retrieved from http://doi.org/10.1017/S0305741008000040

Kim, Y., & Nabar, S. (2007). Bankruptcy probability changes and the differential informativeness of bond upgrades and downgrades. *Journal of Banking & Finance*, *31*(12), 3843–3861. Retrieved from http://doi.org/10.1016/j.jbankfin.2007.02.008

Li, J., Shin, Y. S., & Moore, W. T. (2006). Reactions of Japanese markets to changes in credit ratings by global and local agencies. *Journal of Banking & Finance*, *30*(3), 1007–1021. Retrieved from http://doi.org/10.1016/j.jbankfin.2005.05.026

Norden, L., & Weber, M. (2004). Informational efficiency of credit default swap and stock markets: The impact of credit rating announcements. *Journal of Banking & Finance*, *28*(11), 2813–2843. Retrieved from http://doi.org/10.1016/j.jbankfin.2004.06.011

Poon, W. P. H., & Chan, K. C. (2008a). An empirical examination of the informational content of credit ratings in China. *Journal of Business Research*, *61*(7), 790–797. Retrieved from http://doi.org/10.1016/j.jbusres.2007.08.001

Poon, W. P. H., & Chan, K. C. (2008b). The effects of credit ratings on stock returns in China. *Chinese Economy*, *41*(2), 34–55. Retrieved from http://doi.org/10.2753/CES1097-1475410203

Poon, W. P. H., Chan, K. C., & Firth, M. A. (2013). Does having a credit rating leave less money on the table when raising capital? A study of credit ratings and seasoned equity offerings in China. *Pacific-Basin Finance Journal*, *22*, 88–106. Retrieved from http://doi.org/10.1016/j.pacfin.2012.10.003

Rong, Y. H., Ye, K. S., & Wang, Y. (2010). Strengthen construction of china's credit rating system enhance Shanghai's competitiveness as an international financial center. *Chinamoney*, *100*(2), 29–33.

Stickel, S. E. (1986). The effect of preferred stock rating changes on preferred and common stock prices. *Journal of Accounting and Economics*, *8*(3), 197–215. Retrieved from http://doi.org/10.1016/0165-4101(86)90003-0

Wilson, E. (2006). X Rated: The dirty world of Chinese debt. *Asiamoney*, *17*(3), 20–22.

Wilson, E. (2012). *What's wrong with Dagong? Euromoney*. Retrieved from http://www.euromoney.com/Article/3006007/Whats-wrong-with-Dagong.html

Yamasawa, N. (2008). *China's business cycles and early warning indicators*. JCER Discussion Paper No. 115. Japan Center for Economic Research.

12

How Should Banks Support SMEs to Manage Funding Risks in China? The Role of Relationship Banking

Yajing Liu, Kenya Fujiwara, Toshiki Jinushi and Nobuyoshi Yamori

Abstract

It is broadly recognized in China that funding risks due to a lack of sufficient financial support from banks are the most crucial constraints that prevent the growth of small and medium enterprises (SMEs). In developed economies, such as Japan and European countries, the relationship banking business model is commonly used to help support SMEs to deal with funding risks. In this chapter, we investigate whether the relationship banking business model can be applied in China. This chapter uses the results of a unique survey study that was conducted by Professor Hiroyuki Kato of Kobe University and Professor Tang Cheng of Chuo University. They studied 183 SMEs in Zhejiang Province in China. After cleaning the data, the final sample size for this study was 100 firms. Using this data, we estimated the ordered logistic and OLS models to examine several hypotheses regarding relationship banking. We found evidence suggesting that relationship banking can mitigate funding risks for SMEs in China. Our study suggests that, although Chinese banks are still underdeveloped in terms of providing relationship lending, promoting the relationship banking model may be a significant way to resolve the financial difficulties of Chinese SMEs. It is generally very difficult to test hypotheses regarding relationship banking in China because of a lack of relevant data about Chinese SMEs. Due to our unique data set, which contains relevant information directly provided by Chinese SMEs, we can examine these hypotheses.

Keywords: Bank lending; Chinese SMEs; funding risks; relationship banking; information asymmetries; survey data

Introduction

Small and medium enterprises (SMEs) have played an important role in China's impressive economic growth, but their financial positions are known to be fragile. In particular, when the global financial crisis occurred in 2008 after the failure of Lehman Brothers, many SMEs in China faced sudden large declines in sales. For example, Chinese exports declined sharply following the crisis (Figure 1). According to Figure 2, which shows nominal GDP growth rates since 2001, China's growth rates exceeded 10% from 2003 to 2008, but the growth rate fell below 10% in 2009. These figures demonstrate the large negative impact of the global financial crisis on the Chinese economy as a whole.

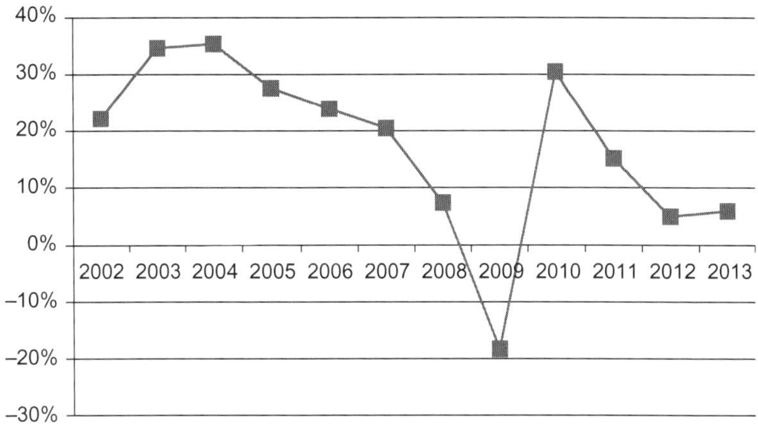

Figure 1: Chinese Exports around the Global Crisis (Changes from the Previous Year). *Source*: National Bureau of Statistics of China, *China Statistical Yearbook.*

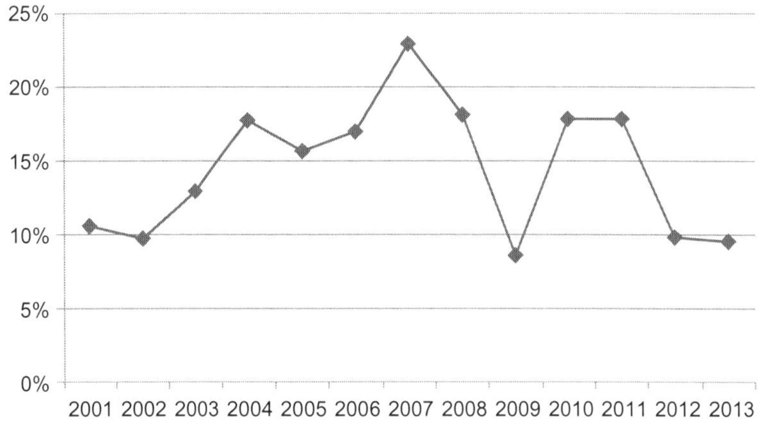

Figure 2: China's Nominal GDP Growth Rate. *Source*: National Bureau of Statistics of China, *China Statistical Yearbook.*

It is understandable that Chinese SMEs, most of which were financially fragile, were seriously affected by the crisis. Under this new economic reality in China, many SMEs actually fell into a serious financial deficit situation, with some even going bankrupt. Firms that record large deficits can continue operating if they can obtain the necessary funds. In other words, the main reason for SMEs' bankruptcies during the crisis period was the lack of financial support from banks, due to the banks' reluctance to extend loans to SMEs that were seriously hit by the crisis.

Financial distress is more serious for SMEs than for big enterprises due to the informational opaqueness that characterizes SMEs. Funding difficulties for SMEs are common not only in emerging countries like China but also in developed countries like Japan, the United States, and European countries. Funding difficulties for SMEs are particularly severe during a crisis period when anxiety about the future is widespread.

Berger and Udell (2002) argue that soft information is different from hard information; they define it as "unquantifiable, unverifiable, and undocumentable information." They note that relationship banking can address the financial difficulties faced by SMEs through the banks' collection of soft information. In developed economies such as Japan, the relationship banking business model is well developed for tackling these difficulties through the gathering of soft information. Relationship banking aims to gather soft information from SMEs — information that is usually difficult to access but helps resolve problems due to asymmetric information — and to provide constant financial support to SMEs; at the same time, as banks and firms have long-term relationships, banks can offer advice to help SMEs develop (Berger & Udell, 1994, 2006; Bharath, Dahiya, Saunders, & Srinivasan, 2011; Petersen & Rajan, 1994).

Relationship banking is one of the main topics in banking literature. Following Petersen and Rajan (1994), many researchers have examined how the relationship between banks and SME borrowers affects the funding conditions of SMEs, including interest rates and maturities. Generally speaking, they have found that relationship banking can mitigate the financial difficulties of SMEs (Angelini, Di Salvo, & Ferri, 1998; Berger & Udell, 1994, 1995; Elsas & Krahnen, 1998; Kim, Kristiansen, & Vale, 2007; Sakai, Uesugi, & Watanabe, 2010).

Since the global financial crisis, many researchers have studied relationship banking. Presbitero and Zazzaro (2011) suggest that increased interbank competition is adverse to relationship lending, while an increase in competition among a large group of small mutual banks may drive banks to further cultivate their extensive relationships with customers. Gobbi and Sette (2012) show that firms with a contraction in credit can get more concentrated lending with greater duration from financial institutions by reducing the number of borrowing financial institutions. Fraser, Rhee, and Shin (2012) find that increased capital market competition may reduce relationship lending activities. However, there are different effects according to the maturity of the loans. Increased capital market competition may reduce long-term relationship lending but increase short-term relationship lending. Uchida, Udell, and Yamori (2012) argue that small banks produce more soft information with relationship lending. Bolton, Freixas, Gambacorta, and Mistrulli (2013) studied how relationship lending and transaction lending vary over the business cycle practically in a crisis. They found that relationship lenders charged larger interest margin of a lending by gathering information about their borrowers before the crisis and then offered more favorable lending terms to help them deal with the crisis, thus reducing the number of defaults. Railienė (2014) argues that relationship banking has changed since the 2008 financial crisis as a result of the distinct change in two conditions, information technology and the economic environment, which affected the value of soft information.

Within the existing literature, we find that there is a lack of research about relationship banking regarding Chinese SMEs. This is mainly due to the unavailability of relevant data; specifically, we need Chinese SME data regarding banking relationships, such as the length of the relationship with the SMEs' main bank or the number of banks from which they borrow in order to examine the hypotheses that previous studies have investigated. For our research, we have been able to obtain a unique data set constructed from a survey study in China's Zhejiang Province. This allows us to investigate the behavior of banks in China with a particular focus on relationship lending for SMEs. In sum, using a unique data set from China's Zhejiang Province, this chapter examines whether the relationship banking model is applicable to China, provides insight into how relationship banking affects financing for SMEs, and assesses how SMEs can obtain financial support from banks.

Our study contributes to the existing literature by examining the unique survey about the environment for bank loans for enterprises, particularly for SMEs. A key contribution of our study is to examine the impact of banking relationships on reducing information asymmetries between lenders and borrowers. We test four hypotheses to analyze the pros and cons of relationship banking for Chinese SMEs comprehensively. Specifically, we examine how Chinese banks and SMEs actually performed relationship lending after the 2008 crisis. As a further contribution of this study, we find that there are clear merits (namely, increasing the accessibility of funds) of relationship banking in China; thus, relationship banking is an effective method for Chinese SMEs to deal with their funding risks. It is recommended that relationship banking be promoted more heavily to provide greater financing opportunities for SMEs.

The remainder of this chapter is structured as follows. The next section describes the current reality for Chinese SMEs and the problems they face with obtaining funds. The section "Theoretical Framework and Hypotheses" discusses the existing literature, which suggests that relationship banking enhances the availability of funds for SMEs and proposes four hypotheses related to relationship banking. The section "Data and Methodology" describes the survey, the equation to be estimated, and the variables and analyzes the regression results. The last section concludes this chapter.

The State of SME Financing and the Problems Faced by SMEs in China

Many startup firms and small businesses have insufficient collateral, such as real assets and financial assets, and the public guarantee system is not yet well developed in China.[1,2] Furthermore, and not limited to China, it is difficult for SMEs to obtain funds directly from financial markets by issuing stocks and securities, partly because security issuers are required to have audited financial statements, which are often cost prohibitive for SMEs.

Therefore, the ability of Chinese banks to screen and monitor borrowers is crucial for tackling financial difficulties related to information asymmetry. However, the ability of Chinese banks to perform this screening is still underdeveloped, as is the infrastructure for SME finance. Currently, there is no credible credit scoring system for SMEs in China: a nationwide credit assessment system for SMEs has been proposed to be put in place before 2020.[3] As it is generally hard for SMEs to get financial support from banks, they are often forced to depend on their own resources and funds provided by families and friends of the firms' managers.

The global financial crisis of 2008 worsened financial environments for SMEs. According to Baidu's 2009 Development Climate Survey about Chinese SMEs, 23.8% of firms cited a lack of funds as the main problem caused by the financial crisis.[4]

To deal with the crisis, the Chinese government implemented several policies that emphasize the creation of a more favorable

1. Under the guarantee scheme, when firms borrow money from banks, the Guarantee Corporation guarantees payback. When firms with the guarantee fail to pay banks, banks can get paid by the Guarantee Corporation. As banks' risks for SME lending decrease, the guarantee scheme encourages banks to extend loans to SMEs. During the global financial crisis, many countries heavily expanded public guarantee schemes. See Organization for Economic Cooperation and Development (2013).

2. For example, 1,458,434 SMEs, or 37.9% of the total SMEs, in Japan used the public guarantee scheme to obtain bank loans in 2013 (Credit Guarantee Corporation of Japan, 2014). See Yamori (2015) for the Japanese public guarantee system.

3. In Japan, the CRD (Credit Risk Database) was founded in March 2001 to collect financial and non-financial data on SMEs.

4. The survey covers 3554 SMEs in 30 provinces that belong to various sectors, including the machine manufacturing industry, the chemical industry, the power industry, the art industry, and the food industry. The survey is available at http://e.baidu.com/2009-02-27/161600215552.html

financial environment for SMEs.[5] Unfortunately, the government's support was not sufficient for resolving the credit constraints faced by many SMEs. In particular, the use of formal finance was still limited. According to the All China Federation of Industry and Commerce (ACFIC) Survey of 2009, over 95% of SMEs could not obtain money from state-owned banks.

Theoretical Framework and Hypotheses

Literature Review: The Positive Side of Relationship Banking

Diamond (1984) and Bhattacharya and Thakor (1992), among others, point out that informational asymmetry exists between lenders and borrowers, which may result in inefficient outcomes. In other words, it is not easy for banks to distinguish creditworthy borrowers from uncreditworthy ones, particularly because SMEs usually do not have audited financial records.

Relationship banking aims to resolve problems related to asymmetric information (Bhattacharya & Chiesa, 1995; Boot, 2000; Petersen & Rajan, 1995; Rheinbaben & Ruckes, 2004). Boot (2000) considers relationship banking to be the provision of a financial intermediary: "i) investing in obtaining customer-specific information, often proprietary in nature; and ii) evaluating the profitability of these investments through multiple interactions with the same customer over time or products." Accordingly, relationship banking is defined in this chapter as follows: (1) banks invest in obtaining customer-specific information (soft information), often proprietary in nature; (2) firms borrow from the same bank over time, obtaining favorable conditions, in exchange for providing soft information.

Previous research has illustrated the merits of relationship banking. Petersen and Rajan (1994) found that firms that build close ties with an institutional creditor will have greater access to financing. Berger and Udell (1995) established that the bank–borrower relationship is an important mechanism for solving the problem

5. See Li (2010) for details.

of asymmetric information; they also found that borrowers with longer banking relationships paid lower interest rates and were required to pledge less collateral. Elsas and Krahnen (1998) studied the availability of house banks for borrowers. Theoretically, house banks are closely related to relationship banking, and these authors found that house banks provide liquidity insurance to borrowers whose ratings have deteriorated unexpectedly. Angelini et al. (1998) investigated the effects of bank–firm relationships on the cost and availability of credit for small firms in Italy. They found that banks with long-term customer relationships will raise their lending rates, but local cooperative banks will not raise the lending rates for their local members. Therefore, closer customer relationships with local cooperative banks can decrease the cost of credit for small businesses. Sakai et al. (2010) investigated how the borrowing costs of firms decrease as they age. They found that interest rates fall as a firm's age advances and the borrower relationship lengthens.

Thus, previous studies have demonstrated that the relationship banking model can mitigate informational problems. We expect that the more banks engage in relationship banking in China, the more Chinese SMEs will be able to obtain sufficient funds from banks. Particularly, whether a Chinese bank will continue to support a small firm that faces a temporary negative shock is critical for its survival.

Under the transaction banking model, banks tend to revise the creditworthiness of borrowers and stop extending loans to firms hit by a serious negative shock because the credit score of the firm is downgraded.[6] Contrary to the transaction banking model, banks employing the relationship banking model may continue to extend loans to a firm if the bank can expect the firm to recover in the future, based on soft information such as the personalities of the firm's managers. Therefore, in terms of considering the

6. Berger and Udell (2002, 2006) classified lending technologies into transaction banking and relationship banking. Subcategories of transaction banking include financial statement lending, credit scoring, asset-based lending, factoring, fixed asset lending, and leasing. Uchida, Udell, and Yamori (2008) investigated the usage of lending technologies by Japanese banks. In this chapter, we focus only on relationship banking; an analysis of transaction banking in China will be the topic of our future study.

funding risks of Chinese SMEs, it is interesting to empirically investigate how Chinese banks actually performed relationship banking during the crisis period.

Following the literature cited, we expect that relationship banking enhances the accessibility of funds for SMEs. We therefore test the following two hypotheses:

Hypothesis 1. SMEs that have a close relationship with banks can receive financial support from the banks. Therefore, firms with a close relationship face fewer difficulties in terms of funding availability.

Hypothesis 2. SMEs that have a close relationship with banks can enjoy more favorable conditions from banks, including paying lower interest rates.

The Soft-Budget Problem and the Hold-up Problem

It should be noted that relationship banking might have a downside. Boot (2000) identifies the soft-budget problem. As a bank cannot deny additional credit to a borrower with a close relationship when the firm falls into a situation of financial difficulty, the bank makes an effort to keep inefficient borrowers afloat. As so-called zombie firms can continue to obtain funds, the efficiency of the economy remains deteriorated. If the soft-budget problem is widespread in Chinese banking practice, promoting relationship banking might hinder the efficiency of the Chinese economy.

Another issue is the hold-up problem. Greenbaum, Kanatas, and Venezia (1989) argue that banks collect soft information through the provision of financial services to firms over a long period of time. Then the banks charge loan rates to maximize their profits because they know that borrowers cannot rely on other lenders that have no soft information about them. Accordingly, the borrowers are forced to pay higher interest rates. Sharpe (1990) also argues that banks use the power of the information monopoly to build their reputations, which leads to higher costs for customers and the hold-up issue. Rajan (1992) presents the costs of the hold-up problem. Banks have bargaining power based on the long-term borrower relationship and can decide how firms finance new projects. Firms cannot choose low-cost funds without the bank's permission, which results in costly financing.

Degryse and Van Cayseele (2000) found that firms that have longer relationships with banks tend to pay higher loan rates, but firms that borrow from more banks are required to pledge less collateral. Ongena and Smith (2001) compared the number of banking relationships held by firms. They found that firms that have relationships with multiple banks reduce the risk of being held up by banks, while firms that have long-term relationships with only one bank can more easily be locked in with lenders. Kano, Uchida, Udell, and Watanabe (2011) used three factors — information verifiability, bank size, and the level of competition in the banking sector — to analyze how relationship lending affects loan contract terms and credit availability. They found that longer relationships with small banks allow firms to obtain the benefits of reduced interest rates and increased credit availability. However, they also found that, as the relationship lengthens, the probability of being required to pledge collateral increases.

Furthermore, Kim et al. (2007) used the life cycle model of borrowing firms to test how bank–borrower relationships reduce the problems of asymmetric information and how this affects interest rates. They found that banks would provide lower interest rates for younger firms, but when firms surpassed the 10-year mark, the interest rates that banks charge tend to increase. This may be indicative of the hold-up problem. Only when a firm reaches 40 years of age does the bank lower its interest rate again. This suggests that the problem of asymmetric information depends on the firm's age.

Thus, we test the following two hypotheses that relate to the demerits of relationship banking:

Hypothesis 3. The soft-budget problem is serious. Namely, inefficient firms that have a close relationship with banks can continue to obtain loans from the banks.

Hypothesis 4. The hold-up problem is serious. Firms that have a close relationship with banks suffer from higher interest rates.

Data and Methodology

Description of the 2010 Survey of SMEs in Zhejiang Province

The data in this chapter come from a survey that investigated the relationships of SMEs with banks in Zhejiang Province, called "A Survey of Firms in the Textile and Cloth Industry in Zhejiang Province."[7]

As part of the survey, representatives of 183 SMEs in the Shaoxing, Ningbo, Jiaxing, Jiashan, and Huzhou areas of Zhejiang Province in China were interviewed.[8] These SMEs were manufacturing firms producing textiles, apparel, footwear, and hats.[9] As part of the traditional economy, the garment manufacturing industry in Zhejiang has a long history and has played an important role in the economic development of the province.

These interviews were carried out from June to July 2010. Therefore, the responses reflect the effects of the global financial crisis, a period in which the difference between the relationship banking and transaction banking models was apparent. The survey questions were divided into five categories: (1) basic information, (2) spatial distribution information, (3) territory evaluation, (4) financial accounting information, and (5) relationships with banks. The response rate was 93.9%. However, 83 firms were omitted from our final sample because of the unavailability of relevant responses. Therefore, our final sample consists of 100 firms.[10]

---

7. This survey is part of a joint study on China conducted by Professor Hiroyuki Kato of Kobe University and Professor Tang Cheng of Chuo University during the period from 2008 to 2012, called "A Study of Urbanization and Regional Economic Development."

8. Zhejiang and Jiangsu provinces and Shanghai belong to the Yangtze River Delta economic area of China, which is the most developed and fastest growing region in China.

9. As the firms are categorized into the textile and clothing industry, we do not employ the industry dummies in the following estimations.

10. In China, firm ownership is believed to be an important determinant for obtaining support from the government as well as banks. Ownership definitions were first published by the State Statistics Bureau of China (SSBC) in 1996. According to the SSBC rules and Zhang, Zhang, and Zhao (2002), the definitions are as follows: *State-owned enterprises* refers to enterprises, government administrative organizations at various levels, and social organizations with state ownership, where the means of production or income are owned by the state.

Model and Data

To test our hypotheses, we estimated the following equations using the data described earlier.

$$\text{Difficulty (Interest)} = \begin{array}{l} \beta_0 + \beta_1\, Years + \beta_2\, Lendingbank\_nums \\ + \beta_3\, Pay\_G + \beta_4\, Growth\_rate + \beta_5\, LA \\ + \beta_6\, Bankloan\_totabili\_ratio + \beta_7\, Collateralized\_loan \\ + \beta_8\, Credit\_loan + \beta_9\, GL + \beta_{10}\, BL + \beta_{11}\, GE + \beta_{12}\, BE \\ + \delta_i\, Earning + \varepsilon_i\, Firmsize + \phi_i\, Bank\_tradeyears + u_i \end{array}$$

To verify our hypotheses, we need proxies for the degree of funding difficulty faced by a firm when it wants to borrow money from banks. We can use the responses to the question "What do you think of the availability of funds from financial institutions?" The respondents were asked to provide an answer based on a scale of 1 to 4, with 1 representing easy access and 4 representing difficult access.

Collectively owned enterprises refers to enterprises and institutions where the means of production are owned collectively, including urban and rural enterprises invested in by collectives and some enterprises that were formerly owned privately but have been registered in industrial and commercial administration agencies as collective units through fundraising from the public. *Privately owned enterprises* refers to enterprises or economic units owned by private individuals, including individually owned private enterprises, jointly owned private enterprises, and privately owned limited liability enterprises. *Shareholding enterprises* refers to economic units registered in accordance with the regulation of the People's Republic of China on the Management of Registration of Corporate Enterprises, with total registered capitals divided into equal shares and raised through the issuance of stocks. Each investor bears limited liability to the corporation depending on the holding of shares, and the corporation bears liability to its debt to the maximum of its total assets. *Enterprises with funds from foreign enterprises or from Hong Kong, Macao, and Taiwan* refers to all enterprises registered as joint-venture, cooperative, sole (exclusive) investment enterprises, or limited liability corporations with funds from foreign enterprises or from Hong Kong, Macao, and Taiwan. *Other enterprises* refers to other ownership enterprises not belonging to the five types described earlier. Note that our whole sample (100 firms) consists of 86 private enterprises, 10 joint enterprises, and 4 other enterprises. As our sample does not include state-owned enterprises or collectively owned enterprises, we do not have to control for the ownership characteristics of the firms in this chapter. Furthermore, as mentioned in this section, we also estimated the equations using a subsample consisting only of private enterprises and found that our main results remained unchanged.

Another dependent variable for this research is the loan interest rate. As the respondents were asked about the difference between their borrowing rates and the official base rates declared by the People's Bank of China, we calculated their actual loan rates and used them for the estimation.

More specifically, to test the merits and demerits of relationship banking in China, methods for measuring the strength of the relationship between firms and banks are crucial. Following previous studies that used the length of the bank–borrower relationship and the number of banks from which firms borrowed, our key independent variables that are relevant to the hypotheses are the number of lending banks (*Lendingbank_nums*) and dummy variables showing the duration of the relationship with a primary bank (*Bank_tradeyears*).

Of course, these variables are not usually available from any public data source. Fortunately, the survey we used includes the relevant information on this matter. The survey asked, "What is the length of your longest relationship with your banks?" Respondents were asked to choose (a) less than 1 year, (b) 1–3 years, (c) 3–5 years, or (d) over 5 years.[11] Among the 100 firms that were used in the following regressions, 5 firms chose (a) less than 1 year; 17 firms chose (b) 1–3 years; 20 firms chose (c) 3–5 years; and 58 firms chose (d) over 5 years. In the estimation, we employed a dummy variable for firms that chose "(a) less than 1 year" (*Under1Y*), a dummy variable for firms that chose "(b) 1–3 years" (*Above_1y_under3ys*), a dummy variable for firms that chose "(c) 3–5 years" (*Above_3ys_under5ys*), and a dummy variable for firms that chose "(d) over 5 years" (*Above5ys*). To avoid collinearity among the dummies, we dropped *Under1Y* from the following estimations.

The survey also provided us with the number of banks from which firms borrowed. Namely, the survey asked, "From how many banks do you mainly borrow?" Respondents were asked to choose (a) 1 bank, (b) 2 banks, (c) 3 banks, or (d) equal to or more

11. The survey offered another choice, "(e) No relationship with bank." We excluded these firms from our final sample because we focused on firms that borrowed money from banks.

than 4 banks.[12] Of the 100 firms, 44 chose (a) 1 bank; 36 chose (b) 2 banks; 13 chose (c) 3 banks; and 7 chose (d) equal to or more than 4 banks. Thus, 44% of respondents borrowed from only one bank. As compared to Japanese SMEs, the survey showed that the number of banks from which Chinese SMEs borrowed is far fewer than that of Japanese SMEs.[13] In the following estimation, *Lendingbank_nums* is defined as the assignment of the value of 1 to firms that chose "(a) 1 bank," the value of 2 to firms that chose "(b) 2 banks," the value of 3 to firms that chose "(c) 3 banks," and the value of 4 to firms that chose "(d) equal to or more than 4 banks."

Furthermore, GL, BL, GE, and BE were also included to test Hypotheses 3 and 4. Here, GL is a cross-term variable, defined as the dummy variable for the most profitable firms (firms recording profits for 2 consecutive years) multiplied by the dummy variable for firms with a relationship with banks of more than 5 years. Profitable firms are creditworthy and are expected to enjoy favorable loan terms such as lower interest rates. Under normal circumstances, the coefficient of GL should be negative in the "Difficulty" and "Interest" equations. However, from the bank's perspective, these firms can afford to pay high interest rates. Therefore, if banks have strong bargaining power, these profitable firms are forced to pay high interest rates. Therefore, if Hypothesis 4 (the hold-up hypothesis) is ture, the coefficients of GL should be positive.

GE is a dummy variable showing the most profitable firms (firms recording profits for 2 consecutive years) as well as firms borrowing from only one bank. Although firms borrowing from a single bank are expected to have a close relationship with that bank, firms may be exploited because they cannot rely on financial

12. Similarly, the survey offered another choice, "(e) don't borrow." We also excluded these firms from our final sample.

13. Regarding Japanese small firms that employed 21–100 persons, 18.7% of firms dealt with 1 bank, 27.0% dealt with 2 banks, 22% dealt with 3 banks, 22.4% dealt with 4 or 5 banks, and 10% dealt with 6 or more banks. See the *Corporate Finance Environment Survey* conducted by the Japanese government's Small and Medium Enterprise Agency in 2003.

resources beyond the incumbent bank. If so, the coefficient for the GE should be positive, and we can conclude that Hypothesis 4 (the hold-up hypothesis) is supported.

BL, defined in the same manner as GL, is a dummy variable for firms with financial deficits for 2 consecutive years and with a relationship with their main bank of more than 5 years. It is natural that firms with BL = 1 are financially weak and face stricter loan terms, including higher interest rates. However, banks might not discipline firms because of their closer relationship with the firms. If low-performing firms having a close relationship with the banks receive support, the so-called soft-budget problem is detected.[14] Therefore, negative coefficients for BL suggest Hypothesis 3 (the soft-budget problem).

BE is similarly defined. Namely, BE = 1 if firms recorded financial deficits for 2 consecutive years and borrowed from only one bank, and BE = 0 otherwise. Like BL, negative coefficients for BE support Hypothesis 3.

The equation contains several control variables. We employ firm age (*Years*), the ratio of accounts payable to sales (*Pay_G*), the growth rate of sales in the last 3 years (*Growth_rate*), the ratio of total liability to total assets (*LA*), the ratio of bank loan to total liability (*Bankloan_totabili_ratio*), a dummy variable for firms that are required by banks to pledge collateral (*Collateralized_loan*), and a dummy variable for firms that could borrow from banks without pledging collateral or guarantees (*Credit_loan*). Furthermore, to control for firms' performance, we add dummies for earnings situations (*E1, E2, E3*, and *E4*): *E1* = 1 if firms had profits in 2 consecutive years, and *E1* = 0 otherwise; *E2* = 1 if firms recorded deficits 2 years ago but had profits last year, and *E2* = 0 otherwise; *E3* = 1 if firms recorded profits 2 years ago but deficits last

14. Under the relationship banking model, banks are expected to support firms that face a temporal negative shock. Therefore, the fact that a firm with deficits borrowed at relatively low interest rates does not imply a lack of discipline and the soft-budget problem. Here, to distinguish temporal shocks from chronic disease, we used the information about deficits for 2 consecutive years as opposed to one-shot deficits. However, we admit that our identification is not perfect.

year, and *E3* = 0 otherwise; and *E4* = 1 if firms recorded deficits in 2 consecutive years, and *E4* = 0 otherwise. To avoid collinearity among the dummies, we dropped *E4* in the following estimations.

Additionally, to control for firm size, we used dummies for firm size (*Firm_B*, *Firm_M*, and *Firm_S*). *Firm_B* = 1 if the sales of the firm are larger than or equal to 400 million Chinese Yuan, and *Firm_B* = 0 otherwise; *Firm_M* = 1 if the sales of the firm are larger than or equal to 20 million Chinese Yuan and smaller than 400 million Chinese Yuan, and *Firm_M* = 0 otherwise; *Firm_S* = 1 if the sales of the firm are less than 20 million Chinese Yuan, and *Firm_S* = 0 otherwise. To avoid collinearity among the dummies, we dropped *Firm_B* in the following estimations.

Table 1 presents the mean, standard deviation, and min/max values of the variables. Tables A1 and A2 summarize the definitions and the expected coefficients.

Results and Discussion

As the "Difficulty" variable is an ordinal variable, ranging from 1 (the easiest) to 4 (the most difficult), we used the ordered logistic estimation for the "Difficulty" equation. However, as the "Interest" variable is a standard scale variable, we used the OLS estimation for the "Interest" equation. As shown in Table 1, the minimum and maximum values of the interest rate were 4.58% and 7.09%, respectively.

The estimation results are summarized in Tables 2 and 3. First, we focus on Table 2, which tests Hypotheses 1, 3, and 4 by estimating the "Difficulty" equations. The left column shows the basic results. A positive and 5% significant coefficient is found for the number of lending banks from which firms borrowed (*Lendingbank_nums*). This suggests that a larger number of lending banks tend to weaken a firm's relationships with the banks, making the firm's financing environment more severe, particularly during the crisis period when our survey was conducted. It is notable that, although firms often make an effort to look for new lenders, these efforts might be counterproductive because they

Table 1: Summary Statistics.

Variables	Observations	Mean	Std. Dev.	Min	Max
Difficulty	100	2.540	0.658	1	4
Interest	100	5.609	0.384	4.580	7.090
Years	100	8.004	4.927	0.600	24.000
Lendingbank_nums	100	1.830	0.911	1	4
BNUM_1	100	0.440	0.499	0	1
BNUM_2	100	0.360	0.482	0	1
BNUM_3	100	0.130	0.338	0	1
BNUM_4	100	0.070	0.256	0	1
Pay_G	100	0.119	0.149	0.001	0.667
Growth_rate	100	0.150	0.130	0.002	1.000
LA	100	0.425	0.263	0.010	0.991
Bankloan_totabili_ratio	100	0.482	0.300	0.031	1.000
Collateralized_loan	100	0.740	0.441	0	1
Credit_loan	100	0.340	0.476	0	1
E1	100	0.760	0.429	0	1
E2	100	0.130	0.338	0	1
E3	100	0.040	0.197	0	1
E4	100	0.070	0.256	0	1
Firm_S	100	0.320	0.469	0	1
Firm_M	100	0.070	0.256	0	1
Firm_B	100	0.610	0.490	0	1
Under_1Y	100	0.050	0.219	0	1
Above_1y_under3ys	100	0.170	0.378	0	1

Table 1: (*Continued*)

Variables	Observations	Mean	Std. Dev.	Min	Max
Above_3ys_under5ys	100	0.200	0.402	0	1
Above_5ys	100	0.580	0.496	0	1
BL	100	0.040	0.197	0	1
BE	100	0.050	0.219	0	1
GL	100	0.460	0.501	0	1
GE	100	0.320	0.469	0	1

destroy the relationship with incumbent banks. Therefore, we note that Chinese SMEs should be cautious when borrowing from new lenders.[15]

The coefficients of the trade duration dummies (*Above_5ys, Above_3ys_under5ys*, and *Above_1y_under3ys*) are negative. Note that, to avoid multicollinearity, we omitted the dummy variable for less than 1 year (*Under1Y*). The negative value of the coefficients means that, as compared to firms with the shortest relationships with banks, firms with longer bank relationships are more likely to enjoy favorable financial environments. In other words, the longer the relationships between banks and firms are, the better the financing environment becomes. These results are consistent with Hypothesis 1, but as the coefficients are insignificant, our conclusion is not strong.

The second, third, and fourth columns of Table 2 examine Hypotheses 3 and 4. Four cross-term variables, GL, BL, GE, and BE, are added to the basic equation. BL and BE test the soft-budget

15. However, we must admit that our test might be biased because of the endogeneity problem (firms facing financial difficulties and being denied new loans by incumbent banks having to look for new lenders).

Table 2: Results of Ordered Logistic Regression with "Difficulty."

Variables	Dependent Variable: Difficulty							
Years	−0.0361	(0.051)	−0.047	(0.052)	−0.0247	(0.052)	−0.0379	(0.053)
Lendingbank_nums	0.583**	(0.273)	0.568**	(0.277)	0.750**	(0.377)	0.740*	(0.389)
Pay_G	−1.56	(1.685)	−1.265	(1.706)	−1.858	(1.706)	−1.392	(1.723)
Growth_rate	4.400**	(2.105)	4.650**	(2.203)	4.376*	(2.343)	4.631**	(2.347)
LA	0.212	(0.919)	0.129	(0.935)	0.575	(0.970)	0.594	(0.987)
Bankloan_totabili_ratio	0.162	(0.830)	0.203	(0.843)	0.355	(0.845)	0.641	(0.875)
Collateralized_loan	−0.612	(0.543)	−0.534	(0.558)	−0.624	(0.547)	−0.468	(0.564)
Credit_loan	−0.865	(0.553)	−0.799	(0.557)	−0.828	(0.560)	−0.701	(0.565)
E1	−1.853**	(0.881)	−1.334	(2.264)	−3.197**	(1.440)	−1.972	(2.396)
E2	−1.409	(1.036)	−1.004	(2.287)	−1.890*	(1.140)	−0.335	(2.415)
E3	1.083	(1.315)	1.663	(2.516)	1.078	(1.343)	3.469	(2.839)
Firm_S	2.032*	(1.156)	1.991*	(1.163)	2.100*	(1.163)	2.092*	(1.183)
Firm_M	1.367	(1.001)	1.266	(1.009)	1.548	(1.018)	1.522	(1.039)
Above_1y_under3ys	−1.172	(1.124)	−1.211	(1.134)	−0.969	(1.159)	−1.047	(1.171)

Above_3ys_under5ys	−0.677	(1.086)	−0.537	(1.098)	−0.801	(1.134)	−0.832	(1.144)
Above_5ys	−1.607	(1.013)	−1.666	(1.027)	−2.702*	(1.503)	−4.070**	(1.734)
BL			1.977	(1.896)			4.086*	(2.277)
BE			−0.994	(2.035)			−0.674	(2.165)
GL					1.397	(1.222)	2.731*	(1.473)
GE					0.531	(0.808)	0.529	(0.830)
Constant (cut1)	−4.799**	(2.026)	−4.388	(2.982)	−4.993**	(2.214)	−3.685	(3.275)
Constant (cut2)	−0.378	(1.975)	0.0598	(2.976)	−0.546	(2.154)	0.89	(3.267)
Constant (cut3)	2.957	(1.993)	3.442	(2.976)	2.847	(2.172)	4.366	(3.287)
Pseudo R^2	0.176		0.184		0.184		0.204	
Observations	100		100		100		100	

Notes: Standard errors in parentheses. Pseudo R^2 measures the model's goodness of fit. *E4*, *Under_1Y*, and *Firm_B* are omitted because of collinearity. Descriptions of the variables are shown in Table A1.
$^{***}p < 0.01$, $^{**}p < 0.05$, and $^{*}p < 0.1$.

Table 3: Results of OLS Regression with "Interest".

Variables	Dependent Variable: Interest							
Years	−0.002	(0.009)	−0.004	(0.009)	−0.002	(0.009)	−0.003	(0.009)
Lendingbank_nums	−0.072	(0.044)	−0.071	(0.044)	−0.103*	(0.060)	−0.095	(0.063)
Pay_G	−0.479*	(0.274)	−0.433	(0.277)	−0.454	(0.280)	−0.418	(0.282)
Growth_rate	0.455	(0.316)	0.598*	(0.355)	0.402	(0.337)	0.495	(0.374)
LA	0.23	(0.154)	0.207	(0.155)	0.218	(0.162)	0.223	(0.162)
Bankloan_totabili_ratio	0.084	(0.136)	0.100	(0.138)	0.086	(0.141)	0.125	(0.145)
Collateralized_loan	−0.034	(0.086)	−0.012	(0.089)	−0.034	(0.087)	−0.007	(0.090)
Credit_loan	0.0796	(0.087)	0.0951	(0.088)	0.0762	(0.088)	0.099	(0.089)
E1	−0.433***	(0.146)	−0.138	(0.355)	−0.379*	(0.221)	−0.168	(0.360)
E2	−0.421**	(0.170)	−0.14	(0.362)	−0.406**	(0.177)	−0.138	(0.376)
E3	−0.357	(0.227)	−0.054	(0.401)	−0.340	(0.230)	−0.004	(0.432)
Firm_S	−0.086	(0.174)	−0.098	(0.174)	−0.080	(0.176)	−0.085	(0.176)
Firm_M	0.147	(0.149)	0.129	(0.150)	0.145	(0.152)	0.139	(0.152)
Above_1y_under3ys	0.097	(0.195)	0.091	(0.195)	0.065	(0.201)	0.067	(0.201)

Above_3ys_under5ys	−0.203	(0.191)	−0.19	(0.193)	−0.237	(0.200)	−0.241	(0.201)
Above_5ys	−0.057	(0.176)	−0.072	(0.177)	−0.097	(0.250)	−0.232	(0.270)
BL			0.388	(0.319)			0.486	(0.362)
BE			0.079	(0.337)			0.025	(0.355)
GL					0.010	(0.199)	0.148	(0.225)
GE					−0.099	(0.128)	−0.079	(0.135)
Constant	5.998***	(0.327)	5.693***	(0.478)	6.085***	(0.352)	5.798***	(0.525)
Observations	100		100		100		100	
R^2*-squared*	0.318		0.33		0.323		0.338	

Notes: Standard errors in parentheses. *E4*, *Under_1Y*, and *Firm_B* are omitted because of collinearity.
***$p < 0.01$, **$p < 0.05$, and *$p < 0.1$.

hypothesis (Hypothesis 3), and GL and GE test the hold-up hypothesis (Hypothesis 4). If the coefficients of BL and BE are negative and significant, it can be speculated that firms with poor financial performance can still obtain financing from banks because of their close relationship with the banks.

According to Table 2, the coefficients for BL are positive and significant at the 10% level only with respect to the fourth column specification, and the coefficients for BE are all negative and insignificant. Given that we failed to find statistically significant negative coefficients for BL and BE, we can safely reject Hypothesis 3. In China, the soft-budget problem that might accompany the relationship banking model is not currently serious.

On the other hand, if the coefficients of GL and GE are positive and significant, it can be speculated that a hold-up problem may exist. This could be problematic, as well-performing firms might find it difficult to obtain cheap bank loans. According to Table 2, all coefficients for GL and GE are insignificant. Given that the coefficients for GL and GE are not statistically significant and not negative, we can reject Hypothesis 4. In China, the hold-up problem is not currently noticeable.

It is notable that the addition of GL, BL, GE, and BE does not alter the signs or significance of *Lendingbank_nums.* Furthermore, the fourth specification of Table 2 demonstrates that the coefficient of *Above_5ys* is statistically significant and negative at the 5% level. That is, firms with longer relationships with banks face more favorable financial conditions than those with shorter relationships. With some reservations, we can say that in China, building stable relationships with banks is a promising way for SMEs to manage their funding risks.

As mentioned in Note 14, our sample consists of 86 private firms, 10 joint enterprises, and 4 other enterprises. Different ownership types will bring different characteristics to firms. Therefore, as a robustness check, we estimated the basic equation using a subsample consisting of only 86 private firms. The coefficient of *Lendingbank_nums* is significantly positive at the 5% level, and the coefficient of *Above_5ys* is significantly negative at the 10% level.

In other words, the result based on the private-firm sample is qualitatively the same as that based on the full sample.[16]

Table 3 reports the OLS regressions on the interest rate, which test Hypotheses 2, 3, and 4. If we obtain positive coefficients for relationship variables, we can support Hypothesis 2. If we obtain negative coefficients, the more lending banks are involved, the easier it is for firms to obtain low-cost funds. In other words, this result suggests that a closer relationship increases interest rates. This is consistent with Angelini et al. (1998) and Degryse and Van Cayseele (2000), among others.

First, we focused on the basic results shown in the left column. The coefficient on the lending bank numbers (*Lendingbank_nums*) is negative but insignificant even at the 10% level. The coefficients for the trade duration dummies (*Above5ys*, *Above_3ys_under5ys*, and *Above_1y_under3ys*) are also insignificant. The duration of the bank–firm relationship does not affect the level of the interest rates.

Next, we add GL, BL, GE, and BE to the basic equation. The second to fourth columns show the results. GL, BL, GE, and BE have no significant coefficients. In sum, we cannot find any evidence that relationships with banks affect interest rates.[17]

Therefore, relationship banking in China is likely to ease the availability of funds without affecting interest rates, although we have some reservations about the results of the "Interest" equation because of the poor performance of the estimation.

Concluding Remarks

SMEs have played an important role in China's economy, but their financial positions are known to be fragile. Management of

16. To save space, we have not reported the results. However, they are available upon request.

17. Furthermore, we estimated the "Interest" equation using a subsample consisting of 86 private firms. We found no significant coefficients regarding *Lendingbank_nums* and trading year dummies (*Above_1y_under3ys*, *Above_3ys_under5ys*, and *Above_5ys*).

funding risks is essential for Chinese SMEs, particularly as the Chinese economy turns the corner of rapid growth and becomes more volatile in the future. As SMEs are not usually eligible to raise funds in financial markets, bank behavior determines the degree of funding risks that SMEs assume.

For example, if banks evaluate borrowers with each new transaction, the availability of funds for SMEs is likely to fluctuate significantly because the performance of SMEs is generally volatile. However, if banks evaluate borrowers based on their future performance, which is predicted using soft information, the availability of funds for SMEs is less likely to fluctuate. For example, when a firm suffers from a temporal negative shock such as the global financial crisis, banks that employ relationship banking as their main business model will continue to support firms, even if it would be difficult to support them based on their current performance. Therefore, as in the case of Japan, to increase the stability of Chinese SMEs, building a close relationship between banks and SMEs seems desirable. However, there is limited research in China to investigate this issue because of the unavailability of relevant data on SMEs.

This chapter aimed to verify the effectiveness of the relationship banking business model for Chinese SMEs during a period of financial distress. Owing to the unique data from China's Zhejiang Province, we could test four hypotheses. Although we did not obtain clear results regarding the effect of relationships on the level of interest rates, we found that a closer bank relationship tends to enhance the availability of funds for SMEs. We also attempted to detect the soft-budget problem and the hold-up problem, which often accompany the relationship banking business model. In this chapter, we did not find evidence suggesting that these problems are serious in China. Therefore, building close relationships between banks and SMEs may not currently lead to serious adverse effects. In conclusion, we recommend that relationship banking be promoted more positively in China.

Finally, we acknowledge that this chapter has several limitations. First, although the survey data enabled us to conduct unique research, we should be cautious in generalizing the results.

How well our sample represents all Chinese SMEs should be investigated. Similar research using survey data from other provinces and periods is needed. Second, there is much room to improve our estimation results. In particular, there are few significant variables in the "Interest" equations. This may suggest that some important variables for determining the interest rate level were omitted.[18] Third, due to the unavailability of data, our proxies for relationship (the length of the relationship and the number of lender banks) are not comprehensive. For example, we noted in our literature review that the degree of multiple interactions (settlement services, demand deposits, time deposits, foreign exchange transaction, shareholder relationship, etc.) is known as a proxy for the strength of the relationship between banks and firms.[19] We must construct a more comprehensive proxy for the strength of the bank–firm relationship. Fourth, we do not control for the character of the banks. Berger and Udell (2002) point out that small banks have a comparative advantage when conducting relationship banking because of their simple organizational structure. Considering banks' characteristics will result in more credible results.

Finally, our study draws on data from 2010, reflecting relationship banking behavior only during the post-crisis period. It would be interesting to test our hypotheses using data during a non-crisis period to see whether our results hold under different economic conditions. Nevertheless, given that SMEs' financing difficulties are not restricted to periods of economic crisis, but rather are heightened during these times, we believe our conclusions are relevant even today.

18. Additionally, we should note that the difference in the loan rates reported by our sample firms is small (only 2.51 percentage points). Our sample firms may be too homogeneous to be distinguished. As another possibility, the Bank of China's regulation may make loan interest rates insensitive to the bank–firm relationship.

19. Furthermore, to produce soft information, face-to-face interaction between firms and banks is crucial. For example, the frequency of meetings between firms and bank officers is a good proxy for future study.

Acknowledgments

The authors wish to thank Professor Takahiro Sato of Kobe University, Professor Hirofumi Uchida of Kobe University, and Professor Fumiharu Mieno of Kyoto University for their useful comments, as well as Professor Tang Cheng of Chuo University, Professor Hiroyuki Kato of Kobe University, and Professor Kai Kajitani of Kobe University for providing us with their survey data set.

References

Angelini, P., Di Salvo, R., & Ferri, G. (1998). Availability and cost of credit for small businesses: Customer relationships and credit cooperatives. *Journal of Banking and Finance, 22,* 925–954.

Berger, A. N., & Udell, G. F. (1994). The benefits of lending relationships: Evidence from small business data. *The Journal of Finance, 49*(1), 3–37.

Berger, A. N., & Udell, G. F. (1995). Relationship lending and lines of credit in small firm finance. *Journal of Business, 68,* 351–381.

Berger, A. N., & Udell, G. F. (2002). Small business credit availability and relationship lending: The importance of bank organizational structure. *The Economic Journal, 112*(477), F32–F53.

Berger, A. N., & Udell, G. F. (2006). A more complete conceptual framework for SME finance. *Journal of Banking and Finance, 30,* 613–673.

Bharath, S., Dahiya, S., Saunders, A., & Srinivasan, A. (2011). Lending relationships and loan contract terms. *Review of Financial Studies, 24,* 1141–1203.

Bhattacharya, S., & Chiesa, G. (1995). Proprietary information, financial intermediation, and research incentives. *Journal of Financial Intermediation, 4,* 328–357.

Bhattacharya, S., & Thakor, A. V. (1992). Contemporary banking theory. *Journal of Financial Intermediation, 3,* 2–50.

Bolton, P., Freixas, X., Gambacorta, L., & Mistrulli, P. E. (2013). *Relationship and transaction lending in a crisis.* Temi di Discussion 917, Bank of Italy.

Boot, A. W. A. (2000). Relationship banking: What do we know? *Journal of Financial Intermediation, 9,* 7–25.

Credit Guarantee Corporation. (2014). *Credit guarantee system in Japan.* Retrieved from http://www.zenshinhoren.or.jp/english/document/anual.pdf

Degryse, H., & Van Cayseele, P. (2000). Relationship lending within a bank-based system: Evidence from European small business data. *Journal of Financial Intermediation, 9*, 90–109.
Diamond, D. W. (1984). Financial intermediation and delegated monitoring. *Review of Economic Studies, 51*, 393–414.
Elsas, R., & Krahnen, J. P. (1998). Is relationship lending special? Evidence from credit-file data in Germany. *Journal of Banking Finance, 22*, 1283–1316.
Fraser, D. R., Rhee, S. G., & Shin, G. H. (2012). The impact of capital market competition on relationship banking: Evidence from the Japanese experience. *Journal of Empirical Finance, 19*, 411–426.
Gobbi, G., & Sette, E. (2012). *Relationship lending in a financial turmoil*. Mo. Fi.R. Working Paper No. 59, Marche Polytechnic University, Ancona.
Greenbaum, S. I., Kanatas, G., & Venezia, I. (1989). Equilibrium loan pricing under the bank-client relationship. *Journal of Banking Finance, 13*, 221–235.
Kano, M., Uchida, H., Udell, G. F., & Watanabe, W. (2011). Information verifiability, bank organization, bank competition, and bank–borrower relationships. *Journal of Banking and Finance, 35*, 935–954.
Kim, M., Kristiansen, E. G., & Vale, B. (2007). Life-*cycle patterns of interest rate markups in small firm finance*. Norges Bank Working Paper.
Li, Z. B. (2010). *The blue book of small and medium enterprises in China: Development, financing service and policies* (pp. 22–34). Beijing, China: China Development Press. (in Chinese).
Ongena, S., & Smith, D. C. (2001). Empirical evidence on the duration of bank relationships. *Journal of Financial Economics, 61*, 449–475.
Organization for Economic Cooperation and Development. (2013). *SME and entrepreneurship financing: The role of credit guarantee schemes and mutual guarantee societies in supporting finance for small and medium-sized enterprises: Final report*. Centre for Entrepreneurship, SMEs and Local Development.
Petersen, M. A., & Rajan, R. G. (1994). The benefits of lending relationships: Evidence from small business data. *The Journal of Finance, 49*, 3–37.
Petersen, M. A., & Rajan, R. G. (1995). The effect of credit market competition on lending relationships. *Quarterly Journal of Economics, 110*, 406–443.
Presbitero, A., & Zazzaro, A. (2011). Competition and relationship lending: Friends or foes? *Journal of Financial Intermediation, 20*, 387–413.
Railienė, G. (2014). The use of IT in relationship banking. *Procedia – Social and Behavioral Sciences, 156*, 569–574.
Rajan, R. G. (1992). Insiders and outsiders: The choice between informed and arm's-length debt. *The Journal of Finance, 47*, 1367–1400.

Rheinbaben, J. V., & Ruckes, R. (2004). The number and the closeness of bank relationships. *Journal of Banking and Finance*, *28*, 1597–1615.
Sakai, K., Uesugi, I., & Watanabe, T. (2010). Firm age and the evolution of borrowing costs: Evidence from Japanese small firms. *Journal of Banking and Finance*, *34*, 1970–1981.
Sharpe, S. A. (1990). Asymmetric information, bank lending and implicit contracts: A stylized model of customer relationships. *The Journal of Finance*, *45*, 1069–1087.
Uchida, H., Udell, G., & Yamori, N. (2008). How do Japanese banks discipline small and medium-sized borrowers? An investigation of the deployment of lending technologies. *International Finance Review (Institutional Approach to Global Corporate Governance*, *9*, 57–80.
Uchida, H., Udell, G., & Yamori, N. (2012). Loan officers and relationship lending to SMEs. *Journal of Financial Intermediation*, *21*, 97–122.
Yamori, N. (2015). Japanese SMEs and the credit guarantee system after the global financial crisis. *Cogent Economics and Finance*, *3*(1). doi:10.1080/23322039.2014.1002600
Zhang, A., Zhang, Y., & Zhao, R. (2002). Profitability and productivity of Chinese industrial firms measurement and ownership implications. *China Economic Review*, *13*, 65–88.

Appendix

Table A1: Definition of Variables.

Variables	Description
Difficulty	Dependent variable: Financing access difficulty level of 1–4, where 4 represents the most difficult access
Interest	Dependent variable: Loan interest rate
Years	Operating years
Lendingbank_nums	The numbers of banks that get loans
BNUM_1	Dummy variable (number of relationships with banks = 1)
BNUM_2	Dummy variable (bank number = 2)
BNUM_3	Dummy variable (bank number = 3)
BNUM_4	Dummy variable (bank number ≥ 4)
Pay_G	Accounts payable/Sales
Growth_rate	The growth rate of sales in the last 3 years
LA	Total liability/Total assets in 2009
Bankloan_totabili_ratio	Bank loan/Total liability
Collateralized_loan	Dummy variable representing whether the firm had a collateralized demand from the bank
Credit_loan	Dummy variable representing whether the firm borrowed without collaterals or guarantees
Earning	Dummy variable expressing the firm's earning level from 2007 to 2009
E1	Dummy variable representing firms that have had profits for 2 years
E2	Dummy variable representing firms who had a financial deficit but began making a profit

Table A1: (*Continued*)

Variables	Description
E3	Dummy variable representing firms that had a profit but became ones with a financial deficit
E4	Dummy variable representing firms that have had a financial deficit for 2 years
Firmsize	Dummy variable representing firm size
Firm_S	Dummy variable for big firms; Firms whose total sales are larger than or equal to 400 million Chinese Yuan (CNY)
Firm_M	Dummy variable for medium firms; Firms whose total sales range from 20 M CNY to 40 M CNY
Firm_B	Dummy variable for small firms; Firms whose total sales are less than 20 M CNY
Bank_tradeyears	Length of service at the same bank
Under1Y	Dummy variable representing less than 1 year
Above_1y_under3ys	Dummy variable representing 1–3 years
Above_3ys_under5ys	Dummy variable representing 3–5 years
Above5ys	Dummy variable representing more than 5 years
GL	E1*Above5ys
BL	E4*Above5ys
GE	E1*BNUM_1
BE	E4*BNUM_1

Table A2: Predicted Signs of the Main Variables.

Variables	Hypothesis 1	Hypothesis 2	Hypothesis 3		Hypothesis 4	
	Difficulty	Interest	Difficulty	Interest	Difficulty	Interest
Years	–	–				
Lendingbank_nums	+	+				
BNUM_1	–	–				
BNUM_2	+	+				
BNUM_3	+	+				
BNUM_4	+	+				
Pay_G	–	–				
Growth_rate	–	–				
LA	+	+				
Bankloan_totabili_ratio	–	–				
Collateralized_loan	–	–				
Credit_loan	–	–	Control	Control	Control	Control
E1	–	–				

Table A2: (*Continued*)

Variables	Hypothesis 1	Hypothesis 2	Hypothesis 3		Hypothesis 4	
	Difficulty	Interest	Difficulty	Interest	Difficulty	Interest
E2	–	–				
E3	+	+				
E4	+	+				
Firm_S	+	+				
Firm_M	–	–				
Firm_B	–	–				
Under1Y	+	+				
Above_1y_under3ys	+	+				
Above_3ys_under5ys	–	–				
Above5ys	–	–				
GL			Control	Control	+	+
GE					+	+
BL	No	No	–	–	Control	Control
BE			–	–		

Notes: HL, BL, GE, and BE are cross variables to test Hypothesis 3 and Hypothesis 4. If the coefficients of BL and BE are negative and significant, this may indicate the soft-budget problem. If GL and GE are positive and significant, this may show the hold-up problem. Descriptions of the variables are shown in Table A1.

13

Risk Management in a Transition Economy: The Chilean Case

Franco Parisi, Sherwood Clements and Edinson Cornejo

Abstract

Over the last decade, the Chilean economy has experienced rapid growth, allowing per capita GDP to rise from $10,700 to $19,887. Additionally, the capital markets size increased over 16%. Given this, it is expected that Chile will be considered a developed country by 2020, according to the Organization for Economic Co-operation and Development (OECD). Chile is in the initial stages of joining the OECD; a process that is expected to accelerate positive changes in the economy. However, in recent years, publicly traded Chilean firms began to face financial scandals causing the upheaval of the regulatory market structures and initiating environmental legislation. These scandals have consistently occurred across all economic sectors and typically have included companies with large market capitalizations and strong risk management procedures. Nevertheless, these mechanisms have proven unsuccessful due to misinformation or information manipulation. The changes to the Chilean economy can be considered as operational risk to its member firms. These risks typically result from inadequate or failed internal processes or people systems, and/or from external events. The radical changes in this transitional economy and the impact on the differing companies involved are good examples that should provide a warning for emerging market economies trying to implement risk management control systems. Unfortunately, agencies such as the Internal Revenue Service and the Securities and Exchange Commission (SEC) in the United States cannot be modeled in the traditional sense in countries similar to Chile. Different authors simplified operational risk management, but this framework is not feasible in emerging economies based solely on the criteria of identification, evaluation, monitoring, and management.

Keywords: Risk management; emerging markets; political risk; transitional economy

JEL classifications: G32; G15; G11; G12

The State of Risk Management in Emerging Markets: The Chilean Case

In emerging markets, risk management is a powerful idea amongst large companies and corporations, but international standards for mitigating risk have not always proven useful. Due to the differences in these emerging market economies and more developed ones at the macro and microeconomic levels, new and different risks must be factored. In this study, we examine the macroeconomic level and can identify the following risks: physical, social, economic, political, and financial and/or exchange rate, operational, technology, and environmental regulatory risk.

Physical Risk

Physical risk, also known as hazard risk, is a serious problem for developing countries due to their differing sizes and locations. The most obvious physical risk is climate. Each country's particular climate impacts corporate global risk within its borders and can have major effects on a given economy. Natural disasters are a common risk. In Chile, earthquakes, floods, and wildfires occur frequently and the impact of these phenomena cannot be diminished or prevented since the government is not sufficiently equipped with resources to protect either their people or businesses. For example, the number of aircrafts available to fight forest fires is minimal in relation to the size of its forest industry and the lack of non-combustible building construction. Additionally, the mining industry is often relevant to economic success, but when rainfall is less than expected the industries excessive water usage can have a major impact on risk management.

Of course these natural risks occur in developed countries and corporations located therein have to handle these risks, but in emerging markets the risk faced is much more critical to their economies. According to Melecky and Raddatz (2011), the output loss for disasters in financially underdeveloped countries appears to be 2–10% of GDP versus, on average, while there is little to no significant loss in financially developed countries. Thus, it is imperative that these climate risks be taken into consideration by the higher levels management teams within companies in emerging markets.

Social Risk

Social risk is an important source of instability for corporations located in emerging markets, as this risk shows how corporate business practices affect the welfare of the public. This risk is latent as it can reveal itself at any moment even when controlled or accounted for by the corporations within each individual country. Primarily, social risk is associated with tribal divisions, especially after the Indigenous and Tribal Peoples Convention in

1989 (ILO-convention 169 or C169), which established the need to protect these tribal cultures' resources, beliefs, and standards of living. Religion risk should be included here, since faith can be a powerful social division in some countries or regions. Expedited methods of communication and a higher degree of readily available knowledge that occur as a nation develops give the implication of tougher social oversight to corporations, which is helpful in limiting this risk. Additionally, social risk can be catalyzed by changes in government regulations and laws as well as improved perceptions of a company and their executives by citizens due to this increased transparency as countries grow.

Population risk, a major concept of risk management, includes birth rate, education level, rural versus urban population distribution, mobility of the workforce, and workforce training within differing industries. Human capital is a key for corporations to grow and prosper and these issues must be examined by risk managers within corporation. Within the mining industry in Chile, the demand for workers is extremely high and companies have been known to train entire households and encourage migration from the southern portion of the country to the north. The mining industry develops ambitious plans to retain these migrated employees often offering lucrative perks such as indoor training facilities. A complication of this migration is labor scarcity for the southern agricultural sector, which is also an important factor to Chile's economy as a whole. Other social risks include lack of adequate health care systems and the population's inferior standards of living are relevant risks for corporations. Measures have been taken in Chile to decrease the health risk among the population working in the agricultural industries include the implementation of standards for sun protection and personal hygiene.

Economic Risk

Economic risk is founded upon the concept that fundamentals of the economy related to state control and intervention may affect the returns on investments for businesses and households. In recent years, there has been a tendency for governments in emerging markets to privatize firms, although there is a slight tendency to renationalize key industries after a short period of privatization. An example of this occurred in Argentina where the government nationalized Yacimientos Petroliferos Fiscales (YPF) from Repsol, a Spanish company. Court litigation ensued with a resulting $5,000,000 settlement in favor of Repsol (Rucinski, Gonzalez, & Gray, 2014). This legal action affirms the notion that risk managers need to be wary of government intervention that can lead to corporate losses affecting the shareholders of the company. Also, protections imposed by a president in an emerging market are a source of economic risk for corporations as these protections can be accompanied by price fixing from within the government. For example, the Argentinian President Cristina Fernández ordered supermarkets to freeze prices on a basic basket of goods for one to three months in order to reduce inflation (Politi, 2013). Not only did this not curb inflation, but it has an effect on the profitability of companies in the retail industry.

Government decisions with regards to infrastructure investment can be an essential factor for corporate decision-making. One such example can be found in Santiago, the capital of Chile. Here, public transportation is privately owned, but the ticket price is regulated by a government agency. This form of subsidy is used by the government to protection vulnerable lower income people using the public transportation system, but portrays economic risks undertaken by managers in the corporate sector. Typically, infrastructure spending is focused on large cities, but on many occasions direct foreign investments are oriented to businesses outside of urban areas. Therefore, due to the lack of funding, some promises by the government to invest in certain regions or zones are not fulfilled quickly leading to economic risks for managers.

In emerging markets, it is important for risk managers to consider certain characteristics of the capital market when assessing economic risk. These include liquidity, depth, self-regulation, transparency, accounting standards, and the reputation of the regulatory agents within each economy. Recently, several scandals in Chile indicated that the capital markets may be manipulated and the regulatory agents were not able to monitor all corporations thoroughly. Although the Chilean capital market is considered reputable, managers' poor decisions betrayed investors and the general public. Economic risk is an issue as the market is not transparent and corporations may also lose credibility with the individual investors. Often, these scandals that emerge in the capital markets can be observed in the volatility of the stock index or individual stock price volatility. For instance, Schwager a Chilean stock's normal volatility is 6.22%, but on a particular day after a scandal the volatility rose to 22%. We will detail 5 of these scandals later in this study.

Political Risk

After the U.S. subprime crisis and resulting economic recession, international investment in emerging markets such as Chile gained popularity. According to the Foreign Investment Committee a total of 100,800,000,000 have been invested in Chile between 2009 and 2013. However, as soon as commodity prices stabilized and returned to the historical levels, international capital flowed out of the country. Now Chile and other emerging countries are facing Balance of Payment issues with high exchange and interest rates and lower asset prices. Under these conditions, the political risk increases regardless of political leader's experience. Remember, "Power tends to corrupt and absolute power corrupts absolutely" (Dalberg, 1887). The concept of the power base in political risk is relevant since democratic election processes now operate in many countries across the globe. However, with this, the disadvantages may include a lack of funding, lack of access to the media, and the arrest and imprisonment of leaders. In emerging markets, presidents with absolute power can make extreme decisions to regulate prices, markets, and the exchange rate. In our example noted earlier, President of Argentina Cristina Fernandez froze food prices and services to fight inflation, but instead generated scarcity (Politi, 2013).

Under political risk, we also note that the legal and regulatory framework of a developing nation is significant. Companies must comply with new laws and regulations that are enacted in order to move forward with operations. For instance, economies in transition will often raise their homeland security and pollution standards in order to meet standards instituted by the OECD. These standards include changes in workers unionization, transparency, tax levels, government deficits, air and water quality, level of education within the population, etc. Risk managers must be knowledgeable of culture and legislation of a given country when their company decides to invest within their borders or they will be subject to hazard.

Just as in real estate, location is also pertinent to risk management in emerging markets. These countries face diplomatic risks when transporting trade goods across the borders from neighboring countries. Chile has an export-oriented economy and during the summer season, fruit exporters face the risk that port unions will block trade flowing through their ports. In addition, shipping vessels carrying vehicles often have to wait days or even weeks to unload their cargo, affording a potential monetary and reputation loss for clients. Regulatory risk is faced by corporations due to underinvestment in or the lack of regulation within utility firms. Public services such as electricity or water may face unnecessary high costs or restrictions in emerging markets. Chilean law favors power producing firms, so the power costs have been growing at a rate higher than productivity in almost all industries. These growing prices have been damaging the Chilean economy in terms of productivity and comparative advantage to other emerging countries, according to the Chilean National Statistical Bureau, INE, the energy cost for the mining industry went up more than 82.94% during the last decade.

Corruption is another important issue with regards to political risk. It may be argued that government and corporate scandals are more frequent in emerging markets, so it is a risk faced by corporations operating within these markets. The final contribution in political risk is both internal and external conflicts in a country; for example, the March of the Penguins, a conflict between students and the federal government in Chile in 2006, where thousands of high school and college students marched, calling for improvements in education and an end to education for profit (Vogler, 2006). This changed the reality of private education and transformed it into a nonprofit sector. During this conflict, international firms with universities in Chile had significant increases in their risk level as the students may have exited these universities and refused to seek a higher education.

At the microeconomic risk level, management firms can face the difficult task of identifying sources of risks, which are discussed here.

Financial Risk

Capital markets in emerging nations can be considered different than their counterparts in developed nations because they may be more volatile, segmented, unpredictable, and thus, companies are financially vulnerable. Regarding the debt markets, financial conglomerates are formed in which a bank finances a portion of the corporations located within and there are implicit agreements with other banks to finance the remaining firms. This type of agreement leads to a lack of transparency and the limited disclosure presents accounting risks. Banks are less regulated and have more discretion with regards to credit analysis. Recently, for example, a Chilean bank granted a loan for $10 million to a small firm with equity capital of $9000. The Chilean regulatory banking agency (Superintendencia de Banco e Instituciones Financieras) approved the loan, but in reality the loan was granted as the firm obtaining the loan was owned by the daughter-in-law of the recently elected president Michele Bachelet. This case and ensuing scandal is known as "Caso Caval" and there is an ongoing a legal investigation into the transaction.[1]

Liquidity with regards to financial institutions is an important issue in emerging markets. The main concern is that liquidity can highly volatile, affecting both the exchange rate and the interest rate for a given country. Due to this, central banks perform an

1. Diario la Tercera, March 6, 2015. The 8.8 magnitude earthquake that struck Chile in February 2010, cost $30 billion, data compiled by the Center for Research on Epidemiology of Disasters (CRED) showed.

important role for each of these nations. In Chile, Inverlink, an investment bank, went bankrupt unexpectedly on February 2003, and the Chilean Central Bank intervened by injecting liquidity into the system. Additionally, the central bank used the state commercial bank "Banco del Estado" to buy Certificates of deposit (CD) from other banks to maintain liquidity in the financial system and keep the Chilean banking system from dissolving.

Operational Risk

In emerging markets, staff culture and work ethic vary and may be volatile. Willingness to strike on short notice for minor issues or nationalist sentiment can be a source of risk. This is especially true in isolated rural areas where income and fringe benefits are lower than the more developed cities. For example, in Chile, in the northern port of Puerto Angamos, workers asked for a lunch hour in their workday or the equivalent in monetary compensation. These were agricultural workers with no employment contracts. This strike occurred during the fruit season and lasted for 21 days, costing the Chilean economy $210 million per day. Unionization, while common in many nations, can lead to operational risks that should be noted by risk managers due to issues such as the agricultural worker's strike. Another risk is pervasive in the Chilean mining industry, as a shortage of skilled local managers and specialized workers make it vulnerable to poaching by competitors. Therefore, companies have developed differing strategies to combat this risk such as continuing education programs to help retain talented workers.

Technology Risk

Technology risk is not a trivial issue in emerging markets. This risk can include such issues as restrictions on hardware imports, incompatibility in communication systems, vulnerability of the communication systems, limited access to technical support and in some cases scarce available of power to run this technology. For example, in southern South America, internet service is less technologically advanced than similar systems in North America, so those southern nations are jointly working towards improved Internet connectivity with larger data capacity and increased speeds. Having these South American nations collaborate is difficult but necessary to overcome the technological risks.

Outsourcing as Management Risk in Emerging Markets

In emerging markets, firms in the raw material industry use outsourcing to control fixed costs and gain flexibility. The risk becomes evident if the firms fail to honor their contracts and do not collaborate. Service standards are met infrequently and post-contractual opportunistic behavior occurs if there is limited reciprocity. Within outsourcing, fraud heightens vulnerability and occurs when management has limited understanding of local practices. Staffs begin to collude and/or political favors are bought locally. For example, transportation unions are often strong in the lesser developed countries of South America, so their bargaining power leads to demands that hinders international investment. This can give the impression of closing the borders mentality and results in less funds flow into the economy. This can be problematic for risk managers of corporations trying to gain entry into the country and is generally due to scarce resources within the emerging markets.

Physical security may be a problem for plants, personnel, and processes. In Chile the demand for security in the mining industry is strong that firms recruit new workers from the local military and law enforcement; taking advantage of their training. In response to this, the government is often forced to increase salaries in their respective departments. This leads to an increase in the standard of living for the trained employees, but hinders possible international investment due to rising costs. Foreign executives need to be adapted to local conditions including procedures compliance with local regulations. Another example from the culture of Chile, it is not uncommon that if the workers are paid on Friday, the company will see a high number of absences on Monday. Also, with political change and new social needs, change may come quickly and suddenly.

Environmental Risk

Environmental risk is also faced by multi-national corporations (MNC) investing in emerging markets. The primary concerns are regulatory changes and the convention 169 of the International Labor Organization (ILO) for indigenous and tribal Peoples.[2] Low government standards or non-enforcement may reduce environmental risk, but poor practices today may lead to problems in the near future. In Chile, in a small region called Caimanes, there is a controversy among the inhabitants and a mining company, Los Pelambres, the Luksic Group. In reaction to this controversy, the firm's costs since 2002. Uncertainty arises from the potential impact that political events can have on the environment, so outside investors may become less confident in providing capital to the area for development. Such is the case of Pascua Lama, a mining company, which is based in both Argentina and Chile. Each of the countries impose different environmental restrictions and mining projects have been stopped consistently for months until environmental resolutions were authorized by Argentina, Chile, or both. The lack of a consistent work schedule increases observable risks such as financial risk due to debt burdens or operational risks due to the loss of workers finding other employment.

Methodology

Emerging markets present a special case for the design and implementation of risk management systems. Specifically, the Chilean economy, a leading country in Latin America, is facing a transition from a developing economy to a fully industrialized nation. With

2. Convention No.169 is a legally binding international instrument open to ratification, which deals specifically with the rights of indigenous and tribal peoples. Today, it has been ratified by 20 countries. Once it ratifies the Convention, a country has one year to align legislation, policies and programmers to the Convention before it becomes legally binding. Countries that have ratified the Convention are subject to supervision with regards to its implementation.

important structural changes in the regulatory business environment and significant changes in its society, citizens are demanding their civil rights and social control. During the last 10 years, Chile has endured rapid economic growth as the subprime crisis has had a minimal effect. This growth can be attributed to fiscal responsibility, high copper prices, and a strong inflow of international capital in both direct and indirect investments. However, the typical management risks such as team, inflationary, exchange rate, commodity price, and interest rate risk amongst others still remain. These risks are not bullet proof in this transitional economy.

Although large firms in Chile have practiced careful risk management strategies, we can identify five specific cases in which the risk management policies were not properly evaluated. In each case, regulatory control by government agencies played a significant role within the organizations. These cases can be identified as: *Schwager S.A.*, *La Polar S.A.*, *Hites S.A.*, *CSVA S.A.*, and *Soquimich*.

Schwager S.A.

Schwager is a case of stock price manipulation which involves the corporation spreading false information (Ullah, Massoud, & Scholnick, 2014). On September 16, 2004, Schwager, a Chilean mining company, stated that its Board agreed to hire the consultant Poch Ambiental SA to assess three possible carbon bond investment projects: (1) afforestation of large areas of desert and other arid land, (2) development of a fuel additive to reduce the effects of air pollution, and (3) a treatment to curb waste and water pollution in fishing areas in the Arauco Gulf. Schwager circulated the announcement publicly throughout various media outlets and initiated a seasoned equity issue. Consequently, its share price increased by 328%, from about CLP 2 to CLP 7.7 (Figueroa, 2012).

The newspaper, *Strategy*, highlights an interview on October 1, 2004 of Schwager's CEO, stated that the share price would be around CLP 100 per share and that the company's projects to reduce emissions were progressing steadily. On this date, the share price reached $CH40. In other words, the news published coincided with a rise in price of 419%. In addition, on June 29, 2005, Schwager reached a joint venture agreement with Empresa Nacional de Petroleo (ENAP) to develop the fuel additive Chiss. The companies agreed on a business plan to market the additive not only nationally, but also on an international basis (Rosenblut, 2011). On June 30, using a Plug Material Event, Schwager sent the text of the agreement and the offer letter referring to the price of the additive Chiss for future trades. The stock price increased by 146%, from an average price of CLP 8.2 in the previous two months to an average price of CLP 20.63 in two months following the announcement (Rosenblut, 2011). However, on August 12, 2005, Schwager unilaterally terminated the agreement with ENAP, a fact that was withheld from the public until November 8, 2005. Coincidentally, the SVS published the terms of the agreement and the stock price fell by 23.8% from the previous day's close. The ruling in the case Schwager is termed "Pump and Dump" (Rosenblut, 2011).

La Polar S.A.

The second case involves La Polar S.A., a retail company specializing in department stores that caters to low- and middle income families. The retailer lost more than $1 billion of its market capitalization due to poor use of credit, but concealed losses with the constant rollover of its debt funding. This practice of unilateral renegotiation involves the company automatically rolling over loans, but in this case the annual interest rate was approximately 250% (Traslaviña, 2013). Rollover is commonly performed on commercial balloon notes in many countries, but La Polar appeared to not pay down the principal on the debt over the term. This business model constitutes the types of bad management practices that risk managers should avoid. The original debt had doubled or tripled with the new 36-month balloon note as it was a unilateral change (Traslaviña, 2013). Additionally, such unilateral renegotiations could raise provisions for loans with loan losses for Chilean banks to between 150 billion and 200 billion Chilean pesos

(Superintendencia de Valores y Seguros [SVS], 2011a), almost 10 times the provisions of 22 billion Chilean pesos made in 2010.

Subsequently, on June 8, the company's closing stock price was CLP 2, 336.2. The next day the closing price was CLP 1, 352.2, posting a loss of 42.1% of its market value in just one day. This drop in the market price came after the company reported unauthorized practices in the management of their loan portfolio that were far from the criteria and parameters established by the company.

Hites S.A.

The decline in La Polar's stock price appears to have been correlated with a negative reaction on the stock price of another retailer in Chile, Hites. This was due to the market suspecting similar, widespread practices in the retail sector. While there was no evidence that Hites practiced a system of unilateral renegotiations, the company used a similar business model to La Polar. When analyzing the abnormal returns of Hite's stock, one may conclude that the market significantly punished the share price of other retail firms in Chile by assuming that they also took part in unilateral renegotiations not surveyed in financial statements (Cornejo & Arias, 2014). According to the results, Hites recorded significant negative cumulative abnormal returns in the following five-day (between −17.44% and −28.72%) and 10-day (between −24.63% and −34.34%) period up to June 9, 2011 (Cornejo & Arias, 2014). Hites appeared to be the company most affected by the momentum in the retail sector.

South American Steamship Company SA (CSAV)

Founded in 1872, South American Steamship Company SA (CSAV) was Latin America's largest shipping company and it ranked amongst the 20 largest shipping companies in the world. In 2009, the subprime crisis in the United States negatively impacted global trade, thus affecting the shipping industry including CSAV. In 2010, transport volumes and freight rates began to increase again and a recovery seemed to be starting. However, in 2011 the maritime containers sector was negatively affected by imbalances between supply and demand, leading to a glut in transport capacity and declining freight rates in many markets. Moreover, oil prices, which accounted for about a third of the maritime containers sector operating costs, experienced a steady increase as compared to the previous 12 years. This combination of factors had a severe financial impact on shipping companies. To combat this unfavorable scenario, shipping companies took a series of measures such as closing trade routes, increasingly detaining fleets, using slower steam freight, and increasing joint operations. This led to a change in the strategic focus from market share to return. In this same context, these negative developments in the container industry reduced operational flexibility, a product of the use of a lower percentage of owned ships versus rented ones. The falling margin of CSVA caused a loss of $1250 million in 2011. Consequently, after the Luksic Group acquired CSAV on Friday, September 2, 2011, the CSVA reported a restructuring plan consisting of inter alia, seasoned equity offerings, and a split into two differing segments: South American Steamship Company (CSAV), in charge of the business of container ships; and American, Air, and Maritime Agencies SA (SAAM), responsible for providing port services and land logistics in different American ports (SVS, 2011b).

Soquimich SA

The last case, Soquimich, is a critical one as it included multiple firms. Soquimich SA, one of the most important non-metal mines in the world, is publicly traded in Chile as well as the United States through American Depositary Receipt (ADRs). On Wednesday, March 18, 2015, media outlets published the announcement of the resignation of three directors: Vice Presidents Wayne Brownlee, José María Eyzaguirre, and Alejandro Montero. These directors were elected by Canada's Potash Corporation of Saskatchewan (PCS), which holds 32% ownership of Soquimich. The news led to a 12.46% decline in the stock price in one day's trading. Therefore, the Santiago Stock Exchange temporarily suspended transactions of Soquimich stock. Parisi and Buchannan (2016) find the use of pyramidal ownership tunneling to related-party transactions as the main issue here. This occurs when a higher level firm moves funds from a lower level firm in the pyramidal chain to expropriate minority wealth.

Soquimich is being investigated for alleged tax offenses associated with illegal campaign financing via false invoices. These are crimes that imply the use of improper influence through peddling and bribery. At a special meeting on Monday, March 16, 2015, the board of Soquimich fired its CEO, who had refused to hand over accounting information requested by prosecutors investigating the alleged crime.

Results

Table 1 provides a summary of the dates and events included in the study.

From the date of the event, a window of 52 weeks and/or one year is constructed to study trends and volatility in the stock market. Then, for each stock, variance and standard deviation of daily returns over the last 52 weeks are calculated. Using the same window, the historical daily average return is also c computed. Thus, we use two statistics to describe the behavior of the stock's return during the last 52 weeks: a measure of average daily return (mean) and a measure of the volatility of daily returns relative to its average value (variance and standard deviation, Markowitz, 1952).

Third, in the context of Risk Management, the potential share losses are estimated by calculating the Value at Risk (VaR), which was established as a widely accepted and important measure of risk (Hull, 2007). However, despite the apparent simplicity of this measure, VaR can be difficult to interpret in some cases (Berkowitz, Christoffersen, & Pelletier, 2011; Linsmeier & Pearson, 2000). The VaR of a portfolio investment is usually defined as the maximum expected loss (resulting from an adverse market movement) with a given confidence level for a certain time period

Table 1: Event Day for Schwager, Mining & Energy S.A., La Polar S.A., Hites S.A., Compañía Sud Americana de Vapores S.A. (CSAV), and Soquimich S.A.

Firm	Event Day	Event
Schwager S.A.	November 8, 2005	It is reported that Schwager unilaterally ended the agreement with ENAP.
La Polar S.A.	June 9, 2011	The company reports on loan rollover and new provisions for loan losses.
Hites S.A.	June 9, 2011	La Polar reports on loan rollover and new provisions for loan losses.
Compañía Sud Americana de Vapores S.A. (CSVA)	September 2, 2012	Corporate restructuring is announced given the new market conditions.
Soquimich S.A.	March 18, 2015	The resignation of three directors who failed to cooperate with the alleged tax investigation.

in the future (Lore & Borodovsky, 2000) and is an attractive measure of risk because it is easy to understand. According to Hull (2007), where VaR is used, the goal is to make a statement as follows: it has an "*X*" percent certainty that you will lose no more than "*V*" dollars in the next "*n*" days. The VaR is based on the assumption of normality of returns, and its calculation requires knowledge of the relevant standard deviation. The VaR for each individual asset is calculated as follows:

In a first approximation, the VaR is estimated for an individual asset *j* (VaR*j*), considering a single risk factor, using Eq. (1).

$$\mathrm{VaR}_j = S_j \times z \times \sigma_{P,j} \times \sqrt{t} \tag{1}$$

This is a standard way to calculate VaR. In Eq. (1), S_j is the spot price of the asset j; z is the critical value of a normal distribution for a given confidence level; $\sigma_{(P,\ j)}$ is the volatility of the price of the asset j; t is the period of maintenance of assets and during which time one is exposed to adverse market movements that can cause losses. Second, to obtain the confidence level, we calculate the estimated VaR_j as the lower limit of a confidence interval of 95% for the daily asset return, according to Eqs. (2) and (3).

$$R_j^{\text{Min}} = \overline{R}_j - z \times \left(\frac{\sigma_j}{\sqrt{n}}\right) \tag{2}$$

In Eq. (2): R_j^{Min} is estimated for the asset j minimum daily return; $\overline{R}_j$ is the average daily return of asset j; z is the critical value of a normal distribution for a given confidence level; σ_j is the standard deviation of daily returns of the asset j; n is the sample size of observations (here, the amount of daily returns).

Then the formula (3) estimates the VaR for individual asset j from the difference between the average daily return $(\overline{R}_j)$ and the estimated minimum daily return $\left(R_j^{\text{Min}}\right)$. The difference between $\overline{R}_j$ and R_j^{Min} indicate the investor's exposure loss, this difference is multiplied by the square root of time (t) to maintain asset j (time during which one is exposed to adverse market movement).

$$\text{VaR}_j = \left(\overline{R}_j - R_j^{Min}\right) \times \sqrt{t} \tag{3}$$

Then VaR_j is estimated from the average daily return $(\overline{R}_j)$ and the standard deviation of daily returns (σ_j), where both statistics are calculated based on historical returns. In this context, it is assumed that the historical average return is a good proxy expected return and that the historical volatility of returns is representative of its future volatility. According to the definition of VaR, one must choose a value for the two parameters in the definition: the level of confidence (of which the value of z is clear) and the maintenance period of the asset (t), where the level of confidence will be a data provided by senior management or the market regulator.

Table 2: Daily VaR Results.

	Schwager	La Polar	Hites	CSVA	Soquimich[d]
Daily return (%)	0.52	−0.01	0.34	−0.34	0.01
σ daily[a] (%)	6.22	1.75	2.19	3.29	1.89
n[a]	214	251	251	251	247
R_j^{Min} (%)	−0.31	−0.23	0.07	−0.75	−0.22
VaR in a day (%)[b]	−0.83	−0.22	−0.27	−0.41	−0.24
Loss (%)	−23.08	−42.12	−4.93	−15.89	−17.05
VaR in a day (CLP)[c]	−1.20	−76	−26	−13	−525
Loss (CLP)	−2.27	−932.64	−29.97	−32.94	−2416.00
Error estimation	**189.17%**	**1227.16%**	**115.26%**	**253.38%**	**460.19%**

Notes: The estimated VaR for a day and the observed losses at the event are shown in the table. Results are expressed in returns (%) and Chilean peso (CLP), for Schwager SA, La Polar SA, Hites SA, South American Steamship Company SA, and Soquimich S.A.
[a]Corresponds to 12 months before the event.
[b]Estimated using Eqs. (2) and (3).
[c]Estimated using Eq. (1). The spot price (St) corresponds to the closing price of the day before the event. It is considered a confidence level of 95%; volatility corresponds to the 12 months prior to the event; and the estimated VaR for a maintenance period of one day.
[d]Stock B Soquimich (SQM-B) Series.

The results for the five cases studied are presented in Tables 2 and 3. Table 2 shows the estimated VaR for one day, in percentage terms (%) — according to Eqs. (2) and (3) — and in Chilean pesos (CLP) — according to Eq. (1).

VaR is estimated for a single day and is written in percentages and compared with the effective event losses. In all cases, the effective loss is greater than the estimated loss by VaR. The risk is underestimated since the effective loses ranged from 115.26% to 1227.16% in relation to the ones estimate. These results are somewhat surprising as, Soquimich, La Polar, and CSVA are publicly traded companies on the Chilean stock market index, but this is an example of the losses that can happen in emerging countries where there is a lack of proper risk management.

Table 3 shows the estimated VaR for different windows of time: one day, one week (five days), one month, and 12 months. The estimated VaR is also compared with the effective losses in each window. It is noted that the observed loss was bigger than the loss estimated by the VaR with the exception of the 12-month window for CSVA stock. As a result, one traditional tool for financial risk management is underestimating the real risk in emerging markets. In Chile these companies were actively traded and scrutinized by investment firms, regulatory agencies and others participating in the market, but managerial risk based on the Chilean transitional economy was underestimated. Considering risk management in emerging or transitional economies as similar to the ones in developed market is a bias conclusions and the traditional tools are not effectives.

Conclusions

In the context of Risk Management, it is typical to estimate the potential loss for a stock or portfolio by calculating the VaR. The VaR of a portfolio investment is usually defined as the maximum expected loss (resulting from an adverse market movement), with a given confidence level for a certain period in the future. However, the VaR may underestimate the risk associated with investments in emerging markets-where new events show up unexpectedly, changing the level of risk in a given company. In this article five cases from Chilean companies whose shares experienced significant increases in volatility were analyzed: Schwager, La Polar, Hites, CSVA, and Soquimich. The results show that the observed loss was greater than the loss estimated by VaR. We expect that the current risk management methodology can be improved by considering the evidence in this article and their listed results. These cases took place under normal macroeconomic conditions in Chile and in almost all case the VaR

Table 3: VaR Estimate for Different Windows.

	Schwager		La Polar		Hites		CSVA		Soquimich	
	VaR (%)	Effective returns (%)	VaR (%)	Effective returns (%)	VaR (%)	Effective returns (%)	VaR (%)	Effective returns (%)	VaR (%)	Effective returns (%)
Event day	−0.83	−23.08	−0.22	−42.12	−0.27	−4.93	−0.41	−15.89	−0.24	−17.05
Event week	−1.86	−25.00	−0.48	−31.59	−0.61	−4.93	−0.91	−12.47	−0.53	−15.86
Event month	−2.04%	−25.16[a]	−0.89	−71.03	−1.24	−15.83	−1.86	−9.18	−1.11	−27.88
Event year	−12.36	−65.43	−3.40	−84.27	−4.30	−46.85	−6.44	−6.38	—	—

The maximum expected loss (VaR) for one day, one week, one month and 12 months is shown. The effective loss (Outcome Observed) for the event day, the week, the month, and year are shown. Results (%) for Schwager SA, La Polar SA, Hites SA, CSVA, and Soquimich S.A. are listed here.

[a]In the case of Schwager, the event occurred on November 8, 2005. The next day, on November 9, the Superintendence of Securities and Insurance suspended the transaction this stock. The stock traded in the stock market one month later, on December 9, 2005.

technique does not hold. In emerging markets such as Chile, there are other factors that are not taken into consideration by the traditional risk management tools.

For all the cases presented in this article, we believe risk mitigation can be improved with greater oversight by regulatory agencies and corporate control. In particular, corporate boards should be independent and, of course, responsible for their actions. We feel implementation is necessary in developing nations because of the lack of access to information leads to inadequate corporate transparency and financial losses as shown in the cases. Such cases may be repeated without proper risk management. Thus, the regulatory requirements of sophisticated capital markets should be transferred to emerging markets to minimize these incidents and more effective risk management is recommended for managers and the market in general, including international investors.

References

Berkowitz, J., Christoffersen, P., & Pelletier, D. (2011). Evaluating value-at-risk models with desk-level data. *Management Science, 57*(12), 2213–2227.

Cornejo, E., & Arias, P. (2014). La Polar S.A.: Manipulación Contable en el sector retail. Paper presented at the XXX Encuentro Nacional de Escuelas y Facultades de Administración (ENEFA), October 22–24, Punta Arenas, Chile.

Dalberg, J. E. E. (1887). Letter to Archbishop Mandell Creighton. *Historical Essays and Studies* (p. 1907). London: Macmillan.

Figueroa, J. P. (2012, June 18). El juicio que podría hundir al dueño de Estrategia por publicar noticias del mercado bursátil en beneficio propio. Reportajes de Investigación, CIPER, Centro de Investigación Periodística.

Hull, J. (2007). *Risk management and financial institutions* (1st ed.). New York, NY: Pearson Education, Inc.

Linsmeier, T. J., & Pearson, N. D. (2000). Value at risk. *Financial Analysts Journal, 56*(2), 47–67.

Lore, M., & Borodovsky, L. (2000). *The professional´s handbook of financial risk management* (1st ed.). Oxford: Butterworth – Heinemann, Reed Educational and Professional Publishing Ltd.

Markowitz, H. (1952). Portfolio selection. *The Journal of Finance, 7*(1), 77–91.

Melecky, M., & Raddatz, C. (2011). *How do governments respond after catastrophes? Natural-disaster shocks and the fiscal stance*. Policy Research Working Paper Series 5564. World Bank, Washington, DC.

Parisi, F., & Buchannan, B. (2016). *Pyramidal ownership, tunneling and propping: Soquimich case, more regulation for dual listed shares*. Working paper.

Politi, D. (2013). *Shop 'Til it Drops*. Retrieved from http://latitude.blogs.nytimes.com/2013/06/11/another-price-freeze-another-shoddy-attempt-by-argentina-to-mitigate-inflation/?_r=0

Rosenblut, V. (2011, March). El Denominado Caso "Schwager": Análisis de Histórica Condena por Uso de Información Privilegiada y Manipulación Bursátil. *Revista Jurídica del Ministerio Público*, N°46, pp. 185–209.

Rucinski, T., Gonzalez, A., & Gray, K. (2014). *Spain's Repsol agrees to a $5 billion settlement with Argentina over YPF*. Retrieved from http://www.reuters.com/article/2014/02/25/us-repsol-argentina-idUSBREA1O1LJ20140225

Superintendencia de Valores y Seguros. (2011a, June 9). Ref: Empresas La Polar S.A. Inscripción Registro de Valores N° 806. Hecho Esencial. Santiago de Chile.

Superintendencia de Valores y Seguros. (2011b, September 2). Ref: Comunica Hecho Esencial. Inscripción Registro de Valores N° 76. Hecho Esencial. Santiago de Chile.

Traslaviña, H. (2013). *Llegar y Llevar: Cómo se Fraguó la Estafa del Siglo* (1ra Edición), Santiago de Chile: Editorial Mandrágora.

Ullah, S., Massoud, N., & Scholnick (2014). The impact of fraudulent false information on equity values. *Journal of Business Ethics, 120*, 219–235.

Vogler, J. (2006). *Chile: The rise of the Penguin revolution*. Retrieved from http://upsidedownworld.org/main/chile-archives-34/330-chile-the-rise-of-the-penguin-revolution

14

Regional Integration and Risk Management of African Stock Markets

Takashi Matsuki, Kimiko Sugimoto and Yushi Yoshida

Abstract

We examine how the degree of regional financial integration in African stock markets has evolved over the last eleven years. Despite increasing regional economic cooperation, the process of stock market integration has been slow. To facilitate growth via developed financial markets but keep financial stability risk at a minimum, further regional integration should be promoted, and mild capital controls on non-African investors may be necessary. A Diebold-Yilmaz spillover analysis is applied to ten African stock markets for the period between August 2004 and January 2015. We examine spillovers among four regions and among individual countries. Regional integration, as measured by total spillovers in Africa, is increasing but remains very low. These spillovers were temporarily heightened during the global financial crisis. Cross-regional spillovers are high between Northern and Southern Africa.

Asymmetric capital controls on African and non-African investors must be considered to foster further regional integration and to mitigate financial stability risk. This is one of the few studies to address the construction of the future architecture of regionally integrated stock markets in emerging countries.

Keywords: African stock markets; capital control; global financial crisis; regional financial integration; risk management; spillover index

JEL classifications: F36; G15; O55

Introduction

The development of financial markets is a prerequisite for promoting economic growth in developing countries. Financial markets promote capital accumulation and technological innovation by reducing the information and transaction costs of economic activities (Levine, 1997). Well-developed stock markets in particular promote economic growth by ensuring investor liquidity, which reduces the risk in long-term investments (Levine & Zervos, 1998b) and provides corporations with opportunities to finance their prospective projects. Moreover, improved risk sharing due to stock market liberalization should decrease the cost of equity capital (Bekaert & Harvey, 2000). In fact, Bekaert, Harvey, and Lundblad (2005) have shown that equity market liberalizations lead to a 1% increase in annual real economic growth.

However, policymakers in emerging economies face challenges in fine-tuning the degree of financial openness for their economies. When they are open only to domestic funds, financial markets in emerging economies lack sufficient funds to boost the economy. When they are open to international investors, financial markets in emerging economies enjoy larger trading volumes and greater liquidity but face the greater volatility risks associated with foreign market conditions.[1] In particular, stock markets in both emerging and less-capitalized developing countries must be designed to weather global financial turmoil, such as those recently experienced after the US subprime mortgage crisis and the consequent and prolonged European sovereign debt crisis.

Financial integration or/and financial openness can be measured in several ways.[2] Capital account openness (or liberalization) is measured de jure by constructing indexes using the IMF's "Annual Report on Exchange Arrangements and Exchange Restrictions" (AREAER) (among others, Chinn & Ito, 2006) or *de facto* by, for example, a country's aggregate assets plus liabilities relative to its gross domestic product (Lane & Milesi-Ferretti, 2007). For financial openness in stock markets for developing countries in particular, Bekaert et al. (2005) provide several de jure measures. The major drawback of these measures is that they are only available on an annual frequency. To capture the gradual progress in financial integration, time-varying correlations calculated from time-series analysis such as VAR or multivariate-GARCH are also widely used (Bekaert & Harvey, 1995; Longin & Solnik, 1995). In this chapter, we focus on African stock markets and apply time-series analysis to examine how financial integration within Africa has evolved over the past eleven years.[3]

The most relevant study for this chapter is the work by Sugimoto, Matsuki, and Yoshida (2014), which analyzes spillovers from stock markets of developed countries, exchange rate markets, and commodity markets to the African region. Rather than examining spillovers from developed countries to African economies, in this chapter, we focus on estimating spillovers within Africa. The sample of countries in this chapter is expanded to 10 countries

1. Ostry, Ghosh, Chamon, and Qureshi (2012) discuss the risk management tools available to cope with the financial-stability risks associated with capital inflows.

2. See Quinn, Schindler, and Toyoda (2011) for a summary and comparisons of these measures.

3. For a survey on financial development and economic growth in Africa, see Murinde (2012). Enisan and Olufisayo (2009) and Ngare, Nyamongo, and Misati (2014) in particular focus on stock market development and economic growth in Africa.

from the seven countries examined by Sugimoto et al. (2014). The 10 African countries are Egypt, Morocco, Tunisia, Kenya, Tanzania, Nigeria, Côte d'Ivoire, South Africa, Mauritius, and Botswana. Moreover, the ten African countries are grouped into four sub-regions, and spillovers among these sub-regions are also examined. For the measurement of spillovers, we apply Diebold and Yilmaz's (2009, 2012) methodology, which simultaneously estimates the spillovers for all possible pairs in a vector autoregressive framework.

From the spillover analysis, we find that regional spillover within Africa was elevated in the wake of the global financial crisis. During enduring turmoil in global markets, regional spillover experienced sharp drops on several occasions and returned to the pre-crisis levels by mid-2013. Only recently has the degree of regional integration in terms of stock market co-movements gradually increased at a steady speed. This recent evidence coincides with regional efforts to consolidate stock markets at the subregional level and to reach agreements for cross-border listings.[4]

Given the strong links of the stock markets of South Africa and northern African border countries with global markets (Sugimoto et al., 2014), an increase in the degree of regional integration indirectly has made stock markets throughout the African region more susceptible to the global shocks. Risk management for this financial stability risk must be introduced. Among the alternative tools available to increase the degree of regional integration within Africa while minimizing spillovers from the global market, we propose mild capital controls only on countries (namely, Egypt, Morocco, and South Africa) that have stronger links to global markets.

The rest of the chapter is structured as follows. The next section briefly describes the development path of financial markets in

4. In fact, there are currently seventeen regional integration arrangements in Africa, eight of which are regional economic communities recognized by the AU (African Union) for pan-African economic and political unification. According to the African Development Bank (2014), all countries except Algeria, Cape Verde and Mozambique overlap in the membership of several regional integration arrangements.

Africa and the current state of sub-regional stock market cooperation. The section "Empirical Methodology for Measuring Return Spillover" describes the econometric methodology used to measure spillovers and discusses how these indices can be used to gauge regional integration. The next section shows the estimation results, and the section "Risk Management in African Stock Markets" discusses the implications for the financial architecture in terms of stock market risk management in the African region. The last section concludes.

Developments in African Stock Markets and Beyond

The development level of stock markets in Africa differs widely among our sample countries. The stock market of South Africa is far larger than those of other African countries in terms of market capitalization values: 612 billion US dollars in 2012 or over tenfold the values of the next largest stock markets in Africa, namely, Egypt, Nigeria, and Morocco (Table 1). The other six stock markets have market capitalization values of less than 20 billion US dollars. Despite the rapid growth of African stock markets recently observed, most remain small and illiquid. Thus, African stock markets represent less than 2% of world market capitalization. However, the ratio of the value of market capitalization to GDP for South Africa is 160%, surpassing the level of Japan (62% in 2012), which is among the most developed markets in the world.

The data availability limits the selection of sample countries; however, the countries are carefully chosen based on geographic diversity. The northern region includes Egypt, Morocco, and Tunisia; the eastern region includes Kenya and Uganda; the western region includes Côte d'Ivoire and Nigeria; and the southern region includes Botswana, Mauritius, and South Africa. By outstanding market size, Egypt, Kenya, Nigeria, and South Africa are candidate sub-regional hub-markets for the northern, eastern, western, and southern regions, respectively (see Table 1).

Table 1: African Stock Markets in 2012.

Country (Region)	Market Capitalization				Traded Values			Listed Companies	Nominal GDP	Per Cap. GDP
	Rank	Value[a]	Growth[c] (%)	/GDP (%)	Value[a]	/GDP (%)	TR[d] (%)	Number	Value[a]	Value[b]
(S) South Africa	1	612,308	129	160	311,778	81.5	55	348	382,338	7314
(N) Egypt	2	58,008	114	22	20,161	7.7	38	234	262,832	3256
(W) Nigeria	3	56,389	494	12	4204	0.9	9	192	462,979	2742
(N) Morocco	4	52,634	300	55	3501	3.6	6	76	95,982	2902
(E) Kenya	5	14,791	254	37	1008	2.5	8	57	40,264	933
(N) Tunisia	6	8887	261	20	1251	2.8	13	59	45,238	4197
(W) Côte d'Ivoire	7	7829	374	32	163	0.7	2	37	78,848	5844
(E) Uganda	8	7294	15,419	36	11	0.1	0.2	10	20,032	551
(S) Mauritius	9	7093	263	62	296	2.6	4	87	11,442	8862
(S) Botswana	10	4588	115	32	113	0.8	3	24	14,537	7255

Source: World Development Indicators 2014.
[a]Million US dollars.
[b]US dollars.
[c]Growth from 2003 to 2012.
[d]Turnover ratio.

Regional integration in Africa in terms of intra-regional trade is progressing. Table 2 provides the status of regional economic union participation, stock market coordination, and cross-border listing. In January 2012, the AU (African Union) summit reached an agreement to establish a Pan-African Continental Free Trade Area by 2017. This decision will accelerate intra-regional trade in goods markets and is expected to foster more active intra-regional transactions in financial markets. The COMESA (Common Market for Eastern and Southern Africa), replacing the 1994 Preferential Trade Area, focuses on the formation of a large economic and trading unit among its 19 member countries, including Egypt in the northern region, Kenya in the eastern region, and Mauritius in the southern region. However, the stock market integration process in Africa lags behind intra-regional trade despite the fact that a regional stock market offers investors the opportunity to share risks across countries. The BRVM (Bourse Régionale des Valeurs Mobilières) in western Africa and the BVMAC (the Bourse des Valeurs Mobilières d'Afrique Centrale) in Central Africa are the only regional stock exchanges, while there exist 25 active stock exchanges in Africa. The eight BRVM member countries and the six BVMAC member countries share a common background: they are all French-speaking countries and use a common currency (CFA francs) pegged to the Euro. The other African countries cannot follow this path. Despite the difficulty faced in coordinating the regulatory and payment systems among existing markets in the region, the EASEA (East African Securities Exchanges Association) and CoSSE (Committee of SADC Stock Exchanges) have initiated talks to integrate their stock markets.

Instead of creating a regional stock market, similar benefits can be partly enjoyed by allowing companies to be listed simultaneously on multiple stock markets. The rightmost column in Table 2 lists the countries that have exchanged an MOU (memorandum of understanding) for cross-border listing. South Africa is most actively engaged in cross-border listing; South Africa has either cross-listed or signed MOUs with Botswana, Egypt, Ghana, Kenya, Malawi, Namibia, Nigeria, Uganda, and Zambia. Kenya is also active in cross-border listing and has made agreements with

Table 2: Regional Economic Integration among Selected African Countries.

	Regional Economic Communities/Union	Stock Market Coordination	Cross-Border Listing
Northern Region			
Egypt	CEN-SAD, COMESA		Kenya, Nigeria, South Africa
Morocco	AMU, CEN-SAD		
Tunisia	AMU, CEN-SAD		
Eastern Region			
Kenya	CEN-SAD, COMESA, EAC, IGAD	EASEA	Côte d'Ivoire, Egypt, Nigeria, South Africa, Uganda; (BRVM, Ghana, Rwanda, Tanzania)
Uganda	COMESA, EAC, IGAD	EASEA	Kenya, South Africa; (Rwanda, Tanzania)
Western Region			
Côte d'Ivoire	CEN-SAD, ECOWAS, WAEMU	BRVM	Kenya, Nigeria; (Ghana)
Nigeria	CEN-SAD, ECOWAS, WAMZ		Côte d'Ivoire, Egypt, Kenya, South Africa; (BRVM, Gambia, Ghana, Sierra Leone)

Southern Region			
Botswana	SACU, SADC	CoSSE	South Africa
Mauritius	COMESA, SADC, IOC	CoSSE	
South Africa	CMA, SACU, SADC	CoSSE	Botswana, Egypt, Kenya, Nigeria, Uganda; (Ghana, Malawi, Namibia, Zambia)

Note: AMU (Arab Maghreb Union), BRVM (La Bourse régionale des valeurs Mobilières), CEN-SAD (Community of Sahara-Sahel States), CMA (Common Monetary Area), COMESA (Common Market for Eastern and Southern Africa), CoSSE (Committee of SADC Stock Exchanges), EAC (East African Community), EASEA (East African Securities Exchanges Association), ECOWAS (Economic Community of West African States), IGAD (Intergovernmental Authority on Development), IOC (Indian Ocean Commission), SACU (Southern African Customs Union), SADC (Southern African Development Community), WAEMU (West African Economic and Monetary Union), WAMZ (West African Monetary Zone).

Côte d'Ivoire, Egypt, Ghana, Nigeria, Rwanda, South Africa, Tanzania, and Uganda. Onyuma, Mugo, and Karuiya (2012) and Irving (2005) detail the development of cross-listing in Africa. Despite the development of cross-listing in Africa, cross-listings do not necessarily take place between neighboring countries. For example, Egypt does not cross-list with other northern countries while cross-listing with countries in the western and southern regions. Cross-listing seems to facilitate coordination between distant markets, whereas the BRVM and EASEA aim to develop stronger links within regional markets.

Despite differences in institutional standards, including exchange systems and legal frameworks, and in broader financial restrictions, such as exchange controls, twelve regional integration arrangements for economic cooperation are in progress (see the first column in Table 2). The collaboration progress of these initiatives is slow; however, many African countries overlap in their membership of various regional communities, and there have been discussions about a pan-African stock exchange at the AU level. Moreover, the successful functioning of three communities seems promising: ECOWAS (Economic Community of West African States), EAC (East African Community), and SADC (Southern African Development Community). ECOWAS held the West African Capital Markets Integration Council in January 2013 and established a technical committee to harmonize listing, trading and settlement rules. EASEA is a member of the Capital Markets Development Committee of the EAC to improve the cross-listing of stocks. Because economic cooperation communities form by geographical proximity, much stronger collaboration across stock exchanges can be expected on a sub-regional basis.

The development of a stock market is dependent on the amount of capital flowing into the market. As most African countries are classified as developing economies, relying only on the capital of domestic investors is not sufficient. Table 3 provides the share of foreign investors in each African stock market. Note that foreign investors include investors from other African countries as well as non-African investors. Keeping that in mind, the largest two stock markets, South Africa and Egypt, receive only 20% of their capital

Table 3: Shares of Foreign Investors and the Most Active Sectors.

	Foreign Investors (%)	Most Active Sectors
Botswana (S)	33	Financial Services and Insurance
Côte d'Ivoire (W)	n.a.	Financial
Egypt (N)	20.5	Telecommunications
Kenya (E)	47	Telecommunication and Technology
Mauritius (S)	29.4	Banks, Insurance and other Finance
Morocco (N)	35	Banks
Nigeria (W)	51	Financial Services
South Africa (S)	16.2	Mining
Tunisia (N)	12.1	Industry
Uganda (E)	n.a.	Banking, Finance and Investment

Note: Figures for foreign investors indicate percentage of foreign investors of the total value traded in 2013. The original source is the African Securities Exchanges Association (2014).

from foreign investors. However, the stock markets in Kenya and Nigeria receive one-half of their capital from foreign countries. Capital flows among African markets should enhance the co-movements of the stock price indices of their markets. Considering the size differences among the stock markets listed in Table 1, the actual value of foreign capital in South Africa is the largest.

Another important aspect of economic integration is monetary integration. There are three monetary unions in Africa: CMA (Common Monetary Area), WAEMU (West African Economic and Monetary Union), and WAMZ (West African Monetary Zone).

The WAMZ aims to establish the West African Central Bank and to launch a single currency; however, the expected launch date, that is, January 1, 2015, has already passed. The member countries of the WAMZ are the Gambia, Ghana, Guinea, Liberia, Nigeria, and Sierra Leone. After launching a single currency, the WAMZ intends to merge with the WAEMU, whose member countries, namely, Benin, Burkina Faso, Côte d'Ivoire, Guinea Bissau, Mali, Niger, Senegal, and Togo, use the CFA franc that is pegged to the Euro. The CMA is the successor to the Rand Monetary Area, and the current member countries are Lesotho, Namibia, Swaziland, and South Africa (see Wang, Masha, Shirono, & Harris, 2007). The smaller members of the CMA issue their own currencies that are pegged to the South African rand (International Monetary Fund [IMF], 2014). Although only at the proposal stage, an eastern African monetary union is also to be established within ten years (see Mougani, 2014 for further details). Regional monetary integration is the strongest form of economic integration, as observed in the Euro area, and could help reduce high transaction costs in Africa. Regional monetary integration in Africa, however, should not affect our empirical investigation of spillovers in the following section because none of the sample countries is a member of the same monetary union or uses the same common currency.

Empirical Methodology for Measuring Return Spillover

First, we provide a brief review of the econometric approaches to investigating inter-market transmissions and discuss the advantages of the Diebold and Yilmaz (2012) methodology. Then, closely following Sugimoto et al. (2014), we provide a brief description of the Diebold and Yilmaz spillover index and introduce a generalized spillover index among African stock markets.

The numerous existing studies that focus on the relationships among the financial markets of different countries are loosely divided into two types, that is, long-run cointegration approaches and short-run GARCH (generalized autoregressive conditional heteroskedasticity) analyses. These methods, however, possess some disadvantages. A cointegration test examines the existence of long-term stable relationships and does not adequately describe the dynamic characteristics of spillovers when such relationships are constantly changing. GARCH models can estimate the complicated dynamics of spillovers. However, two or three variables are the maximum number with which a multivariate-GARCH model can practically achieve a numerical conversion using maximum likelihood estimation.

Accordingly, this chapter focuses on the methodology of Diebold and Yilmaz (2009, 2012), who introduced spillover measures based on forecast error variance decompositions from the traditional orthogonalized and generalized impulse response function and calculated the degree of volatility spillover. This method can investigate a large number of variables simultaneously as well as characterize the rich dynamics of spillovers. Extending their 2009 methodology, Diebold and Yilmaz (2012) then examine volatility spillovers by developing a revised spillover measure based on the generalized impulse response approach of Koop, Pesaran, and Porter (1996) and Pesaran and Shin (1998). The forecast error variance decompositions produced by this version are independent to variable ordering. Accordingly, this chapter uses the new method created by Diebold and Yilmaz (2012). This chapter compliments the study of Sugimoto et al. (2014), which examined six African stock markets along with stock markets in advanced countries, foreign exchange markets, and commodity markets using Diebold and Yilmaz's (2012) methodology.

The Diebold-Yilmaz Spillover Index[5]

The spillover index proposed by Diebold and Yilmaz (2009, 2012) is based on the standard approach to variance decomposition associated with a vector autoregressive model.

5. This subsection heavily borrows from Sugimoto et al. (2014).

Let us consider the following covariance stationary N-variable VAR (p) model:

$$x_t = \sum_{i=1}^{p} \Phi_i x_{t-i} + \varepsilon_t, \quad t = 1, 2, \cdots, T \tag{1}$$

where $x_t = (x_{1t}, x_{2t}, \ldots, x_{nt})'$ is an $n \times 1$ vector of stock returns and $\{\Phi_i, i = 1, 2, \cdots, p\}$ is an $n \times n$ coefficient matrix. ε_t is an $n \times 1$ i.i.d. error vector, where $\mathrm{E}(\varepsilon_t) = \mathbf{O}$ and $\mathrm{E}(\varepsilon_t \varepsilon_t') = \boldsymbol{\Sigma}$ for all t, and $\boldsymbol{\Sigma}$ is a positive definite variance-covariance matrix. Eq. (1) is assumed to meet the condition that all eigenvalues (λ) satisfying the following equations are $|\lambda| < 1$.

$$\left| I_n \lambda^p - \Phi_1 \lambda^{p-1} - \Phi_2 \lambda^{p-2} - \cdots - \Phi_{p-1} \lambda - \Phi_p \right| = 0$$

If this condition is satisfied, Eq. (1) can be rewritten as an infinite order moving average representation.

$$x_t = \sum_{i=1}^{\infty} \mathbf{A}_i \varepsilon_{t-i}, \quad t = 1, 2, \cdots, T$$

where $\mathbf{A}_i$ is an $n \times n$ coefficient matrix, which is expressed as follows:

$$\mathbf{A}_i = \Phi_1 A_{i-1} + \Phi_2 A_{i-2} + \cdots + \Phi_p A_{i-p}, \quad i = 1, 2, \cdots$$

where $\mathbf{A}_0$ is an $n \times n$ identity matrix and $\mathbf{A}_i = \mathbf{O}$ for $i < 0$

By denoting $a_{h,ij}$ for the $i-j$ component of matrix A_h, H-step ahead own- and cross-variance share can be defined as follows:

$$\theta_{ij}(H) = \frac{\sum_{h=0}^{H-1} a_{h,ij}^2}{\sum_{h=0}^{H-1} \sum_{j=1}^{N} a_{h,ij}^2} = \frac{\sum_{h=0}^{H-1} \left(e_i' A_h e_j\right)^2}{\sum_{h=0}^{H-1} \left(e_i' A_h A_h' e_i\right)} \tag{2}$$

where $i = j$ for H-step ahead own-variance share, $i \neq j$ for cross-variance share, and e_i is an $n \times 1$ selection vector that takes 1 for the ith element and 0 otherwise.

Diebold and Yilmaz's (2009) method adopted the Cholesky decomposition of the variance-covariance matrix of error terms ($\boldsymbol{\Sigma}$) to orthogonalize shocks. Therefore, this method depends on variable ordering in variance decomposition, that is, the elements of the decomposed matrix vary with the reordering of variables. In light of this issue, Diebold and Yilmaz (2012) took a generalized impulse response approach to devise a method that is invariant to the ordering of variables. As derived by Koop et al. (1996) and Pesaran and Shin (1998), the H-step ahead forecast error variance decomposition based on the generalized impulse responses is defined as follows:

$$\theta_{ij}^{g}(H) = \frac{\sigma_{ii}^{-1} \sum_{h=0}^{H-1} \left(\boldsymbol{e}_i' \boldsymbol{A}_h \Sigma \boldsymbol{e}_j\right)^2}{\sum_{h=0}^{H-1} \boldsymbol{e}_i' \boldsymbol{A}_h \Sigma \boldsymbol{A}_h' \boldsymbol{e}_i} \tag{3}$$

where σ_{ii} is a standard error term in the ith equation. To normalize the sum of the elements in each row to 1, own- and cross-variance shares are adjusted as follows:

$$\tilde{\theta}_{ij}^{g}(H) = \frac{\theta_{ij}^{g}(H)}{\sum_{j=1}^{N} \theta_{ij}^{g}(H)} \tag{4}$$

Diebold and Yilmaz (2012) define total *gross-sum* spillover as the sum of cross-variance shares for all pairs with G = {1,…, N},

$$S^{\text{sum}}(H) = \frac{\sum_{i \in G} \sum_{j \in G, j \neq i} \tilde{\theta}_{ij}^{g}(H)}{N} \times 100 \tag{5}$$

Note that the term *gross-sum* refers to the inclusion of spillovers in both directions. In Eq. (5), the spillover in which country i affects country j and the spillover in which country j affects country i are both included.

The total gross-sum spillover concept is useful when the research objective is to examine overall spillovers among all sample countries. Two additional concepts enhance the understanding of spillovers among sample countries: directional spillover and subset spillovers. We are also interested in investigating how an individual country interacts with other countries in Africa. The total gross-sum spillover in Eq. (5) can be decomposed into individual gross-sum spillover for country k as follows:

$$S_k^{\mathrm{sum}}(H) = \frac{\sum_{i \in G, i \neq k} \tilde{\theta}_{ik}^g(H) + \sum_{i \in G, j \neq k} \tilde{\theta}_{kj}^g(H)}{N} \times 100 \qquad (6)$$

The first term of the numerator represents the spillover that country k *gives* to other countries and the second term is the spillover that country k *receives* from other countries.

Specifically, in this study, we consider a 10-variable VAR with four groups of markets: North = {Egypt, Morocco, Tunisia}, East = {Kenya, Uganda}, West = {Côte d'Ivoire, Nigeria}, and South = {Botswana, Mauritius, South Africa}. By aggregating individual gross-sum spillovers in Eq. (6) for a sub-region, we obtain the regional gross-sum spillover for region K as follows:

$$S_K^{\mathrm{sum}}(H) = \frac{\sum_{i \in G, j \in K, i \neq j} \tilde{\theta}_{ij}^g(H) + \sum_{i \in K, j \in G, i \neq j} \tilde{\theta}_{ij}^g(H)}{N} \times 100 \qquad (7)$$

where K is a subset of G.

Building on the directional concept of spillovers in Diebold and Yilmaz (2012), Sugimoto et al. (2014) introduce a generalized concept of spillovers from a set of variables to another set of variables. Conceptually, these sets need not be mutually exclusive. For any two sets of variables, $G_1 \subset G$, $G_2 \subset G$, and $G_1 \cap G_2$ may not be empty. We define the spillover from G_1 to G_2 as follows:

$$S_{G1 \cdot G2}^{\mathrm{give}}(H) = \frac{\sum_{i \in G_2} \sum_{j \in G_1, j \neq i} \tilde{\theta}_{ij}^g(H)}{N} \times 100 \qquad (8)$$

Note that this definition can be applied to a single country set as well as to a set that includes all countries. The basic idea of a generalized spillover index is simple and defines spillovers from one set of markets to another set of markets. The spillover index from East to West, for example, is denoted as follows:

$$S^{\text{give}}_{\text{East}\cdot\text{West}}(H) = \frac{\sum_{i\in\{\text{Côte d'Ivore, Nigeria}\}} \sum_{j\in\{\text{Kenya, Uganda}\}} \tilde{\theta}^{g}_{ij}(H)}{10} \times 100 \quad (9)$$

Using this generalized spillover index, we can investigate how stock markets in eastern Africa in an aggregate sense affect stock markets in western Africa altogether. We examine the spillovers at the individual level as well as at the regional level.

Note that with this directional definition of spillover, we redefine gross-sum spillovers in Eqs. (6) and (7) as follows:

$$S^{\text{sum}}_{k}(H) = \frac{\sum_{i\in G,\, i\neq k} \tilde{\theta}^{g}_{ik}(H) + \sum_{j\in G,\, j\neq k} \tilde{\theta}^{g}_{kj}(H)}{N} \times 100 = S^{\text{give}}_{kG}(H) + S^{\text{give}}_{Gk}(H) \text{ and} \quad (10)$$

$$S^{\text{sum}}_{k}(H) = \frac{\sum_{i\in G,\, j\in K,\, i\neq j} \tilde{\theta}^{g}_{ij}(H) + \sum_{i\in K,\, j\in G,\, i\neq j} \tilde{\theta}^{g}_{ij}(H)}{N} \times 100 = S^{\text{give}}_{KG}(H) + S^{\text{give}}_{GK}(H) \quad (11)$$

By the above definitions in Eq. (7) or (11), a region with a greater number of member countries is likely to have a greater value of spillover. To control for the number of countries in region K to compare with other regions, we suggest a measure of *per-giving* regional gross-sum spillover as follows:

$$\text{pg}S^{\text{sum}}_{K}(H) = \frac{\sum_{i\in G,\, j\in K,\, i\neq j} \tilde{\theta}^{g}_{ij}(H) + \sum_{i\in K,\, j\in G,\, i\neq j} \tilde{\theta}^{g}_{ij}(H)}{N\cdot N_K} \times 100 \quad (12)$$

where N_K is the number of member countries in region K.

Similarly, the group-wise spillover index in Eq. (8) can be misleading when comparing groups with different numbers of components because the spillover index between these two groups defined in Eq. (8) in general increases as the number of countries in the groups increases. In our case, the spillover index between

North and South will likely be greater than the spillover index between East and West because the North-South pair consists of six countries and the East-West pair consists of only four countries. To circumvent this aggregation problem, we define a *per-giving-and-receiving* group-wise spillover index, adjusted by the number of combination of pairs:

$$\mathrm{pgr}S_{G1\cdot G2}^{\mathrm{give}}(H) = \frac{\sum_{i\in G_2}\sum_{j\in G_1 j\neq i}\tilde{\theta}_{ij}^{g}(H)}{N(N_1 \times N_2)} \times 100 \tag{13}$$

where N_1 and N_2 are the number of components in G_1 and G_2, respectively. The per-country spillover index from East to West, for example, is:

$$\mathrm{pgr}S_{\mathrm{East}\cdot\mathrm{West}}^{\mathrm{give}}(H) = \frac{\sum_{i\in\{\text{Côte d'Ivore, Nigeria}\}}\sum_{j\in\{\text{Kenya, Uganda}\}}\tilde{\theta}_{ij}^{g}(H)}{10(2\times 2)} \times 100 \tag{14}$$

We also investigate the link within each sub-region. For this purpose, we define a *per-giving-and-receiving* within-group spillover index as follows:

$$\mathrm{pgr}S_{G1\cdot G1}^{\mathrm{give}}(H) = \frac{\sum_{i\in G_1}\sum_{j\in G_1 j\neq 1}\tilde{\theta}_{ij}^{g}(H)}{N(N_1 \times (N_1 - 1))} \times 100 \tag{15}$$

Note that in the denominator, the number of receiving countries is N_1-1, excluding the giving-country. The per-country spillover index within South, for example, is:

$$\mathrm{pgr}S_{\mathrm{South}\cdot\mathrm{South}}^{\mathrm{give}}(H) = \frac{\sum_{i\in\{\text{Botswana, Mauritius, South Africa}\}}\sum_{j\in\{\text{Botswana, Mauritius, South Africa}\}}\tilde{\theta}_{ij}^{g}(H)}{10(3\times 2)} \times 100 \tag{16}$$

For the number of H days ahead forecasts, we choose ten following Sugimoto et al. (2014). The optimum number of p lags in the VAR model is chosen based on the Akaike Information

Criterion (AIC), Bayesian Information Criterion (BIC), and Hanann-Quinn Information Criterion (HQC) among alternative values. The BIC and HQC selected one lag, and the AIC selected three. Based on the parsimonious principle, the lowest one is adopted.

Empirical Results

Data

The daily stock market indices between August 3, 2004 and January 19, 2015 are taken from Datastream, which is maintained by Thomson Reuters. These indices are the Egypt Hermes Financial Index, Morocco All Share Index (MASI), Tunisia TuniIndex, Kenya Nairobi Stock Exchange Index (NSE20), Uganda Stock Exchange All Share Index (ALSI), Nigeria All Share Index, BRVM Composite Index, FTSE/JSE All Share Index, MSCI Mauritius Index, and S&P Botswana Index (BMI). Returns are calculated as $Rt = \frac{P_t - P_{t-1}}{P_{t-1}}$, where P_t is the stock price index on day t.

Return Spillover among African Stock Markets Around Financial Crises

Figure 1 plots the total gross-sum spillover index, that is, the aggregate (excluding own-effect) spillovers of all African stock markets as in Eq. (5). The spillover index moves around the 5–6% level during the first two years and two months, that is, between July 2006 and August 2008. The spillover index gradually increases from 5.85% on August 1, 2008 to 6.92% on September 1, 2008. The spillover index shows abrupt hikes in September and October in 2008; of the ten largest daily changes in the index over the entire sample period, five appear in these two months. Amid the global financial crisis, the spillover index increases around the 14–15% level. In September 2010, the spillover index begins to declines as quickly as it surged in the wake of the global financial crisis; the index decreased from 15.15% on September 1, 2010 to 11.37% on October 1, 2010 and to 9.75% by November 1, 2010.

Figure 1: Total Gross-Sum Spillover (All African Stock Markets Combined).

Note: Spillovers are calculated by the total gross-sum spillovers defined in Eq. (5).

The major underlying cause of this African total spillover index movement is surely the turmoil in the United States and, consequently, in European financial markets as shown by Sugimoto et al. (2014). In this chapter, however, we intentionally omit stock markets in these developed countries from the sample to focus on within-Africa interactions; however, we still find that African stock markets are affected severely by global markets, especially during the financial crisis. In terms of risk management for African financial markets, the current vulnerability to shocks external to Africa, for example, the sharp, nearly three-fold increase in the spillover index value during the financial crisis, must be reconsidered. We take up this issue in the next section.

Developments in Regional Integration of African Stock Markets

Table 4 provides the spillover table for the specific date that is representative of the period spillover plots in previous figures. We

Table 4: Spillover Index by Subsample Periods.

(A) Pre-Crisis (August 4, 2004 to September 12, 2008)											
	EGY	MOR	TUN	KEN	UGA	NIG	BRVM	SAF	MAU	BOT	From Others
EGY	94.1	0.9	0	0.3	0.5	0	0.2	3.9	0.1	0	6
MOR	1.5	94.5	0.3	0.5	0.2	0.1	0.2	1.7	0.1	0.9	6
TUN	0.4	0	98	0	0.3	0.2	0.1	0.1	0.8	0.1	2
KEN	0.4	0.8	0.2	94.8	2.5	0.3	0.4	0.3	0.2	0.2	5
UGA	0.3	0	0.3	5.6	93	0.1	0.1	0.2	0.2	0.2	7
NIG	0	0.2	0.2	0.3	0.1	98.2	0.1	0.6	0	0.2	2
BRVM	0	0.1	0.1	0.2	0.1	0.1	99.2	0.1	0.1	0	1
4SAF	1	0.7	0.1	0.1	0.1	0.4	0	97.4	0.1	0	3
MAU	0	0	0.1	0.2	0	0	0.2	0.2	98.6	0.5	1
BOT	0.1	1.1	0.1	0.2	0.6	0.3	0.1	0.1	0	97.4	3
Contribution to others	4	4	1	7	4	2	2	7	1	2	35
Contribution including own	98	98	99	102	97	100	101	105	100	100	3.50%

Table 4: (*Continued*)

(B) Mid-Crisis (September 15, 2008 to December 31, 2010)											
	EGY	MOR	TUN	KEN	UGA	NIG	BRVM	SAF	MAU	BOT	From Others
EGY	77.8	1.4	1.6	1.7	0.1	0.4	0	14	2.3	0.6	22
MOR	1.7	88.6	1.5	0.8	0.2	1.6	0.3	2.2	3.2	0	11
TUN	2.6	2.1	88.9	0.1	0.2	0	0.6	2.1	3.2	0.3	11
KEN	5.9	3.2	0.6	81.8	1.3	0.5	0.2	6.1	0.2	0.2	18
UGA	1.3	0.9	0.3	16	76.8	0.6	2	1.8	0.3	0.1	23
NIG	1.6	2.7	0.1	0.1	0	93.4	0.3	1.1	0.7	0	7
BRVM	0.3	0.5	0.5	0.4	0.5	0.3	96.5	0.2	0.2	0.6	4
SAF	11.3	2	2	0.3	0.6	0.5	0.2	79.4	3.2	0.6	21
MAU	4.6	3.6	2.9	1.5	0.1	0.4	0.1	5.3	81.3	0.1	19
BOT	0.7	0.2	0.7	0.2	0.3	0	0.6	0.1	0	97.2	3
Contribution to others	30	17	10	21	3	4	4	33	13	2	138
Contribution including own	108	105	99	103	80	98	101	112	95	100	13.80%

(C) Post-Crisis (January 3, 2011 to January 19, 2015)

	EGY	MOR	TUN	KEN	UGA	NIG	BRVM	SAF	MAU	BOT	From Others
EGY	95.4	0.1	0	0.5	0	1	0.1	1.6	0.9	0.3	5
MOR	0.3	98.4	0.2	0.1	0.1	0.1	0.4	0.1	0.3	0	2
TUN	0.1	0.2	98.3	0.3	0	0.1	0.3	0.4	0.1	0.3	2
KEN	1.5	0.1	0.3	91.7	1.7	2.8	0	0.7	1.1	0.1	8
UGA	0.1	0.2	0.1	13.3	84.6	0.9	0	0.2	0.5	0	15
NIG	1.7	0.2	0.3	1.4	0.1	91.4	0.2	2.4	2.3	0	9
BRVM	0.4	0.4	0.5	0.4	0.1	1.1	96.4	0.4	0.3	0.1	4
SAF	0.7	0.1	0.4	0	0.1	1.4	0	96.8	0.3	0.2	3
MAU	0.5	0.3	0.6	0.3	0	1.9	0	2.2	93.8	0.4	6
BOT	0.2	0.1	0.2	0	0	0.2	0.1	0.1	0.1	99	1
Contribution to others	6	2	3	16	2	10	1	8	6	1	54
Contribution including own	101	100	101	108	87	101	98	105	100	100	5.40%

divided the sample into three subsample periods: pre-crisis (August 4, 2004 to September 12, 2008), mid-crisis (September 15, to December 31, 2010) and post-crisis (January 3, 2011 to January 19, 2015). Each cell indicates the percent spillover from the country in the column to the country in the corresponding row. The cells along the diagonal represent own-effects, while off-diagonal cells indicate spillover effects from one market to another. The last column sums the spillovers from other African countries; therefore, the sum of the own-effect (along the diagonal) and this sum equal 100%. For example, for Egypt in the pre-crisis period, the own-effect is 94.1% and the sum of spillovers is 6%. The second cell from the bottom in the last column adds all spillovers for the 10 sample countries, and the last cell scales it to 100% by dividing by 10 (10 countries).

Before the crisis, a 3.50% spillover exists among these ten African stock markets. In other words, most stock market movements, that is, 96.5%, are driven by past own-shocks. In terms of financial integration, this level is much smaller than that found in other geographical areas of developing countries. For example, Diebold and Yilmaz (2010) calculated the total gross-sum spillover among four South American countries to be 18.6% during January 1, 1992 to October 10, 2008. In Asia, the estimated total gross-sum spillover is 31.1% in Sugimoto and Matsuki (2013).[6]

The magnitude of spillovers increases during the turbulent period after the emergence of the crisis, but this is not due to strengthening regional integration. After the initial shock of the global financial crisis dies away in the post-crisis period, total spillover among African stock markets increases to 5.40%. Although this is only a 1.9 percentage point increase, it represents a 59% increase from the pre-crisis period level. Slowly progressing, partly due to the interference of the global financial crisis, African stock markets show only weak evidence of strengthening regional integration.

6. Sugimoto and Matsuki (2013) calculate the spillovers among seven Asian countries and four advanced countries during the pre-crisis period of January 4, 2005 to September 12, 2008. Therefore, spillover among Asian countries is calculated relative to all 11 countries.

The benefits of further promotion of regional integration must be balanced with the heightened risks to the region and with respect to the global market. We discuss this issue in the next section.

Individual Response to the Global Shocks and to the African Regional Integration

Compared to the aggregate index plotted in Figure 1, Figure A1 plots the gross spillover indices for individual African stock markets. For the corresponding country, each index represents the sum of both giving and receiving spillovers from other countries in Africa. The spillovers of most countries respond to the global financial crisis in similar patterns but different magnitudes. There are some exceptions; the spillover indices of Botswana and Uganda do not show sharp increases in September–October 2008 or the following months. The fact that these two stock markets are completely insulated from external shocks is noteworthy, as it implies that financial stability risk may be mitigated below some threshold level of regional integration. According to the 2010 Annual Report on Exchange Arrangements and Exchange Restrictions by IMF, Uganda possessed the least capital controls among ten African countries. The liberalization of capital controls in Uganda may reflect their attempt to overcome their isolation from the rest of Africa.

Table 4 also provides the level of spillovers corresponding to each period for individual countries. By comparing the second rows from the bottom between the pre-crisis (Panel A) and mid-crisis (Panel B) periods, the magnitude of the increase in giving spillovers to other countries can be calculated: the greatest jumps from the pre-crisis level are the 19-fold increases for Mauritius, sevenfold for South Africa, 5.5-fold for Tunisia, and fourfold for BRVM. However, calculating from the rightmost column, the greatest jumps in receiving spillovers from other markets are the 13-fold increases for Mauritius, 10-fold for Tunisia, 7.5-fold for Egypt, and 4.7-fold for South Africa. It is clear that the markets that most influence other stock markets are also most affected by other stock markets.

Similar calculations between the pre- and post-crisis periods (Panel C) provide the degree of regional integration at the individual country level. The countries with the greatest increases in both giving and receiving spillovers represent observed progress in regional integration. These countries are Mauritius (sixfold increase for giving and sixfold increase for receiving), Nigeria (fivefold for giving and 4.5-fold for receiving) and Kenya (2.3-fold for giving and 1.6-fold for receiving). Conversely, Morocco experiences declines in both types of regional spillovers.

Perspectives from the Sub-Regional Level

Figure A2 plots the per-giving gross spillover index for the sub-regional aggregates of African stock markets, corresponding to Eq. (12). Reflecting the responses of individual stock markets in Figure A1, the western region is least affected by the global financial crisis. The northern and southern regions follow the typical pattern of heightened spillovers only during the crisis period. The pattern of the eastern region cannot be categorized as crisis-induced because these spillovers gradually increase during the post-crisis period.

Figures 2–5 show the regional-level spillovers calculated according to Eq. (13) for cross-region and (15) for own-region spillovers. These spillovers are adjusted for the number of countries in both spillover-giving and spillover-receiving countries so that each spillover index is comparable at the level of average bilateral effects. Figure 2 shows how the northern region, which consists of Egypt, Morocco, and Tunisia, has affected other regions as well as itself. The northern region has affected the southern region the most, even more than itself. The temporarily heightened spillovers during the crisis-period apply to all regions except the western region; the spillovers to the western region increased rather gradually during the crisis-period and remained at this high level even as the spillovers to other regions decreased.[7]

7. Moreover, the Jasmine revolution in Tunisia in December 2010, the democratic movements in Egypt in January 2011 and the subsequent social disorders did not affect the spillovers to the rest of Africa.

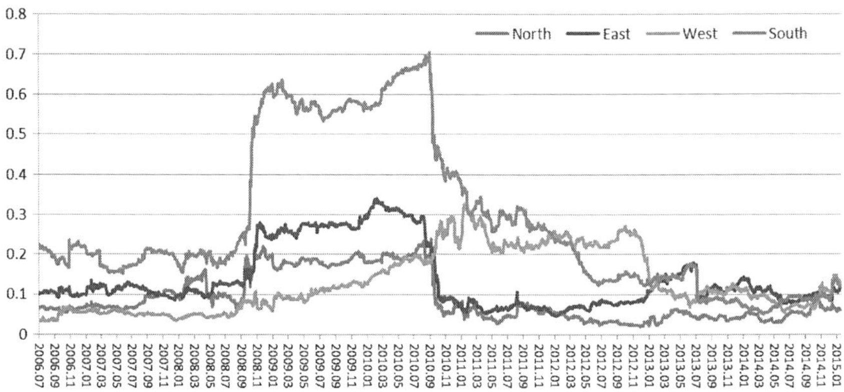

Figure 2: North Spillovers to Four Regions (Give, Per-Giving, and Per-Receiving).
Note: Spillovers are calculated by Eqs. (13) and (15) for cross- and own-region effects, respectively.

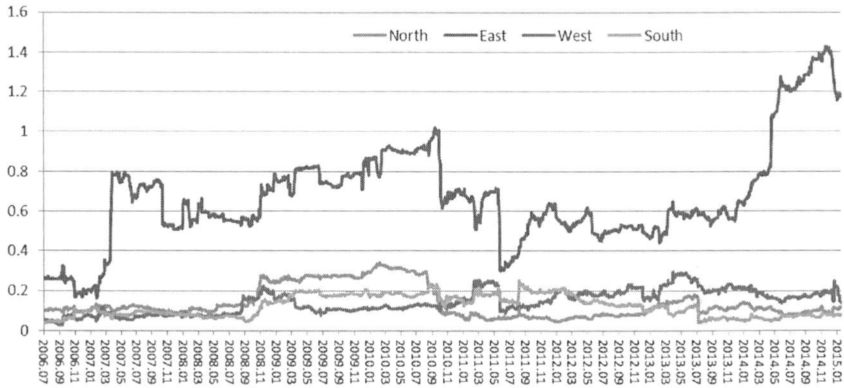

Figure 3: East Spillovers to Four Regions (Give, Per-Giving, and Per-Receiving).
Note: Spillovers are calculated by Eqs. (13) and (15) for cross- and own-region effects, respectively.

Figure 3 indicates the spillovers from the eastern region to other regions and its own-region spillovers. Uniquely, the eastern region is the only region wherein the highest value is the own-region spillover. Note that the scale is exceptionally higher than that of other regions. This high spillover within the eastern region may possibly

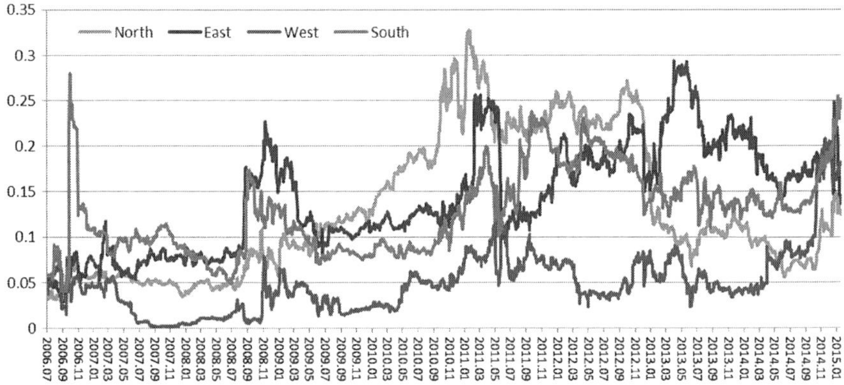

Figure 4: West Spillovers to Four Regions (Give, Per-Giving, and Per-Receiving).

Note: Spillovers are calculated by Eqs. (13) and (15) for cross- and own-region effects, respectively.

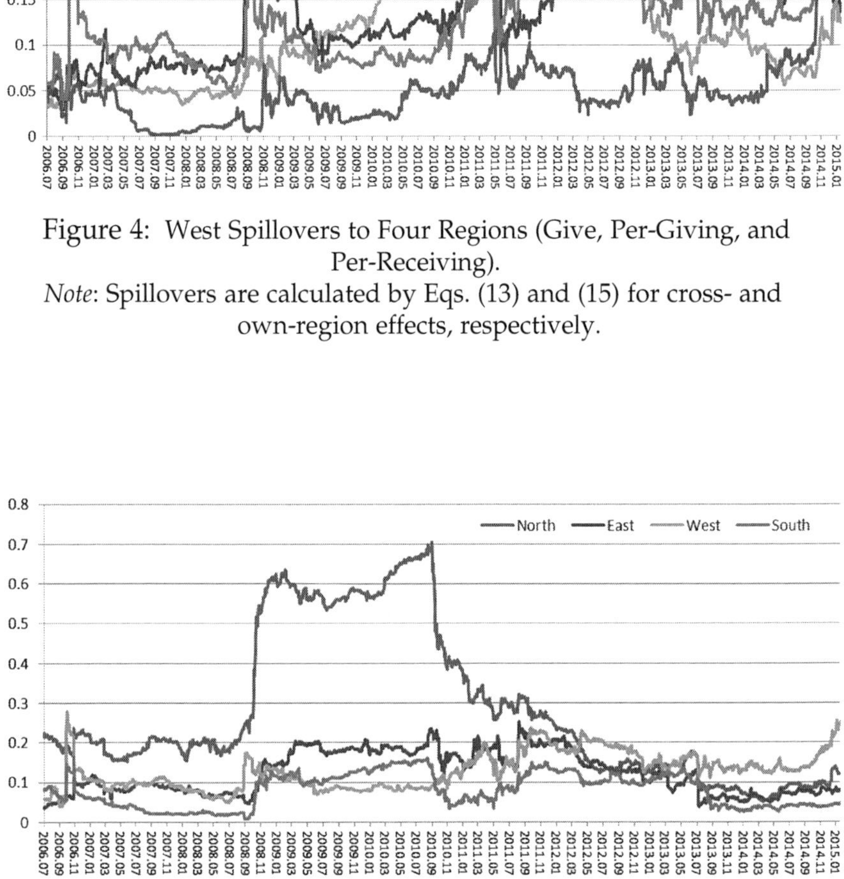

Figure 5: South Spillovers to Four Regions (Give, Per-Giving, and Per-Receiving).

Note: Spillovers are calculated by Eqs. (13) and (15) for cross- and own-region effects, respectively.

be due to the strong ties of EAC members.[8] More specifically, this pattern is solely driven by high spillovers from Kenya to Uganda, as will be shown in Figure 7. The cross-regional spillovers remain relatively stable below the level of 0.3%, even during the crisis period.

Figure 4 shows the cross- and own-region spillovers of the western region. As discussed in the previous subsection, the western region seems the least vulnerable to the crisis. Figure 5 shows the cross- and own-region spillovers of the southern region. The high spillover from the North to South observed in Figure 2 seems bi-directional; the spillover from the South to North is much higher than those from the South to either the East or West.

To summarize the findings above, the following four points are noteworthy: the North and the South link is the strongest; the West has started to be more affected by both the North and South during the recent period than it was during the mid-crisis period; in the East, within-East spillovers are the greatest; and the West is the region with the lowest cross- and own-region effects.

Sub-Regional Integration

We have examined thus far how cross-regional relationships evolved during the period that encompasses the global financial crisis. We now examine the degree of integration within sub-regions. Figures 6–9 show the spillovers among countries within the same region. The spillovers in these figures are calculated as individual spillover adjusted by the number of receiving countries; therefore, each spillover plot represents the (average) bilateral effect and is comparable in scale across figures.

Figure 6 represents the within-region spillovers for each country in the northern region. First, the spillover dynamics of Morocco

8. The introduction of EAC single currency is expected by 2024. Under a currency convertibility agreement between Kenya and Uganda, residents may carry any amount of currency across borders to settle their cross-border transactions. Moreover, in Kenya, pension funds may invest up to 70% of their total assets on the stock exchanges in the EAC countries, compared to 15% in non-EAC countries.

Figure 6: Spillovers within North (Give, Per-Giving, and Per-Receiving).

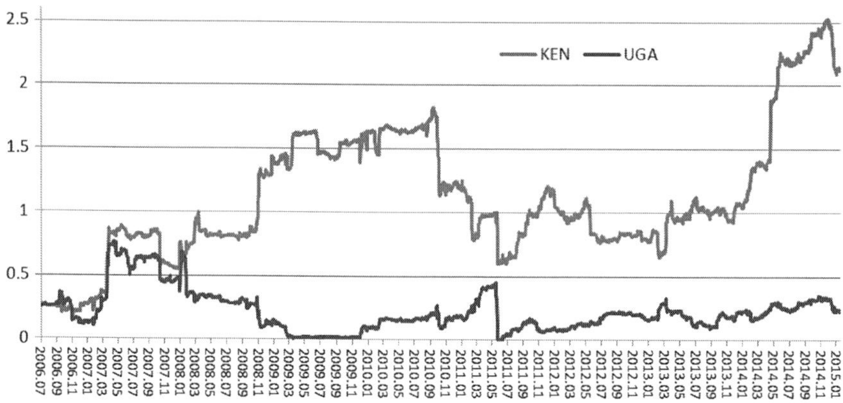

Figure 7: Spillovers within East (Give, Per-Giving, and Per-Receiving).

and Tunisia follow the same pattern throughout the entire sample period; they move in tandem except for small deviations during 2011 and early 2012. The most significant economic tie between these two countries is that they are members of the AMU (Arab Maghreb Union). Second, Egypt seems excluded from the northern region, especially following the crisis. Post-crisis spillover from Egypt to the rest of the northern countries is well below the pre-crisis level in contrast to the influential role of Egypt in other regions.

Figure 7 shows the spillovers between Kenya and Uganda in the eastern region. The striking result is that the spillover from Kenya

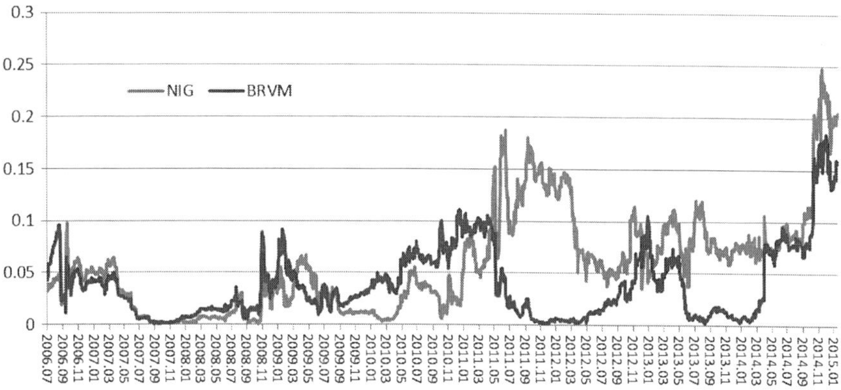

Figure 8: Spillovers within West (Give, Per-Giving, and Per-Receiving).

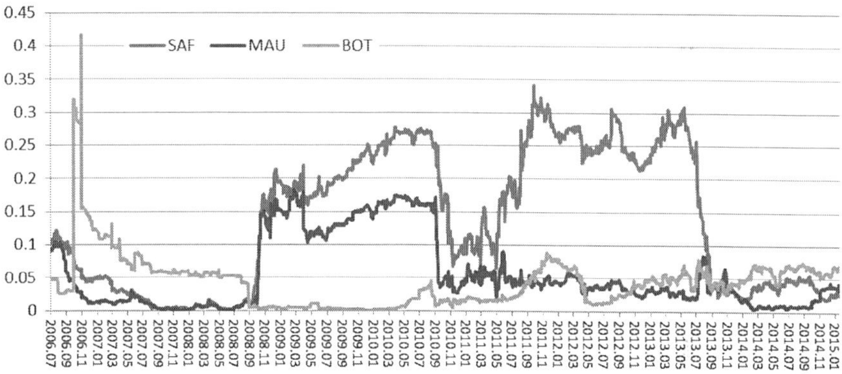

Figure 9: Spillovers within South (Give, Per-Giving, and Per-Receiving).

to Uganda is as six times as high as the highest spillovers observed in other regions and is still increasing in the recent period. Joint membership in the EAC, EASEA, and IGAD (Intergovernmental Authority on Development) and cross-border listing between the two countries explain this increasing integration (see also note 6).

Figure 8 shows the spillovers between Nigeria and Côte d'Ivoire, which represents the western regional stock market. As we have observed in the previous cross-regional figures, the western region seems least affected by the global crisis. The shape of heightened spillovers during the crisis period is blurred in Figure 8. The most distinguishing feature of within-region spillovers in the western region is that both spillovers show an increasing trend during the most recent period. Note that both countries are members of the ECOWAS and signed the MOU on cross-border listings.

The within-region spillovers of the southern countries are shown in Figure 9. The spillovers of Mauritius show the typical pattern observed in this study; a low level during the pre-crisis period, a sudden increase and maintained high level during the mid-crisis, and a sudden decrease and low level in the post-crisis (but slightly higher level than observed during the pre-crisis period). Botswana seems isolated from giving spillovers to other countries in the southern region amid the crisis; instead of increasing, spillovers from Botswana decrease to nearly zero in 2008. The spillovers of South Africa, unlike any other country in Africa, show a two-humped shape. The first hump is like the others associated with the beginning and tapering of the crisis, but the second hump, of the same size and duration, appears between 2011 and 2013.[9]

Considering within-region spillover as a measure of the degree of regional integration, the eastern region shows the strongest links, surpassing the level of the strong cross-regional link between the North and South. The western region shows the most strengthened link during the most recent period. However, regional integration within the North and South remains below cross-regional links, most of which exceed 0.1%.

Regional Hub Interactions

Considering the largest stock market in each region as the regional hub market, namely, Egypt in the North, Kenya in the East,

9. The second hump may be due to the country-specific facts in South Africa during this period. After the World Cup in 2010, South Africa suffered from a recession by decreasing household consumption expenditure because of rand depreciation and steep rise in food prices and by decreasing exports of mineral products because of the seriously repeated mine workers' strikes.

Nigeria in the West, and South Africa in the South, the interrelations among regional hub markets are expected to be higher than those between other pairs of countries. We examine the spillovers among the regional hub markets in Figure A3. The spillovers are calculated as spillovers from an individual country to the other three countries. Crisis effects are observed only for Egypt and South Africa. The degree of spillover from Kenya and Nigeria to other hub markets is unaffected during the crisis period. Regarding the level of spillovers (divided by three to allow comparison with Figures 2–9), we find no evidence that links among hub markets are stronger than links between other pairs.

Risk Management in African Stock Markets

In the previous section, we employed a spillover analysis to observe how financial integration, in terms of stock markets, is progressing in Africa. To reap more benefits from stronger financial integration, African countries can speed the liberalization of current regulations placed on foreign investors, as shown in Table 5. Although it was once universal among economists in the 1990s, the understanding of capital account liberalization of developing economy markets has changed in development economics. Prasad and Rajan (2008) argue that the alleged benefits of economic growth from foreign capital inflows are difficult to identify in empirical studies. In 2012, the IMF also modified its stance on the use of capital controls after the experience of the global financial crisis. The IMF agreed to the use of capital controls when other macroeconomic policy tools are not sufficient to tame temporal macroeconomic instability.

In light of this background, the current process of financial market integration within Africa is worth assessing, and we should discuss whether the opening of financial markets to foreign investors can be beneficial and provides a platform for designing the future stock market architecture in the African region. We begin by reviewing previous studies that investigate the relationships among financial flows, financial development, and economic

Table 5: Capital Controls in African Countries, 2014.

Capital Transactions Controls	BOT	CIV	EGY	KEN	MAU	MOR	NIG	SAF	TUN	UGA
1. Capital market securities	●	●	●	●	●	●	●	●	●	
2. Money market instruments	●	●	●	●	●	●	●	●	●	
3. Collective investment securities	●	●	●	●	●	●		●	●	
4. Derivatives and other instruments		●	●	●		●		●	●	
5. Commercial credits	●	●				●	●	●	●	
6. Financial credits		●				●	●	●	●	
7. Guarantees, sureties, and financial backup facilities		●				●		●	●	
8. Direct investment		●	●	●	●	●		●	●	
9. Liquidation of direct investment										
10. Real estate transactions		●		●	●	●		●	●	●
11. Personal capital transactions		●				●	●	●	●	
12. Commercial banks and other credit institutions	●	●	●	●	●	●	●	●	●	●
13. Institutional investors	●	●	●	●	●	●		●	●	

Note: Information is retrieved from the Annual Report on Exchange Arrangements and Exchange Restrictions 2014, IMF.

growth. Then, we provide recommendations for policy measures for African stock markets that aim to achieve two goals: (1) fostering economic growth via further stock market integration while (2) minimizing the financial stability risk posed by greater foreign investor participation.

Financial Integration, Financial Development, and Economic Growth

Some researchers have argued that the gains associated with financial integration may be negligible or small at best. The numerically calculated welfare gain from financial integration is only a 1% permanent increase in domestic consumption for the typical non-OECD country (Gourinchas & Jeanne, 2006). This rather pessimistic result is obtained because theoretical models assume that countries have the same long-term growth rate and that financial integration only acts as a tool to accelerate convergence. Friedrich, Shnabel, and Zettelmeyer (2013) argue that in addition to financial integration, political integration is important for economic growth; they show that emerging European countries, which have stronger political integration, experience higher economic growth. By observing the recent struggles of financially open developing economies after the crisis, the skeptical view that financial integration leads to little or no growth may gain more support.

One convincing explanation for why some empirical studies do not find a positive relationship between financial market development and economic growth is raised in Rajan and Zingales (1998): financial development may not unequivocally benefit all industries or countries. Rajan and Zingales (1998) argue that the industries that benefit the most from financial development are those that are the most dependent on external finance. Empirical evidence from 41 countries (including five African countries) and 36 industries affirms that industries that rely on external financing grow faster in more developed financial markets. Extending the work of Rajan and Zingales (1998), a threshold argument is introduced by

Prasad, Rajan, and Subramanian (2007), who posit that the positive effect of financial market development is triggered only after a certain threshold. Following a threshold argument, Kose, Prasad, and Taylor (2011) examine 84 countries, including many African countries, to evaluate whether financial openness contributes to growth. They find that there is a threshold level of financial and institutional development that an economy must attain before it can benefit from financial openness.

Taking this empirical result at face value, many of the African countries in our sample have not reached this threshold level, so the benefits of opening their stock markets to foreign investors are negligible. Menyah, Nazlioglu, and Wolde-Rufael (2014) and Andrianaivo and Yartey (2010) have published two studies that exclusively focus on African countries. Menyah et al. (2014) provide direct evidence for 21 African countries. They find that financial development does not affect economic growth in the framework of a panel Granger causality test. Their empirical result is consistent with Kose et al. (2011) because most African countries are currently below the threshold. However, Kose et al. (2011, p. 162, Figure 3) report that South Africa and Egypt have crossed the threshold required to enjoy the benefits of internationally open stock markets. To examine heterogeneous effects of capital account openness on financial development, Andrianaivo and Yartey (2010) examine an expanded sample for 53 African countries and find that the liberalization of capital accounts promotes financial market development only in countries with high incomes and well-developed institutions.

Financial integration, by definition, leads to increased financial/capital flows from foreign economies. Financial flows can take several forms, namely, foreign direct investments (FDI), equity, and debt, and the effect on the domestic economy is not necessarily the same with the three major components of financial flows. FDI is associated with positive spillovers to the host economies from new products, new skills, and efficient management; however, FDI flows are not unconditionally conducive to economic growth. Alfaro, Chanda, Kalemli-Ozcan, and Sayek (2004) find that an FDI variable is not statistically significant in the growth regressions of 51 countries. FDI shows a positive effect only when interacting with financial development variables.

Capital Control, Foreign Banks, and Foreign Investors

How can we reconcile the seemingly contradictory goals of (i) reaping benefits from foreign fund inflows to stock markets, (ii) enjoying economies of scale from regionally integrated stock markets, and (iii) insulating regional markets from heightened volatility, especially financial crises, in foreign markets? One possible answer lies in utilizing some form of capital control in the African region. The IMF's AREAER provides information on regulations in domestic financial markets and capital controls. Table 5 provides the 13 types of capital controls effective in 2014 for 10 African countries. Côte d'Ivoire, Morocco, South Africa, and Tunisia place capital controls on twelve of 13 components, whereas Uganda only has capital controls on two components. Compared to 2010, only three changes in capital controls have occurred: Egypt lifted real estate restrictions and Nigeria lifted one control but imposed a new one. The capital control measures used in the AREAER are known to be persistent partly because they are binary values, as noted by Eichengreen and Rose (2014). The AREAER indicates that many capital controls are already in place for many African countries.

Regarding stock markets, all countries except Uganda have controls on capital market securities. A shortcoming of the AREAER is that it only indicates whether controls exist, that is, it reports a binary variable. There must be substantial differences in the degree of controls among these African countries, as indicated by the widely varying shares of foreign investors listed in Table 3. Foreign investments in African portfolio investment assets, which include both bonds and stocks, are provided in Table 6. The breakdown of foreign investments in African portfolio assets in 2003 indicates that African investors (Egypt, Mauritius, and South Africa) are the top foreign investors in

Table 6: Geographic Breakdown of Total Portfolio Investment Assets.

	Africa	France	Lux	UK	US	Total	Growth	African Share	
								2003 (%)	2013 (%)
Botswana	101	4	118	12	74	320	3.7	77	32
Côte d'Ivoire	79	301	277	1	29	862	8.5	0	9
Egypt	152	426	525	539	2099	5095	4.9	3	3
Kenya	526	18	552	29	0	1789	36.8	49	29
Mauritius	980	11	2784	388	6993	14,955	44.6	7	7
Morocco	119	2200	77	34	403	3151	4.3	0	4
Nigeria	1128	28	1936	468	0	5084	390.9	81	22
South Africa	1706	822	9303	10,745	67,341	112,328	4.1	1	2
Tunisia	0	454	7	0	49	779	6.3	0	0
Uganda	21	0	10	15	61	111	8867.8	0	19

Note: The original source from EQUITY SECURITIES (Derived from Creditor Data), 2013 end of period, CPIS (Coordinated Portfolio Investment Survey) by International Monetary Fund. Africa includes Egypt, Mauritius, and South Africa, and Lux is Luxembourg. Growth = Total in 2013/total in 2003.

Botswana, Kenya, and Nigeria. However, over the last ten years, the dominance of African investors in these markets has faded, and European countries are now the top foreign investors in these countries. In 2013, the United States dominated other foreign investors in Egypt, Mauritius, and South Africa.

In addition to bonds and stocks in capital markets, the banking sector plays an important role in financial markets. Claessens and van Horen (2014) construct a worldwide bank database and provide the shares of foreign banks in each country. Table A1 extracts the foreign bank shares in ten African markets from this database. The presence of foreign banks is especially high in Côte d'Ivoire and Uganda. In terms of the number of banks, 71% in Côte d'Ivoire and 82% in Uganda are foreign.

However, Nigeria, in the western region, abolished the Exchange Control Act in 1995 and is ever-promoting the participation of foreign investors in domestic financial markets. In the eastern region, countries such as Kenya and Uganda are planning to privatize their nationally owned companies and need to redesign their stock markets for the additional liquidity, which is associated with higher foreign investor participation rates. These stock markets in the eastern and western sub-regions are still short on investment funds.

Policy Recommendations for African Stock Markets

One possible solution is to maintain asymmetric standards in the African regions. First, we recommend lifting all of the regulations that currently discourage intra-regional cross-border investments. This requires establishing standards that treat all African investors equally in the region. This should promote greater financial integration in Africa so that stock markets in the eastern and western regions can benefit from the participation of investors who are already active in South Africa, Egypt, and Morocco. The legal definition of an African investor should include African investment banks, which borrow from foreign financial markets. Second, except for South Africa, Egypt, and Morocco, direct participation by foreign investors should be regulated as a safeguard. This measure should mitigate the financial stability risks associated with sudden stops in the stock markets of the eastern and western regions.[10] Third, the investment banks in Africa must be regulated on the basis of the ratio of foreign to total borrowing. Given the expected surge in financial inflows due to the deregulation of investment within Africa, this is another safeguard for insulating African financial markets from foreign shocks. All of these measures promote stronger regional integration in the region.

For these policy recommendations, we would like to quote Kose, Prasad, Rogoff, and Wei (2009, p. 43): "Our view is that, although the risks can never be totally avoided, there are ways to improve the benefit-risk calculus. There is, however, unlikely to be a uniform approach to opening the capital account that will work well for all countries." In agreement with our view, based on findings that capital account openness is less conducive to financial development than trade openness, David, Mlachila, and Moheeput (2014, p. 28) also recommend delaying the promotion of international integration until macroeconomic stability and domestic financial liberalization are achieved.

In addition, the size of cross-border equity trading depends on the efficiency of the information systems adopted in local stock markets. Portes and Rey (2005) find that information proxy variables positively affect cross-border equity portfolio flows, but this evidence is obtained for a sample of developed countries. Moreover, Levine and Zervos (1998a) find that high-quality information on listed firms enhances the positive effect of capital control liberalization on stock market development. Regardless of whether foreign capital flows are solicited, it is imperative that the most efficient and state-of-the-art information technology and

10. Capital flow dynamics are given several names, including sudden stops and capital flight. Forbes and Warnock (2012), Broner, Didier, Erce, and Schmukler (2013), and Calderon and Kubota (2013) investigate the causes of these dynamics, especially those associated with financial crisis. Adler, Djibenou, and Sosa (2014) note the risk management role of domestic investors. They provide empirical evidence that domestic investor repatriation helps ease the effects of the sudden stops and capital flight of foreign investors.

network systems be adopted to promote more regionally integrated African stock markets.

Conclusion

By analyzing spillovers across African stock markets, this chapter examines regional integration in African equity markets and discusses risk management of uncalled financial stability risks. We estimated spillover indices over the period between August 2004 and January 2015. Financial integration within Africa has risen gradually and timidly. A larger well-integrated financial market in Africa would provide opportunities for investors who manage their portfolios in the region as well as entrepreneurs who intend to publically list their companies. At the same time, the recent global financial crisis proves that financial instability brought in from outside Africa is aggravated by increased regional integration.

We discuss whether capital controls provide risk management for financial -stability risk in regional stock markets. Given the strong link between South African and northern country stock markets and global markets, an increase in the degree of regional integration indirectly makes the stock markets in the rest of the African region more susceptible to the global shocks. Risk management of this financial stability risk must be introduced. To increase regional integration within Africa while minimizing spillovers from the global market, among other alternative tools, we propose setting mild capital control on countries with stronger links to global markets, namely, Egypt, Morocco, and South Africa.

Acknowledgments

The authors Matsuki and Sugimoto acknowledge financial support from JSPS Kakenhi Grant Number 24530237 and 25380415, respectively. The author Yoshida acknowledges financial support from JSPS Kakenhi Grant Number 26380295 and the Risk Research Center at Shiga University.

References

Adler, G., Djibenou, M. L., & Sosa, S.. (2014). *Global financial shocks and foreign asset repatriation: Do local investors play a stabilizing role?* IMF Working Paper 14/60, 1-30. International Monetary Fund.

African Development Bank. (2014). *African development report 2014: Regional integration for inclusive growth*, 1–115, Abidjan, Côte d'Ivoire.

African Securities Exchanges Association. (2014). *African securities exchanges association yearbook 2014* (pp. 1–249). Nairobi, Kenya.

Alfaro, L., Chanda, A., Kalemli-Ozcan, S., & Sayek, S. (2004). FDI and economic growth: The role of local financial markets. *Journal of International Economics*, *64*, 89–112.

Andrianaivo, M., & Yartey, C. A. (2010). Understanding the growth of African financial markets. *African Development Review*, *22*(3), 394–418.

Bekaert, G., & Harvey, C. R. (1995). Time-varying world market integration. *Journal of Finance*, *50*(2), 403–444.

Bekaert, G., & Harvey, C. R. (2000). Foreign speculators and emerging equity markets. *Journal of Finance*, *55*(2), 565–613.

Bekaert, G., Harvey, C. R., & Lundblad, C. (2005). Does financial liberalization spur growth? *Journal of Financial Economics*, *77*(1), 3–55.

Broner, F., Didier, T., Erce, A., & Schmukler, S. L. (2013). Gross capital flows: Dynamics and crises. *Journal of Monetary Economics*, *60*, 113–133.

Calderón, C., & Kubota, M. (2013). Sudden stops: Are global and local investors alike? *Journal of International Economics*, *89*, 122–142.

Chinn, M. D., & Ito, H. (2006). What matters for financial development? Capital controls, institutions, and interactions. *Journal of Development Economics*, *81*(1), 163–192.

Claessens, S., & Van Horen, N. (2012). *Foreign banks: Trends, impact and financial stability*. IMF Working Paper 12/10, 1-39. International Monetary Fund.

Claessens, S., & Van Horen, N. (2014). Foreign banks: Trends and impact. *Journal of Money, Credit and Banking*, *46*(S1), 295–326.

David, A. C., Mlachila, M., & Moheeput, A. (2014). *Does openness matter for financial development in Africa?* IMF Working Paper 14/94, 1-37. International Monetary Fund.

Diebold, F. X., & Yilmaz, K. (2009). Measuring financial asset return and volatility spillovers, with application to global equity markets. *Economic Journal*, *119*(534), 158–171.

Diebold, F. X., & Yilmaz, K. (2010). Equity market spillovers in the Americas. In R. A. Alfaro (Ed.), *Financial stability, monetary policy, and central banking* (Vol. 15, pp. 199–214). Santiago: Central Bank of Chile.

Diebold, F. X., & Yilmaz, K. (2012). Better to give than to receive: Predictive directional measurement of volatility spillovers. *International Journal of Forecasting*, *28*, 57–66.
Eichengreen, B., & Rose, A. (2014). Capital controls in the 21st century. *Journal of International Money and Finance*, *48*, 1–16.
Enisan, A. A., & Olufisayo, A. O. (2009). Stock market development and economic growth: Evidence from seven Sub-Saharan African countries. *Journal of Economics and Business*, *61*(2), 162–171.
Forbes, K. J., & Warnock, F. E. (2012). Capital flow waves: Surges, stop, flight, and retrenchment. *Journal of International Economics*, *88*, 235–251.
Friedrich, C., Shnabel, I., & Zettelmeyer, J. (2013). Financial integration and growth – Why is emerging Europe different? *Journal of International Economics*, *89*, 522–538.
Gourinchas, P.-O., & Jeanne, O. (2006). The elusive gains from international financial integration. *Review of Economic Studies*, *73*, 715–741.
International Monetary Fund. (2014). *Annual report on Exchange arrangements and Exchange restrictions 2014*, 1–98, Washington, DC.
Irving, J. (2005). *Regional integration of stock exchanges in Eastern and Southern Africa: Progress and prospects*. IMF Working Paper 05/122, 1-41.
Koop, G., Pesaran, M. H., & Porter, S. M. (1996). Impulse response analysis in nonlinear multivariate models. *Journal of Econometrics*, *74*(1), 119–147.
Kose, M. A., Prasad, E., Rogoff, K., & Wei, S.-J. (2009). Financial globalization: A reappraisal. *IMF Staff Papers*, *56*(1), 8–62.
Kose, M. A., Prasad, E. S., & Taylor, A. D. (2011). Thresholds in the process of international financial integration. *Journal of International Money and Finance*, *30*, 147–179.
Lane, P. R., & Milesi-Ferretti, G. M. (2007). The external wealth of nations, Mark II: Revised and extended estimates of foreign assets and liabilities, 1970–2004. *Journal of International Economics*, *73*(2), 223–250.
Levine, R. (1997). Financial development and economic growth: Views and agenda. *Journal of Economic Literature*, *35*(2), 688–726.
Levine, R., & Zervos, S. (1998a). Capital control liberalization and stock market development. *World Development*, *26*(7), 1169–1183.
Levine, R., & Zervos, S. (1998b). Stock markets, banks, and economic growth. *American Economic Review*, *88*(3), 537–558.
Longin, F., & Solnik, B. (1995). Is the correlation in international equity returns constant: 1960–1990? *Journal of International Money and Finance*, *14*(1), 3–26.

Menyah, K., Nazlioglu, S., & Wolde-Rufael, Y. (2014). Financial development, trade openness and economic growth in African countries: New insights from a panel causality approach. *Economic Modeling, 37,* 386–394.

Mougani, G. (2014). *Challenges toward regional financial integration and monetary coordination in the West African monetary zone and the East African community.* Regional Integration Policy Paper No. 3, 1-62. African Development Bank Group.

Murinde, V. (2012). Financial development and economic growth: Global and African evidence. *Journal of African Economies, 21*(S1), i10–i56.

Ngare, E., Nyamongo, E. M., & Misati, R. N. (2014). Stock market development and economic growth in Africa. *Journal of Economics and Business, 74,* 24–39.

Onyuma, S. O., Mugo, R. K., & Karuiya, J. K. (2012). Does cross-border listing (still) improve firm financial performance in Eastern Africa? *Journal of Business, Economics & Finance, 1*(1), 92–109.

Ostry, J. D., Ghosh, A. R., Chamon, M., & Qureshi, M. S. (2012). Tools for managing financial-stability risks from capital inflows. *Journal of International Economics, 88,* 407–421.

Pesaran, M. H., & Shin, Y. (1998). Generalised impulse response analysis in linear multivariate models. *Economics Letters, 58,* 17–29.

Portes, R., & Rey, H. (2005). The determinants of cross-border equity flows. *Journal of International Economics, 65,* 269–296.

Prasad, E., Rajan, R. G., & Subramanian, A. (2007). Foreign capital and economic growth. *Brookings Papers on Economic Activity, 2007*(1), 153–209.

Prasad, E. S., & Rajan, R. G. (2008). A pragmatic approach to capital account liberalization. *Journal of Economic Perspectives, 22*(3), 149–172.

Quinn, D., Schindler, M., & Toyoda, A. M. (2011). Assessing measures of financial openness and integration. *IMF Economic Review, 59*(3), 488–522.

Rajan, R. G., & Zingales, L. (1998). Financial dependence and growth. *American Economic Review, 88*(3), 559–586.

Sugimoto, K., & Matsuki, T. (2013). *The spillover analysis on the Asian financial markets.* Mimeo, presented at the 13th International Convention of the East Asian Economic Association, Singapore, 2012.

Sugimoto, K., Matsuki, T., & Yoshida, Y. (2014). The global financial crisis: An analysis of the spillover effects on African stock markets. *Emerging Markets Review, 21,* 201–233.

Wang, J. Y., Masha, I., Shirono, K., & Harris, L. (2007). *The common monetary area in Southern Africa: Shocks, adjustment, and policy challenges.* IMF Working Paper, 07/158, 1-63. International Monetary Fund.

Appendix

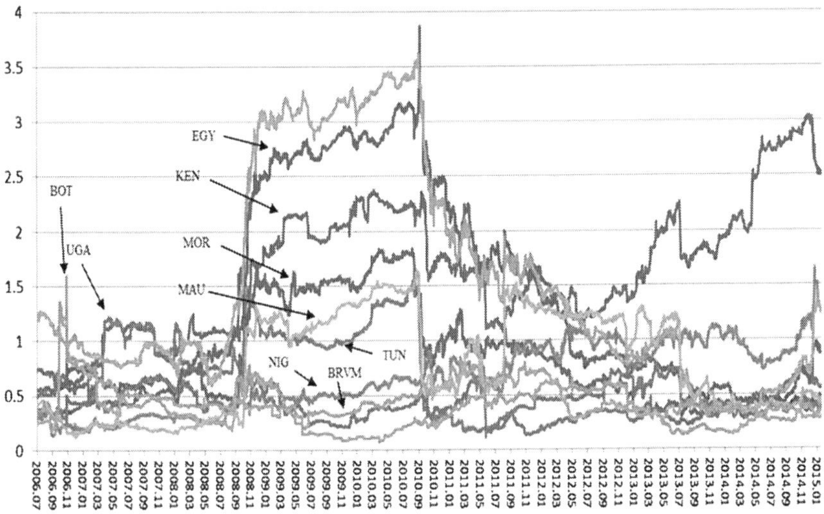

Figure A1: Gross-Sum Spillover (Individual African Stock Markets). *Note*: Spillovers are calculated by the individual gross-sum spillovers defined in Eq. (6).

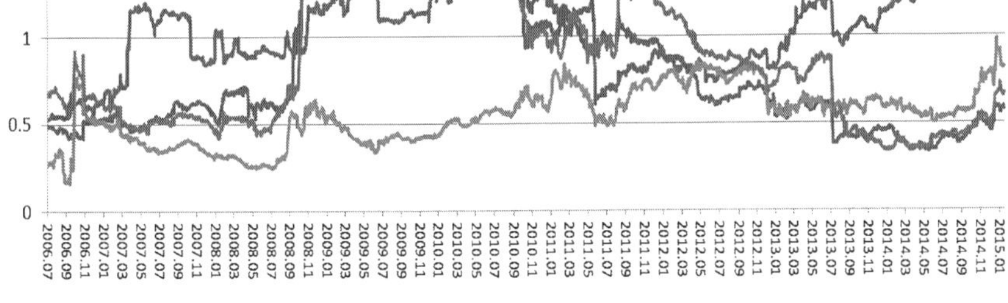

Figure A2: Regional Gross-Sum Spillover (Per-Giving).
Note: The spillovers are calculated as in Eq. (12).

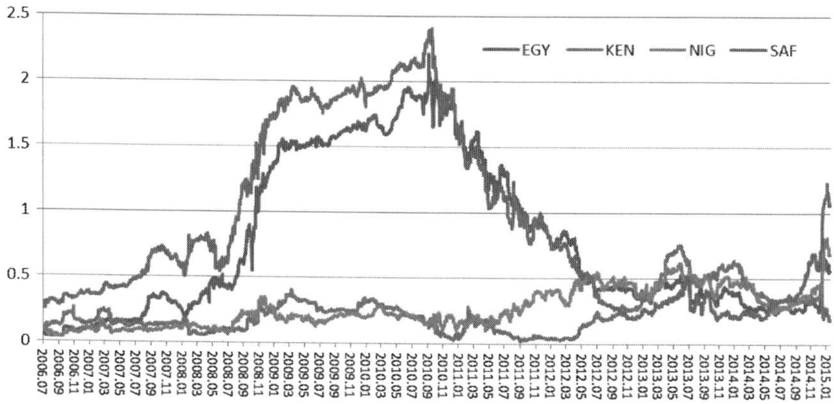

Figure A3: Spillovers of Hub Countries (Give).
Note: Measured as the spillovers an individual country gives to the other three countries.

Table A1: Foreign Bank Shares.

	Percentage of Foreign Banks of Total Banks in 2009	Percentage of Foreign Bank Assets of Total Bank Assets in 2009
Botswana (S)	50.00	66.00
Côte d'Ivoire (W)	71.00	89 (2005)
Egypt (N)	52.00	23.00
Kenya (E)	35.00	44.00
Mauritius (S)	62.00	52.00
Morocco (N)	50.00	34.00
Nigeria (W)	11.00	3.00
South Africa (S)	22.00	22.00
Tunisia (N)	50.00	28 (2008)
Uganda (E)	82.00	89.00

Note: A foreign bank is a bank with 50% or more of shares owned by foreigners. The first column is calculated based on the number of banks. Data are extracted from Claessens and van Horen (2012).

15

Foreign Currency Borrowing in Hungary: The Pricing Behavior of Banks

Zoltán Schepp and Mónika Mátrai-Pitz

Abstract

Over the last decade, foreign currency indebtedness in Hungary has become a systemic financial problem, and its crippling impact on the real economy has been aggravated by its significant constraints on economic policy. In international comparative terms, however, there are certain specific features relating to Hungary which make this issue particularly problematic, and during the financial crisis both exchange rates and interest rates were important factors in increasing the burden on individual households. We present here a case study whereby our research focuses on the causes and determining factors of the pricing of Swiss franc-denominated mortgage loans. Our empirical exercise examines four potential price shocks which might have affected the pricing decisions of credit institutions: foreign currency interest rates, the country risk premiums (measured by Credit Default Swap (CDS) spread), the deteriorating quality of the loan portfolio and the taxes levied on banks. The questions which arise concern the relationship of these costs to the changes in interest rates and the extent to which these cost shocks were passed on by banks to their clients. Empirical evidence based on Vector Error Correction Model (VECM) shows a significant long-run relationship between cost factors and CHF denominated mortgage loans interest rates — with a reasonable sign and magnitude of parameters, but also with moderate forecasting power. Finding a tractable solution to the foreign currency debt trap is only possible if a fair distribution of burdens is achieved, and this should be supported by empirical facts. At the end of the day, all three affected parties (debtors, banks, and the Hungarian State) had made their contribution, but how fair and reasonable the distribution was remains an open issue for further research.

Keywords: Debt pricing/re-pricing; foreign currency indebtedness; systemic risk; unilateral contract modification; vector error correction model; exchange rate depreciation

JEL classifications: D14; G21

Introduction

In Hungary, the demand for external funds was continuously high from the mid-1990s until the economic crisis erupted in 2008. This was due to the attempts made to assist the economy in the "catching-up" process — which involved a massive inflow of foreign capital. As a result of this inflow, the level of foreign currency finance soared in both the private and public sectors, and until 2014 more than 50% of the overall total of loans in business and household portfolios alike is foreign currency-based. In addition, the proportion of foreign debt in the state budget exceeds 40%. The consequences of these high levels emerged in the immediate aftermath of the financial crisis. The increasing value of the Swiss franc and the higher installments resulting from the rising interest rates directly led to higher costs for households (National Bank of Hungary, 2010). Even though they were in a better position than forint debtors had been pre-crisis, they were unaware of the level of risk which they were assuming, and the consequences of this are now jeopardizing financial stability in Hungary. The reasons behind the proliferation of foreign currency lending and possible solutions to the problem are described by Bánfi (2012), and, besides shedding light on the path towards establishing the foreign currency holdings, Erdős (2010) explores the role of exchange rates. In addition to considering causes and effects, the study by Balás and Nagy (2010) examines the possibility of converting foreign currency loans to forints, an issue which has greater international relevance due to the involvement of foreign parent banks. Two newly appeared Hungarian language papers developed a rather analytical framework to understand the consequences of one-sided interest rate changes on FX denominated households loans. Király and Simonovits (2015) found that this might be the decisive factor, taking into account the 50–60% exchange rate depreciation alone HUF loans were associated with even higher *ex post* cost for the borrowers. Radnai (2015) concludes that Hungarian banks where naïve by raising interest rates on CHF mortgage credits, because this in itself might have contributed to the on growing ratio of non-performing loans.

In the related international literature Yesin (2013) focuses on the cross-country characteristics of systemic risk caused by foreign currency borrowing. The Austrian National Bank examines the motives behind borrowing foreign currency denominated loans in nine Central East European countries (Fidrmuc et al., 2011), while the reasons for the late repayment of loans are identified by Beckmann, Fidrmuc, and Stix (2012). The decisive factors of foreign currency lending are also examined by Rosenberg and Tirpák (2009), while Brown and De Haas (2012) study the relationship between foreign assets and foreign currency denominated lending applied to the CEE region. Brown et al. (2011) look at the borrowing of foreign currency by small firms, while Brown et al. (2014) concentrate on the role of information asymmetry in foreign currency lending.

The motivation for this chapter and, consequently, the focus of our empirical analysis differ substantially from those on which earlier studies were based. Over the last couple of years, the relationship between the Hungarian government and the national banking system has been dominated by continuous, intense confrontation, the central issue being that of sharing the financial burden produced by foreign currency loans. There is a consensus that several factors lie behind the problems which emerged. Serious responsibility must be borne by the banking system itself which implemented an aggressive credit policy prior to the outbreak of the crisis in the autumn of 2008. At the same time, borrowers accepted huge risk obligations, and the authorities acted weakly in respect of macro- and micro-prudential issues. There is, however, complete disagreement among the stakeholders as to the balance of responsibility, in addition to which all concerned display a total lack of any intention to co-operate in handling the problem in a socially serious way. Following the outbreak of the crisis, the banking system first attempted to take advantage of its twofold dominant position in relation to their debtors, and, apart from the unhealthy nature of the rapid cut in the loan to deposit ratio, one of the means of dealing with the situation was to pass on the increased costs of refinancing. Starting from the autumn of 2011, the Orbán-administration, backed by a two-thirds parliamentary majority, used their power against the banks. The opportunity of reduced final repayments caused severe losses to banks, as did both the long-term moratorium on evictions and the extended unfavorable exchange rate.[1] Continuing levies on the banks also featured in the government's

1. In the so-called "exchange rate dam," actual interest payment and redemption is calculated with an exchange rate of 180 HUF/CHF which is far lower as the actual market rate (220–250 HUF/CHF). The difference is financed by a new credit with special conditions.

action plan.[2] Nevertheless, it appears that major battles are still to be fought. The aim is that, by the end of autumn 2014, and by means of legal and legislative power, banks have been forced to reimburse their FX-loan clients with a significant proportion of the installments paid, but now deemed illegal.[3] According to the calculations of the Hungarian National Bank, the total losses of the banks could amount to 900 billion HUF (some €3 billion) and this could — very rapidly and for the umpteenth time — force several major, foreign-owned banks to increase their capital base.

Anyhow, the key question is: what use have banks made of their market power and pricing (more precisely: *re-pricing*) freedom to compensate for their unexpected increased costs?

In our previous analysis (in which we applied the SVAR-method) we found that, when pricing domestic CHF residential mortgages, expenses over and above the basic costs appeared in the pricing policy of banks (Pitz & Schepp, 2013). The period examined in that particular study covered the seven years from January 2005 to March 2012, and consequently comprised data collected before and after the crisis. Hence, apart from the structural changes clearly visible from October 2008, changes in bank policy and in actual behavior may justify caution on our part and make it prudent to apply other methods of analysis, concentrating on the aftermath of the crisis. Further, the time which has elapsed gives us the opportunity to analyze the period over a longer and more satisfactory period. This is clearly relevant to the banks' re-pricing freedom in that, in the period when the reference interest of the Swiss franc dropped and continued to decline, the interest on Swiss franc-denominated FX-loans

2. From a bird's eye perspective, the financial transaction tax, the nationalization of Private Pension Funds, limited micro-prudential supervision, and the increased scope of fines on banks can all be regarded as factors in this confrontation. They are not, however, connected to the FX-loan issue in the Government's narrative.

3. In accordance with the decision of the Curia, the highest judicial authority in Hungary, applying a fixed spread (the difference between buying and selling rates) has been declared illegal, and, as Act XXXVIII of 2014 states, banks can only justify their arbitrary raising of interest rates by legal proceedings, and, according to a recent decision by the Hungarian National Bank, retroactive installments must be credited as early repayments, and the resulting refunds are to be made to clients using compound interest rates.

rose — and did not decline even when CDS rates fell. Nevertheless, cost-resistance factors might have been contributed to the fact that, during the legal proceedings, it was problematic for banks to justify professionally the economic legitimacy of the unilateral re-pricing decisions which they made on interest rates of residential mortgages. However, some economic arguments for the banks can be found in the vector error correction model (VECM) presented in our empirical session. The long-term relationship between cost factors and mortgage pricing is significant with reasonable signs, but the explanatory power of the model is still moderate.

The chapter is structured as follows: The next section focuses on the reasons why the pre-crisis accumulation of foreign currency debt in Hungary is such a huge problem in comparison to other CEE countries and then discusses within the country sectoral differences in terms of foreign currency debt (with special attention to households). The section "The Causes of Rising Interest Rates of Swiss Franc Mortgage Loans" continues with the systemic characteristics and consequences of foreign currency indebtedness in Hungary: The deteriorating exchange rate of the Hungarian Forint (HUF) merits special attention, but the level of interest rates on foreign currency denominated loans is of equal importance. In Hungary, interest rates for consumer credit showed a rising trend, despite the reductions in foreign reference rates — which should, after all, govern pricing. The factors which — both in theory and in fact — determine interest rates are also detailed. The section "Empirical Results" presents our empirical research in a VECM framework, where our aim is to identify the factors behind the changing interest rates of Swiss franc-denominated loans of households. We close with a summary of our results and some related policy conclusions.

Specific Features of the Problem of Hungarian Foreign Currency Debt

Important Differences to Other CEE Countries

Despite the fact that foreign currency financing is not only common in Hungary, in our case it is the handling of consequences of accumulated debt that faces greater difficulties.[4] Even if some countries have an even higher level than Hungary's, then, due to their exchange rate system, foreign currency debtors are not directly exposed to the risks. Latvia and Lithuania are good examples since, thanks to their €-linked system, the monetary authority is able to limit the movement of exchange rates. This means that foreign currency debtors enjoy a certain guarantee concerning the risks associated with the exchange rate. Central Banks curb any excessive revaluation or devaluation of the country's own foreign currency reserves and so consumers with accumulated foreign currency debt are not so affected by the consequences of weakening exchange rates, that is, increased installments and debt revaluation. The disadvantage of that system is that it encourages economic stakeholders to take out cheaper foreign currency denominated loans, the risks being borne by the Central Bank. Preserving such a system may involve huge costs in the event of external shocks similar to the crisis of 2008, but, since this problem affects the whole system, it is dealt with at state level (Figure 1).

On the contrary, in Hungary the floating exchange rate encourages economic stakeholders to take into account the risks associated with the volatility of the exchange rate when borrowing. Whether or not they are really capable of successfully evaluating the risks is a very different question, though. In Hungary, the Central Bank had, between 2001 and 2008, applied a *de jure* EUR pegged exchange rate (±15%),[5] but this was replaced by a flexible exchange rate regime after the spring of 2008. The rising demand for foreign currency loans from the mid-2000s was probably partly due to the low volatility of the HUF and its strengthening during

4. For a detailed description of foreign currency debts of Central Eastern European countries, see Hudecz (2012), and for a survey investigation of the interrelatedness of income shocks versus exchange rate driven loan arrears see Beckmann et al. (2012).

5. It is hard to say which regime existed *de facto*, since on each occasion when the exchange rate seemed likely to leave the strong side of the 15% band and approached central parity (HUF 282,36:€1) the Hungarian National Bank increased the base interest rate to strengthen it again and prevent inflationary side-effects.

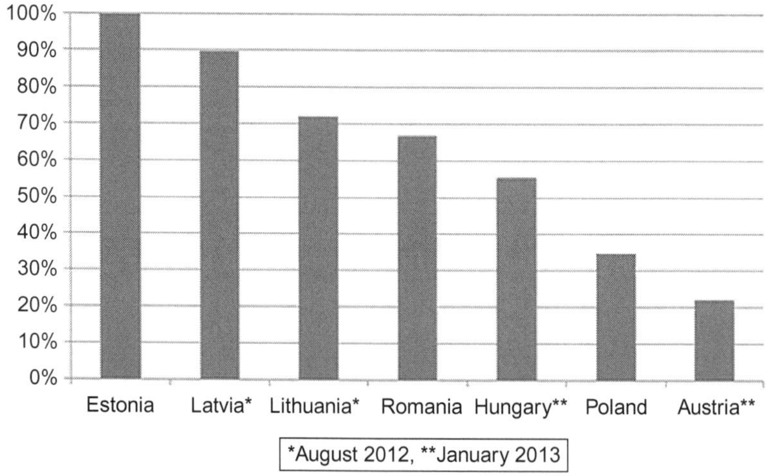

Figure 1: Foreign Currency Loans as a Percentage of Total Household Loans (February 2013). *Source*: National Central Banks.

this period. The current situation shows a reduced credit demand of households, which is clearly due to recent, highly negative experiences. As a consequence of ill-judged risks, the number of debtors who failed to repay their loans on due date has significantly increased, and this is also evident in the increased losses of credit institutions. The poor quality of their loan portfolio reduces banks' funds and their risk-taking potential. This results in a low supply of loan funds, and this lack of funds for lending consequently deepens the recession. The banks responded by offering the opportunity to restructure problematic loans, and so rescheduling repayments resulted in lower installments. This attempt, however, was not crowned with much success, since, despite the more favorable conditions, some of the renegotiated loans became non-performing once more. The government, therefore, intervened with its various debtor-rescue measures which created a way for debtors to repay their foreign currency loans at more favorable exchange rates or to improve their liquidity by rescheduling their debt. The number of non-performing loans is still high, and none of the measures has produced a significant improvement in this respect. In contrast to the benefits to individuals (the cost benefits of foreign currency loans to the debtors and the acquisition of market share by the banks), the risks became evident at society level while central government's handling failed to bring about the desired results.

The risks associated with foreign currency debts are influenced by the foreign currency revenues of economic stakeholders as well as by the nature of the exchange rate regime. Let us take the example of Romania where the amount of foreign currency transferred back to the home country by "guest workers" is significantly higher. The euro income of households provides natural hedge against variable exchange rates, while the denomination of the debt simply aggravates the situation in Hungary. While borrowing in Euros led the way in other countries, the Swiss franc has consistently been the principal foreign currency here, and, although Swiss franc loans were also widespread in Poland and Austria, the proportion was only 25–50% of the domestic currency rate.

The situation in Hungary is clearly worse than in other EU countries with a similar level of foreign currency loans. First, because of the fact that risks are assumed by the individual makes handling the problem more difficult; second, the level of borrowers with natural risk-cover is lower, and third, the level of loans in Swiss francs is high. In addition, the pecuniary position of Hungary towards foreign countries (gross external debt exceeding 90% of GDP with the net figure reaching 40% of GDP)[6] means greater vulnerability and a restricted scope of action.

The Sectoral Character of Foreign Currency Debt in Hungary

In terms of foreign currency debt in Hungary, it is not only households but also the corporate sector and local governments which have been seriously affected. Although the macro-environmental factors which motivate micro-level decisions and distort risk perception are strikingly similar to those applying to households, significant differences are also visible in relation to the micro-aspects

6. Data from end-June 2013.

of detecting or assessing risk. Motivation also involves additional factors, and the approach to the problem by the social and political media (and so the methods of treatment) vary substantially from those applying to residential mortgages — the mass products. Both the similarities and differences were reviewed by Schepp and Pitz (2012), and Mellár's (2014) is also an important reference to on the detrimental effects of the unwholesome combination of fiscal and monetary policy. Let's start with the *common macro-environmental factors*:

- the motivational factors behind foreign currency debt
  - the cost savings expected from foreign currency risk premiums offered on forint-denominated assets
  - the unfavorable features of forint-denominated floating rate loans
    - the excessive interest rates on forint-denominated loans in CEE (Central and East European) comparison terms
    - low and volatile term premium generated by substantial and arbitrary base rate increases by the Hungarian Central Bank (Schepp, 2008)
- distorting factors of risk perception
  - interest rate reactions to fluctuations in monetary policy between 2003 and 2008 (stable HUF/EUR and HUF/CHF exchange rates)[7]
  - from 2002 to 2008, continuous promises of different governments to join the eurozone within the following 5 years, and thus eliminate the greater part of the exchange rate risk
  - distorted competition in the banking sector; intense pressure on the supply side and the systematic ignoring or underestimation of risks arising from lending.

7. In fact: HUF/EUR and HUF/CHF exchange rates seemed to be stationary to that time (see Darvas-Schepp, 2007) which is a quite unique phenomenon.

The general public did not appreciate the risks relating to foreign currency loans for a variety of reasons. These included a total lack of financial culture, information asymmetry, overconfidence (in terms of the behavioral finance), and aggressive selling by banks. At the same time, the huge risks borne by companies and local governments are more directly attributable to poor risk assessment, since both individual loan contracts and bond issues involved a risk-determination and assessment procedure. There were, however, additional factors influencing companies and local governments with no foreign currency income to offset FX borrowings, especially from 2006 to 2008:

- the retention ("own-contribution") needed to obtain grants from EU Structural and Regional Funds
  - Hungary's primary target of "enhancing the quality of life" drove local authorities to apply for EU funds, even if they had no liquid capital, and so they raised the necessary funds by issuing foreign currency bonds with a maturity of 20–25 years
  - In addition to EU subsidies, banks provided FX-loans to fund real estate projects. Although initially this seemed sound, following the onset of the crisis, the weakness of the income-generating capacity of these projects came to light
- the effects of the partial fiscal consolidation carried out by the second Gyurcsány government beginning in the middle of 2006
  - missing demand at companies which had tried to compensate for declining income by the cost-benefits of FX-loans or even by carry trade speculation based on "forward-rate-bias"
  - changes in the terms of financial support and task-sharing to the disadvantage of local authorities — then mostly not of the governing party

- the low interest rates on FX-loans permitted higher capital leverage
    - in terms of Hungarian-owned SMEs, the liquid part of their equity was too low compared to the level of economic activity of the firm pre-crisis and was replaced or supplemented by the relatively cheap, available sources of credit (typically variable interest rate constructed on LIBOR + borrower specific fixed risk premium basis)
    - a substantial number of local authorities had been dealing with chronic financial problems, and so the issue of foreign currency bonds simply aimed to maintain their opportunities for economic activities.

On this basis, it seems rational to accept Király's (2014) approach in which she likens the FX-loan problem to that of subprime loans. In Hungary, FX-loans were given to applicants who, had there been a thorough risk assessment, would not have been offered one — although under those circumstances, they might not have applied. This can be surmised from the fact that these applicants did not ask for a forint loan at the same time.

Vonnák's (2014) empirical analyses of a bank/client database also show that firms in financial difficulties are more likely to opt for higher risk solutions — to choose the Swiss franc instead of the euro, to be precise. Typically, these loans later became problematic. Vasvári's (2013) analysis, in turn, shows a detailed background to local governments debt. Among others, he identifies factors that could motivated the extra risk taking of the local governments by issuing foreign currency denominated long maturity bonds.

Significant sectoral differences can also be seen in connection with the aftermath of FX-loans. While household FX-loans, which were sold as mass products, developed into a serious systemic problem (not yet resolved), new approaches were introduced in respect of the other two affected sectors — in practical terms, comprehensively: in relation to corporate loans, many banks, although they had no legal means to arbitrarily modify contract conditions in the event of repayment difficulties as the crisis struck, in fact tried to organize the modification of credit conditions themselves or drew on new resources. Such adjustments and/or "forintization" could take place legally, and relatively quickly, given the agreement of both parties. The other side of the coin, however, is that, due to the long-term deterioration of business conditions, foreign currency project loans could not be settled in great numbers, and the balance-sheet problems of certain major, foreign-owned banks (e.g., MKB, CIB, Erste and Raiffeisen) reflected this type of loss. The exchange loss in FX-loans of companies who, although weak in terms of credit resources, had survived the 2009–2012 period, were substantially compensated by a decrease in reference interest rates on FX-loans. Since 2013, the serious interest rate reduction policy of the Hungarian National Bank (totaling more than 500 basis points) and its Growth Loan Programme (which allowed FX-loans to be *"derecognized"* at an attractive rate of 2.5%) have aimed to refinance corporate loans. This clearly re-oriented the demand of companies with little or no income in foreign currency towards forint-denominated loans. Banks were motivated by the Central Bank's gradual cutback of passive stocks (e.g., the *de-recognition* of the two-week Central Bank bill).

Eventually, between 2011 and 2014, the government budget, in more steps, took over the cumulative bank liabilities of local authorities in full, the cost amounting altogether to 1344.4 billion HUF (ca. €4.5 billion). No precise data have been made public, but based on the data provided in the National Financial Accounts by the Hungarian Central Bank, since issued, foreign currency liabilities could have amounted to two-thirds of aggregated assets, due to the weakening exchange rate of up to (a substantial) 60%. The convertible (or multi-currency) foreign exchange bonds issued in CHF and EUR between 2006 and 2008 allowed a two- to five-year period of grace for settling accounts with a repayment period of 20–25 years and with an average interest premium of 100 basis points (Aczél & Homolya, 2011). This meant that on account of the reference rate of the CHF and that of the EUR remaining close to zero, the savings on interest could actually have exceeded the realized ("transaction") exchange rate losses originating from the weakening Hungarian currency prior to consolidation. From the perspective of local governments, this can be considered *ex post* as a successful speculation. However, to avoid recurring indebtedness, intensifying legal restraints (the requirement of discretionary governmental licenses) rationally guarantee control over the issue in the future.

Facts and Consequences of Household Foreign Currency Borrowing

In Hungary, foreign currency denominated debt is a systemic problem with a significant constraining impact on the real economy, on monetary policy and on economic policy also. Its importance is highlighted by its sheer volume, but it is also significant due to the consequences of a sudden increase in the resulting repayment burden. Foreign currency debtors had their installments increased following the eruption of the financial crisis, and both the weakening of the exchange rate of the forint and the rising interest rates contributed to this. The weakening exchange rate also increased the current volume of debt. The proportion of foreign currency loans in the total loan volume of households reached 70%, most of which was in Swiss francs. The increase in installments and the sheer volume of debt compelled households to adjust their budgets and during this period the volume of new borrowings by households dropped. The overall volume of foreign currency loans sank below 60% — due partly to the net repayment position which had developed by spring 2009 and partly also to full repayments having been made. Amongst the various types of loan, specifically residential mortgages were of prime importance, since Swiss franc loans accounted for 96% of these. This figure has now fallen to around 80%. The equivalent figure for free-purpose mortgage loans (so-called *mortgage equity withdrawal*) exceeded 98% before it also declined to 80%.

The volume of foreign currency debt was equivalent to some 4000 billion HUF in December 2012, of which residential mortgage loans and free-purpose mortgage loans amounted to 3700 billion HUF. The consequences of this massive foreign currency debt directly affect both the population and the credit institutions, and, due to the pro-cyclic nature of the banking sector, their effects are also felt in the real economy (Horváth et al., 2002). Households had to suffer the unexpected increase in installments, and this resulted in late repayments. The impacts of the suddenly increased repayment burdens were aggravated by the fact that they occurred during the economic recession, when the income of many households was declining. Any inclination to repay the loans was also reduced by the so-called "ethical risk." According to this reasoning, the lack of action in repayment was also due to the fact that households were relying on the state to help them out of their plight. 21% of the volume of housing loans and free-purpose mortgage loans were classified as non-performing or non-paying loans,[8] which means that the debtors were at least 90 days in arrears. This has a twofold negative impact on lending activity. The deteriorating quality of assets increases the risks associated with providing credit, which reduces the willingness of banks to lend as well as narrows the credit supply. In addition, the usual provisions and write-offs associated with bad loans simply remove capital from the credit institutions, and this produces a lower rate of lending capacity and activity. In turn, weak lending activity produces further problems since diminishing investment and consumption hinder economic growth. The factors contributing to the burden on households should, therefore, be taken into account in formulating economic policy decisions.

The Causes of Rising Interest Rates of Swiss Franc Mortgage Loans

Some Important Characteristics of the Hungarian Banking Market

Two factors should be highlighted in respect of the debt burden on the population. In addition to movement in the forint's

8. Based on data from end-June 2013.

exchange rate, the level of interest rates on foreign currency loans also merits attention. One important factor might be the fact that the tax burden as a percentage of GDP can be considered as really high in international comparison (Szigel & Fáykiss, 2012). In Hungary, interest rates on mortgage loans have shown an upward trend despite lower reference interest rates — which should determine their pricing (see Table A1).

The striking data in the study of Darvas (2011) underline that Hungarian households were able to take home currency (so forint rather like Swiss franc) denominated mortgage loans in April 2011 for a more than 50% higher interest rates as people could do that on the similar mortgage EUR mortgage loans in Greece (in a Country *de facto* in bankruptcy).

Prior to the crisis the nature of the competition was likely to play an important role in the evolution of interest rates on loans. Banks have enjoyed a great deal of freedom in setting their rates for consumer credit and on the frequent occasions when re-pricing was under review, individual banks did not compete on the basis of price. The introduction of the annual total percentage rate of charge should have contributed to an easy comparison of credit costs and, consequently, to intensified price competition, but due to the possibility of re-pricing foreign currency denominated loans with variable interest rates, the index failed to fulfill its originally planned function. In their description of the consumer credit market, Banai et al. (2010) underlined the fact that the period from 2002 to 2008 was characterized by risk-based rather than price-based competition in the banking sector. Páles and Homolya (2011) describe the pricing practices of banks and the evolution of the costs of foreign funds during recent years. Their study asserts that the significance of risk-based pricing has increased since 2010, and the inclusion of country risk in pricing has become prevalent. Estimates made by the National Bank of Hungary (2010) suggest that banks have raised the interest rates on Swiss franc-denominated mortgage loans by a much higher margin than reflected in the increased costs of funds and risks post-crisis. The average cost of credit rose, despite the reduction in the reference rate of the Swiss franc, and this, according to the calculations of the Central Bank, could not be justified by the increase in other costs (country risk, deposit margins, swap costs, credit losses). The same report declares that a similarly high rise in the interest rates of the other countries in the region could not be detected. According to the calculations of the National Bank of Hungary (2011), during the first half of 2011 the banks made margins of some 3% on foreign currency mortgage loans over and above the actual costs of funds and risks. This is extremely high when compared to other parts of the region.

Even though margins were high in international terms and banks were able to compete for high-quality clients in terms of price, they still preferred to compete for higher risk clients. One possible explanation for this can be found in the curiously structured market which emerged during the 1990s. On one hand, the leading position of OTP (the biggest Hungarian bank) in lending was hard to disturb and the Postabank was only able to pull itself up to second place in the 1990s on the basis of its deposits, which, in the absence of sufficient market opportunities on the asset side, proved to be unsustainable. On the other hand, there was a certain pressure from the subsidiaries of foreign banks (e.g., CIB, Erste, Raiffeisen) due to the mergers and acquisitions which were expected to follow the country's joining the eurozone — which might mean that only the larger banks would survive. For these two reasons, the Hungarian subsidiaries of foreign parent banks offered new loans by accepting increasingly high risks, as a result of which the banks now have to live with a very poor quality loan portfolio.

We should also ask what other factors have contributed to rising interest rates and whether there are any specific factors where some degree of change might influence their level. It is equally important to ascertain how arbitrary are banks' pricing practices and, consequently, to what extent they need higher level control. Examples of regulatory attempts to improve the transparency of loan pricing have already been seen, although these were crowned by no more than modest success. Within their framework, banks were obliged to guarantee their clients the opportunity to change to schemes linked to reference interest rates, although this was likely to result in higher installments in many cases. The introduction of the relevant regulation (Act CXLVIII entering into force from April 1, 2012) did not modify interest payments on the volume of debt to any significant degree since modifications of contracts were quite rare, and so the role of the reference interest rate and other factors in pricing loans might not be significant in the future either. This regulation is still effective in respect of new loans, so limiting the pricing capacity of credit institutions.

Theoretical Hypotheses Concerning Factors Determining Interest on Loans

In this short section we cite a part of the related theoretical literature. Gambacorta (2008) examines factors influencing the price of loans using examples of Italian banks. He suggests that the level of the interest rate on a loan is a positive function of the real GDP and inflation, since more favorable economic conditions produce a higher demand for loans due to enhanced profitability. According to his study, the costs which indicate the efficiency of banks (monitoring, loan qualification etc.), the risk attached to the loan portfolio and the volatility of market interest rates may also push interest rates higher. The study also shows that a 1% increase in the key interest rate entails an immediate 0.5% increase in the interest on short-term loans — which, after a further quarter, will rise to 0.9%. However, the high proportion of foreign currency loans in Hungary damaged the transmission mechanism (ECB, 2010). On the basis of the interest rate channel, internal demand may be curbed by the burdens of forint loans, and this may reduce inflationary pressure also. In the case of Hungary, however, the rising interest rates of forint loans increased the demand for cheaper foreign currency denominated loans during the period of active foreign currency lending, which further weakened the efficiency of the interest rate channel. The theory of Melitz and Pardue (1973) asserts that only a permanent increase in income may boost the demand for loans, while a temporary rise in income produces the so-called self-financing effect, which, in turn, reduces the demand for loans. There are studies depicting the role of the concentration of the bank sector also which identify a twofold impact with respect to the pricing of loans: the absence of competition produces higher interest rates, while enhanced efficiency may reduce banks' costs (Berger & Hannan, 1989).

The studies investigating the factors determining the "spread" — the margin between interest rates paid on deposits and on loans — also focus on the actual level of interest rates. The significance of the margin is shown by the fact that it indicates the costs of financial intermediation, which ultimately affects the financing of enterprises. The relationship between the development level of the financial infrastructure and growth is investigated and highlighted by several studies (Badjun, 2009). Claeys and Vennet (2008) compared data from banks in East and Central European countries which joined the EU in 2004 with figures from West European banks from the second half of the 1990s. Their results indicate that a higher level of concentration involves wider interest margins in the case of banks in both regions, although, at the same time, larger banks are unable to reap higher interest margins and rely solely on their strong market position. The authors considered capital endowment, access to savings and the ratio of loans to total assets to be significant factors which may all increase the size of the interest margin. The study stated that the correlation between efficiency and the interest margin is negative in the case of West European banks, while the correlation with business cycles is positive. Kasman et al. (2010) also declared — during their study of European countries in the first years of the millennium — that size and efficient leadership might reduce the size of the interest margin. According to the authors, decision-makers should support mergers and market penetration in order to achieve economies of scale and raise efficiency. Foreign participation in the banking system may result in the changing of the interest margin — due directly to the heterogeneous interest rates of member banks or indirectly to enhanced competition. Poghosyan (2010) shows that there is no correlation between foreign ownership and interest margins in Central and East European countries. On the basis of his results, the author concludes that, in order to reduce the costs of financial intermediation, decision-makers should focus on the moderation of loan and market risks, raising the efficiency of banks and enhancing competition. The growth of foreign ownership in itself should not lead to changes in interest margins, although intensified competition and improved performance by banks may reduce financial intermediation costs. The spread issue could be helpful for understanding the exceptionally high home currency interest rates in Hungary, a factor that without doubt contributed to the excess risk taking with foreign currency loans.

This chapter tries to grasp the factors shaping the re-pricing of loans in a totally new way: by identifying the main cost shocks affecting banks. While investigating the factors behind the rising interest rates of Swiss franc-denominated mortgages we shall postulate the hypothesis that Hungarian banks are basically affected by four types of cost shock in pricing foreign currency loans. These are: changing foreign currency interest rates and risk premiums, the changing costs of banks' external funds, the quality of the loan portfolio and the fiscal burden on banks. During our analysis, we shall attempt to find out what relationship exists between these cost shocks and changing interest rates on residential mortgage loans.

Empirical Results

Investigation Database

The data which serve as the basis of the model form a time series from January 2005 until December 2013 with a monthly frequency, and they consist of 108 observations. The time series comprising the interest rates of Swiss franc-denominated loans of households were downloaded from the webpage of the Hungarian Central Bank, which contained the average annualized interest rates weighted with the stock at the end of the given month. Separate investigations were made into housing loans (*housing*) and mortgage equity withdrawals (*mew*). The costs of external funds of banks are shown by the CDS time series illustrating interbank referential loan interest rates and country risks. The basic price component of the total costs of funds (reference yield) fundamentally influences the cost base of the funds of banks. The basic price was estimated by the 3-month Swiss franc LIBOR uncovered interbank interest rate (*chflibor*) available on the webpage of the Swiss National Bank, by using data from the end of the month. Páles and Homolya (2011) concluded — based on oral interviews — that banks mostly used the one-, three- and six-month interbank reference yields to determine basic prices.

One further component of the total cost of funds is the premium which reflects evolving risk-related costs. The study by Páles and Homolya (2011) draws attention to the fact that, for most domestic banks, the premium reflects country risk. The increasing cost of funds due to risk can be seen by the five-year CDS (*cds*) premium showing the sovereign risk of the country. The monthly frequency figures were taken from Reuter's database by averaging their daily data. In our calculations of interest rates — to simplify interpretation — we converted the values of LIBOR and CDS to basis points.

A high-quality loan portfolio is essential in pricing, since an above-average level of non-performing loans forces banks to increase their provisions for losses, and, according to our hypothesis, the resulting costs affect the level of interest rates. Changes in the quality of assets in the banking sector are reflected most accurately in the level of loans rated by banks as doubtful. The data series can be set (on the basis of the data issued by the PSZÁF) by defining the proportion of all loans which cannot be certified as problem-free and which must, therefore, be qualified. All loans which are in arrears, or where some problem is expected regarding the total duration of the loan fall into this category. Since categorization is related to expected problems, this should provide a more accurate picture of the impact on banks of changes in the quality of the portfolio than the categories set up on the basis of the delays (Balás, 2009).

On the basis of the available data, it seems that the quality of housing loans has generally been superior to that of the total volume of loans, although, from the second half of 2010, moratoria came into effect — which inevitably entailed deteriorating quality compared to other types of loan. The most serious deterioration occurred at the end of 2009 and so "Non-payments" appeared in the published accounts of banks roughly a year later. This was in a period when the impacts of the crisis were emerging in the real economy, one result of which was that the readiness or ability of the population to pay also declined. Since the time series of the level of problematic loans is only available quarterly, we based our calculations on the recognized impairment of assets (*impair_hh*), which also shows the losses caused by non-performing loans. The two data series show a strong correlation with each other. Impairment was taken into account as a percentage of the volume of loans. The source of monthly data was the National Bank of Hungary (Magyar Nemzeti Bank, MNB).

We also included in our investigation the banks' liability for corporation tax (advance tax payments during the year and normal tax payments at the year-end), as well as the special bank tax or crisis tax to be paid by financial institutions since 2010. To these we added the direct losses resulting from the so-called *early repayment scheme* (executed with a preferential forex rate), since the crisis tax had, by the end of 2011, produced rather less than budgeted due to this. We further added all costs related to the transaction tax. The data from the Hungarian State Treasury shows the existence of special taxes imposed on banks during previous periods, but their size cannot be compared with the level of the crisis tax.[9] The data are collected from the National Bank of Hungary. The accumulated contributions were measured in relation to the total volume of loans, similarly to impairment.

In Figure 2 we illustrate the changes of the following cost and interest rate measures:

cds: five-year Hungarian CDS premium

housing: interest rate on CHF denominated residential mortgage loans

9. The Special Tax imposed on Credit Institutions and Financial Enterprises was paid by banks during 2005–2006 at an annual level of some 35 billion HUF. Since 2007 this has been replaced by the Credit Institution's Allowance at an annual level of some 13 billion HUF. The specific tax on Financial Organisations has been paid by the bank sector since the second quarter of 2010 amounting to an annual of 120 billion HUF paid in two installments in 2010, and in four installments from 2011 onwards.

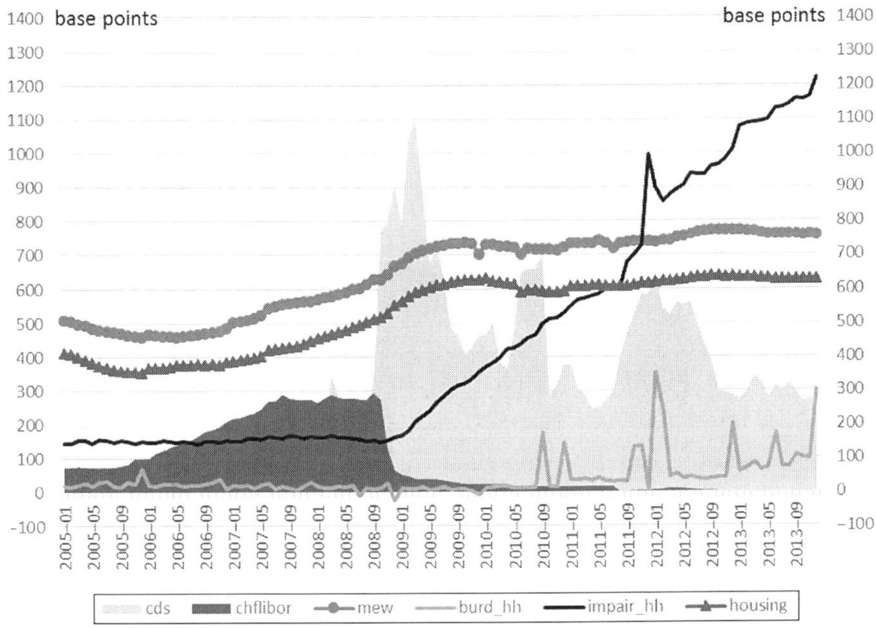

Figure 2: Cost Shocks Affecting Swiss Franc-Denominated Mortgage Loans (% Points). *Source*: National Bank of Hungary, Swiss National Bank, Author's own construction. *Notes*: chflibor: three-month Swiss franc LIBOR uncovered interbank interest rate

mew: interest rate on CHF denominated mortgage equity withdrawal

burd_hh: fiscal burden of commercial banks (as percentage of the loan volume)

impair_hh: recognized impairment of assets (as percentage of the loan volume)

The interest rates on residential housing loans remained below 5% until April 2009 and later reached some 6%, while those for Swiss franc-denominated free-purpose mortgage loans exceeded this by a clear 1% during the period in question. The CDS value showed a significant increase due to the financial crisis during the autumn of 2008, although the premiums then showed a continuous decline and only rose again in 2010 and at the end of 2011.

The impairment of assets, which estimates loan portfolio quality, showed deterioration from 2009. The time series of the fiscal burden shows the serious significance of the crisis tax, the early repayment scheme and the transaction tax.

Even though the empirical tests demonstrate that the first differences in the time series studied do not contain unit roots, any conclusions drawn from our results must be treated with caution due to the relative short sample (limited number of observations) and to the data used. Nevertheless, we still consider that this analysis provides more information than does a simple visual inspection. However arguments in the Hungarian public debate often based on the latter, empirical work with econometric methods is rather an exception.

Vector Error Correction (VEC) Modeling

In our previous work (Pitz & Schepp, 2013) we have concentrated on short-term dynamics, on the indirect interest rate change — inducing effects of cost shocks, and it seems that linkages weakened following the crisis. However, from the borrower's point of view there is a more important open question: to what extent do the cost factors examined by us determine the interest rate level?

To answer this question we employ now the vector error correction (VEC) model which assumes a long-term equilibrium relationship between the variables concerned, and which forecast also changes in interest rates. We ran the model on the available full period (from January 2005 to December 2013) relating to household interest rates (residential mortgage and mortgage equity withdrawals). We use lagged variables indicated by the Likelihood Ratio tests: for housing loans we use a two-lag model and for mortgage equity withdrawals a single-lag model. Because of the long-run nature of relationship assumed we don't use a crisis dummy. In terms of impairment coverage, we take into account only and exclusively the amount that is related to the residential mortgage stock. We are primarily interested to see whether the error correction components are significant, and, if

Table 1: The Coefficients of the Normalized CoIntegrating Vector and Standard Errors.

		Chflibor	Burd	cds	Impair
housing	−1	0.96	−1.73	0.66	0.56
		(0.33)	(0.69)	(0.11)	(0.14)
mew	−1	1.15	−3.53	0.65	0.91
		(0.29)	(0.63)	(0.10)	(0.14)

affirmative, how the cointegrating equation should be interpreted. The contribution of each lagged variable to the forecast is a secondary concern for us. (All variables and quotations like in Figure 2.)

With the Johansen procedure we first estimated the cointegrating equations expressing the long-run dynamic, which indicated a significant relationship for all four cost shocks — normalized version are given in Table 1. Next step was the estimation of VEC models, which involve the lagged values of the variables and also the error correction components represented by the above cointegrating relationship, while a simultaneous estimation procedure was set up in order to forecast changes in interest rates and cost indicators (Table 2).

From these tables, we can draw the following conclusions:

- Error correction components are significant, which indicates the existence of dynamic feedback between cost factors and the complex nature of equilibrium pricing.
- Almost all coefficients in cointegrating vectors are significant, and can, moreover, be explained relatively well:
    - *LIBOR*, that is, the reference rate of interest, appears with point estimates very near to 1 for both loan types — which accords with theoretical expectations. This observation is especially important since the two variables, observed exclusively on their own, move adversely — which is an argument frequently used in public debates in Hungary.

Table 2: The Significant Coefficients of the Estimated VEC Models and Test Results.

Housing	Error Correction	d(Housing (−1))	d(Housing (−2))	C
Coefficient	−0.012	0.237	0.221	1.360
Standard errors	0.005	0.099	0.095	0.542
R^2	0.456			
Adj. R^2	0.392			

Mew	Error Correction	C
Coefficient	−0.020	2.76
Standard errors	0.005	0.77
R^2	0.197	
Adj. R^2-squared	0.148	

- The *CDS* coefficients representing risk premium for both loan types practically coincide which demonstrates that they are reflected in pricing — to an estimated extent of two-thirds. It is relevant to note here also that the sign of risk shocks is positive.
- Concerning fiscal withdrawal (*burd*), although the clerical value of the coefficient does not bear any direct meaning, nevertheless we need to emphasize that its sign is negative in respect of both types of loan. In practice, therefore, the trend in increasing bank burdens did not go hand in hand with the rise in loan interest rates; in fact, the precise opposite occurred.
- Portfolio quality (*impair*) change has considerable higher pricing effects on mortgage equity withdrawals (*mew*) compared to that on *housing* loans. But the estimated 0.91 coefficient is not significantly different from 1, which don't

indicates an overreaction in pricing. Indeed one could argue that housing loan interest rates are spared up to 50% from this type of banks cost shock. Moreover the differences also in line with the observation that mortgage equity withdrawals have a higher non-performing ratio as housing loans.

- In the forecast equations for interest rate changes we found significant and positive constant component in both cases — which implies the existence of pricing factors which are not included in our analysis, and that of cost factors indicating, at the same time, their inelasticity. Due to the huge differences in the explanatory power (R^2 is more as twice higher in the case of housing loans) we conclude that, in respect of mortgage equity withdrawal loans, the role of the omitted variables is greater in emphasis. The lower number of lagged variables considered significant in the forecast also supports this interpretation.

Overall, we can say that the results of the VEC models indicating long-run relationships bring important additional perspectives to the policy conclusions resulting from SVAR-models concentrating on short-term dynamics. On the basis of our estimated cointegrating coefficients, we can also deduce that banks, in the long term, overcame cost shocks in all our four particular dimensions proportionately — or, rather, by cushioning the impact of shocks in their pricing practice of mortgage loans. Even if there are some grounds for the frequently quoted phrase in Hungarian public discussion, "*unfair banking practices*" then these could be traced more appropriately in the validation of factors being only indirectly related to the examined costs as discussed in this chapter. This is indicated by the constant components, the low explanatory power and, in the case of housing loans, the prevailing price persistence.

Result Implications for Economic Policy

Since the year 2000, foreign currency borrowing has become commonplace in several Central- and East-European countries, but nowhere has it become such a central issue of economic policy as in Hungary (except probably Croatia, but the country was not EU member to the time of getting indebted in foreign currency). In addition to the aggressive credit policy of banks and the micro-level weaknesses of risk assessment which involve all participants, the macro-economic and economic policy environment also hinders risk perception. Further, the deficiencies of micro- and macro-level financial regulations and supervision in general — or of those actually in force at the time — account for its spread over several sectors (private individuals, companies, local authorities). Our detailed analysis of the phenomena and a clearer recognition of their complex linkages provide the opportunity for all involved to draw appropriate conclusions for the future.

However, the current problem of household mortgages has now developed a major social dimension, the solution to which could have been given earlier by cooperation among the stakeholders involved, such as the population, the banking system and the government. Instead, in the six to seven years since the crisis erupted, the conflicts inherent in opposing interests have, typically, emerged in the form of direct, bilateral dispute. The banks have frequently made use of their (internationally unique) rights which allow them to modify contract conditions unilaterally, and, in many cases, they have increased interest rates on foreign currency loans by 60–100%. This, together with the huge (40–60%) depreciation of the Hungarian currency, has dramatically increased the burden on the population.

As a consequence of the Act introduced in early Summer 2014 by the newly re-elected Orbán government, banks have to refund during the year of 2015 not only the unilateral interest rate modifications, but also other items, among them the calculated FX bid-ask spread. This generates a burden of approximate €3 billion for the Hungarian banking system. The banks will have an opportunity to prove the legality of their increased interest rates (but not that of their "illegal" existence) within the framework of a court case already filed against the Hungarian state. Apart from evoking, exclusively legal points, such as the precise phrasing of contracts, taking everything into account, it is likely to set the precedent for court cases to prove the cost-side fairness of loan pricing.

On the basis of our empirical analyses (VEC models assuming complex long-run equilibrium pricing dynamics) regarding the banking system at aggregated level, both disputing parties would be able to rely on well-established econometric arguments during the court hearings, which have already started in August 2014. The banks are in a more difficult situation, as the burden of proof lies now on them, and so it will not weigh too much, that proving the unfairness of the pricing decisions would be at least as difficult in the reverse situation.

Summary and Conclusions

Although the high rate of foreign currency borrowing is not exclusive to Hungary, handling the consequences of this debt seems to be particularly problematic in our case, and our situation seems distinctly worse than that of other countries with a similar problem. Not only are the risks assumed by individual stakeholders, so making it more difficult to handle problems, also the proportion of borrowers with good collateral is lower. Furthermore, not only is the proportion of loans denominated in Swiss Francs very high, in addition, the financial position of Hungary in relation to foreign countries produces increased vulnerability and limited scope for action. In respect of the debt burden of the population, the movements in the Hungarian Forint's exchange rate merit special attention, even though interest rate levels for foreign currency loans are also important. In Hungary, interest rates for consumer credit showed an upward trend despite lower reference interest rates which basically determine pricing. The chapter examined the factors affecting the movement of interest rates for Swiss franc mortgage loans. We assumed that movement in the costs of external funds was a fundamental element of pricing, which is mostly shaped by foreign currency reference interest rates and risk premiums. In addition to this, the quality of the loan portfolio and the fiscal burdens of banks produce cost shocks for banks and these will, sooner or later, be passed on to the banks' clients in their loan repayments. By using econometric model, we attempted to determine to what degree the level of interest rates of mortgage loans could be explained by these costs. We performed analyses both on residential mortgage and free-purpose mortgage loans, investigating the existing loan stock. On the basis of the results of our analyses, we can conclude that all four cost types played a role in determining interest rates for housing loans, that is, the cost of banks are more or less accurately reflected in the unilateral interest rates changes (*re-pricing*) by domestic banks.

To the same the significant impact of the CDS supports the hypothesis of risk-based competition. Pricing by banks increasingly reflects the growth of the risk factor, and, since risk-based competition overcame price-based competition, banks were given no incentive to narrow their wide margins. After evaluating our experience of the crisis, it becomes increasingly evident that some form of top-down restriction is necessary in order to maintain the financial stability of the country. Enhanced regulation is justified by the fact that the profit-driven behavior of financial institutions may generate damaging consequences. One specific feature of financial markets is the intense "danger of contagion" which arises from tight symbiosis. Regulation is, therefore, justifiable, but, at the same time, it may reduce the profitability of the banking system while raising the price of financial services. Várhegyi (2010) also draws attention to the ethical risk and competition-distorting effect associated with public bank-rescue attempts. The significance of the creditor role of banks can be understood by the decline in demand and, ultimately, in slower economic growth. Improving weakening creditor activity and relaxing the more strict conditions as part of the adjustment process are rendered more difficult by more expensive funds and inferior debtor quality. Therefore, in order to reduce the repayment burden of existing housing loans, the reduction of the country risk, that is, a predictable economic policy, should be strongly encouraged. Further research directions could be the treatment of structural fractures and the examination of other cost factors. Another question to consider is whether the impact of cost shocks may significantly differ in individual banks — the bank tax calculated on the basis of total assets significantly increased the polarization of banks — and so it would be advisable to create groups on the basis of profitability, for example. At the same time, we are convinced that the empirical analysis of these questions is of fundamental interest to all affected stakeholders (debtors, banks and the Hungarian state). Finding a sustainable exit from the current trap is only possible if a fair distribution of burdens is achieved and this should be supported by a factual knowledge of the situation. However the story seems to fund meanwhile a kind of lucky ending: the mandatory "forintization" of mortgage debt stock was timed at the end of 2014 just before the collapse of the 1.20 CHF/EUR threshold and prevented further serious losses of debtors. In fact EUR reserves of the National Bank of Hungary have been used to manage this huge transaction so the avoided losses could be evaluated as collective gain.

Acknowledgments

We are grateful for the comments and suggestions made by András Balatoni, Elisabeth Beckmann, Péter Benczúr, Péter Cziráki, Zsolt Darvas, Zoltán Gál, Júlia Király, Tamás Mellár, Gábor Rappai, and Zoltán Vásáry, as also for those offered by conference and seminar participants at the Department of Economics and Regional Studies of the University of Pécs, at the 12th Conference of the Hungarian Economic Modelling Association, the 5th Conference of the Hungarian Economic Science Association, at the 12th INFINITI Conference on International Finance, at the 2014 World Finance Conference in Venice, and the RAStaNEWS scientific workshop "Eurozone in the Doldrums." Some of our data were obtained from the MNB database and we are grateful to Dániel Homolya, Réka Pusztai, and Róbert Szegedi for their assistance. The research leading to these results has received funding from the European Union, Seventh Framework Programme FP7/2007–2013 Socio-economic Sciences and Humanities under Grant Agreement No. 320278 – RASTANEWS.

References

Act CXLVIII. (2012). On the Hungarian Export-Import Bank Incorporation and on the Hungarian Insurance Incorporation of Export Credits.

Aczél, Á., & Homolya, D. (2011). Risks of the indebtedness of the local government sector from the point of view of financial stability. *MNB Bulletin*, October, pp. 7–14.

Badjun, M. (2009). Financial intermediation by banks and economic growth: A review of empirical evidence. *Financial Theory and Practice, 33*(2), 121–152.

Balás, T. (2009). A bankrendszer hitelportfóliójának minőségét leíró mutatók összehasonlítása. In: *Jelentés a pénzügyi stabilitásról* (November). háttértanulmány, Budapest.

Balás, T., & Nagy, M. (2010). A devizahitelek átváltása forinthitelekre. *Hitelintézeti Szemle, 2010/5*, 416–430.

Banai, Á., Király, J., & Nagy, M. (2010). Az aranykor vége Magyarországon. *Közgazdasági Szemle, 58*, 105–131.

Bánfi, T. (2012). Causes of foreign currency lending — Possibilities of intervention — Ways of intervention. *Public Finance Quarterly, 2012/3*, 358–370.

Beckmann, E., Fidrmuc, J., & Stix, H. (2012). *Foreign currency loans and loan arrears of households in Central and Eastern Europe*. Oesterreichische Nationalbank Working Papers 181.

Berger, A. N., & Hannan, T. H. (1989). The price-concentration relationship in banking. *Review of Economics and Statistics, 71*, 291–299.

Brown, M., & De Haas, R. (2012). Foreign banks and foreign currency lending in emerging Europe. *Economic Policy: CEPR & CES & MSH, 27*(69), 57–98.

Brown, M., Ongena, S., & Yesin, P. (2011). Foreign currency borrowing by small firms in the transition economies. *Journal of Financial Intermediation, 20*(3), 285–302.

Brown, M., Ongena, S., & Yesin, P. (2014). Information asymmetry and foreign currency borrowing by small firms. *Comparative Economic Studies, 56*(1), 110–131.

Claeys, S., & Vennet, V. R. (2008). Determinants of bank interest margins in Central and Eastern Europe: A comparison with the West. *Economic System, 32*(2008), 197–216.

Darvas, Z. (2011). Debt restructuring in the euro area. A necessary but manageable evil? *Bruegel Policy Contribution, 2011*(7), 1–23.

Darvas, Z., & Schepp, Z. (2007). Kelet-közép európai devizaárfolyamok előrejelzése határidős árfolyamok segítségével. *Közgazdasági Szemle, 54*, 501–528.

ECB. (2010). *Substitution between domestic and foreign currency loans in Central Europe. Do central banks matter?* Working Paper Series No. 1187.

Erdős, T. (2010). Forintárfolyam, kamatszint és devizaalapú eladósodás. Az árfolyam szerepéről. *Közgazdasági szemle, 57*, 847–867.

Fidrmuc, J., Hake, M., & Stix, H. (2011). *Households' foreign currency borrowing in Central and Eastern Europe.* Oesterreichische Nationalbank Working Papers 171.

Gambacorta, L. (2008). How do banks set interest rates? *European Economic Review, 52*(2008), 792–819.

Horváth, E., Mérő, K., & Zsámboki, B. (2002). *Tanulmányok a bankszektor tevékenységének prociklikusságáról.* MNB műhelytanulmányok 23, 2002. február.

Hudecz, A. (2012). Párhuzamos történetek. *Közgazdasági szemle, 59*, 349–411.

Kasman, A., Tunc, G., Vardar, G., & Okan, B. (2010). Consolidation and commercial bank net interest margins: Evidence from the old and new European Union: Members and candidate countries. *Economic Modelling, 27*(2010), 648–655.

Király, J. (2014). *Tézisek a devizahitelezésről* (pp. 1–24).

Király, J., & Simonovits, A. (2015). Jelzáloghitel-törlesztés forintban és devizában — egyszerű modellek. *Közgazdasági szemle, LIXII*, 1–26.

Melitz, J., & Pardue, M. (1973). The demand and supply of commercial bank loans. *Journal of Money, Credit and Banking, 5*(2), 669–692.

Mellár, T. (2014). Deviation from the path to Eurozone accession: Current monetary and fiscal solutions managing macro-imbalances and debt in Hungary. *RAStaNEWS Deliverable* D1.4, 1–24.

National Bank of Hungary. (2010). *Financial Stability Report*, November.

National Bank of Hungary. (2011). *Financial Stability Report*, November.

Páles, J., & Homolya, D. (2011). Developments in the costs of external funds of the Hungarian banking sector. *MNB Bulletin*, October, pp. 61–69.

Pitz, M., & Schepp, Z. (2013). Determinants of the pricing of bank loans: A structural VAR based analysis. *Public Finance Quarterly, 2013*(4), 420–433.

Poghosyan, T. (2010). Re-examining the impact of foreign bank participation on interest margins in emerging markets. *Emerging Markets Review, 11*(2010), 390–403.

Radnai, M. (2015). A lakossági devizahitelek átárazásának bumeránghatása. *Közgazdasági szemle, LIXII*, 113–138.

Rosenberg, C. B., & Tirpák, M. (2009). Determinants of foreign currency borrowing in the new member states of the EU. *Czech Journal of Economics and Finance, 59*(3), 216–228.

Schepp, Z. (2008). Néhány gondolat a változó kamatozású devizafinanszírozás kockázatairól. *Hitelintézeti Szemle, 7*, 67–90.
Schepp, Z., & Pitz, M. (2012). Lakossági devizahitelezés Magyarországon: problémafelmérés és a frankhitelek banki árazásának empirikus vizsgálata. *Műhelytanulmányok* — Pécsi Tudományegyetem Közgazdaságtudományi Kar Közgazdasági és Regionális Tudományok Intézete, 2012(3), 1–49.
Szigel, G., & Fáykiss, P. (2012). Az eladósodás hatása a magyar háztartások pénzügyi és jövedelmi pozíciójára. *MNB-Szemle*, február.
Várhegyi, É. (2010). A válság hatása a magyarországi bankversenyre. *Közgazdasági Szemle, 57*, 825–846.
Vasvári, T. (2013). The financial management of local governments in 2011 in light of the crowding-out effect of their debt service. *Public Finance Quarterly, 2013*(3), 307–333.
Vonnák, D. (2014). *Determinants and riskiness of corporate foreign currency lending: The case of Hungary*. Manuscript, Central European University, 1–35.
Yesin, P. (2013). Foreign currency loans and systemic risk in Europe. *Review, Federal Reserve Bank of St. Louis*, (May), 219–236.

Appendix

Table A1: Representative Interest Rates on New Mortgage Loans[a] (%).

	2005	2006	2007	2008	2009	2010	2011	2012	2013
Bulgaria	n/a	n/a	8.31	9.09	10.09	8.97	8.23	7.51	6.90
Czech Rep.	3.96	4.18	4.69	5.61	5.61	4.90	4.04	3.52	3.26
Estonia	3.27	4.26	5.53	5.83	3.87	3.50	3.42	2.89	2.62
Hungary	13.15	11.05	11.34	11.67	13.15	9.77	10.87	12.66	9.64
Lithuania	3.32	4.06	5.40	5.83	4.17	3.70	3.71	2.97	2.39
Poland	6.98	5.74	6.09	8.05	7.23	6.48	6.70	6.95	5.14
Romania	n/a	n/a	6.60	6.67	7.16	5.31	5.84	5.03	4.73
Slovakia	n/a	n/a	n/a	6.04	5.90	5.24	4.84	4.74	4.10

Source: European Mortgage Federation.

[a]The variable mortgage interest rates at the end of the respective year; in the case of Hungary, the interest rate calculated for the Swiss franc-denominated variable interest rate loan, or, maximum a one-year fixed interest rate loan

16

Intraday Volatility Smiles, Day of the Week Effect, and Risk Management at Borsa Istanbul Stock Exchange

A. Can Inci

Abstract

Intraday volatility characteristics throughout the trading week are examined at the emerging Borsa Istanbul (BIST) stock exchange. Using five-minute (and 15-minute) intervals, accentuated intraday volatility patterns at the microstructure level are examined during the stock market open and close in the morning and in the afternoon sessions. Volatility is highest when markets open in the morning. The second highest is during the afternoon open. The third highest is before the market closes for the day. Volatility before the market close has increased in recent years. These characteristics are seen every trading day. There are also differences: Monday returns are lowest, Friday returns are highest, and Monday morning volatility is highest of the entire trading week. Day-of-the-week and intraday accentuated volatility smile anomalies are jointly investigated using the longest intraday sample period in the emerging country stock exchange literature. Investment companies and professionals can utilize the results for risk management and hedging by avoiding highly volatile opening and closing periods. Arbitrageurs, speculators, and risk takers should trade during these highly volatile periods. Heightened volatility is increased difficulty in price discovery, thus inefficiency. Market participants, exchanges, and public prefer efficient markets. The research presents evidence of trading days, and periods during the trading day, when the exchange becomes more efficient. This is the first research that explores day-of-the-week effect from intraday volatility perspective in an emerging market, and provides useful recommendations in designing risk management strategies at market microstructure level.

Keywords: Market microstructure; accentuated volatility; day-of-the-week effect; Borsa Istanbul; intraday returns; intraday volatility

JEL classifications: G14; D40

Introduction

This chapter examines the impact of the global information flow on the intraday stock market price behavior of emerging country stock markets and the consequences on the risk management of portfolios formed partly with stocks that are part of the stock exchange of the emerging Turkish economy. Global trade, global finance, and international investments have had significant expansion in recent years as a result of the enhancements in integration of markets with the help of easier information access around the world, and with the reduction and partial removal of the frictions of capital flows across borders. Global investors have increased their allocation of funds to emerging country financial markets. In addition to these developments, technological advancements and hardware improvements have enabled much faster trading routines.

The substantial increase in intraday trading activity in this global framework makes it necessary to investigate the impact of global information flow on the intraday stock return performance in emerging country markets in order to develop more sophisticated risk management strategies. Recent research on international finance in the context of this chapter provide evidence of these issues. For example, Jawadi, Louhichi, and Cheffou (2015) study volatility spillover between the United States and the three largest European stock markets (Frankfurt, London and Paris) around the time of the recent subprime crisis making use of intraday data. They find returns and volatility spillover from the United States to European markets and vice versa at different times of the trading day, indicating that the two regions became more dependent during the recent subprime crisis, a finding that supports the contagion hypothesis between the United States and European stock markets. Nishimura, Tsutsui, and Hirayama (2015) study return/volatility spillover from China to Japan with high frequency data. Their findings suggest that China has a large impact on Japanese stocks via China-related firms in Japan. Furthermore, they find evidence that this response has become stronger as the Chinese economy has gained importance in recent years.

In this context, the Istanbul Stock Exchange of Turkey is an excellent example of an emerging country stock market. The Turkish economy has undergone significant transformations over the last 30 years. The "open economy" policy has allowed foreign and global investors to extensively participate in the trading and ownership of the stock shares at the Istanbul Stock Exchange. The Turkish financial markets are heavily influenced by global events and news, especially originating from developed countries such as the United States, the European Union, and Japan. The intraday volatility patterns of the stock returns in the Turkish Stock Exchange would illuminate the information impact on the markets and address how the information is interpreted by market participants. The volatility levels and changes throughout the day during each of the five trading days of the week would also help understand the risk levels in the market and how these risk levels would evolve intraday during each trading day of the week. The intraday volatility patterns would help the design of higher quality risk management strategies for investors. Additionally, the intraday volatility patterns reveal information about the level of market efficiency and therefore, aid domestic and global investors in finding arbitrage opportunities and in controlling the risk exposure of their portfolios.

Market efficiency is generally accepted to be at the semi-strong level in developed country stock markets. Under this level of efficiency, all public information is incorporated into the current stock prices. A particular market behavior that is contrary to semi-strong form market efficiency is called an anomaly. Various anomalies have been documented over the years in the United States and in other developed country equity markets. Two examples of the well-known anomalies are the "day-of-the-week effect" and the "intraday volatility smile" effect.

Day of the week effect refers to the stylized fact that stock returns are not distributed similarly across trading days. For example, the U.S. capital markets exhibit a return behavior where Monday returns are negative, while Friday returns are positive and statistically higher compared to the stock returns in other days. Narayan, Mishra, and Narayan (2014) examine the determinants of the dollar bid-ask spread for each day of the week over the period 1998–2008. They find that there are day-of-the-week effects for certain groups of firms and that the effects of volume and volatility on the spread are mixed, with only some sectors experiencing the day-of-the-week effect. This stylized day-of-the-week anomaly seems to hold in many developed country markets. However, there are also some differences. For example, Japan, Australia, Singapore, France, and Turkey as an emerging country, have Tuesday as the significantly negative return day (as shown by Dubois & Louvet, 1996; Solnik & Bousquet, 1990). Al-Jafari (2012) examines the day-of the week effect at Muscat

Stock Market in Oman and finds no significant evidence of the anomaly.

The common explanation for the negative stock returns on Monday is that pessimistic news and announcements tend to be disseminated during the weekend when the markets are closed in order to avoid a sudden decline in the markets. However, the unfavorable information still influences investors when the markets open on Monday and leads to the disposal of the shares of stocks associated with the negative news. On the other hand, investors tend to consider Friday as a positive day mainly for psychological reasons. Buy orders and open positions with brokers and traders throughout the week are executed on Friday before the end of the work week. This broad purchase activity tends to increase prices on average during Fridays. Finally, the common explanation for the negative stock returns on Tuesdays is the lag effect of pessimistic news in the U.S. stock markets, spilling over to developing country stock markets, or to stock markets whose constituent firms are heavily influenced by the United States Naturally, these explanations do not completely address the anomaly. And each country has additional unique reasons behind the anomaly if it exists there.

Intraday volatility smile is another market anomaly that is seen in developed and developing country stock markets. Belhaj, Abaoub, and Mahjoubi (2015) examine the Tunisian Stock Market for intraday volatility-volume relationship and find inefficiencies. Evidence from these markets generally indicates that accentuated, or heightened, volatility appears when the stock market opens in the morning. High levels of volatility are also seen right before the close of the stock market for the day. During the day, volatility remains at lower levels — thus the shape of intraday volatility resembles a smile. Under rational expectations, volatility should not change statistically during the day, but empirical evidence consistently documents otherwise. The common explanation for accentuated volatility in the morning is the difficulty of market participants in interpreting the accumulated information overnight. And the consensus for the reason behind the heightened volatility before the stock market closes is the pressure that market participants endure in closing out the open positions in their clients' accounts. Accentuated volatility appears in different patterns such as volatility smile or volatility smirk in different stock markets around the world.

The chapter is related to several areas of finance literature. Intraday volatility and day-of-the-week anomalies exhibit different characteristics in developed country markets and in emerging country stock markets. These main differences are presented and the consequences to the risk management practices in emerging country markets are provided in the context of the representative emerging Turkish stock market. Second, the long time series data covers three decades of emerging markets research. The international finance anomalies are investigated and compared to previous emerging market research in order to draw lessons about the history and learning process in the emerging markets literature. Third, the intraday volatility and day-of-the-week anomalies are pieces of evidence against market efficiency, and are, therefore, barriers to effective risk management in the representative emerging market of Turkey. The characteristics of these barriers are investigated in detail throughout the chapter. Fourth, the risk management strategies and policy implications to account for these anomalies are laid out and practical recommendations for future risk management models are provided. Overall, the chapter is a fundamental contribution to risk management in market microstructure in emerging markets.

The goal of this chapter is to investigate and document both the day-of-the-week and the intraday volatility effects simultaneously in an emerging country stock exchange, Borsa Istanbul of Turkey. Turkey is a fast developing country. With the positives and the negatives, Turkey is an excellent representative of an emerging economy. The volatility pattern for each trading day is examined individually at the Turkish Stock Exchange. The patterns and statistical differences are presented. The economic, risk management, and investment interpretations are provided. The dataset used in the chapter is the intraday price and index movements of the most liquid equities traded at Borsa Istanbul. The sample period of 1998–2011 is the longest time series that has been employed compared to previous studies. The long sample period has provided the flexibility to compare the patterns and characteristics between early and recent periods.

The findings indicate that Monday morning intraday volatility is highest for the entire week, implying the additional difficulty that market participants endure in understanding the information accumulated over the weekend. Trades submitted right after the Monday open lead to highest price movements and leads to highest intraday volatilities. Borsa Istanbul has an afternoon break, where trading stops during that time. There seems to be an L-shaped volatility curve in the morning session and a U-shaped volatility curve in the afternoon session for each and every trading day during the week. Intraday volatility is highest every day when the stock market opens in the morning. The next highest volatility is immediately after Borsa Istanbul opens in the afternoon session. The third highest volatility period during the day is right before the close of the market for the day. These observations are reported for every trading day of the week.

The chapter contributes to several strands of finance literature. The market microstructure literature in finance have consistently documented the U-shaped intraday volatility curve in developed country markets. However, the developing country markets exhibit different characteristics. The unique midday break in Borsa Istanbul of the emerging Turkish economy provides interesting volatility patterns that would help explain volatility characteristics in other emerging country stock markets. Second, the sample period used in the study is the longest in the existing literature. The significance of the results and conclusions are stronger compared to most of the existing studies. Third contribution to the literature is that the globalization impact on intraday volatility is addressed in detail, again, by splitting the long sample period into early (1980s and early 1990s) and recent (late 2000s). Fourth, day-of-the-week anomaly is adequately addressed in the emerging Turkish Stock Exchange using the long sample period. The evolution of the anomaly over time is also examined. Finally, the consequences and investment implications of intraday volatility and day-of-the-week effect are addressed. Investment suggestion are provided not only for domestic investment funds and investors, but also for international funds and investors. The suggestions and implications help with the risk management strategies of professional investment companies and funds, as well as individual investors.

With positives and negatives, Turkish economy and the Turkish Stock Exchange are good representatives of emerging country financial systems. There are several policy implications and practical applications that can be drawn from the results presented in the chapter, and these can be adapted in other emerging markets. Risk increases substantially during the 15 minutes when stock exchanges open and close. This is seen every day, but Monday mornings are especially notable. There are several risk management implications: Institutional investors, mutual funds, insurance, and investment companies should avoid these highly volatile periods in order to reduce unnecessary risk exposure. On the other hand, arbitrageurs, speculators, investors with superior information, and risk takers should prefer to trade and take investment positions during these highly volatile periods. As for policy implications, exchange regulators and policy makers prefer efficient markets; hence low volatility. Globalization of markets, opening of economies have increased information and capital flow across borders. These desirable trends also encompass high volatility. Placing auction systems after the market close, as well as before the market open would be one way to reduce volatility and calm down frantic traders. Fast dissemination of information to market participants, interpretation of the information by competent and knowledgeable international finance professionals and sharing through wired and televised finance news agencies would also help reduce intraday volatility. Finally, execution of trades in a fast and fair manner through improved technology, better regulation, and effective monitoring of markets and trades by policy makers are additional policy implications suggested by the results presented here.

The rest of the chapter is structures as follows. Next section provides an overview of the relevant literature. Then the description of the data used in the chapter is provided. The discussion of the empirical results is followed by conclusion.

Literature Review

The day-of-the-week anomaly in stock markets has been investigated numerous times for many countries using different sample periods. In the United States, French (1980), Keim and Stambaugh (1984), and Kohers and Kohers (1995) among many others have consistently reported lower average stock returns on Mondays and higher stock returns on Fridays. For other countries, studies tend to find Tuesday stock returns as the most negative. Examples are Solnik and Bousquet (1990) for the French stock market, Dubois and Louvet (1996) for the stock markets in Japan and Australia, Agrawal and Tandon (1994) for eighteen countries, among other studies. On the other hand, Cinko, Avci, Aybars, and Oner (2015) find no systematic pattern of the presence of the day of the week effect in the 16 developed country indices during 1999–2013.

While there is no uniform consensus in the literature, the general conclusions that have emerged on aggregate are the low stock returns on Mondays in the United States, and low stock returns on Mondays or Tuesdays in stock exchanges of other countries around the world.

Specific studies for the Turkish Stock Exchange also provide evidence of the day-of-the-week effect. Bildik (1998) and Chukwuogor (2006) find negative average stock returns on Tuesdays for the Istanbul Stock Exchange. Bildik (2001) uses 1988–1999 data to report some evidence of negative stock returns on Mondays but concludes that these negative return disappear if Friday returns of the previous week are positive. Balaban (1995) finds evidence for day-of-the-week anomaly for the Istanbul Stock Exchange Index for the 1988–1994 period but also shows that the effect changes direction over time. Oguzsoy and Guven (2003) report low Monday and Tuesday stock returns and dominantly high Friday returns. Yalcin and Yucel (2006) use the modified exponential generalized autoregressive conditional heteroskedasticity in mean (EGARCH-M) modeling technique and find limited evidence that higher returns tend to concentrate around Fridays, whereas volatility is highest on Mondays and lowest on Tuesdays and Fridays.

Overall, the consensus from these studies is lower returns on Mondays and/or Tuesdays, and higher returns on Fridays.

The intraday volatility accentuation anomaly has also been investigated extensively, especially in developed country stock markets. Stoll (2000) shows that noisy trading leads to arbitrary price fluctuations. These fluctuations increase short-term volatility and lead to illiquidity, inefficiency, and ultimately the discouragement of investors from participating in financial markets. Studies such as Madhavan, Richardson, and Roomans (1997), Ozenbas (2006), and Nguyen and Phengpis (2009) find a U-shaped curve in volatility during the day. Ozenbas, Pagano, and Schwartz (2010) and Hussain (2009) examine the quality of price determination and find that large capitalization stocks lead smaller-cap stocks to their new equilibrium values in the United States and the United Kingdom stock markets.

As for developing country stock markets, Choe and Shin (1993) and Tian and Guo (2007) both document two intraday L-shaped volatility patterns; one for the morning trading session, and the other for the afternoon trading session at the Korean Stock Exchange and Shanghai Stock Exchange, respectively. Tissaoui (2012) examines the Tunisian Stock Market and finds evidence of a seasonal U-shaped pattern in return volatility. Bildik (2001) examines intraday return behavior at the Istanbul Stock Exchange using a very limited sample period from 1996 through 1998. Inci (2012) focuses on 100 stocks at Borsa Istanbul, measures volatility using 30-minute estimation periods, and documents volatility patterns during the day.

Intraday volatility results are heavily influenced by the stock market opening procedures. The opening procedures play an extremely important role in facilitating price discovery following the overnight trading break. For example, the NYSE and the Deutsche Börse use a call auction system during the stock market opening to generate liquidity and to execute orders at one price. Using the call auction at the opening is advocated by studies such as Barclay, Hendershott, and Jones (2008) and Chang, Rhee, Stone, and Tang (2008), which find that the market quality of continuous trade increases because of the opening auction.

Short-term volatility patterns provide information about the efficiency of equity markets. Accentuated intraday stock volatility following the opening of the stock market implies the difficulty of market participants in understanding the information cumulated overnight. On the other hand, accentuated volatility before the closing of the stock market for the day indicates the noise trading of market makers trying to clear the order books while executing their clients' trades for the day.

Developed country equity markets have been investigated extensively for intraday price movements and volatility patterns. On the other hand, there has been limited research on emerging country equity markets. The Borsa Istanbul (BIST) Stock Exchange in Turkey is a good representative of an emerging country stock market. The BIST became fully operational in January 1986. The exchange has an unusual trading structure compared to developed country stock markets: there is a midday break. The evolution of the accentuated volatility throughout the trading week at the BIST and the mechanisms placed by market regulators to address the problem are fully examined in this chapter in order to understand how they affect risk management strategies.

The dataset used in this chapter consists of a very long sample period from 1998 to 2011. The most actively traded 30 stocks at the BIST are examined to avoid additional complications and frictions related to illiquid stocks. Intraday volatility is measured using five-minute short intervals with various different techniques. The risk exposure of investment companies and the necessity of hedging protocols for these investment companies are examined. The policy implications for the market regulators are also discussed in the chapter.

Trading hours have changed substantially over the 30 years since the BIST became operational. Currently, trading starts at 9.50 am and ends at 12.30 pm for the midday break. The afternoon session starts at 2.20 pm and trading concludes for the day at 5.30 pm. There are two blind opening auctions before the opening of the stock market in the morning session and before the opening of the afternoon session. Currently, the opening auction is from

9.30 am to 9.50 am; during which order collection is from 9.30 am to 9.45 am and price determination is from 9.45 am to 9.50 am in the morning. In the afternoon, the order collection is from 2 pm to 2.10 pm and price determination is from 2.10 pm to 2.20 pm.

There are approximately 300 stocks traded at the BIST; however, the focus of this chapter is on the 30 largest firms' stocks. These stocks are the most liquid ones at the exchange, therefore, the volatility patterns that are documented are not due to other liquidity frictions. Using five-minute trading intervals, various intraday volatility measures are utilized to investigate and report the existence of strong accentuated volatility right after the market opens in the morning and after the market opens in the afternoon. Accentuated volatility patterns are different during the week. The highest volatility is seen Monday mornings right after when the stock market opens. Evidence of accentuated volatility is also presented right before the close of the stock market for the day, but only during recent years. In 2012, the regulators of the exchange placed a daily clearing call auction system which kicks in every day shortly after the stock market closes. The evidence provided in this chapter indicates that the regulators have made a prudent policy decision for the proper functioning of the exchange.

Trading Hours and Opening Procedures at the BIST

During the normal trading phase, stock market exchanges tend to operate at a high level of market quality. However, there are some phases during a trading day when the informational efficiency and the liquidity are reduced, especially during the opening minutes of the stock market. The lower level of market quality during the opening minutes is mostly related to the preceding non-trading period (Amihud & Mendelson, 1987) and related to the market structure (Stoll & Whaley, 1990) used during the opening minutes. Therefore, the opening procedures play an extremely important role in facilitating price discovery following the trading break overnight, or, over the weekend. Many markets utilize special opening procedures that are designed to provide traders with information related to the market clearing prices. The ultimate goals of these procedures are enhanced liquidity and reduced intraday price volatility around the beginning of the trading session. For example, the NYSE and the Deutsche Börse employ a call auction system during the opening session in order to generate liquidity and to execute orders at one price (Economides & Schwartz, 1995). Studies such as Chang et al. (2008) find that the pre-opening activity of providing indicative bids and offers is informative and improves the market quality during the opening minutes.[1]

There are various trading instruments at the Borsa Istanbul Stock Exchange (BIST), such as ordinary shares (almost all of the volume), ETFs, preference shares, right issues, and ADRs. The stock exchange regulator is the Capital Markets Board of Turkey (CMB). There is no foreign ownership restriction, and foreign ownership has been between 60 and 70 percent of the float over the last decade. Trading at the BIST operates on an order driven system with two blind opening auctions preceding each of the two sessions during the day. The exchange has moved to the call auction system in 2001 before the market opens in the morning. The closing time auction system and the corresponding price determination were implemented in March 2, 2012.

The evolution of the trading hours since the inception of the BIST can be summarized as follows:

1. There are also counter arguments to the call auction system because of potential order imbalances leading to even lower liquidity during the call auction. Camilleri and Green (2009) and others point out the contagion of the disadvantages of the call auction trading mechanism to the regular trading system because of lower liquidity and lower price efficiency. However, call auction system is currently the dominant mechanism utilized in developed country stock exchanges.

January 1, 1986–August 13, 2001: 10 am to 12 pm and 2 pm to 4 pm

August 13, 2001–February 2, 2007: 9.30 am to 12 pm and 2 pm to 4.30 pm

February 2, 2007–September 7, 2007: 10 am to 12 pm and 2 pm to 4.30 pm

September 7, 2007–October 13, 2008: 9.45 am to 12 pm and 2 pm to 5 pm

October 13, 2008–October 19, 2009: 9.50 am to 12.30 pm and 2 pm to 5 pm

October 19, 2009–November 13, 2009: 9.50 am to 12.30 pm and 2 pm to 5.30 pm

November 13, 2009–April 5, 2013: 9.50 am to 12.30 pm and 2.20 pm to 5.30 pm

April 5, 2013–June 10, 2013: 9.45 am to 12.30 pm and 2.20 pm to 5.30 pm

June 10, 2013–Current: 9.35 am to 12.30 pm and 2.15 pm to 5.30 pm

There are two blind opening auctions preceding each of the two sessions before the opening of the market in the morning and in the afternoon. The current opening session is from 9.15 am to 9.35 (the call phase from 9.15 am to 9.30 am is used for order collection, and price determination phase from 9.30 am to 9.35 am is used for producing a consensus share price). The first quotation by the market maker is collected between 9.30 am and 9.34 am and the first quotation is provided by the electronic system at 9.34 am. The afternoon opening session is from 2 pm to 2.15 pm (the call phase is from 2 pm to 2.10 pm for order collection, and the price determination phase is from 2.10 pm to 2.15 pm.).

Data

The sample period is from January 5, 1998 through June 30, 2010 and includes tick-by-tick price and index data during the day for every trading day.[2] The 30 largest and most liquid of the

2. Research involving intraday frequency data tend to use short sample periods due to the intensity of the data. For example, Belhaj et al. (2015) use an intraday data sample from October 2011 through September 2012 even though their daily frequency portion of their paper uses a sample from January 2008 through June 2012. Similarly, Tissaoui (2012) uses intraday data covering the period October 2008 to June 2009. Bildik (2001) examines

approximately 300 stocks of the stock exchange are used for the investigation. Five-minute trading period volatilities of the stock price movements are computed. The price changes from the beginning of the period to the end of the period are used to calculate the volatility variable. In addition to regular returns (ret), log returns (log), the absolute values of the price deviations (abs), and the normalized absolute price differences (nabs) (by dividing the absolute difference with the end price for the interval) are used to compute volatility. Finally, the standard deviations of the differences between the maximum and minimum values of the five-minute periods (maxmin) and the standard deviations of the normalized max-min differences (nmaxmin) (by dividing with the average of the beginning price and the end price of the interval) are used as additional intraday volatility measures.

An alternative set of volatility measures are also calculated using the tick prices in the five-minute intervals. To this end, the tick-by-tick returns (ret), log returns of the tick price movements (log), absolute values of the tick price differences (abs), and the normalized absolute price differences (nabs) (by dividing with the final price) are computed.

Previous studies have reported evolving ecology of the stock markets over time. To examine this important issue for the BIST, the entire sample period is split into two parts: the early sample from January 5, 1998 to March 31, 2004 and the recent sample from April 1, 2004 to July 1, 2010. For robustness, the entire sampling period is also split into three parts: the early sub-sample from January 5, 1998 through February 28, 2002; the middle sub-sample from March 1, 2002 through April 30, 2006; and the

---

intraday return behavior at the Istanbul Stock Exchange using a very limited sample period from 1996 through 1998. Here, the sample period is much longer from 1998 to the middle of 2010. The proprietary data is not readily available and was provided by Borsa Istanbul and covered the range mentioned. The extensive data period cover most of the policy changes in the microstructure of the Turkish Stock Exchange. Therefore, most of the results, conclusions, and comparisons presented in the chapter are representative of emerging country stock markets. The only exception if the introduction of the closing time call auction system. The implications of this policy change can be investigated as a future research project as more data become available.

recent sub-sample from May 1, 2006 to July 1, 2010. The early and recent sub-sample periods are investigated for pattern changes.

There have been numerous changes at the BIST over the years in terms of trading hours, the mechanism of trading, and the opening and closing call auction procedures. Investigation of the early and recent samples addresses the impact of these changes on accentuated volatility.

For each trading day of the week, accentuated volatility during the stock market opening in the morning, during the closing of the stock market before the lunch break, during the stock market opening after the lunch break, and during the closing of the stock market at the end of the trading day are explored statistically. The differences in the volatilities of different intraday periods are presented with point estimates, statistical tests, and graphical plots below. Therefore, the day-of-the-week effect from the intraday volatility perspective and from the risk management perspective are presented and analyzed in the chapter.

Results and Discussion

Table 1 presents the results about the day-of-the-week anomaly analysis. The daily return is measured either using log returns or using the difference between final and beginning stock prices normalized by the beginning stock price. Monday and Tuesday returns are negative and lowest of all the other days. In some measurements, both days' returns are significantly negative. As the week progresses, the returns get more positive, resulting with the highest positive returns on Friday. These results are mainly based on trading day returns. If total returns — including the accumulated changes overnight — are considered and incorporated into price formation; in other words, if consider close-to-close daily returns, as in Panel B, are considered, we first see that the average returns are more positive. This indicates that during the trading day, the markets are more pessimistic about economic news, business announcements, and political events. But the overnight period and the price formation phase before the opening of the stock

Table 1: Daily Returns.

Retlog	N	Mean	Std Dev	Minimum	Maximum	DF	t-Value	Pr > |t|
Panel A. Trading day								
Monday	621	−0.0051	0.0289	−0.1422	0.1061	620	−4.37	<.0001
Tuesday	625	−0.0028	0.0254	−0.1030	0.1280	624	−2.74	0.0064
Wednesday	623	−0.0021	0.0277	−0.1946	0.1282	622	−1.92	0.0551
Thursday	623	−0.0007	0.0273	−0.1432	0.1164	622	−0.67	0.5031
Friday	615	0.0004	0.0247	−0.1031	0.1694	614	0.39	0.6947
Ret	N	Mean	Std Dev	Minimum	Maximum	DF	t-Value	Pr > |t|
Monday	621	−0.0046	0.0287	−0.1325	0.1119	620	−4.03	<.0001
Tuesday	625	−0.0025	0.0255	−0.0979	0.1366	624	−2.41	0.0162
Wednesday	623	−0.0017	0.0274	−0.1768	0.1367	622	−1.6	0.1111
Thursday	623	−0.0004	0.0272	−0.1334	0.1235	622	−0.33	0.7405
Friday	615	0.0007	0.0249	−0.0979	0.1845	614	0.69	0.488
Retlog	N	Mean	Std Dev	Minimum	Maximum	DF	t-Value	Pr > |t|
Panel B. Trading day + overnight [close to close]								
Monday	620	−0.0025	0.0313	−0.1528	0.1284	619	−1.98	0.0482
Tuesday	625	−0.0004	0.0265	−0.0985	0.1503	624	−0.37	0.7102
Wednesday	623	0.0011	0.0302	−0.1924	0.2616	622	0.93	0.3535
Thursday	623	0.0027	0.0294	−0.1369	0.1165	622	2.31	0.0214
Friday	615	0.0035	0.0267	−0.1221	0.1676	614	3.26	0.0012
Ret	N	Mean	Std Dev	Minimum	Maximum	DF	t-Value	Pr > |t|
Monday	620	−0.0020	0.0312	−0.1417	0.1370	619	−1.59	0.112
Tuesday	625	−0.00004	0.0267	−0.0938	0.1621	624	−0.04	0.9689
Wednesday	623	0.0016	0.0305	−0.1750	0.2990	622	1.29	0.1964

Table 1: (*Continued*)

Ret	N	Mean	Std Dev	Minimum	Maximum	DF	t-Value	Pr > $\|t\|$
Thursday	623	0.0031	0.0294	−0.1279	0.1236	622	2.67	0.0078
Friday	615	0.0039	0.0270	−0.1150	0.1825	614	3.55	0.0004

Daily arithmetic average returns are reported for using log differences and using ratios. Panel A reports returns for the trading day. Panel B reports returns that includes overnight changes and before market prices determinations — therefore, from close-to-close of the day.

market contribute positively to the overall average daily return for each day. The ranking of the close-to-close daily average returns are still consistent with the previous result. The week starts with lowest returns and ends up with highest returns. But the negative returns on Monday are not significantly negative. On the other hand, near the end of the trading week, especially on Friday, the returns are significantly positive. These conclusions are consistent with recent studies using stochastic dominance techniques, such as that of Basdas (2011).

Table 2 and Figure 1 explore the core questions of the chapter.[3] Does intraday volatility vary from one trading day to another? Are there any discernable patterns in intraday volatility characteristics? We consistently observe that during the morning trading session, the volatility exhibits a "Smirk" according to the six different volatility measures. The opening five-minute interval generates the highest volatility for every measure for every trading day. The volatility subsides near the middle of the morning trading session, and stays at low levels until the noon break. Thus, the pattern is similar to that of a "smirk." The afternoon trading session starts with high volatilities, but these are not as high as those of the morning opening. Nevertheless, the second highest volatility period is this afternoon session five-minute opening period for each

3. The standard deviation based on log returns are virtually the same as that of regular returns and therefore is not included in the graph.

Table 2: Five-Minute Intraday Volatilities for Each Trading Day of Top 30 BIST Stocks.

Five-Minute Intervals	*N*	abs	log	ret	nabs	maxmin	nmaxmin
Monday							
1st 5 minutes	616	195.30	116.88	116.56	88.27	205.79	90.80
Mid-morning 5 minutes	618	51.88	30.83	30.76	23.53	68.73	26.93
Last 5 minutes before lunch	620	51.44	28.58	28.57	20.25	72.80	23.81
1st 5 minutes after lunch	619	102.90	49.81	49.73	38.53	117.50	41.19
Mid-afternoon 5 minutes	618	55.36	26.90	26.90	18.47	70.85	23.31
Last 5 minutes before close	619	72.23	34.49	34.51	22.85	98.08	25.32
Tuesday							
1st 5 minutes	621	158.37	92.37	93.03	70.14	169.32	76.49
Mid-morning 5 minutes	624	63.80	41.72	42.83	35.50	70.44	22.88
Last 5 minutes before lunch	622	53.27	29.15	29.13	21.16	76.30	24.06
1st 5 minutes after lunch	622	81.68	54.52	54.54	43.58	98.02	45.50
Mid-afternoon 5 minutes	623	63.37	31.09	31.07	22.20	80.78	25.69
Last 5 minutes before close	622	68.22	34.42	34.46	23.13	93.96	26.44

Table 2: (*Continued*)

Five-Minute Intervals	*N*	abs	log	ret	nabs	maxmin	nmaxmin
Wednesday							
1st 5 minutes	621	176.90	104.57	103.12	83.35	191.31	83.57
Mid-morning 5 minutes	619	50.51	28.13	28.12	20.16	71.39	25.49
Last 5 minutes before lunch	619	51.20	28.53	28.53	19.56	71.48	23.69
1st 5 minutes after lunch	612	111.23	58.04	58.08	46.57	118.25	48.99
Mid-afternoon 5 minutes	614	66.92	35.21	35.10	27.79	93.95	27.33
Last 5 minutes before close	614	81.47	33.28	33.32	22.83	107.58	25.06
Thursday							
1st 5 minutes	620	191.85	99.87	99.70	74.86	201.98	76.38
Mid-morning 5 minutes	618	55.60	28.96	28.93	20.22	73.67	24.55
Last 5 minutes before lunch	619	47.47	29.46	29.44	20.56	70.69	23.71
1st 5 minutes after lunch	617	123.48	60.53	60.14	49.68	133.07	52.59
Mid-afternoon 5 minutes	617	77.32	32.73	32.72	24.13	96.44	27.44
Last 5 minutes before close	617	80.34	37.30	37.33	25.81	100.07	26.51

Friday							
1st 5 minutes	613	180.75	91.06	90.91	65.52	186.18	69.71
Mid-morning 5 minutes	614	54.75	26.61	26.61	18.07	73.59	22.77
Last 5 minutes before lunch	614	52.84	30.54	30.59	22.46	71.06	24.67
1st 5 minutes after lunch	612	103.18	53.04	52.85	42.89	114.75	44.14
Mid-afternoon 5 minutes	613	100.30	34.13	34.14	25.78	117.39	27.52
Last 5 minutes before close	612	80.84	34.04	34.10	23.84	105.56	26.64

N is the number of observations; abs is the standard deviation of absolute values of the final and beginning price differences for the period; log is the standard deviation of the log returns expressed in basis points; ret is the standard deviation of the returns expressed in basis points; nabs is the standard deviation of the absolute value of end of period and beginning of period price difference normalized by the final price expressed in basis points; maxmin is the standard deviation of the difference between maximum and minimum values of the trading period; and nmaxmin is the standard deviation of the difference between maximum and minimum values of the trading period divided by the average of the final and beginning prices of the trading period expressed in basis points.

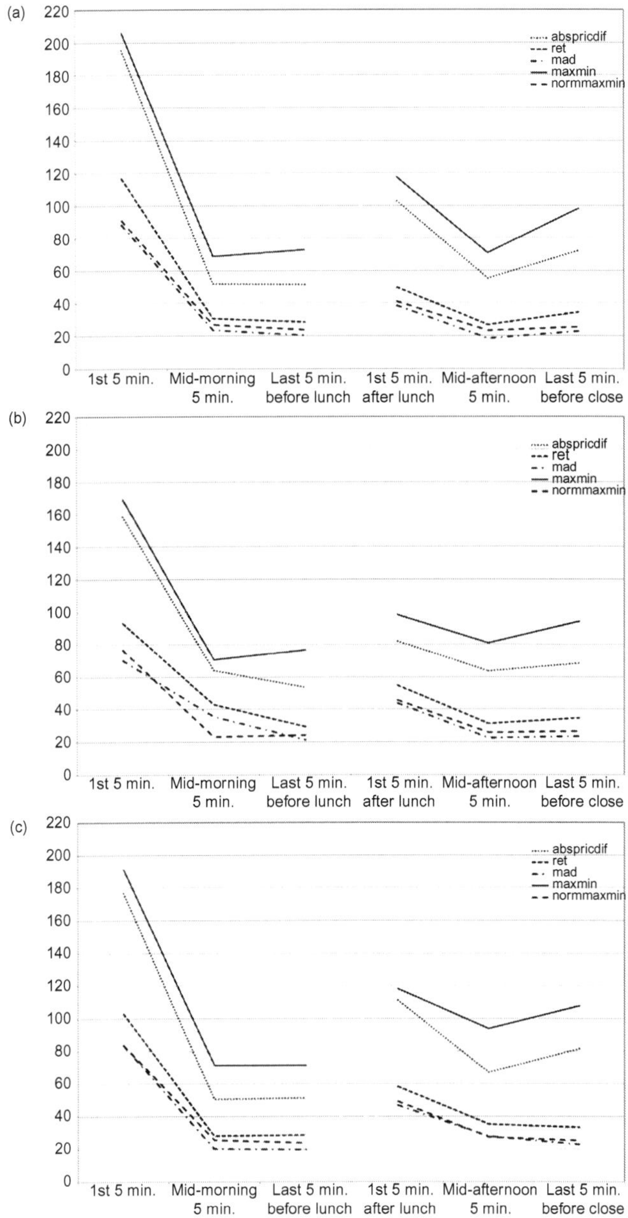

Figure 1: Istanbul Stock Exchange Top 30 Stocks Intraday Volatility. (a) Monday, (b) Tuesday, (c) Wednesday, (d) Thursday, (e) Friday. *Note*: The graph presents Five-minute trading period intraday volatilities for each trading day the top 30 stocks at the BIST exchange.

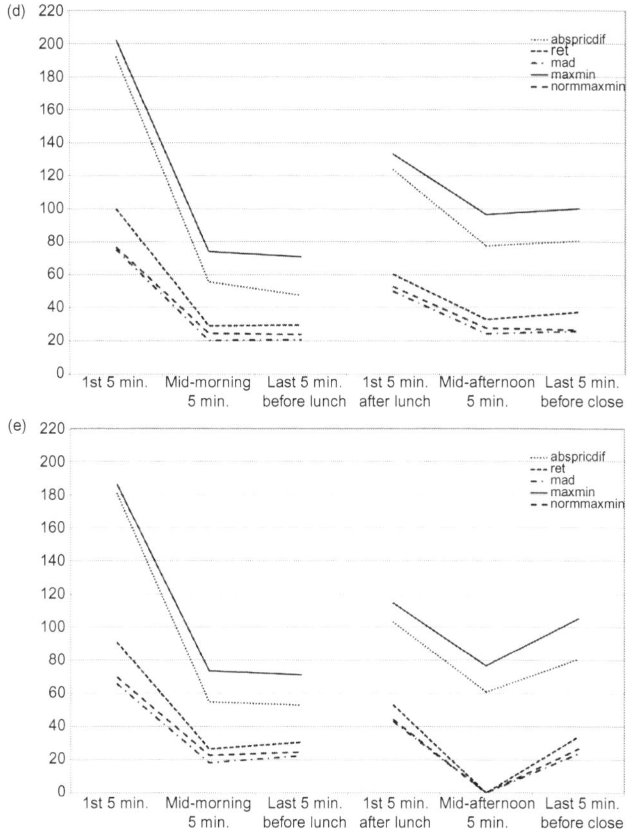

Figure 1: (*Continued*)

and every trading day. In the course of the trading session in the afternoon, the volatility measures get lower. However, there is an increase in volatility for the majority of the measures right before the stock market closes for the day. This increase right before the stock market close is the third highest five-minute volatility period of the trading day. This overall average volatility pattern for the afternoon trading session ends up to be a "Smile."

Table 3 and Figure 2 are about the comparison of volatility values and patterns from one trading day to the next. The focus of the analysis is on the important five-minute opening period in the morning session, where volatility is highest on average for every

Table 3: First Five-Minute Volatility for Every Trading Day.

Five-Minute Intervals	N	abs	log	ret	nabs	maxmin	nmaxmin
Monday	616	195.30	116.88	116.56	88.27	205.79	90.80
Tuesday	621	158.37	92.37	93.03	70.14	169.32	76.49
Wednesday	621	176.90	104.57	103.12	83.35	191.31	83.57
Thursday	620	191.85	99.87	99.70	74.86	201.98	76.38
Friday	613	180.75	91.06	90.91	65.52	186.18	69.71

N is the number of observations. Volatility measures are the same as in Table 2. Morning session opening five-minute average volatilities are reported for each trading day.

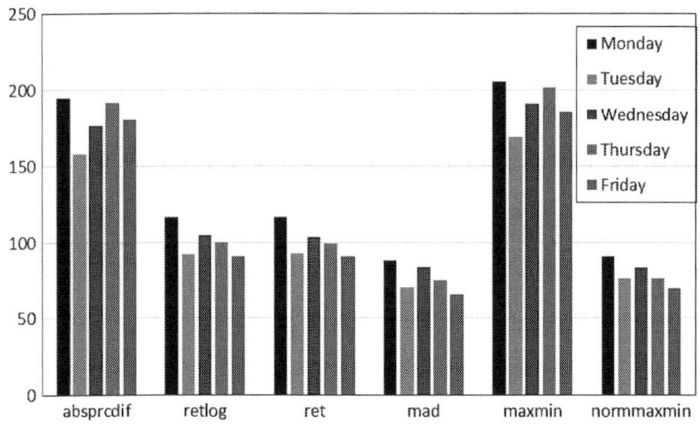

Figure 2: Highest Intraday Volatility (in the Opening Five-Minute Period). *Note*: The graph presents the opening five-minute trading period volatility values for each trading day of the week. The daily volatility values for each measure are clustered together in the figure.

measure and for every trading day. Table 3 clearly demonstrates that Monday morning volatility is highest compared to the morning opening volatilities of the other days. In fact, Monday morning opening five-minute volatility is highest compared to any other five-minute period volatility during the entire week. Figure 2 also clearly demonstrates that the five-minute opening period volatility of Monday morning is higher than any other five-minute volatility during the trading week according to every volatility measure.

While the point estimates of the volatility measures and the graphical representations in Figure 2 clearly show accentuated volatility for the Monday morning opening session, the statistical significance of these accentuated volatility values must be investigated. Table 4 presents the results of F-tests and p-values which compare Monday morning five-minute opening period volatilities to the corresponding volatilities of the other trading days. One can clearly see that Monday volatilities are statistically higher than the volatilities of the other trading days. Statistical difference is not

Table 4: Five-Minute Volatility Significance Tests: f-Values and p-Values.

Monday versus	Tuesday 5 min	Wednesday 5 min	Thursday 5 min	Friday 5 min
abs	1.52	1.22	1.04	1.17
	0.00	0.01	0.66	0.06
log	1.60	1.25	1.37	1.65
	0.00	0.01	0.00	0.00
ret	1.57	1.28	1.37	1.64
	0.00	0.00	0.00	0.00
nabs	1.58	1.12	1.39	1.82
	0.00	0.15	0.00	0.00
maxmin	1.48	1.16	1.04	1.22
	0.00	0.07	0.64	0.01
nmaxmin	1.41	1.18	1.41	1.70
	0.00	0.04	0.00	0.01

The table reports F-test values and p-values of variance equivalence tests of the volatilities of the Monday first period after market open in the morning versus the opening five-minute intervals of the other trading days of the week. The first row is the F-values and the second row includes the p-values. Volatility measures are the same as in Table 2. The shaded area implies that accentuated volatility is not seen; in other words, Monday morning volatility is not statistically higher than the opening five-minute volatility of the particular trading day.

detected for only a couple of measurements. But these shaded insignificant volatility pairs in Table 4 do not exhibit any consistency whatsoever.

The availability of the long time series used in the analyses allows us to split the data into Early and Recent samples and helps us examine whether accentuated volatility characteristics have evolved over time. Studies for the developed stock exchanges have shown the dynamic ecology of the stock markets. The lack of "definitive" evidence of accentuated volatility right before the daily close of the Istanbul Stock Exchange (volatility increases in the final five minutes before the close of the stock market; but overall, it is ranked behind the volatility of the morning open and the volatility of the afternoon open) may be due to the differences and changes in the structure and operation of the exchange during the sample period. Therefore, the entire sampling period is split into two parts: the "Early" sample from January 5, 1998 to March 31, 2004; and the "Recent" sample from April 1, 2004 to July 1, 2010. Table 5 reports the results of this investigation. The first clear conclusion from the table is that the intraday volatility has increased dramatically in the "Recent" period. Therefore, accentuated volatility has become an important concern for the Turkish Stock Exchange in recent years. This accentuated volatility in the "Recent" period is seen each and every trading day.

It is also observed that the Monday opening period dominance of heightened volatility diminishes a little bit in recent years. Accentuated volatility is seen across the board. Thursday and Friday volatilities seem to have increased, especially in the mornings when the market opens.

Evidence reported about the differences in volatility intraday, as well as during certain days of the week indicates the necessity of incorporating these stylized facts while developing risk reduction strategies. Risk exposure of international portfolios can be managed by taking into account of the periods of heightened volatility. These uncertain periods add to the overall risk of the investment portfolio. Executing trades outside of these highly volatile periods would be helpful to avoid unnecessary risk.

Table 5: Early versus Recent Period Volatilities.

	abs	log	ret	nabs	minmax	nmaxmin
A. Early						
Monday	145.94	152.26	151.93	106.43	154.79	106.34
	37.89	36.42	36.40	24.68	48.94	26.45
	60.69	63.60	63.52	46.99	72.74	47.65
	38.43	42.18	42.20	26.19	52.46	25.51
Tuesday	118.25	117.14	118.20	87.53	129.79	93.88
	41.59	37.60	37.56	26.50	49.07	27.55
	60.86	72.03	72.05	55.94	70.20	55.31
	42.59	42.10	42.15	27.53	57.83	27.32
Wednesday	110.38	133.38	131.19	105.46	121.44	102.29
	33.82	36.76	36.76	23.07	47.19	24.73
	62.75	72.59	72.51	56.01	70.60	57.46
	38.83	39.20	39.25	25.73	52.35	25.97
Thursday	128.50	123.23	122.86	90.82	141.02	91.08
	34.77	38.42	38.38	24.80	44.23	26.05
	77.22	74.00	73.41	60.26	90.70	63.27
	40.28	44.06	44.09	29.41	52.42	26.62
Friday	94.04	107.06	106.79	74.34	102.93	79.39
	37.43	40.05	40.11	27.61	48.06	27.30
	66.21	69.07	68.78	55.42	76.33	54.71
	41.55	38.56	38.63	26.10	53.65	25.57
B. Recent						
Monday	227.23	65.68	65.38	47.63	224.19	45.24
	57.52	17.93	17.94	11.49	72.47	11.06
	126.60	30.84	30.76	22.91	129.57	21.06
	85.55	24.90	24.93	16.53	96.97	14.85
Tuesday	176.99	58.86	58.88	40.90	171.12	38.64
	58.02	17.42	17.42	11.08	75.91	10.77
	92.24	28.24	28.26	19.48	96.05	16.70
	78.43	24.31	24.32	14.89	90.50	13.50

Table 5: (*Continued*)

B. Recent						
Wednesday	209.48	64.71	64.52	45.90	212.37	44.28
	59.85	17.25	17.26	11.19	73.17	10.82
	137.68	38.92	39.17	31.04	129.92	28.10
	99.26	26.17	26.22	17.98	110.71	16.00
Thursday	221.20	69.67	69.82	49.11	214.08	46.74
	53.77	16.49	16.51	10.48	71.28	9.88
	147.63	43.12	43.05	34.00	139.14	31.51
	96.55	28.68	28.69	19.50	100.17	16.25
Friday	217.68	72.01	72.04	52.32	203.79	48.78
	61.03	16.88	16.88	11.20	71.32	10.36
	122.28	30.35	30.31	21.54	120.83	18.45
	98.69	27.69	27.73	19.53	110.80	18.49

The table reports five-minute trading period intraday volatilities for the top 30 stocks at the Borsa Istanbul Stock Exchange. Panel A is for the early sub-sample from January 5, 1998 to April 1, 2004. Panel B is for the recent sub-sample from April 1, 2004 to July 1, 2010. The volatility measures are the same as those in Table 2.

The patterns exhibited by the accentuated volatility indicate an L-shaped "Smirk" in the morning and a similar L-shaped "Smirk" in the afternoon during the "Early" sample period. On the other hand, only the afternoon session tends to depict the volatility smile in the "Recent, sample period. Thus, increased volatility in the final five minutes before the daily close of the stock market is only seen in recent years at the Istanbul Stock Exchange.

For the robustness of the results and conclusions of the "Early" and "Recent" sample periods, the entire sample period is also split into three parts. The Earliest and the most Recent periods of this three-way split are re-examined. The results of the volatility measurements for these new sub-samples are reported in Table 6. The original conclusions from Table 5 are confirmed and supported with these new results.

The investigation has focused on volatilities obtained from price changes and returns using the end and beginning of the

Table 6: Robustness: Early (1/3) versus Recent (1/3) Volatilities.

	abs	log	ret	nabs	minmax	nmaxmin
A. Early						
Monday	128.81	153.75	154.08	103.45	146.46	103.55
	42.07	40.65	40.62	26.80	55.84	24.94
	68.88	73.83	73.74	53.33	83.81	51.41
	42.19	46.25	46.27	28.44	60.73	22.03
Tuesday	119.02	120.96	121.28	86.62	136.69	92.18
	47.31	41.79	41.74	28.89	55.94	26.44
	68.31	83.55	83.60	63.73	80.36	59.78
	44.78	44.24	44.30	28.85	65.58	24.37
Wednesday	116.22	149.92	147.07	118.49	132.66	111.77
	37.10	40.64	40.65	24.78	52.98	22.58
	69.18	83.71	83.60	62.68	79.65	62.20
	41.38	43.38	43.43	27.97	59.00	23.37
Thursday	137.83	139.80	139.23	100.91	156.06	99.59
	36.65	43.11	43.07	27.24	48.12	25.16
	88.09	86.52	85.77	67.92	105.80	69.84
	41.40	46.69	46.70	29.73	59.27	23.18
Friday	97.03	119.74	119.46	81.95	110.75	85.06
	40.84	45.95	46.03	29.68	54.97	25.82
	77.61	82.28	81.90	64.78	89.30	60.76
	42.83	40.26	40.31	26.39	60.26	21.76
B. Recent						
Monday	232.73	61.79	61.40	46.94	221.97	44.48
	59.64	17.77	17.77	10.67	71.25	10.78
	143.65	33.93	33.81	25.77	142.70	24.24
	89.31	25.60	25.62	17.04	91.63	15.66
Tuesday	169.52	53.32	53.18	38.05	159.91	36.14
	60.05	17.28	17.29	10.81	75.57	11.26
	103.01	29.63	29.65	20.97	98.90	18.62
	83.44	24.52	24.53	14.87	83.71	13.57

Table 6: (*Continued*)

B. Recent						
Wednesday	182.31	53.81	53.58	38.87	176.37	37.20
	64.94	17.36	17.37	11.07	73.41	10.96
	144.18	41.30	41.70	32.78	132.77	30.52
	111.09	27.05	27.11	19.21	112.15	17.41
Thursday	219.04	64.83	64.94	47.36	206.89	45.78
	57.09	16.30	16.31	10.34	71.39	10.04
	149.53	40.78	40.65	31.28	133.90	28.14
	108.75	31.04	31.06	22.09	100.51	18.40
Friday	226.22	67.30	67.45	50.32	202.66	46.32
	65.36	17.33	17.33	11.22	71.92	10.64
	138.68	33.82	33.78	23.85	131.15	20.48
	109.69	30.87	30.92	21.64	110.31	20.46

The table reports five-minute trading period intraday volatilities for the top 30 stocks at the Borsa Istanbul Stock Exchange. Panel A is for the early sub-sample from January 5, 1998 to March 1, 2002. Panel B is for the recent sub-sample from May 1, 2006 to July 1, 2010. The volatility measures are the same as those in Table 2.

five-minute intervals thus far. Another way to obtain volatility measures is by exploring tick-by-tick price changes during each five-minute interval and by using these tick changes to calculate volatility values. These alternative volatility measurements based on tick-by-tick changes are reported in Table 7. The four alternative volatility measures reported in the table confirm the early conclusions. Monday morning opening five-minute period exhibits the highest volatility. The second highest volatility is seen during the afternoon opening five-minute period, and third highest is seen in the final five-minute period before the close of the stock market for every trading day. These volatility measures also depict the same "Smirk" pattern in the morning trading session and the "Smile" pattern in the afternoon trading session for each and every trading day.

Thus far, five-minute intervals have been used for the accentuated intraday volatility investigation. For further robustness,

Table 7: Five-Minute Tick Return Intraday Volatilities.

	Day of Week	N	absprcdif	retlog	ret	nabs
1st five minutes	Monday	616	195.30	116.88	116.56	88.27
	Tuesday	621	158.37	92.37	93.03	70.14
	Wednesday	621	176.90	104.57	103.12	83.35
	Thursday	620	191.85	99.87	99.70	74.86
	Friday	613	180.75	91.06	90.91	65.52
Last five minutes before lunch	Monday	620	51.44	28.58	28.57	20.25
	Tuesday	622	53.27	29.15	29.13	21.16
	Wednesday	619	51.20	28.53	28.53	19.56
	Thursday	619	47.47	29.46	29.44	20.56
	Friday	614	52.84	30.54	30.59	22.46
First five minutes after lunch	Monday	619	102.90	49.81	49.73	38.53
	Tuesday	622	81.68	54.52	54.54	43.58
	Wednesday	612	111.23	58.04	58.08	46.57
	Thursday	617	123.48	60.53	60.14	49.68
	Friday	612	103.18	53.04	52.85	42.89
Last five minutes before day's close	Monday	619	72.23	34.49	34.51	22.85
	Tuesday	622	68.22	34.42	34.46	23.13
	Wednesday	614	81.47	33.28	33.32	22.83
	Thursday	617	80.34	37.30	37.33	25.81
	Friday	612	80.84	34.04	34.10	23.84

N is the number of observations; abs is the standard deviation of absolute values of the tick price differences during the period; log is the standard deviation of the log returns of tick-by-tick price movements expressed in basis points; ret is the standard deviation of the tick-by-tick price returns expressed in basis points; nabs is the standard deviation of the absolute value of tick-by-tick price differences normalized by the end tick price expressed in basis points.

15-minute intervals are considered next. The volatility results based on these longer periods are reported in Table 8. The volatility values based on these 15-minute intervals reveal that the Monday morning opening 15-minute period again has the highest volatility for the entire trading week. The "Smirk" volatility

Table 8: Fifteen-Minute Intraday Volatilities for Each Trading Day of the BIST Top 30 Stocks.

	Day of Week	N	absprcdif	retlog	ret	mad	maxmin	normmaxmin
First 15 minutes	Monday	618	204.25	133.35	133.10	98.07	240.83	104.77
	Tuesday	621	165.47	109.02	109.82	78.84	202.05	90.35
	Wednesday	621	192.65	125.19	123.87	95.16	229.37	101.02
	Thursday	620	195.68	119.63	119.79	86.25	244.39	113.32
	Friday	613	187.88	105.97	106.41	74.58	225.43	90.43
Last 15 minutes before lunch	Monday	620	68.83	42.14	42.12	30.56	98.36	35.99
	Tuesday	623	84.47	45.02	44.94	32.56	113.26	36.58
	Wednesday	620	76.00	42.65	42.64	30.81	103.33	35.27
	Thursday	619	73.33	43.67	43.60	30.93	104.19	38.85
	Friday	614	76.64	40.44	40.50	28.49	102.96	34.51
First 15 minutes after lunch	Monday	619	151.58	73.61	73.38	55.54	178.67	65.31
	Tuesday	622	130.76	82.57	83.05	61.31	152.13	72.99
	Wednesday	613	144.38	82.04	82.18	60.61	178.57	71.38
	Thursday	617	174.57	86.37	85.90	67.62	196.93	78.39
	Friday	612	151.78	76.37	76.00	57.79	173.25	65.47
Last 15 minutes before close	Monday	619	112.18	50.71	50.64	34.84	142.85	37.59
	Tuesday	622	102.82	51.90	51.95	36.33	134.35	40.68
	Wednesday	614	124.00	52.61	52.58	36.15	157.86	40.51
	Thursday	617	118.06	53.60	53.57	37.28	152.31	40.80
	Friday	612	122.19	49.91	49.97	33.46	157.16	37.45

N is the number of observations; Volatility measures are the same as in Table 2. Morning session opening 15-minute average volatilities are reported for each trading day.

pattern in the morning session is followed by the "Smile" volatility pattern in the afternoon session for every trading day, as before. Volatility values are not that much different from each other for the rest of the trading day based on the 15-minute interval measurements. Monday's overall high volatility is concentrated on the opening quarter hour. Overall, the previous results and conclusions hold according to this alternative volatility design.

Conclusion

This chapter investigates intraday volatility in the context of the day-of-the-week effect at the emerging Borsa Istanbul Stock Exchange. The chapter provides strong evidence of heightened volatility when the stock market opens in the morning trading session, and when the market reopens in the afternoon session. The highest volatility of the trading week is seen on the Monday morning opening session. Volatility measures computed using either the first five minutes or the first 15 minutes of the Monday morning both confirm this conclusion. There is also evidence of increased volatility in recent years, right before the closure of the stock market for the day. Numerous intraday volatility measurements support these findings.

The accentuated volatility of Monday mornings is a natural consequence of the accumulation of information over the weekend. Traders, market participants, and market makers have great difficulty in fully understanding and interpreting this accumulated information when the stock market opens. This confusion and the chaotic trading atmosphere leads to wild price fluctuations and also to the highest intraday volatility of the week Monday mornings. Furthermore, morning volatility is accentuated for each of the other trading days of the week. Information accumulated overnight takes time to be understood. This leads to noise trading and high volatility in the mornings.

We see accentuated volatility when the market reopens in the afternoon as well. Even though the noon break is not long, U.S. markets are about to open during the two-hour noon break in Istanbul Stock Exchange. Information arriving from international markets impacts trading behavior and generates accentuated volatility — even though the levels may not be as high as those in the morning. The globalization of financial markets and reduced friction across borders have contributed to these patterns. International economic and political events do have an impact on the local financial markets of an emerging country with an open economy as seen in Borsa Istanbul.

Finally, some evidence of heightened volatility is also seen before the market closes for the day. The reason for this may be the pressure that market makers and brokers might be having while trying to close out open positions, execute clients' orders, and rebalance investment portfolios. This frantic desire to complete the open trades and clear the order books leads to accentuated volatility before the market closes for the day.

Heightened volatility is an indication of uncertain periods where prices fluctuate significantly. Risk management and hedging strategies should be aware of the results and conclusions of this chapter and take them into account by adjusting trading activity around these highly volatile periods. Taking accentuated volatility patterns into account and avoiding these periods would help in reducing the unnecessary risk exposure and would help with the performance of the investment portfolios.

Accentuated volatility is an evidence of market inefficiency. In recent years, volatility has increased in the final five minutes (and also in the final 15 minutes) before the stock market closes for the trading day. This implies increased inefficiency in recent years at Borsa Istanbul Stock Exchange. The globalization of financial markets in general, and the Turkish economy in particular, have steered the Istanbul Stock Exchange to become more susceptible to changes, events, and news happening around the world. The Exchange regulators have recently implemented a closing auction system in March 2012. The increase in closing period volatility might be harnessed with the implementation of the closing auction system. The full impact of this policy change is an empirical issue for further research in the future.

Turkish economy and the Turkish Stock Exchange are good representatives of emerging country financial systems. Risk increases substantially during the 15 minutes when Borsa Istanbul opens and closes. Monday mornings are especially notable. Risk management implications are (1) Institutional investors, mutual funds, insurance, and investment companies should avoid these highly volatile periods in order to reduce unnecessary risk exposure. (2) Arbitrageurs, speculators, investors with superior information, and risk takers should prefer to trade and take investment positions during these highly volatile periods.

Exchange regulators and policy makers prefer efficient markets; hence low volatility. Globalization of markets, opening of economies have increased information and capital flow across borders. These desirable trends also encompass high volatility. Policy implications are (1) Placing auction systems after the market close, as well as before the market open would be one way to reduce volatility and calm down frantic traders. (2) Fast dissemination of information to market participants, interpretation of the information by competent and knowledgeable international finance professionals and sharing through wired and televised finance news agencies would also help reduce intraday volatility. (3) Execution of trades in a fast and fair manner through improved technology, better regulation, and effective monitoring of markets and trades by policy makers.

Acknowledgments

I am thankful for the helpful comments and suggestions by Huseyin Erkan, David Louton, Efser Mersin, Robert Schwartz, Gregory Sipress, Ben Steil, Bruce Weber, Steve Wunsch, and seminar participants at Bryant University and at the EBES 2015 Istanbul Conference.

References

Agrawal, A., & Tandon, K. (1994). Anomalies or illusions? Evidence from stock markets in eighteen countries. *Journal of International Money and Finance*, *13*, 83–106.

Al-Jafari, M. K. (2012). An empirical investigation of the day-of- the-week effect on stock returns and volatility: Evidence from muscat securities market. *International Journal of Economics and Finance, 4,* 141–149.

Amihud, Y., & Mendelson, H. (1987). Trading mechanisms and stock returns: An empirical investigation. *The Journal of Finance, 42,* 533–553.

Balaban, E. (1995). Day of the week effects: New evidence from an emerging stock market. *Applied Economic Letters, 2,* 139–143.

Barclay, M. J., Hendershott, T., & Jones, C. M. (2008). Order consolidation, price efficiency, and extreme liquidity shocks. *The Journal of Financial and Quantitative Analysis, 43,* 93–121.

Basdas, U. (2011). The day-of-the-week effect for Istanbul stock exchange: a stochastic dominance approach. *Journal of Applied Finance & Banking, 1,* 223–238.

Belhaj, F., Abaoub, E., & Mahjoubi, M. N. (2015). Number of transactions, trade size and the volume-volatility relationship: An interday and intraday analysis on the tunisian stock market. *International Business Research, 8,* 135–152.

Bildik, R. (1998). Day-of-the-week effects in overnight interest rates: Evidence from Turkish money markets. *The ISE Review, 2,* 49–78.

Bildik, R. (2001). Intra-day seasonalities on stock returns: Evidence from the Turkish stock market. *Emerging Markets Review, 2,* 387–417.

Camilleri, S. J., & Green, C. J. (2009). The impact of the suspension of opening and closing call auctions: Evidence from the national stock exchange of India. *International Journal of Banking, Accounting and Finance, 1,* 257–284.

Chang, R., Rhee, G., Stone, G., & Tang, N. (2008). How does the call market method affect price efficiency? Evidence from the singapore stock market. *Journal of Banking and Finance, 32,* 2205–2219.

Choe, H., & Shin, H. K. (1993). An analysis of interday and intraday return volatility evidence from the Korea stock exchange. *Pacific-Basin Finance Journal, 1,* 175–188.

Chukwuogor, N. (2006). Stock market returns analysis, day-of-the-week effect, volatility of returns: Evidence from European financial markets 1997–2004. *International Research Journal of Finance and Economics, 1,* 112–124.

Cinko, M., Avci, E., Aybars, A., & Oner, M. (2015). Analyzing the existence of the day of the week effect in selected developed country stock exchanges. *International Journal of Economics and Finance, 7,* 96–108.

Dubois, M., & Louvet, P. (1996). The day of the week effect: The international evidence. *Journal of Banking and Finance, 20,* 1463–1484.

Economides, N., & Schwartz, R. A. (1995). Electronic call market trading. *The Journal of Portfolio Management, 21,* 10–18.

French, K. R. (1980). Stock returns and the weekend effect. *Journal of Financial Economics, 8*, 55–69.
Hussain, S. M. (2009). *Intraday dynamics of international equity markets.* Ph.D. Thesis. Hanken School of Economics.
Inci, A. C. (2012). Accentuated intraday volatility in emerging markets: The Turkish stock exchange. *Journal of International Finance Studies, 12*, 37–52.
Jawadi, F., Louhichi, W., & Cheffou, A. I. (2015). Intraday bidirectional volatility spillover across international stock markets: Does the global financial crisis matter? *Applied Economics, 47*, 3633–3650.
Keim, D. B., & Stambaugh, F. (1984). A further investigation of weekend effects in stock returns. *The Journal of Finance, 39*, 819–840.
Kohers, T., & Kohers, G. (1995). The impact of firm size differences on the day-of-the-week effect: A comparison of major stock exchanges. *Applied Financial Economics, 5*, 151–160.
Madhavan, A., Richardson, M., & Roomans, M. (1997). Why do security prices change? A transaction-level analysis of NYSE stocks. *Review of Financial Studies, 10*, 1035–1064.
Narayan, P. K., Mishra, S., & Narayan, S. (2014). Spread determinants and the day-of-the-week effect. *Quarterly Review of Economics and Finance, 54*, 51–60.
Nguyen, V., & Phengpis, C. (2009). An analysis of the opening mechanisms of exchange traded fund markets. *The Quarterly Review of Economics and Finance, 49*, 562–577.
Nishimura, Y., Tsutsui, Y., & Hirayama, K. (2015). Intraday return and volatility spillover mechanism from Chinese to Japanese stock market. *Journal of the Japanese and International Economies, 35*, 23–42.
Oguzsoy, C. B., & Guven, S. (2003). Stock returns and the day-of-the-week effect in Istanbul stock exchange. *Applied Economics, 35*, 959–971.
Ozenbas, D. (2006). Pattern of short-term volatility accentuation within the trading day: An investigation of the US and European equity markets. *International Business & Economics Research Journal, 5*, 11–24.
Ozenbas, D., Pagano, M. S., & Schwartz, R. A. (2010). Accentuated intraday stock price volatility: What is the cause? *The Journal of Portfolio Management, 36*, 45–55.
Solnik, B., & Bousquet, L. (1990). Day-of-the-week effect on the Paris bourse. *Journal of Banking and Finance, 14*, 461–468.
Stoll, H. (2000). Friction. *The Journal of Finance, 55*, 1479–1515.
Stoll, H. R., & Whaley, R. (1990). Stock market structure and volatility. *Review of Financial Studies, 3*, 37–71.

Tian, G., & Guo, M. (2007). Interday and intraday volatility: Additional evidence from the Shanghai stock exchange. *Review of Quantitative Finance and Accounting, 28,* 287–306.
Tissaoui, K. (2012). The intraday pattern of trading activity, return volatility and liquidity: Evidence from the emerging Tunisian stock exchange. *International Journal of Economics and Finance, 4,* 156–176.
Yalcin, Y., & Yucel, E. M. (2006). The day-of-the-week effect on stock-market volatility and return: Evidence from emerging markets. *Czech Journal of Economics and Finance, 56,* 258–277.

17

Dynamic Linkages between Hedge Funds and Traditional Financial Assets: Evidence from Emerging Markets

Roland Füss, Dieter G. Kaiser and Felix Schindler

Abstract

This chapter aims to determine whether diversification benefits accrue from adding emerging market hedge funds (EMHFs) to an emerging market bond/equity portfolio, and subsequently whether the type of exposure hedge funds provide is justified by their fees. We use multivariate cointegration analysis to show that the advantages of adding hedge funds to balanced portfolios are limited for the three regions of Asia, Eastern Europe, and Latin America, as well as for the entire global emerging market universe. In summary, we find that emerging market hedge funds are generally redundant for diversifying long-only emerging market investment portfolios with long-term investment horizons. This result also holds when we extend our sample by the global financial crisis in 2008 and 2009 and allow for structural breaks according to the Gregory-Hansen (1996) test. Hence, even during the global financial crisis in 2008 and 2009, when risk diversification was most needed, long-term comovements between hedge funds and traditional assets is, with the exception of the Eastern European region, not disrupted. Because EMHF returns are heavily influenced by the emerging market equity and bond markets, we conclude that the "alpha fees" charged by EMHFs may not always be appropriate for the three main regions under consideration. This also holds, however, to a lesser extent, for a global diversification among hedge funds and traditional assets in emerging markets.

Keywords: Asset allocation; emerging market hedge funds; financial crisis; hedge fund indices; investment strategies; vector error correction model (VECM)

Introduction

The last two decades have seen tremendous growth in hedge funds and emerging market investments, driven largely by international investors. Even in the wake of the 2008–2009 subprime and financial crises, both investment vehicles experienced only a moderate drop in prices with relatively short recovery periods.

The empirical literature generally argues that these alternative investment strategies offer diversification benefits, both within conventional stock and bond portfolios and as stand-alone investments. Hedge funds are usually characterized by investment strategies such as global macro, market neutral, long-short, and short selling (Capocci & Hübner, 2004; Fung & Hsieh, 1999). Emerging markets constitute capital markets in developing countries, that is, countries or regions in the early stages of economic development that are expected to grow rapidly and "emerge" from their less-developed states (Bekaert & Harvey, 2002). Hence, these markets offer investors significant growth opportunities, but may also feature high volatility due to their corresponding political and economic risks (De Santis & Imrohoroglu, 1997).

Financial development in emerging markets is a reflection of the pace of economic expansion (Kuczynski, 1994). Hedge funds in developed markets typically try to either (1) take advantage of temporarily incorrect valuations between different financial instruments or (2) capture alternative risk premia. Emerging market hedge funds (EMHFs) primarily follow a buy-and-hold strategy, as efficient hedging strategies cannot always be applied in emerging markets because of the lack of derivative instruments and the difficulty in building short positions.[1] Another problem emerging market investors may face is low market liquidity, which is also a byproduct of short-selling constraints and capital restrictions (Bris, Goetzmann, & Zhu, 2007).[2] Therefore, EMHFs should exhibit a high beta relative to traditional emerging market investments.

This chapter investigates whether hedge funds differ significantly from traditional emerging market investments. We follow Fung and Hsieh's (2000) line of reasoning, that there is little difference between emerging market mutual funds and EMHFs. More precisely, we explore the long- and short-term relationships

1. In recent years, EMHFs have been able to expand their trading strategies beyond long-biased long-short equity investing. For example, Abugri and Dutta (2009) note that EMHFs have begun to follow distressed, arbitrage, quantitative, and activist strategies. Chen (2011) shows empirically that, by June 2006, 62.7 percent of the EMHFs in the Lipper TASS database were already using derivatives on equities, fixed income, currencies, or commodities. However, this number is rather low relative to other hedge fund strategies. According to Odonnat and Rahmouni (2006), between 20 and 50 percent of EMHFs use leverage.

2. Due to their low market liquidity and the fact that they tend to invest in these markets (albeit alongside institutional investors, mutual funds, and the proprietary trading desks of investment banks), hedge funds are often blamed for emerging market financial crises. In this context, Fung and Hsieh (2000) analyze hedge fund exposure during several major market events. They find that hedge funds are sometimes in a position to exert substantial market impact. Examples are the ERM Crisis in 1992 and the European bond market rally in 1993 and subsequent decline in 1994. At other times, they have little impact, for example, during the stock market crash in 1987, the Mexican peso crisis in 1994, and the Asian currency crisis in 1997.

between hedge funds and traditional financial assets for emerging markets during the pre-crisis period by using multivariate cointegration analysis and vector error correction models (VECM). Additionally, we apply the test developed by Gregory and Hansen (1996) to control for long-term diversification benefits among these investment vehicles during the 2008–2009 financial crisis, that is, under the assumption of a significant structural break. In light of Kotkatvuori-Örnberg, Nikkinen, and Peltomäki (2011), who find that only EMHFs with a regional focus can outperform traditional equity benchmarks, we not only analyze emerging markets as a whole but also specific peer group indices for the Asian, Latin American, and Eastern European regions.

We define EMHFs as funds that invest predominantly in the capital markets of developing countries, irrespective of whether they are located in these regions which is in line the finding by Park (2015) that the alpha is not significantly positive across manager locations even if the proportion of funds with a significantly positive alpha is higher when the fund is not located in the United States but in an emerging market. According to HFR (2011), 423 hedge funds can be classified as EMHFs, with assets of U.S. $114.27 billion under management at year-end 2010. EMHFs can have either a regional focus (e.g., Asia, Latin America, or Eastern Europe), or invest across countries/regions, thus following a broader or more global theme.[3]

3. For the January 2000–December 2003 time period, Teo (2009) demonstrates empirically that EMHFs with a physical presence in the investment region outperform those without one by 5.28 percent per year. See also Orhan and Tekten (2006), who analyze 313 EMHFs and conclude that hedge funds in developing countries achieve two times the average monthly return of global hedge funds. Furthermore, Koh, Koh, and Teo (2003) study 417 Asian hedge funds for the January 1999–March 2003 time period, and empirically show a positive relationship between higher returns and higher assets under management. Moreover, Eling and Faust (2010) show that some EMHFs generate significantly positive alphas, while most emerging market mutual funds fail to outperform their benchmarks. Aragon and Nanda (2012) analyze changes in the risk profile of hedge funds that are related to the fund's incentive contract (consisting of high watermarks, asset flows, and incentive fees). They find significant results for reduced risk-shifting in response to mid-year EMHF performance. Kotkatvuori-Örnberg et al. (2011) provide empirical evidence that EMHFs do

Strömqvist (2007) shows that EMHFs tend to perform better during equity bull markets, but that they are not rewarded with capital inflows for good performance. The incentives for EMHF managers are therefore relatively small compared to other hedge fund strategies, and may even cause excessive risk-taking or prevent experienced money managers from entering the EMHF space. Hence, it seems likely that EMHF managers are running portfolios that are fairly similar to traditional equity portfolios. From this it follows that these managers should only charge "beta fees."[4]

Several studies have investigated the long- and short-term dynamics between hedge funds and financial assets, such as stocks and bonds, for developed countries (Füss & Herrmann, 2005; Füss & Kaiser, 2007; Füss, Kaiser, Rehkugler, & Butina, 2006; Gregoriou & Rouah, 2001).[5] This chapter contributes to the existing literature by focusing on the long-term relationships and short-term dynamics between EMHFs and traditional financial

---

not generally exhibit market timing ability. The findings by Cao and Jayasuriya (2011) mainly support the results by Kotkatvuori-Örnberg et al. (2011) for hedge funds in Eastern Europe and Latin America, in particular, where they do not find positive risk-adjusted excess returns. Aitken, Kilic, and Reid (2015) find also little evidence for hedge funds to time the performance of emerging markets for the period from 1996 to 2013. However, they find evidence of timing ability during the 2008–2009 global financial crises but not during the bull market in the years before the global financial crises. Considering the life cycle of hedge funds, Aggarwal and Jorion (2010) show that there is outperformance during the first two to three years which deteriorates by each additional year of the fund.

4. Interestingly, Abugri and Dutta (2009) show empirically that EMHFs exhibit similar performance patterns to hedge funds that focus on developed markets. Ding, Shawky, and Tian (2009) demonstrate that the emerging market hedge fund strategies have among the smallest assets under management compared to other hedge fund strategies, and that smaller EMHFs underperformed larger EMHFs during the 1994–1997 and 1998–2001 periods but not during the 2002–2005 period. However, the Sharpe ratios achieved by larger EMHFs were higher than those of smaller EMHFs across all three periods.

5. Füss and Herrmann (2005) find no evidence of common stochastic trends among hedge fund strategies and the stock market indices of France, Germany, Japan, North America, or the United Kingdom. Gregoriou and Rouah (2001) examine common stochastic trends among the ten largest hedge funds and equity market indices and find evidence of cointegration for only two. Füss et al. (2006) test for the presence of cointegration among hedge funds and traditional as well as alternative financial assets using multivariate cointegration analysis. Their empirical results suggest that risk-averse investors with long-term investment horizons do not increase risk by including hedge funds in their portfolios.

assets.[6] The analysis of a cointegration relationship between EMHFs and emerging market equities and bonds is especially important because of the similarities between the instruments and strategies used. If there is a strong cointegration relationship between traditional and alternative emerging market instruments, then it would not be justifiable for EMHFs to charge "alpha fees," consisting on average of a 2 percent management fee and a 20 percent performance fee for long-term beta exposure. Moreover, investors would be unable to increase the diversification benefits of their traditional emerging market exposure by allocating additional amounts to EMHFs.

Our empirical results suggest that EMHFs are significantly cointegrated with regional stock and bond markets. Long-term stochastic trends exist among all investment vehicles and regions, with the strongest feedback coming from Latin America. Moreover, even when we include the 2008–2009 financial crisis in our sample and control for structural breaks, hedge funds showed long-term comovements with traditional assets, that is, also during times when diversification was most needed by risk-averse investors. However, in Eastern Europe, we find that hedge funds seem to be disconnected from stocks over both the short and long term. This finding holds during the 2008–2009 financial crisis, where hedge funds showed no comovements with either stock or bond markets in Eastern Europe.

The remainder of the chapter is structured as follows. The next section presents the data we use in our study. We describe the construction procedure and the desmoothing practice of the

6. There is also a strand of the literature that focuses on stock market links between emerging markets and their regional areas. For example, Pan, Liu, and Roth (1999) use a multivariate cointegration approach and find no evidence of common stochastic trends in the equity markets of Australia, Hong Kong, Japan, Malaysia, or Singapore. Garret and Spyrou (1999) investigate the existence of common trends in Latin American and Asian-Pacific equity markets. They note some common trends. But they do not rule out the possibility of long-term diversification benefits because not all countries are part of the region's common trend. For more studies on the interdependence of emerging markets, especially in Asia and Latin America, see Hung and Cheung (1995), Chaudhuri (1997), and Chen, Firth, and Rui (2002).

EMHF indices, and present the investments vehicles' descriptive statistics. The section "Methodology and Empirical Results" introduces the Johansen cointegration test as well as the Vector Error Correction Model (VECM) and discusses the empirical findings. In the subsequent section "Impact of the 2008–2009 Financial Crisis," we apply the Gregory-Hansen (1996) test to control for whether the 2008–2009 financial crisis affects our main results on diversification benefits. The last section summarizes and offers concluding remarks.

Constructing Emerging Market Hedge Fund Indices

To create our indices, we begin with a sample of 2526 EMHFs derived from two hedge fund databases: the *Lipper TASS Hedge Fund* database and the *Eurekahedge Emerging Markets Hedge Fund* database.[7] In order to cleanse out dataset, we exclude duplicate funds, funds of funds, funds with incomplete track records, funds that reported gross rather than net returns, and funds with share classes not denominated in U.S. dollars. After the cleansing procedure, our EMHF universe consisted of 2024 hedge funds.

Next, we control for backfill bias. To do this, we used only EMHF returns after they began reporting to the database (as per Ibbotson, Chen, & Zhu, 2011) for funds where the databases carried this information. For funds where that date was missing, we excluded the first twelve months of observations (following Fung & Hsieh, 2000).

Our final sample consists of 1,817 EMHFs, of which 1060 are alive and 757 have dissolved. Finally, we use the information available in the strategy description of each fund in order to create

7. According to Hakamada, Takahashi, and Yamamoto (2007) and Koh et al. (2003), the databases most commonly used in empirical hedge fund studies such as Lipper TASS, HFR, and CISDM are overly U.S.-centric, and the overlap to the Eurekahedge database is minimal. To avoid this sample bias, the authors suggest using the Eurekahedge database, which operates from Singapore, for empirical EMHF studies.

regional peer groups.[8] This process results in (1) an emerging market composite index containing all EMHFs and (2) region-specific indices for Asia, Eastern Europe, and Latin America.

The data series range from January 2000 through September 2010 in order to avoid structural breaks due to the Asian crisis and the turmoil in the aftermath of the LTCM fund collapse in August 1998.[9] In our first step, we explicitly do not incorporate time series beyond 2007, as EMHFs had net asset outflows in 2008 (U.S. \$7.78 billion), 2009 (U.S. \$8.56 billion), and 2010 (U.S. \$1.55 billion). Furthermore, total assets under management for EMHFs as of the end of 2010 were U.S. \$114.27 billion, still below the year-end 2007 figure (U.S. \$116.70 billion).

Given these dramatic outflows, we expect the attrition rate of EMHFs to be very high and to negatively impact our results. For example, Carpenter and Lynch (1999) show that fund attrition affects performance measures even when the sample includes all non-survivor returns. Eling and Faust (2010) and Abugri and Dutta (2009) also refrained from including data from the financial crisis period in order to avoid the impact of abnormal market volatility following the Lehman bankruptcy. However, we control for this fact by re-estimating our results for the entire sample period until September 2010. We can thus control for the effects of the 2008–2009 financial crisis by using the threshold cointegration approach, as described further in the section "Impact of the 2008–2009 Financial Crisis."

8. We constructed region-specific indices if the sample contained more than 100 funds dedicated to those regions; the Emerging Markets Composite Index also includes EMHFs that invest across various regions. Hence, the only emerging markets region that we were not able to create an index for is the Middle East and Africa.

9. We also applied the Quandt-Andrews unknown breakpoint test to the VECM residuals to check for structural breaks in the data series for 2000 to 2007 (see Table A1). For all regions and the emerging market universe, the test statistics confirm the null hypothesis of no significant structural breaks in our model specifications. Interestingly, cointegration tests with a structural break according to Gregory and Hansen (1996) for the entire period confirm our results, except for Eastern Europe, where no cointegration relationship is found under the assumption of breakpoints during the crisis year 2008.

As of September 2010, the composite strategy sample consisted of 1817 components, with 848 for Asia, 373 for Latin America, and 149 for Eastern Europe. The change in index value for each month represents the equally weighted median of the index components' monthly rate of return at that time. We use the median rather than the arithmetic or geometric mean because hedge fund returns exhibit negative skewness and positive excess kurtosis.

The other financial asset class indices are represented by the *S&P/International Finance Corporation Investable Indices* (S&P/IFCI) and the *J.P. Morgan Emerging Markets Bond Indices* (EMBI) for regional and composite emerging stock and bond markets, respectively. Investable indices only include shares that foreign investors are allowed to invest in, while global indices include all shares.

We use the *S&P/IFC Investable Indices* because some of the funds are located outside the countries they are investing in, and are thus subject to capital restrictions. However, the differences are minimal, as shown by the nearly perfect correlations between IFCG and IFCI index returns.[10] Note that original hedge fund time series are highly autocorrelated because of mark-to-market problems (Kat & Lu, 2002). This autocorrelation bias leads to a gross underestimation of the expected volatility of these types of hedge funds. To obtain a better impression of the true data-generating process of the return series, we use Geltner's (1991, 1993) "desmoothing" formula:

$$r_t = \frac{r_t^* - \alpha r_{t-1}^*}{1 - \alpha}, \tag{1}$$

where r_t and r_t^* are the true underlying but unobservable return and the observed return at time t, respectively. It seems plausible to set α equal to either the autocorrelation coefficient at lag 1, or to the coefficient of an AR(1) process. This adjustment is done so that

10. The correlation coefficients between the returns of the S&P/IFCI and the S&P/IFCG indices for the January 2000 to October 2008 period (when IFCG index covering ends) are Asia 0.98, Eastern Europe 0.98, Latin America 1.00, and Emerging Markets Composite 0.98.

the newly constructed series r_t has nearly the same mean as r_t^*, but with zero first-order autocorrelation (Geltner, 1991, 1993).

Figure 1 shows the monthly total return index levels denominated in U.S.$, with the base date, January 2000, normalized to 100 in log values. The graphs reveal that the financial time series has exhibited similarly increasing trends since the beginning of the 2000s. Hedge funds outperformed stock, but not bond, markets in developing countries until the U.S. subprime crisis emerged in 2006–2007. The only exception is Latin America, where hedge fund performance continued to dominate.

However, stock prices exceeded hedge fund values prior to the 2008 financial crisis, dropping substantially in the aftermath, with the largest losses occurring in Eastern Europe. This large decrease in stock prices may be what disconnects stocks from bonds and hedge funds. In contrast, bond prices showed only a slight decrease in response to the crisis. For Latin America, we note a sharp and steady increase of the hedge fund index; for Eastern Europe, the hedge fund index exhibits more volatility. Finally, we note that the unsmoothed hedge fund composite index suffered the largest losses in 2008, recovering only slightly through the end of our sample period.

Panel A of Table 1 gives the descriptive statistics for the (unsmoothed) hedge fund time series and for the regional stock and bond indices. The highest returns come from Eastern European stock market and hedge funds with an Eastern European investment focus, with annualized average continuously compounded returns of approximately 25 and 23 percent, respectively. In addition, on a risk-adjusted return basis, hedge funds with a regional Latin American focus significantly outperform the other hedge funds. While Eastern European investment vehicles exhibit the highest volatility, the risk-adjusted bond returns are higher than the risk-adjusted returns of the corresponding stock markets for all regions, except Latin America, for which they are close. The Asian and Eastern European bond markets exhibit the highest risk-adjusted returns among all traditional assets.

Almost all investment vehicles exhibit asymmetric return patterns with negative skewness and positive excess kurtosis.

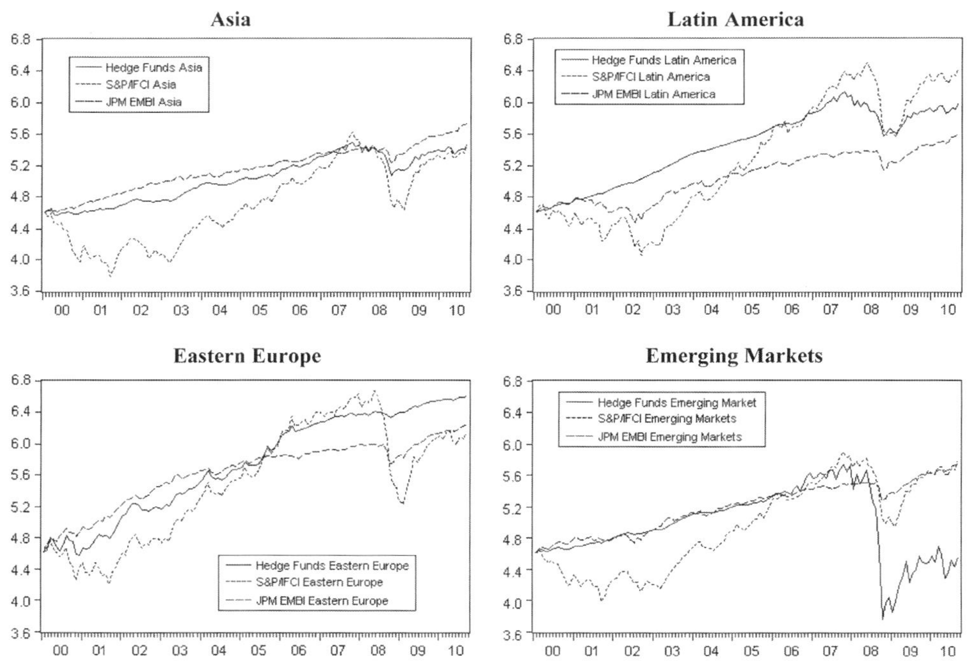

Figure 1: Evolution of Emerging Market Hedge Fund, Stock, and Bond Indices. *Notes*: This figure shows the (desmoothed) hedge fund, stock, and bond market indices in log values for the entire January 2000–September 2010 period. Beginning values are normalized to log(100) at January 2000. The hedge fund series are desmoothed due to the high autocorrelation which leads to underestimation of the volatility compared to the other investment vehicles. They are unsmoothed according to Geltner's (1991, 1993) formula in Eq. (1).

Table 1: Summary Statistics.

	Mean (in %)	Std. Dev. (in %)	Skewness	Kurtosis	J.B. Test
Panel A: Descriptive statistics					
HF Asia	0.89	2.06	−1.16	7.55	104.15***
HF Latin America	1.55	1.74	−1.17	12.99	421.20***
HF Eastern Europe	1.89	4.73	−0.30	4.42	9.46***
HF Emerging Markets composite	1.18	3.44	−0.16	8.56	123.95***
S&P/IFCI Asia	1.02	6.66	−0.31	3.18	1.69
S&P/IFCI Latin America	1.77	7.26	−0.69	3.41	8.18**
S&P/IFCI Eastern Europe	2.11	7.68	−0.34	2.50	2.86
S&P/IFCI Emerging Markets comp.	1.29	5.95	−0.61	2.91	6.06**
JPM EMBI Global Asia	0.83	1.44	−0.41	3.03	2.76
JPM EMBI Global Latin America	0.76	3.28	−0.39	4.38	10.07***
JPM EMBI Global Eastern Europe	1.45	2.90	0.25	3.80	3.61
JPM EMBI Global composite	0.90	2.47	−0.33	3.27	2.06

	S&P/IFCI				JPM EMBI Global			
Hedge Funds:	Asia	Latin America	Eastern Europe	Em.Ma. comp.	Asia	Latin America	Eastern Europe	Em.Ma. comp.
Panel B: Contemporaneous correlations between monthly returns								
Asia	**0.69**	0.60	0.53	0.71	**0.22**	0.29	0.31	0.33
Latin America	0.48	**0.48**	0.34	0.51	0.16	**0.27**	0.20	0.27
Eastern Europe	0.54	0.57	**0.80**	0.63	0.25	0.36	**0.59**	0.45
Em.Ma. comp.	0.41	0.37	0.43	**0.45**	0.19	0.21	0.19	**0.22**

Notes: Panel A shows performance calculations based on monthly continuously compounded total returns for the January 2000–December 2007 period, including 96 observations. Hedge fund data are unsmoothed according to Geltner's (1991, 1993) formula in Eq. (1). Panel B shows the Pearson's correlation coefficients between emerging markets hedge funds and traditional assets for the three regions and the global emerging market universe under consideration.

The bold values on the diagonals show the correlation coefficients between regional hedge fund returns and the corresponding stock and bond market returns. ***, **, and *denote significance at the 1 , 5, and 10 percent levels, respectively (rejection of the normal distribution according to the Jarque-Bera test).

They thus deviate from normality, as shown by the high Jarque-Bera test statistics. Hence, these results suggest that standard deviation is an incomplete measure of risk in a portfolio optimization context, and may lead to suboptimal asset allocation decisions.

Finding the optimal portfolio weights in a mean-variance analysis requires return correlations between assets to be stable over time. Because correlation analysis is valid only for stationary variables, researchers frequently take first differences to force stationarity. However, by doing that, valuable information about possible common price trends can be lost. Cointegration analysis on the prices underlying the return series obviates this problem.

Using conventional correlation analysis as an indicator of dependence among random variables is also problematic, however, as it only measures linear dependence, and hedge funds are typically non-linear functions of traditional markets (Lhabitant, 2002). EMHF portfolios tend to be less complex than their industrialized country counterparts, because trading strategies based on non-linear assets such as options and interest rate derivatives are less common in developing capital markets.[11]

Furthermore, the results of correlation analysis are only meaningful if the multivariate distribution is elliptic (Embrechts, McNeil, & Straumann, 1999, 2002; Kat, 2003). However, as mentioned earlier, most return series exhibit negative skewness and positive excess kurtosis, so the joint distribution is far from elliptic. As a result, the correlation does not exhaust the full interval [−1, +1], which leads to invalid findings of very low dependence, even though the variables are perfectly correlated. The cointegration approach is more suitable in this context because it works directly on asset prices instead of on returns.

Panel B of Table 1 shows the correlation matrix between the hedge fund time series and the stock and bond markets for the specified regions. Note that Asian hedge fund returns are more highly correlated with stock than bond returns, while Eastern

11. Normally, such portfolios exhibit both non-normality fluctuations of the underlying assets and non-linear functions in traditional assets.

European hedge funds exhibit high comovements with both markets. Furthermore, global EMHF returns are more highly correlated with stocks than bonds.

However, despite the aforementioned drawbacks, correlation and cointegration are related but distinct concepts. High correlation does not imply cointegration, and correlation is neither necessary nor sufficient for cointegration between assets. In fact, cointegrated time series can actually have low correlations.

Methodology and Empirical Results

Multivariate Cointegration Analysis

Before applying the Johansen cointegration methodology, we need to test whether the time series are integrated of the same order, or whether each series requires the same degree of differencing to achieve stationarity (Engle & Granger, 1987).

If the hedge fund and financial market index data exhibit a unit root, they are considered integrated of order 1, $I(1)$. If asset returns follow a random walk, temporary shocks to the returns will persist over time, and will not disappear or show evidence of mean reversion. Such behavior inevitably affects the timing of portfolio rebalancing (Gregoriou & Rouah, 2001).

The augmented Dickey-Fuller (ADF) tests (Dickey & Fuller, 1979, 1981; Said & Dickey, 1984) show strong evidence that all time series in levels are non-stationary; the only exceptions are the Eastern European regional hedge fund and bond market indices (at the 10 and 5 percent significance levels, respectively). However, when we use first differences, the null hypothesis of a unit root is rejected at the one percent level for all investment vehicles and regions.[12]

Note also that a constant term or drift parameter is present in all hedge fund, stock market, and bond market return series,

12. The ADF test results are not shown here, but are available from the authors upon request.

except for the S&P/IFCI Asia index. The constant term for the series reflects fluctuations around a mean. These may arise from overestimating returns due to any remaining liquidation bias, especially for the hedge fund indices. We conclude that all financial series are non-stationary in levels but stationary in returns.

We next examine the level of interdependence of the financial series. Cointegration exists when there is a mean reversion in the price spread between the regional EMHF indices and the traditional stock and bond asset categories. We test for the presence of common stochastic trends to evaluate whether hedge funds provide long-term diversification benefits for traditional emerging market portfolios. In the context of portfolio theory, this means that if the value of a fixed weight portfolio of assets with non-stationary prices is stationary, the assets will form a cointegrated set. The set of asset weights within such a portfolio is called the cointegrating vector. Cointegration implies that some long-term equilibrium relationship connects the time series, despite the fact that short-term departures from equilibrium may exist.

The Johansen methodology, a maximum likelihood estimation of a fully specified VECM, allows us to test for the presence of more than one cointegration vector. The n-dimensional cointegrated VAR(k) model in the vector equilibrium correction (VEC) form is as follows (Johansen, 1988, 1991, 1992; Johansen & Juselius, 1990):

$$\Delta X_t = \mu + \Gamma_1 \Delta X_{t-1} + \ldots + \Gamma_{k-1} \Delta X_{t-k+1} + \Pi X_{t-1} + \varepsilon_t, \qquad (2)$$

where μ is an $n \times 1$ vector of intercept terms, ΔX_t exhibits an $n \times 1$ vector of price changes in period t, Γ_i ($i = 1, \ldots k-1$) represents the $n \times n$ coefficient matrix of short-term dynamics, Π is the $n \times n$ long-term impact matrix, and ε_t is an $n \times 1$ *i.i.d.* Gaussian error vector (Maddala & Kim, 1998).

In a portfolio optimization context, cointegrated assets ($\Pi = \alpha\beta'$) imply that mean-variance analysis still applies, but with influences on the conditional moments, which generate a shift in the mean-variance frontier. Thus, the relevance of cointegration for asset allocation depends on the investment holding period, the portfolio rebalancing frequency, and investor risk appetite (Bossaerts, 1988; Lucas, 1997).

For strategic asset allocation with a static (no-rebalancing) long-term investment style, portfolio construction follows weights that correspond to cointegrating vectors in $\beta' X_{t-1}$. The lower long-term volatility of such portfolios makes them particularly attractive for highly risk-averse investors. On the other hand, portfolio managers using tactical asset allocation can anticipate temporary deviations from long-term equilibrium, and can effectively rebalance the portfolio using matrix α (Füss & Kaiser, 2007).

We can use two likelihood ratio test statistics, the trace statistic and the maximum eigen value test, to test for cointegration. The model we choose for these tests has no deterministic trend. But it does have a constant in the cointegration vectors, which agrees with the results of the unit root tests.

The order of the unrestricted VAR models is determined by the Akaike and the final prediction error (Lütkepohl, 1991). Both information criteria indicate a VAR model of order 1 for Asia and Latin America, order 2 for Eastern Europe, and order 3 for the emerging markets composite. Hence, the VECM involves $k-1 = 0$ terms in differences for the Asian and Latin American sample, 1 for the Eastern European sample, and 2 for the emerging market composite sample.

Table 2 reports the cointegration results for the four different regions. For Latin America, Eastern Europe, and the entire emerging market universe, the trace and maximum eigen value tests identify one cointegration vector at the one percent level. Note that, for Asia, trace statistics reject the null hypothesis of one cointegration vector at the one percent level, indicating two cointegration relationships. However, the maximum eigen value tests do not reject the null hypothesis of one cointegration vector at the one percent level. For the Eastern European sample and the entire emerging market universe, a second cointegration vector is found at the five percent level, but we fail to reject $r \leq 2$ at the five percent level. Hence, these results strongly suggest at least one cointegration vector for all regions and markets, but an inconclusive

Table 2: Johansen Cointegration Tests.

Test of Cointegration Rank							
Eigen value	H_0	λ-Trace	5% CV	1% CV	λ-Max	5% CV	1% CV
Panel A: Asia							
0.3406	$r = 0$	68.89**	34.91	41.07	39.56**	22.00	26.81
0.1665	$r \leq 1$	29.33**	19.96	24.60	17.31*	15.67	20.20
0.1189	$r \leq 2$	12.02*	9.24	12.97	12.02*	9.24	12.97
Residual analysis							
Test	LM(1)	LM(6)	LM(12)				
LM test with $\chi^2(9)$	25.846**	4.531	16.178				
p-value	0.002	0.873	0.063				
Panel B: Latin America							
0.4719	$r = 0$	80.31**	34.91	41.07	60.66**	22.00	26.81
0.1550	$r \leq 1$	19.65	19.96	24.60	16.00*	15.67	20.20
0.0377	$r \leq 2$	3.65	9.24	12.97	3.65	9.24	12.97

Residual analysis							
Test	LM(1)	LM(6)	LM(12)				
LM test with $\chi^2(9)$	8.639	8.903	12.580				
p-value	0.381	0.446	0.183				
Panel C: Eastern Europe							
0.3126	$r = 0$	58.11**	34.91	41.07	35.23**	22.00	26.81
0.1664	$r \leq 1$	22.89*	19.96	24.60	17.11*	15.67	20.20
0.0596	$r \leq 2$	5.78	9.24	12.97	5.78	9.24	12.97
Residual analysis							
Test	LM(1)	LM(6)	LM(12)				
LM test with $\chi^2(9)$	23.599*	6.142	11.451				
p-value	0.005	0.756	0.246				
Panel D: Emerging markets composite							
0.4258	$r = 0$	73.81**	34.91	41.07	51.59**	22.00	26.81
0.1780	$r \leq 1$	22.22*	19.96	24.60	18.23*	15.67	20.20
0.0420	$r \leq 2$	3.99	9.24	12.97	3.99	9.24	12.97

Table 2: (*Continued*)

Panel D: Emerging markets composite			
Residual analysis			
Test	LM(1)	LM(6)	LM(12)
LM test with $\chi^2(9)$	60.686**	9.480	12.092
p-value	0.000	0.394	0.088

Notes: The cointegration model is based on a VAR in first differences with no lag (Asia), no lag (Latin America), one lag (Eastern Europe), and two lags (emerging markets), all selected by the Akaike information criterion (AIC) and the final prediction error (FPE). The λ-trace and λ-max statistics are computed under the assumption of no deterministic trend, but with a constant in the cointegrating vector. Critical values for the Johansen test come from Table 1 in Osterwald-Lenum (1992).

** and *denote that the null hypothesis of no cointegration can be rejected at the 1 and 5 percent significance levels, respectively.

result on more than one cointegration vector among the variables.[13]

When the cointegrating vectors are normalized on the first component hedge fund index, we obtain the following long-term relationships:

$$\begin{aligned}
\text{HF Asia} &= 1.22 + 0.23\ \text{Stocks} + 0.64\ \text{Bonds}\\
\text{HF Latin America} &= -6.26 + 0.16\ \text{Stocks} + 1.83\ \text{Bonds}\\
\text{HF Eastern Europe} &= -2.94 + 0.54\ \text{Stocks} + 0.92\ \text{Bonds}\\
\text{HF Emerging Markets} &= 3.35 + 0.07\ \text{Stocks} - 0.23\ \text{Bonds}
\end{aligned}$$

This implies that hedge funds tend to have a positive long-term relationship with the stock and bond markets in all regions. For the overall emerging market universe, we observe a positive long-term relationship with the stock market, and a negative one with the bond market. The large absolute coefficient for the Latin American bond market reflects the higher prominence of the fixed-income market in this region. In general, however, the coefficients of the normalized cointegrating vector indicate that hedge funds mainly share a common trend with the fixed-income market. In summary, the information drawn from these long-term relationships can be useful in developing forecasts of hedge fund values and thus portfolio strategies for traditional assets by explicitly taking hedge funds into account.

The existence of one or more common stochastic trend(s) does not imply that all assets are a driving force, however. It is possible that some hedge fund and conventional asset series do not enter the common stochastic trend. Furthermore, as we discussed earlier, the relevance of diversification benefits depends on the speed of adjustment toward the common trend (Kasa, 1992). Thus, if returns do not react significantly to common trends, their existence will only slightly affect diversification benefits. We test these

13. The residual analysis based on LM test statistics suggests there is no autocorrelation left in the residuals, except for lower lags in the Asian and composite series. The residuals thus support the adequacy of the cointegration analysis models.

interactions between the investment vehicles by analyzing short- and long-term Granger causalities within the VECM framework.

VEC Granger Causality

In a VECM, short-term causal effects are indicated by changes in other differenced explanatory variables, that is, the lagged dynamic terms in Eq. (2) are statistically significant from zero. The long-term relationship is implied by the level terms of the cointegration relationship, that is, the lagged error correction term (ECT). Thus, in the cointegration model, the proposition "X_k does not Granger-cause X_l" in the long term is equivalent to $\alpha_{kl} = 0$. X_l is said to be weakly exogenous for vector β, that is, X_l does not react to equilibrium errors. In addition, in the short term, this proposition is equivalent to $\Gamma_{kl}(L) = 0$, where (L) is the lag operator. In this context, the VECM is useful for detecting short- and long-term Granger causality (Granger, 1969).

To uncover the price relationships among the three investment vehicles within the different regions, we formulate the VECM as follows:

$$
\begin{aligned}
\Delta E_t &= \mu_1 + \gamma_1 Z_{t-1} + \sum_{i=1}^{p} \theta_{1i} \Delta \mathrm{HF}_{t-i} + \sum_{i=1}^{p} \delta_{1i} \Delta \mathrm{Stocks}_{t-i} \\
&\quad + \sum_{i=1}^{p} \lambda_{1i} \Delta \mathrm{Bonds}_{t-i} + \varepsilon_{1t}, \\
\Delta \mathrm{Stocks}_t &= \mu_2 + \gamma_2 Z_{t-1} + \sum_{i=1}^{p} \theta_{2i} \Delta \mathrm{HF}_{t-i} + \sum_{i=1}^{p} \delta_{2i} \Delta \mathrm{Stocks}_{t-i} \\
&\quad + \sum_{i=1}^{p} \lambda_{2i} \Delta \mathrm{Bonds}_{t-i} + \varepsilon_{2t}, \\
\Delta \mathrm{Bonds}_t &= \mu_3 + \gamma_3 Z_{t-1} + \sum_{i=1}^{p} \theta_{3i} \Delta \mathrm{HF}_{t-i} + \sum_{i=1}^{p} \delta_{3i} \Delta \mathrm{Stocks}_{t-i} \\
&\quad + \sum_{i=1}^{p} \lambda_{3i} \Delta \mathrm{Bonds}_{t-i} + \varepsilon_{3t},
\end{aligned}
\tag{3}
$$

where Z_{t-1} is the ECT derived from the cointegrating vector, θ, δ, and λ are the parameters to be estimated, and ε_t are assumed to be stationary random processes with a mean of zero and constant variance.

For each equation in the VECM, we use pairwise short-term Granger causality to test whether endogenous variables can be treated as exogenous by the joint significance of the coefficients of each of the other lagged endogenous variables in that equation. We thus test H_0: $\theta_{11} = \theta_{12} = \ldots = \theta_{1p} = 0$, and the δ_1s and λ_1s using χ^2 (Wald) statistics. The statistic for block exogeneity is the χ^2 statistic for joint significance of all other lagged endogenous variables in the equation. Long-term causality is implied by significant lagged ECT(s), that is, $\gamma \neq 0$.

Table 3 gives the Granger causality and block exogeneity test results. For the Asian region, only the ECT *t*-test is statistically significant at the 1 percent level. This suggests that prices of all investment vehicles can be considered exogenous to the system in the short term, because the price series do not Granger-cause each other. However, bond and stock markets, as well as hedge funds and stock markets, Granger-cause hedge funds and bond prices, respectively, in the long term.

One possible reason for the Asian results is that Asian stock markets are highly developed in terms of liquidity and market capitalization. This may make it difficult to detect any long-term causality with hedge funds. Asian bond markets, on the other hand, are more likely to be underdeveloped, and so may exhibit a dependence on Asian hedge funds.

For the Latin American region, none of the short-term fluctuations in the price series seem to explain movements in the other market segment. However, over the long term, the lagged ECT is highly significant in the equation for hedge funds and for the other assets at a 5 percent significance level. Economically speaking, this implies that, when deviations from the equilibrium cointegrating relationship occur (as measured by the ECT), hedge fund prices and (to a lesser extent) bonds and stocks will adjust to eliminate this disequilibrium.

We also note the presence of long-term bi-directional Granger causality among all investment vehicles. This result again confirms our previous findings from the Johansen test and suggests that

Table 3: VEC Pairwise Granger Causality/Block Exogeneity Wald Tests.

	χ^2 — *Statistics* (for Excluded Variables)				
Dependent Variable	ΔHedge funds	ΔStocks	ΔBonds	Block exogeneity	*t-Statistics* ECT_{t-1}
Asia					
ΔHedge Funds	–	0.94	1.70	2.53	4.31***
ΔStocks	0.04	–	0.86	0.86	1.16
ΔBonds	0.06	0.02	–	0.25	5.66***
Latin America					
ΔHedge Funds	–	1.58	0.00	2.49	8.64***
ΔStocks	0.00	–	0.92	0.93	2.36**
ΔBonds	0.11	0.22	–	0.23	2.53**
Eastern Europe					
ΔHedge Funds	–	1.18	5.38**	8.70**	0.94
ΔStocks	2.09	–	0.08	2.10	1.01
ΔBonds	16.88***	11.81***	–	17.43***	5.20***

Emerging markets composite					
ΔHedge Funds	–	9.82***	1.54	15.93***	7.60***
ΔStocks	6.98**	–	2.23	8.82*	2.72***
ΔBonds	0.76	1.70	–	3.71	3.42***

Notes: All variables except the lagged error correction terms (ECT_{t-1}) are in first difference denoted by Δ. We obtain the ECT from the first cointegrating vector (i.e., the highest eigen value) of the Johansen cointegration test, which is normalized on the hedge fund index. The LM test was used to check the residuals of the VEC models for autocorrelation. The residuals show no evidence of autocorrelation at lag 12 for all equations. The lag orders of the VECM have a constant corresponding to the earlier cointegration models, except for Asia and Latin America, where one lag is included to allow for short-term influences. The lag orders of the VECM have a constant corresponding to the earlier cointegration models. The reported statistic is the block exogeneity Wald-type causality test from the estimated VECM. Block exogeneity refers to the exclusion of all the endogenous variables from the VECM other than the lags of the dependent variable. The figures in the final column are the *t*-statistics that test for the null hypothesis that the lagged ECT is statistically insignificant for each equation.

***, **, and *indicate that the null hypothesis ("no Granger causality") can be rejected at the 1, 5, and 10 percent significance levels, respectively.

Latin American hedge funds are influenced by stock and bond markets, because both are well-developed in the main countries of this region. Furthermore, since the number of hedge funds and their assets under management are decidedly lower in this region, they will tend to be affected more strongly by traditional markets than by Asian hedge funds.

For the Eastern European region, the results appear quite different, that is, the price series are strongly endogenous. Over the short term, fluctuations in stock prices impact the bond market, while we note the existence of bi-directional causality between hedge funds and bonds. The last column in Table 3 shows the long-term relationships among the different investment vehicles, for which only the bond index series acts to eliminate price disequilibrium. Moreover, we can conclude that hedge funds and stocks Granger-cause bonds over both the short and long term.

It is obvious that the diversification benefits from adding EMHFs to an emerging markets bond/equity portfolio are considerably fewer for Asia and Latin America than for Eastern Europe. For the entire emerging market universe, the results of the VEC Granger causality tests suggest that primarily long-term causality channels exist. Both stocks and bonds impact hedge funds to some extent, that is, hedge fund prices can be predicted by other asset categories. In other words, we see that hedge funds and bonds adjust endogenously in different proportions to bring the system back to long-term equilibrium.

Furthermore, hedge funds and bonds exhibit a feedback relationship over the long term in all regions, except Eastern Europe. We also note a uni-directional causality from stocks to bonds in Asia and Eastern Europe, that is, bond market effects are caused by stock market effects. Thus, stocks again lead hedge funds and bonds.

Finally, Figure 2 qualitatively summarizes the findings of the Granger causality tests.

Variance Decompositions (VDC)

To obtain more insight into the structure of dynamic linkages, we examine the variance decompositions of the three investment

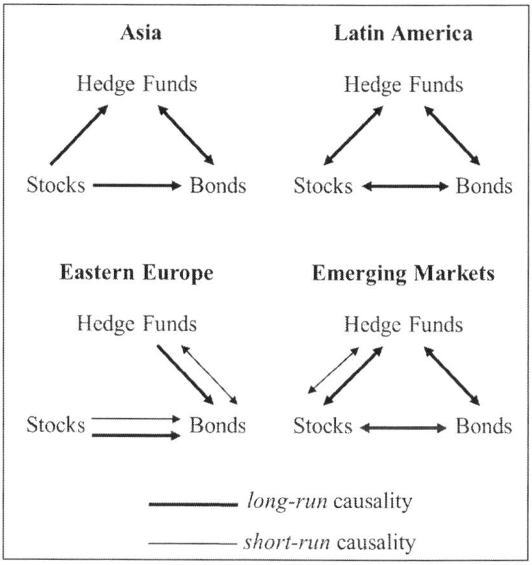

Figure 2: Short- and Long-Term Dynamics among Asset Categories. *Notes*: This figure shows the short- and long-run Granger causality among the three investment vehicles for the three regions and the global emerging market universe. The graphs qualitatively summarize the findings of the Granger causality tests shown in Table 3. The arrows indicate the direction (either uni- or bi-directional) as well as the significance level; thick and thin lines for one and five percent significance level, respectively.

vehicles. The VDC breaks down the variance of the forecast error for each index series into components that can be attributed to each endogenous investment class. This enables us to determine the relative importance of each investment vehicle in generating fluctuations in the others.

Table 4 reports the decomposition of the forecast error variances of each region at the one-, four-, six-, and twelve-month horizons. The order of variables in the VECM matches that of the normalized cointegrating vector. However, we find nearly the same results when the order is changed.

As Table 4 shows, hedge fund prices in Asia, Eastern Europe, and Latin America are relatively exogenous compared to the entire emerging market universe. They are more dependent on

Table 4: Variance Decomposition over 12 Months.

VDC of	Month	Percentage of Forecast Error Variance Explained by Innovation in:					
		ΔHedge F.	ΔStocks	ΔBonds	ΔHedge F.	ΔStocks	ΔBonds
		Asia			Latin America		
ΔHedge F.	1	100.00	0.00	0.00	100.00	0.00	0.00
	4	99.73	0.16	0.12	99.70	0.15	0.14
	6	99.28	0.42	0.31	99.23	0.39	0.38
	12	***96.57***	1.97	1.45	***96.54***	1.77	1.70
ΔStocks	1	49.79	50.21	0.00	24.10	75.90	0.00
	4	48.75	51.24	0.01	24.41	75.58	0.01
	6	48.07	51.91	0.02	24.61	75.36	0.03
	12	***46.06***	**53.85**	0.09	***25.22***	**74.64**	0.14
ΔBonds	1	4.46	0.06	95.48	6.45	36.10	57.45
	4	3.12	0.11	96.77	6.58	35.90	57.52
	6	2.44	0.35	97.21	6.67	35.77	57.57
	12	***1.18***	1.81	**97.01**	***6.93***	**35.35**	**57.71**

		Eastern Europe			Emerging Markets Composite		
ΔHedge F.	1	100.00	0.00	0.00	100.00	0.00	0.00
	4	96.77	1.62	1.61	83.66	15.52	0.82
	6	97.22	1.37	1.41	82.16	16.73	1.11
	12	***98.22***	0.73	1.04	***80.75***	**18.10**	1.61
ΔStocks	1	73.41	26.59	0.00	17.54	82.46	0.00
	4	64.58	35.33	0.09	10.33	89.20	0.47
	6	64.64	35.24	0.12	10.30	89.31	0.39
	12	***66.17***	**33.64**	0.20	***9.82***	**89.87**	0.30
ΔBonds	1	47.87	1.04	51.09	4.31	21.38	74.31
	4	35.81	10.27	53.92	2.34	16.91	80.75
	6	37.45	8.37	54.18	2.11	14.10	83.78
	12	***44.38***	5.42	**50.21**	***1.79***	**11.29**	**86.93**

Note: The Cholesky ordering is based on the normalized cointegration vector (i.e., hedge funds, stocks, and bonds). However, the results do not significantly change if we use the average from all orderings. The numbers in bold-italics in the first column of the values under "Asia", "Latin America" and "Eastern Europe", as well as the entire emerging market universe show the percentage of forecast error variance explained by innovations in hedge EMHF returns after a lag of 12 months. The remaining roman bold numbers highlight economically significant impacts, that is, when the proportion of explained forecast error variance for a lag of 12 months exceeds a threshold of approx. 10 percent.

themselves than on traditional stock and bond markets. In other words, neither a shock to the bond market nor a shock to the stock market tends to impact Asian or Latin American hedge fund prices in the short term, which is consistent with the previous Granger causality findings.

The VDC results also confirm the strong interconnection between European bonds and hedge funds, while Asian hedge funds are highly interrelated with the corresponding stock market. This is supported by Kotkatvuori-Örnberg et al. (2011), who report that Asian EMHFs, for example, invest predominantly in momentum stocks. Investments in those stocks take place when there is enough market liquidity to move in and out of positions quickly, a phenomenon that could be interpreted as positive feedback trading, and could explain the obvious relationship here. Furthermore, Koh et al. (2003) find a positive relationship between holding firm size and Asian hedge fund returns. In contrast, movements in the hedge fund index seem to explain approximately 66 percent and 46 percent (25 percent) of forecast error variance in the Eastern European and Asian (Latin American) stock markets, respectively. Interestingly, note that the proportion of forecast error variance that can be explained by innovations remains nearly unchanged as the time horizon increases, except for the impact of hedge funds on stocks and stocks on bonds for Eastern Europe and the emerging market universe.

For Eastern Europe, movements in hedge funds have a significant and stable impact on bond markets as the time horizon increases. Eastern European hedge funds become significantly interdependent with the stock market. This may be attributable to the Russian market's dominance, which makes it possible to hedge its market risk (through, e.g., shorting index futures). In general, the stock market is highly endogenous for the Asian and Eastern European regions, with 54 and 34 percent of stock market index variance, respectively.

For the emerging market universe, a large proportion of the hedge fund index variance is again due to shocks originating in their own series (81 percent), and, to a lesser extent, to the stock market (18 percent). Table 4 also shows that hedge funds in emerging markets are less influential in determining stock and bond prices. The results indicate that only a small fraction of stock market variance in emerging markets is attributable to hedge fund price movements, while stocks and bonds are highly exogenous.

Impact of the 2008–2009 Financial Crisis

To analyze whether the 2008–2009 financial crisis affects our main results on cointegration relationships, and therefore, on long-term diversification effects, we first test for regime shifts in our sample period. The Gregory-Hansen (1996) test differs from the Johansen test in that the former states the null of no cointegration under the assumption of structural breaks. We can identify regime shifts at various points in time of approximately 16–25 percent (for the 21st–32nd month of the sample period) and 79–85 percent (for the 102nd–110th month). These time periods correspond to the fall of 2001 (terror attacks), and to 2008 (the peak of the financial crisis). The results from Table 5 further show that we can reject the null for all regions except Eastern Europe.

Hence, under the assumption of structural breaks, we find cointegration relationships for Asia, Latin America, and the emerging market universe. The results confirm those of the Johansen test, that hedge funds provide limited diversification effects in the long term. But the result for the Eastern European region suggests that, if there is a structural break, we cannot assume that the cointegration relationship found by the Johansen test will hold. The acceptance of the null of no cointegration for the Eastern European region can be traced back to the disconnection between stocks and other investment vehicles since the beginning of the 2008–2009 financial crisis (see Figure 1). This is also confirmed by our VEC pairwise Granger causalities, which do not show a long-term relationship between stocks and hedge funds. In contrast, slumps in prices of investment vehicles in the other regions occur synchronously.

Table 5: Gregory-Hansen (1996) Test Results.

	Level			Trend			Regime		
	ADF Test	PP Z(*t*)	PP Z(*a*)	ADF Test	PP Z(*t*)	PP Z(*a*)	ADF Test	PP Z(*t*)	PP Z(*a*)
Asia:									
HF–Stocks–Bonds	–4.807**	–4.620	–36.899	–5.140*	–5.629**	–48.556	–4.726	–5.554**	–49.785
Date of structural break:	0.853 Lag 13	0.845	0.845	0.822 Lag 0	0.798	0.798	0.853 Lag 13	0.597	0.233
Latin America:									
HF–Stocks–Bonds	–3.703	–3.635	–22.479	–6.199***	–6.191***	–59.810**	–4.741	–4.760	–37.891
Date of structural break:	0.256 Lag 0	0.240	0.194	0.783 Lag 2	0.791	0.791	0.209 Lag 0	0.209	0.209
Eastern Europe:									
HF–Stocks–Bonds	–4.478	–4.137	–30.536	–5.258*	–4.344	–34.990	–5.201	–5.222	–45.230

Date of structural break:	0.752 Lag 5	0.535	0.791	0.760 Lag 10	0.163	0.163	0.822 Lag 0	0.822	0.822
Composite:									
HF–Stocks–Bonds	−6.644***	−9.006***	−100.99***	−6.279***	−8.810***	−98.112***	−7.137***	−9.051***	−101.25***
Date of structural break:	0.791 Lag 1	0.798	0.798	0.791 Lag 1	0.798	0.798	0.791 Lag 1	0.798	0.798

Notes: Three different model specifications are tested by the Gregory-Hansen (1996) test: A level shift model allows for changes in the intercept only (Level), a model which allows for a shift in level with trend (Trend), and the most general model specification which allows for changes in both the intercept and slope of the cointegration vector (Regime). The null hypothesis of non-stationarity of the residuals and no cointegration, respectively, is tested by the ADF test and the Phillips-Perron (PP) test. The numbers in the first row indicate the values of the corresponding test statistic. The numbers in the second row indicate the estimated date of the structural break as fraction of the analyzed time series in the case of a significant test statistic. The third row indicates the optimal lag length for the ADF test.

***, **, and *indicate significance at the 1, 5, and 10 percent levels, respectively.

Concluding Remarks

This chapter aims to analyze the dynamic linkages between hedge funds and traditional financial assets for the major emerging market regions and thus, whether diversification benefits accrue from adding emerging market hedge funds to emerging market portfolios consisting of stocks and bonds. Without such diversification benefits, one may question whether the "alpha fees" charged by emerging market hedge funds are justified.

To identify diversification benefits, we analyze short- and long-term relationships among the investment classes for emerging markets as a whole, as well as for the Asian, Latin American, and Eastern European regions. Our empirical results suggest that regional EMHFs in Asia, Latin America, and Eastern Europe tend to have positive long-term relationships with emerging market stock and bond markets. Therefore, EMHF returns are heavily influenced by the emerging market equity and bond markets, which leads to the conclusion that the "alpha fees" charged by EMHFs may not be appropriate. However, for global EMHFs, we find a positive long-term relationship with stock markets and a negative one with bond markets.

Short-term linkages among the three investment vehicles are most pronounced between hedge funds and bonds, stocks and bonds in Eastern Europe, and hedge funds and stocks in the emerging market universe. For Eastern Europe, we find a feedback relationship between hedge funds and bonds, and that stocks Granger-cause bonds. However, we find no connection between hedge funds and stocks. The opposite holds for the emerging market universe. Our results indicate a bi-directional relationship between hedge funds and stocks, but no short-run causality between hedge funds and bonds or between stocks and bonds. No short-run causality effects exist among the three investment vehicles in Asia or Latin America.

By extending our sample period to the 2008–2009 financial crisis and controlling for structural breaks in the time series, our previous results are confirmed. In particular, the results for the investment vehicles in Eastern Europe support the aforementioned finding of weak connections between these markets. Hence, returning to our initial question of whether hedge funds should be considered as somewhat redundant securities, we only find portfolio diversification benefits from long investments in hedge funds for Eastern Europe. This result held even during the crisis period, when diversification was most needed and often not available. However, for all other markets, our results for a large sample of different EMHFs in the three primary regions suggest that long-term diversification benefits from investing in hedge funds are limited.

Acknowledgments

We are grateful to Sabri Boubaker, Bonnie G. Buchanan, Duc Khuong Nguyen (editors), and an anonymous referee for valuable suggestions which have significantly improved this chapter. The authors are grateful to Zeno Adams, Greg N. Gregoriou, Daniel Hartmann, Theodore C. Moorman, Joachim Zietz for helpful comments and suggestions on previous versions of this chapter. We of course bear full responsibility for any remaining errors.

References

Abugri, B. A., & Dutta, S. (2009). Emerging market hedge funds: Do they perform like regular hedge funds? *Journal of International Financial Markets, Institutions & Money*, *19*, 834–849.

Aggarwal, R. K., & Jorion, P. (2010). The performance of emerging hedge funds and managers. *Journal of Financial Economics*, *96*, 238–256.

Aitken, A. I., Kilic, O., & Reid, S. (2016). Can hedge funds time global equity markets? Evidence from emerging markets. *Review of Financial Economics*, *29*, 2–11.

Aragon, G. O., & Nanda, V. (2012). Tournament behavior in hedge funds: High-water marks, fund liquidation, and managerial stake. *Review of Financial Studies*, *25*, 937–974.

Bekaert, G., & Harvey, C. R. (2002). Research in emerging markets finance: Looking to the future. *Emerging Markets Review*, *3*, 429–448.

Bossaerts, P. (1988). Common nonstationary components of asset prices. *Journal of Economic Dynamics and Control*, 12, 247–364.

Bris, A., Goetzmann, W. N., & Zhu, N. (2007). Efficiency and the bear: Short sales and markets around the world. *Journal of Finance, 62,* 1029–1079.

Cao, B., & Jayasuriya, S. A. (2011). Market volatility and hedge fund returns in emerging markets. *Applied Financial Economics, 21,* 1691–1701.

Capocci, D., & Hübner, G. (2004). An analysis of hedge fund performance. *Journal of Empirical Finance, 11,* 55–89.

Carpenter, J. N., & Lynch, A. W. (1999). Survivorship bias and attrition effects in measures of performance persistence. *Journal of Financial Economics, 54,* 337–374.

Chaudhuri, K. (1997). Cointegration, error correction and Granger causality: An application with Latin American stock markets. *Applied Economics Letters, 4,* 469–471.

Chen, G.-M., Firth, M., & Rui, O. M. (2002). Stock market linkages: Evidence from Latin America. *Journal of Banking and Finance, 26,* 385–390.

Chen, Y. (2011). Derivatives use and risk taking: Evidence from the hedge fund industry. *Journal of Financial and Quantitative Analysis, 46,* 1073–1106.

De Santis, G., & Imrohoroglu, S. (1997). Stock returns and volatility in emerging financial markets. *Journal of International Money and Finance, 16,* 561–579.

Dickey, D. A., & Fuller, W. A. (1979). Distribution of the estimators for autoregressive time series with a unit root. *Journal of American Statistical Association, 74,* 427–431.

Dickey, D. A., & Fuller, W. A. (1981). Likelihood ratio tests for autoregressive time series with a unit root. *Econometrica, 49,* 1057–1072.

Ding, B., Shawky, H. A., & Tian, J. (2009). Liquidity shocks, size and the relative performance of hedge fund strategies. *Journal of Banking and Finance, 33,* 883–891.

Eling, M., & Faust, R. (2010). The performance of hedge funds and mutual funds in emerging markets. *Journal of Banking and Finance, 34,* 1993–2009.

Embrechts, P., McNeil, A., & Straumann, A. (1999). Correlation: Pitfalls and alternatives. *Risk Magazine*, 12, 69–71.

Embrechts, P., McNeil, A., & Straumann, A. (2002). Correlation and dependence in risk management: Properties and pitfalls. In M. Dempster (Ed.), *Risk management: Value at risk and beyond* (pp. 176–223). Cambridge: Cambridge University Press.

Engle, R. F., & Granger, C. W. J. (1987). Co-integration and error correction: Representation, estimation and testing. *Econometrica, 55*, 251–276.

Fung, W., & Hsieh, D. A. (1999). A primer on hedge funds. *Journal of Empirical Finance, 6*, 309–331.

Fung, W., & Hsieh, D. A. (2000). Measuring the market impact of hedge funds. *Journal of Empirical Finance, 7*, 1–36.

Füss, R., & Herrmann, F. (2005). Long-term interdependence between hedge fund strategy and stock market indices. *Managerial Finance, 31*, 29–45.

Füss, R., & Kaiser, D. G. (2007). The tactical and strategic value of hedge fund strategies: A cointegration approach. *Financial Markets and Portfolio Management, 21*, 425–432.

Füss, R., Kaiser, D. G., Rehkugler, H., & Butina, I. (2006). Long-term co-movements between hedge funds and financial asset markets. In G. N. Gregoriou & D. G. Kaiser (Eds.), *Hedge funds and managed futures – A handbook for institutional investors* (pp. 397–428). London: Risk Books.

Garret, I., & Spyrou, S. (1999). Common stochastic trends in emerging markets. *Manchester School, 67*, 649–660.

Geltner, D. (1991). Smoothing in appraisal-based returns. *Journal of Real Estate Finance and Economics, 4*, 327–345.

Geltner, D. (1993). Estimating market values from appraised values without assuming an efficient market. *Journal of Real Estate Research, 8*, 325–345.

Granger, C. W. J. (1969). Investigating causal relations by econometric methods and cross-spectral methods. *Econometrica, 34*, 424–438.

Gregoriou, G. N., & Rouah, F. (2001). Do stock market indices move the ten largest hedge funds? A cointegration approach. *Journal of Alternative Investments, 3*, 61–66.

Gregory, A. W., & Hansen, B. E. (1996). Residual-based tests for cointegration in models with regime shifts. *Journal of Econometrics, 70*, 99–126.

Hakamada, T., Takahashi, A., & Yamamoto, K. (2007). Selection and performance analysis of Asia-Pacific hedge funds. *Journal of Alternative Investments, 10*, 7–29.

HFR. (2011). *HFR industry report year end*. HFR, Chicago, IL.

Hung, W. S., & Cheung, Y.-L. (1995). Interdependence of Asian emerging equity markets. *Journal of Banking and Finance, 22*, 281–288.

Ibbotson, R. G., Chen, P., & Zhu, K. X. (2011). The ABCs of hedge funds: Alphas, betas, and costs. *Financial Analysts Journal, 67*, 15–25.

Johansen, S. (1988). Statistical analysis of cointegration vectors. *Journal of Economic Dynamics and Control, 12*, 231–254.

Johansen, S. (1991). Estimation and hypothesis testing of cointegration vectors in Gaussian vector autoregressive models. *Econometrica, 59,* 1551–1580.

Johansen, S. (1992). Determination of cointegration rank in the presence of a linear trend. *Oxford Bulletin of Economics and Statistics, 54,* 383–397.

Johansen, S., & Juselius, K. (1990). The full information maximum likelihood procedure for inference on cointegration with applications to the demand for money. *Oxford Bulletin of Economics and Statistics, 52,* 169–210.

Kasa, K. (1992). Common stochastic trends in international stock markets. *Journal of Monetary Economics, 29,* 95–124.

Kat, H. M. (2003). The dangers of using correlation to measure dependence. *Journal of Alternative Investments, 6,* 54–58.

Kat, H. M., & Lu, S. (2002). *An excursion into the statistical properties of hedge fund returns.* Working Paper 0016, Alternative Invesment Researsc Center, Cass Business School.

Koh, F., Koh, W. T. H., & Teo, M. (2003, June). *Asian hedge funds: Return persistence, style, and fund characteristics.* Working Paper. Singapore Management University.

Kotkatvuori-Örnberg, J., Nikkinen, J., & Peltomäki, J. (2011). Geographical focus in emerging markets and hedge fund performance. *Emerging Markets Review, 12,* 309–320.

Kuczynski, P.-P. (1994). Why emerging markets? *Columbia Journal of World Business,* (Focus Issue: Emerging Capital Markets), *29,* 8–13.

Lhabitant, F.-S. (2002). *Hedge funds: Myths and limits.* London: Wiley.

Lucas, A. (1997). *Strategic and tactical asset allocation and the effect of long-run equilibrium relations.* Research Memorandum. Vrije University.

Lütkepohl, H. (1991). *Introduction in multiple time series analysis.* Berlin: Springer.

Maddala, G. S., & Kim, I.-M. (1998). *Unit roots, cointegration and structural change.* Cambridge: Cambridge University Press.

Odonnat, I., & Rahmouni, I. (2006). Do emerging market economies still constitute a homogenous asset class? *Banque de France, Financial Stability Review, 9,* 39–48.

Orhan, M., & Tekten, T. (2006). Hedge fund investing in emerging markets. In G. N. Gregoriou & D. G. Kaiser (Eds.), *Hedge funds and managed futures – A handbook for the institutional investor* (pp. 259–275). London: Risk Books.

Osterwald-Lenum, M. (1992). A note with quartiles as the asymptotic distribution of the maximum likelihood cointegration rank test statistics. *Oxford Bulletin of Economics and Statistics, 54,* 461–472.

Pan, M.-S., Liu, Y. A., & Roth, H. J. (1999). Common stochastic trends and volatility in Asian Pacific equity markets. *Global Finance Journal, 10*, 162–172.
Park, H. (2015). Emerging market hedge funds in the United States. *Emerging Markets Review, 22*, 25–42.
Said, S. E., & Dickey, D. A. (1984). Testing for unit roots in autoregressive-moving average models of unknown order. *Biometrika, 71*, 559–607.
Strömqvist, M. (2007, September). *Should you invest in emerging market hedge funds?* Working Paper. Stockholm School of Economics.
Teo, M. (2009). The geography of hedge funds. *The Review of Financial Studies, 22*, 3531–3561.

Appendix: Test for Structural Breaks

Table A1: Results of the Quandt-Andrews (Unknown) Breakpoint Test.

Statistic	Test Statistic	p-Value
Asia		
Maximum LR F-statistic (2003M05)	5.858957	0.1710
Maximum Wald F-statistic (2003M05)	5.858957	0.1710
Exp LR F-statistic	1.765035	0.0704
Exp Wald F-statistic	1.765035	0.0704
Avg. LR F-statistic	3.216754	0.0370
Avg. Wald F-statistic	3.216754	0.0370
Latin America		
Maximum LR F-statistic (2006M08)	3.459405	0.4645
Maximum Wald F-statistic (2006M08)	3.459405	0.4645
Exp LR F-statistic	0.583956	0.3805
Exp Wald F-statistic	0.583956	0.3805
Avg. LR F-statistic	1.009437	0.3379
Avg. Wald F-statistic	1.009437	0.3379
Eastern Europe		
Maximum LR F-statistic (2003M04)	3.456381	0.4651
Maximum Wald F-statistic (2003M04)	3.456381	0.4651
Exp LR F-statistic	0.778563	0.2759
Exp Wald F-statistic	0.778563	0.2759
Avg. LR F-statistic	1.362951	0.2224
Avg. Wald F-statistic	1.362951	0.2224

Table A1: (*Continued*)

Emerging Markets		
Maximum LR *F*-statistic (2006M07)	4.511994	0.3036
Maximum Wald *F*-statistic (2006M07)	4.511994	0.3036
Exp LR *F*-statistic	0.601248	0.3694
Exp Wald *F*-statistic	0.601248	0.3694
Avg. LR *F*-statistic	0.779147	0.4505
Avg. Wald *F*-statistic	0.779147	0.4505

Note: This table shows the *F*-statistic from the Quandt-Andrews breakpoint for the three regions and the global emerging markets universe. The dates in brackets correspond to the year and month when a structural break in the return series occurred. *P*-values shown in the last column indicate whether structural breaks are statistically significant at conventional levels of 1, 5, and 10 percent.

Part III
Looking Ahead

18

How International Standards Apply to Emerging Countries?

Jocelyn Grira and Chiraz Labidi

Abstract

This chapter discusses the regulatory challenges faced by financial institutions in emerging countries and it presents their specific features compared to financial institutions in developed countries. It offers a practical way of implementing regulatory changes while accounting for emerging countries' specific features. Using a principle-based approach, this chapter builds on the recent regulatory developments in both developed and developing market economies. It relates these developments to industry best practices as well as the current state of the art in risk management and corporate governance. The findings show how the regulation of financial institutions in emerging countries differs from that in developed countries. Different approaches to mitigate the divergences and fill the gaps are discussed. Both regulators and financial institutions in emerging countries will find this chapter offers a practical point of view based on field and industry experience on how to interpret and apply regulations and adopt best practices in risk management in a way that accounts for emerging countries' specific features.

Keywords: International standards; emerging countries; risk management; macroprudential approach; principle-based approach

Introduction

Risk management regulatory frameworks and capital adequacy rules are important parts of the financial institutions environment (Anginer & Demirgüç-Kunt, 2014; Maddaloni & Peydró, 2011). They were designed by international regulatory bodies[1] and implemented by different national jurisdictions. These frameworks (e.g., Basel II/III, Solvency II) were first implemented in developed countries and are currently being implemented in numerous emerging countries. At the industry level, the adjustment efforts and trial-and-error implementation processes were a signal of an initial misunderstanding of the regulatory standards. Implementation delays and adjustments necessarily imply costs for financial institutions. Furthermore, at the country level, national regulators faced several challenges in interpreting the international standards and adapting them to their own national contexts. Both regulators and financial institutions then went through an iterative process where the standards were interpreted, implemented, and adjusted several times during the last few years. These are strong signals that call, first, for a need of clear understanding and interpretation of the international regulation at the national level, and, second, for an efficient implementation of these rules at the industry level (Christmann & Taylor, 2006).

1. National regulators are participatory members of the international standards setters.

Previous studies focus on the implementation of regulatory frameworks in different countries (Calomiris & Powell, 2001; Cumming & Nel, 2005; Engelen, 2005; Jones, 2000). However, no studies have examined how this implementation differs in developed and emerging markets. This chapter complements the literature related to financial regulation and sheds the light on the practical dimensions that differentiate developed from developing countries as well as the challenges they face.

In this chapter, we discuss the standards-setting process starting from the consultation phase at the international level, to the drafting phase, to the communication phase targeting the national regulatory agencies, to the implementation of the finalized standards and suggested revisions, if applicable. Understanding this process is important for the regulators as well as for the industry players. In fact, it allows the regulators to have a participative and, if desired, a more influential role in this process, specifically in the consultation and drafting phases. In also offers the industry a clearer view of how the standards are set and represents a valuable opportunity to help improve the standards, specifically in the revision phase. We also discuss the regulatory requirements related to governance and risk management, and how they apply to emerging countries. We then give an overview of the best practices in risk management and suggest a flexible approach to implement these best practices in emerging countries to account for the differences between developed and developing countries (Barth, Caprio, & Levine, 2013). Finally, we discuss the challenges faced by regulators and financial institutions in relation to regulatory standards and risk management practices, and emphasize the importance of shifting from a compliance-based culture to a risk-based culture in the industry.

This chapter offers the opportunity to improve the understanding of the standards-setting process and allows for bridging regulatory conceptual frameworks to their practical implementations in both developed and developing market economies. It also helps identify the distinguishing characteristics of emerging economies compared to those of developed economies as far as the regulatory dimension is concerned. Finally, it stresses the importance of adopting a culture of risk to enhance the quality of the risk management practices in emerging economies.

Setting International Standards: How It Works

The main objectives of national financial regulators are to maintain the safety and soundness of the financial system and enforce the compliance of financial institutions to laws and regulations. National regulators consist of regulatory and supervisory agencies as well as central banks. They generally rely on the international standard setters (ISS) such as the Financial Stability Board (FSB),[2] the Bank of International Settlements (BIS),[3] and the International Monetary Fund (IMF)[4] to set the international standards, but they actively contribute to the work of these agencies. Setting the standards is a *participatory* and *iterative* process (Figure 1). ISS start by first issuing a proposal, a draft document, for consultancy and comments by the participating members. These members consult the stakeholders of the regulatory

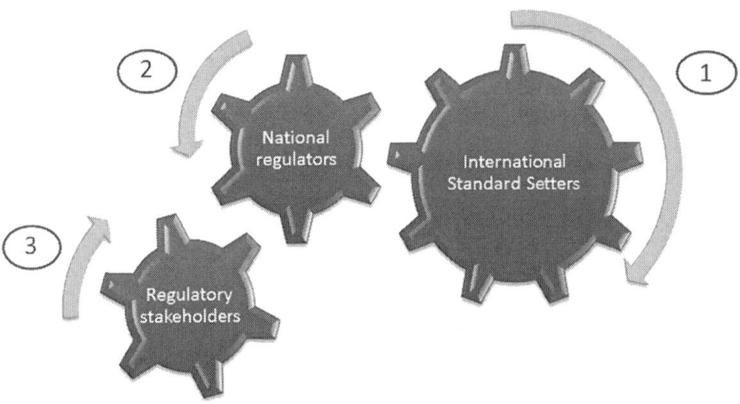

Figure 1: The Standard Setting and Consultancy Process.

2. www.financialstabilityboard.org
3. www.bis.org
4. www.imf.org

process in their jurisdictions: the national regulatory bodies, the central bank, the ministry of finance, the different financial industry groups, and the professional associations. After receiving comments on the proposal, the ISS proceed to the second step, which consists of reviewing the document, adjusting it to account for input from the different groups, and integrating these inputs into the text. The revised proposal is then issued as a first version of the international standards. National regulators interpret them according to their own financial contexts and regulatory environments, and enforce their implementation. Interpretation issues and implementation problems are usually identified at the national level by the supervisory bodies and reported to the ISS by the participating members. Major issues may trigger revisions in the standards; an amended version of these standards is then issued and an adjustment process at the national level may start.

International standards are set at the international level for the different types financial institutions: deposit institutions, commercial banks, insurance companies, pension funds, and so on. National regulatory bodies adopt these standards, interpret them by issuing regulatory principles and requirements based on these standards, and enforce their implementation in the industry within reasonable timelines (Figure 2).

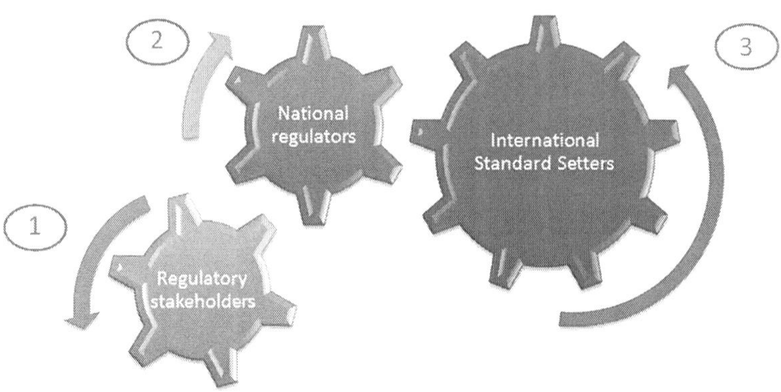

Figure 2: The Standards Reviewing Process.

Setting regulatory standards at the international level is important for several reasons. First, it guarantees consistency among national jurisdictions: the same standards are used to derive regulatory principles and requirements. Second, it prevents regulatory arbitrage resulting from having different rules applied to financial institutions doing business globally. Third, it accounts for the increasing phenomenon of markets integration: having different regulatory requirements would increase frictions and market segmentation, whereas the current tendency moves in the opposite direction. Finally, unique and homogeneous international standards facilitate coordination and common intervention during periods of financial distress.

Several emerging countries are part of the international regulatory bodies mentioned previously.[5] For example, Argentina, Brazil, Mexico, India, Indonesia, and Turkey are active participating members of the FSB, along with the United States, Russia, Australia, China, and other major European countries. Also, the BIS count numerous central banks as full participating members from emerging countries: Algeria, India, Argentina, Brazil, Thailand, Turkey, United Arab Emirates, and so on. Finally, many emerging countries are active members of the IMF. These facts imply that international regulations try to incorporate emerging countries' features, and they account, at least partially, for some of the specifics such as the quality of the regulatory environment, investor protection regulation, and quality of disclosed financial information.

5. The participation of emerging countries in setting international standards is relatively recent and took place for different reasons. First, financial institutions in developed countries urged their peers in emerging countries to enact regulations that would keep equal pressure on the cost of capital in both types of economies and help them remain competitive globally. Second, the emerging countries themselves expressed the importance of taking part in the standards-setting process. Finally, many emerging economies witnessed significant growth in their financial sectors and determined that their regulatory frameworks should be similarly active to maintain the safety and soundness of the financial systems.

A "Beta Version" of International Standards for Emerging Countries

It is important to note that the first international financial regulatory texts were *not* written by and for emerging countries. In fact, the Basel Committee expressly stated that Basel II recommendations were written for G-10 countries, not emerging countries. To fill this gap, the same committee created a set of standards for emerging market economies. The document *Core Principles for Effective Banking Supervision* was drafted in 1997 to address this issue. Large financial holdings, credit rating agencies, and several institutions in developed market economies did not like the duality that existed between regulations applied to developed and developing economies, considering the Basel Accords are the proper standards to implement and work with globally. Their take on the situation was that there were two sets of standards: one for the emerging market economies, more flexible and subject to softer interpretations and another for developed market economies, more prescriptive, precise, and rigid.

The perceived double standards hypothesis proposes several adverse effects on the stability, safety, and soundness of financial systems in emerging countries (Brown & Dinç, 2011). First, the highly technical level of several features of the international standards may pressure national regulators to hire and retain specialized resources to supervise compliance to these new standards. The availability and cost of these resources is challenging for emerging countries. This may lead national regulators to relax the requirements as well as oversight, which could incentivize financial institutions to take more risks. Second, the reliance of international regulations on credit rating agencies may have unfavorable effects on financial institutions in emerging market economies. Whereas large banks can afford to hire rating agencies to rate their debt, this is not the case for smaller financial institutions, which are more predominant in emerging markets. Finally, having two sets of regulations creates regulatory arbitrage opportunities and may incentivize financial institutions in developed market economies to open subsidiaries in emerging market economies to take advantage of regulations that offer implicit subsidies to these institutions.

The document *Core Principles for Effective Banking Supervision* was revised in 2006 and again in 2011 in cooperation with supervisors around the world. The last version of the document dates from September 2012. It states that an adequate balance was achieved in raising the bar for sound supervision while maintaining regulatory principles that are flexible and globally applicable. The concept used to provide flexibility and global applicability is the *proportional concept,* according to which the regulatory assessment criteria accommodate a diverse range of banking systems and are commensurate with the risk profile and systemic importance of a broad spectrum of financial institutions. In other words, countries with complex and systematically important financial institutions have the option to issue regulatory standards that are proportional to the nature, size, and activities of the financial institutions that fall under the supervision of their regulatory bodies. Similarly, countries with relatively simple and systematically limited operations may regulate their financial system accordingly.

Toward an Optimal Regulatory System in Emerging Countries

Designing an appropriate regulation framework for emerging markets is a challenging task. First, an agreement should be made on the regulatory philosophy before designing the regulation. Second, the basic suitable components of an optimal regulatory system need to be identified. Third, an understanding of the main characteristics of the targeted implementation environment is required. The convergence between the specific features of emerging countries and the suitable properties of an efficient regulatory framework that is consistent with the regulatory philosophy then determines the appropriate regulatory system for emerging countries.

The following sections discuss the regulatory philosophy, the basic properties of an optimal regulatory system, and the characteristics of emerging countries' environments.

The Regulatory Philosophy: Toward a Macroprudential and Principle-Based Approach

In the past, developed and developing market economies adopted a microprudential approach to their regulatory framework and supervisory activities. The microprudential approach focuses on individual financial institutions, their solvency, the soundness of their governance mechanisms, and their compliance with rules and regulatory principles (Dobson & Hufbauer, 2001; Rime, 2001). The global financial crisis provides evidence on the failure of the microprudential regulatory approach: regulators now understand that the focus should be wider than on the individual financial institutions and the supervision activities should be more flexible than those dictated by a list of rules. In other words, the focus should be on the system as a whole rather than on the individual institutions, and regulations should be more principle based than rule based. Consequently, a global consensus in favor of a macroprudential, principle-based approach was reached because it seems to be a more adequate philosophy and a much more efficient and flexible tool in preventing system wide collapses (Ho, Palacios, & Stoll, 2012).

A macroprudential approach to regulation allows, first, for a broader understanding of the interconnections among financial institutions in the system, an improved assessment of the firm- and aggregate-level risks to be disclosed to the national regulatory bodies, and a close monitoring of the risks of the financial institutions identified and qualified as *systematically important financial institutions*.[6] Second, the adoption of a macroprudential approach

6. Financial institutions are identified and qualified as *systematically important financial institutions* based on their size, leverage, interconnectedness with other institutions, and degree to which they provide financial services critical to the operation of key markets.

to regulation relies on the *degree of cooperation among national regulators* around the world. In fact, a closer coordination among regulatory agencies allows for a better monitoring of the systemic risks taken by complex and multinational financial institutions. Third, in the same vein, managing systemic risks when they materialize needs not only cooperation among regulatory agencies but also robust *resolution mechanisms* to mitigate the effects of the shock to the financial system as well as the stakeholders. Deposit insurance systems are part of these resolution mechanisms. Finally, the *quality of the institutional environment* plays an important role in facilitating this cooperation and in allowing for an efficient operationalization of the resolution mechanisms during periods of distress. In fact, jurisdiction issues as well as national interests, economic and political, rise in such circumstances. National regulation should then account for its own institutional capacities, structures, and inter-relationships when designing the regulatory framework.

A principle-based approach to regulation allows for an application of the spirit of the rule, rather than the text of the rule itself, and applies mostly to developed market economies. In contrast, a rule-based approach to regulation requires closer and more direct control of the regulated entities and applies mostly to emerging market economies. In fact, regulation in emerging market economies is closer to a compliance-based approach. Because current international standards follow much more the first approach to regulation, emerging market economies would gain from a transition to the principle-based approach. Changing the regulation paradigm, hence migrating from the rules to the principles, requires a fundamental change in the culture of financial players in emerging countries. This necessitates the adoption and implementation of a culture of risk, as will be discussed later in this chapter.

Basic Properties of an Optimal Regulatory System

Large failures and system wide collapses represent worst-case scenarios that regulators want to avoid. Lessons drawn from past experiences have allowed regulatory authorities to improve their supervisory frameworks and tools to prevent such large negative shocks. These shocks usually come from deficiencies in one or more of the following transmission channels that we present under two categories: preventive channels and curative channels.[7]

Preventive Channels

Capitalization levels. Adequate capitalization levels help financial institutions survive negative shocks and avoid default (Barth, Caprio, & Levine, 2004; Rochet, 1999). Regulatory capital requirements are explicitly enunciated in regulatory texts, though national regulators have the flexibility to ask financial institutions to keep their capitalization levels above self-determined target levels. These levels differ across financial institutions depending on their size, risk profile, and operation complexity, and are subject to the approval of regulatory authorities. Severe deviations from these target capitalization levels may trigger regulatory interventions to enforce necessary corrective actions.

Risk measures and tools. The main risks subject to regulatory monitoring in the banking sector are credit, market, and operational risks. Conventional assessment methods are described in the regulatory texts (e.g., Basel Accords) and implemented by financial institutions.[8] Several commercial tools are available on the market and offer an alternative to in-house modeling choices.

In the last few years, the focus has been on liquidity and systemic risks, as a natural response to the recent financial crisis. Regulators now require the implementation of assessment and monitoring tools for these risks, and they have had to adjust their

7. Some channels may be presented in both categories. For the sake of simplicity, we present them in the most relevant category but also discuss how they operate in the alternative category.

8. Regulatory authorities emphasize the importance of implementing risk models, not only for regulatory compliance but also for effective risk assessment and management in day-to-day operations. One important dimension on which regulatory authorities focus is compliance to the "use test," that is, the extent to which the risk measures, models, and tools submitted to regulators for approval are used.

review methods and assessment tools to incorporate these new requirements in their supervisory framework. Regulatory authorities in developed countries have had difficulty finding, hiring, and retaining specialized resources that allow them to achieve these tasks. In emerging countries, both the banking sector and regulatory authorities have a critical need for such resources to help them tackle this challenge.

Sound governance mechanisms. In addition to the quantitative risks discussed above, regulatory authorities closely monitor qualitative risks that affect the financial health of financial institutions. The quality of the governance mechanisms is one of these qualitative risks.[9] Well-governed financial institutions are more likely to resist negative shocks and to perform better in both adverse and normal conditions, other things being equal, and are less likely to experience default or insolvency (Reddy, Locke, & Scrimgeour, 2010).

Much effort is needed in emerging countries as far as corporate governance mechanisms are concerned. Issues such as the lack of independence of board members, lack of skill and experience, unclarity of role definitions for members of the board as well as subcommittees of the board, weak reporting mechanisms, information asymmetry, and the structure of compensation packages and incentives are all important to take into account, and ultimately address, when national regulators undertake supervisory activities.

Transparency and disclosure. Information is a key element in the financial decision-making process (Nier, 2005). Stakeholders use it to assess the value of their financial positions and to adjust, if necessary. Information asymmetry problems may penalize these stakeholders and cause them to make suboptimal decisions (Jordan, Peek, & Rosengren, 2000; Linsley & Shrives, 2005).

9. Other examples of qualitative risks monitored by the regulatory authorities are the quality of the business model, the business environment (competition, elasticity of demand, market shares of each financial player, etc.), the strategic risk, the legal risk (including law suits), the reputational risk.

Information availability and accuracy are even more important in riskier and more volatile markets: the need for complete and accurate information is consequently higher in emerging markets than in developed markets. Therefore, compliance with regulatory requirements related to transparency and information disclosure in emerging markets should be watched more closely as it will improve investor protection and enhance the development of the financial environment and the solvency of financial institutions (Hyytinen & Takalo, 2002).

Curative Channel: Resolution Mechanisms

Government intervention in the recent crisis shows the importance of regulatory agencies in crisis management and failure resolution, even if financial markets interpreted these signals as an implicit subsidy to large financial institutions. The Greek crisis also shows the importance of coordinated government actions. These recent experiences shed the light on the need for robust resolution mechanisms that allow ultimately for ordered failures but also show that these mechanisms are still in of improvement, specifically when it comes to managing failure of the so-called systematically important financial institutions, mostly present in developed market economies.

Resolution mechanisms are a group of coordinated actions taken by the different components of the financial system safety net. Efficient resolution processes rely on having a robust deposit insurance component that works jointly with other components of the financial system safety net: the prudential regulatory and supervisory component, the lender-of-last-resort component (the central banks in most cases), and, generally, the ministry of finance component. This implies the need for regulatory texts to include a clear and explicit description of the resolution mechanisms. This dimension is highly important for developed countries where most large and complex financial institutions evolve. These mechanisms must be supported by a strong accountability framework, an important dimension for emerging countries that need to enhance the quality of their legal and institutional environments.

Characteristics of Emerging Countries' Environments

Corporate Governance

Firms in emerging markets have corporate governance features that are distinct from firms in developed markets. Whereas corporate governance practices are relatively uniform in major developed countries, they are diversified in emerging countries because of the differences in their economic, institutional, legal, and political environments. For example, ownership structures are more concentrated in emerging countries, many firms record a more predominant role of the government in their corporate activities, and many firms are family owned or controlled.

Corporate governance activities in emerging markets are usually the result of (1) "transplantations" from developed countries prompted by the emergence of these countries as major financial players on the international scene and (2) the importance and rapidity of their economic growth. The institutional environment has evolved simultaneously with markets development and economic activity. However, constraints related to political and social contexts have slowed down the evolution of institutional and legal environments, as discussed later, creating a lag between the latter and economic development.

Institutional and Legal Frameworks

Much work has been done on the relation between firm performance and the quality of institutional and legal frameworks. The better the quality, the higher is firm performance. Both the legal framework and the quality of institutions are criteria used to assess the governance of institutions, as discussed previously.

Considering the growing interest of global investors in emerging markets, firms and governments in emerging countries need to enhance the quality of the institutional and legal environments. Investor protection, government efficiency, law enforcement, efficiency of the judicial system, and accountability standards are all important dimensions that need to be improved to attract capital flows and encourage global investors to do business in emerging countries' firms.

Financial Development

Several studies published in the 1990s show the existence of a causal relation between financial development in emerging markets and economic growth. Other important studies show the relation between financial development and corporate governance institutions and practices. In reality, compared to developed countries where the development of the financial sector is mature, the economic growth in emerging countries is marked by the development of the financial sector, followed by a need to improve the quality of firms' environments: institutional and legal environments, business environment, corporate governance and ethics standards, information disclosure standard, and so on.

Information Asymmetry

The growing interest of global investors in emerging market economies is a sustained trend because of the attractive opportunities they offer. This trend is not expected to revert in the next few years. Because information accuracy and availability are major determinants of capital flows in these markets, it is important for both global investors and firms in emerging market economies to improve their disclosure and quality standards to attract and retain capital.

Resources and Infrastructure

Emerging market economies have higher exposure to global investors today than in past years. To remain financially attractive, they have to comply with higher standards for information disclosure and corporate governance. These new business requirements are not cost free. Firms usually have to invest large amounts of money to support their new business environments and offer adequate platforms to communicate with stakeholders. They also have to invest in building and maintaining new capabilities that allow them to compete while complying with the new standards. These investments are considered opportunities that characterize emerging markets economies because they are, for the most part, already being done by their counterparts in developed market economies.

Risk Management

Initially, risk management activities were perceived as a cost center rather than as a revenue center, which generates direct cash flows such as sales in the manufacturing sector and underwriting in the insurance and commercial banking sectors. Risk managers were hired as part of different teams such as R&D, modeling, reporting, or back office, but rarely as a distinct function of the institution.

Financial crises and subsequent regulatory reforms (Basel accords, Solvency directives, and Sarbanes–Oxley Act) have highlighted the importance of risk management as a safeguard and line of defense for institutions, mostly in developed countries. Since the financial crisis, risk management has been integrated into business models and has successfully added value to firms. In contrast, in emerging countries, risk management has been viewed as a compliance function that helps countries cope with new regulatory standards, initially issued by institutions to support regulatory agreements for their projects.

Best Practices

Risk management is the second of three conventional lines of defense, after the top management and before internal audit. Best practices in risk management include:

- At the top management level (the first line of defense):
  - Promotion of sustainable risk–return thinking
  - Adherence to strong risk management vision
  - Reliance on a consistent and ongoing risk monitoring system
- At the risk management level (the second line of defense):
  - Separation of risk management and controls
  - Joint identification of profit drivers and business risk drivers

    - Reporting of risk assessments in a timely manner
    - Integration of risk management across different business units
    - Combination of risk evaluation and risk advising
- At the internal audit level (the third line of defense):
    - Understanding of business functions, risks, and processes
    - Independence of internal audit as far as risk taking and risk management is concerned.

Toward a Culture of Risk

Firms in developed countries realized recently the importance of implementing a culture of risk. New regulatory standards have contributed to the adoption of this culture. In emerging countries, moving from a compliance-based to risk-based philosophy requires the involvement of the firms' leadership, followed by active participation by the business units, and then awareness of all stakeholders that a risk-based culture creates value and strengthens the business model and its chances for success.

Unlike processes, systems, and infrastructures, changing minds and cultures takes time. Firms in emerging markets suffer from a lag in risk management practices and from inadequacies of the regulatory standards to their specific contexts. However, it is only a matter of time before they catch up, taking into account not only the specificities of their business environment but also the necessity to survive in a more integrated and competitive global market.

Conclusion

Originally, developed countries took the initiative of setting the regulatory standards. The recent shocks to the financial world, integration of global markets, and rise of emerging markets as new opportunities shed light on the importance of having a more open and inclusive standards-setting process. These factors have also helped stakeholders, in both developed and developing countries, adopt two new regulation paradigms. The first is the switch of the regulatory philosophy from a rule-based approach to a principle-based approach. The second is the transition of the supervisory framework from a microprudential approach to a macroprudential approach.

Even though regulatory standards are set at the international level, their interpretation and implementation are country specific. In that sense, emerging countries have to take into account their own characteristics when it comes to regulating of their financial sectors. International standards may be viewed as interesting, consistent, and robust guidelines.

Several challenges need to be addressed for emerging market economies to have an adequate regulatory and supervisory framework. Most of these challenges relate to corporate governance issues, transparency and information disclosure, quality of institutional and legal environments, and resource availability. Adopting best practices in governance and risk management is a first step toward an effective change in the current way of doing things. Implementing a culture of risk is the ultimate and critical part of this change: it is a change that emerging market institutions need to embrace, evolving from a mindset based on compliance to one based on risk.

References

Anginer, D., & Demirgüç-Kunt, A. (2014). *Bank capital and systemic stability*. Policy Research Working Paper No. 6948. World Bank, Washington, DC.

Barth, J. R., Caprio, G., Jr., & Levine, R. (2004). Bank regulation and supervision: What works best? *Journal of Financial Intermediation, 13*, 205–248.

Barth, J. R., Caprio, G., Jr., & Levine, R. (2013). Bank regulation and supervision in 180 countries from 1999 to 2011. *Journal of Financial Economic Policy, 5*, 111–219.

Brown, C. O., & Dinç, I. S. (2011). Too many to fail? Evidence of regulatory forbearance when the banking sector is weak. *Review of Financial Studies, 24*, 1378–1405.

Calomiris, C. W., & Powell, A. (2001). Can emerging market bank regulators establish credible discipline? The case of Argentina, 1992–99. In *Prudential supervision: What works and what doesn't* (pp. 147–196). Chicago, IL: University of Chicago Press.

Christmann, P., & Taylor, G. (2006). Firm self-regulation through international certifiable standards: Determinants of symbolic versus substantive implementation. *Journal of International Business Studies, 37,* 863–878.

Cumming, S., & Nel, H. (2005). Capital controls and the lending behaviour of South African banks: Preliminary findings on the expected impact of Basel II. *South African Journal of Economics, 73,* 641–656.

Dobson, W., & Hufbauer, G. C. (2001). *World capital markets: Challenge to the G-10.* Washington, DC: Peterson Institute for International Economics.

Engelen, K. C. (2005). BIS birthday blues: Uneasy times as the Bank for International Settlements turns 75. *International Economy, 19,* 46–51.

Ho, T., Palacios, M., & Stoll, H. (2012). Regulatory principles for the financial system. *Journal of Derivatives, 20,* 19–37.

Hyytinen, A., & Takalo, T. (2002). Enhancing bank transparency: A re-assessment. *European Finance Review, 6,* 429–445.

Jones, D. (2000). Emerging problems with the Basel capital accord: Regulatory capital arbitrage and related issues. *Journal of Banking and Finance, 24,* 35–58.

Jordan, J. S., Peek, J., & Rosengren, E. S. (2000). The market reaction to the disclosure of supervisory actions: Implications for bank transparency. *Journal of Financial Intermediation, 9,* 298–319.

Linsley, P. M., & Shrives, P. J. (2005). Transparency and the disclosure of risk information in the banking sector. *Journal of Financial Regulation and Compliance, 13,* 205–214.

Maddaloni, A., & Peydró, J. L. (2011). Bank risk-taking, securitization, supervision, and low interest rates: Evidence from the euro-area and the US lending standards. *Review of Financial Studies, 24,* 2121–2165.

Nier, E. W. (2005). Bank stability and transparency. *Journal of Financial Stability, 1,* 342–354.

Reddy, K., Locke, S., & Scrimgeour, F. (2010). The efficacy of principle-based corporate governance practices and firm financial performance: An empirical investigation. *International Journal of Managerial Finance, 6,* 190–219.

Rime, B. (2001). Capital requirements and bank behaviour: Empirical evidence for Switzerland. *Journal of Banking and Finance, 25,* 789–805.

Rochet, J. C. (1999). Solvency regulations and the management of banking risks. *European Economic Review, 43,* 981–990.

19

Market Concentration and Bank Competition in Emerging Asian Countries

Hanh Thi My Phan and Kevin Daly

Abstract

This study aims to investigate both market concentration and bank competition of banking across six emerging Asian countries (e.g., Bangladesh, Indonesia, India, Philippines, Malaysia, and Vietnam) over pre and post the 2008 global financial crisis. The conduct parameter approach following the framework suggested by Uchida and Tsutsui (2005) is used to estimate bank competition in these countries. The study employs both seemingly unrelated regression (SUR) and three-stage least squares (3SLS) to estimate simultaneously the system of equations in our model. Generally we find a negative association between market concentration and bank competition across most of the countries in the study suggesting that banks in concentrated markets collude to generate higher profits. Monopolistic competition was the best description of competitive structure of banking across the majority of countries investigated by this study. The study fills the gap in the banking literature by investigating bank competition, concentration, and their relationship across emerging Asian economies over the 2008 global financial crisis. Moreover, several policy implications for banking industry are suggested.

Keywords: Bank competition; market concentration; Asian countries

Introduction

This study contributes to the literature in several respects. Firstly, it fills the gap in the banking literature by investigating bank competition across emerging markets over the recent 2008 global financial crisis. Secondly, the study employs various statistical methods for robustness checks of the results. Thirdly, the study examines the relationships between competition and market concentration across emerging markets banking systems over the 2008 global financial crisis. Fourthly, some policy implications related to market concentration and competition in banking are recommended.

The primary interest of this study is to assess the state of bank competition and concentration across emerging Asian countries by employing the structure conduct performance (SCP) hypothesis. This hypothesis suggests that market structure affects competition and the behavior of banks in setting interest rates which in turn influence banks' performance. The research results suggest a downward trend of concentration levels in banking across Bangladesh, India, Indonesia and Vietnam while the degree of market concentration grew slightly across banking in Malaysia and Philippines. Banks in Indonesia, Malaysia and Philippines continue to operate under monopolistic competition throughout the period covered by our investigation. The Vietnamese banking environment experienced higher marginal cost than price due primarily to non-optimizing behavior of their banks. Indian banks had higher marginal cost than price over 2005–2008 and operated under monopolistic competition over 2010–2012. By contrast, Bangladesh banking has a tendency to operate under conditions of pure monopoly in 2005, monopolistic competition in 2008 while experiencing higher marginal cost than price over 2009–2012. Overall the evidence from this study suggests that competition levels in banking decreased for India and Indonesia where concentration increased. By contrast increased banking competition appears across Bangladesh, Malaysia and Philippines where the latter two markets experienced increases in concentration.

Over the last decade, emerging markets have experienced bank privatization, interest rate deregulation and financial liberalization while their banking structure has become more consolidated (Turk Ariss, 2010). Overall banking across emerging markets has experienced increasing competition from the presence of foreign banks where claimed efficiency advantages include advances in technological capabilities and superior management skills (Berger, Genay, & Udel, 2000; Jeon, Olivero, & Wu, 2011). As mentioned in studies on bank competition by Claessens and Laeven (2004), Jeon et al. (2011), Wu, Jeon, and Luca (2010), Yeyati and Micco (2007), Yildirim and Philippatos (2007), foreign bank entry enhances competition in the domestic banking markets. Furthermore, Williams (2012) found that both foreign bank entry and privatization have increased competition by restructuring domestic banking and consolidating troubled local banks along with decreasing the State's role in banking. In general, emerging markets provide a rich laboratory to study the competitive structure of banking (Turk Ariss, 2010), as testified by several recent studies including Agoraki, Delis, and Pasiouras (2011), Beck, De Jonghe, and Schepens (2013), Fu, Lin, and Molyneux (2014), Marrouch and Turk-Ariss (2014), Nguyen, Skully, and Perera (2012), Soedarmono (2010), Soedarmono, Machrouh, and Tarazi

(2011, 2013) and Tabak, Fazio, and Cajueiro (2012). To test these claimed benefits for emerging markets banking this study employs both the Panzar-Rosse (PR) methodology and the more dynamic Lerner index.

The markets whose banks are the focus of this study are positioned within Asia's fast growing emerging economies. Asian economies have averaged real gross domestic product (GDP) growth of 7.3 percent as opposed to 2.9 percent — for the world's GDP growth over 1980–2010 (Park, 2011). The Asian banking structure changed significantly after the 1997 Asian crisis due to the fast development of banking consolidations as well as an increase in mergers and acquisitions. Since the early 1990s, Asian economies have experienced a significant increase in the arrival of foreign banks with better technological abilities and management skills (Jeon et al., 2011). The growth of foreign bank entry along with changing market structure across emerging markets does raise concerns about competition in the region (Jeon et al., 2011; Turk Ariss, 2010). However, few studies have investigated bank competition in emerging Asian markets such as Beck et al. (2013), Fu et al. (2014), Nguyen et al. (2012), Soedarmono (2010), Soedarmono et al. (2011, 2013), Turk Ariss (2010).

This study investigates bank competition across Asian markets including Bangladesh, India, Indonesia, Malaysia, Philippines, and Vietnam and focuses particularly on these markets banking environment over 2005–2012. The study's innovation is to employ a conduct parameter approach following the framework suggested by Uchida and Tsutsui (2005) and Soedarmono et al. (2011, 2013). For robustness checks of the results, we employ both seemingly unrelated regression (SUR) and three-stage least squares (3SLS) to estimate simultaneously the system of equations in our model. The study also examines the relationship between competition and market concentration over this studied period.

This chapter is organized as follows: the next section reviews the literature on market concentration and competition across banking in both developed and developing countries. The section "Methodology" discusses the methodology and the data. The section "Empirical Results" presents an in-depth discussion about the empirical results. Finally, the section "Conclusions" provides some policy implications that arise from the study.

Market Concentration and Bank Competition: An Overview

Market Concentration

Market concentration is usually considered a proxy for market structure. Market concentration is also an indirect measure of market power based on traditional industrial organization approaches related to banks' behavior and profitability (Casu & Girardone, 2006). The Structure Conduct Performance (SCP) hypothesis by Bain (1951) suggests that greater profitability results from collusion between firms in a concentrated market. According to the SCP hypothesis, market structure affects competition and the behavior of banks in setting interest rates which in turn influence banks' performance. In highly concentrated markets, banks can set lower deposit rates and higher lending rates to get higher spreads which in turn increases their profits. In other words, due to a lower cost of collusion between large banks under more concentrated markets, these banks obtain more market power to set price and earn supernormal profit. Hence, the traditional SCP hypothesis proposes that market concentration is an explanation for bank performance, that is, there exists a positive link between market structure and performance. The SCP hypothesis is based on the assumption that banks in concentrated market collude to get higher profits suggests that concentration and competition in banking is negatively related.

Some dominant pioneering empirical studies on banking lend supports to the SCP hypothesis, for example, Heggestad and Mingo (1977), Lloyd-Williams, Molyneux, and Thornton (1994), Rhoades (1982), Rose and Fraser (1976), Spellman (1981). Besides, Molyneux and Forbes (1995) tested the SCP hypothesis for the European banking during the period 1986–1989. They found that there is a positive and statistically significant relationship between market concentration and bank profitability. Within the context of Asian banking, the SCP hypothesis was tested by Bhatti and Hussain (2010) and Fu and Heffernan (2009). While Bhatti and Hussain (2010) confirmed a positive correlation between market concentration and profitability using annual pooled data from 20 incorporated Pakistani commercial banks over 1996–2004, Fu and Heffernan (2009) showed a significantly negative relationship between market concentration and profitability in the Chinese banking over the second stage of banking reform (1993–2002).

Bank Competition

Approaches to Measuring Bank Competition

The literature on the measurements of bank competition is very large and can be divided into two main streams such as the structural approach and the non-structural approach. The former approach employs market concentration as a measure of competition while the later approach tries to estimate the level of competition directly.

The structural approaches. The structural approaches use market concentration as a measure of competition. Concentration is negatively related to competition based on the traditional structure — conduct — performance (SCP) hypothesis (Bain, 1951) which presupposes that banks operate in highly concentrated markets and have a tendency to collude and thus gain higher profits. This paradigm assumes the more concentrated the market, the more market power banks attain. Therefore, the structural method is based on an assumption that there is a negative relationship between market concentration and bank competition in the banking industry (Fu & Heffernan, 2009). However, the structural approach does not consider differentiation strategies of each bank such as product differentiation. This approach only focuses on the market share of banks rather than competitive behavior of banks (Beck, 2008). As a result, these indicators are viewed as a weak and poor estimate of bank competition (Berger, Levine, & Haubrich, 2004; Claessens & Laeven, 2004, 2005; de Guevara, Maudos, & Pérez, 2005; Maudos & Fernández de Guevara, 2004; Schaeck & Cihak, 2010).

The non-structural approaches — New Empirical Industrial Organization (NEIO). The non-structural approaches, the so-called New Empirical Industrial Organization (NEIO) approaches, have become popular in recent bank studies since they have several advantages over the structural approaches. For instance, the non-structural approaches do not assume the existence of a negative relation between the level of concentration and competition but rather assume contestability in banking competition whereby the degree of potential competition rather than the degree of concentration are investigated. This method does not infer that banks in concentrated market are less competitive because contestability does not necessarily depend on the concentration level but rather on the level of potential competition. In addition, it is not necessary to identify a geographic market because market power can be indicated by individual banks' behaviors (Casu & Girardone, 2006). Therefore, instead of investigating the competitive environment via a structural approach, the NEIO approaches try to measure and estimate the level of competition directly. These approaches evaluate the competitive conditions of the banking industry and the market power via the pricing conduct of banks or observing banks' behavior and estimation of equations related to price and output determination (Coccorese, 2009). Due to the benefits of the NEIO approaches, three techniques for measuring bank competition are often used in empirical studies containing the Panzar-Rosse (P-R) revenue test, the Lerner index approach and the conduct parameter approach.

The H-statistic approach. This approach is based on the Panzar and Rosse (1987) model which estimates a H-statistic to reflect the degree of competition. The H-statistic is also widely used in many empirical studies on bank competition (Casu & Girardone, 2006; Chen, 2009, Mlambo & Ncube, 2011, Masood & Sergi, 2011; Schaeck & Cihak, 2010). This technique aims to evaluate the effect of changes in input prices on banks' revenues and then calculates an H-statistic as the sum of the elasticities of a banks' revenue with respect to all input prices such as price of funds, price of labor, and price of capital from a reduced form revenue equation.

Hence, H-statistic approach needs only information on revenue and factor prices for each bank in the sample rather than data on cost and specific assumptions on market (e.g., product or geography) (Coccorese, 2009). However, a weakness of the Panzar and Rosse H-statistic is that its usefulness only applies when estimating the level of bank competition at the national level rather than at the specific individual bank-level. So, it cannot be employed to evaluate individual bank-level decisions of banks (Turk Ariss, 2010). Furthermore, the H-statistic is considered as a continuous and long run measure under the assumption of long-run equilibrium which is a further limitation of this approach (Liu, Molyneux, & Nguyen, 2012; Schaeck & Cihak, 2010; Shaffer, 2004). There should not be statistical correlation between rates of return and input prices in long-run equilibrium. Hence, this statistic needs to be discussed with some caution if the equilibrium test is rejected (Bikker & Bos, 2008).

The conduct parameter approach. To overcome the H-statistic test's shortcomings, empirical studies used another technique for calculating competition level. This technique estimates a parameter reflecting banks' conduct such as Conjectural Variation Coefficient (Iwata, 1974) or Conduct Parameter (Bresnahan, 1982; Lau, 1982). The advantage of this technique is that it estimates a direct measure of competition that is not based on market structure as well as the assumption of a long-run equilibrium.

The conduct parameter method focuses on banks' behavior via an estimated parameter that represents their degree of market power throughout a mark-up test. The mark-up tests are based on the principle that profit-maximizing banks in equilibrium will select prices at which marginal costs and perceived marginal revenue are equal. This test, therefore, estimates θ which represents the degree of market power of a bank by calculating the deviation of a bank's perceived marginal revenue schedule from its demand schedule. This technique and its variants have been applied in bank competition studies by Brissimis, Delis, and Papanikolaou (2008), Delis, Staikouras, and Varlagas (2008), Delis and Tsionas (2009), Soedarmono (2010), Soedarmono et al. (2011, 2013), Uchida and Tsutsui (2005).

A suggested approach by Uchida and Tsutsui (2005) employed in his research into competition in Japanese banking over 1974–2000 period, referred to as the Cournot-type theoretical framework, provides yearly estimates of the degree of competition. After developing three equations of cost function, inverse demand function, and first order condition of profit maximization, the study estimates simultaneously these equations by multivariate regression and three-stage least square regression. Unlike the method of Bresnahan (1982) and Lau (1982) that estimates a long-run average competition level using time-series data, one of merits of Uchida and Tsutsui (2005) estimation method is to investigate short-term changes in the degree of competition by using panel data, thus this approach can show the trend of competition over a period. Moreover, this approach does not require information on market structure and assumptions regarding market equilibrium.

Lerner index approach. A bank's market power defined as its ability to specify price above marginal cost (Lerner, 1934) is considered as a proxy of bank's competitive behavior. Estimation of a Lerner index pioneered by Lerner (1934) becomes one of the most widely used method to estimate the degree of bank competition at both industry- and bank-level in academic. The conventional Lerner index is calculated by the ratio of the disparity between price (p) and marginal cost (MC) to price (p). This standard indicator that bases on information on costs and prices or average revenues (AR) attempts to estimate banks' conduct as well as their market power. This measure is considered to be *a bank-level and time-varying proxy for market power* (Angelini & Cetorelli, 2003; Coccorese & Pellecchia, 2010; Maudos & de Guevara, 2007). It is, therefore, a more suitable measure of bank competition than the H-statistic or conduct parameter for testing its relationship with bank performance and bank efficiency.

Additionally, Lerner index approach can estimate market power in various markets such as asset market, loan market and deposit market. This method is able to capture the effect of both market concentration and elasticity of demand. Koetter, Kolari, and Spierdijk (2008) found that efficiency-adjusted Lerner indices can assess competitive behavior of the banking markets and other markets, thus they are useful for policies that seek to foster competition over time, and for regulators as well as policy makers to recognize efficient banks in providing bank products and services to customers (Schaeck & Cihak, 2010). However, Vives (2008) suggested that Lerner index cannot measure the level of product substitutability suitably. Moreover, the Lerner index will be bias if either of its two components such as prices and marginal costs is not estimated exactly.

Empirical Studies on Bank Competition

The investigation of competitive structure has become a topical area of research into the behavior of banking. The majority of these studies, however, were conducted in the context of developed countries, especially the United States and European countries, by researchers including Shaffer (1982), Nathan and Neave (1989), Molyneux and Thornton (1994), Vesala (1995), Coccorese (1998, 2004), Bikker and Groeneveld (2000), De Bandt and Davis (2000), Hempell (2002), Bikker and Haaf (2002), Weill (2004), Casu and Girardone (2006), Cipollini and Fiordelisi (2012).

Several studies have estimated the degrees of bank competition using the Panzar and Rosse (1987) H-statistic method within the context of emerging economies, for example, Eastern Europe and Latin America (Gelos & Roldós, 2004), Arab countries, that is, the Gulf Combined Countries (GCC) (Al-Muharrami, Matthews, & Khabari, 2006), South-Eastern European region (Mamatzakis, Staikouras, & Koutsomanoli-Fillipaki, 2005), Sub-Saharan African countries (Chen, 2009), China (Masood & Sergi, 2011), South Africa (Mlambo & Ncube, 2011), emerging Asia and Latin America (Jeon et al., 2011), South East Asia (Liu et al., 2012). Most of findings conclude that emerging banking markets are monopolistically competitive. Similar results are also found in a study by Turk Ariss (2010)for five emerging regions over the period of 1999–2005 using Lerner indices. The author indicated that banks operate under conditions of monopolistically competitive markets in these emerging regions where there are conditions of relatively underdeveloped financial markets and where the essential role of banks are to provide credit. The findings here suggest that banking industries in two regions, namely East/South Asia and Pacific, and Middle East, are less competitive.

In the context of the Latin American banking system, Williams (2012) used the conventional Lerner indices for both loan and deposit markets and efficiency-adjusted Lerner indices for asset markets to estimate market power. The results show that the banking system in Latin America is generally of a monopolistically competitive variety. Similarly, Fang, Hasan, and Marton (2011) concluded that the banking systems of six South-Eastern European transition nations operated under conditions of monopolistic competition in the decade 1998–2008. Pruteanu-podpiera, Weill, and Schobert (2008)also employed Lerner index to calculate the bank competition levels in Czech, a transition country. The results, however, indicate a downward trend as the main trend of banking competition during the transition period rather than a strong development of competition. To investigate whether competition or regulations affected bank risk-taking in transition countries, Agoraki et al. (2011) measured bank market power for a sample of the Central and Eastern European banking systems over the period 1998–2005 using the conventional Lerner index. The results suggest that monopolistic competition is the best description for banking sectors in this region.

The growth of foreign bank entry and changing market structure in emerging Asian markets does raise concerns about competition in banking (Jeon et al., 2011; Turk Ariss, 2010). Claessens and Laeven (2004) and Schaeck, Cihak, and Wolfe (2009) used the Panzar and Rosse (1987) H-statistic to estimate the degree of bank competition for a sample of both developed and developing countries. They found that the structure of banking sectors in some Asian emerging countries is characterized by monopolistic competition. To focus on only Asian banking markets, Soedarmono (2010) examined yearly average market power in ten Asian countries between 1999 and 2007 using the Cournot-type theoretical framework suggested by Uchida and Tsutsui (2005). They found that monopolistic competition best describes the competitive structure of these countries banks over the study period. The findings also suggest that an increase in market power (i.e., a decrease in competition level) appears to predominate across Asian banking over the study period. Soedarmono et al. (2013) estimated bank competition across 11Asian countries over the period 1994–2009 covering both the 1997 Asian crisis and the 2008 financial crisis. They found that competitive structure became monopolistic for almost banking over 2005–2009. Our study adds to the literature on banking across emerging Asian economies by investigating the changes in market concentration and bank competition as well as their relationships over pre and post the 2008 global financial crisis.

Methodology

Measurements of Market Concentration and Bank Competition

To investigate competition across Asian banking and its changes over 2005–2012 which include the 2008 global financial crisis, this study employs a non-structural approach based on explicit information with regards to cost and demand to estimate banks' behavior. The level of banks' market power is reflected via estimates of banks behavior (Coccorese, 2009). The study follows the framework suggested by Delis and Tsionas (2009), Soedarmono et al. (2011, 2013) and Uchida and Tsutsui (2005)to measure competition across emerging markets. Based on the framework developed by Uchida and Tsutsui (2005), bank i is assumed to raise total deposit and short-term funding (d_i) from their depositors, then invest it to total earning assets (q_i) and Government bonds (b_i), and aim to maximize its profit function:

$$\pi_{it} = P_t(q_{it})q_{it} + r_{it}^b b_{it} - r_{it}^d d_{it} - C_{it}(q_{it}, d_{it}) \tag{1}$$

where π are profits of bank i at time t, $P_t(q_{it})$ is inverse demand function for total earning assets, $C_{it}(q_{it}, d_{it})$ is operating cost function. r_{it}^b and r_{it}^d are the yields for bonds and the deposit interest rate, respectively. The bank's problem is to maximize profit:

$$\text{Max}_{b,q,d}\pi_{it} s.t.\ \ b_{it} + q_{it} = d_{it} \tag{2}$$

The first order conditions of the profit maximization are

$$P_t\left(1 - \frac{1}{\eta_t}\theta_{it}\right) = r_{it}^b + \frac{\partial C_{it}}{\partial q_{it}} \tag{3}$$

And

$$r_{it}^b - r_{it}^d - \left(\frac{\partial C_{it}}{\partial d_{it}}\right) = 0 \tag{4}$$

Or

$$r_{it}^b = r_{it}^d + \frac{\partial C_{it}}{\partial d_{it}} \tag{5}$$

where $\eta_t = -(P_t/Q_t)(\partial Q_t/\partial P_t)$ measures the market demand elasticity for total earning assets. $\theta_{it} = (q_{it}/Q_t)(\partial Q_t/\partial q_{it})$ represents the competition degree of bank i at time t and θ_t represents competition degree of banking industry at time t.

Replacing r_{it}^b with $(r_{it}^b + \partial C_{it}/\partial d_{it})$ in Eq. (3) to obtain Eq. (6):

$$P_t\left(1 - \frac{1}{\eta_t}\theta_{it}\right) = r_{it}^d + \frac{\partial C_{it}}{\partial d_{it}} + \frac{\partial C_{it}}{\partial q_{it}} \tag{6}$$

$R_{it} = P_t q_{it}$ is defined as the total revenue of bank i at time t. Like Brissimis et al. (2008), Soedarmono (2010), Soedarmono et al. (2011, 2013), total revenue is the sum of interest and non-interest revenue while total expense is defined as both interest and non-interest expense. These definitions show implicitly the role of both interest and non-interest activities in creating profit of banks. Revenue of bank i generated by total earning assets is specified as:

$$R_{it} = \frac{\theta_t}{\eta_t}R_{it} + r_{it}^d q_{it} + \frac{\partial C_{it}}{\partial d_{it}}q_{it} + \frac{\partial C_{it}}{\partial q_{it}}q_{it} \tag{7}$$

The translog cost function and the revenue function are assumed as follows:

$$\begin{aligned}\ln C_{it} = {} & b_0 + b_1\overline{\ln\ q_{it}} + \frac{1}{2}b_2\left(\overline{\ln\ q_{it}}\right)^2 + b_3\overline{\ln\ d_{it}} + \frac{1}{2}b_4(\ln\ d_{it})^2 \\ & + b_5\overline{\ln\ w_{it}} + \frac{1}{2}b_6\overline{(\ln\ w_{it})}^2 + b_7\left(\overline{\ln\ q_{it}}\right)\left(\overline{\ln\ w_{it}}\right) \\ & + b_8\left(\overline{\ln\ q_{it}}\right)\left(\overline{\ln\ d_{it}}\right) + b_9\left(\overline{\ln\ d_{it}}\right)\left(\overline{\ln\ w_{it}}\right) + e_{it}^C \end{aligned} \tag{8}$$

$$\begin{aligned} R_{it} = {} & \frac{\theta_t}{\eta_t}R_{it} + r_{it}q_{it} + C_{it}\left(b_1 + b_2\overline{\ln\ q_{it}} + b_7\overline{\ln\ w_{it}} + b_8\overline{\ln\ d_{it}}\right) \\ & + C_{it}\frac{q_{it}}{d_{it}}\left(b_3 + b_4\overline{\ln\ d_{it}} + b_8\overline{\ln\ q_{it}} + b_9\overline{\ln\ w_{it}}\right) + e_{it}^S \end{aligned} \tag{9}$$

To reduce multicollinearity, variables with upper bars are calculated by deviations from their means in each time period (Brissimis et al., 2008; Soedarmono et al., 2011; Uchida & Tsutsui, 2005) (Table 1).

Table 1: Definitions of Variables.

Variables	Definition
C	Total expenses
Q	Total earning assets
D	Total deposit and short-term funding
W	Total operating expenses to total assets
R	Total revenue equals sum of interest revenue and non-interest revenue
r	Ratio of interest expenses to total deposits
P	Ratio of total revenues to total earning assets
TA	Total assets
GDP	Real gross domestic product
e	Error term

η_t is captured from the inverse loan demand function as follows:

$$\ln P_{it} = g_0 - \left(1/\eta_t\right)\ln\ q_{it} + g_1 \ln \mathrm{GDP}_t + g_2 \ln \mathrm{IR}_t + g_3 \ln \mathrm{TA}_{it} + e_{it}^D \quad (10)$$

Similar to Delis and Tsionas(2009), macroeconomic variables used in Eq. (10) are GDP instead of GDP growth due to the negative values of GDP growth of Malaysia in 2009.

According to this approach, θ is defined as the conjectural variation elasticity for total banking industry outputs with respect to ith bank's output provides a measure of annual market power. θ is a proxy for bank competition at industry-level. A higher (lower) θ shows a decrease (increase) in bank competition. In theory, values of θ are bound between 0 and 1, where $\theta = 0$ implies perfect competition, and $\theta = 1$ implies pure monopoly, and values of θ in between indicate monopolistic competition. However, $\theta < 0$ implies that marginal cost is higher than price, possibly due to a non-optimizing behavior of banks. In the special case of Cournot competition, $\theta_{i,t}$ = market share of bank i in time t.

Like Uchida and Tsutsui(2005) and Brissimis et al. (2008), the study employs both seemingly unrelated regression (SUR) and three-stage least squares (3SLS) to estimate simultaneously the system of equations including Eqs. (8), (9), and (10). The seemingly unrelated regression (SUR) is able to take into account the correlation among error terms in equations of the system so this method can estimate the system of equations with correlated error terms. However, SUR makes the assumption that the error term and explanatory variables in each equation are uncorrelated. Therefore, if each equation in the system has endogeneous variables on its both sides, this regression will give bias results when estimating such a system. By three-stage least squares, both the endogeneity of the variables in the left hand side and the cross-equation restrictions are considered when the systems of three equations are estimated simultaneously. Moreover, 3SLS regression handles possible correlation between variables in the right-hand side and the error terms, contemporary occurrence of heterokedasticity and correlation between residuals as well (Coccorese, 2009).

For 3SLS, year dummy variables are used to estimate θ_t but time dummy variables for every two years are employed to estimate η_t in both models due to a linear dependence of η on GDP in the Eq. (10). Rank variables of $q_{i,t}$, $d_{i,t}$, $r_{i,t}$, $C_{i,t}$, $P_{i,t}$, $R_{i,t}$, and exogenous variables such as IR_t, $\mathrm{OPL}_{i,t}$, TA_{it}, $w_{i,t}$, GDP_t, and year dummies are used as instrumental variables.

Based on traditional industrial organization approaches which observe the market structure and connect it with banks' behavior and profitability (Casu & Girardone, 2006), market concentration is considered as a proxy for market structure. For measuring the degree of market concentration in emerging Asian banking industries, this study uses four-bank concentration ratio (CRTA) in terms of total assets that is defined as the ratio of the total assets of the four largest banks to the total assets of all the banks in a given year.

Data

To investigate bank competition in emerging banking industries pre and post global financial crisis of 2008–2009, the study uses a sample of commercial banks as these institutions have a tendency to have discretion in their choice of business models across the countries been investigated (Soedarmono et al., 2011). The sample consists of commercial banks in six emerging Asian countries, for example, Bangladesh (36 banks), India (46 banks), Indonesia (40 banks), Malaysia (25 banks), Philippines (24 banks), and Vietnam (32 banks) over 2005–2012.

The study uses panel data instead of time-series data to estimate annual degree of competition, and thus shows the short-term changes in competition level. All bank-specific data was retrieved from Bankscope Fitch-IBCA. For country-specific data, data for the real Gross domestic product (GDP) was collected from World Economic Outlook of International Monetary Fund (IMF). IR is defined as short-term interest rate such as interbank rate (e.g., Bangladesh, India, Indonesia, Malaysia, and Philippines) or benchmark interest rate (for Vietnam) that was collected from Asian Development bank (ADB). Banks that provide insufficient data on the main variables for calculating competition level are excluded from the sample.

Descriptive statistics for all variables are shown in Table 2. In general, the interest rates in these emerging countries were very high, especially in Bangladesh and Vietnam. The averaged interest rates were highest in Bangladesh, followed by in Vietnam (around nine percent). By contrast, Malaysia had the lowest averaged interest rates (around three percent). Total expenses (*C*), total earning assets (*Q*), total deposit and short-term funding (*D*), total revenue equals sum of interest revenue and non-interest revenue (*R*), and total assets (TA) were highest for India, followed by Malaysia but they were lowest for Bangladesh. There were remarkable differences in real gross domestic product (GDP) among countries in the sample. GDP fluctuated from about 28 billion USD for Vietnam to over 192.000 billion USD for Malaysia.

Empirical Results

Bank Competition and Market Concentration across Emerging Asian Countries

Tables 3–8 illustrate the degree of market concentration and competition in banking system across six emerging Asian countries including Bangladesh, India, Indonesia, Malaysia, Philippines, and Vietnam over 2005–2012 using concentration ratios by total assets (CRTA) and values of θ obtaining from simultaneous estimation of equations by seemingly unrelated regression (SUR) and three-stage least squares (3SLS).

Bangladesh

Figure 1 illustrates that the variable θ_t generally displays a downward trend over 2005–2012. Therefore, competition in the Bangladesh banking improved over this period. As shown in Table 3, almost θ_t are statistically significant with the exception of θ_t by SUR in 2006 and θ_t by 3SLS over 2006–2008. θ_t by SUR decreased sharply over 2005–2007 from 1.107 to −0.196. Therefore, banks in Bangladesh had a tendency to operate in the

Table 2: Descriptive Statistics on Variables That Are Used to Estimate Bank Competition.

		Bangladesh	India	Indonesia	Malaysia	Philippines	Vietnam
C	Mean	108	1,661	389	517	235	303
	SD	93	2,286	610	582	287	507
	Min	6	14	4	20	3	0.167
	Max	570	19,372	3,234	3,061	1,400	3,252
Q	Mean	1,156	22,972	4,938	12,634	4,012	3,455
	SD	1,042	31,861	8,643	16,218	5,406	5,313
	Min	64	183	69	284	29	7
	Max	5,860	262,787	53,663	100,411	28,453	28,021
D	Mean	1,173	21,380	4,611	12,736	3,673	3,243
	SD	1,149	29,421	8,222	15,378	4,870	4,955
	Min	71	194	64	182	20	3
	Max	7,630	246,610	47,218	87,228	23,652	26,322
W	Mean	0.024	0.018	0.033	0.017	0.035	0.015
	SD	0.011	0.005	0.013	0.011	0.013	0.005
	Min	0.010	0.007	0.007	0.005	0.012	0.003
	Max	0.097	0.042	0.075	0.112	0.087	0.045
R	Mean	178	2,603	756	1,025	463	444
	SD	147	3,642	1,304	1,177	581	749
	Min	10	22	7	36	5	0.364
	Max	835	30,551	7,723	6,384	2,872	4759
r	Mean	0.068	0.057	0.053	0.026	0.032	0.074
	SD	0.018	0.012	0.020	0.010	0.012	0.032
	Min	0.032	0.028	0.006	0.009	0.010	0.014

	Max	0.173	0.109	0.116	0.101	0.065	0.178
P	Mean	0.156	0.116	0.152	0.095	0.131	0.122
	SD	0.027	0.016	0.043	0.042	0.032	0.037
	Min	0.078	0.085	0.045	0.042	0.053	0.026
	Max	0.245	0.205	0.311	0.420	0.252	0.265
IR	Mean	9.324	6.542	6.687	3.113	5.620	8.873
	SD	2.971	1.528c	1.503	0.498	1.438	2.657
	Min	4.824	3.608	4.037	2.233	4.025	5.917
	Max	13.473	8.422	8.963	3.692	7.825	13.333
TA	Mean	1380	25,639	5,628	15,332	4512	3,883
	SD	1,371	35,577	9,928	18,786	5,929	5,809
	Min	87	217	75	492	34	9
	Max	8,472	290,048	58,232	112,009	30,210	29,634
GDP	Mean	68,139	983,132	226,672	192,033,845	118,068	28,024
	SD	5,703	126,075	34,421	31,949,870	20,573	1,512
	Min	59,389	767,047	178,109	143,803,968	84,446	24,694
	Max	75,208	1145876	271,799	244,930,844	153,303	29,451
Number of banks		36	46	40	25	24	32
Number of observations		288	368	320	200	192	253

Source: Bankscope, Asian Development bank (ADB) and International Monetary Fund (IMF).
Note: R, C, q, d, TA, and GDP are in million of USD; IR is in percent; P, w, r, OPL are ratios.

Table 3: Bank Competition and Market Concentration in Bangladesh over 2005–2012.

	Bangladesh		
	Bank Competition (θ)		Market Concentration ($CRTA_4$)
	SUR	3SLS	
2005	1.107***	0.807***	44.732
2006	0.159	0.242	41.480
2007	−0.196*	0.030	42.260
2008	0.172*	0.142	38.890
2009	−0.195**	−0.148*	35.753
2010	−0.666***	−0.562***	33.887
2011	−0.394***	−0.336***	33.501
2012	−0.522***	−0.483***	30.883
R^2	0.488	0.467	

Source: Author's calculation.
Note: θ is a proxy for bank competition. Values of θ are obtained from simultaneous estimation of equations by Seemingly Unrelated Regression (SUR) and Three-Stage Least Squares (3SLS). There is a negative relationship between θ and degree of competition. So, a higher (lower) θ is associated with a lower (higher) competition level. $\theta = 0$: perfect competition, $\theta = 1$: pure monopoly, $0 < \theta < 1$: monopolistic competition, $\theta < 0$: marginal cost is higher than price. Market concentration is in percent.
*, **, ***Denote statistical significance at the 10, 5, and 1 percent levels, respectively.

conditions of the pure monopoly in 2005 and monopolistic competition in 2006 but the negative value of θ in 2007 implies that marginal cost is higher than price, possibly due to a non-optimizing behavior of banks. θ_t increased and reached a peak at 0.172 in 2008 so banks in Bangladesh seemed to be monopolistic competitive when the global financial crisis happened. However, θ_t decreased dramatically and took on negative values in remaining years. One possible interpretation is that financial reforms in the banking sector such as legal, policy and institutional reforms that have been launched since 1990 enhance competitiveness among banks in the system, however, the recent global financial crisis may result in a slight decrease in competition degrees of banks in the year 2008 when the crisis happened and non-optimizing behavior of banks in later years.

Table 4: Bank Competition and Market Concentration in India over 2005–2012.

	India		
	Bank Competition (θ)		Market Concentration ($CRTA_4$)
	SUR	3SLS	
2005	−0.984***	−1.060***	36.708
2006	−0.670***	−0.704***	35.754
2007	−0.255***	−0.356***	34.614
2008	−0.240***	−0.363***	34.072
2009	0.014	0.017	32.419
2010	0.204***	0.176***	32.037
2011	0.175***	0.182***	31.848
2012	0.269***	0.276***	31.841
R^2	0.621	0.589	

Source: Author's calculation.
Note: θ is a proxy for bank competition. Values of θ are obtained from simultaneous estimation of equations by Seemingly Unrelated Regression (SUR) and Three-Stage Least Squares (3SLS). There is a negative relationship between θ and degree of competition. So, a higher (lower) θ is associated with a lower (higher) competition level. $\theta = 0$: perfect competition, $\theta = 1$: pure monopoly, $0 < \theta < 1$: monopolistic competition, $\theta < 0$: marginal cost is higher than price. Market concentration is in percent.
***Denote statistical significance at the 1 percent level.

Estimated values of θ_t by 3SLS lies between 0 and 1 over 2005–2008 implying that banks in Bangladesh have a tendency to operate under conditions of monopolistic competitive in this period. However, θ_t is statistically significant only in 2005. Similar to the results estimated by SUR, all θ_t by 3SLS takes on negative values which were statistically significant over 2009–2012, thereby suggesting that banks in Bangladesh had higher marginal cost than price possibly because the effects of the global financial crisis.

Table 3 shows that market concentration of the banking in Bangladesh decreased slightly from 44.73 percent in 2005 to 30.88 percent in 2012. The growth of total assets held by four of the country's largest banks (about 14 percent) is lower than the growth of total assets for the whole banking system (about 20 percent). Four of the largest banks could not maintain their market

Table 5: Bank Competition and Market Concentration in Indonesia over 2005–2012.

	Indonesia		
	Bank Competition (θ)		Market Concentration ($CRTA_4$)
	SUR	3SLS	
2005	0.106***	0.089***	57.609
2006	0.083***	0.053***	56.415
2007	0.138***	0.121***	55.539
2008	0.157***	0.149***	54.864
2009	0.142***	0.131***	56.099
2010	0.156***	0.158***	53.938
2011	0.167***	0.157***	52.657
2012	0.184***	0.177***	51.961
R^2	0.920	0.904	

Source: Author's calculation.
Note: θ is a proxy for bank competition. Values of θ are obtained from simultaneous estimation of equations by Seemingly Unrelated Regression (SUR) and Three-Stage Least Squares (3SLS). There is a negative relationship between θ and degree of competition. So, a higher (lower) θ is associated with a lower (higher) competition level. $\theta = 0$: perfect competition, $\theta = 1$: pure monopoly, $0 < \theta < 1$: monopolistic competition, $\theta < 0$: marginal cost is higher than price. Market concentration is in percent.
***Denote statistical significance at the 1 percent level.

shares of total assets over this period because other smaller commercial banks competed away their market shares from the largest banks over a period of time, and thus increased their market shares.

India

By contrast to the banking system in Bangladesh, Figure 2 shows that θ_t in the Indian banking generally followed an upward trend suggesting that there was a decrease in bank competition of this banking over studied period. In addition, Table 4 indicates θ_t took on negative values over 2005–2008 and increased sharply in the first two years from around −1 to around −0.3 but nearly remained constant when the crisis happened. These results suggest that banks in India seemed to operate at non-optimization

Table 6: Bank Competition and Market Concentration in Malaysia over 2005–2012.

	Malaysia		
	Bank Competition (θ)		Market Concentration ($CRTA_4$)
	SUR	3SLS	
2005	1.022***	1.017***	48.317
2006	0.655***	0.630***	51.324
2007	0.526***	0.442***	51.032
2008	0.455***	0.411***	49.855
2009	0.445***	0.438***	50.535
2010	0.324***	0.296***	49.478
2011	0.010	0.002	49.233
2012	−0.347***	−0.375***	49.975
R^2	0.815	0.795	

Source: Author's calculation.
Note: θ is a proxy for bank competition. Values of θ are obtained from simultaneous estimation of equations by Seemingly Unrelated Regression (SUR) and Three-Stage Least Squares (3SLS). There is a negative relationship between θ and degree of competition. So, a higher (lower) θ is associated with a lower (higher) competition level. $\theta = 0$: perfect competition, $\theta = 1$: pure monopoly, $0 < \theta < 1$: monopolistic competition, $\theta < 0$: marginal cost is higher than price. Market concentration is in percent.
***Denote statistical significance at the 1 percent level.

levels before the crisis because they had higher marginal cost than price. In 2008, bank competition had no tendency to decrease dramatically as bank competition over 2005–2007, the Indian banking improved its competition by remaining nearly unchanged competition degrees over 2007–2008 to face with effects of the crisis on the banking system. However, θ_t continued to increase and took on positive values between 0 and 1 over 2009–2012, thereby proposing that competition degrees of the Indian banking followed a downward trend and monopolistic competition is the best description of competitive structure of banking in India over this period. θ_t in 2009 is nearly zero (e.g., 0.014 by SUR and 0.017 by 3SLS) implying the banking system seems to be rather perfectly competitive. However, this finding is insignificant. Table 4 shows that the

Table 7: Bank Competition and Market Concentration in Philippines over 2005–2012.

	Philippines		
	Bank Competition (θ)		Market Concentration ($CRTA_4$)
	SUR	3SLS	
2005	0.890***	0.852***	56.139
2006	0.762***	0.802***	58.480
2007	0.767***	0.773***	58.425
2008	0.616***	0.639***	58.557
2009	0.648***	0.658***	58.279
2010	0.549***	0.590***	59.069
2011	0.497***	0.528***	58.518
2012	0.385***	0.453***	58.976
R^2	0.934	0.939	

Source: Author's calculation.
Note: θ is a proxy for bank competition. Values of θ are obtained from simultaneous estimation of equations by Seemingly Unrelated Regression (SUR) and Three-Stage Least Squares (3SLS). There is a negative relationship between θ and degree of competition. So, a higher (lower) θ is associated with a lower (higher) competition level. $\theta = 0$: perfect competition, $\theta = 1$: pure monopoly, $0 < \theta < 1$: monopolistic competition, $\theta < 0$: marginal cost is higher than price. Market concentration is in percent.
***Denote statistical significance at the 1 percent level.

estimated results of θ_t by SUR and 3SLS are similar. Almost estimated values of θ_t are highly statistically significant at the one percent level except for θ_t in 2009.

Four largest banks hold around one third market shares of the Indian banking sector. The financial sector reforms have allowed the entry of new private commercial banks and foreign banks since 1992. The establishment of new private banks became liberalized. As a result, market concentration decreased slightly over 2005–2012.

Indonesia

Figure 3 shows that θ_t generally increased gradually over 2005–2012. After decreasing over 2005–2006, θ_t became larger until 2008, then θ_t decreased slightly in 2009 before recovering in remaining years. This result proposes that bank competition in Indonesia increased over

Table 8: Bank Competition and Market Concentration in Vietnam over 2005–2012.

Vietnam			
	Bank Competition (θ)		Market Concentration ($CRTA_4$)
	SUR	3SLS	
2005	−0.087	0.112	77.927
2006	−0.199***	−0.266**	72.020
2007	−0.099***	−0.111	59.433
2008	−0.219***	−0.240***	59.689
2009	−0.173***	−0.143***	53.796
2010	−0.156***	−0.131***	48.549
2011	−0.204***	−0.245***	46.203
2012	−0.166***	−0.229***	50.152
R^2	0.728	0.659	

Source: Author's calculation.
Note: θ is a proxy for bank competition. Values of θ are obtained from simultaneous estimation of equations by Seemingly Unrelated Regression (SUR) and Three-Stage Least Squares (3SLS). There is a negative relationship between θ and degree of competition. So, a higher (lower) θ is associated with a lower (higher) competition level. $\theta = 0$: perfect competition, $\theta = 1$: pure monopoly, $0 < \theta < 1$: monopolistic competition, $\theta < 0$: marginal cost is higher than price. Market concentration is in percent.
**, ***Denotes statistical significance at the 5 and 1 percent levels, respectively.

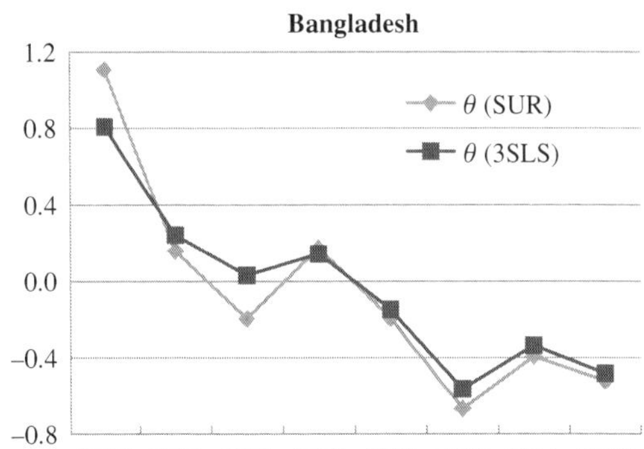

Figure 1: Estimates of θ by Seemingly Unrelated Regression (SUR) and Three-Stage Least Squares (3SLS) for the Bangladesh Banking.

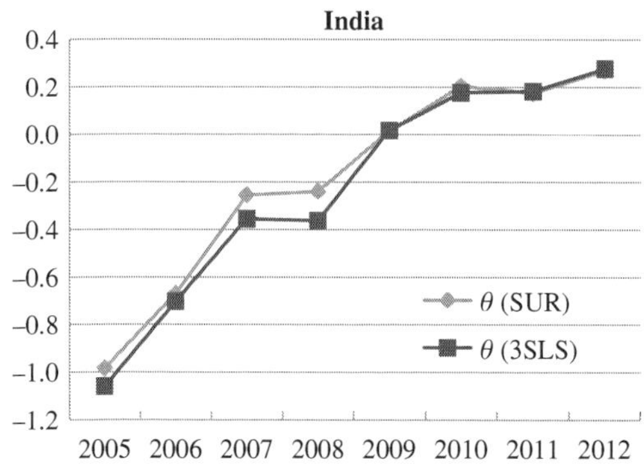

Figure 2: Estimates of θ by Seemingly Unrelated Regression (SUR) and Three-Stage Least Squares (3SLS) for the Indian Banking.

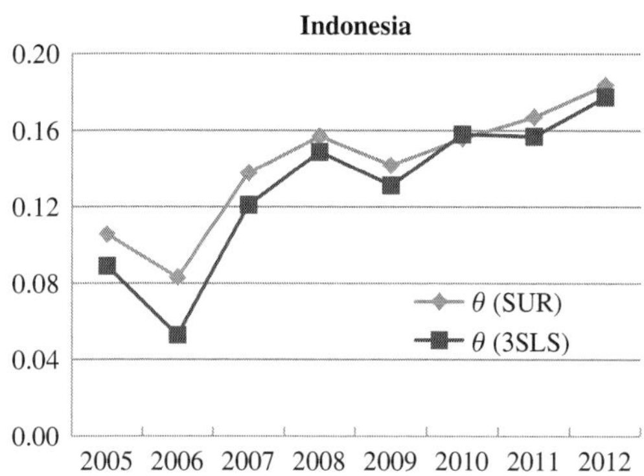

Figure 3: Estimates of θ by Seemingly Unrelated Regression (SUR) and Three-Stage Least Squares (3SLS) for the Banking in Indonesia.

2005–2006 but declined just before the 2008 crisis. Then, bank competition improved in 2009 and decreased over 2009–2012.

Table 5 indicates that the estimated results of θ_t by SUR are slightly higher than those by 3SLS. All θ_t are highly statistically significant at the one percent level. θ_t took on small values from 0.05 to 0.18 over 2005–2012. Therefore, the banking in Indonesia became monopolistically competitive but competition degrees were very strong over this period.

Like competition, market concentration of the Indonesian banking generally had a tendency to decrease over 2005–2012. Four largest banks hold over a half of total market shares of the whole banking. Therefore, banks in Indonesia operated in a highly concentrated market.

Malaysia

In generally, there was a downward trend in θ_t over 2005–2012. Figure 4 shows a sharp decline in θ_t over 2005–2007 and 2009–2012, thus bank competition in Malaysia followed an upward trend in these periods. However, θ_t had tendency to remain constant in three years including 2007, 2008 and 2009. This may be because banks in Malaysia focused on addressing their own problems to contribute to a stable banking system rather than competing with each other so they tend to avoid severe competition over the crisis period.

As shown in Table 6, the estimated values of θ_t by SUR and 3SLS are similar. Almost θ_t are highly statistically significant at the one percent level. θ_t reached unity in 2005 so the banking became pure monopoly. θ_t decreased gradually from approximately 0.6 to 0.3 over 2006–2010 suggesting that banks in Malaysia operate under the condition of monopolistic competition. In 2011, θ_t reached nearly zero, however, this finding is not significant. Then,

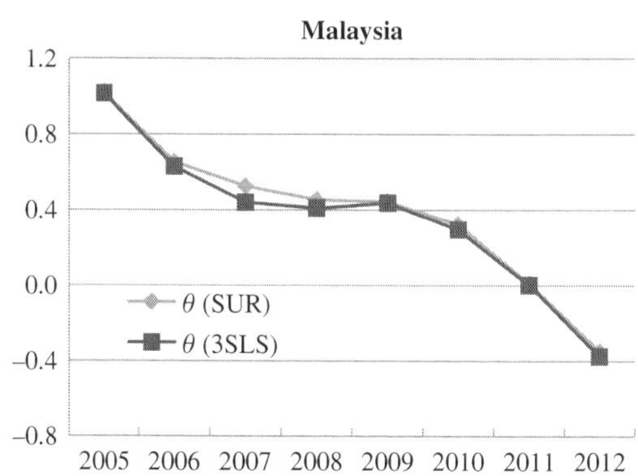

Figure 4: Estimates of θ by Seemingly Unrelated Regression (SUR) and Three-Stage Least Squares (3SLS) for the Banking in Malaysia.

θ_t took on a negative value implying that banks in this country had higher marginal cost than price possibly because banks had non-optimizing behaviors in 2012.

As shown in Table 6, market concentration generally increased slightly from around 48 percent in 2005 to about 50 percent in 2012. However, the concentration levels followed a downward trend over 2006–2011. The changes in market concentration in the Malaysian banking are due to merger, internalization process, liberalization, and globalization (Table 7, Figure 5).

Philippines

Similar to the Malaysian banking, θ_t in Philippines generally decreased, therefore, competition of the banking followed an upward trend during the period of 2005–2012. θ_t declined gradually from approximately 0.9 to 0.4 suggesting that monopolistic competition is the best description of banking competitive structure in this period. All estimated values of θ_t are highly statistically significant at the one percent level for both SUR and 3SLS estimations. While θ_t generally declined, there was a slight increase in θ_t over 2008–2009, thus the recent financial crisis seemed to decrease competition of the banking in Philippines. Market concentration followed an upward trend. Market shares of four largest banks accounted for 56 percent in 2005, then increased

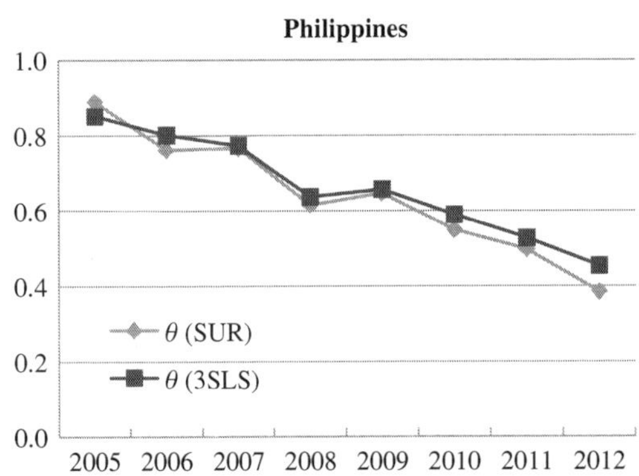

Figure 5: Estimates of θ by Seemingly Unrelated Regression (SUR) and Three-Stage Least Squares (3SLS) for the Banking in Philippines.

to nearly 59 percent in 2012. Therefore, banks in Philippines operated under a highly concentrated market.

Vietnam

Figure 6 illustrates a fluctuation of θ_t of the Vietnamese banking over 2005–2012. θ_t followed a V-shape over 2005–2007. Then, θ_t reached a bottom in 2008 and recovered over 2008–2010. Therefore, competition had a tendency to improve before the crisis but it decreased in two years later. One possible interpretation for this trend of competition is that banks in Vietnam became more vulnerable due to high ratios of non-performing loan especially when the global financial crisis happened. Hence, they had a tendency to focus on addressing their own problems rather than competing with each other. They tend to avoid severe competition over the crisis period. Bank competition improved in 2011 but decreased slightly in 2012 because θ_t reached a new bottom in 2011 before increasing slightly in 2012.

Table 8 shows the estimated values of θ_t by SUR and 3SLS in 2005 are very different (e.g., −0.087 by SUR compared to 0.112 by 3SLS), however, both values of θ_t are not significant. All estimates of θ_t take on negative values and fluctuate within a small range from around −0.1 to around −0.3 over 2006–2012 and they were statistically significant with the exception of θ_t by 3SLS in 2007.

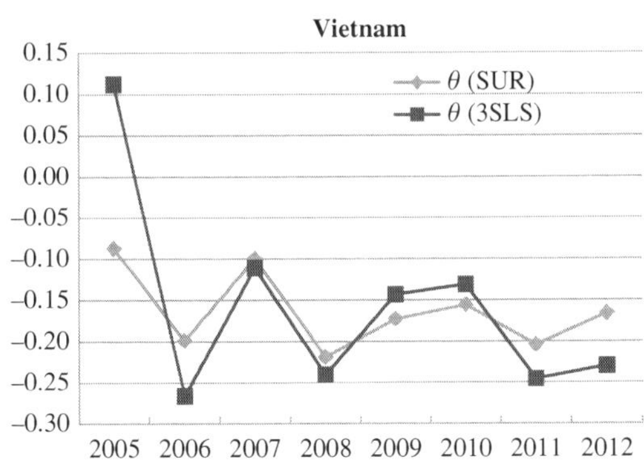

Figure 6: Estimates of θ by Seemingly Unrelated Regression (SUR) and Three-Stage Least Squares (3SLS) for the Banking in Vietnam.

This result suggests that marginal cost was higher than price for Vietnamese banking possibly because banks in Vietnam seem to operate at non-optimizing levels.

Compared to other countries in the sample, Vietnam had the most highly concentrated banking market in two first years with concentration ratios of over 72 percent. Nevertheless, as from the year 2007, the concentration ratios decrease dramatically. There are some main possible reasons to explain these changes. Firstly, the Vietnamese banking system has witnessed a dramatic increase in number of banks mainly due to a remarkable increased presence of foreign banks, especially since 2007 when Vietnam has become a member of the World Trade Organization (WTO). Due to this global integration of Vietnam as well as its WTO commitments, the banking system is more open to foreign investment and removes many barriers to foreign banks. Since January 1, 2011, the playing field for both domestic and foreign banks has been leveled because of the similar treatment to foreign banks' branches as domestic banks such as the same deposit and lending rules or provision of the same services (Ho & Baxter, 2011). Secondly, the strong competition between the joint stock commercial banks and State-owned commercial banks to capture market share lead to a dramatic change in concentration levels.

The Relationship between Market Concentration and Bank Competition

An interesting question is what the relationship between market concentration and bank competition looks like. Hence, we develop a model to examine the influence of concentration and other factors on competition in six emerging Asian countries including Bangladesh, India, Indonesia, Malaysia, Philippines and Vietnam:

$$\theta_{kt}=f(\text{Concentration}_{kt},\text{GDPGrowth}_{kt},\text{Inflation}_{kt},\text{Crisis}_{kt},\text{LOANDEP}_{kt}) \quad (11)$$

where θ is a proxy for bank competition in country k at time t. A higher θ, a lower competition level is. Concentration is a four-bank concentration ratio in terms of total assets. GDP growth and Inflation are the growth of real gross domestic products and inflation rate that are derived from International Financial Statistics of International Monetary Fund (IMF). Crisis is a dummy variable, crisis equals to 1 for the year 2008 and equals to 0 otherwise. LOANDEP is the ratio of loans to deposits. Total deposits and total loans are in million USD and collected from International Monetary Fund (IMF) (Table 9).

The estimated results are presented in Table 10. The coefficient on concentration is significantly positive, implying that concentration is positively related to θ, thus competition among banks across six emerging countries in the studied sample become greater when market concentration decreases. A negative association between market concentration and bank competition in these countries can be explained by the SCP hypothesis that suggests banks in concentrated market can collude to get higher profits. Hence, when market is less concentrated, banks will decrease their collusion and be more competitive. Therefore, the result provides evidence to support the assumptions of SCP hypothesis on negative relationship between concentration and competition in banking.

The coefficient on GDP growth is significant negative at the five percent level. Similarly, the coefficient on inflation is also negative but this finding is significant only when considering θ by seemingly unrelated regression (SUR) as a dependent variable. Thus, GDP growth and inflation promoted bank competition. Crisis and LOANDEP did not affect degree of competition because the coefficients on these variables are not significant.

Conclusions

The study describes movements of market concentration as well as bank competition in banking across the world's fastest economic growing region over the recent global financial crisis. Generally we find a negative association between market concentration and bank competition across most of the countries in the study suggesting that banks in concentrated markets can collude

Table 9: Descriptive Statistics of Variables in Eq. (11).

	θSUR	θ3SLS	Concentration	GDP Growth	Inflation	Crisis	LOANDEP
Mean	0.125	0.121	48.828	6.090	7.123	0.125	0.784
STD	0.447	0.439	11.050	2.028	4.118	0.334	0.153
Min	−.984	−1.060	30.883	−1.513	0.597	0	0.392
Max	1.107	1.017	77.927	11.228	23.120	1	1.005
Number of observations	48	48	48	48	48	48	48

Table 10: The Relationship between Bank Competition and Concentration across Six Emerging Asian Countries.

	Dependent Variable: θSUR		Dependent Variable: θ3SLS	
	Coefficient	*p*-value	Coefficient	*p*-value
Concentration	0.011	0.037	0.012	0.019
GDP growth	−0.063	0.037	−0.065	0.024
Inflation	−0.026	0.099	−0.023	0.118
Crisis	0.084	0.649	0.038	0.831
LOANDEP	−0.434	0.255	−0.478	0.192
Constant	0.472	0.303	0.460	0.293

Note: θSUR and θ3SLS are estimated θ by seemingly unrelated regression and three-stage least squares. θ is a proxy for bank competition. A higher (lower) θ is associated with a lower (higher) competition level.

to get higher profits. Therefore, the result provides evidence to support the assumptions of SCP hypothesis regards the finding of a negative relationship between concentration and competition in banking. The study also investigates changes in bank competition across six emerging Asian countries pre and post the 2008–2009 global financial crisis. Here monopolistic competition appears to best describe the competitive structure of banking across the countries over the crisis.

Some policy implications are suggested from the study which is generally directed toward a strategy of decreased concentration and increased bank competition. Firstly, the policy on mergers and acquisitions should encourage mergers and acquisitions of small-sized and weak financial banks as a means to improve their financial strength and soundness. Secondly, as demonstrated in some studies (Claessens and Laeven (2004), Yeyati and Micco (2007), Yildirim and Philippatos (2007), Wu et al. (2010), Jeon et al. (2011)), more foreign bank entry should be encouraged as this enhances competition by restructuring domestic banking sector and consolidating troubled local banks to change banks' governance as well as decreasing the State's role in the banking markets. Generally our recommendation is to allow increased foreign bank penetration and divestiture of state ownership in banking can heighten competitive pressures in the banking sector. Thus, the main policy lessons drawn from the study is that competitive conditions could be further enhanced by easing regulatory impediments and in the long run, allow more foreign bank participation in an attempt to spur competitive conduct in banking.

In addition, Government policy makers in each country should scrutinize foreign banks' strategy regarding acquisitions and mergers of domestic banks in terms of established criteria related to their strategies to encourage competition and reduce concentration of banking across their respective economies.

References

Agoraki, M.-E. K., Delis, M. D., & Pasiouras, F. (2011). Regulations, competition and bank risk-taking in transition countries. *Journal of Financial Stability*, *7*(1), 38–48.

Al-Muharrami, S., Matthews, K., & Khabari, Y. (2006). Market structure and competitive conditions in the Arab GCC banking system. *Journal of Banking & Finance*, *30*(12), 3487–3501.

Angelini, P., & Cetorelli, N. (2003). The effects of regulatory reform on competition in the banking industry. *Journal of Money, Credit and Banking*, *35*(5), 663–684.

Bain, J. S. (1951). Relation of profit rate to industry concentration: American manufacturing, 1936–1940. *The Quarterly Journal of Economics*, *65*(3), 293–324.

Beck, T. (2008). *Bank competition and financial stability: Friends or foes?* The World Bank.

Beck, T., De Jonghe, O., & Schepens, G. (2013). Bank competition and stability: Cross-country heterogeneity. *Journal of Financial Intermediation*, *22*(2), 218–244.

Berger, D.-K. A., Levine, R., & Haubrich, J. G. (2004). Bank concentration and competition: An evolution in the making. *Journal of Money, Credit and Banking*, *36*(3), 433–451.

Berger, D. R., Genay, H., & Udel, G. F. (2000). Globalization of financial institutions: Evidence from cross-border banking performance. *Brookings-Wharton Papers on Financial Services*, *3*, 23–158.

Bhatti, G. A., & Hussain, H. (2010). Evidence on structure conduct performance hypothesis in Pakistani commercial banks. *International Journal of Business and Management*, *5*(9), 174–187.

Bikker, J. A., & Bos, J. W. B. (2008). *Bank performance: A theoretical and empirical framework for the analysis for profitability, competition and efficiency*. New York, NY: Routledge.
Bikker, J. A., & Groeneveld, J. M. (2000). Competition and concentration in the EU banking industry. *Kredit and Kapital, 33*, 62–98.
Bikker, J. A., & Haaf, K. (2002). Competition, concentration and their relationship: An empirical analysis of the banking industry. *Journal of Banking & Finance, 26*(11), 2191–2214.
Bresnahan, T. F. (1982). The oligopoly solution concept is identified. *Economics Letters, 10*, 87–92.
Brissimis, S. N., Delis, M. D., & Papanikolaou, N. I. (2008). Exploring the nexus between banking sector reform and performance: Evidence from newly acceded EU countries. *Journal of Banking & Finance, 32*(12), 2674–2683.
Casu, B., & Girardone, C. (2006). Bank competition, concentration and efficiency in the single European market. *The Manchester School, 74*(4), 441–468.
Chen, C. (2009). *Bank efficiency in sub-saharan African middle-income countries*. IMF Working Paper No. WP/09/14.
Cipollini, A., & Fiordelisi, F. (2012). Economic value, competition and financial distress in the European banking system. *Journal of Banking & Finance, 36*(11), 3101–3109.
Claessens, S., & Laeven, L. (2004). What drives bank competition? Some international evidence. *Journal of Money, Credit and Banking, 36*(3), 563–583.
Claessens, S., & Laeven, L. (2005). Financial dependence, banking sector competition, and economic growth. *Journal of the European Economic Association, 3*(1), 179–207.
Coccorese, P. (1998). Assessing the competitive conditions in the Italian Banking system: Some empirical evidence. *Banca Nazionale del Lavoro Quarterly Review, 51*(205), 171.
Coccorese, P. (2004). Banking competition and macroeconomic conditions: A disaggregate analysis. *Journal of International Financial Markets, Institutions and Money, 14*(3), 203–219.
Coccorese, P. (2009). Market power in local banking monopolies. *Journal of Banking & Finance, 33*(7), 1196–1210.
Coccorese, P., & Pellecchia, A. (2010). Testing the 'Quiet Life' hypothesis in the Italian banking industry. *Economic Notes, 39*(3), 173–202.
De Bandt, O., & Davis, E. P. (2000). Competition, contestability and market structure in European banking sectors on the eve of EMU. *Journal of Banking & Finance, 24*(6), 1045–1066.
de Guevara, J. F., Maudos, J., & Pérez, F. (2005). Market power in European banking sectors. *Journal of Financial Services Research, 27*(2), 109–137.

Delis, M. D., Staikouras, K. C., & Varlagas, P. T. (2008). On the measurement of market power in the banking industry. *Journal of Business Finance & Accounting, 35*(7–8), 1023–1047.
Delis, M. D., & Tsionas, E. G. (2009). The joint estimation of bank-level market power and efficiency. *Journal of Banking & Finance, 33*(10), 1842–1850.
Fang, Y., Hasan, I., & Marton, K. (2011). Bank efficiency in South-Eastern Europe. *Economics of Transition, 19*(3), 495–520.
Fu, X., & Heffernan, S. (2009). The effects of reform on China's bank structure and performance. *Journal of Banking & Finance, 33*(1), 39–52.
Fu, X., Lin, Y., & Molyneux, P. (2014). Bank competition and financial stability in Asia Pacific. *Journal of Banking & Finance, 38*(0), 64–77.
Gelos, R. G., & Roldós, J. (2004). Consolidation and market structure in emerging market banking systems. *Emerging Markets Review, 5*(1), 39–59.
Heggestad, A. A., & Mingo, J. J. (1977). The competitive condition of U.S. Banking markets and the impact of structural reform. *The Journal of Finance, 32*(3), 649–661.
Hempell, H. S. (2002). *Testing for competition among German banks.* Discussion Paper No. 04/02. Deutsche Bundesbank, Economic Research Centre.
Ho, A., & Baxter, R. A. (2011). *Banking reform in Vietnam.* Retrieved from www.frbsf.org/publications/banking/asiafocus/2011/june-banking-reform-in-vietnam.pdf
Iwata, G. (1974). Measurement of conjectural variations in oligopoly. *Econometrica, 42*(5), 947–966.
Jeon, B. N., Olivero, M. P., & Wu, J. (2011). Do foreign banks increase competition? Evidence from emerging Asian and Latin American banking markets. *Journal of Banking & Finance, 35*(4), 856–875.
Koetter, M., Kolari, J. W., & Spierdijk, L. (2008). *Efficient competition? Testing the "quiet life" of the US banks with adjusted Lerner indices.* Working Paper No. Groningen University.
Lau, L. J. (1982). On identifying the degree of competitiveness from industry price and output data. *Economics Letters, 10*, 93–99.
Lerner, A. P. (1934). The concept of monopoly and the measurement of monopoly power. *The Review of Economic Studies, 1*(3), 157–175.
Liu, H., Molyneux, P., & Nguyen, L. H. (2012). Competition and risk in South East Asian commercial banking. *Applied Economics, 44*(28), 3627–3644.
Lloyd-Williams, D. M., Molyneux, P., & Thornton, J. (1994). Market structure and performance in Spanish banking. *Journal of Banking & Finance, 18*(3), 433–443.
Mamatzakis, E., Staikouras, C., & Koutsomanoli-Fillipaki, N. (2005). Competition and concentration in the banking sector of the South Eastern European region. *Emerging Markets Review, 6*(2), 192–209.

Marrouch, W., & Turk-Ariss, R. (2014). Joint market power in banking: Evidence from developing countries. *Journal of International Financial Markets, Institutions and Money*, *31*(0), 253–267.

Masood, O., & Sergi, B. (2011). China's banking system, market structure, and competitive conditions. *Frontiers of Economics in China*, *6*(1), 22–35.

Maudos, J., & de Guevara, J. F. (2007). The cost of market power in banking: Social welfare loss vs. cost inefficiency. *Journal of Banking & Finance*, *31*(7), 2103–2125.

Maudos, J., & Fernández de Guevara, J. (2004). Factors explaining the interest margin in the banking sectors of the European Union. *Journal of Banking & Finance*, *28*(9), 2259–2281.

Mlambo, K., & Ncube, M. (2011). Competition and efficiency in the banking sector in South Africa. *African Development Review*, *23*(1), 4–15.

Molyneux, P., & Forbes, W. (1995). Market structure and performance in European banking. *Applied Economics*, *27*(2), 155–159.

Molyneux, L.-W. D. M., & Thornton, J. (1994). Competitive conditions in European banking. *Journal of Banking & Finance*, *18*, 445–459.

Nathan, A., & Neave, E. H. (1989). Competition and contestability in Canada's financial system: Empirical results. *The Canadian Journal of Economics / Revue canadienne d'Economique*, *22*(3), 576–594.

Nguyen, M., Skully, M., & Perera, S. (2012). Market power, revenue diversification and bank stability: Evidence from selected South Asian countries. *Journal of International Financial Markets, Institutions and Money*, *22*(4), 897–912.

Panzar, J. C., & Rosse, J. N. (1987). Testing for "Monopoly" equilibrium. *The Journal of Industrial Economics*, *35*(4), 443–456.

Park, C.-Y. (2011). *Asian financial system: Development and challenges*. ADB Economics Working Paper No. 285 (pp. 1–27).

Pruteanu-podpiera, A., Weill, L., & Schobert, F. (2008). Banking competition and efficiency: A micro-data analysis on the Czech banking industry. *Comparative Economic Studies*, *50*(2), 253–273.

Rhoades, S. A. (1982). Welfare loss, redistribution effect, and restriction of output due to monopoly in banking. *Journal of Monetary Economics*, *9*(3), 375–387.

Rose, P. S., & Fraser, D. R. (1976). The relationship between stability and change in market structure: An analysis of bank prices. *Journal of Industrial Economics*, *24*, 251–266.

Schaeck, K., & Cihak, M. (2010). *Competition, efficiency, and soundness in banking: An industrial organization perspective*. European Banking Center Discussion Paper No. 2010-20S.

Schaeck, K., Cihak, M., & Wolfe, S. (2009). Are competitive banking systems more stable? *Journal of Money, Credit and Banking*, *41*(4), 711–734.

Shaffer. (1982). A non-structural test for competition in financial markets. Paper presented at the Proceedings of a conference on bank structure and competition, Federal Reserve Bank of Chicago.
Shaffer, S. (2004). Comment on "What Drives Bank Competition? Some International Evidence" by stijn claessens and luc laeven. *Journal of Money, Credit and Banking*, *36*(3), 585–592.
Soedarmono (2010). Bank competition, institution and economic development: Evidence from Asia during 1999–2007. *Economics Bulletin*, *30*(3), 2119–2133.
Soedarmono, W., Machrouh, F., & Tarazi, A. (2011). Bank market power, economic growth and financial stability: Evidence from Asian banks. *Journal of Asian Economics*, *22*(6), 460–470.
Soedarmono, W., Machrouh, F., & Tarazi, A. (2013). Bank competition, crisis and risk taking: Evidence from emerging markets in Asia. *Journal of International Financial Markets, Institutions and Money*, *23*, 196–221.
Spellman, L. J. (1981). Commercial banks and the profits of savings and loan markets. *Journal of Bank Research*, *12*, 32–36.
Tabak, B. M., Fazio, D. M., & Cajueiro, D. O. (2012). The relationship between banking market competition and risk-taking: Do size and capitalization matter? *Journal of Banking & Finance*, *36*(12), 3366–3381.
Turk Ariss, R. (2010). On the implications of market power in banking: Evidence from developing countries. *Journal of Banking & Finance*, *34*(4), 765–775.
Uchida, H., & Tsutsui, Y. (2005). Has competition in the Japanese banking sector improved? *Journal of Banking & Finance*, *29*(2), 419–439.
Vesala, J. (1995). Testing for competition in banking: Behavioural evidence from Finland. Bank of Finland Studies, E: 1.
Vives, X. (2008). Innovation and competitive pressure. *The Journal of Industrial Economics*, *56*(3), 419–469.
Weill, L. (2004). On the relationship between competition and efficiency in the EU banking sectors. *Kredit and Kapital*, *37*, 329–352.
Williams, J. (2012). Efficiency and market power in Latin American banking. *Journal of Financial Stability*, *8*(4), 263–276.
Wu, J., Jeon, B. N., & Luca, A. (2010). Foreign bank penetration, resource allocation and economic growth: Evidence from emerging economies. *Journal of Economic Integration*, *25*(1), 166–192.
Yeyati, E. L., & Micco, A. (2007). Concentration and foreign penetration in Latin American banking sectors: Impact on competition and risk. *Journal of Banking & Finance*, *31*(6), 1633–1647.
Yildirim, H. S., & Philippatos, G. C. (2007). Restructuring, consolidation and competition in Latin American banking markets. *Journal of Banking & Finance*, *31*(3), 629–639.

20

Possible Unintended Consequences of Basel III on Emerging Markets and Developing Economies: Assessment of Stressed VaR and Effects on Banks' Investment Decisions

Alberto Burchi and Duccio Martelli

Abstract

The recent 2008–2009 financial crisis has led international financial authorities to review the existing regulation; the Basel Committee on Banking Supervision has been thus induced to review the pillars of the Basel Accord (Basel II) in order to strengthen the risk coverage of capital framework

(Basel 2.5 and III). These reforms will help to raise capital requirements for the trading book, which represents a major source of losses for internationally financial institutions, especially during crisis periods. In particular, the Committee has introduced a Stressed Value-at-Risk (SVaR) capital requirement, as a new methodology to evaluate market risk.

This chapter aims to shed some lights on the issues major banks have to face when calculating SVaR in the context of emerging markets, pointing out the differences in adopting an estimation model with respect to another one. Our results show a considerable increase in capital requirements especially when new rules are applied to financial markets with high-risk parameters, such as emerging markets are. The increased cost due to higher capital requirements could be a disincentive to investment in markets with higher risk profiles than the developed markets, taking also into account that diversification benefits deriving from investing in emerging economies have shown a decrease over time. The reduction of institutional investors can thus represent a brake on the process of innovation and evolution of emerging markets.

Keywords: Basel III; Emerging Markets; Developing Economies; Stressed VaR; Banks' Investment Decisions

Introduction

The recent 2008–2009 financial crisis has led international financial authorities to review the existing regulation; the Basel Committee on Banking Supervision has been thus induced to review the pillars of the Basel Accord (Basel II) in order to strengthen the risk coverage of capital framework (Basel 2.5 and III). In particular, in response to higher market risks these reforms will help to raise capital requirements for the trading book, which represents a major source of losses for internationally financial institutions especially during crisis periods. In particular, the Committee has introduced a Stressed Value-at-Risk (SVaR) capital requirement, based on a continuous 12-month period of significant financial stress (Basel, 2009).

The number of studies focused on analyzing challenges related to implementing the SVaR is still scarce. The variety of approaches applied by banks highlights the lack of regulatory guidance. Nevertheless, the changes in the calculation of regulatory capital influence the amount of capital banks need, especially for the operations related to proprietary trading. Therefore, this kind of regulatory intervention impacts, by definition, the decisions of banks in the investment choice.

The methodology consists of implementing several VaR parametric models for the quantification of the SVaR. The approach makes it possible to simulate the process of optimization and evaluation of a financial intermediary that intends to invest in emerging markets.

This chapter aims to shed some light on the issues major banks have to face when calculating SVaR in the context of emerging markets. Specifically, it seeks to identify whether simple or complex models undergo profound changes in the application of the new Basel rules. Our results point out the differences in adopting a model with respect to another one. We expect a considerable increase in capital requirements, especially when new rules are applied to financial markets with high-risk parameters, such as emerging countries are. The increased cost due to higher capital requirements could be a disincentive to invest in markets with higher risk profiles than the developed markets, taking also into account that diversification benefits deriving from investing in emerging economies have shown a decrease over time. The reduction of institutional investors can thus represent a brake on the process of innovation and evolution of emerging markets.

The chapter is structured as follows: the section "Literature Review" summarizes the discussion regarding advantages and disadvantages of the use of VaR methodologies, as methods to estimate market risks, with a particular attention to emerging market countries. The section "The Forecasting of VaR and the Capital Requirement for Market Risks" presents several estimation models related to VaR methodologies (such as historical and parametric simulations, GARCH, EWMA, and TGARCH models) and discuss the importance of minimizing the cost of capital for financial institutions. Thus, the section "The Results of the Empirical Analysis" analyzes the empirical results of the effects of the new capital requirements for market risk in the investment decision-making of banks in emerging market. Finally, the section "Conclusions" reaches some concluding remarks.

Literature Review

In the aftermath of the recent financial crisis of 2008–2009 the Basel Committee on Banking Supervision (2011) has started to revise the existing capital adequacy guidelines, in order to promote a more resilient banking sector raising capital requirements that financial institutions have to hold to face future crisis periods. These rules, better known as the Basel III Accord, aim to improve the regulation, supervision and risk management within the financial sector, especially during periods of financial stress. New regulation is expected to have deeper impacts both at the individual and at the systemic level. On the one hand, increased capital requirements could raise the cost of funding, and thus reduce banks' profitability. This could lead weaker banks, which will find more difficult to find investors willing to lend fresh money, to revise their future strategies (e.g., reducing the risk taken selling parts of their portfolios) or to merge with stronger firms. On the other hand, a lower bank profitability, combined with a persistent low-interest environment, could encourage banks to increase the exposure of their portfolios to those assets and markets, which can likely generate higher returns per unit of risk taken. Emerging markets have been always seen as an excellent opportunity to increase the trading portfolio profitability, while reducing the overall risk through the diversification benefits.

The Basel Committee on Banking Supervision has proposed different measures of market risk, despite the large majority of financial institutions adopt the Value at Risk (VaR). The VaR is defined as the possible maximum loss that a bank can expect, over a given holding period within a certain fixed confidence level.

Unfortunately VaR analysis shows several issues (among others Nielsson, 2009; Rockafellar & Uryasev, 2002). Allen, Boudouk, and Saunders (2004) demonstrate how the assumptions behind these models are not supported by empirical evidence. In particular, traditional VaR analysis assume that risk is randomly distributed (and thus market returns are normally distributed as well), while several papers state that market returns show instead a leptokurtic distribution (among others, Páfka & Kondor, 2001). However, this limit can partially be solved recalibrating the parameters according to a more leptokurtic distribution (such as a logistic distribution), as suggested by Chen (2012). A further limit is that VaR analysis does not take into account the characteristics of the extreme left tail of the distribution after that specific value of loss, despite it can contain useful information in all those cases when market returns do not follow a normally distribution. Finally, VaR models are not able to always fully capture the benefits of portfolio diversification.

However, despite these limitations, VaR analysis still represents the most important tool for evaluating market risk (Macchiarola, 2009). In fact, it is not possible to identify a single limit-free analytical technique for quantifying total risk, when the distribution has fait tails (Farber, 2011). Chen (2014) comes to similar conclusions in his attempt to compare different methodologies (traditional Var, stressed VaR, and expected shortfall): despite the expected shortfall (indicating the average loss when losses exceed the VaR level) has the property of subadditivity, while VaR does not, expected shortfall cannot be backtested, while VaR allows to easily compare forecasts with historical observations (Hull, 2012). That is why financial authorities continue to opt for VaR methodologies instead of for alternative measures of market risk.

However, as Nocera (2009) notices, VaR can be also easily misunderstood and if so, it can put in danger the bank's stability.

Behavioral factors, such as anchoring effect, can also play an important role if VaR is perceived as a point of reference, such as the specific amount of risk that a bank is willing to bear over a certain time horizon (Taleb, 2009): any level of VaR decided at the executive level could in fact encourage traders to align the risk of their portfolios to such level, so to maximize the overall expected return. Besides, a single specific measure of remote loss (i.e., risk) can create a false sense of security among executives, since they do not usually consider what can happen in the extreme left part of the tail (Einhorn, 2008). These behavioral issues affecting both traders and corporate executives could partially explain why financial institutions tend to generally disclose a higher forecast of risk than what actually observed, while adopting a lower level for internal use. Pérignon, Deng, and Wang (2008) propose an explanation more in line with the traditional finance perspective, stating that banks tend to avoid inspections or worse sanctions by financial regulators. However, a conservative approach to the VaR estimation increases the average cost of capital, that is why financial institutions tend to adopt an active and flexible approach in the management of capital requirements related to the trading book (McAleer, 2009).

Unfortunately, due to its limitations, VaR analysis is likely to fail during periods of market stress. For this reason, financial regulators have proposed in the last revision of the Basel Accord a stressed version of VaR analysis, which represents one of the four key elements of the market risk framework (together with an incremental risk charge for default risk, new charges for securitization and a comprehensive risk measure for risks arising from correlation trading) (Bank for International Settlement, 2011). This revised VaR methodology subjects traditional model to a continuous 12-month period of significant financial stress, in order to obtain a more significant threshold, especially during periods of market stress. Despite the easiest way to stress the VaR is using historical data referred to specific past periods of crisis, forecasts can be sensibly different from actual levels of the risk borne by financial institutions, since past performance are not of course a guarantee of future returns.

The VaR analysis has been initially applied to developed countries, but in recent decades, scholars have shown a growing interest in conducting research using emerging markets data. This is mainly due to the fact that emerging markets continue to grow faster than developed ones and attract always more investors (mainly institutional), who are seeking to higher return, while reducing the risk through the diversification benefits. In a recent paper Kearney (2012) highlights the areas of greatest interest and suggests topics for further research. In particular, he documents how market efficiency and risk-adjusted return represent the two main fields of research while conducting analyses on emerging markets.

As stated above, risk measures are crucial in the decision-making process of any financial institution, especially in high-risk markets. However most models currently adopted by banks assume that returns are normally distributed and markets are thus efficient. Unfortunately, when liquidity is low, the assumptions underlying these models do not hold anymore: emerging markets are in fact historically characterized by several market inefficiencies. Hwang and Pedersen (2004), for example, suggest that models, which are able to better capture asymmetry and tail risk in equity returns, should be adopted, in order to better capture market risk of emerging markets.

Thus, analyzing tail risk in emerging markets seems to be crucial: according to Li and Rose (2009) emerging markets are likely to be more dependent on the world market during large joint losses than during large joint gains (i.e., they show similar behaviors to developed markets during periods of market stress). Ignoring tail risk could lead to ignore a significant part of the market risk, especially in all those situations when financial stability is more in danger and when banks and financial regulators needs to know whether their models are keeping risks into adequate account (Berkowitz, 2001). A very well-known case generating misleading results when the standard deviation has been used to capture the market risk (i.e., assuming that market returns were normally distributed) is the demise of Long Term Capital Management in 1998. Since then, emerging markets have changed significantly: unlikely to what investors could think, nowadays diversification benefits are not as significant as they were in the past, despite investors expect to have several advantages from investing in emerging countries. The presence of international financial institutions have made these markets more efficient, so that performance are now more strictly correlated to key variables affecting also developed countries rather than to specific local factors (such as political risk). The raise in the number of professional investors have produced an increase in terms of market efficiency in emerging countries and thus a reduction in the importance of tail risk.

However, despite traditional VaR analysis has been criticized, because it is not able to fully capture market risk (especially in those markets considered less efficient), this methodology is still supported by financial regulators and widespread among financial institutions. Its revised versions, which conveniently keep into account periods of market stress and thus differences in the level of volatility, seem to be the best available compromise between the analytical rigor in thinking and its practical valuation and easy interpretation, also when estimating market risk of emerging countries.

Surprisingly, a recent survey highlights that banks have not reported significant challenges associated with the implementation of SVaR models (Prorokowski & Prorokowski, 2014). As far as peer practices regarding the models used, the majority of the surveyed banks utilize historical simulations and apply both the absolute and relative measures of volatility for different risk factors.

Our study involves advanced methodologies able to detect with greater care the dynamics of risk, limiting the computational complexity. The use of parametric models, supported by a vast theoretical literature, are logical and consistent from an operational point of view and are also solid with the compliance function. However, financial institutions continue to adopt models which are too much simple to take into adequate account all risky factors.

The chapter differs from previous contributions for two main characteristics. First, it focuses on all markets defined "emerging," according to the International Monetary Fund definition (27 countries to be precise), while most scientific research has conducted experiments exclusively regarding developed markets or a very limited number of emerging economies so far. Second, the adoption of an opportunity cost function allows us to quantify the reduction in profits resulting from the rules of prudential supervision. This study thus allows financial institutions to better appreciate the benefits of investing in these specific markets.

The Forecasting of VaR and the Capital Requirement for Market Risks

Defining Value at Risk

Value at risk is a loss that we are fairly sure will not be exceeded if the current portfolio is held over some period of time. VaR has two basic parameters:

- the significance level α (or confidence level $1-\alpha$);
- the risk horizon, denoted h, which is the period of time over which the VaR is measured.

In mathematical terms, the α% h-day VaR is the loss amount (in present value terms) that would be exceeded with only a small probability α when holding the portfolio static over the next h days. (Alexander, 2009)

Hence, to estimate the VaR at time t we need to find the α quantile of the discounted h-day profit and loss (P&L) distribution. Given a sequence of prices of a financial asset $(S_0, S_1, \ldots, S_n)$ the returns during the period t will be:

$$R_t = \ln\left(\frac{S_t}{S_{t-1}}\right) \tag{1}$$

where R_t is the return between the period $t-1$ and t. It is possible to decompose the time series of log-return every time t in a component part of a predictable $C_1(t)$ and unpredictable (random) $C_2(t)$. Then:

$$R_t = C_1(t) + C_2(t) = E(R_t|I_{t-1}) + \varepsilon_t \tag{2}$$

The decomposition allows us to observe that the random variable has a component given by the conditional mean $E(Y_t|F_{t-1})$, where F_{t-1} is the set of information available at the time $t-1$, and a random component ε_t.

Therefore, the distribution of R_t depends on the random variable ε_t. We can assume that it follows a distribution so described:

$$\varepsilon_t = D\left(\mu_t, \sigma_t^2\right) \tag{3}$$

where μ_t and σ_t^2 are the conditional mean and the variance of ε_t and may be estimated through a variety of parametric models, semi-parametric and nonparametric. It follows that the VaR for the variable can be calculated as follows:

$$\text{VaR}_t = E(R_t|F_{t-1}) - \alpha\sigma_t \tag{4}$$

where α represents the critical value of the distribution ε_t to achieve the desired confidence level. It is possible to replace σ_t with alternative measures of conditional variance (Degiannakis et al., 2012).

Guidelines for Estimating VaR from Banking Regulators

In 1974 the central bank governors of the G10 countries created a forum to debate and coordinate best practices for risk management and banking supervision. The crucial action of the Committee was the 1988 Basel Accord which sets core principles for adequate supervision and minimum capital standards and incentivates regulatory convergence and coordination across countries.

The Accord, and its successive 1996 Amendment for Market Risk in the Trading Book, has been progressively adopted into legal regulations by over 100 countries; now the Accord is the global standard for evaluating banking risk. In the 1996 Amendment there was a long technical appendix that responded to the industry calls for the use of internal models, rather than standardized rules, to assess market risk capital. In 2005 the exceptional growth in the market for credit default swaps and collateralized debt obligations lead to an extensive revisions to the assessment of credit risks and the introduction of a capital charge to cover operational. The revision entitled the New Basel II Accord.

The market risk capital requirements under Basel II are largely unaffected from the 1996 Amendment.[1] Under this Accord, exceptional market risks should be monitored in the banking book. However, any additional capital charges for market risks in the banking book are left to the discretion of national supervisors.

The financial crisis of 2007–2008 has severely shocked economies around the world. In response to the lacks in financial regulation revealed by the recent global financial crisis, a new version of the Basel Accords, named Basel III, has been developed since 2010. The new draft is made-up to strengthen bank capital requirements by increasing bank liquidity and decreasing bank leverage. Its implementation, initially planned for the years 2013–2015 has been gradually extended until March 31, 2019.

Accordingly with the Basel Committee, the daily capital requirement should be determined based on the higher level comparing the previous day's VaR and the average VaR of the last sixty days multiplied by a correction factor, which can vary depending on the quality of the estimates generated by the model. It is required to consider the movement of prices equivalent to 10 days. Formally, the capital requirement can be written as follows:

$$\mathrm{CR}_t = \max\left\{ \mathrm{VaR}_{t-1}, (3+k_t)\frac{1}{60}\sum_{i=1}^{60}\mathrm{VaR}_{t-i} \right\} \tag{5}$$

where CR is the capital requirement VaR_{t-1} is the daily VaR estimated decadal based on the previous day $(3 + k_t)$ is the

1. The trading book definition in the Amendment is: the trading book is now defined as the sum of all positions in financial instruments and commodities held either with trading intent or to hedge other items of the trading book. Trading intent may be derived by identifying a clearly documented trading strategy that is approved by senior management, and/or by clearly defined policies and procedures for the active management of the position.

multiplication factor $\frac{1}{60}\sum_{i=1}^{60} VaR_{t-i}$ is the average of VaR of the past sixty trading days.

The multiplication factor k depends on the evaluation of the supervisory procedures regarding risk management adopted by the bank. More exactly, the multiplication factor depends on the result of a procedure for backtesting focusing on the number of cases in which the loss exceeds the VaR in the same trading day. As shown in Table 1, the minimum multiplication factor is equal to 3, which compensates for any errors that may be related to the difficulty of implementing the estimation model, such as oversimplifications, rounding, distortions, and errors due to sample aggregation processes of different positions (Jiménez-Martín et al., 2009). In order to determine the number of violations, obligatory banks compared the VaR on each trading day of the previous year. The calibration factor must be conducted at least quarterly.

The revisions to market risk framework introduces the Stressed VaR (SVaR): it consists of an additional capital requirement calculated in a similar way to the traditional, using the values assumed

Table 1: Multiplication Factor Based on Violations.

Zone	Number of Exceptions	Increase in Scaling Factor	Cumulative Probability
Green Zone	0	0.00	8.11%
	1	0.00	28.58%
	2	0.00	54.32%
	3	0.00	75.81%
	4	0.00	89.22%
Yellow Zone	5	0.40	95.88%
	6	0.50	98.63%
	7	0.65	99.60%
	8	0.75	99.89%
	9	0.85	99.97%
Red Zone	10 or more	1.00	99.99%

Source: Basel (2009).

by the variables in a crisis period, not shorter than one year. The sampling period of stress adopted in the estimation of SVaR must be approved in advance by the authorities. Analytically, the minimum capital requirement is:

$$\mathrm{RC}_t = \max\left\{\mathrm{VaR}_{t-1}, (3+k_t)\frac{1}{60}\sum_{i=1}^{60}\mathrm{VaR}_{t-i}\right\} + \max\left\{s\mathrm{VaR}_{t-1}, (3+k_t)\frac{1}{60}\sum_{i=1}^{60}s\mathrm{VaR}_{t-i}\right\} \quad (6)$$

As in the previous version, the correction factor depends on the result of the backtest performed considering the VaR. Analytically, the SVAR is an additional capital requirement to the one currently in force and not a substitute of it.

The introduction of this procedure leads to a considerable increase in the capital requirement. Under the new formulation, the financial institution must estimate the VaR considering the maximum loss obtained from the model, using the current data and the values associated with the period of crisis identified. It is plausible to assume an increase in the capital requirement stabilized on the level of the most recent financial crisis.

Regarding the estimation method to adopt for the assessment of VaR, the Basel Committee does not put constraints; however, the Committee emphasizes that the choice should fall on a model able to capture all market risks that the bank faces (Basel, 2004).

The Committee defines only guidelines and criteria for the assessment and dissemination of VaR, for example, defining the holding period of reference (holding period) to evaluate the positions in the portfolio of 10 working days and the length of the historical time series of observations used to determine (sampling period), which must be not shorter than one year.

Another key aspect concerns the choice of the confidence interval, which defines the level of protection against adverse changes in market parameters. In this sense, the legislation imposes a level of 99 percent, which is necessary to consider the losses that are expected to exceed 1 percent of cases only.

With regard to the depth and refresh rate of the time series used for estimation, the Basel Committee expects that the first is at least one year, and states that the refresh rate is at least three months, leaving the regulator to increase the frequency in contexts of high volatility (European Banking Autorithy [EBA], 2012).

The Estimation Models

In the analysis, we adopt five different models to estimate:

a. The historical simulation — [HSM];
b. The parametric — [PM];
c. The GARCH (1,1) — [GM];
d. The EWMA — [EWM];
e. The TGARCH (1.1) — [TGM];

The Basel Committee explicitly stated the first two methods. The types 3, 4 and 5 are more complex to use, but allow to obtain estimates of higher precision.

Historical Simulation Models (HSM)

The HSM assumes that the distribution of future returns is constant over time and corresponds to the observed distribution. Given certain distribution in the previous n observations, it is easy to extract the desired percentile (e.g., in a vector of 250 observations, the 99th percentile corresponds to the third worst result). An implicit assumption of historical VaR is that the current portfolio, which is not obviously optimal, would also have been the portfolio of choice during every day of the historical sample.

Parametric Models (PM)

The PM approach is well-known by ease of calculation and understanding. The model assumes a normal distribution of returns R_t. So the VaR observed in the period t is:

$$\mathrm{VaR} = \mu - Z(\alpha)\sigma \tag{7}$$

The VaR is calculated considering estimates of mean and standard deviation of the normal distribution as well as associated values $Z(\alpha)$.

Similar to the historical simulation, the parametric linear VaR models assume that both portfolio and its asset weights to be constant. However, this model makes no reference to a specific historical period. That method adopts a covariance matrix of asset weights or risks factor returns over the risk horizon, how banks forecast this matrix is part of the implementation. It is also possible to use historical data to estimate the matrix, and this methodology is the interpretation of the Basel Committee's recommendations for analyzing data.

GARCH Models (GM)

Going back to the normal distribution of returns, R_t, we can consider the conditional mean of the returns an autoregressive process of order k, AR(k):

$$E(R_t|I_{t-1}) = v_0 + \sum_{i=1}^{k} v_i Y_{t-1} \tag{8}$$

The component ε_t is not predictable and it can be expressed as an ARCH process in the following form:

$$\varepsilon_t = z_t \sigma_t \tag{9}$$

where z_t is the set of independent and identically distributed random variables with mean 0 and variance 1, while σ_t the standard deviation of conditioning ε_t. Engle (1982) introduced the ARCH (q) and expresses the conditional variance as a linear combination of the above terms:

$$\sigma_t^2 = \alpha_0 + \alpha_1 \varepsilon_{t-1}^2 + \cdots + \alpha_q \varepsilon_{t-q}^2 = \alpha_0 \sum_{i=1}^{q} \alpha_i \varepsilon_{t-i}^2 \tag{10}$$

with $\alpha_0 > 0$ and $\alpha_i \geq 0$ for $i = 1, \ldots, q$.

The GARCH model matches up to a generalization of the ARCH model proposed by Bollerslev (1986). Assuming that the conditional variance depends on the number of squares of the errors ε_t^2, and from the series of the variances $\sigma_{t-1}^2, \sigma_{t-2}^2, \ldots, \sigma_{t-p}^2$. The series σ_t^2 according to the GARCH (p, q) equates:

$$\begin{aligned}\sigma_t^2 &= \alpha_0 + \alpha_1 \varepsilon_{t-1}^2 + \cdots + \alpha_q \varepsilon_{t-q}^2 + \beta_1 \sigma_{t-1}^2 + \cdots + \beta_p \sigma_{t-p}^2 \\ &= \alpha_0 + \sum_{i=1}^{q} \alpha_i \varepsilon_{t-i}^2 + \sum_{i=1}^{p} \beta_i \sigma_{t-i}^2 \end{aligned} \tag{11}$$

with $\alpha_0 > 0$, $\alpha_i \geq 0$ for $i = 1, \ldots, q$ $\beta_0 > 0$, $\beta_j \geq 0$ for $j = 1, \ldots, p$.

The GARCH model effectively captures some aspects of financial time series, such as the phenomena of volatility clustering and fat tailed distribution (He & Terasvirta, 1999).

EWMA Models (EM)

A special case of the GARCH family model is the Exponentially Weighted Moving Average (EWMA). The volatility of the time *t* is a weighted average of the estimated volatility and the square of the previous error parameter. The variance of returns is a process with exponential decay:

$$\sigma_t^2 = \lambda \sigma_{t-1}^2 + (1 - t) \varepsilon_{t-1}^2 \tag{12}$$

The EWMA model is a particular case of GARCH (1.1) with intercepts equal to 0, and the sum of the two remaining variables equal to 1. We use a λ equals to 0.94.

TGARCH Models (TGM)

Brooks and Persan (2003) show that VaR models, taking into account the asymmetry of the distributions, tend to generally produce more accurate estimates. TGM gives different weight to the positive observations from the negative ones. Analytically:

$$\sigma_t^2 = \alpha_0 + \sum_{i=1}^{q} \alpha_i \varepsilon_{t-1}^2 + \gamma \varepsilon_{t-1}^2 d_{t-1} + \sum_{j=1}^{p} \beta_j \sigma_{t-j}^2 \tag{13}$$

where d_t is a dummy variable that takes value 1 if $\varepsilon_t < 0$, and 0 elsewhere.

The coefficient γ measures the differential impact on the conditional variance to negative events. The expected sign of γ is positive, then the volatility is higher in correspondence of negative detections and increases as the dispersion of standard deviation.

The Opportunity Cost of Capital Requirements

The extensive literature on VaR focuses primarily on the ability to estimate the percentile of the distribution. From a managerial point of view, the estimate of the expected loss should allow to allocate enough capital to protect the institution from risk. Simultaneously, the managers must operate economically, trying not to distract the scarce resources of capital from profitable activities.

In this chapter, we not only propose to compare the performance of different estimation models in the context of emerging markets, but we plan to evaluate the different approaches in the light of the capital requirements that arise from them. Therefore, we evaluate the model not in terms of violations, but in terms of ability to reduce costs. In order to do that, we introduce a cost function that focuses on the performance not achieved, due to the capital subtracted to the trading activity.

If we denote by ER_t the reserve in excess of the time t, the opportunity cost OC_t is equal to:

$$\mathrm{OC}_t = \mathrm{ER}_t * r_{ptf} \tag{14}$$

with r_{rf} equal to the return of the investment portfolio during the period t.

Concerning the quantification of excess reserves, we identify the capital requirements (CR) set aside to cover market risks.[2]

2. Indeed, the capital requirement identified by the regulatory parameters is the minimum amount that the bank must provide. The bank are not able to update on a daily basis the amount allocated to capital requirement, hence, intermediaries used to assign a fixed amount of capital updated at regular intervals. In order to reproduce this behavior, we can assume that the bank allocate to capital requirements, recalibrating at regular time intervals,

After we quantify the capital that banks must allocate, we can calculate the excess reserves. There are two separate cases of opportunity cost: positive and negative market returns. In the case of negative returns, the excess reserve *ER* is the distance between the return (negative) and the levels of capital set aside. The larger the difference between the two variables, the greater portion of the capital subtracted "unnecessarily" to investment. In the case in which the return exceed, in absolute value, the supplied limit does not have an excess, but a lack of reserves that does not generate opportunity costs.

In the case of positive returns, the opportunity cost is due to the entire reserve, that is, the portion of the allocation of capital. Thus, the occurrence of positive returns, it is not correct to consider the entire difference as excess reserves: the value ER is only estimated reserve.

Figure 1 shows the difference in the approach of the two cases: the broken line represents yields realized, that continues the amount of capital corresponding to the moment of detection. At the time $t = 2$ shown is the excess reserves that occurs on the occurrence of negative returns of the market, while at the time $t = 3$ and $t = 5$ it shows the measure at positive returns, while in the $t = 4$ case of shortage of capital to cover the risks. Analytically:

$$\mathrm{ER}_t = \begin{cases} |\mathrm{DP}_t - \min(0; r_t)| & \text{se } \mathrm{DP}_t < r \\ 0 & \text{se } \mathrm{DP}_t \geq r_t \end{cases} \tag{15}$$

After having defined the cost function, it is also possible to have a measure of daily cost, so to have an evaluation in terms of efficiency of the goodness of the model used. The annual cost for each model is the sum of the total costs incurred during all day observed in the year.

an amount of money that allows not having to make changes to the budget before the next calibration. While recognizing th is a restrictive assumption, it can easily be removed with simple modeling. Therefore, we preferred to analyze this base case to facilitate comparisons between the costs of different models without any further noise.

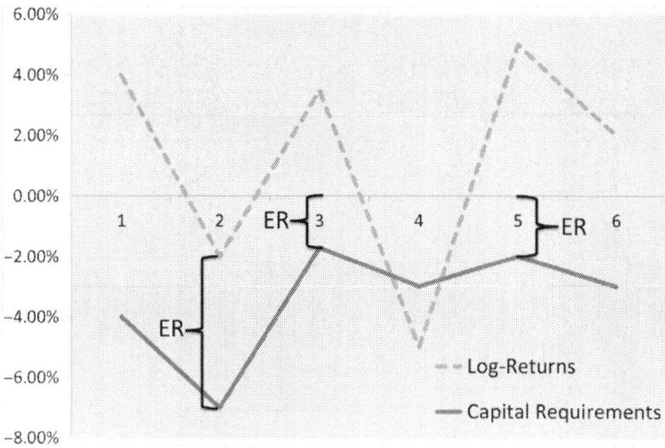

Figure 1: Excess Reserves. *Source*: Our elaboration.

The Results of the Empirical Analysis

Are Emerging Markets a Valid Investment Alternative?

Our data consists of the returns of the financial markets of the emerging countries according to the classification proposed by the International Monetary Fund (IMF). The data sample comprises the log-return of financial assets traded in the stock markets of individual countries. Specifically, the analysis involves the returns of the stock indices representative of the markets. The data covers an observation period of 20 years, from May 1, 1995 to April 30, 2015, for a total of 4971 trading days. Unfortunately, historical time series are not available for all the countries under investigation from the same starting date. Table 2 shows the index selected and the beginning of the observations for each country. To allow a proper comparison of the results, we also use index data, such as the S&P500 and the Eurostoxx50, representing the US and the European market, respectively. The source of all market data is Datastream.

Before analyzing the quantification of capital requirements resulting from different evaluation models, it is appropriate to verify the investment potential of emerging markets. Here, we do not intend to display a conclusive study on the attractiveness

Table 2: Emerging Countries Considered in the Analysis Sample, Benchmark Index of the Stock Market, and the Beginning of the Observations.

Country	Index	Start Date
Argentina	MERVAL	08/10/1996
Brazil	Bovespa	02/05/1995
Bulgaria	SOFIX	05/05/2010
Chile	IPSA	02/01/2002
Colombia	IGBC	09/02/2009
Estonia	OMXT	03/01/2000
Hungary	BUX	02/05/1995
India	S&P BSE SENSEX	02/05/1995
Indonesia	JII	02/05/1995
Latvia	OMXR	03/01/2000
Lithuania	OMXV	03/01/2000
Malaysia	FBMKLCI	01/11/2000
Mexico	IPC	02/05/1995
Pakistan	KSE	02/07/1997
People's Republic of China	CSI 300	02/05/1995
Peru	IGBVL 20	22/06/2009
Philippines	PSE	02/05/1995
Poland	WIGWIG30	04/05/1995
Romania	BET-10	31/10/2000
Russia	RTSI	01/09/1995
South Africa	FTSE/JSE Top 40	29/07/2008
Thailand	SET	02/05/1995

Table 2: (*Continued*)

Country	Index	Start Date
Turkey	ISE-100 (XU100)	02/05/1995
Ukraine	PFTS	03/11/1997
Venezuela	IBC	NA
EURO	EUROSTOXX50	02/05/1995
The United States	S&P500	02/05/1995

Source: Our elaboration.

of these markets; however, a simple analysis of risk-return profiles allow us to appreciate immediately the potential benefits to include these markets in the range of investment alternatives.

Figure 2 shows a graphical representation of the risk-return profile of a sample of the countries under investigation.[3] The space mean-variance is useful to our purpose. For comparison, we also report the data for European and US indices. We divide our analysis into three periods: the whole observation period, the crisis period (2008–2012) and the last five years.

In the definition of emerging markets, they are included countries whose characteristics are not always unique; data reflect this diversity. In Panel A of the figure, it is clear that the majority of the emerging markets of the sample offer a higher return compared to other developed markets. This higher performance is usually associated with a higher variance in returns.

Even more interesting are the data of the crisis period (2008–2012) shown in Figure 2 Panel B. Except for China, Ukraine, and Romania, all emerging countries offered better returns than the European market. The US market, experiencing

3. In order to contain the length of the chapter, we publish just the results referring to major emerging countries, in terms of market capitalization.

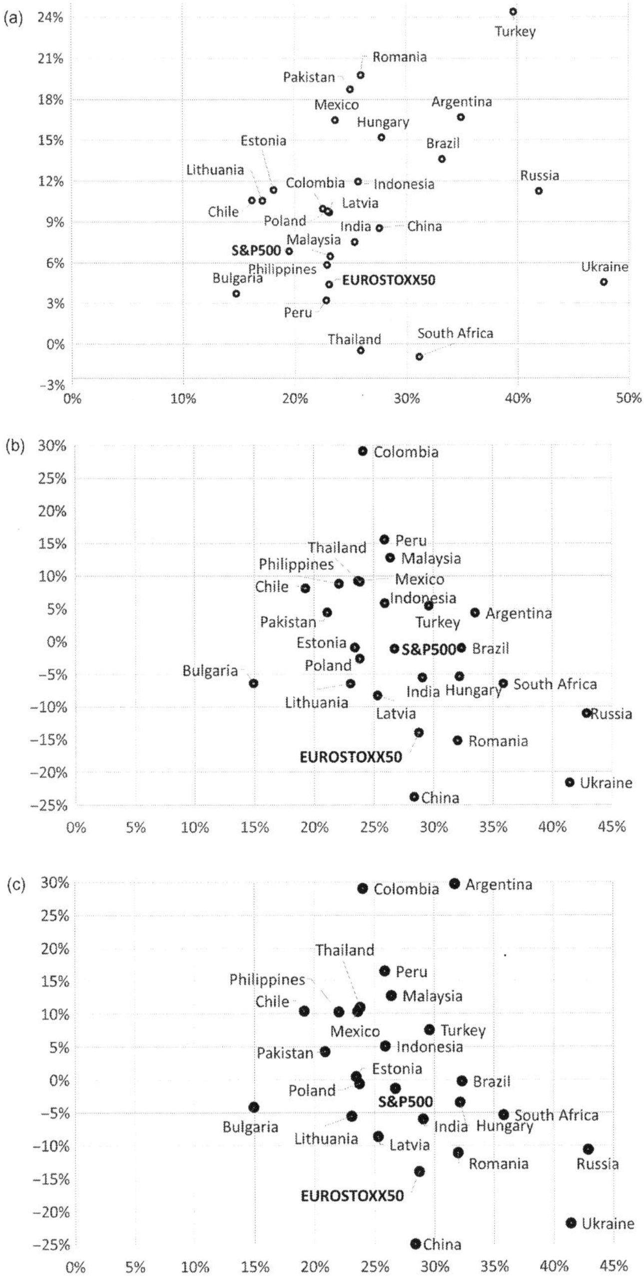

Figure 2: Graphic Representation, in Mean-Variance Space, of Market Indices Analyzed. (A) Complete Sample; (B) Crisis Period 2008–2012; (C) Last 5 Years. *Source*: Our elaboration.

crisis as well, maintained negative performances, combined with a moderate level of risk. This confirms the increased difficulty of Europe to recover to the pre-crisis levels. Emerging markets show mixed results. The presence of a group of indices with higher return and lower risk (top and left) compared to the US market, leading us to affirm the possibility of exploiting this opportunity in a perspective of portfolio diversification, especially in periods of bear markets.

The Figure 2 Panel C shows the last five years, partly overlapped with the final phase of the crisis. The focus allows us to evaluate the ability to recover from a price shock. Also in this period, the data concerning the emerging countries are surprisingly. The European and the US markets are still showing negative returns with a similar level of risk, which is included between 25 percent and 30 percent in terms of standard deviation. The third period shows a certain relative stability in the results, however, it is worth to note that the level of average return for emerging markets has increased and we are observing a concentration of countries with more favorable risk profiles. In other words, in the post-crisis period, emerging markets seem to represent a very attractive risk-return alternative asset class.

Finally, Table 3 shows the correlation matrix between the indexes analyzed. For reasons of space, we only report that about the whole period. Although not constituting a process comparable to the optimization of an investment portfolio, the values of the table demonstrate the concrete possibilities to benefit from the emerging markets in a perspective of risk diversification. The benefits are even more evident when compared with the developed markets that make up the majority of traditional investment portfolios.

The Capital Requirement and VAR Models within the Context of Emerging Markets

This section presents the main results obtained for over 20 years of observations. Figure 2 shows the time series of two portfolios analyzed: High Risk Portfolio and Low Risk Portfolio. It is possible to

Table 3: Correlation Matrix of the Returns of Emerging Markets Analyzed.

	Argentina	Brazil	Bulgaria	Chile	Colombia	Estonia	Hungary	India	Indonesia	Latvia	Lithuania	Malaysia	Mexico	Pakistan	China	Peru	Philippines	Poland	Romania	Russia	South Africa	Thailand	Turkey	Ukraine	EURO	US
Argentina	1.000																									
Brazil	0.544	1.000																								
Bulgaria	0.091	0.043	1.000																							
Chile	0.404	0.537	0.115	1.000																						
Colombia	0.428	0.488	0.076	0.448	1.000																					
Estonia	0.153	0.155	0.219	0.211	0.197	1.000																				
Hungary	0.268	0.265	0.102	0.353	0.356	0.266	1.000																			
India	0.168	0.183	0.157	0.276	0.301	0.243	0.258	1.000																		
Indonesia	0.136	0.125	0.147	0.282	0.222	0.274	0.260	0.312	1.000																	
Latvia	0.056	0.068	0.106	0.118	0.093	0.227	0.100	0.115	0.109	1.000																
Lithuania	0.148	0.146	0.196	0.226	0.214	0.459	0.224	0.232	0.256	0.254	1.000															
Malaysia	0.294	0.409	0.072	0.391	0.514	0.161	0.235	0.247	0.228	0.062	0.135	1.000														
Mexico	0.492	0.616	0.065	0.553	0.474	0.159	0.281	0.206	0.134	0.072	0.147	0.478	1.000													
Pakistan	0.013	0.033	0.112	0.033	0.032	0.058	0.105	0.106	0.077	0.062	0.054	0.021	0.024	1.000												
China	0.037	0.062	0.074	0.137	0.140	0.139	0.072	0.122	0.117	0.061	0.121	0.127	0.037	0.051	1.000											

Peru	0.405	0.510	0.080	0.446	0.493	0.166	0.339	0.263	0.240	0.083	0.176	0.538	0.507	0.021	0.172	1.000										
Philippines	0.106	0.111	0.096	0.168	0.085	0.252	0.213	0.195	0.376	0.127	0.229	0.042	0.123	0.085	0.092	0.089	1.000									
Poland	0.232	0.257	0.115	0.393	0.425	0.300	0.519	0.293	0.286	0.101	0.252	0.299	0.264	0.095	0.071	0.377	0.234	1.000								
Romania	0.181	0.170	0.206	0.224	0.290	0.292	0.318	0.278	0.290	0.167	0.305	0.125	0.198	0.083	0.156	0.212	0.254	0.322	1.000							
Russia	0.276	0.270	0.133	0.335	0.478	0.286	0.436	0.262	0.252	0.121	0.260	0.292	0.273	0.086	0.077	0.419	0.167	0.414	0.310	1.000						
South Africa	0.159	0.153	0.102	0.243	0.064	0.324	0.227	0.242	0.396	0.211	0.358	−0.028	0.207	0.123	0.256	0.066	0.450	0.254	0.355	0.316	1.000					
Thailand	0.174	0.175	0.139	0.273	0.278	0.239	0.235	0.284	0.409	0.109	0.238	0.216	0.185	0.077	0.107	0.242	0.319	0.281	0.264	0.256	0.302	1.000				
Turkey	0.195	0.229	0.039	0.327	0.322	0.173	0.347	0.200	0.170	0.074	0.150	0.163	0.218	0.068	0.046	0.323	0.123	0.339	0.216	0.327	0.186	0.228	1.000			
Ukraine	0.121	0.111	0.171	0.203	0.323	0.167	0.161	0.128	0.137	0.070	0.163	0.146	0.126	0.025	0.076	0.266	0.095	0.204	0.203	0.208	0.209	0.122	0.118	1.000		
EURO	0.000	0.013	0.025	0.020	0.012	−0.004	0.005	−0.004	−0.025	−0.004	0.006	−0.017	0.008	−0.025	−0.007	0.020	−0.005	0.008	−0.017	−0.013	0.009	−0.015	−0.017	−0.007	1.000	
USA	−0.002	0.009	−0.017	−0.008	−0.017	0.023	0.005	0.008	0.037	−0.019	−0.006	−0.009	−0.006	0.007	−0.021	0.014	−0.028	−0.002	0.009	0.033	−0.045	0.026	0.020	−0.042	−0.003	1.000

Source: Our elaboration.

notice the returns generated on a daily basis, the VaR estimates obtained from the models and the corresponding capital requirements. At the beginning of each time series, the first 250 observations have been used to estimate the initial parameters of the models.

In order to estimate the value at risk, we need to identify a period of stress in financial markets that may be approved by the supervisory authority. Our observation period is particularly extended and thus we can identify several moments of bear markets. More precisely, we have selected the three stock market crashes: the 1997 Asian financial crisis, the 2002 stock market downturn and the recent financial crisis of 2007–2008. In order to estimate the value of SVaRs, we use 250 days following the starting date of the chosen crises: July 2, 1997, October 9, 2002, and September 16, 2008.

We estimated the models presented earlier in all countries analyzed in the study. Figure 3 show the graphic representation of the estimates of VaR (99 percent) and Capital Requirements in China, Brazil and India (the countries of the sample with the largest GDP).

The graphs show the difference between VaR and the requirement for prudential supervision. It seems clear that the legislator was inspired to ensure a high capitalization of financial intermediaries neglecting the aspect of a good estimate of potential losses. Regarding the various procedures for estimating VaR, models EMWA, GARCH and TGarch show more evident approximation capacity at the cost of greater complexity of implementation.

The charts show the significant increase in volatility during the period of market stress and the simultaneous worsened of the VaR estimates and associated capital requirements. The changing financial market conditions deserve further investigation about the new features of the standard deviation, or the impacts due to the increased risk on capital requirements.

In the observation period, the occurrence of a crisis, in line with the objectives of the legislature, we have updated the crisis period of reference in estimating the SVaR. The graphs can detect such changes. In all three countries reported it is possible to identify

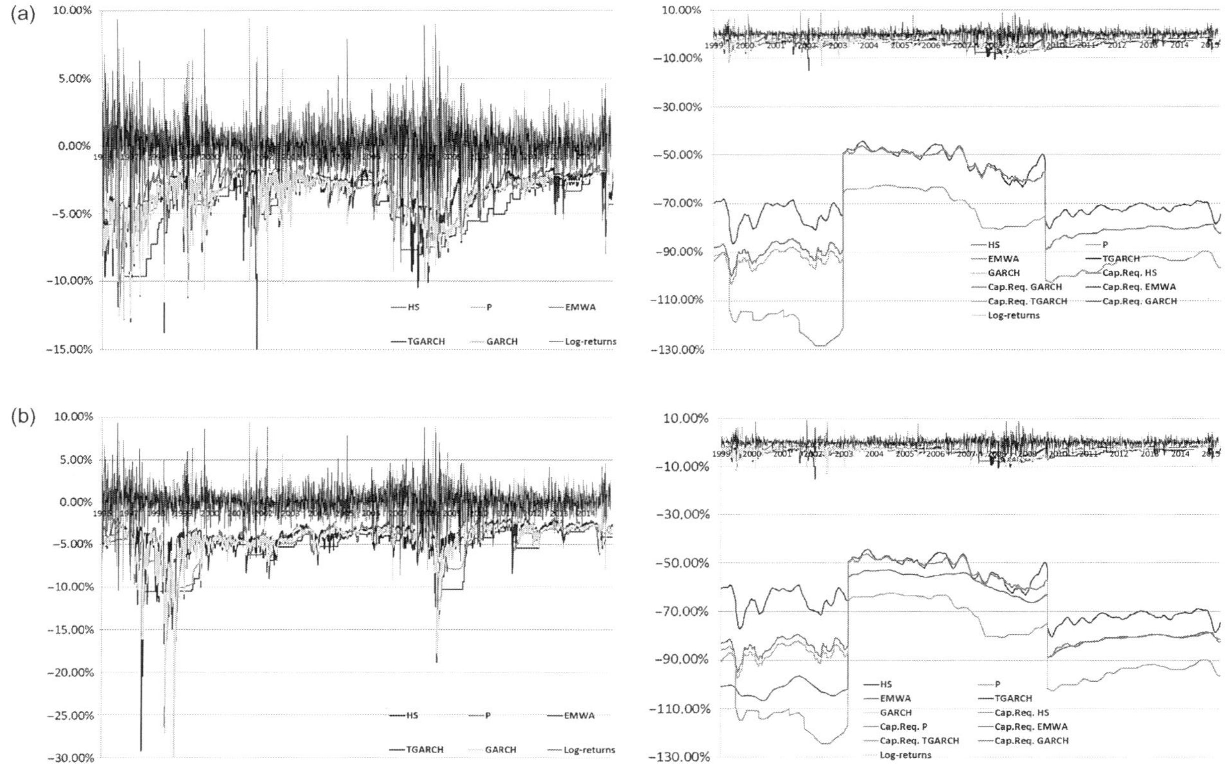

Figure 3: Graphs of the Daily VaR and Capital Requirement Estimated with Different Models. (A) China; (B) Brazil; (C) India. *Source*: Our elaboration.

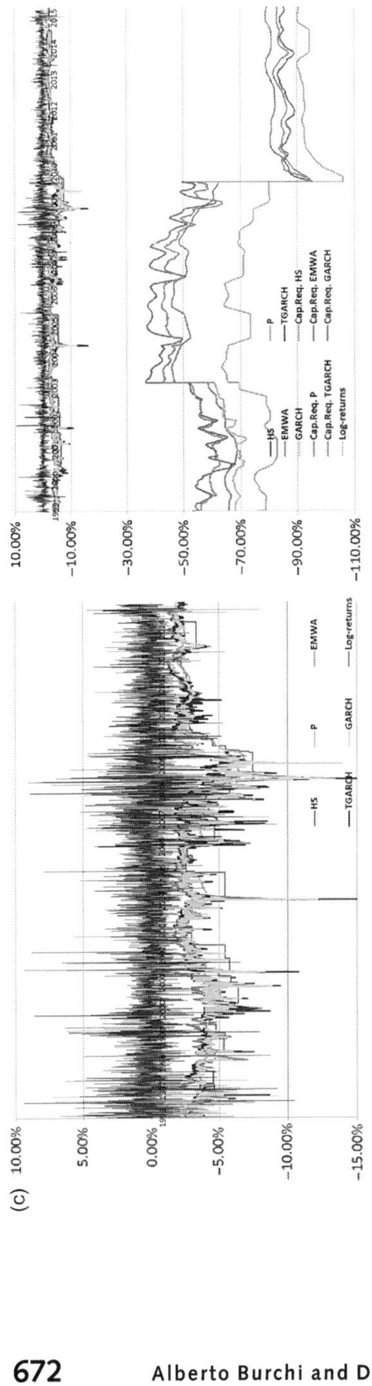

Figure 3: *(Continued)*

two steps in correspondence with changes of the period of references SVaR.

The small distance between the lines of the capital requirement also highlights a sort of flattening of the differences due to the adoption of a model or the other, for the calculation of regulatory capital. The choice of manager of the bank is of greater importance for the reference period rather than the estimation model. In other words, the stressed VaR risk, in its implementation, to be an instrument formally rigorous but "difficult rationale."

The Effects of the New Capital Requirements for Market Risk in the Investment Decision-Making of Banks in Emerging Market

The results of our analysis are shown in the following tables. Table 4 shows the results regarding the quantification of the capital requirement. The value refers to the average regulatory capital throughout the period of analysis, broken down by country and by model estimation.

The analysis of the average capital requirement allows us to highlight which model is more parsimonious. The estimation of HS produces higher results; in other words, the adoption of this process involves a greater capital requirement. On average, the estimated capital with HS is greater than the other models for a value of around 20 percent. Realistically, in period of high volatility, the HS produces estimates of daily VaR often violated. Therefore, the correction factor takes the value 4 for most of the period and remains high until it comes from the time window estimation of the parameter. EWMA, G, TG show minor violations during periods of high volatility, more rapid response on standard deviation and a low number of violations, thereby producing lower capital requirements. We then categorize the models into two groups: the "simple" models, such as HS and P, while the "complex" models are G, E, TG. Such distinction is not due to the mere difficulty of implementation, but also to the different behavior shown in the use for regulatory purposes. The difference

Table 4: Average Value of Capital Requirements, Broken Down by Country and by Model Estimation.

Country	Average Capital Requirement				
	HS	*P*	GARCH	EMWA	TGARCH
Argentina	−128.6%	−96.7%	−93. 2%	−99.0%	−93.2%
Brazil	−89.6%	−78.0%	−71.1%	−52.4%	−71.9%
Bulgaria	NA	NA	NA	NA	NA
Chile	−55.3%	−43.9%	−39.3%	−39.5%	−39.3%
Colombia	NA	NA	NA	NA	NA
Estonia	−62.6%	−44.5%	−44.7%	−45.6%	−44.7%
Hungary	−99.5%	−72.1%	−72.2%	−74.2%	NA
India	−80.3%	−65.3%	−63.0%	−51.9%	−62.7%
Indonesia	−98.9%	−59.6%	−77.8%	−79.1%	−77.8%
Latvia	−76.8%	−50.1%	−38.3%	−37.8%	−33.3%
Lithuania	−55.7%	−43.6%	−38.9%	−41.7%	NA
Malaysia	−31.4%	−21.6%	−12.1%	−13.7%	−12.1%
Mexico	−71.0%	−50.5%	−57.4%	−51.9%	−58.5%
Pakistan	−66.7%	−57.5%	−54.2%	−55.4%	−54.2%
China	−66.7%	−57.5%	−54.2%	−55.4%	−54.2%
Peru	−15.7%	−12.7%	−11.9%	−11.7%	−11.9%
Philippines	−79.1%	−52.7%	−60.3%	−53.2%	−52.7%
Poland	−57.6%	−57.4%	−57.2%	−55.4%	−57.1%
Romania	−76.2%	−59.4%	−59.3%	−53.8%	−58.8%
Russia	−137.5%	−106.1%	−109.5%	−115.3%	NA
South Africa	−125.4%	−111.1%	−76.8%	−63.6%	−76.8%

Table 4: (*Continued*)

Country	Average Capital Requirement				
	HS	*P*	GARCH	EMWA	TGARCH
Thailand	−88.3%	−70.9%	−70.8%	−51.7%	−69.1%
Turkey	−117.4%	−98.8%	−96.1%	−91.2%	−96.4%
Ukraine	−132.6%	−83.7%	−71.7%	−63.5%	−71.7%
Venezuela	NA	NA	NA	NA	NA
EURO	−74.1%	−59.1%	−51.3%	−65.6%	−58.2%
USA	−64.1%	−54.8%	−56.9%	−59.0%	−55.3%

Source: Our elaboration.

between complex and simple models increases in countries with higher risk profiles o in a period of high volatility.

Deepening the analysis to individual markets, it still emerges the high heterogeneity of the countries in the sample. Capital requirements can assume relatively small values, as in the case of Peru and Malaysia, up to so high values that investing in particular markets (such as Turkey or Ukraine) is completely inconvenient, once taken into account the opportunity cost of capital. These extreme values deserve a deeper analysis. For the bank's perspective, values of regulatory capital close to 100% indicate the need to set aside regulatory capital for investing activities equals to capital used in the business division. This involves halving the return on capital of the business. Indeed, the attention of the regulator to protect aspects of profitability appears faint, if we analyze the effects of the introduction of SVaR in financial regulation.

Table 5 shows the results of the regulatory capital required without the adoption of SVaR as in the previous regulation.

Table 5: Average Value of Capital Requirements without the SVaR Provision, Broken Down by Country and by Model Estimation.

Country	HS	P	GARCH	EMWA	TGARCH
Argentina	−25.9%	−19.2%	−18.7%	−18.8%	−18.4%
Brazil	−16.7%	−13.9%	−13.6%	−13.1%	−13.2%
Bulgaria	−10.7%	−8.4%	−7.7%	−7.7%	−7.7%
Chile	−11.7%	−9.1%	−8.5%	−3.5%	−3.4%
Colombia	−15.6%	−11.9%	−11.8%	−11.3%	−11.9%
Estonia	−12.7%	−9.8%	−9.5%	−9.2%	−9.4%
Hungary	−19.5%	−15.4%	−14.5%	−14.2%	NA
India	−16.8%	−13.9%	−13.2%	−13.1%	−13.1%
Indonesia	−19.2%	−14.5%	−14.0%	−13.6%	−13.5%
Latvia	−16.0%	−12.1%	−11.2%	−10.9%	10.7%
Lithuania	−12.2%	−9.3%	−8.7%	−3.6%	NA
Malaysia	−10.8%	−6.9%	−4.8%	−5.4%	−4.8%
Mexico	−15.1%	−12.9%	−11.6%	−12.1%	−11.7%
Pakistan	−17.2%	−13.5%	−12.6%	−12.6%	−12.4%
China	−17.2%	−13.5%	−12.6%	−12.6%	−12.6%
Peru	−10.7%	−8.4%	−7.7%	−7.7%	−11.9%
Philippines	NA	NA	NA	NA	NA
Poland	−15.5%	−12.6%	−11.9%	−11.6%	−11.7%
Romania	−17.2%	−13.2%	−12.4%	−12.3%	−12.2%
Russia	−28.8%	−21.9%	−20.9%	−20.9%	NA
South Africa	−19.3%	−15.0%	−13.2%	−12.4%	−13.0%
Thailand	−17.1%	−14.3%	−13.7%	−12.4%	−13.4%

Table 5: (*Continued*)

Country	HS	P	GARCH	EMWA	TGARCH
Turkey	−25.9%	−21.4%	−20.3%	−19.6%	−20.0%
Ukraine	−26.2%	−17.6%	−15.4%	−15.6%	−14.9%
Venezuela	NA	NA	NA	NA	NA
EURO	−16.1%	−13.4%	−12.3%	−12.7%	−11.9%
USA	−13.1%	−11.0%	−10.2%	−10.3%	−10.1%

Source: Our elaboration.

The introduction of the SVaR analysis leads to a considerable increase in the capital requirement. Under the new formulation, the financial intermediary must estimate the VaR considering the maximum loss obtained from the model, using the parameter associated to the period of crisis. It is plausible to assume an increase in the capital requirement stabilized on the level of the most recent financial crisis. The new methodology results in a lower sensitivity of the capital requirement in respect to the model. The variable that becomes more important is the time horizon, inevitably affected by the crisis period identified in agreement with the supervisory authority.

Finally, Table 6 shows the results, in the same manner, relative to estimated opportunity cost of the capital requirement.

The potential missing profits, which a bank must give up due to regulatory reasons, are noteworthy. On average, the model most favorable to the bank's management produces a reduction in profits of 60 percent during bull market periods, when also the opportunity cost could raise if not properly managed. The increase in the capital requirement for market risk is anticipated by market participants, and welcomed by the scientific community, bankers and supervisors. However, the extreme dimension of this measure seems to punish bankers wishing to invest in riskier markets, such

Table 6: Average Value of the Cost of Capital Requirements, Broken Down by Country and by Model Estimation.

Country	HS	P	GARCH	EMWA	TGARCH
Argentina	−129.9%	−89.7%	−91.6%	−96.4%	−91.6%
Brazil	−92.9%	−79.4%	−78.8%	−70.6%	−78.8%
Bulgaria	NA	NA	NA	NA	NA
Chile	−71.0%	−52.2%	−47.0%	−48.1%	−47.0%
Colombia	NA	NA	NA	NA	NA
Estonia	−73.3%	−51.6%	−53.0%	−55.5%	−53.0%
Hungary	−110.7%	−77.7%	−86.0%	−86.6%	NA
India	−91.9%	−79.4%	−81.5%	−82.3%	−81.5%
Indonesia	−105.5%	−68.8%	−70.2%	−68.3%	−70.2%
Latvia	−88.3%	−63.3%	−59.6%	−62.3%	−59.6%
Lithuania	−92.4%	−55.2%	−47.3%	−53.9%	NA
Malaysia	−50.5%	−35.4%	−18.0%	−19.4%	−18.0%
Mexico	−77.1%	−66.0%	−70.3%	−69.6%	−70.3%
Pakistan	−65.7%	−58.2%	−55.6%	−57.2%	−55.6%
China	−65.7%	−58.2%	−55.6%	−57.2%	−55.6%
Peru	−5.7%	−5.2%	−4.8%	−4.8%	−4.8%
Philippines	−16.1%	−13.0%	−12.2%	−12.2%	−11.5%
Poland	−78.6%	−60.4%	−64.9%	−64.5%	−64.9%
Romania	−116.0%	−81.1%	−81.4%	−89.5%	−81.3%
Russia	−152.5%	−112.5%	−115.9%	−123.4%	NA
South Africa	−125.4%	−111.1%	−76.8%	−63.6%	−76.8%
Thailand	−98.6%	−62.5%	−65.2%	−63.8%	−65.2%
Turkey	−103.2%	−83.6%	−82.6%	−82.1%	−82.6%

Table 6: (*Continued*)

Country	HS	P	GARCH	EMWA	TGARCH
Ukraine	−113.8%	−76.9%	−75.0%	−78.2%	−75.0%
Venezuela	NA	NA	NA	NA	NA
EURO	−81.7%	−61.3%	−68.6%	−72.0%	−68.1%
USA	−87.8%	−64.9%	−71.1%	−76.1%	−71.1%

Source: Our elaboration.

as emerging countries. The precautionary measures may be so large as to discourage potential investors in considering possible investments, as they would see significantly reduce the potential of profitability due to the regulatory provisions.

Conclusions

In this chapter, we analyze 27 emerging markets according to the classification proposed by the International Monetary Fund. Our analysis highlights the potential of investing in these markets in terms of the risk-return profile, since these countries offer better opportunities (or at least equal) compared to developed markets. Emerging markets are not only an alternative, but actually they are still a good opportunity to diversify investment portfolios: the low correlation with the European and the US markets makes it possible to improve the asset allocation of international investors.

However, the study of financial regulation is crucial. In our chapter, we have not only limited our investigations to examine different models for estimating VaR, but also we have investigated the effects of choosing different models for regulatory purposes. Concerning the characteristics of the models, the Basel Committee has provided a procedure to sanction situations that systematically underestimate the level of risk. On a quarterly basis, the verification of the frequency of violations determines a penalty increase with the number of errors. This rule decreases the importance of the ability of the institution in estimating the percentile that represents the value at risk.

However, the lack of incentives to develop and adopt more sophisticated models for estimating the capital requirements is not a valid reason for the completely abandonment of such models. The availability of precise information is an essential prerequisite for effective investment activities; that is why prudential supervision rules should reward the ability of the investors to provide accurate estimates of risk.

The aim of the regulator in introducing the SVaR is clearly the increase the allocation of capital to protect the safety of the bank. This increase is so pronounced that it substantially reduces the profitability of the investment. In other words, when evaluating the return on investments, banks should consider both the capital actually invested, and the capital set aside for supervisory purposes. Since the increase in regulatory capital is more pronounced when markets are high volatile, and taking into account that emerging markets are characterized by a high risk-return profile, financial regulation could be an impediment for financial intermediaries, which consider these markets in their view of investment.

References

Alexander, C. (2009). *Market risk analysis, value at risk models* (Vol. 4). Hoboken, NJ: Wiley.

Allen, L., Boudouk, J., & Saunders, A. (2004). *Understanding market, credit, and operational risk: The value at risk approach*. Malden, MA: Blackwell.

Basel Committee on Banking Supervision. (2004). *Revised international capital framework*. Technical report.

Basel Committee on Banking Supervision. (2009, July). Revision to the Basel II market risk framework. Consultative document.

Basel Committee on Banking Supervision. (2011). *Messages from the academic literature on risk measurement for the trading book*. WP[19]. Basel, Switzerland: Basel Committee on Banking Supervision. Retrieved from http://www.bis.org/publ/bcbs_wp19.pdf. Accessed on July 10, 2015.

Berkowitz, J. (2001). Testing density forecasts, with applications to risk management. *Journal of Business and Economic Statistics, 19*, 465–474.

Bollerslev, T. (1986). Generalized autoregressive conditional heteroskedasticity. *Journal of Econometrics*, *31*, 307–327.
Brooks, C., & Persan, G. (2003). The effect of asymmetries on stock index return value at risk estimates. *The Journal of Risk Finance, Winter*, 29–42.
Chen, J. (2012). *Postmodern disaster theory*. WP[11–17]. East Lansing, MI: Michigan State University College of Law.
Chen, J. M. (2014). Measuring market risk under the Basel accords: VaR, stressed VaR, and expected shortfall. *The IEB International Journal of Finance*, *8*, 184–201.
Degiannakis, S., Floros, C., & Livada, A. (2012). Evaluating value-at-risk models before and after the financial crisis of 2008: International evidence. *Managerial Finance*, *38*(4), 436–452.
Einhorn, D. (2008). Private profits and socialized risk, GARP risk review. Jersey City, NJ.
Engle, R. (1982). Autoregressive conditional heteroskedasticity with estimates of variance of United Kingdom inflation. *Econometrica*, *50*, 987–1008.
European Banking Autorithy. (2012). *Guidelines on stressed value-at-risk (stressed VaR) (EBA/GL/2012/2)*. Retrieved from http://www.eba.europa.eu/regulation-and-policy/market-risk/guidelines-on-stressed-value-at-risk-stressed-var-
Farber, D. (2011). Uncertainty. *Georgetown Law Journal*, *99*(4), 901–959.
He, C., & Terasvirta, T. (1999). Properties of moments of a family of GARCH processes. *Journal of Econometrics*, *92*(1), 173–192.
Hull, J. (2012). *Risk management and financial institutions*. Upper Saddle River, NJ: Pearson.
Hwang, S., & Pedersen, C. S. (2004). Asymmetric risk measures when modelling emerging markets equities: Evidence for regional and timing effects. *Emerging Markets Review*, *5*, 109–128.
Jiménez-Martín, J.-Á., McAleer, M., & Pérez-Amaral, T. (2009). The ten commandments for managing value at risk under the basel ii accord. *Journal of Economic Surveys*, *23*(5), 850–855.
Kearney, C. (2012). Emerging markets research: Trends, issues and future directions. *Emerging Markets Review*, *13*(2), 159–183.
Li, X. M., & Rose, L. (2009). The tail risk of emerging stock markets. *Emerging Markets Review*, *10*(4), 242–256.
Macchiarola, M. (2009). Beware of risk everywhere: An important lesson from the current credit crisis. *Hastings Business Law Journal*, *5*(2), 294–297.
McAleer, M. (2009). The ten commandments for optimizing value-at-risk and daily capital charges. *Journal of Economic Surveys*, *23*, 831–849.
Nielsson, U. (2009). Measuring and regulating extreme risk. *Journal of Financial Regulation & Compliance*, *17*, 156–171.

Nocera, J. (2009). Risk mismanagement. *New York Times Magazine*, January 4, 2009 edition, p. MM24.
Páfka, S., & Kondor, I. (2001). Evaluating the riskmetrics methodology in measuring volatility and value-at-risk in financial markets. *Physica A*, *299*(1–2), 309.
Pérignon, C., Deng, Z. Y., & Wang, Z. J. (2008). Do banks overstate their value-at-risk? *Journal of Banking and Finance*, *32*, 783–794.
Prorokowski, L., & Prorokowski, H. (2014). Compliance with Basel 2.5: Banks' approaches to implementing stressed VaR. *Journal of Financial Regulation and Compliance*, *22*(4), 339–348.
Rockafellar, R. T., & Uryasev, S. (2002). Conditional value-at-risk for general loss distributions. *Journal of Banking and Finance*, *26*, 1443–1471.
Taleb, N. N. (2009). *Report on the risks of financial modeling, VaR and the economic breakdown*. Retrieved from http://www.gpo.gov/fdsys/pkg/CHRG-111hhrg51925/html/CHRG-111hhrg51925.htm. Accessed on July 15, 2015.

21

Before and after the Crisis: A Look at the SMEs in Emerging Economies

Elmas Yaldız Hanedar and Avni Önder Hanedar

Abstract

The aim of this chapter is to understand effects of the recent crisis on the financial constraints that small and medium size enterprises have experienced in emerging economies. Using the firm level survey data provided by the World Bank, a descriptive analysis is conducted by calculating the average of the financial obstacles that the firms had experienced before and after the crisis, and the existence of statistical difference between the two periods is tested. The results indicate that the small and medium size enterprises suffer more from financial constraints relative to large firms. Financial constraints that the small and medium size firms had experienced are largely affected by the recent global financial crisis, relative to the large firms. However, effects of the financial constraints on real variables such as investment, innovation, and research and development expenditures cannot be examined due to data limitations. This chapter contributes to the limited literature of financial constraints experienced by the small and medium enterprises in emerging economies by taking the effect of the recent global financial crisis into account. The novelty of this chapter comes from the dataset: "The World Bank's World Business Environment Surveys," which provides a large sample of emerging countries.

Keywords: Global financial crisis; access to finance; financial constraints; SME; emerging economies; survey data

Introduction

Access to finance is important for firms in order to continue their operations from a micro perspective. From a macro perspective, it is important for the economies to grow as the lack of finance is likely to hamper investments made by firms (Chang, Jia, & Wang, 2010; Fernández, González, & Suárez, 2013; Rahaman, 2011). Ivashina and Scharfstein (2010) show that new loans to large borrowers fell significantly during the recent financial crisis in the United States. The surveys that Campello, Graham, and Harvey (2010) conducted on the financial managers of 1050 firms from 39 countries in Asia, the United States, and Europe show that the financial constraints deepened after the recent crisis. Firms reduced their research and development spending after the crisis. Campello et al. (2010) show that financially constrained large firms had to cut employment as well as tech and investment spending. More specifically, among 1050 firms 903 have reported that they missed attractive investment projects due to credit constraints during the crisis of 2008. Considering these findings, the recent crisis seems to hampered economic growth by diminishing the amount of investments made by large firms.

Previous studies have shown that small and medium enterprises (SMEs) have been suffering more from financial constraints relative to large firms. Opaque information and weak enforcement are the main problems for firm access to finance in emerging economies (Hainz, Weill, & Godlewski, 2008; Menkhoff, Neuberger, & Suwanaporn, 2006; Menkhoff, Neuberger, & Rungruxsirivorn, 2012). Previous evidence indicate that the emerging economies are more vulnerable to crises than advanced and developing economies especially after 1990s (Becker & Mauro, 2006; Husain, Mody, Rogoff, & Kenneth, 2005). Together with the severity of financial obstacles in emerging economies as well as in ordinary times, financial constraints are expected to deepen during a crisis. Using survey data on SMEs in the United Kingdom, Lee, Sameen, and Cowling (2015) address the importance of access to finance for an innovative economy. Lee et al. (2015) also show that the SMEs found it harder to access to finance after the recent crisis. Holton, Lawless, and McCann (2014) use surveys on SMEs from Euro area. According to Holton et al. (2014), the recent crisis has affected the bank credits to SMEs in two different ways. First, the demand for credit by SMEs has decreased due to the economic slowdown. Second, lenders have increased their loan rejections as well as interest rates on loans. As a result of this decrease in bank credits, Casey and O'Toole (2014) show that the SMEs in the Euro area have substituted informal credits for bank finance after the recent crisis. This finding shows that access to bank finance has been difficult for European SMEs after the crisis.

Although there are many studies on developed economies, existing literature does not provide much information for the effects of the recent crisis on the financial constraints that the SMEs have experienced in emerging economies. The aim of this chapter is to rectify this gap by examining the perceptions of SMEs regarding financial obstacles. The novelty of this chapter comes from the dataset that is used: The World Bank's World Business Environment Surveys. This comprehensive dataset provides deep and detailed information not only about SMEs but also about large firms. Moreover this dataset includes both the pre- and post-crisis period for a wide range of emerging economies.

This dataset is suitable to test for the research question in 18 countries that represents the majority of emerging countries, as defined by Standard & Poor's and Morgan Stanley Capital International classifications of emerging markets from 2002 to 2010. The sample covers 41,795 firms, which provides a more comprehensive data set relative to the previous researches.

This chapter contributes to the limited literature by focusing on the financial constraints faced by the SMEs from a wide range of emerging economies. The information related to the degree of financial obstacles for SMEs comes from the answers of SMEs to the following survey question: *"Is access to financing* (e.g., *collateral) a problem for the operation and growth of your business?"* Answers are 0 (no obstacle), 1 (minor obstacle), 2 (moderate obstacle), 3 (major obstacle), and 4 (very severe obstacle). By conducting a descriptive analysis based on this question, results indicate more severe financial constraints for SMEs as compared to large firms in the selected emerging economies. Moreover, the gap between financial constraints perceived by SMEs and large firms seems to increase with the global financial crisis. Results of this chapter indicate the importance of effective government policies on reducing financial obstacles that SMEs experience during crises. As access to finance is improved for SMEs, they will be able to continue operating and make new investments that are essential for a recovery.

The rest of the chapter is structured as follows: the next section presents the literature on financial constraints and SMEs. Data and results are given subsequently, while the last section concludes.

Literature Review

Most of the previous studies on financial constraints are based on developed economies mostly without distinguishing between the sizes of the firms. Campello et al. (2010) use cross country data to examine the effect of the recent crisis in developed economies, while Duchin, Ozbas, and Sensoy (2010), Kremp and Sevestre (2013) and Lee et al. (2015) examine the issue for one single advanced economies, respectively, for the United States, France, and the United Kingdom. Among these three studies Kremp and Sevestre (2013) and Lee et al. (2015) specifically focus on SMEs.

Considering the recent crisis as a negative shock to access to finance for non-financial firms, Duchin et al. (2010) examine the corporate investment behavior subsequent to the crisis by using US firm data, which is available in the Standard & Poor's COMPUSTAT database. Their results indicate that the firms with low cash reserves or with high short-term debt experience higher cuts in their investment spending relative to the financially unconstrained firms. Similar to Duchin et al. (2010), Campello et al. (2010) examine the effects of the recent crisis on corporate investments in Asia, United States and Europe. The surveys that Campello et al. (2010) conducted on 1050 chief financial officers of non-financial public firms from 39 countries, show that these firms began to suffer more from financial constraints after the 2008 crisis. The results show the "*real*" effects of the 2008 crisis, the "*marginal borrowers of the economy*," that is, the financially constrained firms had to cut more investment, technology, marketing, and employment spending relative to the financially unconstrained firms. Accordingly, financial constraints are said to hamper the productive investment projects, leading to the economy missing a higher rate of economic growth for the future. During the crisis, the financially constrained firms withdrew funds from their outstanding lines of credit with the fear of being restricted from future access to those lines of credit.

Kremp and Sevestre (2013) focus on SMEs in France and examine access to bank finance by these SMEs. More specifically Kremp and Sevestre (2013) analyze whether decreased credit volume was a result of the decrease in firms' activity and investment projects or if it was a result of credit rationing stemming from a more cautious behavior of banks in credit allocation. The results indicate that the credits to SMEs have indeed decreased during the recent crisis. However, the reason for this drop in credits to SMEs is the decreasing credit demand by SMEs as they cutback their activity and investment projects.

Using data from over 10,000 UK SMEs in 2007/8, 2010, and 2012, Lee et al. (2015) find that innovative firms have more difficulties in accessing finance because they tend to have riskier business models than other firms. Innovative firms have higher demand for new loans, as they need to finance their new projects or products. Results of Lee et al. (2015) indicate that these firms had even more difficulties in accessing finance during the crisis.

Blalock, Gertler, and Levine (2008) examine the financial constraints that the firms in an emerging economy, Indonesia experienced during the 1997 East Asian financial crisis. More specifically, they distinguish the financial crisis by considering the effect of currency devaluation and banking crisis on firms. Their results indicate that the exporting firms may benefit from a currency crisis as currency devaluation brings higher total sales for this firms. On the other hand, a banking crisis may harm all firms by creating financial obstacles in emerging economies. During economic slowdown default risk of bank credits rise. It is mostly due to the inability of banks to distinguish between the solvent and insolvent borrowers. Moreover, Agung et al. (2001) address the decrease in banks' capitals as the reason of the financial constraints.

On the other hand, Blalock et al. (2008) show that the foreign owned firms have more of an advantage over the domestic owned firms. The reason for this is that foreign owned or multinational firms are able to use internal funds of the parent company during a banking crisis. Accordingly, foreign owned firms were able to increase their capital during the 1997 crisis, while the domestic owned ones could not.

Examining effects of the 1997–1998 Asian crisis and the 2007–2009 global financial crisis in China, Hong Kong, Indonesia, Korea, Philippines, Singapore, and Thailand, Mizen and Tsoukas (2012) show that the sensitivity of the external finance premium, that is, the margin between internal finance, and bank borrowing or equities were greater for the financially constrained firms during the Asian crisis relative to other times. Another country level study is Clarke, Cull, and Kisunko (2012), Clarke et al. (2012) examine how the country and firm level characteristics affected firms' access to finance and the effect of the recent crisis on firms' survival in Eastern Europe and Central Asia. Clarke et al. (2012)

use two different sets of survey data: Financial Crisis Survey[1] and Business Environment and Enterprise Performance Surveys.[2] The results indicate that firms with lower financial obstacles survived the crisis. Moreover, firms in countries where does not have well-established foreign banks have experienced more severe financial constraints during the crisis. Accordingly, foreign banks are found to have a stabilizing effect in the Eastern European and Central Asian regions. Based on these results, Clarke et al. (2012) underline the importance of foreign owned banks for a less risky banking sector. The stabilizing role of the foreign banks are linked to the ability of foreign banks to maintain better lending compared to domestic banks during crises.

Similar to Clarke et al. (2012), Popov and Udell (2012) also use The Business Environment and Enterprise Performance Surveys. The study of Popov and Udell (2012) is closely related to this chapter in terms of the research question and the data set used. Popov and Udell (2012) investigate the credit supply in 16 emerging European countries[3] before and during the financial crisis by using survey data on 10,701 firms in 2005 and 2008. Their findings indicate the importance of the banks' financial conditions for firms' access to credit. The study addresses the effect of the recent crisis which is transmitted by the foreign owned banks (mostly the western European banks). During the crisis, firms working with banks which experienced a decline in equity and Tier 1 capital, as well as losses on financial assets, are identified as credit constrained firms. Moreover, high-risk firms and firms with fewer tangible assets are found to be more sensitive to bank capital shocks.

Joyce and Nabar (2009) is another cross-country study that examines the effects of banking crises and sudden stops in

1. Conducted in six countries in 2009.

2. Conducted in 23 countries from Eastern Europe and Central Asia in 2002, 2005, 2008, and 2009.

3. Albania, Bosnia and Herzegovina, Bulgaria, Croatia, Czech Republic, Estonia, Hungary, Latvia, Lithuania, Macedonia, Montenegro, Poland, Romania, Serbia, Slovenia, and Slovakia

26 emerging economies from 1976 to 2002. The difference of Joyce and Nabar (2009) from the above studies is the macro level data that they use. All the studies summarized above are based on firm level data, while Joyce and Nabar (2009) use country level data. Joyce and Nabar (2009) approximate the sudden stops and banking crises on the investment by gross capital formation as a fraction of GDP. In this study, "sudden stops" are defined as the declines in the net capital inflows that correspond to declines in the financial account of balance of payments and banking crises. Results of Joyce and Nabar (2009) indicate that the sudden stops in emerging economies do not result in significant declines in investments as long as these sudden stops are not accompanied by the banking crises. This study also suggests that the negative effect of the banking crises on the aggregate investment grows as the economy becomes more open to capital flows. Accordingly, the sudden capital outflows are not expected to hamper the real investment as long as the banking system has not collapsed. These results of Joyce and Nabar (2009) imply that emerging economies should strengthen their banking systems in order to cope with the sudden capital outflows that come with globalization.

In addition to the country and firm level studies summarized above, Kroszner, Laeven, and Klingebiel (2007) examine the relationship between the external financial dependence and industrial growth during financial crises in 38 developed and developing economies. Results indicate that the banking crises are more costly for the industries that are dependent on external finance. However, Kroszner et al. (2007) show that the other financial crises, currency crises, or recessions do not yield the same result with the banking crises.

Data

Data used in this chapter come from the World Bank's World Business Environment Surveys. These surveys are conducted by the World Bank Group and the World Bank provides the results of these surveys in a standardised form for both developed and developing 121 countries. The business environment that the firms operate in, economic policy, financial barriers, corruption, and governance are the mainly covered topics in these surveys. As many questions changed over time and varied across countries, many important real variables related to financial constraints are not available, which include research and development expenditures, innovations that the firms made, or the new investments.[4] But the perceptions of firms about the degree of the financial difficulties are available for both the pre and post-crisis period across countries. Stone (1992) underlines the importance of firms' perceptions to evaluate what is really necessary for growth of firms. This dataset provides deep and detailed information, especially concerning the SMEs. Moreover, it includes information from a wide range of emerging economies. More specifically, it helps to answer the research question for 18 countries that represent the majority of emerging countries, as defined by Standard & Poor's and Morgan Stanley Capital International classifications of emerging markets from 2002 to 2010.

Popov and Udell (2012) says "The true extent of the financial crisis and its effect on firm access to finance will only become clear when new, more comprehensive data become available." The dataset that used in this chapter covers 41,795 firms in 18 emerging economies from 2002 to 2010, that is, it is a more comprehensive data set relative to the previous research especially relative to the one that is used in Popov and Udell (2012). Accordingly, this book chapter can be considered as a candidate for the "future research" that Popov and Udell (2012) addressed.

Results

This chapter distinguishes between the large firms and the SMEs based on the number of full time employees. Firms with 101 or

4. Due to data limitations, this chapter is based on descriptive statistics rather than a multivariate regression analysis. This descriptive approach does not take the other factors affecting the access to finance into account.

more full time employees are classified as large firms and are excluded from the sample. Among the surveyed 41,795 firms, 31,216 are SME, while the rest are considered as large firms. The severity of financial obstacles is proxied by the perceptions of the firms regarding the difficulty that they have in accessing to finance. This proxy variable is drawn from the answers of the firms to the following question: *"Is access to finance a problem for the operation and growth of your business?"* Answers are 0 (no obstacle), 1 (minor obstacle), 2 (moderate obstacle), 3 (major obstacle) and 4 (very severe obstacle), this variable is *FIN_OBS*.

As a second step, the sample is divided into two parts, before and after the recent global financial crisis, in order to evaluate the results for SMEs and large firms separately. The results indicate more severe financial constraints for SMEs relative to large firms both before and after the global financial crisis. Before the crisis, the average *FIN_OBS* is calculated as 1.222 for SMEs and 1.151 large firms respectively. After the crisis these values go up by 25 for SMEs and 11 percent for large firms. So, the financial obstacles that SMEs experienced in emerging economies seem to rise by 25 percent after the crisis, while the financial obstacles faced by large firms seem to rise only by 11 percent on average.

Finally *t*-test is employed to evaluate the statistical significance of the difference between mean values of *FIN_OBS* for SMEs and large firms before and after the crisis. The *t*-test is calculated as −3.9502 with 27,722 degrees of freedom, and the corresponding two-tailed *p*-value becomes 0.0001, which is smaller than the critical value of 0.05. This indicates that the SMEs in emerging economies have experienced higher financial obstacles relative to large firms in emerging economies before the crisis. As *t*-test is calculated for the period after the crisis, the value of statistic grows in absolute terms to −8.443 with 10,562 degrees of freedom, and the corresponding two-tailed p-value becomes 0.0000, which is much smaller than the critical value of 0.05. Based on this result, the difference in mean values of *FIN_OBS* between SMEs and large firms are statistically different from zero. This indicates that the SMEs in emerging economies have experienced more severe financial obstacles relative to large firms in emerging economies, and the gap between financial obstacles that SMEs and large firms faced has increased after the global financial crisis.

In Table 2, average values of *FIN_OBS* are calculated by year. The average value of *FIN_OBS* is calculated as 1.30 for SMEs, while it is 1.18 for large firms. The average value of *FIN_OBS* is only 0.02 units higher for SMEs relative to large firms in year 2002. The average *FIN_OBS* is calculated as 1.28 for SMEs, while it is 1.30 for the large firms. The difference between the average values of *FIN_OBS* for SMEs and large firms is always over 0.1 in the remaining years. Together with evidence found in Table 1, these results confirm that the SMEs suffer more from financial constraints relative to large firms. This result is in line with the previous literature that underlines the inability of SMEs in emerging economies to reach external finance. However detailed answers of SMEs presented in Table 3, shows that the number of firms that report access to finance as no obstacle for their operation and growth of their businesses has increased during the crisis period. According to Table 3, 62 percent of SMEs reported access to finance as no problem while the 40 percent of SMEs reported access to finance as no problem on average from 2002 to 2010. The evidence that Kremp and Sevestre (2013) provided shows that the reason of decreasing credits to SMEs during the recent crisis in France is the decline in investments made by SMEs. These two seemingly contradictory findings can be reconciled in the following way: In emerging economies the SMEs suffer more from financial

Table 1: *FIN_OBS* before and after the Global Financial Crisis.

	Before Crisis	After Crisis
SMEs	1.222 [1.318] (21027)	1.537 [1.345] (7922)
Large firms	1.151 [1.307] (6720)	1.284 [1.279] (2642)

Notes: The information regarding the financial obstacles (*FIN_OBS*) is drawn from the answers of SMEs to the following question: "*Is access to finance a problem for the operation and growth of your business?*" Answers are 0 (no obstacle), 1 (minor obstacle), 2 (moderate obstacle), 3 (major obstacle) and 4 (very severe obstacle). Numbers out of the brackets are the average values of *FIN_OBS*. Numbers in squared brackets report the standard deviation, while the numbers in parentheses report the number of observations.

Table 2: Summary of *FIN_OBS* for SMEs and Large Firms.

Year	SMEs			Large Firms		
	Number of observations	Mean	Std. dev.	Number of observations	Mean	Std. dev.
2002	4209	1.286	1.244	1855	1.306	1.271
2003	1925	2.021	1.533	1110	1.627	1.466
2004	2182	1.103	1.315	1172	.746	1.156
2005	2866	1.734	1.291	868	1.623	1.324
2006	9845	.915	1.193	1715	.712	1.078
2007	218	.793	1.202	77	.376	.744
2008	822	1.038	1.259	302	.788	1.121
2009	4742	1.617	1.376	1467	1.520	1.348
2010	2140	1.624	1.252	796	1.127	1.120
Total	28,949	1.308	1.333	9362	1.188	1.301

Notes: This table reports the basic statistical values of *FIN_OBS* for SMEs and large firms by year. The information regarding *FIN_OBS* is drawn from the answers of SMEs to the following question: *"Is access to finance a problem for the operation and growth of your business?"* Answers are 0 (no obstacle), 1 (minor obstacle), 2 (moderate obstacle), 3 (major obstacle), and 4 (very severe obstacle).

constraints as the credit rationing is more severe during crisis times, while SMEs in developed economies refrain from applying new loans as they cut investment spending during crisis periods.

According to results presented in Table 2, the largest gap between the *FIN_OBS* is observed in 2010 while the second largest gap is observed during the crisis. If the gap between SMEs and large firms were not calculated as 0.25, this result could indicate the deepening financial constraints for SMEs relative to large firms with the global financial crisis. Accordingly, these numbers cannot be interpreted as very strong evidence in favor of an increasing gap between the perceptions of SMEs and large firms regarding the financial constraints after the crisis.

Table 3: Answers of SMEs by Year.

	2002	2003	2004	2005	2006	2007	2008	2009	2010	Total
No obstacle	1577	525	1105	734	5299	136	396	1466	541	11779
	(37.5)	(27.3)	(50.6)	(25.6)	(53.8)	(62.4)	(48.2)	(30.9)	(25.3)	(40.7)
Minor obstacle	912	219	303	460	1805	29	182	807	419	5136
	(21.7)	(11.4)	(13.9)	(16.1)	(18.3)	(13.3)	(22.1)	(17.0)	(19.6)	(17.7)
Moderate obstacle	845	321	342	715	1449	25	116	1084	672	5569
	(20.1)	(16.7)	(15.7)	(24.9)	(14.7)	(11.5)	(14.1)	(22.9)	(31.4)	(19.2)
Major obstacle	687	412	308	748	855	18	72	844	319	4263
	(16.3)	(21.4)	(14.1)	(26.1)	(8.7)	(8.3)	(8.8)	(17.8)	(14.9)	(14.7)
Very severe obstacle	188	448	124	209	437	10	56	541	189	2202
	(4.5)	(23.3)	(5.7)	(7.3)	(4.4)	(4.6)	(6.8)	(11.4)	(8.8)	(7.6)
Total	4209	1925	2182	2866	9845	218	822	4742	2140	28,949

Notes: This table reports the numbers of SMEs that answer to the question *"Is access to finance a problem for the operation and growth of your business?"* by choosing one of the answers in the left column, that is, no obstacle, minor obstacle, moderate obstacle, major obstacle, very severe obstacle. The numbers in parentheses are the percentages of SMEs in the corresponding year.

Table 4: Summary Statistics of *FIN_OBS* by Country.

Country	Number of Observations	Mean	Std. Dev.
Brazil	2589	2.472	1.357
Chile	2921	1.077	1.332
China	725	1.197	1.249
Colombia	2509	1.209	1.278
Czech Republic	645	1.571	1.126
Hungary	879	1.283	1.228
India	5048	1.102	1.262
Indonesia	1405	1.144	1.164
Korea. Rep.	482	.898	1.077
Malaysia	544	1.055	1.401
Mexico	2368	.739	1.081
Peru	1250	1.378	1.165
Philippines	968	.926	1.106
Poland	1598	1.717	1.158
Russia	1414	1.554	1.357
South Africa	543	.911	1.243
Thailand	546	1.003	1.334
Turkey	2515	1.489	1.380

Note: This table reports the summary statistics for financial obstacles (*FIN_OBS*) by year. The information regarding *FIN_OBS* is drawn from the answers of SMEs to the following question: *"Is access to finance a problem for the operation and growth of your business?"* Answers are 0 (no obstacle), 1 (minor obstacle), 2 (moderate obstacle), 3 (major obstacle), and 4 (very severe obstacle).

Finally the average value of *FIN_OBS* for 18 countries are presented separately in Table 4. With the average value of 2.472 of *FIN_OBS*, SMEs in Brazil seem to suffer more from access to finance relative to the SMEs in other emerging economies. On the other hand, in another Latin country, Mexico, the average *FIN_OBS* for SMEs is calculated as 0.73. This number shows that the SMEs in Mexico suffered less from financial constraints relative to the SMEs in other emerging economies.

Conclusion

Previous studies have addressed the importance of SMEs in emerging economies while access to finance stands as a major obstacle for SMEs to continue their operations and investments. Because the recent global crisis started in developed economies, there are many studies on the effect of the crisis on financial difficulties that SMEs have faced in developed economies. However, the literature for emerging economies is scant. Popov and Udell (2012) says that *"The true extent of the financial crisis and its effect on firm access to finance will only become clear when new, more comprehensive data become available."* The dataset used in this chapter covers 41,795 firms in 18 emerging economies from 2002 to 2010, that is, it is the most comprehensive data, relative to the previous research especially relative to the one that is used in Popov and Udell (2012).

This chapter compares the effect of the recent global financial crisis on the severity of financial obstacles for SMEs and large firms. The results of descriptive analyses indicate that SMEs have been experiencing more severe financial obstacles relative to large firms in emerging economies. Moreover the gap between financial constraints that SMEs and large firms have faced had increased after the global financial crisis. SMEs perceive more severe financial constraints after the crisis, relative to large firms. It would be interesting to see the effect of this increasing financial constraints during the crisis on the real behavior of firms, such as investment and innovation. However, this issue could not be examined by a multivariate regression analysis due to the data limitations, as the survey includes excessive missing data for questions about investment or innovation. Accordingly, the results in this chapter are based on descriptive statistics rather than a multivariate regression analysis.

Some simple policy suggestions can be drawn from the results of this chapter to mitigate the financial constraints for SMEs in emerging economies. As SMEs in emerging economies seem to suffer more from financial constraints during crisis periods, governments can subsidize banks for lending to SMEs to improve access to finance for SMEs during crisis. At this point maybe supranational entities should have the responsibility to reduce credit constraints of SMEs in this globalized world where a crisis in a country easily triggers another crisis in another country. These proposed policies may reduce the observed differences in access to credit between SMEs and large firms in emerging economies. Financial constraints that SMEs have been experiencing, have been discussed during G20 summits since 2009. Recently, the International Monetary Fund and the European Investment Bank held a workshop[5] aiming to develop policies to improve access to finance by SMEs. As of today, policy makers seem to recognize the importance of access to finance of SMEs.

Acknowledgment

Elmas Yaldız Hanedar appreciates the financial support from Tubitak.

References

Agung, J., Kusmiarso, B., Pramono, B., Hutapea, E. G., Prasmuko, A., & Prastowo, N. J. (2001). *Credit crunch in Indonesia in the aftermath of the crisis: Facts, causes and policy implications*. Discussion Paper. Bank

5. The workshop *"Unlocking SME Financing in Europe and the Role of Capital Markets,"* was held in Brussels October 22–23, 2014.

Indonesia, Directorate of Economic Research and Monetary Policy, Jakarta.

Becker, T., & Mauro, P. (2006). *Output drops and the shocks that matter?* IMF Working Paper No. WP 06/172. International Monetary Fund, Washington, DC.

Blalock, G., Gertler, P. J., & Levine, D. I. (2008). Financial constraints on investment in an emerging market crisis. *Journal of Monetary Economics, 55*, 568–591. doi:10.1016/j.jmoneco.2008.01.005

Campello, M., Graham, J. R., & Harvey, C. R. (2010). The real effects of financial constraints: Evidence from a financial crisis. *Journal of Financial Economics, 97*(3), 470–487. doi:10.1016/j.jfineco.2010.02.009

Casey, E., & O'Toole, C. M. (2014). Bank lending constraints, trade credit and alternative financing during the financial crisis: Evidence from European SMEs. *Journal of Corporate Finance, 27*, 173–193. doi:10.1016/j.jcorpfin.2014.05.001

Chang, P. C., Jia, C., & Wang, Z. (2010). Bank fund reallocation and economic growth: Evidence from China. *Journal of Banking & Finance, 34*, 2753–2766. doi:10.2139/ssrn.1983654

Clarke, G. R. G., Cull, R., & Kisunko, G. (2012). External finance and firm survival in the aftermath of the crisis: Evidence from eastern Europe and central Asia. *Journal of Comparative Economics, 40*(3), 372–392. doi:10.1016/j.jce.2012.01.003

Duchin, R., Ozbas, O., & Sensoy, B. A. (2010). Costly external finance, corporate investment, and the subprime mortgage credit crisis. *Journal of Financial Economics, 97*(3), 418–435. doi:10.1016/j.jfineco.2009.12.008

Fernández, A. I., González, F., & Suárez, N. (2013). How do bank competition, regulation, and institutions shape the real effect of banking crises? International evidence. *Journal of International Money and Finance, 33*, 19–40. doi:10.1016/j.jimonfin.2012.10.002

Hainz, C., Weill, L., & Godlewski, C. J. (2008). *Bank competition and collateral: Theory and evidence.* Bank of Finland Research Discussion Paper No. 27.

Holton, S., Lawless, M., & McCann, F. (2014). Firm credit in the euro area: A tale of three crises. *Applied Economics, 46*(2), 190–211. doi:10.1080/00036846.2013.824547

Husain, A. M., Mody, A., Rogoff, & Kenneth, S. (2005). Exchange rate regime durability and performance in developing versus advanced economies. *Journal of Monetary Economics, 52*(1), 35–64. doi:10.1016/j.jmoneco.2004.07.001

Ivashina, V., & Scharfstein, D. (2010). Bank lending during the financial crisis of 2008. *Journal of Financial Economics, 97*, 319–338. doi:10.1016/j.jfineco.2009.12.001

Joyce, J. P., & Nabar, M. (2009). Sudden stops, banking crises and investment collapses in emerging markets. *Journal of Development Economics, 90*(2), 314–322. doi:10.1016/j.jdeveco.2008.04.004

Kremp, E., & Sevestre, P. (2013). Did the crisis induce credit rationing for French SMEs? *Journal of Banking & Finance, 37*(10), 3757–3772. doi:10.1016/j.jbankfin.2013.05.028

Kroszner, R. S., Laeven, L., & Klingebiel, D. (2007). Banking crises, financial dependence, and growth. *Journal of Financial Economics, 84*(1), 197–228. doi:10.1016/j.jfineco.2006.05.001

Lee, N., Sameen, H., & Cowling, M. (2015). Access to finance for innovative SMEs since the financial crisis. *Research Policy, 44*(2), 370–380. doi:10.1016/j.respol.2014.09.008

Menkhoff, L., Neuberger, D., & Suwanaporn, C. (2006). Collateral–based lending in emerging markets: Evidence from Thailand. *Journal of Banking and Finance, 30*, 1–21. doi:10.1016/j.jbankfin.2004.12.004

Mizen, P., & Tsoukas, S. (2012). The response of the external finance premium in Asian corporate bond markets to financial characteristics, financial constraints and two financial crises. *Journal of Banking & Finance, 36*, 3048–3059. doi:10.1016/j.jbankfin.2012.07.005

Popov, A., & Udell, G. F. (2012). Cross-border banking, credit access, and the financial crisis. *Journal of International Economics, 87*(1), 147–161. doi:10.1016/j.jinteco.2012.01.008

Rahaman, M. M. (2011). Access to financing and firm growth. *Journal of Banking & Finance, 35*, 709–723. doi:10.1016/j.jbankfin.2010.09.005

Stone, A. H. W. (1992). *Listening to firms: How to use firm-level surveys to assess constraints on private sector development*. World Bank Policy Research Working Paper No. 923.

Index